THE COURSE OF MEXICAN HISTORY

THE COURSE OF MEXICAN HISTORY

ELEVENTH EDITION

Susan M. Deeds
NORTHERN ARIZONA UNIVERSITY

Michael C. Meyer
UNIVERSITY OF ARIZONA

William L. Sherman
UNIVERSITY OF NEBRASKA-LINCOLN

NEW YORK   OXFORD
OXFORD UNIVERSITY PRESS

Oxford University Press is a department of the University of Oxford. It furthers the University's objective of excellence in research, scholarship, and education by publishing worldwide. Oxford is a registered trade mark of Oxford University Press in the UK and certain other countries.

Published in the United States of America by Oxford University Press
198 Madison Avenue, New York, NY 10016, United States of America.

Library of Congress Cataloging-in-Publication Data

Names: Deeds, Susan M., author. | Meyer, Michael C. | Sherman, William L.
   Title: The course of Mexican history / Susan M. Deeds, Northern Arizona
      University, Michael C. Meyer, University of Arizona, William L. Sherman,
      University of Nebraska-Lincoln.
   Description: Eleventh edition. | New York, NY : Oxford University Press,
      2017. | Meyer's name appears first on earlier editions. | Includes index.
   Identifiers: LCCN 2017025522 | ISBN 9780190659011 (pbk.)
   Subjects: LCSH: Mexico—History.
   Classification: LCC F1226 .M54 2017 | DDC 972—dc23 LC record available at
      https://lccn.loc.gov/2017025522

9 8 7 6 5 4 3 2 1
Printed by Sheridan Books, Inc., United States of America.

CONTENTS

MAPS AND CHARTS

NEW TO THIS EDITION

Updates to pre-Columbian chapters including recent discoveries at the pyramids of Teotihuacan and on Maya codices (picture writing)

New material on the Spanish conquest of Mexico and native responses to colonial rule

Revisionist interpretations of Santa Anna and the US-Mexican War

Re-evaluation of the Mexican Revolution of 1910 and its aftermath

Expanded coverage of social and cultural history throughout, including discussions of gender history, ethnic groups, local religion, cultural nationalism, environmental change, popular protests, and urban life

Updates on recent political crises and corruption as well as US-Mexico relations

Extended analysis of border issues, including migration and narcotraffic

Reflections and illustrations of Mexico's rich contemporary popular culture, including film, television, music, cuisine, leisure, and sport

PREFACE

In the nearly forty years since the first edition of *The Course of Mexican History* was published in 1979, much has changed in Mexico. Successive editions of the book have noted transformations in the political, economic, social, cultural, and diplomatic history over time. Each addition has also incorporated new and revisionist interpretations of Mexico's past based on the most recent archival research of hundreds of scholars. When the original authors, Michael Meyer and William Sherman, undertook the project of writing a textbook to help college students acquire a deep appreciation of Mexico's past, as well as a nuanced understanding of the present, they could not have anticipated that their collaboration on the subject they themselves found so fascinating would prove so enduring.

Their empathy and appreciation for Mexico's peoples and cultures continue to resonate in the eleventh edition. After the death of Professor Sherman in 1998, Professor Meyer and I collaborated on three more editions of the book. When Michael C. Meyer died in 2007, he left a rich legacy of original scholarship on Mexican history. But perhaps his most lasting contribution is to be found in this fundamental survey text that faithfully maintains his desire to provide sound, up-to-date historical synthesis unencumbered by polemic or theoretical jargon.

For Professor Meyer, the understanding of Mexican history logically began with an understanding of the major political developments that provided a foundation upon which to develop themes of Mexico's socioeconomic and cultural history in the pre-Columbian, colonial, and modern periods. This model has once again served me well for incorporating new materials and perspectives from recent publications to update the basic text. In this edition, I have reorganized the periodization of chapters in the modern era to reflect changes in overall interpretations of the Mexican past. College instructors can supplement our material from the increasingly expansive scholarship that continues to be published on a multiplicity of topics in Mexican history.

The general contours of historical scholarship on Mexico have shifted over the last few decades. Scholars have increasingly called attention to continuities in Mexico's historical experience over time. Changing emphases have illuminated the roles of the popular classes and of women in shaping Mexican history. New cultural approaches have offered alternative insights to explain nation building and the evolution of Mexican national identity. The focus of much of the new scholarship examines the postrevolutionary periods, questioning the degree to which the revolution of 1910 wrought social and political change.

Mexico's place in the world community continues to be remarkable and unique. Even before Mesoamerica was connected to the rest of the globe, it boasted several of the world's most complex civilizations. Distinguished by its significant presence in the Atlantic and Pacific world economies in the colonial period, Mexico later became the first nation to carry out a social revolution in twentieth century. At the turn of the twenty-first century, Mexico once again commanded attention by ending seventy years of one-party rule and embarking on a more politically pluralistic path. Just twelve years later, the return of the Partido Revolucionario Institucional offered poignant testimony to the enormous difficulties of transforming an entrenched political culture.

An even more intractable problem is the drug war that has engulfed Mexico for more than a decade, producing thousands of deaths and disappearances. Recently, migration has topped the list of dilemmas for Mexico to confront. The ties that connect Mexico to the United States have deep historical roots in the border crossings that have evolved for nearly 200 years since Mexico became an independent nation. In this decade, nearly 34 million Hispanics of Mexican origin live in the United States, making meaningful contributions to US society across the political, economic, social, and cultural spectra. Approximately two-thirds of them were born in the United States, and the other third consists of immigrants. The immigrant population expanded significantly after 1970 and then declined in recent years; one-half are undocumented while legal permanent residents and naturalized US citizens make up the other half. As this book goes to press, undocumented Mexicans face a serious crisis, stemming from the 2016 election of Donald Trump as US president. The protracted stalemate in the US Congress which prevented a resolution of the migrant issue resulted in Trump's nationalist and xenophobic agenda. Threats of mass deportations now loom large.

The lessons of history teach us that Mexico will meet future challenges with characteristic creativity, dynamism, and resilience. And, more than ever, US citizens can benefit from understanding the past of their southern neighbor.

During a long relationship with the fine staff at the Higher Education Division of Oxford University Press, the authors of *The Course of Mexican History* have worked with several editors who offered wise counsel. I would like to thank Charles Cavaliere, my editor on the eleventh edition, and the rest of the editorial staff for their skillful guidance and sound editorial judgment. Above all, I am deeply indebted to Catherine Tracy Goode whose professional and editorial skills were crucial to the writing of this edition. I also thank Ana Ortiz Islas who assisted with the illustrations, Rosalba Gasparrini who proofread many chapters, and the many colleagues who suggested changes. Finally, I would like to acknowledge Ross Hassig, Professor Emeritus, University of Oklahoma; Susan Kellogg, University of Houston;

Cynthia Radding, University of North Carolina – Chapel Hill; John W. Sherman, Wright State University; Donald F. Stevens, Drexel University; and Dana Velasco Murillo, University of California – San Diego who shared invaluable feedback with me.

Mexico City   *S. M. D.*
July 2017

THE COURSE OF MEXICAN HISTORY

PRE-COLUMBIAN MEXICO

CHAPTER 1

THE FIRST MEXICANS

There is in Mexican society a pervasive awareness of the ancients. The Indian presence intrudes on the national psyche; it suffuses the art, philosophy, and literature. It lies within the marvelous prehistoric ruins among whose haunted piles the Mexicans seek their origins. It has not always been so. Following the Spanish conquest of the sixteenth century, a combination of the conquerors' ethnocentrism and excessive Christian zeal denigrated most things Indian. At the end of the nineteenth century Mexican political elites saw that the grandeur of the Aztec empire could be invoked to validate their own ambitions, but the great push to revive the indigenous past occurred later during the revolution of 1910, as leaders turned it to the service of a unifying national myth that could transcend the contradictions of an ethnically and culturally divided society. In their search for *mexicanidad*—the spirit of an inclusive Mexican cultural identity—revolutionary intellectuals looked to new configurations of stories, places, and heroes from the past. For several decades talented anthropologists, historians, painters, musicians, novelists, and craftsmen extolled native traditions if not their contemporary reality. Then as cultural nationalism gave way to more nuanced representations of ancient cultures, so did the circumstances of contemporary indigenous peoples pose ever more stark contrasts to the depictions of stunning past achievements. The contradictions were startlingly manifested in the Chiapas insurrection of 1994.

PRE-AGRICULTURAL AND PROTO-AGRICULTURAL MEXICO

At what point or how the first Mexicans appeared on the scene is still debated. The most accepted academic theory is that they are descended from the intrepid hunters who crossed from northwest Asia to Alaska. There may have been several waves of migrants, beginning as early as 40,000 years ago, when sea levels were lower and a land bridge over the Bering Strait facilitated the passage. When a melting trend began around 9000 BC, the migrations likely slowed or ceased.

More recent archaeological discoveries posit new hypotheses that support the idea of sea routes from Asia to North America and a coastal migration pattern down the Pacific coastline. Biological evidence from skeletons and mitochondrial DNA also suggests connections with Polynesian, Japanese, and European peoples (who migrated as far as Siberia). Native Americans offer their own explanations and oppose skeletal dating methods on religious grounds. As new archaeological, genetic, and linguistic discoveries are made, changing and competing understandings about these matters will persist. Advances in the decipherment of hieroglyphic writing will also continue to alter how we divide prehispanic Mexico into chronological periods with distinctive cultural characteristics. The chart below provides a general overview, although not all cultures fit within it and dates vary by group and location.

The early human inhabitants of America were hunters, food gatherers, and sometimes fishermen. They were constantly on the move, searching for food and using crude stone tools. For thousands of years, these early hunters led a precarious existence, with little perceptible improvement in technology until about 10,0o0 BC, when fine pressure-flaked stone points made hunting easier. At this time, the still moist conditions of the late Pleistocene supported lush grasslands and full foliage—ample fodder for animal prey—hairy mammoths, mastodons, giant armadillos, and early ancestors of the bison, camel, and horse. These animals were hunted by men who assailed their prey with missiles—including stone-tipped lances or darts propelled by the *atl-atl*, or "spear thrower." Human remains dating to 13,000 years ago have been discovered in various Mexican sites, most recently in underwater caves near Tulum on the Caribbean coast of the Yucatán Peninsula. These predate the 10,000-year-old "Tepexpan Man" (who, as it turned out, was a woman), discovered in the 1940s just north of Mexico City in the village of Tepexpan. Mammoth bones with stone points lodged in the ribs, lying adjacent to flint knives, dating to more than 20,000 years ago, offer another kind of evidence for human habitation. The earliest hunter-gatherer sites have been unearthed in Puebla and Oaxaca.

Around 7500 BC, a drying-up phase began: rainfall was less frequent, and the rich plant life gradually yielded to sparse vegetation; the lakes shriveled up; and the huge beasts that had provided a plentiful supply of meat eventually became extinct as their sources of food and water disappeared. Ancient Mexicans were again back to eating insects, lizards, snakes, rodents, and anything else remotely edible, to supplement their diet of seeds, roots, nuts, berries, eggs, and shellfish. The audacious killer of mammoths gave way to the hunter of small game.

As meat consumption fell to less than 21 percent of the diet by 4000 BC, collection of plants increased. And over several millennia maize cultivation developed as *teosinte* grass underwent genetic alteration to produce small corn cobs. Maize became the basis of the Mexican diet. We know, for example, that as early as 5000 BC primitive farmers practiced rudimentary agriculture at Tehuacan in the modern state of Puebla, although we have no precise data for the domestication of corn. By at least 2000 BC, maize, along with previously domesticated beans and squash, had become a widespread source of human sustenance in Mesoamerica, or Middle America, as indicated by the presence of grinding stones for the making of meal.

40,000–7000 BC	*Pre-Agricultural:* Nomadic hunters and food gatherers.
7000–1500 BC	Archaic (*Incipient Agricultural*): Slowly evolving domestication of food plants; nascent village life; development of primitive skills.
1500 BC–AD 150	*Formative or Pre-Classic:* Elaboration of farming, villages, and pottery; appearance of chiefdoms, public architecture, solar calendar, and long-distance exchange.
AD 150–900	*Classic:* The florescence of ancient Mexican civilization with state-level societies ruled by kings and priests; elaboration of cities and monumental architecture; intensification of agriculture; increased social stratification; advancement in artistic expression, literacy, and science.
AD 900–1521	*Post-Classic:* Growth of city-states and empires; expansion of commerce; intensification of Late Classic trends in sacrifice and warfare; development of metallurgy; final destruction of Indian states by Spanish conquest.

PERIODS IN PRE-COLUMBIAN MEXICO

The farmer was evolving; but there was great variation in this process throughout Mexico, and hunting and gathering continued to be practiced to differing degrees, even solely by some nomadic groups. But in central and southern Mexico, barring disasters common to all tillers of the soil, a fairly reliable source of food allowed populations to grow and to find leisure time for experimentation, to develop and refine skills and talents. Weavers of baskets and mats began to shape clay, a most important development.

THE FORMATIVE PERIOD

Ancient garbage dumps are to the archaeologist what documents are to the historian. From those piles of refuse scientific investigators patiently assemble pictures of early societies. Much has, of course, long been reduced to dust; and whatever use early inhabitants made of wood, hides, and woven reeds must be left to speculation. But instruments of flint, obsidian, and various kinds of stone survive; and some pottery has left us indelible traces of early cultures.

By 2000 BC the rough outlines of a Mesoamerican identity had begun to form. "Mesoamerican" refers to a loosely defined cultural tradition that characterized much of pre-contact Mexico and Central America. In the Formative period, its fundamental common characteristics were the dependence on maize agriculture and the evolution of an agricultural technology that used a wooden digging stick. Agriculture advanced with the beginning of irrigation, terracing, fertilizers, and raised fields. Implements of stone and wood facilitated cultivation of fields by farmers, who built huts of branches, reeds, and mud nearby. A simple village life with incipient political and social orders evolved. Subsequently, cliques emerged to control both power and wealth. Increased exchange of goods among different societies developed as a result of distinctive products and artisan specialties. In addition, varied climate and geography yielded regional fruits, vegetables, woods, stone, and other items of value, such as shells, jade, cotton, and turquoise. This spreading trade naturally led to cultural exchanges as well.

Artists began to create ceramics that were both esthetically pleasing and functional. Clay figurines, usually of females, were produced in great numbers. Among them were those of Tlatilco, in the Valley of Mexico, where artists rendered charming figurines of the type known as "pretty lady," with delicate and beautiful faces. The eyes are almost slanting and the hairdos sometimes elaborate. The figures have tiny waists and bulging thighs. At the same time, a fascination with the deformed manifested early the Mexican idea of duality, for other small clay figurines represented dwarfs, hunchbacks, and the diseased. Some figurines are of interest for their depiction of everyday life—nursing babies, dancing, playing, and performing acrobatics. Through them we gain some idea of popular pastimes, the use of jewelry, and clothing. Still other pieces were made in the images of animals and gods whose forms suggest ritual purposes related to natural forces and dependence upon the products of the earth.

During the Late Formative period agriculture was further enhanced by the use of terracing and raised fields. One form of the latter was the *chinampa*, the so-called floating garden, rectangular areas constructed by building up layers of mud and aquatic vegetation in a shallow lake.

Although textile manufacturing had evolved, it is likely that, in the more temperate zones anyway, people went about nude, or almost so. Clothing was apparently worn more among the upper classes than the lower, as were sandals, jewelry, and other adornments. Individual expression and vanity were evident in the dyed hair and elaborate coiffures of aristocratic women.

Ceramic figurine of a dancer from Tlatilco, near Mexico City.

As villages grew in size and society became more complex, serious decisions had to be made by those who were most knowledgeable. Increasing reliance on agriculture made people aware that their security depended upon the blessings of nature. The mysteries of the universe were associated with the supernatural and, as in other ancient cultures, gods of nature came to be worshipped. Vagaries of the elements were equated with capricious gods. When rain failed, for example, supplication was made to the angry deity through a priesthood that acquired a predominant position. This presumed special relationship with the gods, astutely cultivated by the priests, gave them a certain mystique and a hold over the community. In order to pay due reverence to the gods and to ensure their cooperation in providing rain and sunshine, priests ordered the construction of mounds, on top of which offerings were made. As the structures became larger and more elaborate, advanced permanent architecture evolved. By the Middle Formative (1200–400 BC) some impressive sites were already in evidence.

OLMEC CULTURE AND INFLUENCE

For many years, archaeologists exclusively associated the early development of complex society in Mesoamerica with the Olmec culture of the Gulf coast lowlands in southern Veracruz and Tabasco. They believed it to have been the "mother culture" that profoundly influenced later Classic period civilizations. In the past few decades, scholars have learned more about the Olmecs, whose sites of San Lorenzo, Veracruz, and La Venta, Tabasco, offered tantalizing clues for reconstructing their development. From simple village cultures, Olmecs and other simultaneously evolving groups developed societies with distinctive art forms, economic specialization, new forms of religious life, and the building of large platforms and mounds with temples. Although Olmec culture evolved in the propitious natural setting of the coastal villages of the Gulf coast, it was distributed over several phases (dating from about 1500 BC to the Christian era).

Massive public construction seems to have begun at San Lorenzo by 1350 BC, where we find the Olmec "pudgy babies," or dolls, and motifs like the serpent mouth. The site also came to have a drainage system, a ball court, and the colossal stone heads for which the Olmecs are most well known. Some of these spectacular sculptured heads—embellished likenesses of rulers—were over nine feet high and weighed as much as 40 tons. By about 850 BC, San Lorenzo was eclipsed by the island site of La Venta, where elites mobilized labor and directed construction of this city of monumental architecture for over 400 years. Their tombs have furnished many artifacts of Olmec culture including large mosaic masks and elegantly carved jade figurines. Early Olmecs revered the alligator, representing the earth, and the shark, representing the sea. Elites added the serpent as a symbol of rule, along with were-jaguars. One theory holds that these supposed were-jaguars were actually symbols related to women and their healing powers. Olmecs also had a god for precious, life-giving corn.

The Olmec and some contemporary cultures in the highland valleys of Mexico seem to have been the originators of the elite-commoner class divide that came to characterize Mesoamerican societies. Elites commanded resources from commoners, who grew maize. Elites also developed the long-distance trade in obsidian, jade, cacao, and other items that

This handsome basalt stone carving from the Gulf coast Olmec culture is known as "The Wrestler."

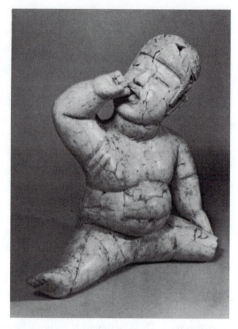

Genderless "pudgy babies" like this hollow ceramic figurine (13.5 inches in height) may represent Olmec lineages or gods, or perhaps even effigies of infants destined for sacrifice.

helped to spread Olmec influence. Their impact on surrounding and later cultures can also be seen in the advancement of terracing in agriculture and a calendrical system that meshed ritual and solar calendars. Speculation persists about whether Olmecs developed the first writing system, but discoveries since the 1990s have strengthened the hypothesis that they did. These include a cylindrical ceramic stamp and a tablet called the Cascajal block, the latter dated about 900 BC, found in the Veracruz lowlands. Both have incised glyphs that are still being studied.

Other Mesoamerican societies developed sophisticated polities in the Late Formative period that had features in common with the Olmec: the building of public structures, the rapid growth of villages, the development of calendrical and writing systems, craft specialization, and long-distance trade. The nature of the exchanges between them is not well understood, but archaeologists now believe that although Olmec characteristics may have been widespread, they were not singular. "Sister cultures" may have evolved comparable traditions and technologies independently. Similar types of Pre-Classic architecture and ritual symbols have been found in sites throughout central and southern Mexico in the present-day states of Mexico, Morelos, Guerrero, Oaxaca, and Chiapas.

New centers with temple-pyramid complexes like that at Cuicuilco, located on the outskirts of present-day Mexico City, and at lowland Maya locations to the south emerged in the Late Formative period (400 BC–AD 200). Some of the new sites would develop into great hubs

Several colossal Olmec stone heads have been discovered. This one, more than eight feet high, is covered with what appears to be a helmet.

of the Classic world in Mexico. On a hilltop in the Valley of Oaxaca, the site of Monte Alban expanded into an urban center administering much of the surrounding countryside. And in the Valley of Mexico, Cuicuilco's destruction by a volcano in the first century AD encouraged rapid urban growth at nearby Teotihuacan. Above an area of natural caves—considered sacred in Mesoamerican religion—its inhabitants constructed huge pyramids dedicated to the moon and the sun. By the end of the Formative period, the civic–religious complex at Teotihuacan had amassed the technology and central authority necessary for the creation of one of the splendors of the world.

RECOMMENDED FOR FURTHER STUDY

Adams, Richard E. W. *Prehistoric Mesoamerica*, 3d ed. Norman: University of Oklahoma Press, 2005.

Adams, Richard E. W., and Murdo J. MacLeod, eds. *The Cambridge History of the Native Peoples of the Americas*, Vol. II: *Mesoamerica*. New York: Cambridge University Press, 1998.

Bernal, Ignacio. *The Olmec World*. Translated by Doris Heyden and Fernando Horcasitas. Berkeley: University of California Press, 1969.

Blake, Michael. *Maize for the Gods: Unearthing a 9,000-Year History of Corn*. Berkeley: University of California Press, 2015.

Carmack, Robert M., Janine Gasco, and Gary H. Gossen. *The Legacy of Mesoamerica: History and Culture of a Native American Civilization*. Upper Saddle River, NJ: Prentice Hall, 1996.

Coe, Michael, and Richard A. Diehl. *In the Land of the Olmec*. 2 vols. Austin: University of Texas Press, 1980.

Diehl, Richard A. *The Olmecs: America's First Civilization*. London, UK: Thames and Hudson, 2004.

Flannery, Kent V., ed. *The Early Mesoamerican Village*. New York: Academic Press, 1976.

Flannery, Kent V., and Joyce Marcus, eds. *The Cloud People: Divergent Evolution of the Zapotec and Mixtec Civilizations*. New York: Academic Press, 1983.

Grove, David C. *Discovering the Olmecs: An Unconventional History*. Austin: University of Texas Press, 2014.

Guernsey, Julia. *Sculpture and Social Dynamics in Preclassic Mesoamerica*. New York: Cambridge University Press, 2012.

MacNeish, Richard S. *The Origins of Agriculture and Settled Life*. Norman: University of Oklahoma Press, 1991.

Miller, Mary Ellen. *The Art of Mesoamerica, from Olmec to Aztec*. London, UK: Thames and Hudson, 1986.

Pohl, Mary E. D., K. O. Pope, and C. Von Nagy. "Olmec Origins of Mesoamerican Writing." *Science*, 298/5600 (2002): 1984-1987.

Pool, Christopher A. *Olmec Archaeology and Early Mesoamerica*. New York: Cambridge University Press, 2007.

Rodríguez Martínez, María del Carmen, et al. "Oldest Writing in the New World." *Science*, 313/5793 (2006): 1610-1614.k

Sharer, Robert J., and David C. Grove. *Regional Perspectives on the Olmec*. New York: Cambridge University Press, 1989.

Stark, Barbara L., and Philip J. Arnold III, eds. *Olmec to Aztec: Settlement Patterns in the Ancient Gulf Lowlands*. Tucson: University of Arizona Press 1997.

Tate, Carolyn. *Re-Considering Olmec Visual Culture: The Unborn, Women, and Creation*. Austin: University of Texas Press, 2012.

Taube, Karl A. *Olmec Art at Dumbarton Oaks*. Washington, DC: Dumbarton Oaks Research Library and Collection, 2004.

Wolf, Eric. *Sons of the Shaking Earth: The People of Mexico and Guatemala—Their Land, History, and Culture*. Chicago, IL: University of Chicago Press, 1974.

CHAPTER 2

MESOAMERICA'S GOLDEN AGE:
The Classic Period

The Mesoamerican culture region flourished over the first millennium AD, most visible in the monumental architecture of cities and the refinement of calendrical and astronomical knowledge. As the Roman empire crumbled in Europe, Mesoamerica was resplendent.

THE FLOWERING OF CITIES

The period from AD 150 to 900 has been viewed as a "golden age" of intellectual and artistic endeavor. Because of the many societies under consideration, the Classic cannot be put into any simple chronological framework.[1] Some sites, such as Teotihuacan and Monte Alban, developed Classic features much earlier. Most Classic cultures declined in the ninth century, but some persisted as late as AD 1000.

One is struck by the grandiose scale of human endeavor in those centuries, most notable in the stunning architecture but also by the excellence of the ceramics, sculpture, and murals. Religion was the cohesive force in an increasingly stratified society, and kings invested with sacred power exacted both labor and tribute from the masses. It was a time of great vigor, with the proliferation of crafts and skills necessary to provide for complex communities. The leadership was dedicated to a sense of order in propitiating the gods, made possible by an apparently strict adherence to regimentation. Pressures to provide sustenance for a burgeoning population led to more careful consideration of planting cycles, which in turn produced exact calculations of the seasons. Even more important was the Mesoamerican belief that all things—gods, people, animals, plants, mountains, even cities—were alive and that their movements could be timed to account for all life events. Consequently, there developed a sophisticated knowledge of astronomy and mathematics, which made possible precise calendrical markings. Mesoamericans devised a highly sophisticated calendar system that included a 365-day solar count as well as a ritual calendar and counts of many other celestial bodies.

---

1 With only a tiny fraction of the thousands of known archaeological sites in Mexico having been scientifically excavated, the complexities of charting can be appreciated.

Why is this boy laughing? Such unrestrained joy is characteristic of the thousands of ceramic pieces found at the site of Remojadas in the state of Veracruz. Unique for their expressiveness, the figurines have triangular, flattened heads and teeth that are often filed to points.

A howling coyote, another delightful piece from the Remojadas culture, AD 300-900. Indian artists frequently displayed a touch of whimsy in their works.

Farming became scientific; abstract thinking soared. The intellectuals in ancient Mesoamerica apparently arrived at the revolutionary concept of the zero cipher well before its arrival in Europe in 1202 AD, when it was introduced by Arab mathematicians. Despite their advanced understanding of astronomy and math, they made almost no practical use of metals, relying instead upon chipped stone like flint for cutting tools. However, the sharpness of the prismatic blades they crafted from obsidian (volcanic glass) required sophisticated skills virtually unknown today. Although Mesoamericans were aware of the wheel (used in children's toys), the lack of draft animals meant that there was no practical use for wheels in transport.

In some places Mesoamericans were able to raise structures to the height of 230 feet that have stood for some fifteen hundred years. What many have described as their technical limitations was equaled by their ingenuity. In lowland areas, massive blocks of cut stone were most likely transported on river rafts from quarries to distant cities, and logs may have been used in other zones. For lifting the pieces high in the air some clever engineering devices were utilized. Armies of laborers toiled for years on public works projects. An architectural design tradition evolved to take earthquakes into account in the highlands, but technical perfection in construction tended to be subordinated to an irresistible propensity for the esthetic. Though capable of exact measurements, they avoided harsh angles unpleasing to the eye. If the result was agreeable to humans, the purpose, it is clear, was to please the gods.

For many years archaeologists believed that these building complexes were not true cities but only ceremonial centers inhabited by priests, rulers, and their retainers. Today it is universally agreed that Classic centers were true cities and that urbanism is a defining Mesoamerican characteristic. Elites lived in the most luxurious chambers of palace compounds nearest the primary ceremonial complexes or major avenues, which consisted of temple-pyramids, tombs, observatories, and acropolises. Other urban features include ball courts, steam baths, and causeways. Surrounding the city core in a concentric pattern were the apartment complexes of artisans who specialized in craft production as well as those of other middling occupational groups such as petty officials, soldiers, and merchants. Laborers, farmers, and others of the commoner class lived even further out, in modest thatched-roof huts of wattle and daub construction. There they farmed the land, hunted, fished, carried the burdens, and performed all sorts of tasks necessary to support the aristocracy. During festivals, religious in nature, or on market days, masses of people tended to gather in the central precincts.

These Mesoamerican cities functioned first and foremost as administrative and religious centers whose architecture and spatial design attempted to replicate the order of the universe and the hierarchical relationships that linked humans and super naturals. Teotihuacan in central Mexico was truly remarkable for its size and religious importance. The marvelous stone cities of the Classic period were conceived for an impression of grandeur and laid out in breathtaking expanses. The architects were true artists, interposing grand courtyards to offset with horizontal lines the massive vertical projections. As Monte Alban dramatically testifies, they blended their creations with nature and composed with stone and textures that reflected the sunlight.

Although city size, population density, and spatial arrangements varied among Classic centers, there is no question that concentrated populations in so many sites had an incalculable impact on culture. The arts thrive with greatest vigor in an urban milieu, and intellectual growth is enhanced as well. At the same time, the stratification of society is inevitable. So, too, is a central administration to maintain order, promote public works, provide justice, set regulations—to perform, in short, on a more simplified scale, the functions familiar to city administrators of our own times. Great plazas and avenues were paved, buildings were plastered and painted, subterranean tile drainage systems were provided, waste was disposed of, domestic water supplies were channeled, and the staggering problems of food supply were met. Marketplaces were also a feature of cities, although we know less about how exchanges functioned.

Traditionally, scholars viewed the Classic period as having been devoted to moderation and comparative serenity, with order imposed by dominant centers such as Teotihuacan and Monte Alban. These powers, like city-states, carved out spheres of influence that were tolerated by others. We now realize that warfare and human sacrifice were very much a part of the Classic and that conquest explains why certain city-states were able to exercise sway over surrounding territory. Although much of the evidence for the prevalence of sacrificial practices comes from the Maya area, excavations in central Mexico testify to mass executions of warriors and other captives. Classic cities once thought to have lacked fortifications were often built on defensible hilltops. In the art of the Classic, we find images of soldiers, weapons, and slaves. The wide dispersion of a pan-Mesoamerican culture resulted not only from peaceful exchange but also from forceful impositions. The ruling class consisted not only of powerful priests but also of warriors.

The conventional view of relative tranquility has been most discredited in the case of the Classic Maya. Because of important revelations as a result of improved deciphering of Maya hieroglyphic script, the characteristics of Classic societies have been dramatically reassessed. The Maya genius in art, architecture, and science remains clear; nevertheless, the romanticized version of a society ruled by a benevolent and intellectual priesthood, shunning violence and conquest, now rings hollow. Scholars have revealed that aggressive Maya kings during the Classic period regularly made war on their neighbors for both ritualistic and materialistic motives. The most valued prize was another king, who would be humiliated over a period of time, subjected to exquisite tortures, and finally decapitated. These kings, with a profound sense of history, erected monuments to commemorate their victories and to record their lineage. Maya kingdoms tended to be small in scale, controlling limited territory; but at times regional states were able to subdue larger areas and exercise power over several hundreds of thousands. Various constellations of Maya states formed blocs or were interdependent in terms of trade and defense, but the Maya were not politically unified as a whole.

A unifying element in Classic societies was religion. Shaman-priest kings derived their authority from the gods. Priests were guardians of scientific and genealogical knowledge, and, along with other cultural leaders like scribes and painters, they held high social status and provided guidance to those below. The pantheon of gods included the omnipresent rain god Tlaloc and Quetzalcoatl, the "Feathered Serpent." To the god of the sun and goddess of the moon were added deities to celebrate the beneficence of fire, corn, and the butterfly.

In these polities social cleavage was implicit. There was an order in which everyone had an assigned place. In this respect social stratification was like that in other parts of the world, except that the commoners who supplied tribute in goods and labor may have benefited more from the calendrical knowledge of their rulers, which helped to ensure good harvests. Families thus had their daily needs met, and rulers enjoyed the surpluses. We cannot know how willingly the masses performed their obligatory duties, but as warfare increased, states commanded loyalty as long as they could provide a measure of security.

After a spectacular run of several centuries, the Classic world in Mesoamerica began to deteriorate. Just why the great centers fell is still a mystery, although some theories have wide acceptance; in the case of the Maya, drought has emerged as a main factor. While some of the cities went into gradual decline, others, it appears, met a sudden, violent end. Pressures of various kinds impinged on ordered ways: aggressive nomadic tribes on the peripheries and wars between kingdoms played a role in some cases. Demand for increased food supplies, the result of population pressures, crop failures, and possibly soil exhaustion, was another cause. Perhaps an internal disruption was occasioned by a peasants' revolt against the ruling classes, bred by excessive demands or the priests' inability to mediate successfully with the all-important nature gods. Or were there plagues of some kind? The reasons no doubt vary from place to place, and there may well have been a combination of factors. Scholars lean more and more to explanations that stress overpopulation, environmental destruction, and increasing warfare. In any event, the golden age came apart after a long period of human intellectual and cultural achievement.

Small, hairless *techichi* dogs from Colima were bred for the table and were also used as foot-warmers. Molded in various poses, these ceramic pieces are usually in the form of a vessel.

Poised for action, another Colima figure may represent either a warrior or an athlete.

A bearded musician sings and keeps rhythm with rasps. The clay figure, from the state of Nayarit (AD 300-900), is about twenty inches in height.

TEOTIHUACAN AND ITS SUCCESSORS

Classic Mexico had many important centers, but at least three dominant polities exercised great influence over surrounding regions—Teotihuacan, Monte Alban, and some Maya centers. The most important city of its time was the immense urban complex of Teotihuacan, "the Place of the Gods," as the Aztecs were to call it later. The overall expanse measured perhaps twelve square miles, in the core of which was the ceremonial center occupying about two square miles. Surrounding this precinct were the sumptuous quarters of the rulers and their retainers, and on the outer fringes the masses resided in apartments and rude dwellings that have long since disappeared. The population of the city at its height of prosperity remains in dispute, but it may have had as many as 160,000 inhabitants, making it one of the largest cities in the world at the time. Long after its fall the site was held in reverence and awe by succeeding cultures, and owing to the grandiose dimensions of its structures, the Aztecs considered it to have been built by a race of giants.

The origins of the Teotihuacanos are unknown, but the destruction of nearby Cuicuilco in the first century AD coincided with the emergence of Teotihuacan as a powerful kingdom in the central Valley of Mexico. Exceptional urban planning created a colossal city of avenues, a grid system of streets, plazas, markets, temples, palaces, apartment complexes, waterways, and drainage systems. Its main thoroughfare was the Avenue of the Dead, 150 feet wide and stretching over two miles. It connects the Pyramid of the Moon, the Pyramid of the Sun, and the Ciudadela (Citadel), a ceremonial plaza that covers nearly 40 acres. The most striking monument is the splendid Pyramid of the Sun, measuring over 700 feet at the base lines and rising about 215 feet high. The truncated structure covered a sacred cave reminiscent of origin myths and served as a base for the elevation of a temple on top. In Mesoamerica, caves were considered sacred and seen as entrances to an underworld, perhaps a dark, watery void from which humankind emerged. The summit, reached after an ascent of 268 steps, offers the breathless viewer a commanding sweep of the surrounding valley. Even so, what we see today is a pale replica of the former magnificence of the Pyramid of the Sun. Its construction probably occupied 10,000 workers for two decades. Excavations under the smaller Pyramid of the Moon have yielded animal and human skeletal remains, suggesting it functioned as a religious sacrificial space. The Ciudadela was flanked by fifteen low pyramid mounds. Near one end is the Temple of Quetzalcoatl, its incline studded with carved stone projections of the Feathered Serpent and Tlaloc that seem as phantasmic as medieval gargoyles. Linking the Ciudadela and the temple is an underground tunnel (discovered in 2003) that has yielded thousands of artifacts, including statues, jewelry, and obsidian knives.

Teotihuacan must have been a bustling metropolis, teeming with porters carrying goods to the marketplace, laborers erecting temples, artisans busily engaged with their crafts, and here and there the sober presence of the elegant lords. Along the main avenue were various kinds of edifices covered with lime stucco, painted, and polished. Walkways and courts were paved. Of the one hundred palaces, the largest had an estimated three hundred rooms. Some of the salons contained bright frescoes.

The Pyramid of the Sun at Teotihuacan dominates the extensive ruins of the ancient city.

The dominance of Teotihuacan was so extensive that some scholars have discussed it in terms of an empire, believing its hegemony, based in part on its monopoly of obsidian so necessary to daily life and ritual, to have been as broad as that of the later Aztecs. In any event, its trading network reached from parts of northern Mexico down into Guatemala, and artisans from Monte Alban, Mayan city-states, and other distant places resided there, crafting exotic goods. Foreign ambassadors and trade missions occupied special quarters in the city. Undoubtedly heavily influenced by Teotihuacan, nonetheless Monte Alban and the Maya culture remained independent of this metropolitan power. Within its sphere, the impact of that great city consisted not only of its cultural imperialism with respect to art and architecture but also of its religious significance. Although much of what we know about Teotihuacan was transmitted by later cultures who revered it, religion and warfare were central to its governance. Its pantheon of gods included Quetzalcoatl, representing fertility, as well as deities of warfare, sun, rain, and other aspects of nature. According to the later Aztecs, gods had sacrificed themselves at Teotihuacan to sustain the sun, thus initiating their cosmos—the Fifth Sun—that required continuous blood sacrifice.

For some reason, perhaps related to an agricultural debacle, decline set in, inviting incursions on the northern frontier. About AD 650 a weakened Teotihuacan suffered desecration and partial burning—apparently by its own inhabitants. The fall of the mightiest center was the first casualty in the gradual decay of the Classic world in Mexico.

With the Teotihuacano culture dissipated, central Mexico lost its focus. A number of other states emerged but commanded smaller spheres of influence. Cholula in the modern state of

Carved stone images of the rain god Tlaloc and Quetzalcoatl on the Temple of Quetzalcoatl at Teotihuacan.

Puebla was a holy city and a large center of considerable importance. While tradition has it that 365 Christian chapels were later built over the ruins of "pagan" temples, the actual number is closer to 70. The nature of the city's relationship with Teotihuacan is not entirely clear, but it seems to have been close. The center was dominated by its massive pyramid, the largest single monument in pre-Columbian America, with a total volume greater than that of Egypt's Pyramid of Cheops. It was a sanctuary of Quetzalcoatl, and many of the refugees from Teotihuacan fled to Cholula, which continued to flourish until it fell to invaders about AD 800.

Other successor states like Xochicalco in Morelos and Cacaxtla in Puebla were built on mountaintops and manifest the alarming escalation of militarism that developed in Mexico in the Late Classic period. Striking combinations of Teotihuacan and Maya influences are revealed at these sites, nowhere more graphically than in the beautifully painted murals that have been discovered at Cacaxtla since the 1970s.

El Tajín in Veracruz had extensive influence along the Gulf coast. A dramatic example of its unique architecture is the Pyramid of Niches, of which there is one for each day of the year. The vigorous life at Tajín included bloody rites that anticipated the terror of the

Detail of a plumed serpent head. The eyes at one time held red jewels, long since plucked out by vandals.

Post-Classic period. The ball game *ollama* was an ancient tradition that became an obsession with these lowland peoples. Most of the prominent centers in Mexico had ball courts, and Tajín had no fewer than eleven. Along each side of the court (which could vary considerably in length, according to the culture) was a wall on which a stone ring was fixed. Two teams played, the object being to keep the seven to eight-inch solid rubber ball out of the opponents' possession and, if possible, to hit the ball through one of the rings. Scoring was exceedingly difficult, not only because the ring was small and high but also because the players could not hit the ball with their hands. Often they were allowed to use only their hips, although rules differed according to time and place. The athletes wore padding in vulnerable spots as the flying ball could kill if struck with sufficient force. Contests were played with great enthusiasm, and on some occasions large sums were wagered. Ollama was more than a game, however; it was a sacred ritual in imitation of the movement of celestial bodies and associated with human fate. On occasion, the teams represented political factions. So seriously was the contest taken that the losing captain was sometimes sacrificed, as scenes on the architectural friezes depict. In another variation, the losers became slaves of the victors.

Not as well researched and understood are the peoples who created monumental architecture and exquisite artifacts of ceramic, jade, and stone in the Occident (west Mexico, including Nayarit, Jalisco, and Colima). Sharing characteristics and some gods with other prehispanic Mesoamerican cultures, these groups also created distinctive works, including shaft tombs, circular pyramidal structures and plazas, wetland gardens, and copper tools.

And to the north, the cultures and cities that evolved in Zacatecas (Chalchihuites and La Quemada) likewise had Mesoamerican features related to monument-building and warfare, but scholars disagree about their origins and place in regional networks.

MONTE ALBAN

From its lofty eminence 1,300 feet above the valley floor, Monte Alban, the creation of the Zapotecs, dominated surrounding Oaxaca for centuries. Less grand in scale than its contemporary Teotihuacan, it was nevertheless spacious, literally sculpted out of a mountaintop more than 3,000 feet long and half again as wide. Urban construction was carried out at great cost in human effort because all materials, even water, had to be hauled up the mountainsides. Many temples, platforms, and low pyramids, along with sunken patios, stood adjacent to its great paved plaza. Surrounding the center were many separate *barrios* (neighborhoods) of houses terraced into the hillsides. The early evolution of Zapotec urban society at Monte Alban between 500 and 100 BC reflects Olmec-like features. At the top of the social hierarchy that strictly separated nobles and commoners sat a hereditary king and a hereditary high priest. The king controlled noble administrators who ruled the surrounding towns in Oaxaca. By the fourth century, higher population density and military strength had been created through colonization, conquest, and alliance building to bring more distant provinces into Monte Alban's tribute-paying orbit. Skilled diplomacy enabled the Zapotecs to coexist

The Pyramid of Niches, El Tajín, state of Veracruz.

A ball court at Monte Alban. The ball game of ollama (*tlachtli*) was played in many different cultures, although the rules and courts varied somewhat.

peacefully with Teotihuacan, but between AD 400 and 800 Monte Alban lost its dominant position in Oaxaca as subject towns—especially those in more defensible positions and better agricultural locations—grew in size and asserted their autonomy. In decentralized fashion, through Zapotec marriage alliances with neighboring Mixtecs at Mitla, both groups continued to exercise influence in Oaxaca for many centuries, enduring to the present day.

THE MAYA

Although the Maya in the Pacific coastal plain and highland areas created marketing and ceremonial centers with temple architecture as early as 400 BC, their greatest florescence came later, occurring between AD 250 and 800, primarily in the southern lowlands of present-day Yucatán, Guatemala, and Honduras.

The Classic Maya had many important centers, no one of which completely dominated the others. A number of regional states, each composed of a capital city and subject towns, competed with each other, expanding and contracting over time in response to changing fortunes of war and trade. Defeated kingdoms supplied rulers for sacrifice and tribute in goods and slaves to conquering cities. Trade with Teotihuacan was accompanied by bride exchanges and the incorporation of art and architectural styles from this northern neighbor. The Petén in northern Guatemala could be said to be the heartland of the Classic Maya, but they also lived in the Mexican states of Chiapas, Tabasco, Campeche, and Yucatán, as well as in Quintana Roo. The development of Classic Maya centers reflected an increasing emphasis on the lineage of hereditary kings, supported by a noble class of warriors and intellectuals; below them artisans, skilled laborers, and peasant farmers produced the luxury items enjoyed by the aristocracy as well as the basic staples of maize, beans, and vegetables that sustained the entire society. We know much more about the lifestyles of elites who are depicted through a variety of Maya art forms. Their esthetic sensibilities appear in elaborate ornamentation in dress and jewelry (often fashioned from jade), cranial deformation that flattened and slanted the head both front and back, filed teeth, and extensive body tattooing.

For many years, archaeologists believed the lowland Maya cities to have been primarily ceremonial, reasoning that the surrounding jungle could not have supported large populations with slash-and-burn agriculture. Extensive archaeological excavation demonstrated, however, that these areas were densely populated and that the Maya also used raised fields, terracing, and kitchen gardens to augment the production of corn and other foodstuffs. They also utilized plentiful local limestone for building. Like Teotihuacan and Monte Alban, the Maya had a vigorous ceramic tradition and produced lovely polychrome bowls and cylinders that recorded mundane events. In their murals and bas-reliefs, however, they tended less to the geometric designs of central Mexico and more to the depiction of the human form, often rendered with superb draftsmanship. In 2001, archaeologists discovered in the northern Petén what is thought to be the oldest intact Maya mural. Over 2,000 years old, its red, black, and yellow colors depict the resurrection of the corn god and provide clues to the nature of Maya kinship and society. The great fluidity and exuberance of Maya art give it a baroque quality, whether in stone or stucco. Of the fascinating codices, only four survived the ravages of time, climate, insects, and the fires of Spanish clergymen.[2]

The Maya stand as the premier scientists of ancient America, noted for their independent invention of a positional numeration system based on the mathematical concept for zero. Just as impressive were their achievements in calendars and writing. Like other Mexican calendars, theirs had 365 days; in addition, a ceremonial calendar had 260 days. The two calendars coincided every fifty-two years when the cycle of life was believed to be renewed. In 1996 some Maya scholars found an inscribed plaque in southern Mexico that led to the erroneous interpretation that the Mayas had predicted the world would come to an end on December 21, 2012. Of course the date passed without incident, but it had fueled a frenzy of apocalyptic thinking, despite the fact that scholars had carefully explained the reasons why the inscription had been so misinterpreted.[3] It is true that the Maya accurately observed and recorded the movements of celestial bodies to aid in predicting future phenomena, but they did not prophesy the end

---

2   Only about two dozen pre-Columbian codices survive; these are screenfolds made of deerskin, cotton cloth, or bark paper featuring illustrations or hieroglyphic text. They variously include calendrical and other scientific data, prophecies, and information on dieties and rulers. Three of the Maya codices are named after the cities where they are housed: Dresden, Madrid, and Paris. The fourth, the Grolier Codex, long believed to be a fake, was authenticated in 2016 and is the earliest, dating from the thirteenth century.

3   See, for example, Matthew Restall and Amara Solari, *2012 and the End of the World: The Western Roots of the Maya Apocalypse* (Lanham, MD, 2011).

An overview of Monte Alban in Oaxaca, showing its platforms and expansive plazas.

Incised on stone slabs, curious figures who seem to be dancing are a feature of Monte Alban. They are called *danzantes* and are believed to represent the bodies of slain enemies.

Principal Archaeological Sites

of the world. Coincidentally in 2012, another archaeological discovery in a remote corner of northeastern Guatemala revealed wall paintings dating from the ninth century that depict the oldest known Mayan calendar and provide more evidence to counter doomsday fears.

The Maya also inscribed hieroglyphic texts on stone pillars (stelae), facades, and stairways. These inscriptions recorded historical events and were intended to highlight the ancestral privilege of Maya kings (and occasionally queens, probably ruling as regents for minor sons) who were also the incarnation of local sacred knowledge. In ceremonies of self-mutilation, Maya rulers ritually shed blood from their own penis, ear, lips, and tongue, symbolically manifesting the life force that also substantiated their lineage and power. They were particularly obsessed with engraving their triumphs in stone. Recent progress in deciphering Maya writing has revealed that highly learned scribes, responsible for recording these histories, ranked at the highest levels of Maya society.

The extensive pantheon of Maya deities included four lords who held the earth and sky apart at the four cardinal directions. Life had emerged from an underworld of darkness and death due to the sun deity's daily travels through a triple-layered cosmos. Many Maya gods, bearing human or animal attributes, have been identified. They regularly embody the dualism common to Mesoamerican cosmology—that a deity may have both male and female, or both benevolent and malevolent, attributes.

The metropolis of the Maya Classic was Tikal, with a population of about fifty thousand. It is one of the earliest sites, settled in the Formative period long before AD 292, the date of its

In dark hardwood, this unusual carving known as the Mirror Bearer depicts a dignified Maya worthy. It dates from the sixth century.

earliest inscription. Set in a clearing of Guatemala's Petén jungle, Tikal is dominated by six great pyramids, including the tallest of any in the Maya civilization, towering 230 feet. The inner precinct covers more than a square mile, with other ceremonial edifices surrounding the core for a considerable distance. Aside from the usual temples, palaces, plazas, and ball courts, Tikal had ten reservoirs and was beautified by artificial lakes.

The Maya designed their temple-pyramids architecturally and artistically to proclaim the power of the site and glorify the rulers. Their brilliantly decorated masonry, roof combs, statuary, and interior murals exhibit highly sophisticated craftsmanship. The cultural achievements of the Maya, from astronomy and calendars to architecture, art, and writing, were fruits of their understanding and legitimation of a complex cosmic order.

As the largest of the Classic Maya city-states, Tikal and Calakmul were rivals in dominating large areas of the Maya lowlands in which Dos Pilas played an important role. Recent excavations have also highlighted the importance of the affluent trading center of Cancuen on the Pasión River in Guatemala. Other major Classic era kingdoms included Copan in Honduras and Piedras Negras in Guatemala. Yaxchilan, in the modern state of Chiapas, is known for its great central plaza, a thousand feet long. Palenque (Chiapas), though relatively small, is considered the gem of the Maya cities because of its exquisite sculpture. The bas-relief work there shows the art in its highest form. Although of minor importance in most respects, Bonampak (Chiapas) contains the most illustrious of the Maya murals, brilliantly depicting the aftermath of a battle, captives, and sacrifice.

Although central Mexican pyramids are usually solid, without interior chambers, to the south temple-pyramids of the Maya sometimes contain tombs like the one shown here at Palenque's Temple of the Inscriptions.

The Temple of the Sun at Palenque is framed by thick jungle growth.

A superb stucco head with an elegant headdress found at the Temple of the Inscriptions at Palenque.

A pot-bellied, seed-filled ceramic rattle from the Maya culture on the small island of Jaina, off the coast of Campeche.

Of the same Maya culture is this whistle, in the form of an embracing couple.

There may have been no one cause for the decline of Classic Maya centers that began around 750 AD, scattered as they were over considerable distances, although drought seems to have been a key factor. One hypothesis posits climate change and suggests that the Mayas' exploitation of seasonal wetlands may have induced drought and rising temperatures. Explanations have tended to highlight demographic and ecological stress resulting from rapidly growing populations and intensification of agriculture. Population densities may have been as high as six hundred per square mile in some places. It is also possible that commoners rose up in rebellion against increasing demands from their overlords as well as food shortages. But there is growing evidence that warfare—which escalated dramatically in the Late Classic along with human sacrifice—played a significant role. Foreign intrusion from other Maya areas probably capitalized on the instability that prevailed after AD 800. By 900 most of the southern lowland cities were abandoned as many Mayas fled north to the Yucatán Peninsula. Others moved back into the surrounding countryside where they and their descendants have continued to farm for centuries and today number some 20 million people. Their "lost" cities were reclaimed by the jungle until archaeologists began to excavate the lichen-mottled ruins nearly 1,000 years later. Thus, the Classic world in Mesoamerica folded, but in its demise loomed alarming portents of what was to follow.

RECOMMENDED FOR FURTHER STUDY

Adams, Richard E. W., ed. *The Origins of Maya Civilization*. Albuquerque: University of New Mexico Press, 1978.

Bassie-Sweet, Karen. *At the Edge of the World: Caves and Late Classic Maya World View*. Norman: University of Oklahoma Press, 1996.

Bricker, Harvey M., and Victoria R. Bricker. *Astronomy in the Maya Codices*. Philadelphia, PA: American Philosophical Society, 2011.

Coe, Michael D. *Mexico: From the Olmecs to the Aztecs*. London, UK: Thames and Hudson, 1994.

Cowgill, George L. *Ancient Teotihuacan: Early Urbanism in Central Mexico*. New York: Cambridge University Press, 2015.

Culbert, T. P., ed. *The Classic Maya Collapse*. Albuquerque: University of New Mexico Press, 1977.

Doolittle, William E. *Canal Irrigation in Prehistoric Mexico: The Sequence of Technological Change*. Austin: University of Texas Press, 1990.

Fash, William L., and Leonardo López Luján, eds. *The Art of Urbanism: How Mesoamerican Kingdoms Represented Themselves in Architecture and Imagery*. Washington, DC: Dumbarton Oaks Research Library and Collections. Cambridge, MA: Harvard University Press, 2009.

Florescano, Enrique. *The Myth of Quetzalcoatl*. Translated by Lisa Hochroth. Baltimore, MD: Johns Hopkins University Press, 1999.

Foster, Michael S. *Greater Mesoamerica: The Archaeology of West and Northwest Mexico*. Salt Lake City: University of Utah Press, 2010.

Freidel, David, Linda Schele, and Joy Parker. *Maya Cosmos: Three Thousand Years on the Shaman's Path*. New York: William Morrow & Co., 1993.

Graulich, Michel. *Myths of Ancient Mexico*. Norman: University of Oklahoma Press, 1997.

Houston, Stephen D. *The Life Within: Classic Maya and the Matter of Permanence*. New Haven, CT: Yale University Press, 2014.

Houston, Stephen, David Stuart, and Karl Taube. *The Memory of Bones, Body, Being, and Experience among the Classic Maya*. Austin: University of Texas Press, 2007.

Joyce, Arthur A. *Mixtecs, Zapotecs, and Chatinos: Ancient Peoples of Southern Mexico*. Hoboken, NJ: Wiley-Blackwell, 2009.

Joyce, Rosemary. *Gender and Power in Prehispanic Mesoamerica*. Austin: University of Texas Press, 2000.

King, Eleanor M., ed. *The Ancient Maya Marketplace: The Archaeology of Transient Space*. Tucson: University of Arizona Press, 2015.

Kubler, George. *Art and Architecture of Ancient America*. Harmondsworth, UK, and Baltimore, MD: Pelican, 1984.

Marcus, Joyce, and Kent V. Flannery. *Zapotec Civilization: How Urban Society Evolved in Mexico's Oaxaca Valley*. London, UK: Thames and Hudson, 1994.

Miller, Mary Ellen, and Karl Taube. *The Gods and Symbols of Ancient Mexico and the Maya: An Illustrated Dictionary of Mesoamerican Religion*. London, UK: Thames & Hudson, 1993.

Proskouriakoff, Tatiana. *Maya History*. Edited by Rosemary A. Joyce. Austin: University of Texas Press, 1993.

Restall, Matthew, and Amara Solari. *2012 and the End of the World: The Western Roots of the Maya Apocalypse*. Lanham, MD: Rowman & Littlefield, 2011.

Scarborough, Vernon L., and David R. Wilcox. *The Mesoamerican Ballgame*. Tucson: University of Arizona Press, 1991.

Schele, Linda, and David Friedel. *A Forest of Kings: The Untold Story of the Ancient Maya*. New York: William Morrow & Co., 1990.

Sharer, Robert J., ed. *The Ancient Maya*, 6th ed., Stanford, CA: Stanford University Press, 2005.

Stuart, David. *Palenque: Eternal City of the Maya*. London, UK: Thames & Hudson, 2008.

CHAPTER 3

TIMES OF TROUBLE
Post-Classic Mexico

The order imposed by Teotihuacan's dominance during the Classic period gave way to a fragmentation of power among the transition centers in areas north of the Mayas. Our knowledge of the history of the Valley of Mexico between AD 650 and 900 is imprecise, but a high incidence of movement and migration characterized the waning decades of the Classic period, when aggressive city-states—Cholula, Xochicalco, and El Tajín—vied for control, but none succeeded in bringing about unity and order.

The Post-Classic era began about AD 900 and lasted until the Spanish conquest in the early sixteenth century. New states had significant commercial interests, as evidenced by the expansion of market systems. In fact, a key feature of the Post-Classic was the increase of long-distance exchange and the overall economic integration of Mesoamerica. An example of the first, if not the latter, was the far distant regional center at Paquimé/Casas Grandes in northwest Mexico (with links to the US Southwest), where Mesoamerican features and artifacts were manifest. New technology could be seen in cotton quilted armor and the bow and arrow but, in general, technological innovation slowed. Although metallurgy was introduced, its use was limited. The inhabitants fashioned gold and silver into beautiful jewelry, and used copper in the manufacture of various tools and to cover the tips of arrow shafts.

In an even more striking change during the Post-Classic, the militaristic propensities of the Late Classic continued to grow, enhancing the prestige of warriors and fostering the conquest of tribute-paying subjects. Human sacrifice proliferated as both elites and commoners became convinced that only the offering of massive and sustained quantities of the life force of blood to the gods could prevent cosmic disaster.

Another change occurred in the Post-Classic and proved to be a boon for later historians. For this period we have more written records in which individuals appear with more clarity. But although there are now pegs upon which to drape our historical fabric, accounts are manifestly shot through with myths; thus, some details vary with the telling, and many versions are vague and fragmentary at best.

THE TOLTECS

The great city of Teotihuachan, situated in the northeastern part of the valley of Mexico, had served as a buffer between "civilized" Mexico and the nomadic peoples of the north. With the fall of that stronghold, however, vigorous warriors from the arid lands beyond breached the frontier. The northern tribes, consisting of many diverse groups, were known by the generic term *Chichimecs,* a designation that later came to be construed by Spaniards as peoples lacking the culture of settled society and thus "barbaric." Some of these groups were hunter-gathers, but according to legend the more agricultural Tolteca-Chichimeca from southern Zacatecas swept into the central valley at the beginning of the tenth century led by Mixcoatl (Cloud Serpent), a skilled warrior who swiftly scattered his demoralized opponents. After establishing his capital at Culhuacan and successfully extending his power, the resourceful Mixcoatl was assassinated by his brother, who seized leadership for himself. Mixcoatl's pregnant wife fled into exile, where she died upon giving birth to a son. The boy received the name Ce Acatl Topiltzin (Ce Acatl meaning "One Reed," the year of his birth, perhaps AD 947), and he would become the cultural hero of foremost proportions in ancient Mexico. He became a devotee of the ancient god Quetzalcoatl and later, as a high priest of the cult, he assumed the name of his deity.

It is important to note, however, that our knowledge of Toltec history derives primarily from Aztec post-conquest accounts in which Tula figures prominently in their origin myths. The legend of Topiltzin-Quetzalcoatl comes from these sources and includes the idea that this priest-god was of fair complexion and bearded, that he abhorred human sacrifice, and that he had left cross-like signs along his journey of exile. Many scholars question the reliability of these stories recorded after the conquest by Aztec elites, working with Spanish priests. Their interpretations served to explain the conquest as preordained by a Christian god.

The legend asserts that upon reaching manhood, Topiltzin-Quetzalcoatl killed in single combat his uncle, Mixcoatl's assassin, and made himself lord of the Toltecs. Topiltzin-Quetzalcoatl eventually removed his capital some fifty miles northwest of the present Mexico City to an area of obsidian deposits. There, around AD 968, he founded the splendid city of Tula (Tollan), the most important urban center in the long interim between the fall of Teotihuacan and the later rise of Aztec Tenochtitlan. The Toltecs continued to incorporate northern nomads and gradually absorbed more urban Mesoamerican characteristics. From their new capital they played a key role in the obsidian trade, used for making blades and other tools, and asserted power over the surrounding area. Although their limited hegemony lasted only about two centuries, their prestige was such that the name "Toltec" pervaded the consciousness of the land for five hundred years.

Less extensive in area and population (40–60,000) than Teotihuacan, Tula was certainly more grandiose than its ruins today indicate. The brilliant plumage of exotic birds decked palace interiors, sheets of gold, jewels, and rare seashells lined various salons. Residents' ears were soothed by the sweet singing of pet birds. This version of paradise on earth was embellished in the retelling over the centuries; it accounts, in part, for the curiously persistent Toltec mystique.

The honeyed tradition notwithstanding, all was not peace and light at Tula. Two religious traditions evolved in the period of Toltec rule, emblematic of conflict in Mesoamerican society. The ancestral supreme deity of the Toltecs was the fearsome and unpredictable

Tezcatlipoca or Smoking Mirror because of his association with obsidian, as well as the night sky and fate. His adherents resented the exaltation of the foreign god Quetzalcoatl (associated with knowledge and creativity) introduced by Topiltzin. The deity-impersonator priests of Tezcatlipoca bided their time, conspiring against the heresy.

They sought by various deceits to discredit the high priest of Quetzalcoatl. According to one account, Tezcatlipoca, in disguise, gained entrance to the house of Topiltzin, who was ill. At first the ruler refused an offer of "medicine," which was, in fact, the strong drink of pulque, made from undistilled cactus juice. Finally persuaded to take a sip, the innocent Topiltzin found it pleasing and asked for more. At length inebriated by five cupfuls, the lord of Tula awoke the next morning on a mat beside his sister. Having broken his priestly vows and disgraced himself by the sins of drunkenness and incest, he prepared to go into exile after almost twenty years of enlightened rule.

The reign of Topiltzin-Quetzalcoatl at Tula thus came to a close, but he does not disappear from history. He and his followers dispersed to the south, some remaining in the holy city of Cholula and others continuing on to Maya areas around 987. One legend relates that Topiltzin-Quetzalcoatl coasted down a river to the sea in a raft of serpents, after which he flashed into the heavens to become the morning star.

Another account had more serious, actually ominous, implications. When Topiltzin and his partisans left Tula for their long odyssey, they marked their way by shooting arrows through saplings, leaving signs that resembled crosses. Later he sent word that he would return from where the sun rose to take back his rightful throne in the year Ce Acatl, which recurred cyclically. By some accounts, he was of fair complexion and bearded. All of this would be of immense significance when, five centuries later, the Spaniards appeared on the eastern horizon. The year was 1519—and Ce Acatl.

Meanwhile, with the success of the militant Tezcatlipoca faction at Tula, a new order of things evolved. While the reputation of the Toltecs as great architects was secure (the Aztecs

The ingenuous Topiltzin-Quetzalcoatl is deceived by the crafty Tezcatlipoca.

Giant stone warriors at Tula were manifestations of the militaristic spirit that came to dominate the Toltecs.

named them Toltecs, meaning "Artificers"), a new and grotesque image of them was revealed in later works. Themes of death and destruction are evident in the Chacmools—reclining human figures with basins on their stomachs to receive human hearts—and a "serpent wall" that shows rattlesnakes devouring human skeletons. Towering statues of impassive warrior figures, sixteen to eighteen feet tall, appeared on top of temples, and friezes symbolized the military orders of the jaguar and eagle, the latter shown devouring human hearts. Tula nourished two traditions that persisted until the coming of the Spaniards—an excess of human sacrifice and the forceful conquest of other states. Yet many questions persist about the size and nature of the alleged Toltec "empire."

From the late eleventh century to 1156, drought and famine struck the Toltecs. Wars and internal social conflict further weakened the state until, in desperation, the people even turned to the worship of their enemies' alien deities. Evidence of fire throughout the site may explain the onset of the Toltec diaspora, with people spreading in many directions. The collapse of Tula was significant for Mexico: once again the northern buffer zone between the sedentary peoples of the valley and the northern semi-nomads remained unguarded. Not long after, new groups descended upon this wonder of the Post-Classic world and subjected Tula to brutal desecration.

THE ZAPOTECS AND MIXTECS

To the south, following the abandonment of Monte Alban in Oaxaca, the Zapotecs remained a vigorous culture with many important centers including their capital at Zaachila. Mitla, built at roughly the same time as Tula, was a comparatively small religious and military base. What one sees there, however, is a jewel of Mexican architecture. Surrounding a modest courtyard are white temples with walls of marvelous design—thousands of small pieces of cut stone, fitted together with a precision requiring no mortar, form mosaics of dazzling geometric patterns. Opening off the patios are subterranean passages leading to crypts. Although the site occupies an exposed area, set apart some distance is the hill fortress, a grim reminder of the intense warfare that had overtaken Post-Classic Mexico.

To the areas west and north of the Zapotecs were a remarkable people who inhabited the mountainous regions, the Mixtecs, or "Cloud People." The Mixtecs were certainly influenced by the Toltecs, some of whom apparently infiltrated after the fall of Tula. By the thirteenth century the Mixtecs penetrated eastward into Zapotec territories, and, primarily by marrying into the Zapotec royalty, they eventually came to dominate their neighbors. At times they occupied many of the Zapotec sites, including Monte Alban and Mitla.

Mixtec artistic achievements are extraordinary in the exquisite decoration of their temple complexes. Among the treasures they gave us is the richest collection extant of picture *códices*, for example the Selden Codex. These pictographic books are executed in brilliant colors on deerskin (the books of the Maya and others were made of both deer skin and vegetable fiber). They offer valuable historical sources that chronicle centuries of conquering dynasties, genealogies, and warfare. Following the appearance of metallurgy around AD 1000, the Mixtecs became, in addition, the foremost jewelers in Mexico, fashioning delicate pieces in gold and silver.

A palace at Mitla.

Detail of the palace showing the intricate geometric designs formed by precision stone cutting.

THE POST-CLASSIC MAYA

Coincident with the final disintegration of the Maya Classic period by around AD 900, a rising Maya cultural phenomenon appeared on the peninsula of Yucatán. That peninsula is a limestone shelf, flat with some rolling, brush-covered hills, a land without surface rivers. With its thin soil and dependence for water on the *cenotes*, the sinkholes created by the collapse of underground caverns, it seems an unlikely location for an agricultural people. Maya groups had inhabited Yucatán for many centuries BC, but their achievements had not matched those of the southern Maya who flourished during the Classic era.

Beginning in the tenth century, the ancestral Yucatec Maya culture was transformed by outside influences of peoples stigmatized as "foreigners." Some of the newcomers were undoubtedly refugees from the deserted Classic areas. The invigorating force that gave impulse to the new hybrid style in Yucatán appears to have been Toltec, but the nature of the relationship between Tula and the dominant early Post-Classic center of Chichen Itza is still disputed. One explanation holds that the banished Topiltzin-Quetzalcoatl and his followers actually made it to Chichen Itza in 987 and imposed Toltec rule. Others believe that the northern attributes may have been brought earlier by coastal Putun and Chontal Maya invaders who had been heavily influenced by non-Maya cultures of the Gulf coast and central Mexico.

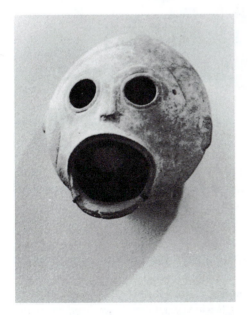

This unusual ceramic vessel, created in the Classic Period, is in the form of a stylized monkey wearing a startled expression.

A Mixtec vase from Zaachila. Representations of death were and still are common and are often treated lightly.

Zapotec bat god (Dios Murciélago).

From about 900 to 1150, Chichen Itza allied with the cities of Mayapan and Uxmal, although it dominated the alliance as a result of its successes in trade and military exploits. Warfare and human sacrifice were common, but whether they actually increased as a result of central Mexican influence is unknown. Certainly these practices were already widespread among the Yucatecan Mayas' neighbors to the south in the Late Classic. The art and architecture of Chichen Itza evoke the militant spirit of Tula with warrior motifs, images of the Feathered Serpent, the forest of columns, and Chacmools. Among the monuments of Post-Classic Maya centers, those of Chichen Itza are the most widely known. Like the sculptures, they are esthetically less pleasing than works of the Classic Maya. Uxmal, however, has structures of great beauty. Many consider its Palace of the Governor to be the most elegant of prehispanic architecture.

During the period of Toltec influence, curious Chacmool figures appeared at Chichen Itza.

Mesoamerican influence promoted the inclusion of Quetzalcoatl (called "Kukulcan" by the Maya) in the pantheon of local deities. Among the most important were the fire god Itzamna, the rain god Chac, and the gods of corn and the sun. Into the great Sacred Cenote, a well measuring some two hundred feet across at the mouth, victims (although infrequently the virgins so dear to modern tradition) were cast, along with jewels and other valuables, to appease the rain god. Although ritual practices remained strong, religious elites began to lose political and cultural influence to rising merchants engaging in a wider variety of commodity trading.

By the end of the eleventh century, Chichen Itza fell from dominance, due in part to environmental factors. Eventually in the twelfth century, Mayapan, in the interior north of the Yucatán peninsula, rose to fill the void. A mercantile emphasis characterized this shift, overshadowing esthetic endeavors undertaken in earlier Mayan cities. A new area of burgeoning trade (e.g. salt, cacao, cotton) in Caribbean and Gulf coast areas commenced and persisted until the arrival of the Spaniards. Mayapan fell around 1450, after suffering drought, plagues, and hurricanes. Over time, environmental factors and warfare compromised agrarian

A great ball court in the Maya style at Chichen Itza. Scores were seldom made by knocking the ball through the high ring. This city had six ball courts, one of which, the largest in Mesoamerica, measures 480 by 120 feet.

sustainability and political stability in the absence of new technologies, but changes varied across time and region from Yucatán to the south.

Elsewhere, in the highland Maya areas of Guatemala, other groups had established kingdoms. Their Quiche and Cakchiquel warriors would pose a formidable challenge to conquering Spaniards in the sixteenth century. The newest interlopers in Maya areas might well have been seen as the latest variation on an older, cyclical pattern of conquest. At any rate, arriving Spaniards found few vestiges of former Maya grandeur, but rather decentralized polities and villages in which merchants still traded and commoners continued their familiar traditions of maize cultivation, family rituals, and community life. When we refer to the collapse of Maya "civilization," we must remember that Mayas number some 7 million people today.

Detail of the carved stone ring.

A heavily padded Maya ball player is portrayed in this graceful sculpture from Jaina.

A reconstruction of Chichen Itza shows the broad thoroughfare leading from the Temple of Kukulcan to the Sacred Cenote (well).

The Temple of Kukulcan, also known as "El Castillo."

Despite their amazing skills, the Maya architects never developed the true arch; however, a corbeled vault of the type pictured here served much the same purpose. This is the magnificent Palace of the Governor at Uxmal, measuring more than 320 feet in length and 25 feet in height.

RECOMMENDED FOR FURTHER STUDY

Blomster, Jeffrey, ed. *After Monte Albán: Transformation and Negotiation in Oaxaca, Mexico.* Boulder: University Press of Colorado, 2008.

Byland, Bruce E., and John M.D. Pohl. *In the Realm of Eight Deer: The Archeology of Mixtec Codices.* Norman: University of Oklahoma Press, 1994.

Diehl, Richard A. *Tula: The Toltec Capital of Ancient Mexico.* London, UK: Thames and Hudson, 1983.

Flannery, Kent V., and Joyce Marcus. *The Creation of Inequality: How Our Prehistoric Ancestors Set the Stage for Monarchy, Slavery, and Empire*. Cambridge, MA: Harvard University Press, 2012.

Flannery, Kent V., and Joyce Marcus, eds. *The Cloud People: Divergent Evolution of the Zapotec and Mixtec Civilizations*. New York: Academic Press, 1983.

Fox, John W. *Maya Postclassic State Formation*. New York: Cambridge University Press, 1987.

Kelemen, Pál. *Art of the Americas, Ancient and Hispanic*. New York: Crowell, 1969.

López Austin, Alfredo. *The Myth of Quetzalcoatl: Religion, Rulership, and History in the Nahua World*. Translated by Ruth Davidson with Guilhem Olivier. Boulder: University Press of Colorado 2015.

Masson, Marilyn, and Carlos Peraza Lope. *Kukulcan's Realm: Urban Life at Ancient Mayapán*. Boulder: University Press of Colorado, 2014.

Mastache, A. G., Robert Cobean, and Dan Healan. *Ancient Tollan: Tula and the Toltec Heartland*. Boulder: University Press of Colorado, 2002.

Minnis, Paul E., and Michael E. Whalen, eds. *Ancient Paquimé and the Casas Grandes World*. Tucson: University of Arizona Press, 2015.

Monaghan, John. *The Covenants of Earth and Rain: Exchange, Sacrifice, and Revelation in Mixtec Sociality*. Norman: University of Oklahoma Press, 1995.

Robertson, Donald. *Mexican Manuscript Painting of the Early Colonial Period*. Norman: University of Oklahoma Press, 1994.

Sabloff, Jeremy. *Archaeology Matters: Action Archaeology in the Modern World*. Walnut Creek, CA: Left Coast Press, 2008.

Sanders, William T., Jeffrey R. Parsons, and Robert S. Santley. *The Basin of Mexico: Ecological Processes in the Evolution of a Civilization*. New York: Academic Press, 1979.

Schroeder, Susan. *Chimalpahin and the Kingdom of Chalco*. Tucson: University of Arizona Press, 1991.

Sharer, Robert J. *Daily Life in Maya Civilization*. Westport, CT: Greenwood Press, 1996.

Smith, Michael E., and Frances F. Berdan, eds. *The Postclassic Mesoamerican World*. Salt Lake City: University of Utah Press, 2003.

Spores, Ronald. *The Mixtecs in Ancient and Colonial Times*. Norman: University of Oklahoma Press, 1985.

Thompson, J. Eric S. *The Rise and Fall of Maya Civilization*. Norman: University of Oklahoma Press, 1966.

CHAPTER 4

THE RISE OF THE AZTECS

The high Valley of Anahuac—the Indian name for the Valley of Mexico, meaning "near the water"—was a compelling lure to wandering peoples seeking a more abundant life. With its equable climate and system of interconnecting lakes bordered by forests full of wild game, it was especially attractive to the nomads of the arid north. Because of its central location, the valley had been, from ancient times, a corridor through which tribes of diverse cultures passed—and sometimes remained. This cultural mélange produced a rich environment for the exchange of ideas and skills. Moreover, traders and merchants introduced exotic products from the coasts and other regions, thereby adding to the variety of life. At the same time, frequently hostile alien groups periodically upset the lake country with violence. In the twelfth century, new city-states developed in the Valley of Mexico, interacting with each other, sometimes peacefully, sometimes aggressively. Throughout Mesoamerica, the links between polities multiplied in shifting relationships of exchange and political domination. In this network, central Mexico occupied the most influential position.

AZTEC PREDECESSORS

With the power vacuum created by the collapse of Tula in the twelfth century, several groups of Nahuatl-speaking Chichimecs entered the valley from the north. By the early thirteenth century the valley teemed with activity and became increasingly crowded. It was an age of anxiety and tension. The first invader groups quickly staked out their claims, and later arrivals found little available space. The early Chichimecs settled in the proximity of established towns populated by remnants of Toltec refugees whose culture retained more complex Mesoamerican features. The phenomenon so familiar in history occurred: the recently arrived hunter-gatherers gradually adopted the more advanced ways of their sedentary neighbors.

Most prominent of the early invader chieftains was Xolotl (Divine Dog), who arrived with his people in 1244. These Chichimecs established themselves at Tenayuca and came to dominate this northern part of the valley through aggressive warfare based on the use of the bow and arrow. Under Xolotl (1244–1304), the crude northerners adopted features of the surrounding sedentary towns, imitating their dwellings, clothing, and agricultural practices. In 1246, they conquered the prestigious city of Colhuacan, and Xolotl married his son No-paltzin (Revered Prickly Pear) to a princess of the vanquished Toltecs. As their standing grew, their Nahuatl language was becoming the *lingua franca* of the valley.

The Tepanecs, other invaders who had arrived in the valley in 1230, recognized Xolotl as overlord. For their service as mercenaries, the Tepanecs received land grants enabling them to extend their influence from their capital of Atzcapotzalco on the western side of Lake Texcoco. The key figure of Tepanec expansion was Tezozomoc who made Atzcapotzalco the most powerful center in the valley in the fourteenth century. Employing deceit, dynastic marriages, violence, and treachery, this tyrant expanded Tepanec territory with the conquests of Tenayuca, Colhuacan, Xochimilco, and Cuauhnahuac (now Cuernavaca). Tezozomoc vanquished the city of Texcoco in the early 15fifteenth century and brutally skewered its ruler Ixtilzochitl with spears in full view of his young son, Nezahualcoyotl (Hungry Coyote), who was concealed in a tree. Through the politics of terror, the Tepanecs broadened their sovereignty in the valley.

THE AZTEC RISE TO POWER

The irruption of the Chichimecs from the arid north included one group that engages our attention above all others. While they called themselves the *Mexica* (pronounced "May-sheeka"), they have become more commonly known as the Aztecs. No tribe of record had more humble beginnings and rose to such heights in so short a time. Over the long view of prehispanic Mexico, they must be regarded as upstarts, latecomers on the scene. The last of the important nomadic groups to enter the valley, they began to acquire some notoriety about two hundred years prior to the Spanish conquest, but their rise to great power occurred less than a century before the advent of Cortés in 1519.

The origins of the Aztecs are apparently found on an island they called Aztlan, somewhere to the northwest of the valley, from which many tribes wandered southward. Historical accounts for the first decades following their departure from Aztlan, evidently in AD 1111, are fragmentary and unreliable for, once secure, the Aztecs destroyed all the records and reconstructed their history with accounts favorable to themselves. Like other Nahua groups who entered the valley before them, the Aztecs eventually evolved official histories linking their migration stories with marriages that established (however spuriously) their prestigious Toltec connections.

The Aztecs' great search for the promised land logically enough led them toward the verdant intermontane basin of Anahuac, but they arrived there only after many decades of wandering. Somewhere along the way they came to conceive of themselves as a messianic people, the chosen of the gods. They pressed on, inspired by visions of their imperial destiny and by the persistent twitterings of their strange hummingbird god. Their supreme deity was Huitzilopochtli (hummingbird on the left), god of war who slew his sister Coyolxauhqui after she killed their mother, Coatlicue. He then proceeded to devour Coatlicue's heart.

At length these nomads made their way into the Valley of Mexico, where they found a cold reception. To begin with, other groups had already carved up all the lands into various city-states, and perceived the Aztecs as unwelcome squatters, a boorish, uncouth lot, disposed to all sorts of vulgarities. Held in disdain, the more refined farming residents of the valley encouraged the newcomers to keep moving. It seems as if the Aztecs purposely sought to anger others with some repugnant habits (which included gruesome human sacrifices) and their outrageous practice of stealing their neighbors' wives. But however much the interlopers repulsed the farming peoples of the valley, they also learned (sometimes the hard way) to entertain a healthy respect for them. The Aztecs were a young, vigorous people, hungry and ambitious. They were also superb warriors, whose fighting abilities did not go unnoticed by the ruling warlords of the valley. Consequently, it was as allies exploiting the tenuous balance of power in Anahuac that the Aztecs first achieved recognition.

From the 1270s to the year 1319 the Aztecs maintained a precarious existence, occupying the hill of Chapultepec (now a park in Mexico City). They continued in their aggressive ways, and the leaders of some of the principal towns decided to deal with them once and for all. They drove the intruders from Chapultepec and sacrificed the Aztec chief and his daughter. The survivors escaped by concealing themselves in the rushes along the lakeshore until it was safe to come out.

Now subject to Coxcox (Pheasant), the ruler of Colhuacan, the Aztecs received some land to settle. But what land! They found themselves living in a gully acrawl with rattlesnakes, no doubt to the amusement of their enemies. But, according to legend, the Aztecs liked rattlesnake meat, and they devoured the vipers with gusto. Still, it was not the promised land, and the restless Aztecs bided their time. Their chance came when Coxcox agreed to give them their liberty and better land in exchange for assistance in a war against the town of Xochimilco. Aztec leaders delivered to the shocked Coxcox proof of their deeds—sacks containing 8,000 ears cut from the slain Xochimilcas.

Although the king of Colhuacan hastily gave them their freedom, the Aztecs did not go away. They asked the Colhua lord for his daughter, who would be made the Aztec queen and would be treated as a goddess. Coxcox unwittingly agreed, whereupon the Aztecs, in a move calculated to assert independence from their overlords, sacrificed and flayed the princess. When her father attended the banquet in his honor, he was horrified to find that the entertainment included a priest-dancer dressed in the skin of his daughter. Having finally had enough, Coxcox raised an army that scattered the Aztecs, who took refuge once more among the reeds of the lake.

Again the Aztecs showed their adaptability and turned the situation to their advantage. They found that in the marshy edges of the lake no one bothered them, for the place was considered unsuitable for dwelling. It was, however, a region abundant in waterfowl, fish, and other edible creatures. Furthermore, it was of some strategic placement, located at a point where three kingdoms merged. Huddled in those swamps, the dogged Aztecs drew on their resources and, finding strength and unity in adversity, they stiffened their resolve.

Unmolested, in about 1325 the Aztecs occupied a small isle, counseled by the prophecy of Huitzilopochtli that attributed significance to a place where an eagle with a serpent in its beak perched on a cactus. They began to acquire, through trade, the materials they needed to enlarge their foothold, and they dredged the lake bottom to form more surface soil. From such inauspicious beginnings, and with considerable ingenuity and great labor,

The founding of the Aztec capital of Tenochtitlan, as depicted in the Codex Mendoza.

they eventually created the great city of Tenochtitlan. From that island redoubt they later built connecting causeways, which could easily be defended, to the mainland. It was an inspired defensive concept, flawed only by the eventual dependence on mainland Chapultepec for drinking water. Aqueducts conveying water could be cut.

Meanwhile the furious activity of the Aztecs and the development of the island came to the attention of Tezozomoc, the Tepanec strongman of Anahuac, who brought them under his sway and used them in their traditional role of mercenaries. Tezozomoc made unreasonable demands of tribute from the Aztecs, and even humiliated them, but he was astute enough not to push them too far. Gradually he accepted them as minor partners and eventually allowed Tenochtitlan to establish a royal dynasty. In 1377, the young Acamapichtli became ruler of the Aztecs. By the time Tezozomoc finally died, in 1426, the Aztecs, his apt disciples, were flourishing.

About this time the Aztecs elected as their leader Itzcoatl (Obsidian Snake), whose energetic rule led to Aztec independence and the expansion of trade. Following a power struggle in 1428, Tenochtitlan allied itself with the *altepetl* (city states) of Texcoco and the weaker Tlacopan against the Tepanecs. This Triple Alliance would soon control central Mexico. Izcoatl's reign firmly established Huitzilopochtli, Quetzalcoatl, and Tezcatlipoca as the supreme Mexica deities.

THE AZTEC EMPIRE

Although the feverish drive of the Aztecs ultimately carried them to dominance of the alliance, Texcoco maintained its position of equality for some time. To considerable extent Texcoco's strength was owing to the brilliance of Nezahualcoyotl (Hungry Coyote, ruled 1418–72), one of the most remarkable figures in the history of Mexico. While so many are remembered for their military exploits, the illustrious Nezahualcoyotl commands attention for his cultural refinement. A man of his times, he steadily increased his influence through military force, but he had esthetic sensibilities as well. Renowned for his philosophical verse, this "poet king of Texcoco" embodied the talents of a wise legislator and a principled judge. In addition, he was an engineer who was instrumental in the construction of a great aqueduct, which brought water to Tenochtitlan from the mainland, and of a long dike across the lake. A scholar and bibliophile, his Texcoco, "the Athens of Anahuac," had libraries housing thousands of manuscripts, which tragically Spaniards later destroyed. The city, with its gardens, royal baths, and beautiful temples represented the finest expression of culture in an age otherwise marred by cruelty, intrigue, and almost constant warfare. When Nezahualcoyotl died, in 1472, his son Nezahualpilli, who had many of his father's qualities, became ruler of Texcoco. But the city came increasingly under the influence of Tenochtitlan.

After Itzcoatl died, in 1440, his nephew, Moctezuma I (Moctezuma Ilhuicamina) became sovereign of the Aztecs. Even before taking power, Moctezuma had become a prominent general, and during his reign of twenty-eight years he launched his armies to smashing victories as the Aztec dominions were extended to the south and northeast. Beyond this explosive growth of territory and tribute, the Aztec state took on more formal characteristics and began to achieve remarkable cohesion. At the same time, a genuine Aztec art style evolved as one manifestation of the extension of imperial ambitions.

A population explosion fueled by in-migration of other groups had begun in the valley in the mid-fourteenth century, leading to an intensification of agriculture. This expansion was followed by plagues and floods in the middle of the fifteenth century that produced catastrophic famine. After several years of near-starvation, during which increasing resort to human sacrifice failed to placate the gods, Aztec rulers promoted chinampa agriculture and sought to expand their control over fertile lands. Moctezuma I's successor, Axayacatl (1469–81), conquered new provinces, gaining control of transport routes and towns

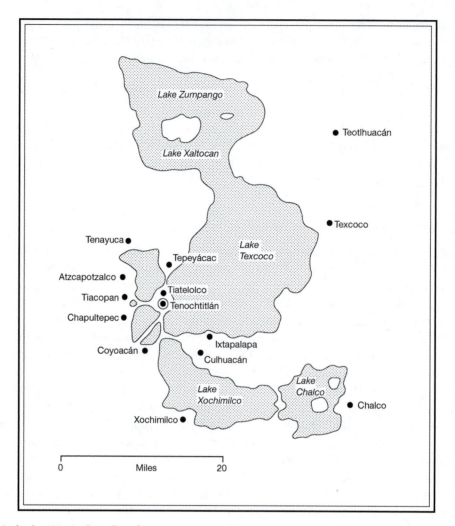

Principal Lake Cities in the Valley of Mexico during the Aztec Period

required to pay tribute. A brave leader who fought furiously alongside his common soldiers, Axayacatl lost a leg in one of his battles. He successfully brought neighboring Tlatelolco with its great marketplace under Mexica control, but failed to conquer the Tarascan
empire to the west, forcing him to build border fortifications to keep the enemy at bay. He
was succeeded by his brother Tizoc, whose lack of military success was accompanied by a
loss of tributaries.

Under the leadership of of Tizoc's successor Ahuitzotl, the great warrior king, from 1487
to 1502, the Aztecs conquered the valley of Oaxaca and pushed far down the Pacific coast
to Soconusco. In the first year of his reign, Ahuitzotl oversaw the dedication of an impressive new temple erected to honor the god Huitzilopochtli. In a ceremony lasting four days
sacrificial victims taken during campaigns were formed in four columns, each stretching

This sculpture of a female deity is reflected in an Aztec obsidian mirror with a wooden frame.

three miles. By some estimates, as many as twenty thousand human hearts were torn out to please the god. Prominent guests, selected from allies and tributary towns, were invited to be impressed (and intimidated) by the might and glory of Tenochtitlan. In the frenzy of this ghastly pageant, exhaustion finally overcame the priests. The militant reign of Ahuitzotl, with its pageants of political terror, closed in 1502 when he accidentally struck his head on a stone lintel while trying to escape a flood.[1]

By this time, the Aztec yoke included several hundred city-states or ethnic kingdoms with varied arrangements in tribute obligations. While a city-state, or altepetl, acquiesced to Aztec tutelage in a material sense, its inhabitants retained a sense of cultural or ethnic distinctiveness, grounded in their singular tribal migration history and leadership. Recent study has suggested that the impressive expansion of Aztec hegemony in the first half of the fifteenth century was masterminded by Tlacaelel, who advised his brother Moctezuma I and succeeding rulers. Depicted in native histories written after the conquest as brave, but also cunning, unscrupulous, and brutal, Tlacaelel served as a strategist for building Aztec political power and military dominance through the expansion of warfare and human sacrifice.

---

1 In 2007, Mexican archaeologists reported the possible discovery of Ahuitzotl's tomb in the Templo Mayor complex, under a stone monolith representing the Aztec earth deity, Tlaltecuhtli, symbol of the Aztec life and death cycle. Such a significant find would be the first of its kind since Aztec kings were believed to have been cremated. The discovery revealed many exquisite offerings fit for a king. Subsequent excavations in the Templo Mayor have uncovered sacrificial stones and mass burials, but not that of Ahuitzotl.

A fine example of Aztec stone sculpture.

The central basin of Mexico was firmly under Aztec control, but in some areas of the center and south where the Aztecs had won military victories, for example, in Oaxaca, rebellions by Mixtec and Zapotec city-states erupted frequently. Even closer to home, several mountainous zones to the east and south harbored independent states—most notably that of Tlaxcala. And to the west, the Tarascans never succumbed to Aztec domination.

The Tarascan empire comprised a score of city-states in the modern state of Michoacán, with its capital at Tzinztuntzan on Lake Pátzcuaro. By trading with areas along the Pacific coast and becoming highly militarized, the Tarascans built a strong state capable of resisting the Aztecs. After Axayacatl's army was soundly defeated in 1479 by a large Tarascan force relying heavily on archery and some copper weapons, the Aztecs pulled back from frontal assaults on the Tarascan empire.

The independent state of Tlaxcala was founded by one of the early Chichimec tribes in the region east of the mountains lining the Valley of Mexico. At various times the Tlaxcalans were allies of the Aztecs, but the relationship became increasingly hostile as Tlaxcala forged a confederacy with several other city-states and strengthened its army with mercenary soldiers from areas defeated by the Aztecs. In addition to preserving autonomy, the Tlaxcalans wanted to keep the Aztecs from taking over their trade in salt, cotton, and other items with the Gulf coast. The Aztecs seem to have been content to try to keep the Tlaxcalans isolated and to engage them in periodic low-intensity warfare designed to wear them down and to obtain sacrificial victims.

Known as "Flower Wars," these battles, also practiced with other hostile states, came to form the main basis of the relationship between Aztecs and Tlaxcalans. A culture of war was not new to Mesoamerica, but the Aztecs had taken it to unprecedented levels. Warfare had two main purposes: to increase the number of tribute-payers and to obtain captives for sacrifice. Neither objective would be served by killing large numbers of foes in battle. As the Aztecs' hold on key areas intensified, Flower Wars with recalcitrant city-states provided the opportunity for the revered class of warriors to gain experience and to show their superiority. Military orders such as the jaguar and eagle knights accumulated prestige in these ritualized battles and obtained brave prisoners to be offered to the gods. Although these ceremonial engagements took place by invitation, the contests between Tlaxcalans and Aztecs only fed their enmity—a fact that would have ominous consequences with the arrival of the Spaniards in 1519.

In 1502 the ill-starred Moctezuma II was elected to succeed Ahuitzotl. He reigned as the most absolute of Aztec lords, governing with great authority and enjoying the deference due a demigod. Educated to be a high priest, he later proved his valor on the field of battle. Under his reign, further expansion of the empire was hindered by the Tarascans on the west while the vast, sparsely populated north promised little reward. And, in the Maya lowlands to the south a weakly developed market system meant that tribute would be difficult to exact. Moctezuma II tried with limited success to wipe out pockets of resistance in mountainous areas and to consolidate control within the empire, but social unrest and internal conflicts may have been eroding the loose bonds holding the realm together. Nevertheless, in the bustling, well-organized metropolis of Tenochtitlan where commerce and artistic endeavors flourished, the emperor lived in splendor for seventeen years. Then, quite suddenly, the Aztec world was turned upside down.

RECOMMENDED FOR FURTHER STUDY

Berdan, Frances F., et al. *Aztec Imperial Strategies.* Washington, DC: Dumbarton Oaks, 1993.

Caso, Alfonso. *The Aztecs: People of the Sun.* Norman: University of Oklahoma Press, 1958.

Clendinnen, Inga. *Aztecs: An Interpretation.* New York: Cambridge University Press, 1991.

Durán, Fray Diego. *The Aztecs: The History of the Indians of New Spain.* Translated, with notes, by Doris Heyden and Fernando Horcasitas. New York Orion Press, 1964.

Gillespie, Susan D. *The Aztec Kings: The Construction of Rulership in Mexican History.* Tucson: University of Arizona Press, 1989.

Hassig, Ross. "Aztec and Spanish Conquest in Mesoamerica." In *War in the Tribal Zone: Expanding States and Indigenous Warfare,* edited by R. Brian Ferguson and Neil L. Whitehead, 83–102. Santa Fe, NM: School of American Research, 1992.

Hodge, Mary G., and Michael E. Smith, eds. *Economies and Polities in the Aztec Realm.* Austin: University of Texas Press, 1993.

León Portilla, Miguel. *The Aztec Image of Self and Society: An Introduction to Nahua Culture,* edited by José Jorge Klor de Alva. Salt Lake City: University of Utah Press, 1992.

Matos Moctezuma, Eduardo. *The Great Temple of the Aztecs*. New York: Thames and Hudson, 1988.

Padden, Robert C. *The Hummingbird and the Hawk: Conquest and Sovereignty in the Valley of Mexico, 1503–1541*. New York: Harper Collins, 1988.

Sahagún, Bernardino de. *Florentine Codex: General History of the Things of New Spain*. Translated by Arthur J. O. Anderson and Charles E. Dibble, 13 parts. Salt Lake City and Santa Fe, NM: University of Utah Press and School of American Research, 1950–82.

Schroeder, Susan. "The Mexico that Spain Encountered." In *The Oxford History of Mexico*, edited by Michael C. Meyer and William H. Beezley, 45–72. New York: Oxford University Press, rev. 2010.

_____. *Tlacaelel Remembered: Mastermind of the Aztec Empire*. Norman: University of Oklahoma Press, 2016.

Smith, Michael E. *The Aztecs*, 3rd ed. Hoboken, NJ: Wiley-Blackwell, 2011.

CHAPTER 5

AZTEC SOCIETY AND CULTURE

It is one of the paradoxes of history that violence and artistic development are entirely compatible within the same society; brutality coexists with refinement and justice. Aztec society offers a good case in point. We have seen the emergence of a state committed to a policy of war and a cosmovision that demanded blood sacrifice; it is also true that Aztec society and culture embodied some remarkably enlightened codes of conduct and justice, sensitive accomplishments in the arts, an orderly administration, and behavior that was uniquely puritanical in outlook. In many respects it constituted civilization of the highest order.

AZTEC RELIGION

The mutually reinforcing relationship between Aztec cosmology and imperial policy bears examination. Aztec ideology certainly incorporated long-standing aspects of Mesoamerican religions, but it is probable that fifteenth-century rulers added political considerations recasting migration history and myth in order to facilitate and legitimate their conquests. The Aztec rationale for human sacrifice had its origin in a cosmic view that encompassed the demands of their god Huitzilopochtli, lord of the sun and god of war, as well as a myth of solar struggle. They believed that the sun and earth had been destroyed in a cataclysm and recreated four times and that, in their age of the fifth sun, final destruction was imminent. That fate was, understandably, to be avoided as long as possible, and the Aztecs believed that special intervention through Huitzilopochtli would serve their interests.

Furthermore, the Aztecs accepted the view of a natural cycle: the sun, along with the rain, nourished the plant life that sustained human life; therefore humans should give sustenance to the sun and rain gods. Ancient deities had sacrificed themselves to the sun, and mere mortals could hardly decline the same honor. The highest expression of piety was the giving of life itself, and captured warriors, women, children, and slaves were the most valuable of these gifts. In practice, the ritual offering to the sun god involved the removal of a palpitating human heart for presentation to Huitzilopochtli. Without such expressions of reverence,

A temple is burned in this Indian painting, signifying the end of a fifty-two-year cycle. From the Codex Telleriano-Remensis.

Aztecs feared that the sun might not rise to make its way across the sky. Of course, the need for sacrificial blood served militant expansionism.

Human sacrifice was not the sole preserve of Mesoamericans as many ancient cultures of the Old World had also practiced it earlier. Sacrifice was to the Aztecs a solemn, and necessary, religious ceremony for the purpose of providing the nourishment and renewal that enabled the gods to maintain balance in the cosmos. The offering itself became a living god in the performance of the rite. Likewise, occasional indulgence in ritual cannibalism as a means of acquiring the attributes of the enemy was not an Aztec novelty.[1]

---

1   Frank Lestringant, *Cannibals* (Berkeley, CA, 1997), examines the universality of sacrifice and cannibalism in real and symbolic forms, including the Eucharist. The extent to which cannibalism was practiced is a topic that continues to excite debate among scholars. The argument that it satisfied a dietary need for protein has

Aztec New Fire Ceremony from the Codex Borbonicus.

These rituals followed strictly prescribed procedures in a complex ceremonial system. The most familiar sacrificial ceremony took place atop a high temple, where the victim was spread-eagled over a stone, his back arched. While his limbs were held by four assistants, the priest went in under the rib cage with an obsidian knife to remove the heart. There were variations, according to the god to be honored. Those dispatched for the god of fertility were bound and shot full of arrows, the falling drops of blood symbolizing the falling of spring rain. Those honoring the fire god were drugged and then placed in fire. Metaphors of warfare and sacrifice pervaded Aztec thought.

The Aztecs perceived themselves as living in an insecure world, in a conflict between order and chaos, at the mercy of the elements and at the edge of doom. Natural calamities in their fragile universe were occasioned by the gods' displeasure. Most Mesoamericans believed themselves surrounded by strange and harmful forces: as human beings were at one with nature, a person could suddenly be transformed into a hawk, a coyote, a fish, or even a tree or a rock. The souls of the dead could haunt or inspire the living. Since individuals were at the mercy of the gods, their best safeguard was to take no chances and adhere to carefully prescribed rules and rituals.

Huitzilopochtli was the predominant god, but many others were paid homage. The ancient deities of Tlaloc (rain) Tezcatlipoca (the favorite of the warriors), and Quetzalcoatl (revered by the intellectual priests) represent only a few of the more prominent gods worshipped for their special benefactions. Favored gods of conquered peoples were readily incorporated into a swelling Aztec pantheon of deities. Among these was Tlazolteotl, the deity of filth, who represented a set of beliefs and ritual practices that linked the earth, fertility, sexual

been discredited, but at least one historian asserts that it constituted an efficient and practical way of disposing of the bodies of sacrificial victims. Shawn W. Miller, *An Environmental History of Latin America* (New York, 2007), 36-40.

The goddess Tlazolteotl is shown here giving birth to the god of maize.

relations, waste (excrement), uncleanliness, and indulgence. She could give absolution for sexual transgressions but more importantly served to moderate excess and prevent disease.

There was a version of afterlife, but it was not the same for all. Mothers who died in childbirth went to a special heaven. Warriors who fell in battle or who were sacrificed by the enemy went to a paradise with perfumed clouds, to accompany the sun in its daily passage; or they could find a new life as a hummingbird, destined to spend eternity among fragrant blossoms, but most went to Mictlan, which required the soul to take an arduous journey through nine downward levels. In the Aztec sacred cosmos, the home served a place of power in which women's roles in childbirth were comparable to men's as warriors.

Intense spirituality pervaded Tenochtitlan, and religious observances occurred daily from birth to death. They had many holy days during which celebrations, both solemn and joyful, took place. Some festivities included singing and dancing, along with children parading in garlands of flowers. Ritual activities included feasting, fasting, bloodletting, and human sacrifice—all part of Aztec beliefs that conjoined life and death in a continuous cycle. It is difficult for modern observers to understand how the elaborate ritual complex reconciled the patterns of daily life with the violence of bloodshed implicated in Aztec beliefs.

AZTEC SOCIETY

While Aztecs were nomadic and relatively few in number, their social structure was simple; the majority were peasants or warriors, and the handful of priests and war leaders enjoyed comparatively few perquisites. Following the settlement of Tenochtitlan, however, a rapidly expanding population, a diversified economy, and the organizational demands of the imperial system led to a more complex class structure.

Naturally, the royal family was the most noble of all, and it was a large group. While the supreme ruler or emperor had one principal wife, he had many others as well. The numerous royal offspring proliferated greatly. It is said that Nezahualpilli of Texcoco had two thousand wives and 144 children. Moctezuma II, with one thousand women, once had one hundred fifty pregnant at the same time. The Aztec system of polygyny applied only to the noble class. It has been argued that the incorporation of women from other polities, whether as slaves, concubines, or wives, was an important factor in creating a more flexible society that attenuated the development of a rigid class structure. At the same time, the lived experience of these women has been shown to have been fraught with tension, jealousy, and concern over the fate of their children. Kings were chosen from the royal family but, in the complex polygynous system, the heir apparent was not fixed and could be a son, brother, nephew, or other male relative of the previous king. Noblewomen enjoyed varying degrees of status and respect, related to their importance in forging political alliances and strengthening royal legitimacy. Although they were increasingly denied leadership roles as the empire expanded, Aztec women of all classes should be viewed through the lens of a complementary gender system in which male and female roles were appreciated as different but essential to the functioning of society, and wherein women had property and other legal rights.

In addition to royal families, others of noble status (*pipiltin*) could include high priests, prominent military officers, and influential government leaders such as judges and tax collectors. Sons of nobles enjoyed an advantageous position to achieve their fathers' rank, but nobility (outside of the royal family) was not an inherited right. One had to distinguish oneself in service in order to enjoy the privileges of the aristocracy. Considerable variation in wealth and prestige among the nobility could be observed in the range of luxuries they enjoyed, for example, in clothing, jewelry, housing, foodstuffs, and servants. In the late Aztec period, an elite class with landed estates, a kind of incipient feudal aristocracy, was apparently in the process of formation.

Able-bodied males were expected to bear arms. As Inga Clendinnen made clear: "To be born a male in Tenochtitlan was to be designated a warrior. . . . What compelled the Mexican imagination were the men who were prepared to play the end game, to accept and embrace that final ritual of violent death."[2] Distinction in battle was one way in which a commoner might rise to high status. In order to achieve the cherished rank of warrior, a youth had to take a prisoner. If he succeeded in capturing or killing four of the enemy, he was entitled to share in the booty. Perhaps more important, he was allowed to dress in the distinctive adornments of the military elite. Conceivably, he could become a member of the prestigious military orders—the Eagle Knights or Jaguar Knights—and thus enjoy the luxuries of noble status.

Another avenue for mobility came through trade. The merchants of Tenochtitlan ranged far and wide. The long-distance traders, the *pochteca*, organized and led caravans as far as Central America, often passing through hostile country. The pochteca were as brave as they were shrewd and often depended on both their wits and courage to evade dangers. Some

---

2   Inga Clendinnen, *Aztecs: An Interpretation* (New York, 1991), 112, 149.

of them knew foreign languages and customs and served as diplomats and spies for the Aztec militarists. The pochteca imported to the capital exotic and profitable goods, including slaves displayed in the markets along with many tribute commodities demanded by the Aztecs. They lived in their own district and formed a separate group altogether. They had their own guild-like associations, their special deity, and their own courts. Within their section of the city they frequently gave sumptuous banquets and enjoyed other luxuries. Not of the nobility, they nevertheless carried influence and commanded respect.

Along with the ruling nobility, priests, scholars, artists, and scribes enjoyed high status as part of an educated elite that nurtured literary traditions within the altepetl. They kept historical annals, genealogies of rulers, writings on philosophy and astronomy, and tribute records in their pictorial books. The sacerdotal life began with training young boys (or girls destined to be priestesses) in a monastery school, or *calmecac*. Priests were expected to lead exemplary lives, and they spent long hours in prayer, fasting, and penance. Most of the priests led modest lives of service; those who advanced through the hierarchy, however, enjoyed the status of nobles and many of its perquisites. Aside from routine religious duties, each priest had a specialty, such as music, painting, teaching, dancing, or assisting at sacrificial rites. Some priests were also warriors. Priests were the guardians of morality, and some of their admonitions are not unlike scriptural injunctions, such as a man who looks too curiously on a woman commits adultery with his eyes.

The great majority of the people (about 90 percent) formed the class of commoners (*macehualtin*). These farmers, laborers, minor craftsmen, servants, vendors, and petty functionaries of an altepetl were organized into ward districts or rural villages called *calpollis* (*barrios* to the Spaniards). Each of these subunits consisted of several households and had a temple dedicated to its patron deity and a school. It was a close-knit organization with loyalties much like those of an extended family. Each calpolli had lands apportioned to family heads who could use fields but did not own them. Members of the calpolli worked together, played together and, in times of war in the absence of a standing army, were called up to fight together as a unit. The people elected a veteran warrior who served as military commander of the district and was responsible for their welfare and good order. A new class of landless peasants (*mayeques*) emerged as nobles required increased labor for their expanded landholdings.

At the bottom of the socioeconomic scale were the slaves. Aztec slavery differed from the slave system most familiar to us, inasmuch as slaves had certain rights and bondage was not passed from parent to child. Some, in fact, served as slaves only for a specified term, either in payment of a debt or as punishment for a crime. In bad times people sometimes sold themselves or their children into slavery to avoid starvation. Some slaves were favored as concubines, and all slaves could intermarry with free persons. Little stigma was attached to some conditions of slavery; the mother of the emperor Itzcoatl, in fact, had been a slave. In a different category were those captured in war and destined for sacrifice. The class of slaves may have been growing at the time of the Spanish conquest, another sign of the widening social gap.

Aztec society's concern with education was singular for its time. After a period of regimented home schooling, instruction was compulsory for children in order to make them productive and worthy members of society. Two main types of schools existed. Children of the nobility usually attended the *calmecac*, run by the scholarly priests, in preparation for the priesthood or some high office in the state. Occasionally a talented son of a commoner gained entrance. In a vigorous intellectual regimen, young boys studied religion, astronomy, philosophy, history, poetry, rhetoric, oratory, singing, and dancing, among other disciplines. History was passed on by oral traditions committed to memory. Picture writing depicted certain dramatic scenes that gave continuity and jogged the memory, but the fine details were transmitted from one generation to another by the retelling.

Most children attended one of the commoners' *telpochcallis*. Laypersons gave both boys and girls practical instruction in basic subjects. Here, fifteen-year-old boys learned the rudiments of warfare, and those who went on to excel in the profession of arms could do well for themselves; others had to be content with learning trades or lesser skills. Girls were instructed in the responsibilities of the household and motherhood. It should be noted that although Aztec society increasingly rewarded military skill, women maintained valued complementary roles, not only domestic but also in agriculture, trade, and religion. The highest political and religious offices were restricted to men, but most deities had androgynous characteristics, in recognition of the vital female contribution to fertility and the sustenance of the universe.

Women played key roles in the performance of routines that upheld society as well as in the transmission of values, teaching moderation and frugality. They exercised religious power as healers and midwives. In addition to making food and clothing for their families, they sold produce in the markets. Their weaving skills were especially valuable as the textiles they wove from maguey fibers and cotton constituted a massive part of the tribute collected by Aztec officials. Women could own property, and males and females inherited equally from their fathers and mothers.[3]

In the home, parents imposed strict discipline. The birth of a child occasioned celebration and florid speeches. Babies received gifts according to gender: for females, there were weaving tools, cooking utensils, and brooms, while males were given bows and arrows and farming implements. A child was named in hopeful anticipation of its character—the boys usually given names indicating military prowess and the girls' names denoting beauty and delicacy, such as Rain Flower or Water Bird. In the home children learned not only proper deportment but also how to perform daily tasks. When children were young some indiscretions were tolerated, but by the age of eight they were considered to be responsible and infractions brought harsh punishment. Although parents were ordinarily tender and loving, wayward children were castigated by whippings, scratching with thorns, or being forced to inhale the smoke of a fire into which chile peppers had been placed. It is reasonable to suppose that most children behaved themselves. Girls worked in the household until they were sixteen to eighteen, when they married; boys took mates in their early twenties. Marriage was sacred and monogamy was the rule, at least for commoners.

A morally rigorous aspect of Aztec society derives from how they conceptualized the sacred. Because alcohol and drugs provided paths for opening an individual up to the supernatural,

---

3　For more on women, see the articles by Louise Burkhart and Susan Kellogg in *Indian Women of Early Mexico*, eds. Susan Schroeder et al. (Norman, OK, 1997).

Prehispanic Mexican women ground their corn with stone *mano* and *metate* and made tortillas much as many do today. From the Florentine Codex.

ritual control of intoxicants such as pulque was deemed necessary to avoid dangerous displays of sacred power. Drunkenness could be a capital offense, although older people were allowed to become inebriated. Sexual activity and physical prowess also provided other vehicles of the sacred and, like alcohol and drugs, entailed strictly prescribed behaviors.

Aztec society demanded moral conformity, and violators of the code, as well as criminal offenders, were dealt with firmly. For minor offenses punishment was correspondingly light, as in the case of petty theft, which called for restitution of the property. But since personal dignity was highly prized, any public humiliation, such as the cutting of one's hair, was a great insult to pride. Several offenses, including murder, perjury, rape, abortion, incest, fraudulent business practices, grand larceny, and treason, could bring the death penalty. This may seem unduly harsh, but the legal codes were designed to forestall the conversion of individual wrongdoing into general social disorder.

The Aztec legal system was complex, with multiple levels and arenas of jurisdiction that served different constituencies. The legalistic society had need for many judicial officials to prepare the multitude of carefully documented lawsuits. Judges in the great marketplaces maintained fairness in business transactions and settled disputes. Selected for their integrity and virtue, judges had great authority and could arrest even the highest dignitaries, for before the law all were equal. Expected to be absolutely impartial, if a judge accepted a bribe or favored a noble over a plebeian, he could be executed.

Duty and responsibility, as well as danger, increased with one's rank, and they imposed special restraints. Because self-control was considered a mark of good breeding and nobility, the upper classes were subject to standards different from those of the lower classes. In contrast to most systems, where the upper classes have a favored position before the law, Aztec aristocrats were dealt with more harshly than plebeians. An offense that might bring a whipping or public humiliation for a commoner could mean death for a noble. A salient example of justice for the wayward nobility may be observed in the notorious case of one of Nezahualpilli's wives (a daughter of Mexica ruler Axayacatl) who was unfaithful. She and three of her lovers were publicly executed.

Aztec medical practices were generally on a par with those in Europe and, in some respects, superior. Doctors knew how to set broken bones and dislocations and to treat dental cavities. They even performed brain operations. Like their European counterparts, Aztec healers attributed disease to both supernatural and natural causes. Also like Europeans, they practiced bleeding as a treatment, but their most common, and often effective, cures were plants and herbs, delivered through a bewildering variety of brews, powders, poultices, purges, and pastes. Years after the conquest, a Spanish physician cataloged some fifteen hundred different plants whose medicinal properties were utilized by the Indians. The conquerors adopted native medicines, many of which are still popular in rural Mexico today.

Because Aztec society was largely agricultural in character, the daily routine of most people directly involved the growing of food. Aside from the many chinampas that ringed the island city, producing up to seven harvests annually, there were extensive plantings along the shores of the lakes. The diet remained much as it had been for centuries, with a base of corn, beans, chile, and squash. It also included a wide variety of other vegetables and melons, cactus fruit, and amaranth, in addition to many fruits imported from tropical regions. Commoners ate some meat, but the nobles, who liked to hunt for sport, consumed more and of a greater variety, for example, venison, peccary, pheasant, and turkey. A special treat was the small hairless dog fattened for the table. Cacao from the tropics was made into a chocolate drink, and traders brought avocados and many other exotic delicacies. Fish was a favorite when available.

AZTEC POLITICAL HEGEMONY

The limited resources of the valley did not suffice to meet the needs of Tenochtitlan, Texcoco, Tlacopan (the allied altepetl that made up the Triple Alliance), and other valley communities. Moreover, there was an increasing demand for luxuries from other provinces. To satisfy the necessities and desires for both raw materials and consumer goods, Aztec realms were extended. The so-called Aztec empire was really a loose coalition of over 500 subject city-states or altepetl that paid tribute to the imperial center. The Aztecs used marriage alliances to bolster the network of tribute obligations and discourage revolt, but they did not impose their own political system in conquered areas. Rather, the collection of tribute, which kept the valley culture prosperous, was their main concern.

Tributes included a wide variety of commodities, among them cacao, cotton textiles, feathers, precious stones, jaguar skins, eagles, shells, dyes, cloth, gold, silver, sandals, and corn and other foodstuffs, as well as jewelry. Imperial ambassadors were stationed in tributary towns to steward and collect goods. Towns conquered by the Aztecs had to provide soldiers and slaves and to recognize the imperial courts of appeal. But they were also allowed considerable autonomy. If the conquered peoples agreed to submit to Aztec sovereignty, the Aztecs did not much interfere with their internal affairs and their customs, respecting their local deities, religious practices, and traditions.

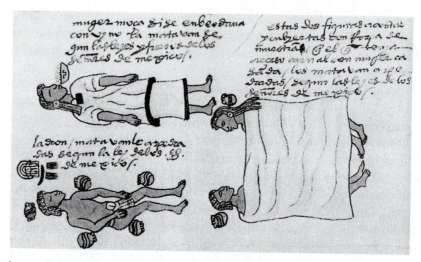

A girl has been put to death for drunkenness and a thief has been executed by stoning. Adulterers are shown wrapped together in a sheet and then stoned to death. From the Codex Mendoza.

An older woman is legally allowed to partake of the intoxicant ocli (pulque). From the Codex Mendoza.

Aztec political organization rested lightly on tributary towns, provided they were cooperative. In fact, it may be said that the Aztecs' policy of relative autonomy for subject provinces was a weakness in their political system. The subject peoples continued to be foreigners within the empire, which remained a conglomeration of tributaries with many different languages, customs, and religions. The provinces paid tribute under duress, but their primary allegiance was to their altepetl, or local polity. Thus, the empire lacked genuine unity and was honeycombed with discontent, a circumstance that would be fatal in the years ahead.

After the death of Nezahualcoyotl of Texcoco in 1472, the Triple Alliance had little significance, and Tenochtitlan gathered to itself almost all the power and most of the tribute.

Aztec justice was strict, and it often imposed the harsher punishment on high officials. Here an erring functionary is being strangled. From the Florentine Codex.

Consultation with other rulers became superfluous, and the emperor came to be elected from among the royal family by an increasingly elite group of military men with royal lineage. Surrounded by a small circle of military advisors, the monarch, whose selection was also seen as divinely ordained, grew even more powerful by the sixteenth century.

AZTEC ART, MUSIC, AND LITERATURE

The Aztecs borrowed much of their art from others and put their own stamp on it. The Mixtecs exerted strong influence on Aztec gold and silver work, pottery, and pictographs. We have few examples of Aztec murals, but we do have beautiful painted manuscripts and pictorial maps, many rendered after the conquest. An outstanding example is the Mapa de Cuauhtinchan No. 2, from the 1540s, with its hundreds of images that shed light on sacred knowledge, origin myths, ethnic and power relationships, and acculturation. Not only esthetically appealing, writing with pictures was vital to the persistence of community, ethnic identity, and solidarity after the conquest.

Aztec ceramic work was good but not superior. They did excel, however, in stone sculpture. "Aztec carvers created one of the world's strongest sculptural traditions with powerful conceptions that both impress and intimidate."[4] Monumental in size and weight, Aztec stones adorned ritual precincts to commemorate victories and conquests, to hold sacrificial blood, and to represent mythical-historical events. For the Aztecs, the religious images sculpted in stone were both animate and divine.

---

4   Elizabeth Hill Boone, *The Aztec World* (Washington, DC, 1994), 131.

This fearsome image of the goddess Coatlicue, mother of Huitzilopochtli, stands over eight feet high.

The artisans who made the gold and silver jewelry were also superb craftsmen. It is therefore lamentable that almost all of their work was either lost or destroyed during the Spanish conquest, for the conquerors valued raw gold but all too often did not appreciate the fine workmanship. Equally impressive was the art of the lapidarists; from precious jadeite, turquoise, and other stones they fashioned fine jewelry and mosaics. Most unusual were the artists who worked with feathers. The Aztecs put great value on the long green plumes of the quetzal bird that lived in the highlands of Chiapas and Guatemala, but the feathers of many other birds, too, were woven into mosaics of wonderful patterns

A realistic stone sculpture of an Aztec Eagle Knight. His helmet is shaped like an eagle's head; knights of the orders of the Jaguar and Coyote were adorned with distinctive costumes, headgear, and insignia.

and colors. Only rare examples remain, the most spectacular being the great headdress of Moctezuma II.

Poetry and song constituted artistic expressions that connected people with the gods. Aztec music was composed primarily for ceremonial purposes, and accompanied by dancing. Instruments consisted of flutes, whistles, rasps, rattles, trumpets, conch shells, and drums vital for providing rhythm. Musicians were highly regarded because of their accompaniment in the religious rituals. Powerful lords were patrons to composers who created

Musicians played important roles in religious and civic observances. From the Florentine Codex.

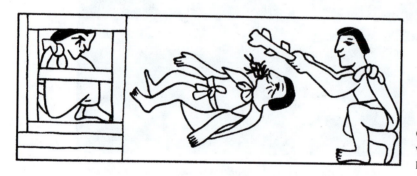

Careless musicians were sometimes punished by death.

ballads recounting the nobles' military exploits. As no written form for recording music had developed, musicians had to memorize a wide repertoire for the many ceremonies that often went on for hours and could include variations. At the same time, as Robert Stevenson points out, "Imperfectly executed rituals were thought to offend rather than appease the gods, and therefore errors in the performance of the ritual music—such as missed drum beats—carried the death penalty."[5]

5   Robert Stevenson, *Music in Mexico: A Historical Survey* (New York, 1971), 18.

Aztec lyrics were often eloquent, moving, and sentimental. Flowers served as a key metaphor for the Aztecs in relationship to fertility, birth, and sexuality. In this verse praising a goddess, the poet likened the blooming of a golden flower to the beginning of life itself:

The yellow flower has opened,
Our mother has opened like a flower.
She came from Our Place of Beginning . . .
Butterfly of Obsidian. . . .[6]

Like the short life of a bloom, however, life on earth was also fleeting. Poets sometimes addressed themselves to the proper role of artists and appealed to the public at large to assume a responsible and dignified posture. Like poets the world over, they often waxed philosophical and examined the meaning of life:

Truly do we live on earth?
Not forever on earth; only a little while here.
Although it be jade, it will be broken,
Although it be gold, it is crushed,
Although it be quetzal feather, it is torn asunder.
Not forever on earth; only a little while here.[7]

THE CITY OF TENOCHTITLAN

Aztec architecture, like Aztec art, borrowed much from other Mesoamerican civilizations. Buildings were basically elaborations of forms that went all the way back to Teotihuacan. But while many pre-Aztec structures survive in amazingly good condition, Tenochtitlan was thought to have been completely demolished by the Spaniards. However, excavations since 1978 have revealed important archaeological findings, including parts of the Templo Mayor (main temple) and monumental sculptures like the magnificent disk of the dismembered Coyolxauhqui. We do have, moreover, enough descriptions of Tenochtitlan from both native and Spanish contemporary accounts to appreciate what the city looked like.

By the time Moctezuma II was elevated to power in 1502, the island capital of Tenochtitlan was a most impressive city. With the estimate of 150,000 to 200,000 residents accepted by most scholars, the Aztec capital was one of the largest cities in the world. Only four cities of Europe—Paris, Venice, Milan, and Naples—had populations of 100,000 or more at the time. Seville, had a population in 1520 of around 40,000; and by 1580, when it was the largest city in Spain, it had only slightly over 100,000. The amazement of the Spanish conquerors at their first sight of Tenochtitlan is therefore understandable. Cortés wrote of

---

6　Quoted in Frances Gillmor, *Flute of the Smoking Mirror: A Portrait of Nezahualcoyotl, Poet-King of the Aztecs* (Albuquerque, NM, 1949), 23.

7　Quoted in Miguel León Portilla, *Aztec Thought and Culture: A Study of the Ancient Nahuatl Mind*, trans. Jack Emory Davis (Norman, OK, 1963), 7.

The center of Tenochtitlan, reconstructed by Ignacio Marquina from descriptions of Spanish conquerors and surviving Aztec monuments.

"the magnificence, the strange and marvelous things of this great city," which itself was "so remarkable as not to be believed."[8] In the Valley of Mexico, an area of some three thousand square miles, there were about fifty different cities by the second decade of the sixteenth century. If we take into account "greater" Tenochtitlan, with its many satellite communities on the lakeshores, the area surely held one of the heaviest concentrations of population in the world at the time.

By the early sixteenth century the island comprised about five square miles, densely settled, and occupied much of the present center of Mexico City. It was a metropolis swarming with activity. Some sixty thousand people gathered daily in its buzzing marketplaces, the most important of which was Tlatelolco, to barter for foodstuffs, cloth, and utilitarian wares. Cacao beans and cotton textiles served as forms of currency. The core of the city, corresponding to the extensive plaza of today (the Zócalo), had the Templo Mayor, a great double pyramid dedicated to Huitzilopochtli and Tlaloc, along with the royal palaces and other large structures. Adjacent to the main complex, in 2017 archaeologists uncovered the base of a massive circular temple dedicated to the wind god. Built at the end of the fifteenth century, it towered over a ball court where neck vertebrae have been found, presumably the remains of sacrificial victims who may have been defeated competitors. To the shock of conquering Spaniards, the royal center boasted a giant stone rack, the *tzompantli*, that displayed many thousands of human skulls.

---

8   Hernán Cortés, *Hernán Cortés: Letters from Mexico*, trans. and ed. A. R. Pagden, introd. J. H. Elliott (New York, 1971), 101-2.

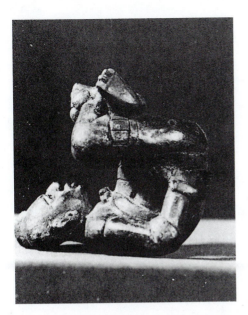

A ceramic foot juggler from Oaxaca, ca. AD 300.

From that central precinct enclosing about 125 acres, the city extended out to the residences of the nobles, often of two stories and containing as many as fifty rooms and patios. Beyond were districts with the modest adobe dwellings of the commoners. The city was interlaced with stone-edged canals, which served as thoroughfares for thousands of canoes carrying people and goods. Paralleling the canals were streets for pedestrians. The Aztecs loved flowers that along with trees and other plants decorated many luxurious gardens. Aside from the royal botanical garden that displayed almost all species of plant life in the empire, zoos housed practically all the animals and snakes of the country, as well as a large aviary full of all varieties of domestic birds. Large ponds were maintained for swans, ducks, and egrets. Moctezuma's snakes, eagles, and jaguars lived in cages, reportedly consuming 500 turkeys daily. Hundreds of people labored daily to maintain these gardens and zoos.

Five shallow lakes interconnected to form a network—two freshwater lakes in the south drained into the brackish water of Lake Texcoco. Three long causeways joined the major island city to the shores: one stretched southward to Ixtapalapa, branching off with a road to Coyoacan; another causeway went west to Tlacopan, with an offshoot to Chapultepec; and a third made a connection to the north with Tepeyacac. These broad thoroughfares, twenty-five to thirty feet wide, were cut at intervals by drawbridges. Within the city itself many canals were spanned by stout bridges across which, according to Cortés, ten horsemen could ride abreast.

Compared to other cities in the world at the time, Tenochtitlan was remarkably clean. There was good drainage, and night soil and garbage were hauled away in canoes. A crew of a thousand men swept and washed down public streets every day. Cleanliness was considered essential, and people bathed often, many once a day. Owing at least in part to good sanitation and clean air, Aztec society was healthy.

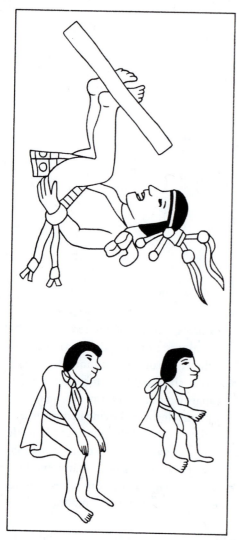

An Aztec foot juggler, from the Florentine Codex. Also shown are a hunchback and a dwarf, for whom the Indians had affection.

MOCTEZUMA II

Moctezuma II reigned over a territory roughly the size of Italy. His domains included the modern states of Mexico, Morelos, Puebla, Hidalgo, most of Veracruz, much of Oaxaca and Guerrero, as well as the coast of Chiapas. They contained scores of "provinces," stretching from arid highlands to the sweltering tropics. If, as some authorities believe, all of Mexico had a population approaching 30 million,[9] it was more populous than any country in Europe. France, the largest, had about 20 million, and Spain, 10 million at most.

With his immense authority, prestige, and luxurious style of life, Moctezuma II wielded enormous power. Hundreds of nobles and three thousand servants attended him in his huge

---

9   Sherburne F. Cook and Woodrow Borah, *The Indian Population of Central Mexico, 1531-1610* (Berkeley, CA, 1960); Sherburne F. Cook and Woodrow Borah, *The Aboriginal Population of Central Mexico on the Eve of the Spanish Conquest* (Berkeley, CA, 1963).

palace. Each day he was presented with a choice of a hundred different dishes, although he ate sparingly, taking his meals behind a screen. For his pleasure he had an unlimited number of women and he was entertained by the antics of dwarfs, jesters, tumblers, acrobats, musicians, and dancers. No one dared look him in the face or touch him, and it was forbidden to turn one's back on him. Moctezuma was indeed the epitome of royalty, held as semi-divine, exalted far above any of the earliest Aztec rulers. Nevertheless, he came to be portrayed in the aftermath of conquest as a tragic figure, undone by historical forces beyond his control.

Before the Spanish arrived, Moctezuma was known for his bravery and successful military campaigns into Mixtec and Maya areas. In addition, his deep knowledge of Mexican history and respect for tradition factored into his successful rule. Yet these same issues would play a role in the collapse of the Aztec state. Aside from his religious convictions, Moctezuma was pensive and sensitive; he was also an amateur "wizard" who made use of astrology, perhaps as a means of lifting the shadow of historical inevitability. Or did he truly believe, as the pervasive myth claims, that the great Quetzalcoatl would return, as he had promised, to take back his rightful throne?

Just when Moctezuma learned of the presence of white men in the New World is not entirely clear. It is no doubt true that word of the Spaniards, who had been in the Caribbean for several years, drifted to the mainland. Perhaps he was not yet unduly concerned. Cuba, in fact, lay dangerously near—but it was not part of the Aztec world. Moctezuma's agents almost certainly informed him that Spaniards had landed on the Yucatán Peninsula in 1517 and that others the following year were making their way up the Gulf coast. Indians reported seeing "towers or small mountains floating on the waves of the sea." Meanwhile, strange phenomena, construed by the emperor's priests as evil portents, had occurred, if we are to believe self-interested post-conquest sources. Lightning, unaccompanied by thunder, "like a blow from the sun," damaged a temple. A strange bird was found with "a mirror in its head," in which Moctezuma saw a host of foreign warriors. In 1517 a comet appeared "like a flaming ear of corn . . . it seemed to bleed fire, drop by drop, like a wound in the sky."[10] Then, in the spring of 1519 (the Aztec year Ce Acatl), the emperor received a courier bearing ominous paintings—they depicted the encampment on Aztec shores of strangers, bearded white men with crosses.

RECOMMENDED FOR FURTHER STUDY

Anderson, Arthur J. O., and Susan Schroeder, eds. *Codex Chimalpahin: Society and Politics in Mexico Tenochtitlan, Tlatelolco, Texcoco, Culhuacan, and Other Nahua Altepetl in Central Mexico: The Nahuatl and Spanish Annals and Accounts Collected and Recorded by Don Domingo de San Antón Muñón Chimalpahin Quauhtlehuanitzin.* Norman: University of Oklahoma Press, 1997.

Berdan, France F. *Aztec Archaeology and Ethnohistory.* New York: Cambridge University Press. 2014.

Berdan, Frances F., and Patricia Anawalt, eds. *The Codex Mendoza,* 4 vols. Berkeley: University of California Press, 1992.

Boone, Elizabeth Hill. *The Aztec World.* Washington, DC: Smithsonian Books, 1994.

_____. *Cycles of Time and Meaning in the Mexican Books of Fate.* Austin: University of Texas Press, 2007.

_____. *Red and Black: Pictorial Histories of the Aztecs and Mixtecs.* Austin: University of Texas Press, 2000.

Broda, Johanna, David Carrasco, and Eduardo Matos Moctezuma. *The Great Temple of Tenochtitlan: Center and Periphery in the Aztec World.* Berkeley: University of California Press, 1987.

Brokaw, Galen, and Jongsoo Lee, eds. *Fernando de Alva Ixtlilxochitl and His Legacy.* Tucson: University of Arizona Press, 2015.

---

10   Miguel León Portilla, ed., *The Broken Spears: The Aztec Account of the Conquest* (Boston, MA, 1972), 4-6, 13.

Brumfiel, Elizabeth, and Gary M. Feinman, eds. *The Aztec World*. New York: Abrams, 2008.

Burkhart, Louise. *The Slippery Earth: Nahua-Christian Moral Dialogue in Sixteenth-Century Mexico*. Tucson: University of Arizona Press, 1989.

Carrasco, David. *City of Sacrifice: The Aztec Empire and the Role of Violence in Civilization*. Boston, MA: Beacon Press, 2000.

Carrasco, David, and Scott Sessions, eds. *Cave, City, and Eagle's Nest: An Interpretive Journey through the Mapa de Cuauhtinchan No. 2*. Albuquerque: University of New Mexico Press, 2007.

Clendinnen, Inga. *Aztecs: An Interpretation*. New York: Cambridge University Press, 1991.

Cook, Sherburne F., and Woodrow Borah. *The Aboriginal Population of Central Mexico on the Eve of the Spanish Conquest*. Berkeley: University of California Press, 1963.

_____. *The Indian Population of Central Mexico, 1531-1610*. Berkeley: University of California Press, 1960.

Cortés, Hernán. *Hernán Cortés: Letters from Mexico*. Translated and edited by A. R. Pagden, with an introduction by J. H. Elliott. New York: Orion Press, 1971.

Gibson, Charles. *The Aztecs under Spanish Rule*. Stanford, CA: Stanford University Press, 1964.

Gillmor, Francis. *Flute of the Smoking Mirror: A Portrait of Nezahualcoyotl, Poet-King of the Aztecs*. Albuquerque: University of New Mexico Press 1949.

Hassig, Ross. *Polygamy and the Rise and Demise of the Aztec Empire*. Albuquerque: University of New Mexico Press, 2016.

Keen, Benjamin. *The Aztec Image in Western Thought*. New Brunswick, NJ: Rutgers University Press, 1971.

Lee, Jongsoo. *The Allure of Nezahualcoyotl: Pre-Hispanic History, Religion, and Nahua Poetics*. Albuquerque: University of New Mexico Press, 2008.

León Portilla, Miguel. *Aztec Thought and Culture: A Study of the Ancient Nahuatl Mind*. Translated by Jack Emory Davis. Norman: University of Oklahoma Press, 1963.

_____, ed. *The Broken Spears: The Aztec Account of the Conquest of Mexico*. Translated by Lysander Kemp. Boston, MA: Beacon Press, 1972.

_____. *Fifteen Poets of the Aztec World*. Norman: University of Oklahoma Press, 1992.

Lestringant, Frank. *Cannibals: The Discovery and Representation of the Cannibal from Columbus to Jules Verne*. Berkeley: University of California Press, 1997.

Matos Moctezuma, Eduardo, and Leonardo López Luján. *Monumental Mexica Sculpture*. Mexico City: Fundación Conmemoraciones, 2010.

Miller, Shawn W. *An Environmental History of Latin America*. New York: Cambridge University Press, 2007.

Nichols, Deborah L., and Enrique Rodríguez-Alegría, eds. *The Oxford Handbook of the Aztecs*. New York: Oxford University Press, 2017.

Offner, Jerome A. *Law and Politics in Aztec Texcoco*. New York: Cambridge University Press, 1983.

Olko, Justyna. *Insignia of Rank in the Nahua World: From the Fifteenth to the Seventeenth Century*. Boulder: University Press of Colorado, 2014.

Ortiz Montellano, Bernard R. *Aztec Medicine, Health and Nutrition*. New Brunswick, NJ: Rutgers University Press, 1990.

Pasztory, Esther. *Aztec Art*. New York: Harry N. Abrams, 1983.

Pennock, Caroline Dodds. *Bonds of Blood: Gender, Lifecycle and Sacrifice in Aztec Culture*. New York: Palgrave Macmillan, 2008.

Schroeder, Susan, Stephanie Wood, and Robert Haskett, eds. *Indian Women of Early Mexico*. Norman: University of Oklahoma Press, 1997.

Sigal, Peter H. *The Flower and the Scorpion: Sexuality and Ritual in Early Nahua Culture*. Durham, NC: Duke University Press, 2011.

Stevenson, Robert. *Music in Mexico: A Historical Survey*. New York: Thomas Y. Crowell, Co., 1971.

Zantwijk, Rudolf van. *The Aztec Arrangement: The Social History of Pre-Spanish Mexico*. Norman: University of Oklahoma Press, 1985.

Zorita, Alonso de. *Life and Labor in Ancient Mexico: The Brief and Summary Relation of the Lords of New Spain*. Translated, with an introduction, by Benjamin Keen. New Brunswick, NJ: Rutgers University Press, 1962.

COLLIDING WORLDS

CHAPTER 6

THE SPANISH INVASION

Let us try for a moment to imagine," the late Ramón Iglesia wrote, "the astonishment of the inhabitants of a small island called Guanahani one morning when they beheld three shapes out there in the water, three immense hulks, out of which issued several . . . beings . . . of light complexion, their faces covered with hair, and their bodies . . . covered with fabrics of diverse pattern and color."[1] We might surmise that, in 1492, the natives of the Caribbean fancied Columbus and his men to be exceedingly strange beings. The invaders were also surprised but even more disappointed, for they found little sign of the precious metals, valuable spices, and other wealth they had sought, and no indication of the fabulous Asian kingdoms they had anticipated. The native inhabitants, whom they nonetheless called "Indians," were swiftly relegated to the status of "others," less worthy of respect.

SPANISH LEGACIES AND CARIBBEAN TRIALS

Later voyages to the "New World" (or the "Indies") dampened even the most optimistic spirits. Consequently, the Caribbean islands attracted relatively few settlers as expeditions were financed with borrowed capital that could not easily be paid back in the absence of profitable trade goods. Columbus, who was happier sailing about than governing waspish colonists, let administrative matters slide, thus giving the Spanish crown a pretext for removing him as governor of Santo Domingo, the name of the New World colony, and revoking the generous terms earlier granted him. Ultimately, the great discoverer was sent back to the mother country in chains.

Royal officials then took charge, but the bickering continued. Nearby islands were explored, some were settled, and Indians were put to work washing the streams for gold, which provided lucrative income for a few in the early years. Beyond that, and small profits from agriculture, there seemed little opportunity. Others began to explore elsewhere—up to the coast of Florida, to Central America, and down to South America.

---

1   Ramón Iglesia, *Columbus, Cortés and Other Essays,* trans. and ed. Lesley B. Simpson (Berkeley, CA, 1969), 8.

"Well, they look pretty undocumented to me."

A *New Yorker* cartoon from 2006 reimagines the scene described by Ramón Iglesia.

Who were these Spaniards who came to conquer? Their own past embodied a history of conquest. Under the control of the Roman empire from the first to the fifth centuries AD, Iberia underwent subsequent invasions by Visigoths and then Muslims, who arrived from north Africa in the eighth century. Over a period of nearly eight centuries Iberians reclaimed lands from the Muslims, but the kingdoms that emerged were diverse in cultural and linguistic traditions. At the dawn of the age of expansion, a single Spanish monarchy had not yet coalesced to unite the various Iberian kingdoms (except for Portugal, an independent polity since the twelfth century). The largest of these, Castile, provided much of the initiative that bound the future Spain loosely together by the sixteenth century, and it was from Castile that the New World ventures would be launched. Queen Isabel of Castile, strengthened by her marriage to King Fernando of Aragón in 1469, worked vigorously to mold judicial and administrative institutions intended to counter the power of both the nobility and a strong tradition of municipal autonomy. Tensions between the monarchy, the nobility, and the towns would persist for some time in the peninsula while in the Americas the crown more rapidly curtailed the entitlements and autonomy of its early emissaries.

But even in the New World this was not an easy task. Spanish conquistadors were strongly influenced by the legacies of the Reconquista (Reconquest) of the peninsula from the Muslims, which had only recently been finalized in 1492 with the defeat of the rulers of Granada. The Reconquista had fostered a quasi-medieval cultural legacy in which military conquest, religious crusading, and the accumulation of booty and property were inextricably linked and mutually reinforcing. The legacy found expression in the New World, especially in the religious justification for military conquest and the strong role that would be played by the Roman Catholic Church in advancing the goals of the Spanish crown. Tales of chivalry and dreams of prizes to be won also traveled to the Americas in the minds of adventurers, but they were tempered by a changing economic milieu. By the end of the fifteenth century, the inroads made by mercantile capitalism meant that these aspiring conquistadors had to seek private funds to finance their expeditions. The need to recoup their investments provided even greater incentive for them to claim the customary material and political rewards from the monarchy they served.

In the peninsula privilege was reserved for the nobility, who comprised about 10 percent of the population; but only a small segment of this class held noble titles or great wealth. Most of the nobility consisted of untitled *caballeros* and *hidalgos*. Commoners made up the other major social subdivision, but they were also diverse in terms of income and status. The majority were peasants who worked for the nobility in agriculture and stock-raising, although some possessed their own land. The commoner group also included professionals, clerics, artisans, and merchants. People of all classes lived in and identified with towns and cities because civilized (politically ordered) living was exclusively urban. Society was also categorized in terms of religion: Christians, Jews, and Muslims. Where religious tolerance had once existed under Muslim rule, however, it disappeared at the turn of the sixteenthth century, when the Catholic monarchs expelled Jews (1492) and Muslims (1502) who refused to convert to Christianity.

The Castilian monarchy's efforts to consolidate power rested on a narrow agricultural economic base, with production concentrated in grain, sheep, olive oil, and wine. Economic contraction, in turn, led to a more concerted search for guaranteed income via government and other bonds, which led to even less investment in productive enterprises and continuing contraction. The overall economic and social milieu encouraged the untitled nobility and even commoners to look elsewhere for social advancement, and their pretensions were fueled both by the past—the cultural heritage of the Reconquista—and the future—the potential offered by the New World "discoveries." Although frequently led by minor nobles, the majority of conquistadors were commoners among whom skilled artisans like carpenters, stonemasons, and blacksmiths proved crucial assets in the logistics of conquest. The tensions between their ambitions, economic difficulties in Spain, and the slowly evolving bureaucracy of the crown dominated the early colony in Mexico.

From the Caribbean, the crown conducted the first experiments in imposing and inventing systems and institutions. The seat of royal government was on the island of Santo Domingo, but the larger island of Cuba held out more promise. Conquered in 1511, Cuba proved disappointing. But the royal government sanctioned the implementation of an institution called *encomienda* that rewarded conquerors with the labor of subjected groups. At least in the Indies they had natives working their modest farms or, if they were lucky, mining for gold. However, one of the tragic consequences of the European occupation of the islands was a catastrophic loss of life among the Indians, partly because of fatigue and mistreatment but mostly because of their vulnerability to diseases to which they had no previous exposure or immunity. Epidemics of smallpox, measles, and other illnesses spread quickly among the natives, causing widespread death. With the great decline in the Indian population, a labor shortage ensued, prompting Spaniards to initiate what became a massive world trade in African slaves.

Governor Diego Velázquez of Cuba sent out an expedition in 1517 for the purpose of trading and finding other Indians to be enslaved. Under the command of Francisco Hernández de Córdoba, the party of three ships sailed west and touched the coast of Yucatán, thought at first to be an island. Further exploration revealed the existence of cultures more organized than those of the Caribbean, with people dressed in cotton fabric who tilled prosperous fields and lived in stone houses. In their brief contact with the natives the Spaniards heard of gold and silver in the land, and they also saw the first signs of human sacrifices. After a cautious initial reception, the Spaniards were attacked by a large, fierce army of warriors; in the ensuing battle 50 of the Europeans were killed.

Despite the ferocity of the Yucatec warriors, the tantalizing references to gold fired the Spaniards' cupidity and Governor Velázquez prepared to pursue the encouraging prospects. In 1518 he dispatched his nephew, Juan de Grijalva, with four ships and two hundred eager men to investigate further. After five months, the expedition returned home with some small gold objects and stories of a wealthy lake kingdom in the interior dominated by a great lord—Moctezuma of the Aztecs. Believing his nephew to have acted too cautiously and sensing the potential for riches and power, Velázquez commissioned the bolder, thirty-four-year-old Fernando[2] Cortés to undertake this venture.

FERNANDO CORTÉS

Cortés was a native of the arid province of Extremadura, the region from which so many of the prominent conquistadors came. Born in 1485 into an old, honorable family of slender means, the frail boy grew into a robust youth, often into mischief. Not much interested in the law career his family wished for him, he chose to seek his fortune in the Spanish Indies by preparing to sail with a large fleet. An amorous adventure frustrated his plans however: he fell off a wall outside a bedroom and narrowly escaped death from a wrathful husband. Injured and ill, he missed the sailing. Later, when he did catch a ship to the New World, it was 1504, and Cortés was nineteen.

After accompanying Velázquez in the conquest of Cuba in 1511, Cortés settled there in Santiago de Baracoa, where he raised livestock. His Indian servants mined enough gold for him to enter into a trading partnership. With an official position in local government, Cortés was a secure and respected member of the community. Had it not been for the indecision of the governor's nephew, Fernando Cortés would likely have ended his days in obscurity.

---

2   Cortés's first name is often shown as Hernán or Hernando, but he seems to have preferred Fernando.

Cortés began recruiting a company of men following the pattern of earlier expeditions from Spain, as a group of investors in the Yucatán enterprise. They contributed money, supplies, weapons, and skills as an investment on future returns. Velázquez became apprehensive about Cortés's ambitions and canceled the expedition. He ordered the arrest of his aspiring rival. Alerted to the danger, Cortés addressed his men, promised them riches and glory, and then prepared to sail immediately. At muster, he counted five hundred fifty men, perhaps one hundred of whom were sailors, along with several Cuban natives and some Africans. The soldiers were divided into eleven companies, each with a captain, and put aboard eleven small vessels. Sixteen scarce and expensive horses were put on board, as well as some small cannon. All of this had put Cortés and his men heavily in debt. But on February 18, 1519, they set sail as adventurers, to gamble on the potentially lucrative outcome.

THE INITIAL RECEPTION

After weathering stormy seas, the ships put in at the island of Cozumel, where friendly natives told them of two white men who lived in nearby Yucatán. Cortés made contact with one of them, Jerónimo de Aguilar, a survivor of a shipwreck in 1511 en route from Panama to Santo Domingo. The other was thoroughly assimilated into Indian society, but Aguilar was overjoyed to be among his own again. His knowledge of the native language and local customs would be of great assistance to the Spaniards in the months ahead.

Later, at Potonchan (Tabasco), the local natives resisted Cortés's overtures for peace and attacked with abandon. After a bloody contest, Cortés took the city by force. In this and other fights the Spaniards suffered many wounded and several men were killed. The Indians, on the other hand, lost two hundred men. Little gold was found, but the natives said that people to the west had great amounts of it. After lecturing the Indians on their need for salvation through Christianity and describing the magnificence of the king of Spain, Cortés accepted a gift of twenty young maidens and continued up the Gulf coast.

When they got near the present city of Veracruz, the Spaniards met people who spoke a tongue foreign to Aguilar. However, one of Cortés's young maidens, baptized Marina, was able to communicate with them. Her role as a cultural intermediary in the conquest proved to be of great significance. Doña Marina, as she became known to her contemporaries (and Malinche to Mexicans who consider her part in the conquest as treasonous) became Cortés's interpreter and adviser. More than that, she was later his mistress and bore him a son. As a small child she had been given to or stolen by merchants who sold her to people of the south, and consequently she knew not only her native Nahuatl but one of the Maya languages as well. She communicated with the Indians, passing on the words in Maya to Aguilar, who then translated into Spanish for Cortés.

Realizing that the Indians would report to Moctezuma, Cortés had his men perform a mock battle to impress them. He then asked the local chief to send greetings to Moctezuma and to tell the Indian ruler that the Spaniards desired to travel to his great city. Although Tenochtitlan lay two hundred miles into the interior, swift runners quickly relayed the report to Moctezuma, who had already received drawings of their ships. The emperor's reaction is not known, but early Spanish accounts propagated the myth that he feared that Quetzalcoatl,

The chapel-de-fer, or "kettle-hat," was a helmet popular with the Spanish infantry.

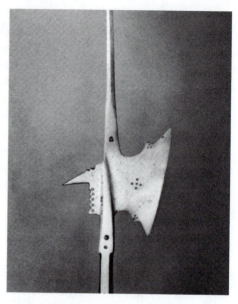

A halberd of the type used by the conquistadores.

An elaborate Spanish stirrup of the seventeenth century.

A warhorse of the sixteenth century was sometimes fitted with a chamfron, like the one shown here.

Fernando Cortés (1485–1547) dressed in the half armor used in battle. Full armor was not as heavy as one might think, but it did make the wearer very warm. Most Spaniards eventually adopted use of Indian layered-cotton protection.

or his emissaries, had returned to take the throne. For the moment, the Aztec king sent word that he rejoiced in the coming of the strangers. He sent rich presents but declined to meet with Cortés because he was ill and could not make the long journey. Moreover, it was out of the question for Cortés to come to see him because the trip through rugged mountains and deserts was too rigorous. Beyond these hardships, the Spaniards would have to pass through dangerous enemy territories. In this fashion Moctezuma wished Cortés well, as if to dismiss him—all of which disheartened the Spanish captain not one bit. He replied by message that he would not think of missing the opportunity of greeting the great emperor to deliver a message from his king.

Meanwhile, Cortés was well aware of his own tenuous legal position. Spaniards were not allowed to go off exploring on their own but only with official permission. Since Cortés had ignored the revocation of the governor's commission to him, he was dangerously close to treason. Thus, following another precedent from his homeland that allowed towns limited autonomy, he sought to clothe his actions with a veneer of legality.

With that in mind, he founded a settlement called La Villa Rica de la Vera Cruz (today Veracruz), according to established ceremony, in the king's name, with the procedure duly noted by witnesses. Cortés appointed town councilmen and other appropriate municipal officials and resigned his leadership. The officials of Veracruz then proceeded to elect him captain and *justicia mayor* with authority in military matters, pending royal orders to the contrary. Then on June 20, 1519, the council sent a petition to the Spanish crown (the only known original Spanish document to survive from that pivotal year), requesting recognition for the town of Veracruz and new titles for Cortés. They asked the king to give Cortés the right to grant encomiendas to his company, as well as to block Velázquez from seeking profit from the expedition he had tried to thwart.

To gain the loyalty and goodwill of his men, Cortés turned over to them all the supplies and equipment, which, he said, had put him seven thousand ducats in debt. In keeping with the generosity of the moment, the men agreed that, after the king's share of 20 percent—the *quinto*—was deducted, their captain would receive one-fifth of the remaining spoils.

THE TOTONACS AND A MUTINY SUPPRESSED

Pushing on to the Totonac city of Cempoala, the Spaniards were enthusiastically greeted by citizens bearing flowers and fruit. The obese ruler, who had sent regrets that he was too heavy to travel to meet them, complained of Aztec tyranny and gave Cortés a detailed description of Tenochtitlan. He suggested an alliance of the Spaniards with the victims of the oppressors.

Cortés agreed to stand by the Totonacs and told them to send word to potential allies to be prepared. Cortés then directed other Indian towns to stop tribute payments to the Aztecs. His army, strengthened by the arrival of a ship from Cuba bearing sixty Spaniards and nine horses, Cortés made plans to press inland. In order to maintain a coastal base, a fortress and houses were built at Veracruz, to be staffed by the ill, wounded, and older men. Cortés wrote the king, telling of his progress to date, assuring him of his devotion, and sending most of the treasure accumulated to that point. He added that he needed help, requesting financial assistance. The town council wrote another letter to the king, asking that the election of Cortés be confirmed. A ship with the letters, treasure, and two delegates sailed for Spain in late July 1519.

Anticipating the dangers and hardships that lay ahead, some men, especially the followers of Cuban governor Velázquez, plotted mutiny. Cortés learned of the conspiracy and, after a trial and confessions, he hanged two of the leaders and severely punished others. Nonetheless he knew he must maintain discipline and prevent mutiny under stressful conditions. Cortés was regarded as fearless by his men with whom he shared all the fatigues, privations, wounds, fevers, and narrow escapes from death and sacrifice. He now arranged to give the weak-hearted no alternative and the disloyal no opportunity to desert. Alleging the unseaworthiness of the ships, he instructed loyal pilots to strip the vessels and then scuttle them as quietly and quickly as possible. His audacity brought the army close to mutiny, and some no doubt questioned his sanity; but by this bold stroke he cut off all means of retreat. There was now no question of the Spaniards' course—they would have to conquer the mighty Mexica or die in the attempt. So Cortés led his men and indigenous allies into the heart of the Aztec empire.

THE TLAXCALANS AND REPORTS TO MOCTEZUMA

Moctezuma's depiction of the hardships before the Spaniards was only slightly exaggerated, for the march upcountry would take them some two hundred miles, on a rough and twisting path, from the steamy tropics to the chilling highlands, where they would find the Aztec capital above seventy-five hundred feet. Aside from the wild terrain, there was indeed danger from enemies—both those hostile to the Aztecs and those who acted under the orders of the wily emperor himself.

Leaving one hundred fifty men and two horses at Veracruz, Cortés departed the city in the middle of August with four hundred troops, hundreds of Cempoalan allies, the remaining horses, and three cannon. As they pushed inland the Spaniards were well received by towns subject to Moctezuma, for the emperor had ordered them to be friendly. Cortés sent some of the Cempoalans ahead to make amicable contact with the Tlaxcalans, known to have an adversarial relationship with the Aztecs. But the Tlaxcalans, aware of the communications between Cortés and Moctezuma, were suspicious and engaged in several skirmishes with the intruders, killing two of their horses. The word now spread that the beasts were mortal, a loss of psychological advantage for the invaders.

Meanwhile, noble envoys from Moctezuma arrived to reaffirm the emperor's friendship and willingness to pay a yearly tribute to the king of Spain, provided Cortés halted his ascent to the interior. In case appeasement would not work, Moctezuma also ordered his agents to sacrifice captives whose blood the "gods" might wish to drink.

The European animals with Cortés at first terrified the natives. Later descriptions compared horses to deer and also depicted beasts who snorted and bellowed as their muzzles spilled over with foam. Although Cortés seems to have utilized war dogs little in battle, the swift greyhounds and huge mastiffs, which weighed as much as 200 pounds, intimidated the natives, one of whom recorded that

> their dogs are enormous, with flat ears and long, dangling tongues. The color of their eyes is a burning yellow; their eyes flash fire and shoot off sparks. Their bellies are hollow, their flanks

long and narrow. They are tireless and very powerful. They bound here and there, panting, with their tongues hanging out. And they are spotted, like a jaguar. . . . They raised their muzzles high; they lifted their muzzles to the wind. They raced on before with saliva dripping from their jaws.[3]

Receiving descriptions of all these strange and unnerving things, the emperor summoned priests to call on the supernatural to stop the Spaniards. And finally, when these strategies failed to halt the Spaniards' advance, he commanded his people to offer gifts to the strangers. Surrounded by warriors who counseled resistance, Moctezuma had not ruled out force, but his gifts to Cortés suggest another explanation. Gift exchanges between rulers were customary gestures of reciprocity. But, the particular precious items sent to Cortés—feather headdresses, other ceremonial clothing, and weaponry—symbolically signaled another intention: to sacrifice the recipient.

As much as Cortés had tried to manipulate Indian rivalries and the discontent of tributaries, he still did not fully understand the complexities of native governance. Quite aware of the precariousness of the Spaniards' situation, he must have breathed a sigh of relief when the Tlaxcalans finally pledged their support. What he did not know was how close Xicotencatl, the commander of the Tlaxcalan forces, had come to convince the other nobles to oppose the newcomers. This would not be the first or the last time that the Spaniards would be saved by a fortuitous political decision in a factionalized situation over which they had no control.

THE CHOLULA MASSACRE

Moctezuma, who had been kept abreast of these developments by his agents, warily waited to see what the Spaniards would do next. His seeming reluctance to attack the invaders stemmed in part from military and logistical weakness. It was now late September 1519, a few months short of the harvest necessary to sustain the imperial economy and provide food to supply large armies and of the dry season that could make roads passable.

At this point Cortés chose to proceed with his Indian supporters to Cholula, a former Tlaxcalan ally only recently brought into the Aztecan orbit. Cortés may have been manipulated by Tlaxcalan and Cempoalan allies into attacking the Cholulans, who initially received him in friendship. A Spanish version of the story holds that the Cholulans secretly planned to bottle up the Spaniards in the city and attack them. Warned either by Tlaxcalan allies or by Doña Marina, allegedly informed of the plot by a Cholulan woman, the Spanish captain now moved to an unprovoked preemptive strike. He gave a prearranged signal to his men, who were poised for the attack, and the guns raked the main plaza, cutting down the unsuspecting citizens. Cortés gave orders to spare women and children, but in the ensuing five-hour battle some six thousand Cholulan warriors were killed. Much of the ancient holy city was burned and then put to the sack by the Spaniards' Indian allies, who richly savored the defeat of their old enemies.

Whatever the reasons for Cortés's decision to attack, certainly the massacre at Cholula was a turning point, for Moctezuma, stunned at the Spaniards' prescience, now seemed to have despaired of stopping them from entering Tenochtitlan.

---

3   Miguel León Portilla, ed., *The Broken Spears: The Aztec Account of the Conquest of Mexico*, trans. Lysander Kemp (Boston, MA, 1972), ix, 31, 41.

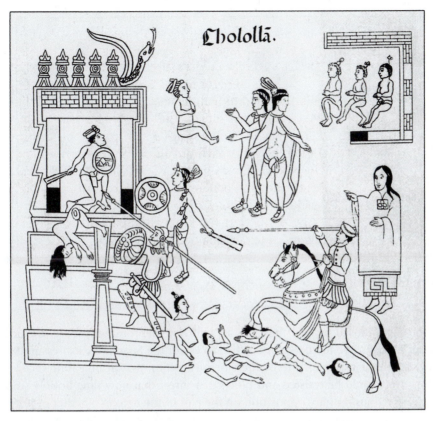

The Cholula massacre as depicted by a sixteenth-century Indian artist in the Lienzo de Tlaxcala.

INTO THE VALLEY OF ANAHUAC

The emperor reluctantly invited Cortés to an audience. The Spanish commander and his men made their way toward the valley, observed by incredulous natives, one of whom later preserved the striking impression made by the aliens.

> They came in battle array, as conquerors, and the dust rose in whirlwinds on the roads; their spears glinted in the sun, and their pennons fluttered like bats. They made a loud clamor as they marched, for their coats of mail and their weapons clashed and rattled. Some of them were dressed in glistening iron from head to foot; they terrified everyone who saw them.[4]

The Spaniards climbed to the high pass between the spectacular volcanic peaks of Popocatepetl and Iztaccihuatl. As they began the descent into the valley, they saw laid out in the distance before them the grand prospect of the lake cities. In that breathless moment, viewing one of the most awe-inspiring sights humans have ever seen, the soldiers experienced a tense excitement from the drama of the occasion and all that it promised but also a chilling realization of the audacity of their scheme. None was more alive to the peril than the captain.

---

4   Ibid., 41.

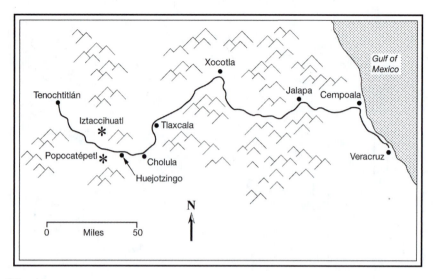

Route of Cortés

As the army moved toward the lake, an embassy of prominent lords, including the young Cacama, lord of Texcoco, approached to escort the Spaniards, expressing Moctezuma's regrets that he was unable to be there because of illness. Cacama announced that the Spaniards' way would be resisted and blocked, a threat that now rang hollow since there had been no serious military opposition on the part of the Aztecs. Whether or not the emperor was demoralized by prophecies he decided to face Cortés in the stronghold where he might contain the Spaniards.

On November 8, 1519, Indians of the valley flocked to observe the entrance of the newcomers, who descended on Ixtapalapa, which anchored the longest causeway. From that beautiful city the Spaniards could look straight down the thoroughfare to where the red and white towers of Tenochtitlan rose out of the water and the torches of the temples shimmered on the lake. Proceeding down the causeway, the Spanish force of about four hundred, with their six thousand native allies, moved through throngs of the curious who lined the way with their canoes. At length the party crossed the bridge that gave access to the city and there, under a canopy of green, gold, and silver and attended by a splendid retinue, was the lord of the Aztec empire. Moctezuma leaned on the arms of two nephews. Clothed in gorgeous finery, the fifty-two-year-old emperor was of dignified mien, with longish hair, a sparse moustache and chin whiskers. As he walked forward, servants placed mantles on the ground so that the royal sandals did not touch the earth. Following him was a magnificent procession of two hundred courtiers.

The bearded captain, dressed in shiny armor and bright European fabrics, dismounted and strode forth to embrace Moctezuma; but the nobles restrained him, signifying that the emperor's person was not to be touched. Instead, the leaders saluted each other and exchanged gifts. Then Moctezuma courteously received Cortés and offered the Spaniards palatial accommodations.

A TEST OF WILLS

By incredible good fortune, having made their way into the Mexica stronghold, the Spaniards spent several days wandering about the city, taking in the marvelous sights, much like any tourists in a foreign land. They admired the palaces with their cedar-lined chambers, the gardens, and the canals. Other scenes had quite the opposite effect: they were aghast at the great rack festooned with human skulls, and the priests, their long hair matted with dried blood, were repulsive to them. The visitors were properly fascinated by the zoo, as Bernal Díaz del Castillo noted, but as for "the infernal noise when the lions and tigers roared, and the jackals and foxes howled, and the serpents hissed, it was horrible to listen to and it seemed like a hell."[5]

Moctezuma and his nobles visited their guests' quarters often to see to their needs. This attention and gracious hospitality notwithstanding, the peril of the situation was not lost on Cortés, who realized that they were in fact trapped—if Moctezuma chose to make it so. Outside their luxurious palace the Spaniards were surrounded by a multitude of Indians who could rise on signal to ensnare them. The Spanish soldiers manifested their anxiety to Cortés, who considered making Moctezuma a hostage. Cortés himself reported that he accused Moctezuma of preparing to massacre the Spaniards in Tenochtitlan and made him a prisoner. The emperor would continue to rule his people and would be treated with the greatest respect. Meantime he was to counsel calm and patience among his people because any outbreak of hostilities would result in his death. Whether or when Cortés took Moctezuma prisoner is not certain, but the emperor continued to interact with the Spaniards while also meeting with his advisors and worshiping at the great temple. In circumstances of unpredictability, he counseled peace and continued to treat with Cortés who presented himself as a powerful friend should nearby city-states defect from their alliance with Tenochtitlan.

Many in the high Aztec nobility of warrior and priests did not share Moctezuma's approach of generosity and hospitality to the Spaniards. They were incensed at Cortés's demands that human sacrifice cease and pagan idols be smashed, to be replaced by crosses and images of the Virgin Mary. After some six months, outraged priests roused the populace and joined the warriors in calling for an armed offensive against the Spaniards. Moctezuma advised Cortés, with the greatest urgency, to leave the city. The pleased ruler told Cortés that the Spaniards could leave immediately—he had received word that a fleet of eleven ships stood off the shore at Veracruz.

THE NARVÁEZ EXPEDITION

In Cuba, Diego Velázquez seethed with anger against Cortés and grew more bitter with news of his protégé's success. To Velázquez, Cortés's deeds represented a blatant act of rebellion. He assembled a large force to pursue the rebel captain and arrest him. Under the command of Pánfilo de Narváez, the expedition included not only a sizable complement of foot soldiers but also eighty horses.

---

5   Bernal Díaz del Castillo, *The True History of the Conquest of New Spain, 1517-1521*, trans. A. P. Maudslay, intro. Irving Leonard (New York, NY, 1958), 213.

Making port at Veracruz, Narváez ordered two soldiers and a priest to the garrison, now under the command of the capable Gonzalo de Sandoval, to demand submission. Sandoval arrested the three of them and sent them off to Cortés. Narváez then landed his troops and proceeded instead to Cempoala, where the Totonacs, assuming the newcomers to be associates of Cortés, lavished gifts and provisions on them. Narváez convinced the Cempoalans and agents of Moctezuma that Cortés and his men were traitors. He assured them that, after Cortés was taken, all Spaniards would leave the country and the emperor would again rule as before. Moctezuma, unknown to Cortés, responded with presents and encouragement to Narváez, shrewdly exploiting the quarrel between the two Spanish forces. For the first time since the strangers arrived, the besieged ruler found himself in a favorable position. With good fortune, the white men might kill each other off.

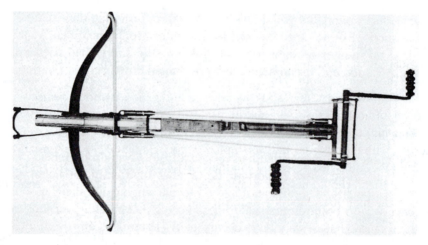

A crossbow with windlass of the type used in the conquest. Because of its devastating force, popes forbade its use against Christians; but it was used very effectively in wars against Muslims and natives of the New World.

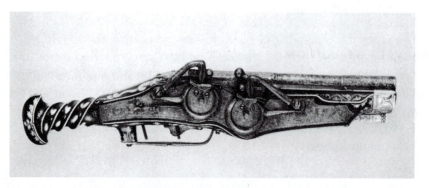

A wheel-lock pistol of the sixteenth century. This one belonged to Charles V.

On first learning of the large Spanish expedition on the coast, Cortés had a sense of foreboding—it was an army roughly twice as large as his own. After failing to win Narváez to his side, Cortés mustered his followers. He told them that Narváez and his men had dishonored them by insults and were trying to steal what they had won with their sweat and blood. The captain selected some volunteers to accompany him to Veracruz and asked Moctezuma to assure the safety of the Spaniards left behind. Leaving Pedro de Alvarado in command of about eighty men in the city, Cortés departed for the coast with the same number. In Cholula he was joined by one hundred twenty of his men who had been settling a town on the lower Gulf coast.

In a rapid march Cortés soon put his men on the outskirts of Cempoala, arriving under cover of darkness. He attacked suddenly, at midnight during a driving rainstorm, and in the confusion and darkness he gained the advantage. It appears that many of the newcomers were less than anxious to resist Cortés. After a frenzied skirmish, Narváez took a pike in the eye and surrendered.

The swift and decisive action of Cortés, against a much larger force, served to enhance his prestige among the Indians as well as with the men of Narváez. Using diplomatic skill and bribery, Cortés now showed generosity to the defeated soldiers, most of whom he had known in Cuba. They were eager enough to join him when they were promised their share of the spoils. But as Cortés set out for the return to Tenochtitlan, a battered messenger brought news of disaster—the Aztecs had risen up and Alvarado and his companions were pinned down in their quarters.

THE SPANIARDS BESEIGED AND THE NIGHT OF SORROW

Alvarado gave permission to the nobles of Tenochtitlan to celebrate an important festival, that of Toxcatl in honor of Huitzilopochtli. The Spaniard agreed to the singing and dancing, but there was to be no human sacrifice. There are conflicting versions of the tragedy that subsequently occurred. We assume, in any event, that the reduced Spanish garrison was edgy, especially since Narváez had sent provocative messages to the Aztecs, inciting them to rebel against the men of Cortés.

According to Alvarado, he was informed that the ceremonial dance to the war god was a prelude to an attack on the Spaniards, who were to be sacrificed. Therefore, he determined to strike first. Others have maintained that he simply overreacted to rumors without basis in fact or, more unlikely, that Cortés had sanctioned such an attack, reminiscent of Cholula, before he left the city. Whatever the truth, during the festivities the Spaniards blocked the four exits from the square, drew their swords, and rushed the celebrants. There followed a wild and bloody scene in which the Indians, caught unarmed and without escape, had little chance. In a short time thousands of Aztec nobles, the cream of the warriors, fell under Spanish steel. After the Spaniards retreated to their quarters, they were besieged by a multitude of grief-stricken and enraged Indians.

Cortés reacted swiftly with forced marches to the valley in order to lift the siege. Approaching Tenochtitlan, he found a strangely silent city, showing little sign of activity. He fired a cannon and was heartened to hear a return boom. He entered Tenochtitlan unopposed with about one thousand soldiers, one hundred cavalrymen, and two thousand Tlaxcalan war-riors. Although he gained the palace without difficulty, it soon became clear that the Aztecs had simply allowed him to walk into a trap.

The Spaniards preferred fighting in wide open spaces where they could deploy their guns to advantage and charge their horses into enemy ranks. Confined in the city, hemmed in by buildings that afforded protection to the natives, they were less effective. The Aztecs made repeated assaults on the Spanish position, finally resorting to what resembled suicide squads. The cannon put shot into them at close range, while the harquebuses, falconets, and crossbows took a frightful toll—and still fresh relays came. After twenty-three days and with food supplies and munitions dwindling, Cortés persuaded Moctezuma, who was still held hostage, to urge the Aztecs to desist. The ruler mounted the rooftop to draw attention and began to speak. He was struck down and died three days later.

There are two versions of his death. The Spanish version is that he was stoned, per-haps accidentally, by his own people. But it is more likely that Moctezuma was strangled or stabbed to death by Spaniards. Because of his failure to effectively oppose the Spanish inva-sion, Moctezuma has been viewed in Mexican histories as too indecisive. We cannot know what motivated the emperor, but he had not shied from battle before.

Surrounded by tens of thousands of their adversaries, after failing in negotiations with the Aztec ruling class and his men badly mauled from the fighting, Cortés decided to make a break for it that night, June 30, 1520. The chosen avenue for escape was the Tlacopan (Tacuba) cause-way which, though said to have been two miles long, was the shortest of them. The Aztecs had removed the bridges spanning the gaps in the causeways, so Cortés ordered the construction of a portable bridge, which was to be carried by forty Tlaxcalan warriors. The treasure acquired earlier from Moctezuma was divided, with each man allowed to take what he wished for his share. Some foolishly weighted themselves down with precious metals and jewelry, which later hampered their movements and contributed to their capture or death.

Sandoval, who had returned to Tenochtitlan with Cortés, was put in charge of the lead columns, while Alvarado was given command of the rear guard which included most of the Narváez force. Cortés elected to lead a flying squad of one hundred men, ready to shift to any weak point. At midnight they stole quietly out of the palace, the horses' hooves wrapped in cloth to muffle their movements. A pitch-black sky and light rain helped obscure the figures but made the footing treacherous. It was early in the morning of July 1, 1520, the *Noche Triste*, or "Night of Sorrow," as it came to be known in Spanish history.

Moving carefully over the causeway, the Spaniards were able to place their bridge over the first channel and cross. According to one version of their flight, an old woman drawing water from a canal suddenly spotted them and cried out, but it is more likely that sentries sounded the alarm with blasts on their conch shells. The Aztecs came pouring out of the darkness. Thousands of warriors fell on the escapees, and some Spaniards in the rear retreated only to be killed later. Other Indians flanked the causeway in their canoes and shot into the mass. The Spanish formations broke as each man tried to save himself.

With great effort the bridge was thrown across the second breach, but under the strain of fleeing cavalry and foot soldiers, the bridge collapsed, throwing into confusion and panic those who followed. Cortés and his cohorts raced for the mainland, forced to swim the remaining breaks in the causeway. The unit in gravest danger was the rear guard, for it was taking the brunt of the Aztec charge. Alvarado's mare had fallen under him and he now stumbled over the masses of the dead choking the breaches and crossed on the bodies. As the enemy closed, Alvarado, who was a powerful athlete, sprinted toward the last open channel, placed the point of his lance, and, according to legend, made a tremendous vault that carried him over to safety.

In that terrifying night, the most drastic reversal of Spanish arms in the conquests of the New World, at least four hundred fifty of Cortés's men died[6] and more than four thousand of the steadfast Indian allies fell. Forty-six of the horses lay sprawled along the littered causeway. The survivors gained the mainland, where, according to tradition, Fernando Cortés was so moved by the disaster that he sat under a great tree and wept. He soon learned of another calamity—a convoy of Spaniards and their allies traveling from Veracruz to join him had been captured at Zultepec in western Tlaxcala. Powerless to rescue them, he discovered their fate months later.[7]

THE SPANIARDS REGROUP

As the Spaniards and their allies retreated north (the most strategic route) to go around the lake to get to Tlaxcala, they received help from some towns but also fought several battles, in which more Spaniards and Tlaxcalans lost their lives. Uncertainty prevailed when the survivors (about four hundred fifty Spaniards with twenty horses) reached the Tlaxcalan stronghold after five days; there they were allowed to nurse their wounds and regroup. They were aided by at least three factors. (1) Although Tlaxcalan support was by no means assured even though they had incurred more enmity from the Aztecs, Cortés secured it by promising them spoils of a war along with exemption from tribute. (2) It was the rainy season and the Aztec farmer-soldiers could not be called up in numbers great enough to mount a major offensive. (3) Furthermore, the Aztec leadership was in disarray, with factions competing for power. Many in the top warrior class had perished in the fighting, and Cuitlahuac, Moctezuma's brother, died of smallpox soon after being raised to the throne.

So along with the promise of indigenous fighters, the Spaniards had a silent, deadly, and totally unexpected ally in the land: one of Narváez's men came to Mexico infected with smallpox, which spread quickly with devastating consequences to the Indians. Tens of thousands of Spanish allies and foes, including many nobles, were carried off by the disease. Some have questioned whether Spaniards may have infected with syphilis by natives because a virulent form of it appeared in Europe soon after the conquest, although similar types of spirochetes were already present there. In any event, Europeans were not decimated by New World diseases. The dwindling Aztec leadership selected a nephew of Moctezuma, the eighteen-year-old Cuauhtemoc, as the new ruler. Official mourning ceremonies for their lost

---

6   Bernal Díaz del Castillo, who was present, wrote that on the Night of Sorrow and in the next five days, during which the Aztecs pursued them, over 860 Spaniards died. Ibid., 321.

7   After the Aztec fall of Tenochtitlan, his men discovered that fifteen Spaniards and perhaps several hundred allies (including fifty women and ten children) had been ritually sacrificed and eaten over a period of months, stark evidence that not everyone had capitulated to the Spanish advance. Their resistance turned out to have been futile as the town and its people were then destroyed.

Cuauhtemoc (1502?-1525), the last Aztec emperor, as he appeared to a post-conquest Indian artist.

kings slowed preparations for dispatching the Spaniards once and for all. In the interim, Cortés was laying plans for a return to Tenochtitlan. He would assault it by water as well as by land. To that end he set carpenters to work constructing launches in sections that could be carried from Tlaxcala across the mountains by native porters and assembled on the lake shore. The vessels would be fitted for both sails and oars.

THE FALL OF TENOCHTITLAN

Cortés was well aware that for his strategy to work it was crucial to attract allies in the cities adjoining the lake. Fortuitous events aided him in negotiating a pact with Iztlilxochitl, a son of Nezahualpilli who had begun a rebellion against the ruler of Texcoco; together they took this city without bloodshed. After making his headquarters there in December 1520, over the next few months Cortés and his allies succeeded in winning the support of the surrounding area through the use of diplomacy and force. By April, reinforced by new arrivals from Veracruz, he counted nine hundred Spaniards, of whom eighty-six had horses, a hundred and eighteen carried crossbows and harquebuses, and all were armed with swords and daggers. Some wielded pikes and halberds, most had shields, and many wore some form of protective armor. There were fifteen bronze cannon and three heavy guns of cast iron. Supporting the Spaniards were native legions numbering many thousands of warriors. Cortés now dispatched Juan de Sandoval to Tlaxcala to escort the launches. Sections of the thirteen vessels were carried over the mountains by 8,000 porters, while another two thousand bore provisions. The long procession, stretching out almost six miles, arrived at the Spanish camp at Texcoco without grave incident.

The small Spanish fleet was crucial to their strategy, for if the causeways could be commanded, all transportation and communication to the island could be cut off. Moreover, the Aztecs could be prevented from attacking the Spaniards from their canoes. Cortés chose to command the fleet in person. Those fighting on land were assigned to three commanders, each of whom was to secure a causeway. On May 10, 1521, they began the siege, and with help from favorable winds they overpowered hundreds of Aztec canoes. Spanish boats penetrated canals on the edges of the city, after which the attackers set fire to many houses. With the success of the operation on water, Alvarado and Cristóbal de Olid charged down the causeways to engage the defenders of the barricades and bridges.

Furious fighting continued for weeks, for although the attackers were able to penetrate sections of the city, they could not easily hold positions. They were assailed by warriors who rained arrows and stones on them from the flat rooftops while others engaged them in hand-to-hand combat. The advantages of horse and cannon were greatly reduced in the close street fighting. Cortés concluded, to his regret, that he must level the city. Accordingly, his men began the systematic destruction of the great temples and palaces that afforded his adversaries protection.

Early on, the aqueducts had been cut and the launches swept the lake to prevent water, food, and reinforcements from reaching the besieged defenders. Still, in the face of heavy casualties, disease, and a lack of food and drinking water, the Aztecs held out, resigned to the warrior's death. Attempts to effect a truce failed. Finally, in a last concerted offensive, the Spaniards and their native allies overran the Aztec position. In the savage finale Cortés and Alvarado backed the survivors to the wall, and Tenochtitlan fell on August 13, 1521.

An Aztec Jaguar Knight dressed for battle, wearing a pelt and wielding an obsidian-edged war club.

A mounted Spaniard in full armor.

Taken by Cortés, Cuauhtemoc then touched the dagger in his adversary's belt and spoke: "I have done everything in my power to defend myself and my people, and everything that it was my duty to do, to avoid the pass in which I now find myself. You may do with me whatever you wish, so kill me, for that will be best."[8]

When the tumult subsided and the dust settled, there remained a scene of desolation: the beautiful metropolis effectively smashed, the gardens flattened, and the canals filled with rubble. The destruction of one of history's grandest cities was accompanied by bravery and suffering on both sides. Aside from their superior weapons and armor, the Spaniards derived great advantage from some 200,000 Indian allies, their horses, the spread of smallpox, and a favorable psychological atmosphere. They benefited enormously from their deployment of native allies in tactics of all-out warfare that ignored the traditional ceremonial formalities of Aztec combat.

Brilliant as it was in certain respects, Aztec civilization thrived on militarism; therefore, the character of its fall was consistent with its rise. And it was poetically apt that its last great warrior-king was Cuauhtemoc, whose name translates as "Falling Eagle" or, in another sense, "Setting Sun."

RECOMMENDED FOR FURTHER STUDY

Bassett, Molly H. *The Fate of Earthly Things: Aztec Gods and God-Bodies*. Austin: University of Texas Press, 2015.

Brian, Amber, Bradley Benton, and Pablo García Loaeza, eds. *The Native Conquistador: Alva Ixtlilxochitl's Account of the Conquest of New Spain*. University Park: Pennsylvania State University Press, 2015.

Cerwin, Herbert. *Bernal Díaz, Historian of the Conquest*. Norman: University of Oklahoma Press, 1963.

Chance, John K. *Conquest of the Sierra: Spaniards and Indians in Colonial Oaxaca*. Norman: University of Oklahoma Press, 1989.

Cook, Noble David, and W. George Lovell, eds. *Secret Judgments of God: Old World Diseases and Colonial Spanish America*. Norman: University of Oklahoma Press, 1991.

Cortés, Hernán. *Hernán Cortés: Letters from Mexico*. Translated and edited by A. R. Pagden, with an introduction by J. H. Elliott. New York: Orion Press, 1971.

Crosby, Alfred W. *The Columbian Exchange: Ecological and Cultural Consequences of 1492*. Westport, CT: Greenwood Press, 1972.

Cypess, Sandra. *La Malinche in Mexican Literature from History to Myth*. Austin: University of Texas Press, 1991.

Díaz del Castillo, Bernal. *The True History of the Conquest of New Spain, 1517-1521*. Translated by A. P. Maudslay with an introduction by Irving Leonard. New York: Grove Press, Inc., 1958.

_____. *The History of the Conquest of New Spain*. Edited by David Carrasco. Albuquerque: University of New Mexico Press, 2008.

Elliot, John H. *Imperial Spain, 1469-1716*. New York: St. Martin's Press, 1962.

Gardiner, C. Harvey. *The Constant Captain: Gonzalo de Sandoval*. Carbondale: Southern Illinois University Press, 1961.

_____. *Naval Power in the Conquest of Mexico*. Austin: University of Texas Press, 1956.

Hassig, Ross. *Aztec Warfare: Imperial Expansion and Political Control*. Norman: University of Oklahoma Press, 1988.

---

8   Quoted in Francisco López de Gómara, *Cortés: The Life of the Conqueror by His Secretary* (Berkeley, CA, 1964), 292.

_____. "The Collision of Two Worlds." In *The Oxford History of Mexico*, edited by Michael C. Meyer and William H. Beezley, 73-106. New York: Oxford University Press, rev. 2010.

_____. *Mexico and the Spanish Conquest*. Norman: University of Oklahoma Press, 2006.

Iglesia, Ramón. *Columbus, Cortés and Other Essays*. Translated and edited by Lesley B. Simpson. Berkeley, University of California Press, 1969.

Kamen, Henry. *Philip of Spain*. New Haven, CT: Yale University Press, 1997.

Karttunen, Frances. *Between Worlds: Interpreters, Guides, and Survivors*. New Brunswick, NJ: Rutgers University Press, 1994.

León Portilla, Miguel, ed. *The Broken Spears: The Aztec Account of the Conquest of Mexico*. Translated by Lysander Kemp. Boston, MA: Beacon Press, 1972.

Liss, Peggy. *Isabel, the Queen: Life and Times*. New York: Oxford University Press, 1992.

López de Gómara, Francisco. *Cortés: The Life of the Conqueror by His Secretary*. Berkeley: University of California Press, 1964.

Lynch. John. *Spain, 1516-1598: From Nation State to World Empire*. Oxford, UK: Blackwell, 1992.

Matthew, Laura E., and Michel R. Oudijk, eds. *Indian Conquistadores: Indigenous Allies in the Conquest of Mesoamerica*. Norman: University of Oklahoma Press, 2007.

Nader, Helen. "The Spain that Encountered Mexico." In *The Oxford History of Mexico*, edited by Michael C. Meyer and William H. Beezley, 11-44. New York: Oxford University Press, rev. 2010.

Padden, Robert C. *The Hummingbird and the Hawk: Conquest and Sovereignty in the Valley of Mexico*, 1503-1541. New York: Harper & Row, 1970.

Parker, Geoffrey. *Imprudent King: A New Life of Philip II*. New Haven, CT: Yale University Press, 2014.

Prescott, William H. *History of the Conquest of Mexico*. New York: Bantam Books, 1967.

Restall, Matthew. *Seven Myths of the Spanish Conquest*. New York: Oxford University Press, 2003.

Restall, Matthew, and Felipe Fernández-Armesto. *The Conquistadors: A Very Short Introduction*. New York: Oxford University Press, 2012.

Schroeder, Susan et al. *Chimalpahin's Conquest: A Nahua Historian's Rewriting of Francisco López de Gómara's "La Conquista de México."* Stanford, CA: Stanford University Press, 2010.

Schwartz, Stuart, ed. *Victors and Vanquished: Spanish and Nahua Views of the Conquest of Mexico*. New York: Bedford/St. Martin's, 2000.

Schwaller, John F., with Helen Nader. *The First Letter from New Spain: The Lost Petition of Cortés and his Company, June 20, 1519*. Austin: University of Texas Press, 2014.

Todorov, Tzvetzan. *The Conquest of America: The Question of the Other*. New York: Harper & Row, 1984.

Townsend, Camila. "Burying the White Gods: New Perspectives on the Conquest of Mexico." *American Historical Review* 108/3 (2003): 659-87.

_____. *Malintzin's Choices: An Indian Woman in the Conquest of Mexico*. Albuquerque: University of New Mexico Press, 2006.

CHAPTER 7

THE SETTLEMENT OF NEW SPAIN

The conquerors withdrew to nearby Coyoacan, leaving the Aztecs to remove their dead. The Spaniards decided to build a new city over the ruins of Tenochtitlan, and soon armies of native laborers under the direction of not only Spanish architects and artisans but also indigenous elites, laid the foundations for the splendid city of Mexico. Many continuities in the lived experience of prehispanic daily life persisted as new features were added. Try as they would, Spanish officials and Franciscan friars could not completely erase indigenous influences as material and cultural exchanges evolved. New civic and religious rituals often showed traces of indigenous celebratory practices.

INDIAN SLAVERY AND THE ENCOMIENDA SYSTEM

For Spaniards, the conquest had been the result of a great effort by individual adventurers who received no pay for their work. Many had gone into debt to outfit themselves for the enterprise; all had suffered hardships and had seen companions die horrible deaths; almost all had been wounded. But the treasure for which they had endured so much proved to be a pittance. Some of the survivors of the Noche Triste had escaped with a few valuable objects, but the bulk of the riches had been lost in the lake waters.[1] Of the spoils, a horseman received as his share only about a hundred gold pesos, one-fifth of the cost of a horse. Foot soldiers, who constituted the bulk of the army, received even less. As the mood of his companions grew uglier, Cortés relented and allowed the torture of Cuauhtémoc and other lords, hoping thereby to learn the location of any remaining hoard of riches. The royal feet of the nobles were oiled and held over fire. Despite their agonies, they gave no information, for there was no cache—or at least none has ever been found.

How, then, were the conquerors to be rewarded? Invariably the first answer to this question came in the form of human bodies. Indians were initially often brutally enslaved and

---

1 In 1981, several feet underground in Mexico City a crude gold bar was found. Quite possibly it was dropped on the retreat.

forced to perform labor in appallingly inhumane tasks. The Aztecs, of course, had slaves, so the practice was not new to their subject populations, although the Spanish rationale was different (and would be challenged by legal scholars). Cortés saw that Aztec practices provided other avenues to wealth, and he moved to secure the tribute rolls of the Aztec empire, which contained paintings identifying the subject towns along with the kinds and amounts of tribute paid to Tenochtitlan. There were 370 such towns, each having yielded to the Aztec emperor one-third of its production. Thus, the Spanish captain acquired knowledge of the population, the geography, and the economy—not to mention the tribute that the conquerors could now enjoy. In order to calm his irate soldiers, Cortés agreed, with some misgivings, to distribute the Indian towns to them as rewards.

There was a precedent for this practice; in the Caribbean Islands, Spaniards had been granted native villages for their profit. As originally conceived, this system, the encomienda, was seen as the best solution for all concerned. The individual deserving Spaniard (the *encomendero*) received the tribute of the Indians, as well as their free labor, in return for which the natives were commended to the encomendero's care. He was to see to their conversion to Christianity, to ensure good order in the village, and in all ways to be responsible for their welfare. Theoretically it was thought that this system could better acculturate, control, and protect the Indians. What happened in practice was quite another matter as the system, subjected to every imaginable abuse, kept the Indians in a state of bondage, although not chattel slavery. Indians were overworked, separated from their families, cheated, and physically maltreated. The encomienda in early decades was responsible for creating economic and social tragedies that persisted in one guise or another into modern times.

The tremendous loss of Indian lives, attributable at least in part to slavery and the encomienda, offered grim warnings. Moreover, the Spanish crown wanted the tribute for itself and thus sought to maintain direct control over the Indians to retain them as royal vassals. Yet because the crown did not have the fiscal resources to compensate those who had won extensive territories and millions of people for Spain, the king acceded the awarding of indigenous labor and tribute through the encomienda. Nonetheless, he was never at ease with the arrangement and from the first sought the means to bring all Indian towns under royal control. The struggle between the crown and the individuals who held encomiendas dominated much of the suxteenth century.

THE SPREAD OF CONQUEST

Even before the fall of Tenochtitlan, Cortés had sent small parties to explore the land's resources. They returned with information on sources of gold and silver and reported on the location of natural ports and timber for the construction of ships. Once he had secured the valley, Cortés lost no time in dispatching expeditions in all directions to bring other inhabitants in the country under Spanish control. He was impelled to do so for various reasons: to gather more information about the people and the land, to satisfy a consuming interest in the existence of a strait through the continent to Asia, and to dominate as much territory as possible before rivals staked their claims. His time was short, for the crown had ordered an agent to take over the government and to arrest him. By August 1521 Cristóbal de Tapia had arrived, but he was intimidated by partisans of Cortés and withdrew. The conqueror meanwhile sent the king word of his defeat of the Aztecs, after which Cortés was forgiven his insubordination.

During the course of the next several years Spanish forces under many different lieutenants overran Mexico, parts of Central America, and a piece of what is now the southwestern United States. In doing this, they had a particular advantage. Just as in the earlier conquest of the Aztecs, they were able to recruit indigenous co-conquerors who accompanied them in the thousands. Among these were Tlaxcalans, Purépecha, and Otomí who were crucial to the planting of new colonies; for their services they received special privileges. The use of different ethnic groups in military conquest had also been a feature of late prehispanic expansion, but these multi-directional flows of migration increased under Spanish rule. Although the conquest of the Mexica-Aztecs had taken a relatively short time, the Spaniards

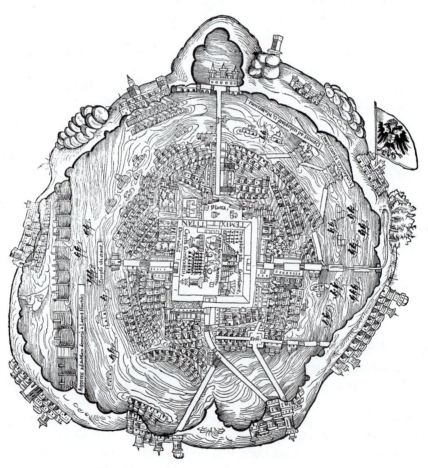

An early map of "Temixitan" (Tenochtitlan). Probably drawn at the request of Cortés, it appeared in the Latin edition of his Second Letter, printed in Nuremburg in 1524. In order to ingratiate himself. Cortés wrote five long letters to the king in which he related the progress of the conquest.

soon discovered that bringing under their sway the entire land was a vastly more difficult enterprise, not least because of the geographical features that characterized Mexico.

They were already familiar with the southern part of Mexico's land mass, which stretched along the eastern coast from the flat lowlands of the Yucatán Peninsula to Veracruz. They had made the climb from the coast to the valleys of Puebla-Tlaxcala and then up through the peaks to the southeast of Tenochtitlan and down into the central Valley of Mexico. Much of Mexico's terrain is, in fact, mountainous. The explorers who ventured northward sailed along the Pacific coast as far as modern-day British Columbia or followed a central plateau (*altiplano*) bordered by the Sierra Madre Occidental on the west and the Sierra Madre Oriental on the east. Both chains stretch to the current Mexican border with the United States. On their coastal sides they drop sharply down to relatively narrow Pacific and Caribbean plains, respectively. Much of north central and northwest Mexico is semi-arid, and the precipitous canyons of the Sierra Madre Occidental do not offer inviting human habitats.

The Spaniards who undertook the campaigns into southern territories similarly encountered highly broken terrain consisting of mountains and valleys. The manifold variations in elevation explain why Mexico experiences so much climatic differentiation, even though two-thirds of its land mass lies in tropical latitudes. Southern coastal areas, on both the Caribbean and Pacific sides, experience hot and humid weather, tropical rain forest in some areas, and occasional hurricanes; but between these coasts rise the highest mountains and valleys, where the climate becomes cooler as altitude increases. The basin floor of the Valley of Mexico lies within a comfortable temperate zone, while the mountains that surround it have a colder climate. Latitude and altitude (and the El Niño phenomenon in the Pacific) also influence rainfall patterns in the annual cycle of wet (warm) and dry (cool) seasons. Compared to the north, southern Mexico receives greater amounts of precipitation with less annual variability. This is why indigenous peoples formed the most concentrated sedentary communities in central and southern Mexico.

In moving out from the center (the Valley of Mexico), Spaniards encountered difficult terrain and diverse ecosystems with considerable climatic variations in temperature and rainfall, factors that influenced their efforts at conquest. Where they found more mobile peoples whose agriculture was circumscribed by aridity or other climatic factors (as in the north), they tended to have trouble subduing them. Highly centralized states strongly dependent on a dominant capital are vulnerable, tending to disintegrate quickly when the center falls. Hence, the collapse of the imperial capital of Tenochtitlan was tantamount to the surrender of almost all towns under the city's control, and much of central Mexico automatically fell to the invaders. There were many other areas of Mexico, however, outside the Aztec pale. Some threw in with the Spaniards early, and some came around as the Spaniards gained in reputation. But other groups that had successfully resisted the Aztecs rejected Spanish overlordship as well. While none could command forces comparable to those of the Aztecs, their more fragmented political structure made conquest difficult. Fighting the loosely organized indigenous groups of Mexico presented the same frustrations and vexing problems that confront those dealing with guerrilla tactics in modern warfare.

Cortés was eager to plant settlements with a view to legitimizing his actions. In 1521 he sent Gonzalo de Sandoval to Coatzacoalcos (later called Puerto México but now known also by its Indian name) to settle that region and establish better communications with the islands. The same year Luis Marín departed for Oaxaca, where he encountered little success in his attempt to pacify the Zapotecs in hill country. He was more fortunate farther south in Chiapas, remaining until 1524 to establish a town; however, in 1527, the Chiapanecos rebelled, and the territory had to be reconquered by Diego de Mazariegos.

The governor of Jamaica, Francisco de Garay, had earlier been granted a royal commission to govern the Pánuco region north of Veracruz on the Gulf coast. Hoping to prevent what they considered an incursion, Cortés and Alvarado used force and diplomacy to convince Garay to withdraw. Meanwhile Cristóbal de Olid, one of Cortés's closest friends and confidants, was sent to western Mexico in 1522. After a cordial reception in Michoacán, he explored the Pacific coast, but in Colima he was stiffly opposed and forced to pull back.

Aware that expeditions from Panama were pushing northward up into Central America, Cortés moved to seize control first. Rumors circulated of cities rivaling Tenochtitlan in size and wealth, and in late 1523 Alvarado was ordered into the Maya territory of Guatemala, accompanied by Nahua, Zapotec, and Mixtec allies who stayed on, imprinting their own Mesoamerican influences. After some arduous campaigns, he drove into El Salvador and conquered that region as well. For Alvarado's brilliant, though bloody, accomplishments, a grateful Spanish king appointed him governor and captain general of the lands he had won.

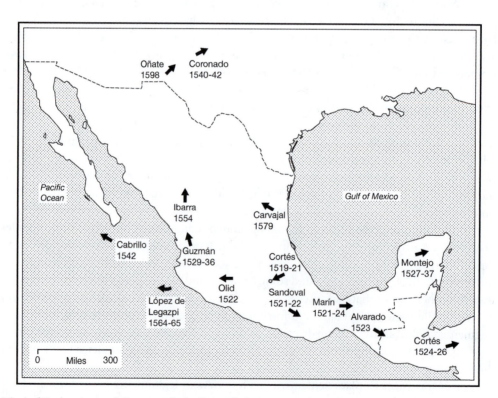

Principal Explorations and Conquests in the Sixteenth Century

Shortly after Alvarado's departure from Mexico, Olid set sail to secure Honduras, stopping by Cuba for provisions. At this point Olid threw off loyalty to his captain and made common cause with the enemy, Governor Velázquez. When Cortés learned that Honduras was to be taken in the name of Olid and Velázquez, he was furious. He dispatched a punitive expedition, then decided to go down himself. It was the most costly decision the conqueror ever made.

Departing Mexico with a party of Spaniards mostly mounted, along with many Indian allies, musicians, tumblers, acrobats, and some young Spanish noblemen, Cortés headed to the Gulf coast and then cut southward across unknown country. The journey took them through Tabasco, Campeche, and the base of Yucatán. Because they were not following native trade routes, they encountered few settlements and had to survive off the wilderness. Great numbers of porters collapsed from exhaustion, and many of the horses perished. Indians and Spaniards alike contracted fevers and dysentery, and all suffered from near starvation. Though lacking the drama of the Aztec conquest, the Honduras march exceeded the earlier enterprise in sheer hardship. For months the expedition cut its way through thick jungles, waded in swamps, and crossed swollen rivers. Once, within a distance of fifty miles, the Spaniards were forced to build fifty bridges, one of which, by Cortés's account, required a thousand trees. During this disastrous march a tragic episode occurred. Cuauhtémoc and

The flamboyant Pedro de Alvarado (1485–1541), Cortés's lieutenant and the conqueror of Guatemala.

several other native lords had been taken along as hostages lest, in the absence of Cortés from Mexico, they encourage a native rebellion. When they allegedly attempted to foment an uprising among the Indians on the expedition, all, including Cuauhtémoc, were summarily tried and hanged.

At last Cortés and his men stumbled into Honduras, only to find that all had been in vain, for the advance punitive party had beheaded the rebel Olid and returned to Mexico. After spending some time trying to establish a settlement in his name, the captain set about returning, this time wisely traveling by sea. The nineteen-month venture was a remarkable feat of exploration and endurance but a fiasco in all else.

CORTÉS IS DISCREDITED

Before departing for Honduras, Cortés had entrusted the government to the hands of royal treasury officials, with Alonso de Estrada in charge. Estrada was an honorable judge, but he found it difficult to govern the various factions that had formed and finally lost control. Because the expedition to Honduras remained out of contact for so long, the rumor spread in Mexico that Cortés and the others had perished. Encouraged by word of Cortés's death, various factions moved to dispossess his followers of their encomiendas and other privileges, which were then handed over to supporters of corrupt treasury officials. A time of anarchy for all, Indians were especially maltreated.

The usurping governors ordered funeral ceremonies for Cortés and his men and then granted permission for the "widows" to remarry. When one of the wives, Juana Ruiz de Marcilla, criticized the action and heaped scorn on the officials, she was given one hundred lashes in public. Cortés later paid her great honors, carrying her on his horse and addressing her as "Doña." Most detrimental for the captain (irreparably damaging, as it turned out) were the accusations made against him in dispatches sent to Spain, in which he was charged with having hidden Aztec treasure for himself, misusing crown funds, and cheating the royal treasury in other respects. The reports also cast doubt on his loyalty to the king. The dramatic news that Cortés was alive caused his men to rise up and seize the usurpers, who were thrown in cages and put on public display. Cortés's return to Mexico had a calming effect on political strife, but his reputation was not so easily restored.

The charges against the conqueror were never substantiated, but they planted seeds of suspicion. Moreover, the allegations provided a convenient pretext for which the crown may well have been thankful. At precisely the time Cortés was campaigning against the Aztecs, Emperor Charles V, the king of Spain, faced a revolt of his nobles at home; and although he was able to prevail, he retained a distrust of the fractious Spanish nobility. Thus, Charles viewed with some concern the concentration of so much prestige and power in the hands of a budding aristocracy in the New World, especially since these "nobles" were rough adventurers and far distant from his royal armies in Europe. Crown policy had been to ease explorers and conquerors from political power but, for the sake of appearances, the crown sought pretexts to void earlier signed agreements. Hence, Columbus's maladministration of Española had given the crown an excuse to replace him. And now the accusations against Cortés would serve the same purpose.

Charles V (1500–58), king of Spain and Holy Roman Emperor, reigned during the decades of the Spanish conquests of the New World.

Receiving word of the defeat of the Aztecs, the king had appointed the conqueror as governor and captain general of New Spain in 1522. As an administrator, Cortés, in addition to moving energetically to explore the land and seek ports for further discoveries, began to develop the economy. He undertook the search for mines, introduced European plants and livestock, and promoted commerce. His active encouragement of marriages between his lieutenants and daughters or widows of Indian nobles strengthened Spanish claims to indigenous wealth. He issued ordinances to implement in the colony, sought ecclesiastics and educators, and in many respects acted as an enlightened governor should. While he probably commanded sufficient respect and fear among both Spaniards and Indians to seize the land as his own, the evidence is that he remained stoutly loyal to his sovereign. The king and his council did not, however, ignore the allegations made against the conqueror by enemies both at court and in Mexico, and they decided to suspend him for the time being at least. Royal officials were sent to supplant Cortés's authority. Growing increasingly frustrated and disgusted, he resolved to lay his case before the king in person.

With a grand retinue of Indian nobles, exotic Mexican plants and animals, and rich gifts for Charles V, Cortés arrived in Spain in 1528. His entrance caused a great sensation, and he was received with considerable fanfare. Charles V, pleased with his gifts and charmed by the conqueror's gallant manner, was satisfied that most of the rumors of misconduct were false or exaggerated. He allowed Cortés to choose for his encomiendas twenty-two towns, and the captain proceeded to select some of the richest settlements in the land. He received 23,000 Indians in encomienda, was confirmed as captain general, along with the grand title of the Marqués del Valle de Oaxaca. Nonetheless, he was not confirmed as governor of New Spain, and he took this slight as a special rebuke.

THE ADMINISTRATION OF NEW SPAIN

Prior to the settlement of Mexico, there were few Spaniards in the Indies. The territories under Spanish control were small and required little attention from Spain. Ferdinand and Isabella appointed counselors for matters pertaining to the New World and turned their full attention to more pressing matters in Europe. In 1503, shortly before her death, Isabella created the Casa de Contratación, a house of trade to deal with affairs of the Indies, especially with regard to commerce, shipping, and emigration to the colonies. Juan Rodríguez de Fonseca, the bishop of Burgos, was given prime authority for making overseas policy.

The situation changed considerably, however, following the conquest of Mexico, with its extensive lands and millions of people. Shortly thereafter Central America was penetrated, and early reports on Peru and other South American lands promised even more far-flung colonies. Affairs in the New World now clearly required a more broadly organized administration. Consequently, in 1524 Charles V created a supreme body called the Council of the Indies. This committee, composed of able, high-ranking Spaniards, would oversee all aspects of the colonies, both counseling the king and acting on his behalf.

Earlier, in 1511, the crown created in Santo Domingo a court of appeals so that matters of justice could be handled in the Indies instead of being referred to Spain. But the three judges of that body, called the *audiencia*, came to have broader duties. Traditionally, audiencias in Spain were courts of justice only, but in the New World they assumed executive and legislative functions as well. The judges (*oidores*) in Santo Domingo were the most powerful individuals in the Indies. The lack of good government in New Spain moved the crown in 1527 to establish a similar court in Mexico. Four experienced judges in Spain were appointed, but two died before taking office. The president of the audiencia was Nuño de Guzmán, a lawyer from a noble family with powerful connections.

Guzmán joined the two surviving judges in Mexico in early 1529. The rule of these three judges proved to be blatantly abusive and corrupt. As an adherent of Governor Velázquez of Cuba, Guzmán was a dedicated enemy of Cortés and, with the conqueror absent in Spain, the audiencia moved against his followers. Once again their encomiendas were taken, and some were removed from official positions. It was a time of graft, corruption, and injustice for Indians and Spaniards alike.

Meanwhile, a bishop, Juan de Zumárraga, had arrived in Mexico City. Although he bore the title "Protector of the Indians," the judges refused to recognize his authority and prevented the Indians from seeking help from him or any other clergyman. Angered by the chaos and iniquities engendered by the misrule, Zumárraga bravely preached a sermon condemning the oidores, which brought threats against his life. All correspondence critical of the government was intercepted before it reached Spain, until the bishop traveled to Veracruz and entrusted a letter to the crown to a faithful sailor who smuggled the message aboard a departing vessel. As it became clear to Guzmán that his days were numbered and fearing imminent arrest by royal agents, he set off in late 1529 for the west of Mexico, hoping to regain the royal confidence by a spectacular conquest of new territories.

Guzmán invaded Michoacán with a large force of Spaniards and thousands of native auxiliaries. He cut a bloody path through the west, burning villages, murdering chiefs, enslaving the Indians, and abusing them in every manner. One of the most brutal incidents saw the Tarascan king dragged behind a horse until he was almost senseless and then burned alive. The soldiers pressed north, lured by tales of a bountiful island ruled by attractive Amazons, tales fabricated by the natives to induce their tormentors to move on. Quite aside from his depredations, Guzmán explored and conquered a large area, all the way up to southern Sonora. Altogether he founded five cities.

Juan de Zumárraga (1468–1548), a Franciscan, was the first bishop and archbishop of Mexico.

The extensive western region was isolated from central Mexico and was later created as the separate administrative territory of New Galicia, over which its conqueror was appointed governor. But Guzmán's apparently psychopathic behavior caught up with him at length. After his long odyssey, notable for its duration no less than its savagery, Guzmán was ordered in 1533 to appear before a new audiencia to answer charges. In 1538 he was sent to Spain, where he spent the next two decades of his life as a virtual prisoner of the court.

While Guzmán was terrorizing the hinterlands of the west, the southeast region of Yucatán, the area first sighted in 1517 by Spaniards from Cuba, remained outside Spanish control. Its conquest had been unsuccessfully attempted in 1527 by Francisco de Montejo, an early companion of Cortés. The enterprise went badly because of unfavorable terrain and a lack of local provisions, but mostly because of the indomitable resistance of the Maya, as well as Spaniards' failure to understand Maya political institutions. After nine years of stalemate in Yucatán, the conquest was renewed in 1537, and Montejo's son and nephew, both of whom were also named Francisco, brought most of the region under Spanish control by 1542, when the city of Mérida was founded. In 1547 a serious insurrection broke out, and many Spanish settlers were killed before calm was restored. After two decades of conflict, the conquest of Yucatán was finally effected.

After the fiasco of the first audiencia, the king and the Council of the Indies were more circumspect in their choice of oidores. They chose wisely in the appointment of Sebastián Ramírez de Fuenleal, who had served as both president of the Audiencia of Santo Domingo and bishop of that island. A man of the highest integrity and proven abilities, he stood in contrast to his predecessor in Mexico. He was joined in Mexico City by fellow judges of uniformly high quality, including Vasco de Quiroga, who would distinguish himself later in other undertakings. Within five years (1530–35) these learned magistrates wrought significant changes in the troubled colony. Bringing to bear the full weight and authority of the crown and maintaining a busy schedule, they proceeded to correct many abuses. A semblance of order was restored, and ordinances designed to improve the conditions of the Indians were passed, despite the failure of most encomenderos to obey. The crown also moved to eliminate any threat from the powerful Cortés. Under investigation for encomienda abuses, he was deprived of various properties and privileges. Cortés remained the most prestigious individual in New Spain, but in 1535 even that status was challenged with the arrival of a viceroy.

The king and the Council of the Indies had decided by 1528 that New Spain needed a ruler who would personify the dignity and authority of the crown and offset Cortés's influence. Such a person would have to be a great nobleman, jealous of his honor and above staining his name with acts of avarice and injustice, one whose competence and loyalty to the king were beyond question. After all, he would literally be a "vice-king." Cortés, who aspired to the post, had neither the desirable lineage nor the administrative experience for the high honor. Furthermore the very qualities that brought him success as a conqueror—audacity, independence of thought, and imagination—were anathema to the centralized bureaucracy of an absolute monarch.

The appointment went to Don Antonio de Mendoza, the count of Tendilla, and he proved to be an excellent choice. An able ambassador to Rome, Mendoza was scion of one of Spain's most distinguished families and related to the royal house itself. He received his commission as viceroy in 1530, but the press of personal affairs prevented his arrival in Mexico until 1535. The viceroy's charge was to observe all matters of consequence affecting the colony except judicial affairs, which would continue as the province of the audiencia. He had special orders to increase crown revenues and to ensure good treatment of the Indians. He was also vice-patron of the church and responsible for the defense of New Spain. Allowing the viceroy a good salary as well as perquisites that included a palace and a personal guard, the crown purposely sought to enhance the prestige of the office.

Don Antonio de Mendoza (1492?-1552) served as first viceroy in New Spain, from 1535 to 1550.

IN SEARCH OF FABLED CITIES

During the 1520s and 1530s many fantastic tales circulated about wondrous lands in the New World. Among the more intriguing was the so-called Northern Mystery, which embraced not only the persistent myth of the Amazons but also stories of the Seven (Golden) Cities of Cíbola. Speculation about fabulously rich kingdoms in other parts of the New World was rife, and it is not strange that men were ready to believe them. Had not the first rumors of Tenochtitlan and the dazzling Inca empire (conquered in the early 1530s) appeared just as fanciful?

Pánfilo de Narváez, the one-eyed casualty of Veracruz, commanded a fleet to Florida in 1528, hoping to discover the fabled lands of Apalachee. After an overland expedition, Narváez failed to make contact with his supply ships, and he and his men tried to reach Mexico by sailing makeshift boats down the Gulf coast. Most of them perished, but a few made the Texas coastline. In the end only four survived: Alvar Núñez Cabeza de Vaca, two other Spaniards, and Esteban, a black slave. For years they wandered among the Indians of the present-day Southwest of the United States, sometimes as slaves, sometimes as respected medicine men. In 1536, after many travails, they reached the northern Mexican outpost of Culiacan, where they were received with astonishment by their fellow countrymen.

Having spent so much time in the north, they were plied with questions when they returned to Mexico about the Seven Cities, of which they had heard vaguely. These tales caused excitement, and prominent men scrambled for the privilege of undertaking the great search. Perhaps just as important were the accounts told by Aztecs about their homeland Aztlan, somewhere in the north, giving rise to the idea that a great city, comparable to Tenochtitlan, existed to the north. The viceroy sensed an opportunity for an expedition that might overshadow the achievements of Cortés, so of course he kept the rights for himself. But he took the precaution of sending an advance party, guided by Esteban, under the command of a Franciscan friar named Marcos de Niza. Pushing ahead of the main party, Esteban met an ironic end, for, having survived so long among the northern tribes, he apparently angered some Indians, who killed him.

Distraught by this news, Marcos de Niza proceeded with extreme caution. He reportedly viewed from a distance one of the Zuni villages in New Mexico, which he later related as larger than Tenochtitlan. Moreover—so he said—local chiefs told him that the city he saw was the smallest of the seven. In kindness to the friar, it must be said that sometimes, toward sunset, the fading light in that part of the country casts a rosy glow, and there may have been pieces of reflective quartz stuck in the adobe walls of the two-story dwellings he saw from afar; so it is possible that he imagined he saw something truly marvelous. In any case, Spaniards and Nahuas in Mexico wanted to believe in the existence of such cities, and preparations were eagerly made for the adventure. Those who had missed the earlier conquests would now have their chance.

Mendoza chose his friend, Francisco Vázquez de Coronado, the governor of New Galicia, to lead the well-equipped expedition. In 1540, 336 Spaniards, with hundreds of Indian allies and about 1,000 horses and swine, moved out with high expectations. When they saw the mud village at the end of a grueling march, they vented their frustration by slaughtering

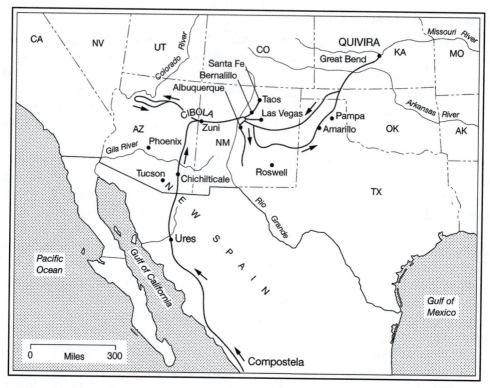

Route of Coronado's Expedition, 1540–42

Zunis unwilling to cooperate with them during a time of ritual celebration. From other Pueblo Indians, they learned of "the Land of Quivira," some distance away but even more wonderful than the legendary cities of Cíbola. Their hopes raised, off they went.

The natives whose villages were being destroyed soon found that the best way to get rid of the unwelcome intruders was to tell them that, while they had no wealth, there were abundant riches *más allá*—farther on. Relying on such information, the Spaniards wandered aimlessly for months, finally reaching the vicinity of Wichita, Kansas. Now greatly disheartened, having seen only a few villages scattered over a vast prairie and some "shaggy cows" (buffalo), the miserable survivors dragged themselves back to Mexico. Still the organization of natives in pueblos, supported by the myth of Aztlan, fueled the possibility of further exploration. In 1542 a party commanded by Juan Rodríguez de Cabrillo sailed up along the shoreline of California. Seeing little to interest them, Spaniards would not settle California for several centuries. That same year Mendoza dispatched Ruy López de Villalobos to the Philippines (named for prince Philip), but the expedition failed to return to Mexico.

The Vázquez de Coronado mission occasioned serious problems of another sort. When the expedition left western Mexico a good number of Spaniards who had settled New Galicia went along, leaving the frontier sparsely occupied by Christians and militarily weakened. Conscious of the situation, the Indians, who harbored resentments going back to the cruelty of Nuño de Guzmán, were roused by their shamans to rebel. The ensuing Mixtón War (1540–41) was the most serious revolt prior to Mexico's struggle for independence. The whole frontier was aflame. Natives attacked isolated Spanish ranches and then fortified themselves on well-stocked hilltops called *peñoles*, from which they could not be dislodged.

When the governor of New Galicia failed to subdue the rebels, he turned for assistance to Pedro de Alvarado, who had sailed up from Guatemala on his way to explore the Pacific. Courageous to a fault, Alvarado rashly ignored the advice to wait for reinforcements. A furious counterattack by the Indians produced a panicked Spanish retreat, during which a horse fell on Alvarado, crushing him. The great rebellion ended only after the viceroy himself took the field at the head of a strong army, comprised primarily of central Mexican Indian allies. Nonetheless, frontier wars in the north continued over the next three centuries.

THE LAST YEARS OF CORTÉS

Meanwhile Cortés, having been excluded from the search for the "Northern Mystery" and feeling insulted by his treatment from the viceroy and the audiencia, returned to Spain in 1540 to put his grievances once again before the king. Charles V was abroad, however, and crown representatives gave the marqués a cool reception. The crisis of instability appeared to have been resolved in the colony, and with the royal bureaucracy entrenched and functioning well, government officials saw no need to humor the conqueror. Cortés spent his last years in frustration. He was about to return to New Spain when, in 1547, he fell ill. Shortly thereafter, at age sixty-two he died in a village outside Seville. In 1556 his bones were deposited in Mexico, according to his wishes.

Though the last two decades of Cortés's life were fraught with disappointment, there is no greater example of a legend about the rise to fame and fortune in the history of the New World. Notwithstanding his diverse talents, without the aid of indigenous allies and disease, he would never have gained immortality as one of the greatest military figures of the ages. He married into one of Spain's most noble families, was awarded a high title himself, and became one of the richest men in the Spanish empire. As a symbol of Spain's might and the exploitation of indigenous peoples, his image later became tarnished, first with Mexico's independence from Spain and later with the revolution of 1910, which aspired to rehabilitate the indigenous past. The image of destroyer displaced that of heroic leader.

Few of his fellow conquerors attained Cortés's status and wealth in the colonial period, but many established themselves as part of New Spain's upper class. When the immediate wealth they had hoped to carry home to support a life of leisure did not materialize, they comforted themselves by acquiring native labor and property locally. For most of them, the new lifestyle represented a significant step up from their modest origins.

STABILITY UNDER VICEROY MENDOZA

Despite the reversals of the ill-fated Coronado expedition and the costly Mixtón War, by 1542 the colonial government was closer to achieving stability and order. The viceroy had begun to review information from indigenous accounts of their past, for example in the case of the Purépecha in Michoacán, to sort out the interethnic rivalries. There was good cause for optimism, for Mendoza was a firm and capable viceroy and the audiencia he worked with was responsible. Bishop Zumárraga was an energetic and positive complement to civil government. Yet there was brewing in Spain a reform movement that was destined to inflame passions once again. Bartolomé de Las Casas, a powerful Dominican friar and an indefatigable lobbyist on behalf of Indian liberties, went to Spain from Guatemala where he had observed the worst atrocities against Indians. He successfully convinced the crown to introduce legislation aimed at curtailing abuses of the natives, whose numbers had declined drastically. He was appointed the Bishop of Chiapas, where he became an icon for indigenous liberty centuries later.

The New Laws of 1542–43 called for, among other things, the freedom of natives who had been unjustly enslaved and the easing of labor requirements. Most threatening from the standpoint of the Spanish conquerors, the laws eroded the encomienda system, for encomiendas awarded to conquerors and first settlers were to revert to the crown on the death of the original encomendero. News of the provision caused a great outcry among the encomenderos, who remonstrated bitterly that they would have nothing to leave their children. Surely, they insisted, the king could not be so ungrateful to those who had won and settled lands larger than Spain itself.

The continuance of the encomienda system was regarded in Mexico, even by many royal officials, as vital to the maintenance of the colony's prosperity, for without it, it was feared, many Spaniards would leave. In fact, most ecclesiastics also favored its retention, seeing it as the best instrument for control of the Indians. Furthermore, tribute and labor helped support various charities, educational facilities, and religious institutions. Many Spaniards held that natives under crown control were abused more by royal agents than by encomenderos. When an official investigator, Francisco Tello de Sandoval, was sent from Spain to help implement the New Laws, he found widespread opposition in the colony.

Tello de Sandoval and Viceroy Mendoza, assessing the situation and fearing a general revolt, exercised the prerogative of withholding the laws. Under the circumstances, they probably chose wisely: when the viceroy in Peru insisted on imposing the ordinances, a serious insurrection ensued, which took his life and embroiled the colony in civil war for years. Finally, giving way to the outraged encomenderos, the crown modified the laws in 1545 by removing the offending limitation to the encomiendas.

Although the crown had retreated, it still intended to reform the encomienda system. In 1549 it ordered that encomenderos could no longer avail themselves of the free labor of their Indians but would have to be content with their tributes only. In the same year there was a flurry of excitement when a small group of Spaniards plotted to overthrow the government. They were tried, found guilty, and summarily hanged.

By 1550, as Mendoza's rule of nearly fifteen years came to a close, the colony was well implanted and thriving. In the crown's view Mendoza was the ideal administrator. His dreams of extending Spanish realms into rich areas (that did not exist) were unrealized, but his contributions in other respects were impressive. The part played by Mendoza was of crucial importance because, as the first viceroy, he established patterns that would be followed by his successors. He left a growing economy and a capital that had already assumed the appearance of a beautiful city distinguished for its cultural life. He established order and stability; he founded schools, hospitals, and charitable foundations; he attempted to foster religion and justice. Because of his government, royal authority began to be stamped on New Spain. The colony had survived the turbulent first three decades of its life.

RECOMMENDED FOR FURTHER STUDY

Adorno, Rolena, and Patrick Charles Pautz. *Alvar Núñez Cabeza de Vaca: His Account, His Life, and the Expedition of Pánfilo de Narváez.* Lincoln: University of Nebraska Press, 1999.

Afanador Pujol, Angélica Jimena. *The "Relación de Michoacán" (1539–1541) and the Politics of Representation in Colonial Mexico.* Austin: University of Texas Press, 2015.

Aiton, Arthur S. *Antonio de Mendoza, First Viceroy of New Spain.* Durham, NC: Duke University Press, 1927.

Altman, Ida. *Emigrants and Society: Extremadura and America in the Sixteenth Century.* Berkeley: University of California Press, 1989.

_____. *Transatlantic Ties in the Spanish Empire: Brihuega, Spain, and Puebla, Mexico, 1560–1620.* Stanford, CA: Stanford University Press, 2000.

_____. *The War for Mexico's West: Indians and Spaniards in New Galicia, 1524–1550.* Albuquerque: University of New Mexico Press, 2010.

Bolton, Herbert E. *Coronado: Knight of Pueblos and Plains.* Albuquerque: University of New Mexico Press, 1949.

Chamberlain, Robert S. *The Conquest and Colonization of Yucatán, 1517–1550.* Washington, DC: Carnegie Institute of Washington, 1948.

Chipman, Donald E. *Moctezuma's Children: Aztec Royalty under Spanish Rule, 1520–1700.* Austin: University of Texas Press, 2005.

_____. *Nuño de Guzmán and Pánuco in New Spain, 1518–1533.* Glendale, CA: Arthur H. Clark Company, 1966.

Clendinnen, Inga. *Ambivalent Conquests: Maya and Spaniard in Yucatán, 1517–1570.* New York: Cambridge University Press, 1987.

Elliott, John H. *Empires of the Atlantic World: Britain and Spain in America, 1492–1830.* New Haven, CT: Yale University Press, 2006.

Flint, Richard, and Shirley Flint. *Documents of the Coronado Expedition, 1539–1542.* Albuquerque: University of New Mexico Press, 2012.

Gruzinski, Serge. *Images at War: Mexico from Columbus to Blade Runner, 1492–2019.* Durham, NC: Duke University Press, 2001.

Jones, Grant D. *The Conquest of the Last Maya Kingdom.* Stanford, CA: Stanford University Press, 1998.

_____. *Maya Resistance to Spanish Rule: Time and History on a Colonial Frontier.* Albuquerque: University of New Mexico Press, 1989.

Krippner-Martínez, James. *Rereading the Conquest: Power, Politics, and the History of Early Colonial Michoacán, 1521–1565.* University Park: University of Pennsylvania Press, 2001.

Levin Rojo, Danna A. *Return to Aztlan: Indians, Spaniards, and the Invention of Nuevo México.* Norman: University of Oklahoma Press, 2015.

MacLachlan, Colin M. *Imperialism and the Origins of Mexican Culture.* Cambridge, MA: University of Harvard Press, 2015.

Matthews, Laura E. *Memories of Conquest: Becoming Mexicano in Colonial Guatemala.* Chapel Hill: University of North Carolina Press, 2012.

McEnroe, Sean F. *From Colony to Nationhood in Mexico: Laying the Foundations, 1560–1840.* New York: Cambridge University Press, 2012.

Mundy, Barbara E. *The Death of Aztec Tenochtitlan, the Life of Mexico City.* Austin: University of Texas Press, 2015.

Quezada, Sergio. *Maya Lords and Lordship: The Formation of Colonial Society in Yucatán, 1350*. Translated by Terry Rugeley. Norman: University of Oklahoma, 2014.

Reséndez, Andrés. *A Land so Strange: The Epic Journey of Cabeza de Vaca*. New York: Basic Books, 2007.

Restall, Matthew. *Maya Conquistador*. Boston, MA: Beacon Press, 1998.

Schroeder, Susan, ed. *The Conquest All Over Again: Nahuas and Zapotecs Thinking, Writing, and Painting Spanish Colonialism*. Brighton, UK: Sussex University Press, 2011.

Schwartz, Stuart, B. *Sea of Storms: A History of Hurricanes in the Greater Caribbean from Columbus to Katrina*. Princeton, NJ: Princeton University Press, 2015.

Warren, J. Benedict. *The Conquest of Michoacán: The Spanish Domination of the Tarascan Kingdom in Western Mexico, 1521–1530*. Norman: University of Oklahoma Press, 1985.

Weber, David J. *The Spanish Frontier in North America*. New Haven, CT: Yale University Press, 1992.

LIVING IN THE VICEROYALTY

CHAPTER 8

THE IMPERIAL SYSTEM ENTRENCHED

THE POLITICAL ADMINISTRATION OF NEW SPAIN

"Do little and do it slowly" had been Viceroy Mendoza's stated philosophy of administration. It was an attitude less than acceptable to reformers but consistent with royal wishes. The sixteenth-century viceroys, facing many crucial situations, were allowed considerable latitude, but their successors in the seventeenth century were reined in by later kings and their councils. Yet given the difficulty of communication and the time lapse between a request for instructions and the response from Spain, a certain amount of autonomy was implicit. Correspondence between colonial officials and the crown was necessarily slow because for much of the colonial period ships sailed only once a year between Mexico and Spain. It was common for authorities in New Spain to wait many months for guidance. Consequently, high officials often made important rulings on their own, pending royal approval. When a crown order seemed contrary to the best interests of the local situation, a viceroy sometimes noted, in all deference, *Obedezco pero no cumplo* (I obey but do not execute). The process of government was further bogged down by the endless detailed reports, requiring action, sent to Spain by officials, clergymen, and private subjects.

Colonial policy of the Hapsburgs was ponderous and inefficient. But sluggish as the bureaucracy was, the crown concerned itself less with competence than with loyalty. Unable to micromanage a far-flung empire, the Hapsburgs were willing to relinquish considerable control to local elites who could keep the peace in the crown's name. The preoccupation with conformance and fidelity also manifested itself in the system of checks and balances. Officials were encouraged to comment on and criticize the performance of others. The viceroy was the most powerful individual, but as the judges of the audiencia reported directly to the king and the Council of the Indies and were often at odds with the viceroy, they were a restraint on the viceroy's actions. Moreover, treasury officials and various other bureaucrats, as well as clergymen, members of town councils, and private individuals, contributed their complaints. As a result, the crown was exposed to a wide spectrum of opinion on the operation of colonial administration.

To ascertain the true state of affairs, the crown occasionally sent a royal inspector (*visitador*) to make an on-the-spot investigation (*visita*). The crown visitador had great authority on arrival; he usually assumed rule of the colony for the tenure of his inspection which could take weeks or months. The visita was sometimes undertaken in response to a specific set of charges emanating from the colony, but in other instances it was more routine in nature. In some instances the visitador traveled incognito, taking officials by surprise, before adequate cover-ups could be arranged. At other times the imminent arrival of the inspector became known in time for precautionary measures on the part of local officials. Visitadores, usually men trained in the law, were responsible for correcting abuses and instituting reforms. Another mechanism for judging the performance of the viceroy and other high functionaries was a judicial review, or trial, known as a (*juicio de*) *residencia*. A residencia usually came at the end of an official's term of office. Notice of an impending review was made public so that all within the official's jurisdiction with grievances could bring charges.

The admirable institutions of the visita and the residencia were models that might well profit all governments. Unfortunately, like so much in Spanish administration, there existed a wide breach between theory and practice. Witnesses were sometimes bribed or intimidated, perjury and obfuscation were common, and judges were occasionally bought. Furthermore, despite the long lists of allegations posted—and testimony that often convincingly established the official's guilt—relatively few were punished in accordance with their crimes. In the early years of Spanish rule in western Mexico, Spanish colonists flagrantly defied laws in their bloody, internecine battles. Heavily reliant on the allegiance of far-removed colonial officials, the crown frequently winked at their greed and misdeeds.

Various restrictions were imposed on officials with a view to averting corruption. They were forbidden to hold encomiendas or to participate in commercial activities as well as other undertakings that presented a conflict of interest. Although certainly one finds many officials of integrity, the infractions were numerous. In essence, a weak Hapsburg state governed informally through mechanisms that rewarded New Spain's elites by allowing them to exploit Indians and maximize profits. The crown was satisfied as long as they kept the peace and remitted a modicum of returns to the imperial government. Corruption was furthered by the introduction in the sixteenthth century of the sale of public office. At first limited to local appointments, the practice was extended in the seventeenth century to include the highest positions, including treasury officials, oidores, and even viceroys.

Of the sixty-two viceroys who served in New Spain, almost all came from the high nobility and were born in Spain. Men born in the New World could attain this highest office (Mexico had three in the seventeenth century), but as sons of high nobles serving as viceroys themselves, they were not identified as locals. Most viceroys proved reasonably good rulers; a few were truly outstanding. The colony was fortunate that the first viceroys, Mendoza (1535–50) and Luis de Velasco (1550–64), were capable administrators who set New Spain on firm footing. Thereafter, the quality of their service fluctuated, and many seventeenth-century viceroys proved less talented. Palace intrigues and corruption reached a high point under the administration of the Duque de Alburquerque during the first decade of the eighteenth century. Easily bribed, he collaborated with contraband traders to enhance his personal finances and liberally rewarded his partisans. Only after he left office did the crown indict him for misconduct and force him to pay an enormous fine. His successors in the eighteenth century proved to be more trustworthy and effective representatives of the king.

It is more difficult to assess the character of the oidores of the audiencias. As the functions of the courts expanded, more judges were added. With the settlement of western lands, the new audiencia Nueva Galicia was created in 1548. It usually had four or five oidores, while the Audiencia of Mexico counted ten by the late eighteenth century, plus other lawyers. Since the appointments of judges were for life, they developed strong local ties, prompting speculation as to their impartiality.

The same cannot be said for the provincial officials. As new territories were colonized and towns founded, it became impossible to govern outlying provinces from the capital. The crown formalized subdivisions of administration and created many smaller administrative districts within the audiencia jurisdictions. Such districts were administered by officials known variously as *corregidores, alcaldes mayores,* or *gobernadores,* whose territories of jurisdiction were called *corregimientos, alcaldías mayores,* or *gobiernos.* Since few differences existed among the duties of these officials, a brief discussion of the position of corregidor serves to describe the others as well. Corregidores were responsible for the good order of their districts, but their judicial and legislative responsibilities were limited as they were subject to higher authorities in all matters. In the early years of the system these positions often went to conquerors or their sons, or other early settlers, as a form of pension in lieu of encomiendas. As can be imagined, most appointees had little or no training for administrative posts and were poorly paid. It came to be accepted that these provincial officials would supplement their salaries where they could—which usually meant cheating the natives or other lower-class groups.

Luis de Velasco I (1511–64), the second viceroy of New Spain, served until his death. He continued the prudent policies established by his predecessor Mendoza.

Most notorious were *corregidores de indios*, whose responsibility it was to administer Indian towns. The natives had been gathered into new villages to facilitate their conversion, taxation, and acculturation; and the corregidor de indios was charged with the good order of those under his jurisdiction in those towns paying tribute to the crown rather than to individual encomenderos. These Spanish supervisors, or their agents, collected the king's tributes in the "crown towns" and supposedly guaranteed justice. In fact, they numbered among the greatest enemies of the Indians, defrauding them in a variety of ways, often in collusion with the native governors. In addition to forcing Indians to produce cloth, which they then sold at a profit, corregidores acted as petty traders, compelling natives to buy goods from them at elevated prices. These practices were known as the *repartimiento de mercancías*.

Distinct from the royal authorities were those in municipal government. Beginning with the founding of Veracruz in 1519 by Cortés, as Spanish towns were established, a town council was immediately formed. In the earliest years Cortés simply appointed many local administrators, but it became customary for them to be elected annually. The municipal council, called the *cabildo* (or *ayuntamiento*), consisted of members known as *regidores*. These councilmen numbered anywhere from four or five in smaller communities up to fifteen in late colonial Mexico City. A council usually had two senior officials, called *alcaldes ordinarios*, who had some judicial powers and more importance than the regidores who were simply councilors.

The cabildos were responsible for such purely local matters as defending the town, keeping the peace, controlling prices, allocating lots, cleaning streets, and seeing to drainage, water supplies, public food, and a multitude of other concerns. Generally speaking, the cabildos of the various towns represented the interests of the local elites, frequently in conflict with the wishes of the crown.

Positions in the cabildos were awarded to the highest bidders, even though consideration was supposed to be given to those with the best credentials. Such posts were cherished because of the distinction they offered in the community, not to mention the opportunities for making profits on the side. As a result, membership in the cabildos came under the control of certain families who held proprietary interest in them for generations. Since the seats were often sold in perpetuity, they were passed on from father to son. By the late colonial period fifteen regidores in Mexico City owned their positions. Cabildos tended to be composed largely of elite *criollos* (Mexican-born Spaniards).

Administration of Indian towns was modeled after that of the Spanish communities, but practices varied widely. In areas where an Indian nobility existed before contact, regidores were commonly chosen from among them. Indian towns also had a local governor (*gobernador*) who oversaw the activities of the cabildo and aided it in collecting tribute, apportioning village lands, and dispensing justice. Native leaders had to engage in a delicate balancing act in order to satisfy the demands of the local Spanish officials or clergymen without alienating their fellow Indians. Failure to maintain this balance could result in their removal by Spanish authorities or violence against them by local villagers. As time went on, in most parts of central and southern Mexico hereditary leaders found their political and/or economic privileges eroded in some measure.

The degree to which indigenous communities preserved some autonomy and maintained ethnic distinctiveness is a topic that has attracted the attention of many scholars of the colonial period, some of whom have benefited from the survival of native language documents in Nahuatl and other Indian languages, to study Indian cabildos, land tenure, religious beliefs, and cultural practices. Outcomes were tremendously mixed, but indigenous peoples devised many ways to defend themselves and to perpetuate pre-conquest hierarchies and ways of life throughout the colonial period. Some Nahua communities created "primordial" titles, which recorded collective visions of their evolving histories and attempted to substantiate their claims to land. Sometimes they could ignore the new demands by feigning ignorance or by bribing officials, but many more learned how to maneuver in the Spanish world of institutions. Indigenous intellectuals in central and southern Mexico created written texts in their own languages and made other visual representations to establish the claims of the communities. In their interactions with colonial officials and institutions, they frequently exercised an effective role in the reformulation of community politics and practices that preserved traditions and afforded some autonomy, for example, in matters of taxation and land tenure, into the eighteenth century. In other areas where Indians had not lived in permanent pueblos before the conquest, Spanish civil and religious officials congregated them in villages and exerted strong influence over their government. Although it was not uncommon to find outsiders and individuals of mixed race occupying the position of governor after a couple of generations, even these communities found means of resistance and incorporated new mechanisms to strengthen ethnic vitality and religious traditions.

DISTURBANCES DURING THE "COLONIAL SIESTA"

By the middle of the sixteenth century, the Spanish imperial system had been established and the bureaucracy spread its net. Even though order was steadily imposed, the next two and a half centuries cannot accurately be depicted as a "colonial siesta." Challenges to Spanish hegemony came from both outside and inside New Spain. Internal contestation emanated from all levels of society.

Even elites plotted rebellion when their interests were threatened, as an episode of the 1560s demonstrates. Anticipating the eventual loss of their encomiendas, a group of young criollos in Mexico City began to talk loosely of assassinating oidores and other high officials, throwing off allegiance to the crown, and making Martín Cortés king of Mexico. Don Martín was the only legitimate son of the conqueror and his heir. Because his active role in the conspiracy could not be proven, Martín escaped the fate of its leaders, whose heads were cut off and displayed on pikes. For most of the colonial period, however, the upper classes sought redress or influence through cooperation with the royal officials or through the courts. At least until the middle of the eighteenth century, they tended to enjoy considerable autonomy as long as they could maintain local order and furnish the crown its share of colonial profits. They forged a political culture in which they used extravagant public ceremonies to reinforce allegiances to empire and church, quite strikingly in the self-designated "very noble and very loyal city" of Puebla de los Angeles. But local elites also choreographed these rituals to vie for power among themselves.

Intra-elite squabbles occasionally resulted in violence. For example, in 1624, bitter animosities among viceregal, audiencia, and religious authorities, which reflected rivalries between Mexican- and Spanish-born Spaniards (*peninsulares* or *gachupines*), set against a background of bad harvests and rising food prices, eventually erupted in mob violence from the lower classes, who supported the archbishop in the elite dispute. More than seventy people died in the upheaval, and the viceroy was recalled to Spain.

Popular urban protests continued to manifest themselves over food shortages, prices, or taxation in Mexico City and provincial capitals. In 1692, a crisis brought on by severe food shortages, the result of crop failures, was exacerbated by the rumor that authorities had connived to corner the grain market to their profit. The resentment of the Indians and *mestizos*—persons of mixed Spanish and Indian blood—burst into destructive riots during the celebration of Corpus Christi in which the viceregal palace was burned and looted (see cover image). Other government buildings were destroyed, along with 280 shops and stalls, before the viceroy's troops finally restored order through harsh measures.

Authorities had to contend with various natural calamities over which they had little control, for example earthquakes, epidemics, and crop failures. Especially destructive were the many floods that plagued the capital in the colonial period. The Aztecs had carefully managed the lake ecosystem not only for agriculture (for example with chinampas) and pasture, but also for transport of foodstuffs and other goods. They controlled flooding through a system of dikes (causeways) and canals. This arrangement did not suit the Spaniards' construction plans and commercial endeavors; for them the answer was to dry up the lakes by draining them. The demands of an early modern economy and new ideas of property ownership were paramount. The solution called the *desagüe* required a massive investment of back-breaking native labor, supervised by European engineers and natives with knowledge of the wetland environment. Many solutions were tried over the next centuries in the ongoing attempt to carry water out of the valley, producing an environmental calamity. Over time, structures built in unstable, marshy foundations have experienced sinking, and Mexico City still faces chronic flooding and a shortage of fresh water.

Although urban riots were not a daily occurrence, violence was. For the growing numbers of mixed-race and marginalized peoples, poverty could serve as a powerful motivation for petty theft. Racial and gender tensions frequently erupted in domestic abuses, crimes of passion, and personal violence. In the colonial Mexican countryside, insecurities, tensions, and resistance to exploitation were also vented in personal violence, witchcraft, village riots, and even rebellions in peripheral areas.

EXPANSION INTO NORTHERN MEXICO

Violent resistance to Spanish intrusion was the primary response of the nomadic and semi-sedentary indigenous groups in northern Mexico. While much of central and southern Mexico was under Spanish control by the middle of the sixteenth century, the wide expanses of the north remained unsettled by the newcomers. Interest in the northern frontiers had quickened, however, with the discovery of silver ore in the 1540s, setting off a rush into the Zacatecas region. Within a few years mining camps appeared in many locations, but Chichimec warriors made supplying the camps difficult and dangerous. The long distances between Spanish settlements and the isolated mining camps offered the Indians ample opportunity to strike the mule trains. For half a century the indomitable northern tribes resisted the Spanish advance, and the fighting subsided only in the last decade of the sixteenth century when Viceroy Luis de Velasco II, with the help of missionary clergy and indigenous allies from central Mexico who established colonies, inaugurated a policy of conciliation. In return for annual supplies of cattle and clothing, many of the natives were persuaded to put down their arms.

Although some Franciscans had preceded them, in the seventeenth century the Jesuits forged northward, following Spanish explorers and miners like Francisco de Ibarra into the northwestern areas of Sinaloa, Durango, and Chihuahua that became known as Nueva Vizcaya (New Biscay). Eventually they pushed all the way to Baja California and Arizona. Their attempts to resettle semi-sedentary Indians in permanent mission villages invariably met with rebellion, either within a generation or two or later in the colonial period.

In many of these cases Indians, for example the Yaquis, did settle in mission towns where, despite a reduction in their numbers due to epidemic disease, they used innovative strategies of resistance and accommodation to persist as discrete ethnic groups. Others, like many of the Tarahumaras, chose flight into remote mountainous areas where they eluded incorporation into the Spanish realm for much of the colonial period.

In the 1570s the viceroy commissioned several expeditions to settle northeast Mexico, resulting in the 1577 founding of Saltillo (Coahuila), which became an important trading outpost. Finding little mineral wealth and dispersed, non-sedentary Indians who put up a tenacious resistance, the settlers ruthlessly turned to enslaving bands of natives who were forced to work on Spanish ranches. Another solution proved more effective when the viceroy promoted the establishment of a Tlaxcalan colony, San Esteban, adjacent to Saltillo in 1591. The Tlaxcalans received land grants and special privileges, serving as military allies to Spaniards; they were also intended to help settle and acculturate hostile Indians. Other such colonies were established later around Spanish centers like Monterrey which was founded in 1596.

In the 1590s the viceroy also sent out more expeditions to the far north earlier traversed by Vázquez de Coronado. Following the march of Juan de Oñate in 1598, an outpost was established and Franciscan friars worked to convert the sedentary Indians at San Juan, Taos, and other pueblos. In 1609, two years after the English colonized Jamestown, the northern capital was planted at Santa Fe. Nevertheless, the extensive region of New Mexico remained sparsely populated by Europeans, other than some friars, a few soldiers, and a scattering of miners, traders, and ranchers, along with various officials. The outpost served to assert a tenuous hold on the land in the face of French expansion from the east.

While the Spanish endeavored to colonize and conquer new lands in what today is Mexico, they never left behind the idea of finding a direct route to the markets of Asia, brimming with spices, textiles, and porcelains. Mexico, uniquely positioned between the Atlantic and Pacific, proved an advantageous place from which the new empire could connect to Asia. Moreover, despite the Spanish desire for gold, the discovery of vast silver mines across North and South America positioned them for trading success with the Chinese; controlling the largest trading economy in the early modern period, China's economy had been silver-based since the mid-fourteenth century. The Spanish made various early attempts to find a western passage to Asia, first in 1519 when the crown sent Ferdinand Magellan who sailed across the Atlantic to the shores of Brazil (territory claimed by the Portuguese) and then down the coast. After a year of calamities, his ships found the passage at the tip of South America that became the Strait of Magellan and reached the Philippines in March 1521. In 1543 the viceroy of New Spain dispatched Ruy López de Villalobos who sailed from Acapulco to the islands he named *las Islas Filipinas* after the Spanish king.

It was the difficulty of returning to Mexico directly across the Pacific that delayed Spanish efforts to establish a colonial presence in Asia. This changed in 1565 with the expedition of Miguel López de Legazpi and the friar Andrés de Urdaneta. Sailing straight west from Acapulco to the Philippines was a relatively easy journey of about three months. In the summer of 1568, Urdaneta set out to find a satisfactory route back to mainland New Spain across the Pacific. By following the easterly prevailing winds and currents he took his ship further north before dropping down to sail along the California coast to arrive in Acapulco in just over four months. Although Villalobos had claimed the islands, they were not under Spanish control. While Urdaneta was sailing east, Legazpi and his soldiers explored and fought for Spanish dominance, ending in the conquest of Maynila, the "Place of the Water Lilies," designated by Legazpi as the capital of the Spanish Philippines in 1570. With a colonial foothold and a direct route of return, Spaniards wasted no time in launching the famous Manila galleons, making one voyage a year (almost every year from 1571 to 1812), consisting of one to four ships. Vast amounts of Mexican silver reached Asia in payment for such prized goods as

The Pacific port of Acapulco in a 1671 Dutch engraving.

Chinese silks and porcelain, Indonesian spices, and Indian cottons. In addition to commodities, sailors, merchants, and bureaucrats arrived in mainland New Spain on the ships, along with eight thousand Asian slaves (principally from the Philippines and regions of India).

The China trade piqued new interest in the coast of California, where the galleons first sighted the mainland of North America. In the 1590s Sebastián Vizcaíno explored the coastline with indifferent success. In 1602 another expedition under his command produced a commendable chart of California waters, and Vizcaíno founded the port of Monterey, but there was still no compelling reason to make a serious attempt to colonize California.

RIVALS IN THE NEW WORLD

A growing concern of Spanish authorities was the encroachment of foreigners on the fringes of New Spain, by both land and sea. A French force led by the Chevalier de La Salle journeyed southward from Canada in the 1680s into the region of Texas where, it was rumored, a settlement was planted. In response, Spaniards began to occupy Texas, and in 1698 a Spanish fort was established on the Gulf coast at Pensacola (Florida).

A more serious threat was posed by foreigners on the seas. North European powers had never accepted the pope's division of the New World, which gave most of it to Spain; especially following the growth of Protestantism, they challenged Spain's hegemony. Pirates, often with the blessings of their sovereigns, aggressively attacked Spanish property. French interlopers were cruising the eastern coastline of South America little more than a decade after Columbus's first voyage. The ship sent by Cortés carrying Aztec treasure to Charles V had been seized by French corsairs when it was in sight of Iberian shores. Later the French moved closer to the source, attacking Spanish ships in American waters and looting ports. Along the Gulf coast, from Yucatán to Tampico, French filibusterers raided with little opposition. In 1561 they sacked the town of Campeche and a decade later seized valuable treasures from a Franciscan convent in Yucatán.

Somewhat later the English, too, appeared off Mexican shores. In 1567 John Hawkins sailed boldly into the port of Veracruz under pretext of repairing his ships, but he actually planned to sell his cargo of black slaves in defiance of laws that forbade Spanish trade with foreigners. Hawkins was trapped by an incoming Spanish fleet bearing a new viceroy. Despite a gentleman's agreement for a truce, the viceroy brought his ships to bear and peppered the English vessels, allowing only two of Hawkins's nine ships to escape. The captured English corsairs were given sentences at labor, and later some were tried and burned by the Inquisition, not for piracy but for heresy. The defeat of Hawkins amounted to a great feather in the viceroy's cap, but the Spaniards would pay dearly for it, as Hawkins's cousin Francis Drake escaped on one of the English ships. Before long *El Draque* took his vengeance, becoming the terror of the Spanish Indies, raiding with considerable success in both the Caribbean and the Pacific, and driving the Spaniards to distraction.

From the middle of the sixteenth century until the end of the eighteenth, English and French corsairs attacked the coasts of Yucatán and Campeche many times, though the rewards were often modest. Some of the small, isolated ports were so poorly defended that they could be taken by a handful of pirates. In Pacific waters both the English and Dutch were active, the most successful of them Thomas Cavendish, who captured a richly laden Manila galleon.

The most vicious attack, however, occurred not at sea but on land. In 1683, after laying careful plans, a Frenchman known as "Lorenzillo" led a force of about 1,000 ruffians of mixed nationalities to the strongly fortified port of Veracruz and infiltrated the city under cover of night. More than six thousand local citizens were rounded up, held inside the churches, and denied food and water for three days and nights. Many were horribly tortured, and most of the females, of all ages, were raped. The pirates carried off about one million dollars worth of loot.

By the end of the seventeenth century the viceroyalty of New Spain stretched out over a vast expanse of territory. It embraced all land on the mainland north of Panama, extending up to New Mexico, the islands of the Caribbean, and even the Philippines. Ostensibly all these far-flung regions were under the control of the viceroy; in actual practice, his authority was nominal for the more remote areas were effectively beyond his reach. Central America,

A Spanish shield of the seventeenth century.

the islands of the Caribbean, and the Philippines had their own audiencias, which were for all intents and purposes autonomous.

Spain itself, after boasting the richest and most powerful empire in the world during the sixteenth century, lost predominance in the early decades of the seventeenth century. But the Spanish empire remained intact and relatively prosperous, thanks to an administrative system that relied less on a rational bureaucracy in the modern sense than on informal networks of exchange and on the public performance of viceregal power.

RECOMMENDED FOR FURTHER STUDY

Bolton, Herbert E. *Rim of Christendom: A Biography of Eusebio Francisco Kino, Pacific Coast Pioneer*. New York: Macmillan, 1936.

Borah, Woodrow. *Justice by Insurance: The General Indian Court and the Legal Aides of the Half-Real*. Berkeley: University of California Press, 1983.

Burkhart, Louise M. *The Slippery Earth: Nahua-Christian Moral Dialogue in Sixteenth Century Mexico*. Tucson: University of Arizona Press, 1989.

Burkholder, Mark A. "An Empire beyond Compare." In *The Oxford History of Mexico*, edited by Michael C. Meyer and William H. Beezley, 115–49. New York: Oxford University Press, 2000.

Candini, Vera S. *Dreaming of Dry Land: Environmental Transformation in Colonial Mexico City*. Stanford, CA: Stanford University Press, 2014.

Cañeque, Alejandro. *The King's Living Image: The Culture and Politics of Viceregal Power in Colonial Mexico*. New York: Routledge, 2004.

Carte, Rebecca A. *Capturing the Landscape of New Spain: Baltasar de Obregón and the 1564 Ibarra Expedition*. Tucson: University of Arizona Press, 2014.

Cline, S. L. *Colonial Culhuacan, 1580–1600: A Social History of an Aztec Town*. Albuquerque: University of New Mexico Press, 1986.

Connell, William F. *After Moctezuma: Indigenous Politics and Self Government in Mexico City, 1524–1730*. Norman: University of Oklahoma Press, 2011.

Deeds, Susan M. *Defiance and Deference in Colonial Mexico: Indians under Spanish Rule in Nueva Vizcaya*. Austin: University of Texas Press, 2003.

Farriss, Nancy M. *Maya Society under Colonial Rule. The Collective Enterprise of Survival*. Princeton, NJ: Princeton University Press, 1984.

Folsom, Raphael. *The Yaquis and the Empire: Violence, Spanish Imperial Power, and Native Resistance in Colonial Mexico*. New Haven, CT: Yale University Press, 2014.

Gerhard, Peter. *The North Frontier of New Spain*. Princeton, NJ: Princeton University Press, 1982.

Gibson, Charles. *The Aztecs under Spanish Rule: A History of the Indians of the Valley of Mexico, 1519–1810*. Stanford, CA: Stanford University Press, 1964.

Giráldez, Arturo. *The Age of Trade: The Manila Galleons and the Dawn of the Global Economy*. Lanham, MD: Rowman & Littlefield, 2015.

Gruzinski, Serge. *The Conquest of Mexico: The Incorporation of Indian Societies into the Western World, 16th–18th Centuries*. Cambridge, UK: Polity Press, 1993.

Hanna, Mark G. *Pirates Nests and the Rise of the British Empire, 1570–1740*. Chapel Hill: University of North Carolina Press, 2015.

Haring, Clarence H. *The Spanish Empire in America*. New York: Oxford University Press, 1947.

Haskett, Robert. *Indigenous Rulers: An Ethnohistory of Town Government in Colonial Cuernavaca*. Albuquerque: University of New Mexico Press, 1991.

————. *Visions of Paradise: Primordial Titles and Mesoamerican History in Cuernavaca*. Norman: University of Oklahoma Press, 2005.

Himmerich y Valencia, Robert. *The Encomenderos of New Spain, 1521–1555*. Austin: University of Texas Press, 1991.

Horn, Rebecca. *Postconquest Coyoacan: Spanish-Nahua Relations in Central Mexico, 1519–1650*. Stanford, CA: Stanford University Press, 1997.

Jones, Oakah L. *Nueva Vizcaya: Heartland of the Spanish Frontier*. Albuquerque: University of New Mexico Press, 1988.

Kellogg, Susan. *Law and the Transformation of Aztec Culture, 1500–1700*. Norman: University of Oklahoma Press, 1995.

Kessell, John. *Pueblos, Spaniards, and the Kingdom of New Mexico*. Norman: University of Oklahoma Press, 2008.

Lane, Kris E. *Pillaging the Empire: Piracy in the Americas, 1500–1750*. Armonk, NY: M.E. Sharpe, 1998.

Liss, Peggy Korn. *Mexico under Spain, 1521–1556: Society and Origins of Nationality*. Chicago: University of Chicago Press, 1975.

Lockhart, James. *The Nahuas after the Conquest: A Social and Cultural History of the Indians of Central Mexico, Sixteenth through Eighteenth Centuries*. Stanford, CA: Stanford University Press, 1992.

McDonough, Kelly S. *The Learned Ones: Nahua Intellectuals in Postconquest Mexico*. Tucson: University of Arizona Press, 2014.

Mecham, J. Lloyd. *Francisco de Ibarra and Nueva Vizcaya*. Durham, NC: Duke University Press, 1927.

Megged, Amos, and Stephanie Wood, eds. *Mesoamerican Memory: Enduring Systems of Resistance*. Norman: University of Oklahoma Press, 2012.

Owensby, Brian. *Empire of Law and Indian Justice in Colonial Mexico*. Stanford, CA: Stanford University Press, 2008.

Poole, Stafford. *Juan de Ovando: Governing the Spanish Empire in the Reign of Philip II*. Norman: University of Oklahoma Press, 2004.

Powell, Philip W. *Soldiers, Indians, and Silver*. Berkeley: University of California Press, 1969.

Ramos, Frances L. *Identity, Ritual, and Power in Colonial Puebla*. Tucson: University of Arizona Press, 2012.

Ramos, Gabriela, and Yanna Yannakakis, eds. *Indigenous Intellectuals: Knowledge, Power, and Colonial Culture in Mexico and the Andes*. Durham, NC: Duke University Press, 2014.

Rosenmüller, Cristoph, *Patrons, Partisans, and Palace Intrigues: The Court Society of Colonial Mexico, 1702–1710*. Calgary, Canada: University of Calgary Press, 2008.

————, ed. *Corruption in the Iberian Empires: Greed, Custom, and Colonial Networks*. Albuquerque: University of New Mexico Press, 2017.

Ruiz Medrano, Ethelia. *Mexico's Indigenous Communities: Their Lands and Histories, 1500–2010*. Boulder: University Press of Colorado, 2010.

Ruiz Medrano, Ethelia, and Susan Kellogg, eds. *Negotiation within Domination: New Spain's Indian Pueblos Confront the Spanish State*. Boulder: University Press of Colorado, 2010.

Seijas, Tatiana. *Asian Slaves in Colonial Mexico: From Chinos to Indios*. New York: Cambridge University Press, 2014.

Tavárez, David. *The Invisible War: Indigenous Devotions, Discipline and Dissent in Colonial Mexico*. Stanford, CA: Stanford University Press, 2011.

Terraciano, Kevin. *The Mixtecs of Colonial Oaxaca: Nudzahui History, Sixteenth through Eighteenth Centuries*. Stanford, CA: University of California Press, 2001.

Townsend, Camilla, ed. *Here in This Year: Seventeenth-Century Nahuatl Annals of the Tlaxcala-Puebla Valley*. Stanford, CA: Stanford University Press, 2010.

Weber, David J. *The Spanish Frontier in North America*. New Haven, CT: Yale University Press, 1992.

Wade, Maria F. *Missions, Missionaries, and Native Americans: Long-Term Processes and Daily Practices*. Gainesville: University Press of Florida, 2009.

Wood, Stephanie. *Transcending Conquest: Nahua Views of Colonial Mexico*. Norman: University of Oklahoma Press, 2003.

CHAPTER 9

THE COLONIAL ECONOMY

SPAIN'S ECONOMIC POLICIES

Mexico, as the colony of New Spain, existed for the benefit of the mother country. At least that was the view of the Spanish crown's economic advisers. Like other European colonial powers, Spain subscribed to the economic philosophy of mercantilism, which held that the purpose of a colony was to make the mother country stronger and more self-sufficient. If a colony did not return such advantages to the mother country, it could be more of a liability than an asset. There were other considerations, both religious and strategic, but profit was no doubt the primary consideration.

Spain's colonial economic policies were protectionist in the extreme, which meant that the economy in New Spain was restricted by limitations imposed by the imperial system. Thus, the natural growth of industry and commerce was significantly impeded because man-ufacturers and merchants in Spain were protected from the competition of those in the colony. In accord with the classic pattern, the Spanish Indies were to supply Spain with raw products, which could be made into finished goods in the mother country and sold back to the colonists at a profit. In the case of Mexico, silver would become the main export to Spain, where it promoted inflation and Spanish imperial wars.

In the early years of the colony, whites lived parasitically off many Indians and a substan-tial number of Africans, but the picture changed considerably after a time. The importance of the encomiendas in the overall economy of New Spain did not last long, for not many of those who came after the conquerors received grants of Indian village labor. Within a short time the encomenderos formed but a small minority of the Spaniards in Mexico. Of perhaps eight hundred first-generation encomenderos, their numbers dropped to just over five hundred by the mid-sixteenth century, and at the beginning of the seventeenth century, there were only about fifty left in central Mexico. Most of the encomienda towns reverted to the crown for lack of legitimate heirs.

In all events, even in the sixteenth century the majority of the encomenderos had en-comiendas that offered only modest incomes. It is true, however, that the more prominent conquerors had large numbers of tributaries, and such men were prosperous, especially if they diversified their interests. The wealthiest of all was Fernando Cortés, who had many rich towns. He also held real estate and engaged in commercial transactions in New Spain as well as in other colonies; he raised blooded horses and other stock and experimented with the production of silk; and he had interests in mining, shipbuilding, sugar processing, and farming.

Meanwhile many more Spaniards poured into the colony and, contrary to the view often held, most of them had to work as officials, clergymen, merchants, artisans, miners, ranchers, lawyers, physicians, teachers, or sailors. Despite official attempts to encourage Spanish farmers and laborers to emigrate to America, almost none did. As a consequence, the necessary physical labor was performed by Indians, blacks, and those of mixed races. It has often been noted that the true wealth discovered by the Spaniards consisted of the millions of natives whose labor kept the colonies functioning. In the years following the conquest a good number of Indians were slaves, either because they were already in that category in their own societies or because they were enslaved by Spaniards for continued resistance to Spanish authority. Slaves were often worked to the point of exhaustion and usually had short lives. Owing to the bitter protests of Spaniards of conscience—most notably the Dominican friar Bartolomé de Las Casas—Indian slavery was finally abolished in the 1550s, but it persisted long after in New Spain's far north.

The percentage of Indians who were truly chattels was relatively small; those assigned to encomiendas constituted a far greater number in the early period. In addition to the tribute owed to their encomenderos, Indians were required to contribute labor under a regulated system. Often the encomendero rented the services of his Indians to merchants and others, who drove them mercilessly. In 1549 the labor obligation was abolished, and labor in lieu of tribute was forbidden. Without slaves and forced labor, who would carry out the necessary tasks of labor? The policymakers in Spain reasoned that if Indians were paid a fair wage for their work and if they were treated humanely, they would volunteer. But few among the dwindling number of Indians stepped forward to assume the burden.

Consequently, the crown decreed a system of forced labor called the *repartimiento*, or *cuatequil* (the Nahuatl name for a similar structure employed by the Aztecs to extract labor). Under this system each adult male Indian had to contribute about forty-five days of labor a year, usually a week at a time at various intervals. Only a small percentage of the men from any village were to be absent simultaneously, and the head of a family was to have time free to cultivate his own fields. Provisions stipulated that each laborer would be paid for his work and treated with consideration. In practice, however, Indians were mistreated, forced to work excessive hours, and cheated of their pay. Labor drafts often took entire villages away from their own fields at planting or harvest times. Laws in the early seventeenth century decreed the abolition of repartimiento, but it persisted, especially in the northern and southern fringes of New Spain, until the end of the colonial period.

In central Mexico, the frequent labor shortages caused by Indian population decline were met with a variety of labor practices that included repartimiento, black slavery, sharecropping, and wage labor. Wage labor sometimes turned into debt peonage when money or goods were advanced to individuals by an employer and not repaid quickly. In some cases,

A Spanish overseer directs Indian laborers on a sugar plantation in this painting by the modern muralist Diego Rivera (1886–1957).

employers could hold these workers in perpetual servitude by continuing to advance credit, but the system could also work to the advantage of laborers who could accumulate debt and resources and then move on to another place. The degree of force that employers could exert varied according to time, place, and the available labor pool, but coercive debt peonage was probably not widespread in the colonial period.

One onerous labor practice was a carryover from prehispanic times, when everything that had to be moved was transported on the backs of porter or tamemes. Despite a legal limit of fifty pounds for each load, it was not uncommon for tamemes to be forced to carry twice that weight over mountain passes. Prominent Spaniards arriving at Veracruz were conveyed to the capital two hundred miles distant in sedan chairs carried by Indians. So many carriers succumbed to fatigue that a royal decree ordered the increased use of mules and horses and the opening of roads for carts. But the sight of men bent under staggering loads remained familiar.

MINING

The lands of the Spanish Indies belonged to the Spanish sovereigns personally, but their subjects were allowed to exploit the land at the pleasure of the rulers. The royal quinto (fifth) of American riches applied to Indian treasure, precious metals and jewels, and the sale of slaves, to cite a few examples. The crown was, therefore, no less anxious to promote the search for gold and silver than the most avaricious colonist. The search for precious minerals continued unabated and ultimately succeeded. It was silver, however, not gold, that provided the great wealth of colonial Mexico. By the early 1530s silver was being mined in various locations, but not until a quarter-century after the fall of Tenochtitlan was a great strike made. Between 1546 and 1548 the fabulous silver deposits of Zacatecas were revealed, and within a few years more rich mines operated in Guanajuato, San Luis Potosí, Pachuca, and other sites. Later silver strikes in Parral and Chihuahua spurred settlement in the far north during the seventeenth and eighteenth centuries.

The great wealth of the mines dramatically transformed the economy of the colony. Mining camps, some of which became the important cities we see today, sprouted in many locations in northern Mexico. By the early years of the seventeenth century Zacatecas had become the third largest city in the colony, surpassed only by the capital and Puebla. A few miners became very wealthy and lived in ostentation. Other entrepreneurs made their fortunes by supplying those who flocked to the mining camps seeking silver. Commerce was profitable for merchants who risked taking their goods over the dangerous trails, past unsubdued Indians. Others established stores and provided diverse services for the miners. Equally prosperous farmers furnished the food that was so much in demand in the barren north. At first cattle and sheep were driven north in herds, but eventually ranchers saw the wisdom of establishing ranches in the vicinity of the mines; this was the genesis of the great livestock spreads of northern Mexico.

Until the late eighteenth century when Guanajuato became the chief producer, most silver was mined in Zacatecas and areas further north, where no large sedentary Indian populations existed. Even so, Spaniards first tried to enslave local Indians or force them to work in repartimiento. Conditions were onerous far underground in the dark, damp shafts with the danger of floods or explosions. Workers climbed up crude ladders to haul out the heavy ores. Some succumbed to early death and others tried to flee. In this situation, miners turned to recruiting Indians from western and central Mexico with promises of pay and exemption from tribute, prompting an inflow of free native laborers, along with Africans and mixed-race peoples, that continued throughout the colonial period. Pay was probably the best in the early years of wage labor and often included ore sharing. The mines at Zacatecas thrived, generating a third of Mexico's silver with some five thousand laborers at the height of production in the seventeenth century. These workers built the city center where Spaniards lived, at the same time creating their own communities around the outskirts. Many of these barrios knit together people who had ethnic and linguistic affiliations, and some were multi-ethnic. At least in the case of Zacatecas, over time they created municipal and religious institutions that afforded them a measure of autonomy and civic pride. The evolution of mining towns, their conditions, and their interethnic relationships varied across time and space with the mix of free and coerced labor.

Silver proved to be a blessing and a curse for the Spanish. While they valued gold above silver, the vast silver mines across their colonial possessions fed the dominant Asian markets, filtered through European exchanges or sent directly across the Pacific on the Manila galleons. New Spain was the nexus between the Atlantic and Pacific economies, and silver allowed for the importation of diverse luxury goods as well as more mundane commodities. Moreover, silver apparently stimulated Mexico's internal economy because so much of it—perhaps half—was used to buy goods produced in New Spain. While the viceroyalty of New Spain had a thriving economy based on silver exports, this same commodity proved to be the bane of the Spanish on the peninsula. Unregulated flows of bullion through the royal treasury at first created a boom economy in the sixteenth century, but the bubble burst by the end of the century leaving Spain with soaring inflation and falling silver receipts. Through the mixed use of smelting and mercury amalgamation processes, mining output fluctuated throughout the colonial period. From the seventeenth century on, less silver apparently reached the coffers of the crown as it was increasingly employed in the local economy, used to purchase European or Asian trade goods, or siphoned off in contraband trade.

Indian *tamemes* were the traditional bearers of cargo, transporting goods to all corners of the colony. From the Florentine Codex.

AGRICULTURE AND RANCHING

Although mining was the most salient enterprise, agriculture remained the basic occupation in all parts of New Spain. It was, of course, absolutely essential for the sustenance of the colony, and most agricultural production went to domestic consumption. To the variety of foods native on the land, the Spaniards introduced an assortment of plant life—citrus and other fruits, wheat, sugarcane, and many edibles to enrich the colonial diet. Early Spanish settlers were given, in addition to town lots for residences, small garden plots outside of town for their own needs, to be cultivated by Indian farmers. The natives had their own personal lands, held privately or in common, to provide food for themselves.

Colonists were allowed to grow what they wished as long as their production did not conflict with interests in Spain. Often, they ended up having to pay inflated prices for imported necessities that could easily have been grown in Mexico. Wine and olive oil, for example, were not luxuries but staples. They were considered essential to the traditional Spanish table, and wine was necessary for Catholic mass. Yet so great were the profits to producers and middlemen in Spain that the growing of vines and olive trees was largely forbidden in the colonies. One significant exception occurred in the far north, where the crown allowed the development of a wine industry at Parras (in modern-day Coahuila). In this area, where the soils were favorable and water was available, descendants of the conquistador Francisco de Urdiñola, Jesuits, and Tlaxcalan colonists produced wine primarily for a limited and isolated northern market. As a supplemental beverage, beer was brewed in Mexico as early as 1544.

A panoramic view of a silver-mining operation.

Export crops constituted an important part of royal income. Hides were an early important export. Essential to the booming textile industry in Europe were good dyes, and Mexico produced one of the best with the native product cochineal. This red dye was of considerable value and convenient for export because of its compact nature. It was extracted from tiny insects found in the nopal cactus, which was soon planted in extensive tracts. Another profitable dye was the blue extracted from the indigo plant. Cacao, the source of a prized beverage in the pre-conquest period (while it also served a form of currency), eventually caught the fancy of Europeans, providing yet another valuable export for Spain. Both vanilla and henequen constituted additional products of some importance. After Cortés introduced sugar in 1524, plantations and mills flourished in the warmer climes of the colony. Comparatively modest Mexican exports of sugar added to the diversity of New Spain's economy. Black slaves commonly toiled in sugar and indigo production.

Most agricultural produce was consumed locally, and the staple crops were corn and wheat. Indians continued to produce corn for subsistence and for the market, but eventually Spanish *haciendas* (agricultural estates) supplied the bulk of maize consumed in urban areas. They also produced large quantities of wheat in the areas of Puebla and the Bajío (Guanajuato and Querétaro). At the same time, Indians could also be required to plant fruits, vegetables, and grains introduced by the Spaniards.

The Spanish introduction of livestock had the most far-reaching implications for indigenous peoples. They were most likely to raise chickens, pigs, and sheep for themselves; and their communities often owned at least a few head of cattle. While animals introduced more protein into the Indian diet, in the predominantly unfenced terrain, they also caused great harm to Indian crops. The ranching industry developed throughout Mexico, but the largest

This graceful aqueduct at Querétaro was built between 1729 and 1739. With seventy-four arches, it is eighty-five feet high at one point and carried water to the city over a distance of five miles.

livestock spreads evolved in the north, where the land was marginal for cultivation. The stockmen's guild, the *mesta*, branded and regulated multiplying herds.

Travelers reported seeing herds of as many as one hundred fifty thousand head, and in the region of Zacatecas more than two million sheep grazed in summer pastures. Even though beef was inexpensive, colonists consumed much more of the costlier mutton. Sheep thrived better in the north than cattle, and their wool brought very good returns on investments.

Large Mexican estates are usually associated with the vast haciendas of the north, but in central and southern Mexico, important, though smaller, landholdings engaged in the growing of sugar, henequen, and other agricultural products. The conquerors were often rewarded with tracts of land consisting of twenty to a hundred acres, and many were able to add to their holdings. Thus, the acquisition of large estates began in earnest in the late six-teenth century, especially after the devastating epidemic of the 1570s that took thousands of Indian lives and facilitated the claiming of their lands. Individuals with the capital neces-sary for an enterprise appealing to royal interests either received land outright or purchased it at a low price. Large acreage was necessary for cattle and sheep to forage. One entrepreneur of the northern frontier began putting together parcels in 1583, and by his death, in 1618, the family estates stretched over 11,626,850 acres. In many instances hacienda owners ac-quired land from Indians, by either purchase, fraud, or coercion.

While it is traditional to assume that a large percentage of Indian lands were lost to the Spaniards, in fact, the natives retained sufficient ancestral holdings at least until the population began to rebound at the mid-seventeenth century. After that, land and water disputes multiplied between Indian towns and between Indian towns and Spanish haci-endas. Indigenous litigants learned to use the courts and not infrequently succeeded in retaining water rights through compromises which assigned hours or days to contending parties during which they could access shared water. Although there were regional varia-tions, haciendas and villages coexisted in a kind of synergy that allowed Spaniards to profit modestly in a chronically weak domestic market and Indian villages to preserve some autonomy and land.

The new agricultural systems that emanated from what has been called the "Columbian exchange" of plants and animals produced varying effects throughout the colony. On the one hand, the introduction of livestock like cattle, sheep, goats, pigs, and chickens and new plant species (including vegetables and fruits) increased the amount of food and the general caloric intake of all groups. On the other hand, the imports could have negative effects on Mexican ecosystems. Livestock were particularly invasive as they proliferated in ungrazed grasslands and overran Indian fields and commons. Erosion and damage from overgrazing and the transhumance of sheep were already apparent by the end of the 16th century. In the Valle de Mezquital, north of Mexico City, desert vegetation quickly took over from the grasslands that had supported what has been termed a "plague" of sheep. Reduction in pasturelands curbed the raising of livestock for a time in the sev-enteenth century, but production climbed again in the eighteenth to supply the mines and growing urban populations with meat and leather. Furthermore, silver production required great quantities of charcoal for smelting, resulting in the almost total deforesta-tion of mining areas.

INDUSTRY AND COMMERCE

With industry so closely regulated to prevent competition with Spain, Mexico made little in the way of manufactured goods. What they produced was mainly for internal consumption. Mining of silver and the cultivation of dyestuffs, cochineal and indigo, provided for a healthy export economy. But an export economy cannot exist without an internal economy to feed, clothe, and entertain the labor force. Internally, all manner of meat, vegetables, and grains were sold in the markets, tobacco and alcohol were locally produced, while textile production made up the majority of the true manufacturing. Iron working and ceramics (*talavera*) constituted small segments of manufacturing, while the processing of sugar and cacao made these raw material ready for sale. Most luxury goods were imported through Spanish merchants, although olive oil and wine were the main items of Spanish origin. Merchants in the colony imported expensive fabrics, porcelains, and spices from China, India, and northern Europe.

The crown instituted all manner of regulations to restrict manufacturing in the colonies, in order to prop up a failing Spanish economy that had little in the way of a manufacturing base. Wine and olive oil could not be legally produced in the colonies, although some enterprising monks in northern missions planted vineyards. Textile producers on the peninsula, especially of wool and silk, often lamented their small market share in New Spain even though the crown forbade production of fine cloth there. But cheaper, better quality materials imported from Asian and European markets fed the demand of the silver-rich viceroyalty in New Spain regardless.

Still many products for everyday use came out of small industries in Mexico. Cotton and woolen cloth was manufactured in *obrajes*, the textile mills that existed in various locations, especially Mexico City, Puebla, and Querétaro. Since few could afford imported finery, local mills proliferated, with more than eighty by 1571. Until the eighteenth century, when the powered mills of Europe flooded the markets with cheap cloth, Mexican obrajes employed thousands of workers to meet the growing demand for textiles. Conditions in the obrajes varied, but in some cases workers were virtually imprisoned in sweatshops.

Other manufactured items were produced by the many artisans in the colony, among them tailors, blacksmiths, cobblers, candle makers, and goldsmiths. Guilds, or *gremios*, existed or each of these crafts. Well established by the late sixteenth century, the guilds fixed the quality of goods and influenced prices. Non-Spaniards could join the gremios, but only whites could attain the rank of master. In a more positive sense, the gremios protected of their members, making provisions for those who suffered accidents and illness, and extended help to widows. They actively promoted religious celebrations and philanthropic undertakings for the community. Eventually about one hundred guilds existed in Mexico City. A professional merchants' guild, the Consulado, was established in the capital in 1592. It functioned to arbitrate commercial disputes, to protect the interests of merchants, to establish rules of business conduct, and to foster the interests of the community.

The Casa de Contratación (House of Trade), located in the city of Seville which served as the official entrepôt for all traffic with the Indies, supervised the imperial commercial system. As in industry, the institution imposed tight controls on commerce in order to benefit the crown above all. Everything and everyone going to or coming from the colonies theoretically passed through officials who checked all papers with care. Of course, the closed system encouraged contraband exchanges that cannot be measured with any precision. Traders in the city of Seville sent to the colonies a wide variety of goods—expensive fabrics, hats, wax for candles, wine, liquors, vinegar, olive oil, paper, steel and iron implements, fruit preserves, and other items. Trade in Asian merchandise, theoretically controlled by officials in Seville, in practical terms was managed from New Spain. This trade proved especially lucrative for the great Mexico City silver merchants, who also served as brokers in the exchanges of Peruvian silver and Asian goods.

All products destined for the Spanish Indies were required to go on Spanish ships with Spanish crews to facilitate the collection of duties, inspection of goods, and the

The city of Puebla was (and is) famous for its excellent ceramic products. Pots and tiles are richly decorated and glazed in the styles known as *majolica* and *talavera*. *Above right,* A typical seventeenth-century Puebla bowl. *Above left,* Mudejar influence is evident in this vase. *Right,* This flowerpot is of a Chinese type.

enforcement of legal restrictions. Cargoes were channeled through the two official ports of entry: Veracruz for the Atlantic and Acapulco for the Pacific. Local officials exercised a great deal of control over these processes and often used that to the benefit of merchants, accounting for part of the contraband trade. For example, in the early eighteenth century, the top official in Acapulco frequentlyregistered large quantities of goods arriving on the galleons as "gifts" from merchants in Manila to their counterparts in mainland New Spain to elide the fact that the local merchants were forbidden to import from the Asian markets. Ships sailing to and from the New World went in annual convoys, once a year in the Pacific and up to four times a year in the Atlantic. Because of pirates, the convoys traveled with armed escort vessels in the Atlantic. An increase in the number of ships and frequency of the voyages from the sixteenth to the eighteenth centuries responded to the growing economy of New Spain.

The arrival of the fleet in Veracruz and the galleons in Acapulco were momentous events marked by large fairs visited by merchants from across New Spain and beyond. In Veracruz, the prevalence of yellow fever and malaria discouraged any sizable permanent population, but when the fleet arrived tents bristled on the beach almost overnight, as great numbers of buyers came to negotiate in the colorful trade fair that ensued. In some years the cargoes were taken to Mexico City to avoid the pestilential airs of the port. Eventually the fair relocated inland to the higher, more salubrious climate of Jalapa, which had the added advantage of being a safer depository for silver destined for Spain.

Once a year the Manila galleon arrived to Acapulco, usually in January. The ships were laden with rich luxuries including silks, cottons, porcelains, furniture, spices, perfumes, incense, and other goods destined to be sold at a large fair that brought many to this Pacific-coast port. This fair created a cottage industry to support the increased population and the provisioning of the ships for the return voyage to Manila. Officials attempted to control prices, made sure that the silver that left the port city was certified, and supervised the inspection and provision of the ships. Moreover, they contracted with local elites to provide food from their haciendas, arranged extra lodgings for the influx of merchants, and organized the transport of people and goods to Mexico City and beyond. The government officials often relied on the repartimiento obligations of indigenous communities who negotiated payment in specie and goods. For a few months a year, Acapulco served as the center of commerce in New Spain, allowing for the development of a local economy to support the importation of goods destined for markets across the viceroyalty.

In the capital, a diverse population, ethnically and economically, met to buy locally produced goods and luxury merchandise imported from Asia and Europe. While the majority of the population could not afford to partake of the luxury goods to a great extent, the market was sufficiently strong to increase imports throughout the colonial period. The main plaza of Mexico City was the commercial hub with multiple markets always crowded with shoppers—serving poor, middling, and elite consumer populations. (See the cover image.) On the lower end of the scale, the Baratillo market was a space to buy secondhand and illegally procured items, often held up as an example of vice in the capital. After 1703, the Parian market, named after a similar one in Manila, was the place to go to see and buy Asian imports. Villages throughout Mexico had their own small public markets with few imported

Loading merchandise onto a Spanish galleon in Manila.

Muleteers (*arrieros*) were a familiar sight on the roads of New Spain.

goods; Indians were limited consumers of Spanish goods. They continued to weave their own cloth and produce utilitarian wares, prompting the forced sale of goods practiced so venally by the corregidores.

THE RESULTS OF SPAIN'S POLICIES

In addition to its profits through mining and agricultural exports, the Spanish crown realized revenues through retention for itself of monopolies on such items as mercury, gunpowder, salt, pulque, and, in the eighteenth century, tobacco. The crown's quinto was eventually reduced to a tenth, but it still constituted a substantial source of royal income. As the encomienda system withered away, more Indian villages came under the crown, to whom tribute was paid. Although tribute in the early years was rendered in kind, Spaniards increasingly demanded it in coinage as a way of forcing the Indian economy into the marketplace. Indians then had to sell their produce or their labor to get cash. But for the most part, under Hapsburg rule, villages had some latitude to reconstitute hybrid communities of their own making. The king's treasury also benefited from the sale of licenses, offices, and land and from the various taxes paid by the colonists. Altogether there were about sixty different taxes, of which the most detested was the *alcabala*, a sales tax payable on almost everything sold. At first only 2 percent of the item's value, the alcabala went as high as 14 percent during Spain's wars of the eighteenth century, although colonial subjects had become adept at avoiding payment of this tax. The *almojarifazgo* was a tax of 7.5 percent on all imports and exports, so the crown was paid twice for goods moving between Spain and its colonies, for a total income of 15 percent.

Despite the reduction in the labor force that resulted from the Indian demographic decline, production of silver apparently did not drop drastically in the seventeenth century. Nor did the excessive and arbitrary economic controls of the Hapsburgs necessarily stifle local incentive and growth. A greater share of royal revenues remained in the colony, and population revival after 1630 contributed to a rise in craft production as well as more regional specialization in agriculture and manufacturing. According to most economic historians, a growing transoceanic trade with Europe and Asia in the end did not foster a profound capitalist transformation in New Spain's primarily agrarian economy, where domestic relations of production changed little and an oligarchy controlled limited markets.[1] Nonetheless, by the last decades of the seventeenth century, change was in the offing with a modest expansion in mining, agricultural production, and commerce. In the next century, the Spanish Bourbon kings would take advantage of this transitional phase as a base for transforming the colonial economy.

---

1 In contrast, the historian John Tutino has argued that the economic development of the Bajío region was crucial to the development of global capitalism in the early modern period. John Tutino, *Making a New World: Founding Capitalism in the Bajío and Spanish North America* (Durham, NC, 2011).

A piece-of-eight minted in Mexico in 1609. Such coins were used mainly for trading with Spain for manufactured goods or purchase of Asian spices and silks carried by the Manila galleon.

RECOMMENDED FOR FURTHER STUDY

Bakewell, Peter J. *Silver Mining and Society in Colonial Mexico: Zacatecas, 1546–1700*. New York: Cambridge University Press, 1971.

Barrett, Elinore M. *The Mexican Colonial Copper Industry*. Albuquerque: University of New Mexico Press, 1987.

Barrett, Ward. *The Sugar Hacienda of the Marqueses del Valle*. Minneapolis: University of Minnesota Press, 1970.

Borah, Woodrow. *Early Trade and Navigation between Mexico and Peru*. Berkeley: University of California Press, 1954.

————. *New Spain's Century of Depression*. Berkeley: University of California Press, 1951.

Boyer, Richard. "Mexico in the Seventeenth Century: Transition of a Colonial Society." *Hispanic American Historical Review* 57/3 (1977): 455–78.

Brockington, Lolita Gutiérrez. *The Leverage of Labor: Managing the Cortés Haciendas in Tehuantepec, 1588–1688*. Durham, NC: Duke University Press, 1989.

Castro, Daniel. *Another Face of Empire: Bartolomé de las Casas, Indigenous Rights, and Ecclesiastical Imperialism*. Durham, NC: Duke University Press, 2007.

Chevalier, François. *Land and Society in Colonial Mexico: The Great Hacienda*. Berkeley: University of California Press, 1963.

Cuello, José. "The Persistence of Indian Slavery in the Northeast of Colonial Mexico, 1577–1723." *Journal of Social History* 21/4 (1980): 683–700.

Dusenberry, William. *The Mexican Mesta: The Administration of Ranching in Colonial Mexico*. Urbana: University of Illinois Press, 1963.

Frank, Andre Gunder. *Mexican Agriculture, 1521–1630. Transformation of the Mode of Production*. New York: Cambridge University Press, 1979.

Giráldez, Arturo. *The Age of Trade: The Manila Galleons and the Dawn of the Global Economy*. Lanham, MD: Rowman & Littlefield, 2015.

Goode, Catherine Tracy. "Merchant-Bureaucrats, Unwritten Contracts, and Fraud in the Manila Galleon Trade." In *Corruption in the Iberian Empires: Greed, Custom, and Colonial Networks*, edited by Christoph Rosenmüller. Albuquerque: University of New Mexico Press, 2017.

Harris, Charles H., III. *A Mexican Family Empire: The Latifundio of the Sánchez Navarro Family, 1765–1867.* Austin: University of Texas Press, 1975.

Hassig, Ross. *Trade, Tribute, and Transportation: The Sixteenth-Century Political Economy of the Valley of Mexico.* Norman: University of Oklahoma Press, 1985.

Hoberman, Louisa. *Mexico's Merchant Elite, 1590–1660.* Durham, NC: Duke University Press, 1991.

Israel, J. I. "Mexico and the 'General Crisis' of the Seventeenth Century." *Past and Present* 63/1 (1974): 33–57.

Kicza, John E. *Colonial Entrepreneurs: Families and Business in Bourbon Mexico City.* Albuquerque: University of New Mexico Press, 1983.

Konove, Andrew. "On the Cheap: The Baratillo Marketplace and the Shadow Economy of Eighteenth-Century Mexico City." *The Americas* 72/2 (April 2015): 249–278.

Konrad, Herman W. *A Jesuit Hacienda in Colonial Mexico: Santa Lucia, 1576–1767.* Stanford, CA: Stanford University Press, 1980.

Ladd, Doris. *The Making of a Strike: Mexican Silver Workers' Struggles in Real del Monte, 1766–1775.* Lincoln: University of Nebraska Press, 1988.

Leiby, John S. *Colonial Bureaucrats and the Mexican Economy.* New York: Peter Lang, 1986.

Lipsett-Rivera, Sonya. *To Defend Our Water with the Blood of Our Veins: The Struggles for Resources in Colonial Puebla.* Albuquerque: University of New Mexico Press, 1999.

Melville, Elinor G. K. *A Plague of Sheep: Environmental Consequences of the Conquest of Mexico.* New York: Cambridge University Press, 1994.

Melville, Elinor G. K., and Bradley Skopyk. "Disease, Ecology, and the Environment." In *The Oxford History of Mexico*, edited by Michael C. Meyer and William H. Beezley, 203–34. New York: Oxford University Press, rev. 2010.

Meyer, Michael C. *Water in the Hispanic Southwest: A Social and Legal History, 1550–1850.* Tucson: University of Arizona Press, 1984.

Miller, Shawn W. *An Environmental History of Latin America.* New York: Cambridge University Press, 2007.

Patch, Robert W. *Maya and Spaniard in Yucatan, 1648–1812.* Stanford, CA: Stanford University Press, 1993.

Radding, Cynthia. *Landscapes of Power and Identity: Comparative Histories in the Sonoran Desert and the Forests of Amazonia from Colony to Republic.* Durham, NC: Duke University Press, 2006.

Riley, G. Micheal. *Fernando Cortés and the Marquesado in Morelos: A Case Study in the Socioeconomic Development of Sixteenth-Century Mexico.* Albuquerque: University of New Mexico Press, 1973.

Salvucci, Richard J. *Textiles and Capitalism in Mexico: An Economic History of the Obrajes, 1539–1840.* Princeton, NJ: Princeton University Press, 1988.

Schurz, William L. *The Manila Galleon.* New York: Dutton, 1939.

Seijas, Tatiana. *Asian Slaves in Colonial Mexico: From Chinos to Indios.* New York: Cambridge University Press, 2014.

_____. "Inns, Mules, and Hardtack for the Voyage: The Local Economy of the Manila Galleon in Mexico." *Colonial Latin America Review* 25/1 (2016): 56–76.

Semo, Enrique. *The History of Capitalism in Mexico: Its Origins, 1521–1763.* Translated by Lidia Lozano. Austin: University of Texas Press, 1993.

Simpson, Lesley B. *The Encomienda in New Spain.* Berkeley: University of California Press, 1960.

Taylor, William B. *Landlord and Peasant in Colonial Oaxaca.* Stanford, CA: Stanford University Press, 1972.

Tutino, John. *Making a New World: Founding Capitalism in the Bajío and Spanish North America.* Durham, NC: Duke University Press, 2011.

Van Young, Eric. *Hacienda and Market in 18th-Century Mexico. The Rural Economy of the Guadalajara Region, 1675–1820.* Berkeley: University of California Press, 1981.

Velasco Murillo, Dana. *Urban Indians in a Silver City: Zacatecas, Mexico, 1546–1810.* Stanford, CA: Stanford University Press, 2016.

West, Robert C. *The Mining Community in Northern New Spain: The Parral Mining District.* Berkeley: University of California Press, 1949.

CHAPTER 10

THE COLONIAL CHURCH

A traveler in colonial Mexico approaching the outskirts of a town first saw in the distance a bell tower rising over all other structures. Before long he would hear the tolling of bells resounding over town and countryside. In the streets priests, friars, and nuns mingled prominently in the crowds. If the physical presence of the church was everywhere, in other ways, too, it was the most pervasive of colonial institutions, and none left its imprint more deeply on the culture.

CHURCH ORGANIZATION

Because of its expulsion of the Muslims in Spain and its "discovery" of the New World, the Spanish crown was granted extraordinary privileges by the papacy. In effect, through the royal patronage (*patronato real*) Spanish kings headed the Roman Catholic Church in their domains. While this conferred great power and prestige, it also imposed many responsibilities. And, significantly, it meant that the church became an arm of the state.

Church organization consisted of two distinct branches—the secular clergy and the regular clergy. The secular group consisted of priests who served under their bishops. The regulars were missionaries under the separate authority of the superiors of their various orders; the Franciscans, Dominicans, Augustinians, and others. Fueled by a desire for status and wealth, the Spanish conquest was also legally justified by its Christian mission—the saving of souls. And most Spanish conquerors were devout in their religious observances, confessing their sins and praying frequently, especially in times of danger. Cortés demonstrated his pious fervor in his adamant insistence, even in threatening circumstances, that Indians cast down their idols, forbear from human sacrifices, and abandon their old gods. His zeal more than once jeopardized the safety of the Spaniards, and he had to be restrained by his own priests.

In 1527 the Dominican Julián Garcés arrived in Tlaxcala to assume his duties as the first bishop in the land. That same year another bishopric was created for the city of Mexico, and the following year Juan de Zumárraga, a Franciscan friar, arrived as bishop. With the

Typical fortress-like construction is apparent in this sixteenth-century Dominican monastery at Tepoztlán, Morelos. There are some striking Renaissance details in this important structure.

additional title "Protector of the Indians," Zumárraga not only established the form of the early secular church but also took an active part in alleviating the sufferings of the Indians, a policy that brought him into conflict with encomenderos and Spanish officials. A Christian humanist and wise administrator, Zumárraga served as a stabilizing factor in the early years of the colony. He was elevated to archbishop of Mexico shortly before his death in 1548.

An event of considerable significance was said to have occurred in 1531. According to tradition, a newly converted Indian by the name of Juan Diego beheld a vision of the Virgin, who commanded him to have a temple built in her honor.[1] After this legend was popularized in the mid-seventeenth century, first criollos and later many Indians embraced the devotion of the Virgin of Guadalupe. The latter occurred when the church undertook a deliberate

---

1   Despite controversy regarding his existence, Juan Diego became Mexico's first Indian saint on July 30, 2002. Stafford Poole, *The Guadalupan Controversies in Mexico* (Stanford, CA, 2006).

evangelization campaign in the eighteenth century that emphasized the Virgin's indigenous, dark-skinned features. Since modern times, Guadalupe has become a symbol of liberation and of cultural fusion, not only in Mexico but in all of Latin America. The shrine to Guadalupe at Tepeyac in the northern part of Mexico City attracts many thousands of pilgrims each year on December 12.

As the Spaniards spread out over the land, new bishoprics emerged: seven were established in the sixteenth century, one in the seventeenth century, and two in the eighteenth. They were staffed by large numbers of priests who ministered to the needs of all segments of society.

THE RELIGIOUS CONQUEST

Meanwhile the evangelizing work of the regular orders had begun. In 1521 Cortés requested that missionaries be sent, and in 1523 three lay brothers arrived, the most remarkable of whom was Pedro de Gante. The following year twelve Franciscan friars landed at Veracruz and walked barefoot to the capital. One of them, lame and tattered, was Father Toribio de Benavente, who was given the affectionate name of Motolinía, "the Poor Little One," by Indians. He became one of the most renowned churchmen in Mexico's history. As monasteries were built to accommodate their activities, other Franciscans traveled to the colony. Friars of the Dominican order arrived in 1525. Distinguished for their intellectual discipline, the Dominicans had long been powerful in Spain, where they were associated with the Inquisition. In the colonies, Dominicans like Las Casas campaigned for more just treatment of Indians.

The Augustinians reached Mexico in 1533 and proceeded to construct some of the finest monasteries in the land. All of these orders flourished early: by 1559 there were thirty Franciscan houses with 380 religious; 210 Dominicans labored out of forty houses; and 212 Augustinians had forty houses. Other orders, including those of nuns, had convents as well. The fruit of their activity is astounding; Motolinía claimed (no doubt with considerable exaggeration) that as early as 1537 some 9 million Indians had been baptized, 4 million of them by the Franciscans alone.

Founded years after the conquest, the Jesuits entered Mexico only in 1571, when other religious groups were well established in the center and the south. In their first years they occupied themselves with educating the sons of Spaniards and soon won the reputation of being superior teachers. But they also taught Indian children, and within a few years they undertook the task of converting natives on the northern frontiers. After establishing their first missions in Sinaloa, Durango, and Chihuahua, later Jesuits, such as Fathers Eusebio Francisco Kino and Juan Manuel de Salvatierra, carried their evangelization efforts to Sonora, Arizona, and Baja California. In addition to teaching Indians the Christian doctrine, by resettling them in villages, missionaries hoped to get them to adopt Spanish agriculture, animal husbandry, and crafts. Eventually missions could sell their surplus production to local markets, and the congregated Indians could be drafted for repartimiento labor. Franciscans continued this work in New Mexico, Texas, and California until after the end of the colonial period.

The Virgin of Guadalupe as protectress of Mexican children in twentieth-century barrio art, Ciudad Juárez.

Throughout Mexico, then, the clergy took up the challenge of conversion and undertook initial efforts in any given region with great dedication and zeal as priests learned local languages and often faced hostility. The clergy's efforts to train selected young native men in Spanish and Christian doctrine meant that early the church was able to produce confessional manuals and other religious writings in Indian languages, predominately Nahuatl and Maya. Native elites also staffed the offices that assisted the clergy, and were key to the fashioning of local Catholicisms that were unique to individual and cultural references in catechisms and ritual performances. Over time local religions blended and layered the Christian and the native. One manifestation of this phenomenon was the conflation of the Catholic patron saint with a local deity. In particular, Saint James (Santiago) and the Virgin Mary came to have powerful connotations as protectors of Indians. At the same time, Christian images (for example, the Crucifixion) could easily be misconstrued by the natives as they sought to place them in familiar contexts. These images became living sources of solace and healing for many over time.

In churches and in religious celebrations, native ritual, myth, and history continued to be layered with Catholic themes and motifs. By the end of the colonial period, indigenous peoples did not always distinguish between what was native and imported in their local religion. But for many of them, the ability to borrow and blend had served as protection and resistance against the complete eradication of their cultures. Some local pre-conquest devotional practices were kept alive primarily through oral transmission but also by pictorial texts created by native communities to substantiate their claims regarding hierarchies and land tenure. Many practices overtly Christian in symbol ironically served to bolster indigenous identity and local community autonomy. In diverse local ways, Indians became devoutly attached to their churches and to the miraculous images and shrines they claimed as their own. Even when devotional practices or cults seemed to transcend Catholic orthodoxy, officials were wont to turn a blind eye if these did not stray too far from sanctioned beliefs.

Indians were more likely to adopt those introductions by the clergy that could enhance their material conditions, such as tools and additions to the diet. Local fiestas or feast-day celebrations were especially popular, as they liberated Indians from their labors and were associated with feasts that enabled them to consume more of their own production. Religious plays, music, and dancing served as evangelical tools and often accompanied these festivals. Accustomed to public ritual, indigenous people modified and adapted ceremonies such as those of Corpus Christi, Todos Santos, and Holy Week.

Indian *cofradías*, created to promote particular religious devotions, also served the purpose of enabling Indians to manage their own economic resources. Although cofradía holdings varied widely, they commonly included some livestock and perhaps small properties that were rented out. In some places, they functioned as credit institutions, lending modest amounts to members. Conflicts between parish priests and cofradías over control of these resources erupted frequently. Many priests complained that Indians used cofradía assets for unauthorized purposes and that the fiestas they sponsored were too extravagant and libertine.

RELIGIOUS DISPUTES AND COLONIAL PIETY

From the beginning, clergymen in Mexico became embroiled in bitter disputes. Ecclesiastics and encomenderos competed for control of the Indians, while friars and priests tried to protect the natives from the abuses of Spaniards. The clerics construed them as bad Christians who corrupted Indian morals in addition to mistreating them physically and exacting exorbitant tributes. Spanish civilians, in turn, regarded many of the ecclesiastics as hypocrites who were guilty of the same crimes of which they accused others. Within the church itself there were other quarrels over evangelical methods and territorial jurisdiction. On occasion the disputes ended in violence.

An anonymous Mexican artist of the early eighteenth century rendered this St. Michael.

Some acrimonious disputes between ecclesiastical and civil authorities involved not only lesser figures in the provinces but even archbishops and viceroys. One of the most notorious and scandalous episodes took place in the 1640s between the Jesuits and the bishop of Puebla, Juan de Palafox, who also held a number of high civil posts and served briefly as viceroy. This contest involving the wealth and power of the Jesuits became a cause célèbre in which several important people were excommunicated and a Jesuit school was almost burned. For the moment the Jesuits were victorious and the powerful bishop was withdrawn. Eventually, however, the secular arm of the church gained the upper hand in Mexico, as the crown consciously strove to weaken the influence of the regular orders.

Finally, some clergymen felt discriminated against because of the social circumstances of their birth. As in the civil bureaucracy, most of the higher positions were denied to those of Spanish blood born in Mexico. Yet, by the seventeenth century the majority of Mexican clerics were criollos. Nearly all elite families provided at least one son or daughter to some branch of the church, along with the income to support him or her. For some women, life as a nun provided a desired alternative to marriage as well as a means to devote themselves to God and perhaps even acquire an education. Since most Spaniards were faithful Catholics, they also left pious bequests to the church. Thus, the church became wealthy, the owner of extensive rural and urban properties (which it rented out) throughout Mexico. In the absence of banks, the church became a major lending institution, extending credit to elites. In addition, a good deal of church wealth went into the construction of opulent places of

The eighteenth-century baroque Sanctuary of Nuestra Señora de Ocotlán, Tlaxcala.

worship, but it was also used to finance the colony's only social services: the charitable institutions such as hospitals, schools, and orphanages that were run by the various orders and cathedral chapters.

The good works of the church must be measured against the personal behavior of clerics. In general, the regular orders were regarded as more dedicated—primarily because they were better educated—than the secular clergy. Reports accused priests of taking mistresses, imbibing to excess, gambling, soliciting in the confessional, and engaging in commerce. Others were charged with exacting excessively high fees for the sacraments and subjecting Indians to harsh punishments. As the primary agents of social control, at least until the eighteenth century, parish priests and missionaries were expected to use or condone corporal punishment to compel the obedience of their charges. And although the majority of priests observed their vows, lived modestly, and worked to foster improvements in the physical plant of their domains, charitable activities were less in evidence. They customarily extracted resources from their parishioners, serving to benefit not only the church but often themselves.

By the seventeenth century, the humility and simplicity evident in earlier decades yielded to a more material and increasingly profane mode of behavior that may be attributed to a decline in interest as the novelty of the crusading spirit wore thin and routine set in. Then, too, in a practical sense the challenge was less in terms of numbers, for the Indian population had declined drastically. The humanistic efforts of the early church to provide education and social services to Indians gradually gave way to less zealous, more avaricious priests who, along with corregidores, conspired to extract resources from the natives. Still,

Detail of San Francisco Acatepec. The tiles are green, yellow, and blue, bordered by red brick.

The tiled domes of Iglesia del Carmen in Mexico City.

some priests played a broker role, defending their flocks out of either common interests or altruism. And on the fringes of New Spain, missionaries conscientiously persisted in their evangelical labors, often among hostile non-sedentary groups of Indians.

Throughout the colonial period, the organized church continued to provide a vocation and income for thousands of Mexican clerics. At no time, however, did they constitute more than a fraction of a percent of the total population. Perhaps more than half lived in Mexico City and other sizeable cities like Puebla and Valladolid. Several convents for Indian nuns were established in the middle colonial period, and in the 18teenth century, Indian males could be admitted to the priesthood. At the end of the colonial era, there were about two thousand nuns and slightly over seven thousand priests (of whom about 40 percent belonged to the regular orders).

THE INQUISITION

Religious affairs assumed a more somber cast in 1571 with the formal entrance of the Holy Office of the Inquisition. With its roots in the Middle Ages, the Inquisition was employed in Spain when Ferdinand and Isabella were striving to achieve political and cultural unity in the state. These "Catholic kings" saw conformity as essential, equated Christianity with the very soul of Spain, and viewed heresy astreason. The crown forced Jews to convert or leave, along with the remaining Islamic peoples, and later on Protestants were forbidden in Spanish realms. The Inquisition functioned essentially to maintain the purity of the faith and to preserve religious orthodoxy. Since proper morality was so inseparable from correct religious behavior, the Inquisition's broader mandate became the enforcement of social conformity.

Although emigrants to the New World were screened with care, some heretics slipped by. Particularly suspect were *conversos*, or New Christians, that is, those of Jewish origins who had converted to Christianity; and the Inquisition endeavored to root out "crypto-Jews" in New Spain. Some unfortunate Protestant corsairs underwent trial for heresy. Moreover, the Inquisition tried many colonists, including clergymen and even persons in high official positions, for purely moral offenses.

The Inquisition also exercised control over printed matter that entered the colony, concerned primarily with works that dealt with liberal, "dangerous" ideas, which it was feared would corrupt and lead astray the unsophisticated Indians as well as Spaniards. However, many prohibited writings, including those of the eighteenth-century French and English Enlightenments, found their way into the private libraries of educated people, among whom were a good number of clergymen.

Before the formal establishment of the Inquisition, bishops had exercised inquisitorial powers and their jurisdiction included Indians charged with false worship. The most notorious case involved Don Carlos of Texcoco, who was accused of idolatry, though his outspoken statements allegedly contained political and social overtones. Bishop Zumárraga found the noble guilty and, in 1539, had him burned at the stake. This and other examples of excessive zeal, along with the realization that conversion would not occur overnight, helped convince the crown that the conquered peoples should not be tried as heretics. Instead, after 1570, suspicion of idolatry was to be investigated by local clerics under diocesan organization, and royal officials would administer suitable punishments, often corporal but short of the death penalty.

The Inquisition headquarters in Mexico City.

The great majority of Inquisition cases involved more mundane aspects of the lives of the non-Indian population. Thousands of cases investigated the misappropriation of supernatural power through the fraudulent manipulation of Christianity or practices of magic, witchcraft, and superstition. Another large portion pertained to sexual transgressions such as bigamy, solicitation in the confessional, cohabitation, fornication, and sodomy. In indigenous villages, as in Spanish towns, local rivalries often played into accusations of heretical behavior. For historians, Inquisition cases provide rich information about social and ethnic relationships, popular beliefs, and petty rivalries. For example, cases of blasphemy reveal a great deal about masculinity and the social structures of male authority. Accounts from

Inquisition records also show that folk customs from Indian and African religions as well as local religion in Spain were often manifest in the popular piety of diverse ethnic groups. In trying to correct popular and traditional practices, the Inquisition applied a range of punishments (including floggings, fines, and forms of public humiliation), but as the colonial period progressed, Inquisition officials often threw out charges and lightened penalties

The frontispiece of a treatise against heresy printed in Spain in 1519. Much of colonial publishing dealt with religious subjects.

Baroque façade of the Jesuit seminary of San Javier, Tepotzotlán.

through confession and penitence. The reach of the Inquisition was not all pervasive and was often tempered by local relationships and conditions. Well-educated high Inquisition officials, both civil and religious, tended toward moderation in imposing punishments.

Those who paid the extreme penalty had been convicted, in most cases, of the serious crime of heresy, often compounded by "obstinancy"—that is, the refusal to recant. The relatively few prisoners sentenced to burning at the stake were often strangled first. The solemnity of official proceedings notwithstanding, *autos da fé* assumed a carnival spirit for which elaborate preparations were made. People came from near and far to jeer at the parade of those who carried candles and wore penitential garb with pointed hoods, as well as to regard the special ceremony reserved for those consigned to the stake. From the reviewing stand the viceroy, bishops, and other high dignitaries, with their ladies, viewed the macabre spectacle.

Carved wooden mask used in a dance celebrating the Christian victory over the Moors.

The first auto da fé in the colony took place in 1574. Sixty-three prisoners had been judged, of whom five were burned and most others flogged. Eight more autos occurred in the next twenty years. But perhaps the most sensational proceeding involving crypto-Jews concerned Don Luis de Carvajal, the colonizer and governor of Nuevo León, who was accused in 1590 of harboring relatives who practiced Jewish rites. Over the next fifty years some members of his family were incarcerated or burned at the stake. The high point of autos da fé occurred between 1646 and 1649, when 216 people were tried for heresy.

The Inquisition became in later times, less concerned with spiritual matters. As an instrument of royal policy, it served in the eighteenth century to check dissident political elements. Both of the liberal priests who led the struggle for independence from Spain in the early nineteenth century were tried by the Inquisition before being turned over to secular authorities for execution. The tribunal persisted almost to the end of the colonial period and was not abolished until 1820.

Although the Inquisition affected relatively few people living in the colony, the Catholic church in its many branches exercised enormous influence over most inhabitants. The church touched the lives of those in New Spain from baptism to burial. Altogether some 12,000 churches were built in the colony during the three centuries of Spanish rule. To the Spaniards the church was a link with the mother country, a familiar and comforting association that made them feel less alien in the New World. It has been argued that considerations of honor and piety motivated them to support the church lavishly "almost to the point of their own economic suicide."[2] A deep spirituality also inspired local Catholicisms in Indian communities. Indians engaged in the solemn ceremonies that connected them with whatever sense of the cosmic they had evolved; the tolling of chimes and tinkling of bells, the incense, and the burning candles could arouse a sense of reverence and awe. Outside the churches, native peoples savored the singing, dancing, eating, and drinking of the fiestas with their noisy and colorful displays of fireworks and pageantry. Above all, "local religious practices sought to explain and domesticate Spanish colonial rule. Indians sought access to the Spaniards' spiritual knowledge and power in order to fortify the connection between the sacred and profane in ways that responded to the overshadowing importance of natural forces in their lives."[3] Studies of Indian peoples have increasingly downplayed the role of the Catholic church as an oppressive cultural monolith, highlighting instead how popular Catholicism bolstered the persistence of indigenous identity and community formation.

RECOMMENDED FOR FURTHER STUDY

Bauer, Arnold J. "The Colonial Economy." In *The Countryside in Colonial Latin America*, edited by Louisa S. Hoberman and Susan M. Socolow, 19–48. Albuquerque: University of New Mexico Press, 1996.

Boone, Elizabeth Hill, Louise M. Burkhart, and David Tavárez, eds. *Painted Words: Nahua Catholicism, Politics, and Memory in the Atzaqualco Pictorial Catechism.* Washington, DC: Dumbarton Oaks Research Library and Collection, 2017.

Brading, D. A. *Mexican Phoenix, Our Lady of Guadalupe: Image and Tradition across Five Centuries.* New York: Cambridge University Press, 2001.

Brescia, Michael M. "Liturgical Expressions of Episcopal Power: Juan de Palafox y Mendoza and the Tridentine Reform in Colonial Mexico." *The Catholic Historical Review* 90/3 (2004): 497–518.

Bristol, Joan Cameron. *Christians, Blasphemers, and Witches: Afro-Mexican Ritual Practice in the Seventeenth Century.* Albuquerque: University of New Mexico Press, 2007.

Burkhart, Louise M. *Before Guadalupe: The Virgin Mary in Early Colonial Nahuatl Literature.* Austin: University of Texas Press, 2001.

Cervantes, Fernando. *The Devil in the New World: The Impact of Diabolism in New Spain.* New Haven, CT: Yale University Press, 1994.

Christensen, Mark. *Nahua and Maya Catholicisms: Texts and Religion in Colonial Central Mexico and Yucatan.* Stanford, CA: Stanford University Press, 2013.

Chuchiak IV, John F., ed. *The Inquisition in New Spain, 1536–1820: A Documentary History.* Baltimore, MD: Johns Hopkins University Press, 2012.

Clendinnen, Inga. "Disciplining the Indians: Franciscan Ideology and Missionary Violence in Yucatán." *Past and Present* 94 (1982): 27–48.

Curcio-Nagy, Linda A. "Faith and Morals in Colonial Mexico." In *The Oxford History of Mexico*, edited by Michael C. Meyer and William H. Beezley, 143–74. New York: Oxford University Press, rev. 2010.

---

2   Arnold J. Bauer, "The Colonial Economy," in *The Countryside in Colonial Latin America*, eds. Louisa S. Hoberman and Susan M. Socolow (Albuquerque, NM, 1996), 46.

3   William B. Taylor, *Magistrates of the Sacred: Priests and Parishioners in Eighteenth-Century Mexico* (Stanford, CA, 1996), 62.

Deeds, Susan M. *Defiance and Deference in Colonial Mexico: Indians under Spanish Rule in Nueva Vizcaya.* Austin: University of Texas Press, 2003.

Díaz, Mónica. *Indigenous Writings from the Convent: Negotiating Ethnic Autonomy in Colonial Mexico.* Tucson: University of Arizona Press, 2010.

Farriss, Nancy. *Crown and Clergy in Colonial Mexico, 1759–1821.* London, UK: University of London Press, 1968.

Greenleaf, Richard E. *The Mexican Inquisition of the Sixteenth Century.* Albuquerque: University of New Mexico Press, 1969.

_____. *Zumárraga and the Mexican Inquisition, 1536–1543.* Washington, DC: Academy of American Franciscan History, 1961.

Gruzinski, Serge. *Man-Gods in the Mexican Highlands: Indian Power and Colonial Society, 1520–1800.* Stanford, CA: Stanford University Press, 1989.

Hackel, Steven W. *Children of Coyote, Missionaries of Saint Francis: Indian–Spanish Relations in Colonial California, 1769–1850.* Chapel Hill: University of North Carolina Press, 2005.

Hanke, Lewis. *Bartolomé de Las Casas: Bookman, Scholar, and Propagandist.* Philadelphia: University of Pennsylvania Press, 1952.

Hordes, Stanley M. "The Inquisition as Economic and Political Agent: The Campaign of the Mexican Holy Office against the Crypto-Jews in the Mid-Seventeenth Century." *The Americas* 39/1 (1982): 22–38.

Hu-Dehart, Evelyn. *Missionaries, Miners and Indians: Spanish Contact with the Yaqui Nation of Northwestern New Spain, 1533–1820.* Tucson: University of Arizona Press, 1981.

Jackson, Robert H. *Frontiers of Evangelization: Indians in the Sierra Gorda and Chiquitos Missions.* Norman: University of Oklahoma Press, 2017.

Lavrin, Asunción. *Brides of Christ: Conventual Life in Colonial Mexico.* Stanford, CA: Stanford University Press, 2008.

_____. "The Role of the Nunneries in the Economy of New Spain in the Eighteenth Century." *Hispanic American Historical Review* 46/4 (1966): 371–93.

Lopes Don, Patricia. *Bonfires of Culture: Franciscans, Indigenous Leaders, and Inquisition in Early Mexico, 1524–1540.* Norman: University of Oklahoma Press, 2010.

Mann, Kristin Dutcher. *The Power of Song: Music and Dance in the Mission Communities of Northern New Spain, 1590–1810.* Stanford, CA: Stanford University Press, 2010.

Megged, Amos. *Exporting the Catholic Reformation: Local Religion in Early-Colonial Mexico.* Leiden, Netherlands: E. J. Brill, 1996.

_____. *Social Memory in Ancient and Colonial Mesoamerica.* New York: Cambridge University Press, 2010.

Melvin, Karen. *Building Colonial Cities of God: Mendicant Orders and Urban Culture in New Spain.* Stanford, CA: Stanford University Press, 2012.

Miller, Mary Ellen, and Barbara E. Mundy, eds. *Painting a Map of Sixteenth-Century Mexico City: Land, Writing, and Native Rule.* New Haven, CT: Yale University Press/Beinecke Library, 2012.

Nesvig, Martin Austin. *Forgotten Franciscans: Works from an Inquisitorial Theorist, a Heretic, and an Inquisitorial Deputy.* University Park: Pennsylvania State University Press, 2011.

_____. *Ideology and Inquisition: The World of the Censors in Early Mexico.* New Haven, CT: Yale University Press, 2009.

_____, ed. *Local Religion in Colonial Mexico.* Albuquerque: University of New Mexico Press, 2006.

Osowski, Edward W. *Indigenous Miracles: Nahua Authority in Colonial Mexico.* Tucson: University of Arizona Press, 2010.

Palafox y Mendoza, Juan de. *Virtues of the Indian/Virtudes del indio.* Translated by Nancy H. Fee. Lanham, MD: Rowman & Littlefield, 2009.

Peterson, Jeanette Favrot. *Visualizing Guadalupe: From Black Madonna to Queen of the Americas.* Austin: University of Texas Press, 2014.

Phelan, John L. *The Millennial Kingdom of the Franciscans in the New World: A Study of the Writings of Gerónimo de Mendieta*. Berkeley: University of California Press, 1956.

Poole, Stafford. *The Guadalupan Controversies in Mexico*. Stanford, CA: Stanford University Press, 2006.

_____. *Our Lady of Guadalupe: The Origins and Sources of a Mexican National Symbol, 1531–1797*. Tucson: University of Arizona Press, 1995.

_____. *Pedro Moya de Contreras: Catholic Reform and Royal Power in New Spain, 1571–1591*. Norman: University of Oklahoma Press, rev. 2011.

Ricard, Robert. *The Spiritual Conquest of Mexico*. Berkeley: University of California Press, 1966.

Riley, James D. "The Wealth of the Jesuits in Mexico, 1670–1767." *The Americas* 33/2 (1976): 226–66.

Sandos, James A. *Converting California: Indians and Franciscans in the Missions*. New Haven, CT: Yale University Press, 2004.

Scheper-Hughes, Jennifer. *Biography of a Mexican Crucifix: Lived Religion and Local Faith from the Conquest to the Present*. New York: Oxford University Press, 2010.

Schroeder, Susan, and Stafford Poole, eds. *Religion in New Spain*. Albuquerque: University of New Mexico Press, 2007.

Schwaller, John F. *The Church and Clergy in Sixteenth-Century Mexico*. Albuquerque: University of New Mexico Press, 1987.

Schwartz, Stuart B. *All Can be Saved: Religious Tolerance and Salvation in the Iberian Atlantic World*. New Haven, CT: Yale University Press, 2008.

Sigal, Peter. *From Moon Goddesses to Virgins: The Colonization of Yucatecan Maya Sexual Desire*. Austin: University of Texas Press, 2000.

Solari, Amara. *Maya Ideologies of the Sacred: The Transformation of Space in Colonial Yucatan*. Austin: University of Texas Press, 2013.

Taylor, William B. *Magistrates of the Sacred: Priests and Parishioners in Eighteenth-Century Mexico*. Stanford, CA: Stanford University Press, 1996.

_____. *Marvels and Miracles in Late Colonial Mexico: Three Texts in Context*. Albuquerque: University of New Mexico Press, 2011.

_____. *Shrines and Miraculous Images: Religious Life in Mexico before the Reforma*. Albuquerque: University of New Mexico Press, 2010.

Temkin, Samuel. *Luis de Carvajal: The Origins of Nuevo Reino de León*. Santa Fe, NM: Sunstone Press, 2011.

Totorici, Zeb, ed. *Sexuality and the Unnatural in Colonial Latin America*. Berkeley: University of California Press, 2016.

Truit, Jonathan. "Courting Catholicism: Nahua Women and the Catholic Church in Colonial Mexico City." *Ethnohistory* 57/3 (2010): 415–444.

Villa-Flores, Javier. *Dangerous Speech: A Social History of Blasphemy in Colonial Mexico*. Tucson: University of Arizona Press, 2006.

Wake, Eleanor. *Framing the Sacred: The Indian Churches of Early Colonial Mexico*. Norman: University of Oklahoma Press, 2010.

CHAPTER 11

COLONIAL SOCIETY
Race, Ethnicity, Class, Gender, and Identity

To understand the structuring of society in New Spain requires us to take into consideration concepts of race, ethnicity, gender, religion, and lineage. Race refers to dividing people into groups based on biological and genetic factors while ethnicity signifies people who share cultural traits. In Spain, the term *raza* was used, but by the sixteenth century it came to be identified with purity of blood (*limpieza de sangre*) relating to religion. Those who had unblemished old Christian lineage (free of Jewish or Muslim blood) possessed limpieza de sangre. It is important to note that this designation was predicated on maintaining control over Spanish women's bodies to procreate within this lineage group. These concepts could be challenged in New Spain where the mixing of different biological groups or races complicated the hierarchical ordering of society by creating multiple ethnic identities, based on cultural and economic factors.

The fact that few conquistadors took their wives to Mexico meant that from the beginning they mixed freely with female natives and later with black slave women producing children of mixed blood (*mestizos* or *mulatos*). But those who were theoretically mestizo did not constitute a uniform category. The children of Spanish and native parents could be distinguished by whether their ethnicity (cultural traits) derived from the Spanish or Indian parent. Early on, those who were raised in the household of the Spanish father took on predominantly Spanish characteristics and could even be considered criollos (Spaniards born in New Spain). But since many of the unions between Spaniards and Indians were fleeting (often the result of rape), their children assumed cultural identities that were primarily indigenous. The offspring of Spanish-African unions were mulatos, but they had lower status juridically because black blood was often associated with slavery in early modern Europe. Blood was seen as a means through which moral and spiritual qualities were passed on.

Later unions of the mixed children themselves resulted in additional distinctions making for a confusing system of categorization with scores of racial and ethnic designations. Eventually mixed-race groups were lumped together in the catch-all classification of *castas*. In a rapidly changing milieu, however, racial and ethnic identities did not remain static, and the social hierarchy evolved through changing legal rationales as well as lived experience. Factors such as kinship, place of residence, and occupation could facilitate the ability of individuals to sidestep norms and stereotypes. Initially, Spanish authorities tried to order society by establishing separate legal codes for Spaniards and Indians, but this division was untenable in light of widespread *mestizaje* (racial mixing). Over time purity of blood became more linked to the modern idea of race, related to observable physical features like skin color as well as traits perceived to be inherent in them. At the same time, social categorization often deviated from the laws that tried to fine-tune it with fixed labels, as individuals and groups found ways to maneuver in fluctuating economic and cultural experiences. And even in a gender system which required that social ordering be transmitted through marriage and family, placing a particular burden on women, sexuality did not always adhere to prescribed norms. The following sections convey some of the distinctions within organizing categories as well as the fluidity that characterized New Spain's society in the evolution of classes.

SPANIARDS

The elite of society in the post-conquest colony consisted of the more than two thousand Spaniards in Mexico in 1521. As the conquerors and first settlers, they were lords of the land, yet few were born with the proverbial silver spoon in the mouth. While a considerable number of conquerors were hidalgos from the nobility, more often than not they had little wealth. Their options were limited because their pretensions to hidalgo status prevented them from taking employment deemed unworthy of their class. A career in law might enable one to find a place in the royal bureaucracy, but it required a university education. Alternatives lay in the church or the army. Owing to the long history of warfare in Spain, by the early modern period a warrior could attain social standing. In the colonial world a military occupation continued to be honorable, but one's social status also depended on other factors. Elites developed a system of honor in which attitudes regarding occupation, lineage, and behavior were prescribed and adjusted to ensure their superior social status. Of course, the majority of the conquerors came from the working class, and many of them had trades. In the early post-conquest period, barely literate tailors, carpenters, masons, cobblers, seamen, and the like found themselves part of an aspiring aristocracy.

The heyday of the conquerors and their unfettered access to Indian labor and other rewards were short-lived. Soon the colony was invaded by a different type of Spaniard, educated and well connected in the mother country. Royal officials with legal training entered to look after the crown's interests, and private lawyers arrived to involve themselves with the interminable lawsuits that arose. Cultured men of the church were expected to set a higher moral and intellectual tone. Most of these newcomers had a more elevated social status than the conquerors, and they were favored at the royal court. Spanish immigrants were not of one mind or loyalty as they brought with them their regional and local customs and prejudices. For example, many Basques who were instrumental in the colonization of northern Mexico saw themselves as ethnically distinct from and even superior to other Spaniards.

With the phasing out of conquest society, the remainder of the colonial period would be dominated in circles of influence by men sent from the Spanish peninsula—the peninsulares, or *gachupines*, as they were sometimes derisively called by those born in Mexico. The peninsulares held the best positions in the civil and ecclesiastical hierarchies for much of the colonial period. They also were found, along with criollos, in the most lucrative occupations as miners, merchants (especially long-distance traders), and landowners; but as time wore on, emigrant Spaniards of modest means attained those levels only through wealthy relatives or marriage into influential criollo families. Other later arriving Spaniards did not easily acquire the economic means to rise in social status. It is estimated that during the three centuries of colonial rule between two hundred fifty thousand and three hundred thousand Spaniards entered Mexico, but their numbers were never large at any one time.

CRIOLLOS

The second level of potential privilege accrued to those of Spanish blood born in Mexico. These criollos were by physical appearance indistinguishable from the peninsulares, but the mere fact of their New World birth prejudiced their status. It was commonly held by those born in Europe that America's environment was somehow detrimental, that the climate was enervating and corrosive, and that Spaniards born in Mexico might even be tainted by Indian blood. They were also deemed to be potentially less loyal to the mother country.

The criollos, despite their secondary rank, actually occupied a relatively favorable position in the society of New Spain; merely by virtue of their light skin they were considered superior to the darker masses below them. They could rise to respectable levels in church organization and to lower- and middle-rank posts in the royal bureaucracy, and they came to dominate local government in the cabildos. In fact, during the seventeenth and early eighteenth centuries some criollos succeeded in attaining the highest offices of both church and government, and eventually a number also held high military rank. Nevertheless, distance from the power centers in Spain and the less prestigious academic degrees of the colony prevented their having equal opportunity.

Year	Whites	Comments
1521	2,329	peninsulares
1529	8,000	peninsulares
1560	20,211	peninsulares and criollos
1570	57,000	peninsulares and criollos
1646	114,000–125,000	mostly criollos
1770	more than 750,000	mostly criollos
1793	1,095,000	70,000 of these were peninsulares

WHITE POPULATION OF NEW SPAIN

Still, criollos made up the largest segment of New Spain's economic elite as *hacendados*, or owners of large agricultural estates, miners, and merchants. Their dominance in the cabildos abetted their economic pursuits. The special social prestige attached to landholding also helped to confer upon criollos a prominent place in the social hierarchy. Despite their superior numbers, that prominence would be eroded in the latter decades of the eighteenth century, with fateful results.

MESTIZOS AND CASTAS

During the conquest some friendly caciques gifted women to the Spaniards, and other native females either joined the conquerors by choice or were taken forcibly. These women cooked for their men, nursed their wounds, carried their belongings, and shared their beds. Many such liaisons were fleeting, but others ripened into long, comfortable arrangements. In the early, hopeful years the conquerors visualized advantageous marriages with Spanish women. But when, as happened in most cases, circumstances prevented their returning to Spain in desirable style, they remained in Mexico, where their relative positions were sounder. Other Spaniards already had wives in Spain or in the Caribbean and, although by law they were obligated to send for them, by one pretext or another many avoided doing so. In 1551, according to the bishop of Mexico, there were 500 married Spaniards in his diocese whose wives languished outside the colony. Meantime most of these men took native partners, and some even remarried, thereby risking trial for bigamy.

In the early post-conquest years, crown and church encouraged unmarried Spaniards to wed Indian noblewomen and to legitimize their illegitimate children. Such marriages served the interests of both groups since they provided Spaniards peaceful access to Indian lands and also allowed segments of the indigenous nobility to retain oversight of their property and to benefit from it. The most noteworthy, but certainly not the only, example of such liaisons was a daughter and principal heir of Moctezuma, who before 1525 wedded three times; the second and third were her marriages to the last two Aztec emperors. After she converted to Christianity and took the name Isabel, Cortés arranged her fourth marriage (she was just seventeen years old) to a conquistador and granted her the largest encomienda in the Valley of Mexico. When her husband died shortly thereafter, Doña Isabel lived in Cortés' household where she had a daughter with him. In her fifth marriage to a Spanish associate of Cortés, she gave birth to a son, just before her husband died. In 1532, she was wed for the sixth time to another conquistador. This marriage lasted until her death in 1551 and produced five more children. All her children inherited parts of her holdings and some made advantageous marriages, including her out-of-wedlock daughter who married Juan de Tolosa, the discoverer of rich silver deposits in Zacatecas.

As the numbers of Spanish women arriving in Mexico with their fathers, brothers, and uncles slowly increased, the situation changed. By midcentury, there were also a number of mestizo daughters of conquistadors of marriageable age, and after that time, few Spaniards or criollos married Indian women. Financial considerations were important factors in marriage; a woman of property had a decided advantage, often to the exclusion of certain other qualities. A widow of an encomendero, for example, seldom remained unmarried very long. If she happened to be an Indian or mestiza, she might well be more attractive to a poor Spaniard than a penniless Spanish woman. If an encomendero died leaving no son or widow to inherit his Indian villages, the encomienda passed to his eldest daughter. If single, she was required to marry within a year in order to keep the encomienda. As time went on, however, it was much less likely that non-Spanish women would possess such high status.

The proportion of mestizos and other mixed-blood castas increased rapidly in Mexico, surpassing the number of Spaniards in the seventeenth century. It is difficult to generalize about their status, which varied according to time and place, influenced by such factors as physical characteristics, gender, the ability to acquire skills or property, and cultural identity. The mestizo children who were legitimized by their conquistador fathers fared the best in terms of rank.

To take a notable case, Don Martín Cortés was the son of the captain and Doña Marina. Technically he was a mestizo, but such was the standing of his father that he was considered to be a Spaniard. Fernando Cortés took his mestizo son with him to Spain, where Martín was made a knight of the prestigious Order of Santiago and a page to the prince (later Philip II). Pedro de Alvarado's mestizo daughter also had high social status; she married a cousin of the duke of Alburquerque, one of Spain's most powerful nobles.

The majority of the mestizos, however, could not aspire to high status. A high percentage were illegitimate (not infrequently the result of rape) and the term *mestizo* was synonymous with bastard for much of the colonial period. Informal liaisons between Spanish men and casta or Indian women continued to be commonplace. Mexico (as elsewhere in Spanish America) had a high rate of illegitimate births across all racial groups in urban areas. At the same time, Indians in rural zones had the highest ratio of legitimate births.

Castas (along with some poor Spaniards) could be found in a wide variety of occupations, working as domestic servants, apprentices, artisans, petty entrepreneurs and traders, muleteers, and common laborers. Being lower on the social scale did not necessarily translate into deference. In fact, the record is replete with examples of individuals who challenged their subordination by protesting unfair treatment in the courts; by occasionally attempting to "pass" to a different ethnic category in asserting a corresponding occupational or cultural identity; by verbally and physically abusing superiors; by calling on magic to bring retribution against oppressors; or by migrating to other regions.

INDIANS

Central Mexico alone (roughly equal to the size of France) may have had a pre-conquest population as high as 25 million, and for many decades the Indians of Mexico vastly outnumbered all other racial groups in New Spain. Then their numbers declined catastrophically. Waves of devastating epidemics swept over the land, and after a century of Spanish occupation, during which many died from overwork and maltreatment, only about a million natives remained. From their lowest number around 1630 the indigenous population began to increase slowly. By the end of the colonial period the Indians were still the largest ethnic group, but not by so vast a percentage.

As a conquered people the natives were exploited by the victors. At first Spaniards used the Indian nobility to do their bidding, and noble caciques could maintain higher status

Year	Indians	Plague Years	Comments
1519	25,200,000		
		1520	smallpox
		1529	measles
1532	16,800,000		
		1545	matlazáhuatl (typhus?); Indian deaths est. 800,000
1548	6,300,000		
1568	2,650,000		
		1576	matlazáhuatl; Indian deaths est. 2,000,000
1580	1,900,000		
1595	1,375,000		
1605	1,075,000		
1625–50	1,000,000		lowest point of Indian population

INDIAN POPULATION OF CENTRAL MEXICO: CONTACT TO MID-SEVENTEENTH CENTURY

Sources: Figures to the year 1605 are based on the research of Sherburne F. Cook and Woodrow Borah: *The Indian Population of Central Mexico, 1531–1610* (Berkeley, 1960), and *The Aboriginal Population of Central Mexico on the Eve of the Spanish Conquest* (Berkeley, 1963). Their counts, especially those prior to 1568, are considered much too high by some scholars.

within indigenous societies at least for a time. For the most part, however, the Spaniards saw the Indians as an inferior people. Some enlightened ecclesiastics and a few royal officials pleaded the Indian cause; they appealed to Christian ethics, emphasized the natives' positive qualities, and pressed for humane treatment. All too many Spaniards, however, considered Indians to be lazy, disposed to vices, devious, and backward. They were deemed *gente sin razón* (people without reason) as opposed to non-Indian *gente de razón* (people with reason).

Legally Spain considered Indians to be minors and wards of crown and church, commending their care and supervision to clergymen and officials. Yet, because of their tutelary status, the Indians were, at least in some respects, protected and given consideration. The crown and the church showed concern for the Indians' welfare, and laws were passed for their benefit. The flexibility of the Spanish legal system allowed Indians to pursue litigation as a way to defend their interests. They filed lawsuits, and a surprisingly large number were settled in the Indians' favor in the General Indian Court (Juzgado General de Indios) or in other tribunals. Indigenous leaders mastered Spanish legal concepts and vocabularies, using them to advance their interests related to land, labor, native hierarchies, and local governance.

Ultimately, however, the colony's welfare depended upon the labor of the Indians, so they were forced to serve the interests of the Spaniards. But they hardly did so with total acquiescence. The responses of native peoples to Spanish colonialism were so varied as to defy categorization, but whether the response was aggressive or accommodative, the intent was to preserve familiar structures and to maintain whatever balance was necessary for living in harmony with the natural world and for assuring an adequate material subsistence. We know, for example, that Nahua peoples resisted linguistic and other forms of acculturation for generations while asserting their rights to ancestral lands through fabricated "titles" that would have resonance in the Spanish legal system. In central western Mexico, indigenous heirs of the Tarascan empire strengthened communal sovereignty over time. In general, indigenous groups in central and southern Mexico succeeded in using the courts to protect substantial portions of their land. They were less effective in resisting recruitment of their labor and the variety of means devised by Spaniards for extracting resources from their communities. Corregidores or alcaldes mayores collected tribute through Indian middlemen, forced sales of unwanted merchandise on Indian communities, and exacted graft payments. At the same time, their links to market systems gave rise to class divisions within indigenous villages.

Despite the constant drain on Indian economies, local Indian leaders consistently sought ways to keep control of their own resources and production. Sometimes they were able to do this through *cofradías* (confraternities dedicated to the cult of a saint), which owned property and livestock. In addition to keeping some of their foodstuffs in the community, cofradías

Eighteenth-century "casta paintings" depicted the many combinations of mixed race marriages and their children. This one, from an anonymous artist, is entitled *Español e india, mestizo.*

served as a source of local credit. Indian villages exercised varying degrees of control over the *caja de comunidad* (community chest) that supported local government. Imposed by Spaniards, both of these "broker" institutions provided pathways for indigenous communities to devise inventive strategies for manipulating local assets. The degree to which these were successful often depended upon the relative power of the local priest and how easily he could call upon Spanish coercive power to thwart unwelcome indigenous initiatives.

In peripheral areas, more aggressive resistance was initially the response of less sedentary peoples to Spanish intrusion. Some, like the Apaches in the north, adopted the Spanish horse and preyed upon Spanish cattle to successfully avoid subjugation. Eventual defeat and resettlement in pueblos followed for most semi-sedentary northern Indians, but even then, they chose flight and other evasive tactics such as foot-dragging, false deference, sabotage, pilfering, gossip, and slander to resist total incorporation. Rebellion continued to be an option, either for resisting the early stages of incorporation when their worlds were turned upside down (the case of the Tepehuanes and Tarahumaras of Durango and Chihuahua in the 17th century) or for peoples who found the accommodations they had worked out with their oppressors for generations to have been violated.

No widespread rebellion affected Mexico in the colonial period, and aggressive resistance in more densely populated Indian areas was mostly restricted to single village riots, which increased as the eighteenth century progressed, and burgeoning Indian populations put new strains on resources, including land and water. These protests were often directed against the excessive demands of individual Spanish officials or priests. Some villagers struggled to maintain cohesive communities, remaining in the pueblos where they cultivated small plots of land and retained many traditional linguistic and cultural practices. Growing numbers, however, left to find work in Spanish haciendas and mines. In some cases, they found advantageous situations under the protection of their *patrones* (bosses), but the loss of communal ties and the failure to substitute compensatory social relationships could also result in despair and alcoholism.

In varying degrees, then, indigenous communities and peoples survived conquest and epidemic disease and went on to conserve features of their cultural patrimony by deliberately and selectively taking from European techniques and beliefs what could be most usefully adapted to indigenous ways. Of course, the effectiveness of resistance could be thwarted when native populations declined drastically, when natural resources were valuable enough to bring heavy Spanish might to bear, or when indigenous middlemen sided with their exploiters.

AFRICANS AND MULATOS

During the conquest half a dozen blacks fought with the Spanish forces. In the Caribbean an expanding sugar economy resulted in the importation of large numbers of African slaves, and eventually many were taken to Mexico. At first most slaves were personal servants imported by prominent men, who often had three or four in their household staffs. Less fortunate were those slaves assigned to hard labor, especially in the mines. As a consequence of the declining Indian population, one hundred twenty thousand or more slaves entered Mexico between 1519 and 1650. But blacks were expensive, while natives cost little. Accordingly, slaves from Africa used for labor were put where they could produce returns justifying their high purchase price. In the early years of silver mining, they made up perhaps as much as a third of the labor force. Later they labored extensively in the tropical sugar-producing regions and in obrajes. Considered more reliable than Indians, blacks were often trained for important skilled positions and sometimes put in charge of native workers as overseers in mining operations, small factories, and ranches. In the latter capacity, they were sometimes accused of exploiting the Indians. Other blacks became accomplished artisans, bringing their masters good profits. It was not uncommon for the slave to be given a share of the profits, which eventually allowed him or her to purchase freedom. And despite often arbitrary and unjust treatment of slaves, owners not infrequently manumitted them, especially domestic slaves, women, and children, in their wills.

Afro-mestizos or mulatos, offspring of the union of Spaniards and blacks, could also improve their circumstances, both because they were Hispanicized and because their Spanish fathers could ease the way for them by making sure they were free. Otherwise, the mulato would inherit the status of his or her mother according to law and would be a slave if she were one. Nonetheless, by the late sixteenth century many free blacks and mulatos populated the colony. At least one historian has argued that in the early colonial period, a significant number of those labeled mulato were actually Afro-indigenous; in northern Mexico they were usually designated as *coyotes* or *lobos*.

Approximately two hundred thousand Africans entered Mexico during the colonial period. It appears that by around 1560 there were almost as many blacks as whites in New Spain. Especially in urban areas, elites enhanced their social prestige by having a retinue of black and mulato slaves engaged in domestic service and craft production. Slaves were often rented out to other Spaniards. The importation of slaves diminished at mid-seventeenth century, when the official slave trade to New Spain ended. Recent research on slavery in New Spain has revealed a remarkably rich composite picture of African experiences. Despite constraints on their freedom and the perception that they were naturally rebellious, promiscuous, and prone to producing harm through witchcraft, most Afro-Mexicans cast themselves as loyal subjects of the crown and faithful Catholics. Slaves and free Afro-Mexicans established families and kinship ties through marriages to partners within and outside of their ethnic groups, and they fashioned social networks that reinforced a distinctive cultural identity. They used institutions created by Spaniards—for example, free black militias and religious confraternities—to acquire status and honor. Their interactions with other groups varied across urban and rural landscapes, but their contacts with natives and castas were by and large harmonious.

From the early years of Spanish occupation, black slaves in Mexico had frequently run away from their masters, sometimes joining Indians in isolated regions. Apprehension that blacks would incite a general rebellion abounded, but most fears seem to have originated from the belief that they had special witchcraft powers. Few slave insurrections occurred, although both slaves and free blacks were often accused of inciting natives to raid ranches and assault mule trains in remote areas. In response, runaway slaves (maroons, or *cimarrones*) were hunted down by bounty hunters and punished with floggings, castration, or hanging if they had committed serious crimes.

Around the beginning of the seventeenth century the threat of black resistance centered in the eastern region, especially near Veracruz. There an elderly slave named Yanga had held out in the mountains for thirty years. In 1609 the viceroy sent an army of 600 men against Yanga, whose camp had 80 men and some women and children. The viceroy's soldiers were given some lessons in guerrilla maneuvers by Yanga and, when the skirmishing finally ended in a standoff, the government agreed to treat with the black rebel. It was an extraordinary concession on the part of royal authority, and Yanga's struggle was one of the most successful instances of black resistance in the New World. He and his followers remained free by agreeing to cause no more trouble and to help track down other runaways. Not long afterward an independent black town, San Lorenzo de los Negros, was founded near modern Córdoba.

Through manumission and the purchase of freedom by slaves themselves, black slavery declined considerably over generations, particularly as the indigenous population rebounded in the seventeenth century making up a larger percentage of the labor pool. Although toward the end of the colonial period there were more than half a million Afro-Mexicans, only around ten thousand would be considered blacks by Spanish authorities due to mestizaje. Of those, perhaps only six thousand or so were slaves by 1800, mainly congregated in the environs of Veracruz and Acapulco. By far the majority of Afro-Mexicans had become integrated into the larger casta segment of society.

OTHER GROUPS

Crown policies severely restricted the flow of foreigners into the Mexican colony, but this hardly put a damper on desire of many Europeans to make the journey. During the union of the Spanish and Portuguese crowns (1580–1640), a substantial number of Portuguese crossed the Atlantic to New Spain. Included in their ranks were some converted and crypto-Jews. The Spanish relied heavily on the Portuguese who controlled the international slave trade, an economic relationship that lasted long after the union of the crowns dissolved. Other Europeans—Italian, French, German, English, and Greek—also went to New Spain; those who were Catholic usually fared better than Protestants. Many were merchants, participating in the lucrative Atlantic and Pacific trading routes where silver was exchanged for all manner of luxury goods, but some were specialists and scientists invited by royal officials.

Asians in the Spanish colonies were collectively labeled as *chinos*, although this Spanish legal category hardly represented the diversity of populations coming from regions of India, China, Japan, the Southeast Asian islands. They entered New Spain through the port city of Acapulco, usually on the Manila galleons; it has been estimated that at least fifty thousand chinos came to the colony, predominantly in the seventeenth century. They mainly settled in Mexico City, Puebla, and Veracruz as well as several areas of the west coast (including Guerrero and Michoacán). While most came as individuals, as sailors on the galleons, merchants, government officials, laborers, or servants, one extraordinary visit was chronicled in the writings of Chimalpahin. In 1610, in a period of open foreign relations, a diplomatic mission of Japanese officials left for New Spain to negotiate trade relations, investigate mining, and promote peaceful dealings. This was followed by an even larger embassy of 150 Japanese who traveled through New Spain en route to Europe in 1614.

Chinos, from many parts of Asia, found work as artisans, musicians, craftsmen, butchers, tailors, and coachmen; they were most likely to be merchants or barbers. The Parian market in the central plaza of Mexico City was home to the largest concentration of Asian merchants in the colony, selling imported goods to the residents of the capital. As barbers, they not only cut hair and shaved faces, but also performed medical services like bloodletting and basic dentistry. Spanish peninsular barbers fought against the growing influence of the chinos in this industry, as they came to dominate these services.

Beyond the influence of the many Asians who journeyed to the shores of Mexico, luxury products such as silks, porcelains, and spices transformed consumption patterns in cities like Mexico City, Puebla, and Guadalajara where local artisans produced furniture, talavera, and paintings with an Asian esthetic. For example, the famous *biombos* (folding screens) that depict the conquest of Tenochtitlan and an early map of Mexico City were a Japanese art form adapted to and painted in the colonial context. Initially, biombos were some of the first art objects imported into New Spain while other Japanese-produced screens were given as gifts during the embassies described above. Eventually, the biombo was adapted by artists in New Spain, who created works of art inspired by Asian forms for a colonial audience.

Not all Asians came to Mexico voluntarily, with approximately 8,000 imported as slaves before the practice was outlawed in 1700. Transported first to the Philippines by Portuguese, Chinese, and Malay vessels, they became part of the cargo of the Manila galleons on the journey from Manila to Acapulco. They hailed from diverse places: the Philippines, Timor, Burma, Ceylon, India, and even Africa having been transported across the Indian Ocean. Those from the Philippines, the only Spanish colony in Asia, were categorized as *indios chinos*, a special designation that gave them a legal position closer to indigenous peoples rather than other chinos. This was especially significant in the late seventeenth-century debates about the abolition of indigenous slavery in the Spanish empire, which ended the practice of enslaving Asians on the basis of their indigenous status (although not all Asian slaves were in fact indios chinos).

A *biombo*, created in New Spain and located in the Museo Franz Mayer, depicts a map of Mexico City at the end of the seventeenth century.

The most famous of the Asian slaves was Catarina de San Juan; originally from the west coast of India, she was sold into slavery in the markets of Manila in the early the seventeenth century. Arriving in Acapulco in 1619, she made her way to Puebla as the property of a Portuguese slave merchant. There as a domestic servant, owned by her masters, she lived in an urban environment where she was afforded some freedoms, particularly to attend church where she found her calling. Granted her freedom upon the death of her masters she desired to become a *beata*, or laywoman of the church. Stymied by the priest she worked for who forced her into marriage, she finally was able to take vows once widowed. Her conversion to Christianity and the obstacles she overcame to practice her faith led her to be seen as a popular saint, still revered today in the city of Puebla. She is better known as the *china poblana*, although this association has little to do with the real Catarina. Developed in the late nineteenth century, an elite, nationalist fashion trend that mixed different ethnic elements (embroidered blouses, distinctive skirts, and fancy shawls) adopted Catarina and her "Mughal" background to promote the Mexican fashion trend.

Racial diversity in Mexico was well advanced before the close of the sixteenth century. White remained the color of privilege, but the number of castas far outstripped the European population before the eighteenth century. Since even the criollo sector was not free of race mixture, money could sometimes buy status regardless of color. And although elites endeavored to maintain a race-based hierarchy, there was a substantial divide between how people were categorized and how they understood themselves. The racially mixed castas

The only extant image of Catarina San Juan from the seventeenth century.

Contemporary *chinas poblanas* from the Festival de la China Poblana, Puebla, Mexico, 2013.

habitually contested the boundaries of their subordination creating a popular culture that transcended ethnic divisions, as they simultaneously reinforced and challenged colonial prescriptive norms.

WOMEN AND FAMILY

The power to negotiate was not a solely male preserve despite the constraints of the Spanish Catholic patriarchal system through which men theoretically exercised control over the sexuality, reproductive capacities, labor power, and public conduct of women. The ideal woman was chaste, pious, and submissive, living under the supervision and protection of her father or husband. However, we should note that such a prescriptive behavior code varied across ethnic and class lines. While women of status who defied these norms stained the honor and threatened the racial purity of the family, the promiscuous sexual behavior of men was seen as a natural component of male virility and authority (*machismo*). Domestic abuse was a result of patriarchal and honor codes and its predominance in daily life has been documented.

In spite of the arbitrariness of this system, Spanish women could inherit from their fathers, and they enjoyed control over property they owned before they married. For elite families, carefully arranged marriages were crucial to enhancing status and wealth. Widows and unmarried older women not infrequently administered estates and businesses. Some women elected not to marry, choosing instead the religious vocation of the convent. Life as a nun was not as constraining as one might guess. Many elite Spanish nuns enjoyed material comforts in convents, attended by their servants. Although most chose the profession for primarily spiritual reasons, others elected conventual life for the possibilities it offered for education, self-expression in the arts, escape from worldly danger, or belonging to a supportive community. In some cases, nuns contributed to the economic support of the convent by making candies and other confections. Other Spanish women transgressed the norms by engaging in informal liaisons, but they often did so in the hope of securing a promise of marriage.

Lower-class casta women were even less easily held to the rules, not surprisingly because they were often objects of men's sexual advances. Their virginity did not command the same respect as that of elite women. Unmarried mestizas and *mulatas*—frequently single heads of households—worked as street vendors, maids, cooks, washerwomen, midwives; a significant number, along with indigenous women, sold produce in their own stalls in the markets. By the eighteenth century, increasing numbers of rural Indian women were migrating to Mexico City to seek domestic work.

Rural indigenous women were more likely to be married and engaged in performing agricultural labor, domestic chores, and perhaps a skill like weaving or potting. Although Indian women had held significant religious and political positions in earlier pre-contact societies, those who came under the more stratified organization of imperial rule found their roles circumscribed even before Spanish contact. At contact, Indian women throughout Mexico performed crucial social and economic functions that paralleled and complemented those of men. Complementary gender relations defied Catholic patriarchal norms during much of the colonial period and worked to moderate sociocultural change. The tendency of native societies to recognize and even venerate women's contributions to shared duties was eroded by the late colonial period, resulting in diminished legal status, but not always economic power.

Across the ethnic spectrum, women typically engaged in contesting and negotiating their status through a variety of channels including the church, the courts, and petty witchcraft. Moreover, their activities contributed importantly to the maintenance of families—the critical social unit in all sectors of society. Families were a site for the transmission of cultural values and a supportive base for forging political and social connections. Extended families and godparents (*compadres*) constituted networks that could provide access to advantageous marriages and economic influence for elites, as well as a safety net for the lower classes. In the final analysis, the complexities of the intersections of race, class, and gender determined the lived experiences of women and men in colonial society.

POPULATION FIGURES

Tenochtitlan had a population of perhaps 200,000 at the advent of the Spaniards, but the Christian city that arose on its ruins began with far fewer people. In 1560 Mexico City had about eight thousand Spaniards. By 1574 there were around 15,000 Spaniards, in addition to a large Indian population and significant numbers of blacks and mixed bloods. By 1810 Mexico City had more than 150,000 souls; the largest city in the Western Hemisphere, it still had a much smaller population than that boasted by the Aztec capital at the time of the conquest.

Population figures for the colony as a whole are especially suspect because of the difficulty of counting people in so many isolated villages and spaces. Some generalizations can be made. From its nadir of about one million at the mid-seventeenth century, the Indian population of central Mexico began to recuperate and probably tripled by the end of the colonial period despite continued cycles of epidemic disease. In southern Mexico (especially in Oaxaca and in Maya areas), the indigenous population also continued to constitute the largest segment, while in the north some indigenous groups disappeared altogether and the rest were outnumbered by non-Indians.

Castas rapidly increased in numbers after the mid-seventeenth century to compose nearly a third of the total at the end of the eighteenth. As noted earlier, few pure blacks remained, although many Afro-Mexicans could be counted within the mestizo sector. Analyses of a major census undertaken in 1793 suggest that a substantial number of mestizos claimed criollo status. At independence in 1821, almost exactly three hundred years after the conquest, the total population of Mexico had reached 6 million. What is striking is that the population had nearly doubled since the mid-eighteenth century. In 1821, about 60 percent were Indians, mixed races made up nearly a fourth, blacks less than one percent, and Spaniards (predominantly criollos) between 15 and 20 percent. Of course, regional variations in those proportions were striking, with marked differences between rural and urban areas and between central-southern Mexico and the north.

RECOMMENDED FOR FURTHER STUDY

Anderson, Arthur J. O., Frances Berdan, and James Lockhart, eds. *Beyond the Codices: The Nahua View of Colonial Mexico*. Berkeley: University of California Press, 1976.

Bennett, Herman L. *Africans in Colonial Mexico: Absolutism, Christianity, and Afro-Creole Consciousness, 1570–1640*. Bloomington: Indiana University Press, 2003.

————. *Colonial Blackness: A History of Afro-Mexico*. Bloomington: Indiana University Press, 2009.

Boyer, Richard. *Lives of the Bigamists: Marriage, Family, and Community in Colonial Mexico*. Albuquerque: University of New Mexico Press, 1995.

Carrera, Magali M. *Imagining Identity in New Spain: Race, Lineage, and the Colonial Body in Portraiture and Casta Paintings*. Austin: University of Texas Press, 2003.

Carroll, Patrick J. *Blacks in Colonial Veracruz: Race, Ethnicity, and Regional Development*. Austin: University of Texas Press, 1991.

Chance, John K. *Conquest of the Sierra: Spaniards and Indians in Colonial Oaxaca*. Norman: University of Oklahoma Press, 1989.

Chandler, D. S. *Social Assistance and Bureaucratic Politics: The Montepíos of Colonial Mexico, 1767–1821*. Albuquerque: University of New Mexico Press, 1991.

Christensen, Mark, and Jonathan Truitt, eds. *Native Wills from the Colonial Americas: Dead Giveaways in a New World*. Salt Lake City: University of Utah Press, 2015.

Cook, Noble David, and W. George Lovell, eds. *Secret Judgments of God: Old World Diseases and Colonial Spanish America*. Norman: University of Oklahoma Press, 1991.

Cook, Sherburne F., and Woodrow Borah. *The Aboriginal Population of Central Mexico on the Eve of the Spanish Conquest*. Berkeley: University of California Press, 1963.

————. *The Indian Population of Central Mexico, 1531–1610*. Berkeley: University of California Press, 1960.

Cooper, Donald. *Epidemic Disease in Mexico City, 1761–1813*. Austin: University of Texas Press, 1965.

Few, Martha. *Women Who Live Evil Lives: Gender, Religion and the Politics of Power in Colonial Guatemala*. Austin: University of Texas Press, 2002.

Fisher, Andrew B., and Matthew O'Hara, eds. *Imperial Subjects: Race and Identity in Colonial Latin America*. Durham, NC: Duke University Press, 2009.

Franco, Jean. *Plotting Women: Gender and Representation in Mexico*. New York: Columbia University Press, 1989.

Giráldez, Arturo. *The Age of Trade: The Manila Galleons and the Dawn of the Global Economy*. Lanham, MD: Rowman & Littlefield, 2015.

Gosner, Kevin, and Deborah E. Kanter, eds. *Women, Power, and Resistance in Colonial Mesoamerica*. Special Issue, *Ethnohistory* 42/4 (1995).

Gradie, Charlotte M. *The Tepehuan Revolt of 1616: Militarism, Evangelism, and Colonialism in Seventeenth-Century Nueva Vizcaya*. Salt Lake City: University of Utah Press, 2000.

Gutiérrez, Ramón. *When Jesus Came, the Corn Mothers Went Away: Marriage, Sexuality, and Power in New Mexico, 1500–1846*. Stanford, CA: Stanford University Press, 1991.

Haslip-Viera, Gabriel. *Crime and Punishment in Late Colonial Mexico City, 1692–1810*. Albuquerque: University of New Mexico Press, 1999.

Herrera, Robinson A. *Natives, Europeans, and Africans in Sixteenth-Century Santiago de Guatemala*. Austin: University of Texas Press, 2003.

Hoberman, Louisa. "Bureaucracy and Disaster: Mexico City and the Flood of 1629." *Journal of Latin American Studies* 6/2 (1974): 211–30.

_____. *Mexico's Merchant Elite, 1590–1660*. Durham, NC: Duke University Press, 1991.

Israel, J. I. *Race, Class and Politics in Colonial Mexico, 1610–1670*. New York: Oxford University Press, 1975.

Jackson, Robert H. *Indian Population Decline: The Missions of Northwestern New Spain, 1687–1840*. Albuquerque: University of New Mexico Press, 1994.

Johnson, Lyman L., and Sonya Lipsett-Rivera, eds. *The Faces of Honor: Sex, Shame and Violence in Colonial Latin America*. Albuquerque: University of New Mexico Press, 1998.

Kanter, Deborah E. *Hijos del Pueblo: Gender, Family, and Community in Rural Mexico, 1730–1850*. Austin: University of Texas Press, 2008.

Katzew, Ilona, and Susan Deans-Smith, eds. *Race and Classification: The Case of Mexican America*. Stanford, CA: Stanford University Press, 2009.

Kellogg, Susan. *Weaving the Past: A History of Latin America's Indigenous Women from the Prehispanic Period to the Present*. New York: Oxford University Press, 2005.

Kellogg, Susan, and Matthew Restall, eds. *Dead Giveaways: Indigenous Testaments of Colonial Mesoamerica and the Andes*. Salt Lake City: University of Utah Press, 1998.

Landers, Jane. *Black Society in Spanish Florida*. Urbana: University of Illinois Press, 1999.

Lavrin, Asunción, ed. *Sexuality and Marriage in Colonial Latin America*. Lincoln: University of Nebraska Press, 1989.

_____. "Women in Colonial Mexico." In *The Oxford History of Mexico*, edited by Michael C. Meyer and William H. Beezley, 235–61. New York: Oxford University Press, rev. 2010.

Lewis, Laura A. *Hall of Mirrors: Power, Witchcraft, and Caste in Colonial Mexico*. Durham, NC: Duke University Press, 2003.

Lipsett-Rivera, Sonya. *Gender and the Negotiation of Daily Life in Mexico, 1750–1856*. Lincoln: University of Nebraska Press, 2012.

Martin, Cheryl E. *Governance and Society in Colonial Mexico: Chihuahua in the Eighteenth Century*. Stanford, CA: Stanford University Press, 1995.

Martínez, Maria Elena. *Genealogical Fictions: Limpieza de Sangre, Religion, and Gender in Colonial Mexico*. Stanford, CA: Stanford University Press, 2008.

Mörner, Magnus. *Race Mixture in the History of Latin America*. Boston, MA: Little, Brown, 1967.

Palmer, Colin A. *Slaves of the White God: Blacks in Mexico*. New York: Cambridge University Press, 1976.

Patch, Robert W. "Indian Resistance to Colonialism." In *The Oxford History of Mexico*, edited by Michael C. Meyer and William H. Beezley, 175–202. New York: Oxford University Press, rev. 2010.

Pizzigoni, Caterina. *The Life Within: Local Indigenous Society in Mexico's Toluca Valley, 1650–1800*. Stanford, CA: Stanford University Press, 2013.

Powers, Karen V. *Women in the Crucible of Conquest: The Gendered Genesis of Spanish American Society, 1500–1600*. Albuquerque: University of New Mexico Press, 2005.

Proctor III, Frank T. *"Damned Notions of Liberty:" Slavery, Culture, and Power in Colonial Mexico, 1640–1769*. Albuquerque: University of New Mexico Press, 2010.

Radding, Cynthia. *Wandering Peoples: Colonialism, Ethnic Spaces, and Ecological Frontiers in Northwestern Mexico, 1700–1850*. Durham, NC: Duke University Press, 1997.

Reff, Daniel. *Disease, Depopulation, and Cultural Change in Northwestern New Spain*. Salt Lake City: University of Utah Press, 1991.

Restall, Matthew, ed. *Beyond Black and Red: African-Native Relations in Colonial Latin America*. Albuquerque: University of New Mexico Press, 2005.

_____. *The Black Middle: Africans, Mayas, and Spaniards in Colonial Yucatan*. Stanford, CA: Stanford University Press, 2009.

_____. *The Maya World: Yucatec Culture and Society, 1550–1850*. Stanford, CA: Stanford University Press, 1997.

Restall, Matthew, Lisa Sousa, and Kevin Terraciano, eds. *Mesoamerican Voices: Native Language Writings from Colonial Mexico, Oaxaca, Yucatán, and Guatemala*. New York: Cambridge University Press, 2005.

Roth-Seneff, Andrew, Robert V. Kemper, and Julie Adkins, eds. *From Tribute to Communal Sovereignty: The Tarascan and Caxcan Territories in Transition*. Tucson: University of Arizona Press, 2015.

Sanabrais, Sofia. "From *Byōbu* to *Biombo*: The Transformation of the Japanese Folding Screen in Colonial Mexico." *Art History* 38/4 (September 2015): 778–791.

Schroeder, Susan, ed. *Native Resistance and the Pax Colonial in New Spain*. Lincoln: University of Nebraska Press, 1998.

Schroeder, Susan, Stephanie Wood, and Robert Haskett, eds. *Indian Women of Early Mexico*. Norman: University of Oklahoma Press, 1997.

Schwaller, Robert C. *Géneros de gente in Early Colonial Mexico: Defining Racial Difference*. Norman: University of Oklahoma Press, 2016.

Seed, Patricia. *To Love, Honor, and Obey in Colonial Mexico: Conflicts over Marriage Choice, 1574–1821*. Stanford, CA: Stanford University Press, 1988.

Seijas, Tatiana. *Asian Slaves in Colonial Mexico: From Chinos to Indios*. New York: Cambridge University Press, 2014.

Slack, Edward R., Jr. "The *Chinos* in New Spain: A Corrective Lens for a Distorted Image." *Journal of World History*, 20/1 (2009): 35–67.

Socolow, Susan M. *The Women of Colonial Latin America*. New York: Cambridge University Press, 2000.

Sousa, Lisa. *The Woman Who Turned into a Jaguar, and other Narratives of Native Women in Archives of Colonial Mexico*. Stanford, CA: Stanford University Press, 2017.

Stern, Steve J. *The Secret History of Gender: Women, Men, and Power in Late Colonial Mexico*. Chapel Hill: University of North Carolina Press, 1995.

Totorici, Zeb, ed. *Sexuality and the Unnatural in Colonial Latin America*. Berkeley: University of California Press, 2016.

Tuñón Pablos, Julia. *Women in Mexico: A Past Unveiled*. Austin: University of Texas Press, 1999.

Twinam, Ann. *Public Lives, Private Secrets: Gender, Honor, Sexuality, and Illegitimacy in Colonial Spanish America*. Stanford, CA: Stanford University Press, 1999.

_____. *Purchasing Whiteness: Pardos, Mulattos, and the Quest for Social Mobility in the Spanish Indies*. Stanford, CA: Stanford University Press, 2015.

Uribe Urán, Victor M. *Fatal Love: Spousal Killers, Law, and Punishment in the Late Colonial Atlantic*. Stanford, CA: Stanford University Press, 2015.

Velasco Murillo, Dana, Margarita Ochoa and Mark Lentz, eds. *City Indians in Spain's American Empire: Urban Indigenous Society in Colonial Mesoamerica and Andean South America, 1530–1810*. Brighton, U.K.: Sussex Academic Press, 2012.

Velasco Murillo, Dana. *Urban Indians in a Silver City: Zacatecas, Mexico, 1546–1810*. Stanford, CA : Stanford University Press, 2016.

Vinson III, Ben. *Bearing Arms for His Majesty: The Free-Colored Militia in Colonial Mexico*. Stanford, CA: Stanford University Press, 2001.

Vinson III, Ben, and Matthew Restall, eds. *Black Mexico: Race and Society from Colonial to Modern Times*. Albuquerque: University of New Mexico Press, 2009.

Von Germeten, Nicole. *Black Blood Brothers: Confraternities and Social Mobility for Afro-Mexicans*. Gainesville: University Press of Florida, 2006.

Yannakakis, Yanna. *The Art of Being In-Between: Native Intermediaries, Indian Identity, and Local Rule in Colonial Oaxaca*. Durham, NC: Duke University Press, 2008.

Yetman, David A. *The Ópatas: In Search of a Sonoran People*. Tucson: University of Arizona Press, 2010.

Zeitlin, Judith Francis. *Cultural Politics in Colonial Tehuantepec: Community and State among the Isthmus Zapotec, 1500–1750*. Stanford, CA: Stanford University Press, 2005.

CHAPTER 12

CULTURE AND DAILY LIFE
IN NEW SPAIN

EDUCATION

When Don Antonio de Mendoza arrived in Mexico fourteen years after the fall of Tenochtit-lan, he was greeted by, among others, an Indian boy who recited in classic Latin. The amused viceroy soon learned that the energetic friars had begun to Hispanicize the natives through education. It was a plan encouraged by both crown and church for, quite aside from senti-ments of altruism, there were practical considerations. The sincere design to Christianize the conquered people was best achieved through their understanding Spanish; moreover, it hastened their assimilation of Spanish ways.

In Spain a broad educational system was not seen as a responsibility of the state. Educa-tion was, rather, an individual concern, usually involving only those of the privileged class, while instruction itself was the province of the church. Only on the university level did the crown evince strong interest, primarily to prepare young men for careers in the bureaucracy. The church was equally concerned with higher education in order to instruct clergymen, who would in turn run the schools in the colonies, as in Spain.

One is struck by the cultural vitality in the early years of a conquest society that was in so many ways both turbulent and rustic. The impulse to refinement came from learned clergymen primarily because educated laymen were usually involved in government, law, or other professional interests. Therefore the intellectual and cultural attainments of the Span-ish colony are attributable primarily to the religious orders.

The first prominent educator in Spanish Mexico was Pedro de Gante, a Franciscan lay brother and illegitimate relative of Charles V. By 1524 he was teaching Indian boys, and later he founded the famous school of San José, where under his direction hundreds of native youths received primary instruction and adults were taught trades. While the children were drilled in Latin, music, and other academic subjects, the elders became the colony's masons, carpenters, blacksmiths, painters, and sculptors. Gante put their skills to good use, person-ally supervising the building of one hundred chapels and churches.

The school of Santa Cruz de Tlatelolco was founded in 1536 by Viceroy Mendoza and Bishop Zumárraga. With such powerful patrons it became the outstanding Indian school and aimed at the higher instruction for the sons of nobles, through whom it was thought Spanish culture would more easily be passed on to commoners. Aside from the fundamentals of reading and writing, courses were offered in Latin, rhetoric, logic, and philosophy, as well as music and native medicine. Taught by learned humanists, the youths received excellent European instruction, and they in turn aided the friars in schools and church.

The most appealing figure in early education was Vasco de Quiroga, whose practical approach to education was distinct. A man of varied interests, Quiroga was a humanist, lawyer, and a judge in the second audiencia. But his fame rests on his personal crusade to benefit the conquered peoples. Using his own capital, the aging lawyer established his first hospital-school of Santa Fé in 1531-32, on the outskirts of Mexico City. Shortly thereafter he moved to Michoacán, near Lake Pátzcuaro in the area of the old Tarascan kingdom. There, in the region so troubled since the depredations of Nuño de Guzmán and by the continued savage in-fighting among Spaniards, the benevolence of Quiroga (Tata Vasco) aimed to inspire trust from the natives. Intrigued by Thomas More's *Utopia*, Quiroga attempted, with considerable success, to create an ideal society in the New World. He formed communities in which the Indians received training not only in religion but also in practical arts and crafts as well as in the rudiments of self-government. Each person worked six hours a day, sharing and contributing equally to the common welfare. Appointed bishop of Michoacán in 1537, Quiroga continued to lead a productive life until he was nearly ninety. With his death the utopian villages declined, but he had established some fine traditions that persisted, and descendants of his specialized artisans ply their crafts still.

Other Indian schools included the Jesuit San Gregorio Magno that trained Nahuas from 1586 to 1767. Concern for abandoned or orphaned mestizos led to the opening in 1547 of the orphanage school of San Juan de Letrán. But in the end the attempts to educate young

The Colegio de Santa Cruz de Tlatelolco.

Indians and mestizos were limited in scope. What had begun on such an auspicious note fell largely into neglect and apathy set in. After several decades of association with their conquerors, many of the natives grasped the language and customs of the Spaniards, and the danger of large-scale rebellion seemed past. Educating Indians and mestizos was not given priority until later in the colonial period.

The early education of Indians fell mostly to the Franciscans while the Jesuits and Augustinians predominated in instructing criollos. Though many Spanish conquerors were uncultured, their sons inherited a social position that called for some measure of refinement. Consequently, tutors schooled young children at home, and primary schools existed in Spanish communities of any size. Religious orders established a number of secondary schools (*colegios*). The most prestigious of such schools was the elite Jesuit Colegio de San Pedro y San Pablo, founded in 1576 and supported by profits from efficient Jesuit haciendas. Its graduates were equal, and sometimes superior, to those of the University of Mexico. An Augustinian institution, established a year earlier by the prominent intellectual Alonso de la Veracruz, also provided superior studies. In addition excellent seminaries for training priests maintained a high level of scholarship, among them San Ildefonso and Tepotzotlán, both of which belonged to the Jesuits.

The Royal and Pontifical University of Mexico was created in 1553 at the petition of Viceroy Mendoza and Bishop Zumárraga, making it the first university to function in the New World. Founded with the aim of educating criollos for the clergy and other professions, the university modeled itself on the Spanish University of Salamanca, with which it was supposed to be equal in rights and privileges. With an excellent faculty, it would produce many of New Spain's leading literary figures, scientists, lawyers, medical doctors, and theologians. During the colonial period the university granted around 30,000 bachelors' degrees and over 1,000 masters' and doctorates. Late in the colonial period, in 1791, another university was founded in Guadalajara.

Females enjoyed fewer opportunities for education. As early as 1534 nuns created schools for girls. Indian girls, under the tutelage of Gante, were taught mainly how to be good wives in the Spanish manner. In 1548 the Caridad school was established for orphaned mestizas, and in the late sixteenth century schools were founded for young criolla women.

SCHOLARSHIP AND LITERATURE

Perhaps the most remarkable aspect of scholarship in the colony began not long after the conquest with the diligent studies made by friars, among whom were a number of non-Spanish Europeans educated in France, Flanders, or other countries. Their inquiries into the nature of the native peoples and the land were truly phenomenal.

Cortés described the conquest itself in his famous letters to the king which have been translated into several languages and appear in many editions. A more popular account, however, remains the *Historia verdadera de la conquista de la Nueva España*, written by Bernal Díaz del Castillo, a footsoldier in Cortés's army. Díaz later moved to Guatemala, where he wrote his richly detailed, personalized account years after the events. He has left us a work that, with its simple prose and graphic descriptions, has become a classic of its kind.

Especially noteworthy are scholarly studies of the Indians: Motolinía's *Historia de los indios;* the Spanish judge Alonso de Zorita's *Breve y sumaria relación de los señores de la Nueva España;* and the magisterial *Historia general de las cosas de la Nueva España* (Florentine Codex) by Father Bernardino de Sahagún, a compendium of Aztec life that forms a basis for our knowledge of Nahua peoples, but with the primary aim of gathering knowledge useful for conversion. Anticipating modern anthropological practice, Sahagún worked with native informants to record their history in Náhuatl and Spanish. Many other important works of the sixteenth century, including church histories, offer eloquent testimony to the evangelical zeal, intellectual curiosity, industry, and painstaking scholarship of these early historians.

Although the scholarly studies of the sixteenth century were outstanding, valuable works appeared later as well. In the early seventeenth century, Chimalpahin, descended from Nahua royalty and educated by Franciscans, wrote detailed accounts of the pre-contact period as well as annals of Mexico City's daily religious and cultural life in his own time. A significant eighteenth-century work is the *Historia antigua de México* by the celebrated Jesuit Francisco Javier de Clavijero, a native-born Mexican considered to be the founder of modern Mexican historiography. Another erudite Jesuit was Francisco Javier Alegre, accomplished in many fields but best known for his history of the Jesuits in New Spain.

No matter what their motives, clergymen preserved Indian histories, customs, and languages. They created dictionaries and grammars so that Indians could read and write in their own languages. Many of the friars became proficient in three or four native tongues. There were fewer scholars of note in other disciplines, although some excelled in studies of the flora, fauna, and medicines of Mexico. The crown occasionally sponsored research: in 1571 the royal cosmographer was ordered to take a census, study eclipses, and undertake both a general and a natural history. The towering figure in scientific thought was Carlos de Sigüenza y Góngora, a criollo of universal renown during the seventeenth century. He

Carlos de Sigüenza y Góngora (1645-1700) was an eminent
scholar of wide-ranging scientific and historical interests.

studied to be a Jesuit at Tepotzotlán but was expelled for an infraction of the strict rules. Poet, historian, mathematician, astronomer, and antiquarian, he exemplifies the scientific curiosity that would flourish especially toward the end of the colonial period.

Leaving aside chronicles of the conquest, literary achievements in New Spain began with the *Dialogues* of Francisco Cervantes de Salazar, who extolled the beauty of Mexico City and the quality of the university. The brightest literary light of all, however, and holding first place in the hearts of Mexicans, was a woman, *Sor* (Sister) Juana Inés de la Cruz (1651–95). Apparently of high but illegitimate birth, Sor Juana grew from a child prodigy who amazed intellectuals at the viceregal court into a beautiful, graceful young woman with astonishing talents. An early exponent of women's rights, she lamented the disdain with which female efforts were greeted and the subordinate position of women generally. Her disenchantment was well expressed in one of her poems:

Hombres necios que acusáis	Ah stupid men, unreasonable
a la mujer sin razón,	In blaming woman's nature,
sin ver que sois la ocasión	Oblivious that your acts incite
de lo mismo que culpáis;	The very faults you censure.
. . . .	. . . .
¿Cuál mayor culpa ha tenido,	Which has the greater sin when burned
en una pasión errada:	By the same lawless fever:
la que cae de rogada	She who is amorously deceived,
o el que ruega de caído?	Or he, the sly deceiver?
¿O cuál es más de culpar,	Or which deserves the sterner blame,
aunque cualquiera mal haga:	Though each will be a sinner:
la que peca por la paga,	She who becomes a whore for pay,
o el que paga por pecar?[1]	Or he who pays to win her?

At the age of eighteen she stunned her admirers by ignoring favorable prospects of marriage and her privileged position at court when she entered a convent. She devoted the rest of her life to contemplation, intellectual exercises, correspondence with Spanish writers, and the writing of prose and lyric poetry, surpassed by only a few in the "Golden Age" Spanish-speaking world. Sor Juana, the first great poet in the New World, composed passionate, almost erotic, love poems of great beauty.

Late in the colonial period, however, Mexico produced another major literary figure in José Joaquín Fernández de Lizardi. His satirical *El Periquillo Sarniento* (translated as *The Mangy Parrot*) [1816], a picaresque depiction of life in early nineteenth-century Mexico, is widely considered to be the first true novel written in Spanish in Latin America.

Mexico City had a printing press by 1537-39. In the latter year the first book was printed in the colony, a religious tract written in both Nahuatl and Spanish by Bishop Zumárraga. Before the century was out, about 220 books had been produced in the capital, although

---

1   *Chicano Literature: Text and Context*, trans. Robert Graves, eds. Joseph Sommers and Antonia Castañeda Shular (Englewood Cliffs, NJ, 1972), 10-11.

no other Mexican city had a press until a century later. Scholars estimate that during the colonial period some fifteen thousand volumes were printed in Mexico, among them books in at least nine different Indian languages. In addition to many religious studies, publications included dictionaries, grammars, accounts of navigation, descriptions of natural phenomena like earthquakes, and works on medicine, methods of teaching reading, and simple arithmetic. In the second half of the sixteenth century at least twelve liturgical books containing music were published; in the same period only fourteen came out of presses in Spain.

Despite the theoretical threat of censorship, books were available in considerable variety, and some large and excellent private libraries existed in New Spain. When Vasco de Quiroga died in 1565, he had accumulated more than six hundred volumes, and in her convent Sor Juana was surrounded by four thousand of her own books. By the seventeenth century the College of Discalced Carmelites had twelve thousand volumes. Probably the finest library in the New World, however, at least by the eighteenth century, was the one originally started by Bishop Juan de Palafox y Mendoza in Puebla.

The literate public without means, however, had limited reading material, for there were no public libraries and, until late in the colonial period, no newspapers. Communication within the colony was, for the general populace, mainly rumor, gossip, and the information brought by travelers. In early times official announcements emanated from the public square by a town crier, following the ringing of church bells, drum beats, or the blast of trumpets. Eventually broadsides could be found tacked up in public places. The curious were drawn to such places no more by official pronouncements than by the graffiti that showed up mysteriously. These *pasquines* offered a way of venting displeasure with government or excoriating personal enemies. Usually in rhyme, they were witty, sarcastic, and frequently risqué. No one was safe from these lettered shafts, and the more prominent the victim, the sweeter the vengeance. Although illegal, they could no more be prevented than the scrawls that decorate our public walls today.

News from Spain and other parts of Europe came with the annual fleet, at which time enterprising printers published sheets with the "latest" information. For domestic events of high interest, such as a pirate attack in Campeche or a destructive earthquake in Oaxaca, a special sheet might be run off. Sigüenza y Góngora published a periodical, *Mercurio Volante*, beginning in 1693. It was not until 1805, however, that a daily newspaper—the *Diario de México*—was offered to the public.

MUSIC

Music was performed formally in the viceregal court and before bishops and wealthy, cultured ladies and gentlemen of various occupations. Elegies were composed to mourn the deaths and celebrate the lives of kings and viceroys. In the early eighteenth century Manuel Zumaya wrote the New World's first opera, *La Parténope*, staged in 1711.

More importantly music composed a vital part of life for everyone in the colony. Music had been important to the Aztecs, especially for ritual ceremonies, and musicians held a respectable status in the Indian community. Spanish clergymen soon found that the

Indians' love of music offered an expedient through which the natives could be attracted to Christianity. They staged religious plays in Nahuatl in which music had a place. However, the indigenous interpretations in these performances played into the creation of hybrid forms of Christianity. At the same time, the singing of the mass connected music to the Spaniards' religion. Natives enjoyed performing, not only because of the enjoyment and the prestige involved but also because performers were, at least part of the time, exempt from paying tribute. By 1576 about 10,000 Indians sang at services, and although most were men, women also participated later in the colonial period, especially in the northern missions.

In the beginning, Indians sang a cappella or accompanied by native instruments, but organs were later introduced from Spain. Before long the variety of European instruments arrived, and local musicians became familiar with sackbuts, clarinets, rebecs, violas, bassoons, lutes, guitars, cornets, and so forth. Indians quickly learned to make such instruments, and even the great organs. Native artists also reproduced choir books, complete with illuminated letters. In addition, Spanish masters encouraged Indians to compose music, which they did with considerable skill.

The church discouraged some Indian music identified with paganism, replete with the "obscene motions and lewd gestures" of native dances. To complicate matters, uninhibited dancing found new life with the introduction by black slaves of dances from the Caribbean. Clerical admonitions notwithstanding, provocative dances like the *sarabunda* and the *chacona* continued to be popular. In the eighteenth century the Inquisition protested the *jarabe gatuno*, "so indecent, lewd, and disgraceful, and provocative, that words cannot encompass the evil of it. The verses and the accompanying actions, movements, and gestures, shoot the poison of lust directly into the eyes, ears, and senses."[2]

Yet the church did not discourage all forms of frivolous amusement. Enjoying sensational popularity was the *villancico*. Originally a type of traditional Spanish Christmas carol usually sung in church, the villancico developed in Mexico as a popular song for festive occasions. In the seventeenth century it emerged, like the contemporary baroque taste in art, as an exuberant display of lightheartedness. Felicitous lyrics celebrated not only saints' days but also the rites of spring and the emotions of profane love in startlingly modern form.

ARCHITECTURE

Creative expression in colonial Mexico was achieved in architecture through European styles and by Indian laborers and craftsmen. The Catholic church dominated building projects designed to evangelize, glorify God, and provide solace as well as preparation for salvation. Naturally enough, Spaniards tried to create buildings in the colony similar to those in Spain, and in the early years an essentially Gothic medieval style predominated. It was, nevertheless, modified in Mexico: churches assumed a fortresslike appearance because of the threats

---

2   Robert Stevenson, *Music in Mexico: A Historical Survey* (New York, 1971), 184.

of Indian attacks; the danger of earthquakes called for buildings with thick walls, often supported by great flying buttresses; and the humid tropics required provision for better ventilation. The apocalyptic views of the Franciscans are also evident in the defensive elements. As the sixteenth century progressed, Renaissance styles, plateresque and mannerist, were the norm. Moreover, architecture in Mexico took on a distinctively local character because building materials in the colony offered more color. In wide use were the red, porous *tezontle* pumice, the local whitish limestone, and a green stone found in Oaxaca. As the bright Puebla (*poblano*) style emerged, polychrome Talavera tiles came to be used extensively and in some cases dominated the façades of buildings. Indian influence crept in as native craftsmen insinuated their motifs in carvings and paintings. And because even the large churches could not accommodate the great crowds of Indian worshipers, broad courtyards and "open-air chapels" became a familiar sight.

The first century of architecture in Mexico saw a *mestizaje* of styles, in which Gothic, Renaissance, and *mudéjar* (Moorish) features merged and led to forms loosely described as baroque. The intricate plasterwork of the plateresque resembled the art of silversmiths. Monasteries of the friars had a simplicity that contrasted with the massive, richly ornate cathedrals. The great cathedrals stand out by virtue of sheer bulk, but those of Mexico City and Puebla, designed by the same architect and competing in excellence, are especially noteworthy structures. Begun in 1563, the cathedral of Mexico City occupied teams of craftsmen for a century and even then was not completed until the late colonial period. That of Puebla, considered by many the finer of the two, was laid out around 1575 and dedicated in 1649. Its dome provided more light to accent the interior ornamentation, a pattern widely copied throughout New Spain. Other features of the evolving Mexican baroque included the distinctive *retablo* (altarpiece) façades with twisted columns and brightly colored stone and plaster work.

Civil architecture fared less well over the centuries. We know that splendid buildings arose—palaces of the viceroy and bishops, offices of the audiencia and ayuntamiento, and various other government structures. But some were destroyed, and the original forms of others were altered by later constructions. It is sad, too, that the Renaissance mansions of the conquerors have almost all disappeared, although we gain some appreciation of their elegance from the residence of Francisco de Montejo in Mérida and the modified palace of Cortés in Cuernavaca. The monumental palace of the Condes de San Mateo de Valparaíso in Mexico City has an impressive central courtyard framed by four huge, lowered arches.

The Mexican baroque has been called an art of paradox by the late Mexican cultural critic, Carlos Fuentes—a "criollo" style that fuses elements of the Old World and the New and represents continuous cultural negotiation between Indian artisans and clergy throughout the colonial period. As it developed, it gave way to what some have called "ultra" baroque—that is, a style dominated by a profusion of decorative effects. Surfaces were encrusted with decoration, and façades and altarpieces were choked with riotous detail. The baroque gloriously celebrated the optimism and prosperity of criollo society. The many baroque churches still seen today continue to awe the visitor with their splendor and abundance of ornamentation.

The church and convent of San Agustín, Hidalgo.

Perhaps the excesses of the baroque ultimately exhausted the senses and led to a reaction. The severe, formal neoclassic represented a sober turn, devoid of the color and fantasy that have generally characterized Mexican art from the marvelous Maya façades to the brilliant murals of the twentieth century.

SCULPTURE AND PAINTING

Sculpture was, to a great extent, an adjunct to architecture. Sculptors, many of whom were Indians and mestizos, rendered in stone and plaster the incredibly complex designs of ceilings and façades, and they carved wooden altarpieces, images of saints, and other adornments that contributed to the grandeur of the art of New Spain. Most of these artists remain anonymous, but one prominent sculptor deserves mention. Manuel Tolsá, a Spaniard, created the admirable equestrian statue of Charles IV affectionately known as "the Caballito." Prominently on display in Mexico City today in front of the National Art Museum, it is regarded as one of the finest works of its kind in the world.

The first European painter in Mexico was a companion of Cortés who painted his captain at prayer. With the construction of churches and monasteries, friars and Indians trained in Gante's school painted tempura murals on their walls. Good examples of these early efforts have been preserved at Acolman, Cuernavaca, and Actopan. Also to the first decades belong the post-conquest codices, painted, with official encouragement, by Indian artists. The codices that survive have not only invaluable historical importance but genuine artistic qualities as well. For the most part, however, native painters shed earlier artistic traditions as they were pressed into studios for training in the realism of the Spanish school.

Painting advanced in quality with the arrival in 1566 of the Flemish master Simón Pereyns. He gathered around him a talented group of criollo artists who painted canvases in the Spanish manner. European mannerist and baroque styles evolved in the second century of colonial rule. One of the best-known of seventeenth-century painters is Cristóbal de Villalpando, whose brilliantly colored and shadowed paintings of religious themes grace churches throughout Mexico. Some of the canvases, such as those in the sacristy of the Cathedral of Mexico, cover entire walls. Although Villalpando was influenced by Peter Paul Rubens, many of his compositions have inventive features. Luis Juárez also painted many images for convents and monasteries.

Cathedral of Mexico.

In the seventeenth century more opportunities opened for the studio artist who prospered through rich patrons. The prominent and wealthy adorned their residences with paintings, and portraits were in great demand. One may weigh the skills of those portraitists in the paintings of the viceroys, most of whom stare down from the walls with grim and baleful countenance. Many such portraits by Nicolás Rodríguez Juárez and his brother Juan were produced at the end of the seventeenth century. By the eighteenth century painters like Miguel Cabrera prospered, satisfying the egos of the silver barons and others who sought to be preserved for posterity (see his portrait of Sor Juana in the color section of this book). Elites also coveted Asian art, for example in the imported porcelain vases and in the ceramics produced in the colony that used Chinese motifs. Especially eye-catching were imported lacquered chests and desks with mother-of-pearl inlays. Spaniards also emulated the Japanese practice of painting on folding screens (biombos), commissioning both religious and pastoral scenes.

The most originally Mexican category of painting can be seen in the casta paintings that depicted the myriad of hybrid racial classifications that resulted from mestizaje. They typically show a male from one ethnic group with a female partner from a differing ethnicity, and their racially blended offspring, with a label that states these categories (see illustration in the color photo section of this book). In addition to the fluidity of the *sistema de castas* depicted in these images, the proliferation of casta paintings also reveals an ongoing, deep-seated concern by elites with behavioral prescriptions regarding marriage and interracial relations.

A water tower at Teoloyucan, with its flared buttresses, one of the many remaining monuments to colonial artisans.

Second-story façade of the sixteenth-century residence of Francisco de Montejo in Mérida, Yucatán.

Currents of change in Spain at the end of the eighteenth century prompted the establishment of the Art Academy of San Carlos in Mexico City. It was dedicated in 1785 to train artists in new styles consonant with the neoclassic turn, but its early years witnessed conflict between art administrators in the colony and in Spain over hierarchies and styles.

DAILY LIFE

The poverty, exploitation, injustices, and general misery of the lower classes notwithstanding, colonial life was not a scene of unrelieved tragedy. Religious festivals and public spectacles honoring Spanish rulers provided welcome diversions for many. Colonial elites intended to use ritual performances to inculcate the correct forms of religious observance and to demonstrate to subordinates their proper place in the social hierarchy. Nonetheless, popular celebrations had a way of taking on a life of their own. They often fostered unruly behavior and veiled forms of social protest, and occasionally they became the sites of riots—for example, the 1692 tumult in Mexico City that took place during the celebration of Corpus Christi. Even in less agitated moments, the viceregal capital offered a variety of diversions.

Visitors to Mexico City who recorded their impressions usually commented on its fine buildings and broad, straight avenues. In the seventeenth century, travelers asserted that everything one could desire was available, including abundant supplies of foods that were both delicious and inexpensive. Daily more than one thousand boats and three thousand mules carried in provisions from outlying provinces. Foreigners remarked on the excellence of the city's construction, laid out in a grid pattern with plazas, fountains, and sidewalks. An Englishman living in Mexico City in 1625 estimated that the capital had fifteen thousand coaches, some trimmed with gold, silver, and Chinese silk.

Color, of which Mexicans have always been especially fond, was what struck the foreigner's eye. Color was everywhere, from the flower gardens and blossoming trees, to the textured hues of walls, to the kaleidoscope of the great open markets where bright exotic fruits and vegetables vied with polychrome tiles and pottery, brilliant native textiles, and jewelry. An astonishing variety of goods abounded in the marketplace, where thousands of people gathered to bargain and exchange gossip. A motley population thronged the streets, their rich skin tones adding to the mosaic of color. Dark habits of the ecclesiastics heightened the bright sashes of university students and the dress of criollo dandies who paraded in plumed, scarlet taffeta hats, ruffled laces, and velvet capes. A dignified worthy clothed in severe ebony might be accompanied by black slaves attired in blue or yellow breeches, with white silk stockings.

Both men and women wore jewels in the street, and it was not uncommon to see hatbands set with pearls and diamonds. Occasionally the procession of the viceroy or archbishop with his retinues passed, causing a mild sensation. Women, who were just as fashion conscious as men, flaunted exquisite cloths from Asia and the richest textiles from Europe. Wealthy ladies frequently observed modesty by making their way through the streets in veiled palanquins, sedan chairs borne by slaves. Visitors were especially taken by beautiful mulata women wearing expensive silks and sparkling gems, despite sumptuary laws that were passed from time to time to prevent them from dressing like whites. Women of various classes applied rouge and eye makeup.

Beneath all the finery and cosmetics, however, were people who aged quickly and who enjoyed fewer of the beauty aids available to serve the vanities of our times. In close conversation with a colonist one would become aware of a strong musty odor, a smile marred by missing or rotting teeth, and a face scarred and pitted. At least on social occasions some were considerate: a strong perfume might disguise the infrequency of bathing, and offensive breath could be tamed by chewing cloves or licorice.

Among the more unfortunate elements of society were the many vagabonds who roamed the colony. They lounged around city streets, living by their wits and making a general nuisance of themselves in both urban and provincial areas. These *picaros*, so charmingly presented in literature, were a threat to the colonial order, much to the dismay of the authorities. Vagabonds came from all racial groups. Many suffered from disease, poverty, and official neglect. Dressed in filthy rags, syphilitic victims displayed open sores, grotesque tumors, and maimed limbs. The blind joined other indigents outside churches to collect alms. The church made modest attempts to provide care for them and regularly dispensed food and small sums of money. In the countryside vagabonds often lived illegally in Indian villages, forcing villagers to support them and sometimes seizing their women.

All these social types, elegant and rustic, were part of daily scenes in streets that were alternately muddy or dusty, depending on the season. Cursing mule drivers prodded their braying beasts along, stirring up clouds of dust or making quagmires, while other herders pushed swine, sheep, or turkeys through the crowds. Peddlers hawked their wares, Indian servant women carried jugs of water from the public fountains, and tamemes bent under the loads that almost obscured them. Eventually some streets had cobblestones, but gutters remained like open sewers, strewn with garbage and an occasional dead dog. If color delighted the eye, stench assailed the nostril. But such aromas and unsanitary conditions were, after all, not much different from those in other parts of the world at the time. The filth did pose a serious health problem, however, and the government moved to keep the capital cleaner. The pigs that ran loose in the streets and scavenged for food were relied upon less fully after an ordinance of 1598 provided for twelve teams of two Indians, with mule carts, to collect refuse from city streets every day. Public buildings, including storehouses and jails, had to be cleaned every four months. There was little improvement in sanitary conditions throughout the colonial period, however, and swine, mongrel dogs, and vultures continued to be counted on to help keep streets clean, at least until they themselves fouled them.

At the center of elite social life was the viceregal court, although bishops and wealthy laymen often rivaled the court in extravagant entertainment. For the cultured elite there were the latest plays, music, and literature from Spain and clever conversation in the salons. Some recitals and performances were private, but a great many appealed to the general public. Dancing enjoyed popularity with all, from the formal balls of the wealthy to the more spontaneous, often earthy, dances of the lower classes. Irreverent and worldly theatrical performances and puppet shows, mostly performed by itinerant troupes on urban streets or in rural towns, attracted people from all classes. Bullfighting, introduced shortly after the conquest, found wide favor with all segments of society. An archbishop in the early seventeenth century was such an *aficionado* that he had his own private bullring on the grounds of the archiepiscopal

Late seventeenth-century ceramic fountain from Puebla suggesting Chinese influence.

A Puebla vase decorated in Chinese style, late seventeenth century.

Flower pot of the style commonly used in the halls and patios of colonial houses.

Tiles from Puebla were commonly used on building façades.

palace. The more intellectual enjoyed chess, and all classes played cards. Almost everyone was addicted to the vice of gambling as they waged at dice, cards, horse races, cockfighting, or any contest available for betting purposes. Primarily men indulged in such diversions, but new arrivals to the colony were shocked to see criolla women of presumed high social standing dealing cards with males. For the aristocrats there were jousting and other games played on horseback, and they rode to the hunt with their greyhounds and falcons.

Leisure time was abundant for many urban dwellers; colonists enjoyed multiple holidays, with dozens of religious festivals annually. Individuals celebrated their saints' days, and towns had their special saints to be honored as well. Colonial Mexicans enjoyed holy days to the fullest. Solemn religious rites, processions, and sometimes penance were followed by fireworks, feasting, singing, dancing, and no small amount of drinking—which in turn often led to fighting. Gentlemen might settle accounts of honor with a duel; the lower classes would more likely find satisfaction informally and immediately with knives or machetes. A favorite—and healthier—diversion at parties (during which daughters were watched by hawk-eyed chaperones) involved the throwing of eggshells filled with confetti or of hollow wax balls containing perfume water. All of this was conducted with great merriment and a consuming interest in sweetmeats and the opposite sex. A cherished ritual of the elite youth manifested itself in the daily *paseo*, in which the young men gathered around five o'clock in Mexico City's Alameda Park. These popinjays arrived in fancy carriages or perhaps mounted on purebred horses, attended by black slaves suitably dressed to display their young masters' elegance. Young ladies arrived in much the same fashion, for the same purpose.

Other events demanded celebration. The birth of a royal child, a royal marriage, the coronation of a new king, the arrival of a new viceroy or archbishop, or a great victory over one of Spain's enemies, called for constructing triumphal arches and merrymaking. The most glorious of spectacles were the *mascaradas,* often planned far in advance and summoning the most creative talents to assure sensational (and sometimes bizarre) effects. The essential part of the show was the grand parade, in which place in the procession reflected the colonial social hierarchy. It might lead off with Indian caciques decked out in traditional native garb, followed by dignitaries of the church in their rich vestments, high royal officials mounted on superb horses with silver trappings, and university faculty members in their gaudy robes. Parades boasted decorated floats, clowns, acrobats, jugglers, and musicians. Some individuals were masked (from which the ceremonies took their names), wearing costumes representing mythical or historical figures, while others personified Pride, Greed, Lust, or perhaps one of the virtues.

Sometimes the mascarada was sponsored, at great cost, by a wealthy individual and other times by the state, but the organizers aimed to surpass previous extravaganzas. No expense or labor was spared—even to the extent of importing camels and ostriches for the parade, to the great delight of the spectators. In the eighteenth century Mexico City officials, increasingly alarmed by the profanity and disorder of these spectacles, began to severely curtail celebrations. Public ritual no longer served the interests of state authority and social control.

The impression should not be left that colonial society witnessed a continual round of parties and sport. The foregoing observations of colonists at play pertain mostly to large centers like Mexico City and Puebla. Smaller towns had similar amusements but on a scale less grand and carried off with less flair. Occasions such as saints' days in small communities called for celebrations and processions that were simple but lively, and the custom of the paseo—which has persisted into modern times—saw the gathering of young people of more humble aspect in village plazas. Local celebrations might consist of little more than a mass followed by fireworks and drinking to stupefaction.

Life in the colony also had its grim aspects. Domestic violence was common and sometimes deadly when jealousy was involved. Women who did not conform to their proscribed roles or took lovers could be dragged out of their homes and publicly humiliated by having their faces

The picturesque Alameda Park in the center of Mexico City was first laid out in 1593 during the rule of Viceroy Luis de Velasco. Over the years, its tree-lined pathways and fountains became a haven for small vendors, but in 2012 it was refurbished with additional flower gardens and fences to keep out the petty sellers and to gentrify it as a place for people to meet and stroll.

cut or being whipped in flagrant cases of female immorality. City streets at night were the preserve of men, and they seldom went out without arms or companions to defend themselves against frequent assaults and theft. Rural brigandage was a plague to all. In the sixteenth century there were almost no inns, and Indian villages were required to furnish food and lodging for itinerant peddlers and traders. Later on, crude lodgings and taverns served wayfarers.

A traveler might expect to see criminals hanged by the roadside and left as a warning to others. Death by hanging was decreed for some crimes, and for especially serious offenses, such as treason, the body of the culprit was drawn and quartered, with the head and limbs prominently and gruesomely displayed. Mutilation of limbs, the severing of a hand or foot, the crushing of a foot in a diabolical device known as "the boot," and other tortures were employed on occasion. Officials also administered floggings of one hundred to two hundred lashes, but sentences to terms of hard labor were more frequent. Those of high social position, however, usually avoided humiliating and cruel punishment, escaping with fines or sometimes jail sentences.

A greater danger to New Spain than crime was disease. Epidemic diseases like smallpox and measles persisted in cycles throughout the colonial period, with higher morality for indigenous peoples. Other virulent epidemics took their toll on all groups. *Matlazahuatl*, variously identified as typhus or plague, appeared in the sixteenth century, followed by cycles in the seventeenth and the particularly devastating pandemic of the late 1730s which was most lethal among groups who lived in the least sanitary conditions. Yellow fever, which infested the port cities like Veracruz, similarly affected all groups. Inhabitants of New Spain also experienced illnesses still common today, for example, digestive disorders, heart failure, kidney stones, rheumatism, venereal disease, and gout.

Effective treatment for such diseases as smallpox and measles would have to wait until vaccines were developed much later. Inoculation with the smallpox virus was first used in Mexico during the 1779-80 epidemic, along with traditional measures like quarantine and special hospitals. To treat other, less lethal maladies, throughout the colonial period medical practices combined European methods and a variety of regional indigenous remedies. European medicine did not advance much in the early modern period beyond an understanding of anatomy, and bleeding and purging continued to be standard cures. For this reason, indigenous herbal remedies often proved more effective. Administered by local healers, over time indigenous and mixed-race women became the primary practitioners, often doubling as midwives. The latter served as the primary attendants in childbirth long after the medical establishment began to modernize methods of delivery in the eighteenth century.

Crown officials established hospitals from the early sixteenth-century in Mexico City; by 1580 there were six of them, established to treat different ethnic groups, as well as an asylum for the insane. Given the rudimentary state of Spanish medical practice, these hospitals and others established later throughout the viceroyalty were widely seen as places where the extremely ill went to die. Before the seventeenth century, when a professorship of surgery and anatomy was established at the university, "surgeons" as they called themselves consisted primarily of barbers (a good number of whom were Asians). The crown also established an examination board, the Protomedicato, to license physicians, surgeons, pharmacists, and phlebotomists, but oversight was lax until the late eighteenth century when medical practices began to modernize. As the dying looked to religious rituals for comfort, people in New Spain learned to live with death, maintaining contact with their departed relatives through ceremonies and offerings on the Día de los Muertos (All Soul's Day).

Far from being the vulgar backwater peninsular Spaniards supposed, New Spain had a vibrant and diverse cultural life, especially in the larger cities. Scholarship and learning advanced primarily through the clergy with support from viceregal and church officials. At the same time a rich patchwork of popular culture and popular piety evolved throughout the viceroyalty, often linking people of diverse ethnic groups. By 1700 it had a uniquely Mexican character, with customs and traditions so firmly impressed on society that the patterns are still evident today.

RECOMMENDED FOR FURTHER STUDY

Bailey, G. A. *Art of Colonial Latin America*. London, UK: Phaidon Press, 2005.

Beezley, William H., Cheryl E. Martin, and William E. French, eds. *Rituals of Rule, Rituals of Resistance: Public Celebrations and Popular Culture in Mexico*. Wilmington, DE: Scholarly Resources, 1994.

Burkhart, Louise. *The Slippery Earth: Nahua-Christian Moral Dialogue in Sixteenth-Century Mexico*. Tucson: University of Arizona Press, 1989.

Charlot, Jean. *Mexican Art and the Academy of San Carlos, 1785-1915*. Austin: University of Texas Press, 1962.

Curcio-Nagy, Linda. *The Great Festivals of Colonial Mexico City: Performing Power and Identity*. Albuquerque: University of New Mexico Press, 2004.

Donahue-Wallace, Kelly. *Art and Architecture of Viceregal Latin America, 1521-1821*. Albuquerque: University of New Mexico Press, 2008.

Edgerton, Samuel. *Theaters of Conversion: Religious Architecture and Indian Artisans in Colonial Mexico*. Albuquerque: University of New Mexico Press, 2001.

Fields, Sherry. *Pestilence and Headcolds: Encountering Illness in Colonial Mexico*. New York: Columbia University Press, 2008.

Few, Martha. *For All Humanity: Mesoamerican and Colonial Medicine in Enlightenment Guatemala*. Tucson: University of Arizona Press, 2015.

Florescano, Enrique. *Memory, Myth, and Time in Mexico: From the Aztecs to Independence*. Austin: University of Texas Press, 1994.

Gibson, Charles. "Writings on Colonial Mexico." *Hispanic American Historical Review* 55/2 (1975): 287-323.

Gutiérrez, Ramón, et al. *Home Altars of Mexico*. Albuquerque: University of New Mexico Press, 1997.

Hernández Sáenz, Luz María. *Learning to Heal: The Medical Profession in Colonial Mexico, 1767-1831*. New York: Peter Lang, 1997.

Katzew, Ilona. *Casta Painting: Images of Race in Eighteenth Century Mexico*. New Haven, CT: Yale University Press, 2004.

Kubler, George. *Mexican Architecture of the Sixteenth Century*. 2 vols. New Haven, CT: Yale University Press, 1948.

Lanning, John Tate. *Academic Culture in the Spanish Colonies*. London, UK: Oxford University Press, 1940.

León Portilla, Miguel. *Bernardino de Sahagún: First Anthropologist*. Norman: University of Oklahoma Press, 2002.

Leonard, Irving. *Baroque Times in Old Mexico: Seventeenth-Century Persons, Places, and Practices*. Ann Arbor: University of Michigan Press, 1971.

_____. *Don Carlos de Sigüenza y Góngora, A Mexican Savant of the Seventeenth Century*. University of California Publications in History, vol. 18. Berkeley: University of California Press, 1929.

Lockhart, James, Susan Schroeder, and Doris Namala, eds. *Annals of His Time: Don Domingo de San Antón Muñón Chimalpahin Quauhtlehuanitzin*. Stanford, CA: Stanford University Press, 2006.

Lomnitz, Claudio. *Death and the Idea of Mexico*. New York: Zone Books, 2005.

Martin, Cheryl E. *Rural Society in Colonial Morelos*. Albuquerque: University of New Mexico Press, 1985.

McAndrews, John. *The Open-Air Churches of Sixteenth-Century Mexico*. Cambridge, MA: Harvard University Press, 1965.

Merrim, Stephanie. *The Spectacular City, Mexico, and Colonial Hispanic Literary Culture*. Austin: University of Texas Press, 2010.

Mullen, Robert J. *Architecture and Its Sculpture in Viceregal Mexico*. Austin: University of Texas Press, 1997.

Paz, Octavio. *Sor Juana. Or, The Traps of Faith*. Translated by Margaret Sayers Peden. Cambridge, MA: Harvard University Press, 1988.

Robertson, Donald. *Mexican Manuscript Painting of the Early Colonial Period: The Metropolitan Schools*. New Haven, CT: Yale University Press, 1959.

Ronan, Charles E. *Francisco Javier Clavijero, S.J.: His Life and Works*. Chicago, IL: Loyola University Press, 1977.

Schroeder, Susan. *Chimalpahin and the Kingdoms of Chalco*. Tucson: University of Arizona Press, 1991.

Sommers, Joseph, and Antonia Castañeda Shular, eds. *Chicano Literature: Text and Context*. Translated by Robert Graves. Englewood Cliffs, NJ: Prentice Hall, 1972.

Stevenson, Robert. *Music in Mexico: A Historical Survey*. New York: Thomas Y. Crowell, Co., 1971.

Taylor, William B. *Drinking, Homicide and Rebellion in Colonial Mexican Villages*. Stanford, CA: Stanford University Press, 1979.

Toussaint, Manuel. *Colonial Art in Mexico*. Translated and edited by Elizabeth W. Weismann. Austin: University of Texas Press, 1967.

Warren, Fintan B. *Vasco de Quiroga and His Pueblo Hospitals of Santa Fé*. Publications of the Academy of American Franciscan History, vol. 10. Washington, DC: Academy of American Franciscan History, 1963.

Will de Chaparro, Martha. *Death and Dying in New Mexico*. Albuquerque: University of New Mexico Press, 2014.

REFORM AND REACTION

The Move to Independence

CHAPTER 13

THE BOURBONS RESTRUCTURE NEW SPAIN

EARLY BOURBON REFORMS

The nadir of Spain's fortunes by the late seventeenth century was nowhere better exemplified than in the person of the king himself. Inheriting the throne in 1665 at age four, Charles II was feeble in mind as well as body and was even in maturity clearly incompetent to rule. This wretched king, called in all kindness *El Hechizado*, "the Bewitched," sought desperately in off moments to hang himself with his bedclothes. While exorcists tried to drive out his devil, advisers made policy of sorts.

Charles was the last of the Spanish Hapsburgs, and there was justifiable concern over the matter of succession. Despite two marriages, the king did not sire an heir. Who, then, would rule the Spanish Empire after his anticipated early demise? Then, as now, there was considerable intermarriage among the various royal families of Europe, and relatives floated their pretensions to the Spanish throne. In the end the Austrian and French factions emerged as the two strongest claimants and their diplomats maneuvered for years. Finally, as Charles II's days grew short, he named as his successor Philip of Anjou, a grandson of Louis XIV of France. The line of Spanish Bourbons began in 1700 with the rule of Philip V (1701–46). The Austrian party and its allies contested Philip's crowning during the long War of the Spanish Succession (1701–13), but the final outcome saw the Bourbons established in Spain.

Philip inherited a debilitated Spain, wracked by foreign wars and internal revolts. Even as he was forced to devote resources to the ongoing war, the new king began to take measures to put Spain on a firmer administrative and financial footing. He applied many of the administrative policies that other Bourbons had used in France, and his centralization of authority proved effective in some areas. An immediate concern was the strengthening of the Spanish army and navy. Philip undertook a program of rehabilitation with some success.

He then turned to the internal economy in which productivity had languished for much of the previous century, at least until the 1670s when agricultural yields and commerce showed modest growth.Heavily indebted to foreigners, much of Spain's trade with the colonies was in the hands of non-Spanish merchants. Furthermore, silver remittances to the

Charles II (1661–1700). The death of this unfortunate king, the last Spanish Hapsburg, precipitated the War of the Spanish Succession.

metropolis from New Spain had declined throughout the seventeenth century, despite the fact that the colony's mining economy had begun to bounce back after 1670.

As his government began to bring some order to Spain, Philip also looked to his colonies with an eye to improving their economies for the financial benefit of the empire and as compensation for Spain's territorial losses in Europe. As one of his first measures, he appointed the Duque de Alburquerque as viceroy of New Spain. Entrusted with the task of dislodging the networks of patronage and clientelism that dominated the silver trade, the viceroy quickly ran afoul of local commercial interests. When they subverted his efforts, he acquiesced and became involved in contraband trade himself.

Philip's efforts in opening up trade experienced more success. In 1702 a royal decree allowed two ships a year, instead of one, to sail from Manila to Acapulco. The volume of Asian trade carried by the Manila galleons has yet to be determined by scholars, but this route was a valuable conduit for silver that complemented the transfer of silver pesos to Asia via Europe, highlighting New Spain's importance in both the Atlantic and Pacific. The antiquated trading system was further improved in 1717 when the official port for the New World trade formally moved from Seville to Cádiz, which had better facilities. This was an important break in the monopoly of vested interests. In 1740 the crown suspended the fleet system, which had operated so inefficiently for two centuries. With the threat of piracy having subsided and smuggling rampant, there seemed little point in restricting both merchants and consumers. In case of war, however, privateers could freely attack Spanish shipping and, in fact, the fleets were revived later, sailing off and on until their final abolition in 1789. Although these colonial economic reforms were modest enough, along with other changes they signaled the Bourbon interest in economic development that would benefit the imperial state.

SHIFTS IN THE COLONIAL ECONOMY

In the second half of the century, the pace of change accelerated. Following the relatively calm reign of Ferdinand VI (1746–59), Spain had a dramatic resurgence under one of its greatest sovereigns, Charles III (1759–88). A devotee of the Enlightenment philosophies then current in Europe, Charles not only introduced important reforms within Spain but also moved to restructure the colonies. To that end, in 1765 he dispatched to New Spain José de Gálvez with the powers of visitor general. Gálvez energetically undertook a long tour of the colony, and over the next five years he compiled important information that led to the formulation of several new policy initiatives in New Spain. The Bourbons determined to extract more wealth from the colony by stimulating mining production, creating a loyal but efficient bureaucracy to collect taxes, and appropriating a share of the church's immense assets in money and rural and urban properties.

Charles' attempts to expand trade and increase revenues produced mixed results. The tax structure was modified to make collection more efficient and, by 1780, New Spain was exporting more silver to the metropolis. New ports opened in Mexico, and the crown sanctioned trade between the colonies, but efforts to break the merchant monopolies in Mexico and Cádiz met with formidable resistance. In the end, vested interests defeated the reform party in Charles' government that tried to reduce Spain's dependence on foreign merchants, bankers, and manufacturers.

Nonetheless, Spain did profit from the rise in silver production, collecting about 250,000 silver pesos between 1760 and 1810. This had a negative impact in New Spain, however, by reducing liquidity and disrupting commerce in the internal economy. The silver boom was partially attributable to royal policies but probably derived more from improved management, stable or declining labor costs that resulted from greater exploitation of workers, the discovery of new lodes (especially in Guanajuato), and a rise in the value of silver. Mining output increased at an annual average of nearly two percent throughout the century, although this growth came in spurts (with peaks in the 1770s and 1790s) and alternated with periods of stagnation. Mexico alone produced about as much silver as the rest of the world. Between 1690 and 1822 Mexico minted over 1.5 billion pesos in silver and some 60 million in gold.

By the late colonial period there were about three thousand mines in the colony, although most had been abandoned and many of those being worked were small operations. In 1774, thirty-five sizable mining camps existed, of which only a few produced most of the silver. Mines could be worked with increased efficiency because of blasting techniques and better mechanisms for draining water that permitted deeper mine shafts. The great Valenciana (Guanajuato) reached into the earth some two thousand feet, deeper than any other mine in the world. The continuing use of smelting, however, caused considerable deforestation through the production of charcoal.

Important as precious metals were, however, the general production of the colony increased considerably in other ways, too. Always profitable, cochineal dye was the second most valuable export during the eighteenth century. Produced primarily in Oaxaca, as many as thirty thousand Indians labored in the industry. Another important commodity was sugar; by 1774 the town of Córdoba (Veracruz) alone had more than fifty sugar mills, employing mostly black slaves. Toward the close of the century the colony produced around twenty-five thousand tons of sugar annually, of which some two-thirds were exported. The city of Puebla was a manufacturing center of note, specializing in both textiles and ceramics. It sent more than a million pounds of cloth a year to the capital and in 1793 had forty-six shops producing pottery and glass. Eventually, cheap contraband textiles and falling wages in Mexico stunted the manufacture of cloth. A lucrative crop by the late eighteenth century was tobacco; Mexico City and Querétaro each had factories employing about 7,000 workers. The many other export commodities included hemp, cacao, vanilla, and hides. Few manufactured goods were exported from the colony but rather circulated internally; 93 percent of exports consisted of silver, cochineal, and various agricultural products.

By the second half of the eighteenth century New Spain had become by far the most prosperous of Spain's holdings. Around 1800 the port of Veracruz had a trade in excess of 30 million pesos annually. By 1810 New Spain contributed nearly three-fourths of the profits from all the Spanish American colonies. Phenomenal demographic growth tripled the size of Mexico's population between 1700 and 1821, increasing the potential of the internal market. But this transformation did not result in positive economic growth for all sectors. Wages lagged and prices rose. The need to boost production of staple crops put pressure on the land, and larger owners began to encroach upon the tracts of weaker owners in some areas. More workers were employed in the production of goods for Mexican consumption—in agriculture, ranching, minor industry, and local commerce—than in export commodities. The following table indicates how the main economic sectors contributed to overall production.

Source	Value in Pesos	Percentage
Agriculture	106,285,000	56
Manufactures	55,386,000	29
Mining	28,451,000	15

VALUE OF NEW SPAIN'S ANNUAL PRODUCTION, CA. 1810

Source: David A. Brading, *Miners and Merchants in Bourbon Mexico, 1763–1810* (Cambridge, 1971), 18.

Royal income derived from Mexican taxes, duties, and monopolies increased steadily over the eighteenth century by more than two percent each year. In the last three decades of colonial rule royal receipts rose even higher as the Spanish crown exacted hefty voluntary and forced loans from individuals and institutions in the colony to pay for its involvement in European conflicts. Although the Bourbon reforms channeled more capital to the metropolis, the gains were limited by persistent mercantilist structures in trade and manufacture. Spain itself never moved beyond a primarily agrarian economy and narrow tax base.

REFORM OF COLONIAL ADMINISTRATION

International rivalries among colonial powers in the eighteenth century led to wars that were fought in various theaters, including the New World. The power of Great Britain and its expanding colonies in North America was perceived in Madrid as a threat to the Spanish Indies, and not without reason. Thus, in 1762, during the Seven Years' War, Charles III authorized a professional standing army for New Spain. The troops were few in number, but the addition of various militia groups, including a number if free blacks, brought the armed forces in 1810 up to roughly thirty-three thousand, of whom no more than a third were regular soldiers.

During his inspection tour José de Gálvez became acutely conscious of the defenseless northern borders. Spanish settlement had pushed northward slowly during the seventeenth century, but even by the mid-eighteenth century, Spaniards had barely penetrated Arizona and Texas with a handful of missions and even fewer presidios. Problems with hostile Indians—especially Comanches and Apaches who had become more mobile and aggressive with Spanish horses and firepower—inhibited colonization. Franciscans under Fray Junípero Serra began founding missions in California in 1769,[1] but in general the northern lands remained sparsely settled and vulnerable to encroachments by other powers. Even though the French threat to Texas ended in 1762 when Spain acquired Louisiana from France, British expansion presented a menace, as did the appearance of Russian ships in California waters.

One result of the increasing international tensions was that viceroys and other high officials appointed in the last decades of the colonial period were often men with military training

---

[1] Pope Francis canonized Serra in September 2015 in spite of protests from California Indians that the Franciscan had severely mistreated their forbears in his zeal to extirpate indigenous culture. Serra is the first Catholic saint to be canonized on US soil.

and experience. But even they were too far removed from the distant north to render effective defense of the frontiers. Therefore Gálvez planned an independent military government for the north. After he returned to Spain and was appointed to the powerful post of minister of the Indies, he created, in 1776, the position of commandant general of the Provincias Internas (Interior Provinces). The new territorial organization of the commandancy general embraced the present north Mexican states as well as Texas, greater New Mexico, and California. The commandant general oversaw the military and political administration of this large area, and in the early years he was independent of the viceroy, reporting directly to the king. His main goals were to increase Spain's military presence in order to stem foreign incursions and to bring frontier Indian groups under Spanish control. Despite considerable bureaucratic wrangling, the second goal was partially achieved in the 1780s when the commandant and his officers succeeded in using diplomacy and gifts ("peace by purchase") to fashion temporary alliances with Comanches, Navajos, Utes, and Apaches. Relative peace with Indians and the failure of a serious European threat to materialize facilitated modest settlement of the borderlands. Yet the culture that evolved in the north, where warfare and violence persisted, displayed social and gendered features that distinguished it from central and southern Mexico.

The bureaucracy of the colony, seen by the crown as inefficient and corrupt, also came under the careful scrutiny of Gálvez, and he did effect some profound changes for New Spain's administration. Since the first decades of settlement, alcaldes mayores and corregidores had been notorious as the worst tormentors of the Indians. Their inadequate salaries had always encouraged extralegal commercial activities, and by the early eighteenth century

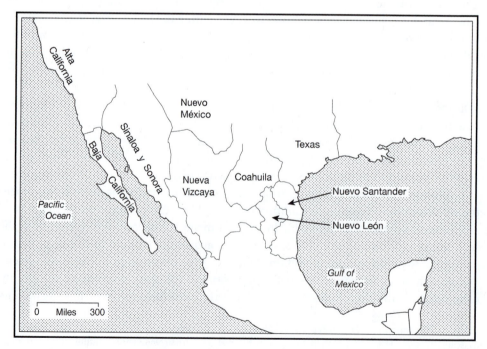

Interior Provinces (Late Eighteenth Century)

these officials received no salaries at all. Instead, they were expected to engage in business ventures. In effect, they were petty merchants who lived by purchasing the products and labor of the natives cheaply and forcing them to buy, at inflated prices, goods that they neither needed nor wanted. Gálvez proposed that such officials be replaced by others called *intendants* and their lieutenants or *subdelegados*. In 1786 Charles III agreed to the appointment of twelve intendants and over a hundred subdelegados to replace some two hundred governors, alcaldes mayores, and corregidores in Mexico.

Implicit in the reforms decreed by the Bourbons were centralization and the imposition of unity, order, and efficiency. And paramount to the reorganization was the firm and effective management of crown revenues. The intendants sent to New Spain were charged with controlling royal monopolies, collecting taxes, improving royal roads for transporting commodities, and overseeing the whole range of treasury interests in the colony, including suppression of smuggling. More than that, however, they had broad responsibilities to improve general administration in their districts, called "intendancies," including such matters as justice, public facilities, and defense. Peninsulares would now be the exclusive candidates for the positions of intendant and audiencia judge, and for the most part they were experienced, educated, and capable administrators. They enjoyed considerable prestige and had ample authority in their large districts. The same could not be said for the subdelegados who, unlike the intendants, did not receive adequate pay and resorted to the tactics of extortion that had been employed by the corregidores. Indians, therefore, did not find the change to be beneficial, but more importantly, the creation of the new offices engendered the resentment of both the oidores and the viceroys, many of whom saw their own authority circumscribed as a consequence.

CHURCH REFORMS

If the Catholic church had always functioned as an administrative complement to the state, the Bourbons determined that it must do so more as an underling than as a privileged associate. The change in policy was not an attack on the spiritual power of the church. Rather the crown was concerned about the extent to which the various branches of the church had come to monopolize control of land and property in Mexico.

Above all, it was the Jesuits who stuck in the monarch's craw. The Society of Jesus had distinguished itself in various ways, especially in educating and missionizing, but it had also grown powerful and wealthy. The Jesuits were also believed, unfairly in the case of New Spain, to be too closely aligned with the pope and susceptible to political intrigue against monarchies. For these reasons, the Portuguese and French kings had expelled the Jesuits from their realms at mid-century.

In 1766 the Jesuits were accused of fomenting a popular riot against Spain's prime minister. The following year, without warning, the crown suddenly expelled them from all Spanish kingdoms. Sealed orders were opened throughout the Spanish empire on the same day in 1767, ordering the expulsion of the Jesuits forthwith and decreeing the confiscation of their properties. Colonists were stunned by this bold move of the crown. Initial shock gave way to outrage on the part of many criollos who had been educated in Jesuit colegios, and in a half-dozen communities violent demonstrations by criollos and Indians protested the action.

New Spain was notably affected by the expulsion. The crown took over Jesuit assets, reported to be worth some 10 million pesos. The Jesuits had maintained the best schools in the colony, with twenty-three colegios and many seminaries staffed by distinguished faculties. Their graduates, especially those of San Ildefonso, were some of the most prominent men in Mexico, including audiencia judges. Bourbon decrees targeted not only the Jesuits, but also eroded some of the powers of the Inquisition and, perhaps more significantly, the authority (both temporal and moral) of local parish priests. Reforms imposed on nunneries sought to impose tighter regulations on nuns, especially those who had chosen this life for reasons other than spiritual and lived in separate, sometimes lavish quarters.

In a broader attempt to wrest functions of social control from the clergy and to impose orthodoxy on popular religiosity, the crown imposed restrictions on the frequency of public celebrations and the lavish spending on public ritual. Church leadership also attempted to stem the "baroque" excesses of religious and cultural practices, calling for a reformed piety that downplayed ritual in favor of Christian contemplation and emphasized individual morality as a requisite for salvation as well as simplicity in art, music, and architecture. Nonetheless, peoples of all classes clung to familiar devotional practices that filled sacred spaces with lavish ornamentation, performances, and pomp.

Other more secular efforts aimed to promote godliness, virtue, cleanliness, and frugality as a means of curbing public disorder. Crown officials implemented measures to clean up the city streets by beautifying them and clearing them of prostitutes, vagabonds, and animals. In part, this was a measure to improve health and sanitation. Royal authorities took aim at another health hazard by ordering that the dead be buried in public cemeteries rather than in churches (in ceremonies deemed too ostentatious). Efforts at moral reform also included limiting the number of lower-class drinking establishments and discouraging popular pastimes like bullfighting, gambling, and street theater.

THE EFFECTS OF BOURBON REFORMS

A confluence of factors brought about significant change in the colony of New Spain by the time of the death of Charles III, in 1788. Still, change is not necessarily progress, and it is necessary to consider who actually benefited from the "reforms." On the whole, the economic reforms stimulated increased production in the colony, but they did not constitute a profound capitalist transformation, and draining the colony of silver was a detriment to the internal economy. Market demand grew along with demographic recuperation as the Indian population doubled in the eighteenth century while non-Indian numbers tripled. At the same time, rural working people experienced a drop in real wages and incomes as the century progressed. In addition, the crown gave itself certain monopolies that inevitably hurt some elites. The king's exclusive control over tobacco, for instance, took great sums of money out of private hands and displaced a large number of individuals involved in its production and marketing. But the monopoly was an important part of the imperial policy of restructuring since these new crown revenues went to the support of the professional army. The pulque monopoly also put local merchants out of business, while the surtax imposed on this drink of the plebeian class outraged the populace.

Political reforms were equally mixed blessings. What had been envisioned as a more centralized, tighter colonial administration became in the end an expanded bureaucracy in which the number of highly paid officials quadrupled. Furthermore, almost all the intendants were Spaniards, and they replaced many criollos who were persons of importance in their localities and who had come to regard the positions as their preserve. The result increased resentment on the part of criollos against the peninsulares. The commandancy general brought slightly better administration to the borderlands without, however, effecting any profound change. Throughout the colony power, like wealth, was redistributed, creating new vested interest groups. As the prerogatives of the viceroys and audiencia judges diminished, the intendants and tax collectors assumed considerable influence. One administrative reform may have countered the effects of excluding criollos from high political office. The creation of new local militias to repel foreign threats and control local disturbances provided an opportunity for Mexican-born Spaniards to acquire prestige and power.

In summary, the Bourbons were successful in extracting more resources from the colony of New Spain, but they were unable to capitalize on them. Although Bourbon Spain wished to create a modern nation-state, it did not have the will or means to make the necessary changes in modes of production and labor relations. Nor did it help that Spain squandered much of its new wealth in European political and military machinations. In the end, debts would bankrupt the treasuries of both Spain and New Spain. Charles III was succeeded by a son lacking in wisdom; political affairs on the European continent would ultimately engulf

The Mining College (Colegio de Minería), designed by Manuel Tolsá, was constructed at great cost between 1797 and 1813. One of Mexico's handsomest colonial buildings, it has 238 rooms, thirteen stairways, eleven fountains, and seven courtyards. Its grandeur is an indication of the importance of silver mining in the late Spanish period.

Spain; and these and other events would foster a growing disenchantment among the colonists in New Spain. Since the royal intent was to benefit Spain, not the colonists, tradition-bound monarchs of the eighteenth century saw no plausible benefits in social reform. Quite to the contrary: the year following the death of Charles III the French masses rose up in the name of social justice, beheaded their king, and went on the rampage. The shudder that passed through the royal courts of Europe was felt in Madrid as well.

RECOMMENDED FOR FURTHER STUDY

Archer, Christon I. *The Army in Bourbon Mexico, 1760–1810*. Albuquerque: University of New Mexico Press, 1977.

Arnold, Linda. *Bureaucracy and Bureaucrats in Mexico City, 1742–1835*. Tucson: University of Arizona Press, 1988.

Barr, Juliana. *Peace Came in the Form of a Woman: Indians and Spaniards in the Texas Borderlands*. Chapel Hill: University of North Carolina Press, 2007.

Baskes, Jeremy. *Indians, Merchants, and Markets: A Reinterpretation of the Repartimiento and Spanish-Indian Economic Relations in Colonial Oaxaca, 1750–1821*. Stanford, CA: Stanford University Press, 2001.

_____. *Staying Afloat: Risk and Uncertainty in Spanish Atlantic World Trade, 1760–1820*. Stanford, CA: Stanford University Press, 2013.

Beebe, Rose Marie, and Robert F. Senkewicz. *Junípero Serra: California Indians and the Transformation of a Missionary*. Norman: University of Oklahoma Press, 2015.

Blyth, Lance R. *Chiricahua and Janos: Communities of Violence in the Southwestern Borderlands, 1680–1880*. Lincoln: University of Nebraska Press, 2012.

Booker, Jackie R. *Veracruz Merchants, 1770–1829: A Mercantile Elite in Late Bourbon and Early Independent Mexico*. Boulder, CO: Westview Press, 1993.

Brading, David A. *Miners and Merchants in Bourbon Mexico, 1763–1810*. New York: Cambridge University Press, 1971.

Burkholder, Mark A. "The Council of the Indies in the Late Eighteenth Century: A New Perspective." *Hispanic American Historical Review* 56/3 (1976): 404–42.

Castleman, Bruce A. *Building the King's Highway: Labor, Society, and Family on Mexico's Caminos Reales, 1757–1804*. Tucson: University of Arizona Press, 2005.

Connaughton, Brian E. *Clerical Ideology in a Revolutionary Age: The Guadalajara Church and the Idea of the Mexican Nation, 1788–1853*. Calgary, Canada: University of Calgary Press, 2003.

Córdova, James M. *The Art of Professing in Bourbon Mexico: Crowned-Nun Portraits and Reform in the Convents*. Austin: University of Texas Press, 2014.

Crosby, Harry W. *Antigua California: Mission and Colony on the Peninsular Frontier, 1697–1768*. Albuquerque: University of New Mexico Press, 1994.

Cutter, Charles R. *The Legal Culture of Northern New Spain, 1700–1810*. Albuquerque: University of New Mexico Press, 1995.

Deans-Smith, Susan. *Bureaucrats, Planters, and Workers: The Making of the Tobacco Monopoly in Bourbon Mexico*. Austin: University of Texas Press, 1992.

De la Teja, Jesús Frank. *San Antonio de Béxar: A Community on New Spain's Northern Frontier*. Albuquerque: University of New Mexico Press, 1995.

_____, and Ross Frank, eds. *Choice, Persuasion, and Coercion: Social Control on Spain's North American Frontiers*. Albuquerque: University of New Mexico Press, 2005.

De la Torre Curiel, José Refugio. *Twilight of the Mission Frontier: Shifting Interethnic Alliances and Social Organization in Sonora, 1768–1855*. Stanford, CA: Stanford University Press, 2013.

DeLay, Brian. *War of the Thousand Deserts: Indian Raids and the U.S.-Mexican War*. New Haven, CT: Yale University Press, 2008.

Frank, Ross. *From Settler to Citizen: New Mexican Economic Development and the Creation of Vecino Society, 1750–1820*. Berkeley: University of California Press, 2000.

Garner, Richard L., and Spiro E. Stefanou. *Economic Growth and Change in Bourbon Mexico*. Gainesville: University Press of Florida, 1993.

Haas, Lisbeth. *Saints and Citizens: Indigenous Histories of Colonial Missions and Mexican California*. Berkeley: University of California Press, 2013.

Hackel, Stephen W. *Junípero Serra: California's Founding Father*. New York: Hill and Wang, 2012.

Hämäläinen, Pekka. *The Comanche Empire*. New Haven, CT: Yale University Press, 2008.

Hamnett, Brian R. *Politics and Trade in Southern Mexico, 1750–1821*. New York: Cambridge University Press, 1971.

Jackson, Robert H., ed. *New Views of Borderlands History*. Albuquerque: University of New Mexico Press, 1998.

Jacobsen, Nils, and Hans-Jürgen Poole. *The Economies of Mexico and Peru during the Late Colonial Period, 1760–1810*. Berlin, Germany: Colloquium Verlag, 1986.

Larkin, Brian. *The Very Nature of God: Baroque Catholicism and Religious Reform in Bourbon Mexico City*. Albuquerque: University of New Mexico Press, 2010.

Marichal, Carlos. *Bankruptcy of Empire: Mexican Silver and the Wars between Spain, Britain, and France, 1760–1810*. New York: Cambridge University Press, 2007.

McAlister, Lyle N. The *"Fuero Militar" in New Spain, 1764–1800*. Gainesville: University Press of Florida, 1967.

Mörner, Magnus. *The Expulsion of the Jesuits from Latin America*. Boston, MA: Little, Brown & Co., 1967.

Offutt, Leslie F. *Saltillo, 1770–1810: Town and Region in the Mexican North*. Tucson: University of Arizona Press, 2001.

O'Hara, Matthew D. *A Flock Divided: Race, Religion and Politics in Mexico, 1749–1857*. Durham, NC: Duke University Press, 2010.

Ouweneel, Arij. *Shadows over Anáhuac: An Ecological Interpretation of Crisis and Development in Central Mexico, 1730–1800*. Albuquerque: University of New Mexico Press, 1996.

Rosenmüller, Christoph. *Patrons, Partisans, and Palace Intrigues: The Court Society of Colonial Mexico, 1702–1710*. Calgary, Canada: University of Calgary Press, 2008.

Shelton, Laura M. *For Tranquility and Order: Family and Community on Mexico's Northern Frontier, 1800–1850*. Tucson: University of Arizona Press 2010.

Stein, Stanley J., and Barbara H. Stein. *Apogee of Empire: Spain and New Spain in the Age of Charles III, 1769–1789*. Baltimore, MD: Johns Hopkins University Press, 2003.

Thomas, Alfred B. *Teodoro de Croix and the Northern Frontier of New Spain, 1776–1783*. Norman: University of Oklahoma Press, 1941.

Thomson, Guy C. P. *Puebla de los Angeles: Industry and Society in a Mexican City, 1700–1850*. Boulder, CO: Westview Press, 1989.

Tutino, John. *Making a New World: Founding Capitalism in the Bajío and Spanish North America*. Durham, NC: Duke University Press, 2011.

Viqueira Albán, Juan. *Propriety and Permissiveness in Bourbon Mexico*. Translated by Sonya Lipsett-Rivera and Sergio Rivera Ayala. Wilmington, DE: Scholarly Resources, 1999.

Voekel, Pamela. *Alone before God: The Religious Origins of Modernity in Mexico*. Durham, NC: Duke University Press, 2002.

Weber, David. J. *Bárbaros: Spaniards and Their Savages in the Age of Enlightenment*. New Haven, CT: Yale University Press, 2005.

CHAPTER 14

SOCIETY AND STRESS IN THE LATE COLONIAL PERIOD

DISTRIBUTION OF WEALTH

Wealthy colonials seemed even less attuned to the tensions of the late colonial period as they accumulated greater riches. A disproportionate number of the wealthiest were peninsulares who had made good in America, but there were many prosperous criollos as well. Great fortunes were made in mining, such as those of the counts of Regla, Valenciana, and Bassoco. From his origins as a poor immigrant from Spain, Pedro Romero de Terreros, the future Conde de Regla, began as an apprentice to his merchant uncle. He used family connections to build up capital and invest in mining, hitting the bonanza with Real del Monte in Pachuca, eventually becoming the wealthiest man in the colony, perhaps even the world, at the time. His other investments included land and the production of pulque; he founded the Monte de Piedad, Mexico's national pawnshop; and he was a generous benefactor of the church. In the late eighteenth century Valenciana sometimes took a net profit of more than a million pesos annually, quite aside from his millions tied up in land and various other interests. Bassoco, elevated to count only in 1811 after a gift to the government of two hundred thousand pesos, accumulated assets worth some 3 million pesos.

These mining barons, along with some wealthy ranchers and merchants, frequently made generous gifts to the crown, which in gratitude conferred on the donors cherished titles of nobility—usually that of *conde*, less often that of *marqués*. Some prominent men had to be content with knighthood in one of the prestigious military orders. During the eighteenth century about fifty titles of nobility were granted to residents of New Spain, most of them after 1750.

But while these titles appealed to the vanity of the recipients, many of the rich were more genuinely philanthropic. They contributed large sums of money to religious organizations, funded charities, and financed the construction of schools, hospitals, and ornate churches. They also sponsored festivals and cultural events for the enjoyment of the community. In times of pestilence the rich often paid for medicines, and when famine struck they distributed large supplies of grain and other foods. Unfortunately these gestures often amounted to little more than tokens, for some catastrophes were overwhelming. A subsistence crisis in 1785–86 resulted in hundreds of thousands of deaths due to starvation and disease.

Among the most powerful men of Mexico were a number of rich hacendados in the north. As missionaries, miners, and soldiers penetrated the frontier, most of the Indians were gradually pushed back and land came into the possession of wealthy and influential ranchers. Much of the northeast region consisted of semi-desert and could be acquired at low cost; in 1731 the marqués de Aguayo purchased 222,000 acres in Coahuila from the crown for a paltry two hundred fifty pesos. Within four decades his family controlled over 14.5 million

Considered the most complete example of Mexican baroque is the exquisite church of Santa Prisca in Taxco. Built between 1751 and 1759, its cost was underwritten by the mining baron Don José de la Borda.

acres, some of which were patrolled by the marqués's private cavalry to protect the livestock from marauding Indians. The Sánchez Navarro family also amassed huge holdings. Aside from running sheep, cattle, and horses, they engaged in mining, agriculture, and commerce. Their *latifundio*, eventually covering an area almost as large as the country of Portugal, was the largest ranch in Spanish America.

The increased prosperity of some was reflected not only in ornate religious edifices but also in the many impressive public buildings. In Mexico City today one can still see enough of them, along with private mansions, to appreciate the grandeur of the capital in the late colonial era. The spectacular House of Tiles, covered on the exterior and the interior with tiles said to have been brought expressly from China, is a modern landmark. Once the residence of the Conde del Valle de Orizaba, it is today a restaurant.

The colony, and especially the capital, benefited from the improvements made by one of the greatest viceroys, the second count of Revillagigedo (1789–94). Among his many innovations were the paving and lighting of streets intended to reduce accidents and crime. He is remembered also for having ordered an important census, for improving the postal service, and for sponsoring scientific and artistic projects. To promote public order, he mandated that city officials restrict unauthorized gatherings and street performances of music and dance. Although these efforts did not succeed in eradicating popular customs, they did serve to reinforce racial hierarchies and draw spatial boundaries between social groups.

The aristocracy of the eighteenth century differed from its counterpart of the two preceding centuries primarily in the matter of style rather than attitude. Later aristocrats were

The magnificent colonial residence, rising four stories, is a good example of baroque architectural style. Built in the eighteenth century for the Count of San Mateo de Valparaíso, it was later used as a palace by Emperor Agustín I (Iturbide). Subsequently it served as a hotel and today it is beautifully maintained by a bank.

A rural scene of a hacendado and his foreman.

A spirited mount and fine clothing typify this scene of rural landowners in the early nineteenth century. The Mexicans' equestrian skill and love of fine horses have long been known.

wealthier and more cosmopolitan. Some had studied and traveled in Europe. They adopted continental fashions, the women appearing on festive occasions in expensive gowns and elaborate coiffures, the men in knee breeches, tricorn hats, and, on formal occasions, powdered wigs. To some extent Mexican high society had, like that of Spain, become "Frenchified" through tastes acquired with the Bourbon accession. Also in imitation of European styles were the fancy dress balls and salons in which the elite discoursed on the new philosophies emanating from France and England and conversed about art, literature, music and, inevitably, the economy and politics. Poetry was read and scientific papers were presented. Gossip and expressions of horror at the vulgarities of the masses spiced these displays.

In rural New Spain, where Indians predominated, new tensions appeared. Many of the natives in remote areas, and particularly in southern Mexico, had scarcely been acculturated into Spanish society, but in the rural communities conflicts escalated between indigenous and nonindigenous peoples. Village riots had long been commonplace, but they took on new urgency at the end of the eighteenth century as outsiders expanded their political and economic influence in predominantly Indian villages.

This imposing residence, built in 1528, had been altered by the counts of Santiago de Calimaya by 1770. Today it is the Museum of the City of Mexico.

The Casa de Alfeñique ("Sugar-candy House"), an eighteenth-century showplace in Puebla, a city of many co-lonial treasures.

SOCIAL UNREST

The proliferation of wars during the eighteenth century, far from the shores of Mexico, occa-sioned little more than casual notice, enlivened perhaps by the personal account of a Span-ish veteran. But interest increased with the successful revolt of the English colonists to the north and the outbreak of the French revolution. Later came news of the alarming success of black slaves who overthrew their French masters in Haiti and declared their independence. Informed criollos could hardly fail to observe that in both hemispheric revolts, colonial populations smaller than Mexico's had thrown over imperial powers greater than Spain. But criollos also recognized that their own society was far more heterogeneous than either the United States or Haiti.

The opulence if the rich stood in glaring contrast to the majority who lived in more modest conditions, if not poverty. Indians and castas comprised five-sixths of the total population, but these groups were far from homogeneous. Castas constituted a particularly diverse lot because racial and ethnic hierarchies were not rigidly fixed in practice. Their individual occupational, physical, and cultural circumstances could generate flexibility or immobility in the social system. By the same token, this was true for Indians and Spaniards; class divisions existed within these categories. Most indigenous peoples still had tribute or labor obligations.

A portrait of an aristocratic lady by Miguel Cabrera (1695–1768).

As a whole, the lower classes suffered periodic epidemics and famines, especially in the the worst years between 1779 and 1784. Prices shot up and remained high; the rate of inflation increased. Wages stagnated and fell behind the price increases of basic commodities. To make matters worse, a prolonged wage-price squeeze ran from 1782 to 1816 and probably played a role in late colonial popular uprisings.

Indigenous peoples who still lived in villages sought to preserve community solidarity. When their numbers dropped after conquest, their lands became more vulnerable to sale, rental, or other forms of appropriation by outsiders. Demographic recuperation created new tensions by the mid-eighteenth century, and land values rose. Pueblos increasingly came into conflict with each other and with neighboring estates over access to land and water. Local grievances over land and the payment of taxes (tribute, tithe, and other ecclesiastical duties) frequently erupted in violence, although it was usually confined to the village level. Food shortages and rising prices after 1808 aggravated local tensions, but indigenous protest centered primarily on the defense of local community resources and identity. By this time, the demographic recovery among Indians most likely had slowed due to increased pressures on land.

Scarcity of land could drive Indians to seek work outside their pueblos. A considerable number were attracted to the expanding economy of the Bajío region (parts of Guanajuato, Querétaro, Michoacán, and Jalisco). The cities of this fertile wheat-producing area also boasted a sizable textile industry and some of the richest silver mines. But even there subsistence crises and inflated prices limited opportunities toward the end of the eighteenth century, and indigenous miners, hacienda workers, and artisans found their wages insufficient to meet their needs and obligations.

A typical scene along a provincial road.

Lower-end castas also suffered from the economic vagaries of the late eighteenth century, which included rising unemployment and inflation. Along with blacks and Indians, many casta groups shared the indignities of poverty and discrimination. Together this underclass nursed resentments against the privileged Spanish colonists. Because they were so dispersed, their occasional violent protests did not represent a cohesive threat before the nineteenth century. Some of the disaffected harbored a vague hope that the Spanish king would intervene to punish their local oppressors. They were occasionally attracted by messiahs who wandered the countryside, making millenarian prophecies of a better future and often extorting money from community funds. Popular ideology in Indian communities drew on a mixture of indigenous and imposed traditions, but it clearly differentiated between Indians and outsiders in ethnic and cultural terms. In the face of new changes that threatened rural community values, collective anxieties multiplied to produce more protest and violence, still quite localized.

Criollo grievances, on the other hand, lent themselves to more coordinated expression through local societies and literary clubs established in the eighteenth century to discuss economic innovations that might boost colonial economic production as well as other enlightened ideas of the day. Criollos, in theory, held a secondary position. The peninsulares, or gachupines, had enjoyed special privileges and occupied favored positions in church and state. There was a certain logic in this, as peninsulares tended to have more education and administrative experience. Beyond that, an official with strong ties to the mother country tended to be more loyal to the interests of Spain. Few criollos, on the other hand, had ever seen Spain; and by birth, education, cultural milieu, property, and familial relationships they naturally identified strongly with New Spain. As officials, they might succumb to the temptation of favoring their countrymen, perhaps at the expense of royal interests.

Still, in the seventeenth and early eighteenth centuries the crown appointed some criollos to high office, and others were able to purchase posts put up for bidding. A number even served as judges in the audiencias as well as in other powerful positions. By 1769 at least eight of the twelve members of the Audiencia of Mexico were criollos. They were even more successful in obtaining rank in the church. This promising state of affairs came under some change during the reign of Charles III, who agreed with Gálvez that the colonists' participation in government should be restricted. As a result the number of criollos in the audiencia of the capital had declined by 1780 to only four of sixteen, and later there were even fewer. Criollos could, however, secure rank in the military; by the close of the eighteenth century of a total of 361 officers in the regular regiments 227 were criollos, and in the militia they held 338 commissions of 624 officer positions.

The distinctions they perceived between the gachupines and themselves became increasingly galling to the criollos. Far from accepting the stigma of congenital inferiority that Spaniards had placed on them, however, the criollos asserted their self-worth more vocally in the eighteenth century. Charges of colonial degeneracy supported by some of the pseudoscientific theories of European naturalists were energetically refuted by criollo patriots in the *Gaceta de Literatura*, as well as by the historian and collector Lorenzo Boturini in his 1746 book *Idea de una historia general de la América Septentrional* which extolled the native past and criollo patriotism. Criollos also drew on the work of the exiled Jesuit Father Clavijero, who accurately described New Spain's geography, flora, and fauna and highlighted the region's positive characteristics and achievements. There was reason for pride in their land; foreign travelers had affirmed that Mexico City compared favorably with Spanish cities, even Madrid.

One immediately noticeable difference expressed itself in the language, now losing its Castilian lisp and enriched by Indian words and diminutives. The Mexican diet was distinctive; the architecture of Spain had been modified; customs and dress had acquired their own traits. The Mexican ambience had influenced literature, art, and music. The people, the landscape, the flora, and the fauna were not a replica of Spain. What was originally Spanish had been altered, and while the Spaniards showed disdain for the corruption of Spanish culture, the native-born began to celebrate their homeland. Shunning the socially tainted designation of *criollo*, they considered themselves *americanos* or *mexicanos* and took to satirizing the inequities and absurdities of colonial policies in verse and song.

Despite the grumbling, only the most radical of colonists entertained serious consideration of rebellion against Spain. Others complained about the imposition of new taxes and the administrative changes that burdened them. But while some criollos had been hurt by royal economic policies, others had prospered and, all things considered, the native-born Spaniards were better off than ever before. Most still felt a personal relationship to the monarchy and most were devoted to the church which, in addition to attending to their spiritual needs, had been lending them money.

What the criollos really wanted was to be on an equal footing with the peninsulares or, better yet, somehow to replace them altogether. Socially elevated by virtue of complexion and lineage, most criollos wanted to maintain the racial hierarchy. Their attitudes toward the lower masses were no less critical than the peninsulares' opinion of the criollos. In no way did the criollos advocate social equality for those below them. As the visiting German scientist Alexander von Humboldt observed in the late colonial period, "In America, the skin, more or less white, is what dictates the class that an individual occupies in society. A white, even if he rides barefoot on horseback, considers himself a member of the nobility of the country."[1] Rebellion evoked the specters of anarchy and race war in which the colored masses, who made little distinction between gachupín and criollo, might rise against all white persons.

CHURCH AND STATE

Crown policies that had aimed to diminish the traditional power, wealth, and prestige of the church did not always sit well with criollos, and many were particularly rankled by the crown's expulsion of the Jesuits—those teachers and defenders of their *patria chica* (local world). In the end, some criollos benefited from the opportunity to acquire former Jesuit properties, but many more would be affected negatively by the Act of Consolidation of 1804.

After the expulsion of the Jesuits, the crown continued to complain about the extensive urban and rural properties held by branches of the church. Royal officials claimed these holdings were not being used to their potential, thus obstructing government efforts to stimulate

---

1   Quoted in Magnus Mörner, *Race Mixture in the History of Latin America* (Boston, MA, 1967), 55–56.

the economy. Therefore, in 1804 the crown required the church to call in all the loans it had made using charitable funds. Royal officials would receive the principal and pay interest on it. Many of these loans had been made to criollos in the form of mortgages, and most colonists were hard-pressed to come up with the cash to pay them off. The Act of Consolidation represented a serious threat to the interests of a substantial portion of the Mexican elite since about half of the colony's available capital was tied up in these loans. Nonetheless, several million pesos were collected within a few years, financial structures were debilitated, and some criollos were reduced to financial ruin.

The act, although intended to solve liquidity problems, also severely constrained the activities of the church and embittered many clerics in the process. In particular, the lower echelon of parish priests became alienated as their perquisites were threatened, and they communicated their disillusionment with crown policies to their flocks. Another source of disenchantment for the masses lay in the church hierarchy's cooperation with Bourbon officials in curtailing popular religious celebrations and devotions, at a time when the devotion to the Virgin of Guadalupe flourished as a form of popular religious nationalism.

CONSPIRACIES IN NEW SPAIN AND CONFUSION IN SPAIN

Resistance to Spanish domination took many forms throughout the colonial period. Most often it transpired through small acts of defiance, but a number of rebellions and conspiracies challenged Spanish rule before the outbreak of insurgency in 1810. Some posed serious threats to Spain's hegemony, while others were trivial affairs. At least in a few there was mention of independence, but such movements were considered aberrations and slightly insane by the general populace. Most of the disturbances found their origins in local grievances and lacked broad support. However, some of the Indian rebellions attracted numerous ardent followers— with violent and bloody consequences. Examples of native rebellions that occurred many generations after contact are rare, but they did occur. In the northern province of New Mexico, the Pueblo Revolt of 1680 drove out the Spaniards for more than a decade; Tzeltal Mayas shook the colonial system in Chiapas in 1712; the Yaqui Rebellion of 1740 slowed Spanish expansion in Sonora; and a Maya insurrection led by Jacinto Canek threatened Yucatán in 1761. In each of these cases, discontent spilled outside the village to encompass larger ethnic groups when Indians saw their way of life overwhelmingly threatened. The excesses and abuses of elites had violated the many accommodations they had already made to colonial rule. Messianic leadership that drew on native and Christian beliefs also played a role in these revolts.

Grievances abounded in the last decades of the eighteenth century, but sporadic and localized late colonial protests by castas and Indians did not yet provide the catalyst for widespread rebellion. Neither were criollos ready for a complete break with Spain.

In 1794, the popular Viceroy Revillagigedo was replaced by the vain, corrupt marqués de Branciforte. His appointment aroused anger, ventilated in September in wall posters appearing in the capital. The messages acclaimed the ideals of the French revolution, and rumors of a plot spread throughout the city. In at least two cases, different configurations of peninsulares and criollos did, in fact, plot to overthrow Spanish rule, but few colonists entertained radically liberal designs.

María Luisa of Parma, the queen of Spain, painted by Goya. At age fourteen she married her cousin, who became Charles IV.

Ultimately the deterioration of Spain's position in Europe brought on a crisis. At the death of his father, in 1788, Charles IV had become king, and he quickly lent weight to the commonplace that great men seldom beget sons of their equal. He was inept and had little apparent interest in ruling the empire. His subjects grew weary of him and impatiently awaited the succession of Prince Ferdinand. The queen also tired of him and found solace in the intimate company of a handsome provincial guardsman named Manuel de Godoy. The clever, ambitious Godoy maneuvered himself at the age of twenty-five into the rank of prime minister. He then proceeded to make a series of unwise alliances, which finally encouraged the invasion of Spain in 1808 by the troops of Napoleon Bonaparte. When Madrid fell to the French army, Charles IV and his son became prisoners, and shortly thereafter the king abdicated in favor of the prince, making Ferdinand VII a king without a throne. Napoleon appointed his own brother Joseph to rule over Spain, while much of the country resisted. Some Spanish patriots formed a government in exile in the fortified city of Cádiz.

When news of the king's capture and the occupation of Spain by the French reached New Spain, confusion reigned as to who was to rule the colony. Joseph Bonaparte as sovereign was unthinkable, but what was the logical alternative? Although a few saw the situation as a golden opportunity to gain independence, the majority of the colonists advocated the formation of a caretaker government to run affairs in the name of Ferdinand VII until such time as the king was released. The viceroy seemed the obvious person to assume rule in Mexico, but the audiencia insisted on sharing power. Eventually, in cities throughout the Spanish American colonies, the cabildos asserted their own claims. They argued that historically, when a legitimate ruler was lacking, provisional bodies, or *juntas*, formed to manage local affairs. Following such a bold proclamation, several members of the cabildo of Mexico City were arrested.

Viceroy José de Iturrigaray had shrewdly assessed the developments, looking for a compromise that would please the criollos while keeping New Spain under Spanish control. When he signaled he would allow criollos to form an assembly, Spaniards from the audiencia and the heavily peninsular merchant guild decided to act. On the evening of August 15, 1808, a small band of Spaniards forcibly removed the viceroy from his palace and packed him off to Veracruz to await passage to Spain, where he was later imprisoned. The peninsulares also arrested half a dozen prominent criollo leaders. Replacing Iturrigaray was Pedro Garibay, a senile field marshal in his eightieth year who had to contend with various militant factions.

The instability of government in 1809 only added to the anxieties arising from a threatening economic picture. Insufficient rain fell that summer, and the resulting shortage of corn caused prices in some areas to triple their normal level. The consequences were far-reaching, affecting, for example, mining production, since there was too little food for draft animals, and workers had to be laid off. Interrupted commerce with the occupied mother country further dislocated the Mexican economy. Taken altogether, it was a time of confusion and stress.

Among the more sophisticated criollos in Mexico City the mood remained conservative. They might question the traditional order, but rebellion against the crown was a painful and perhaps frightening thought since it evoked the possibility of mob rule. Attitudes in the provinces were somewhat different. More isolated from ritual and pomp, more independent, and more closely identified with the land, criollos in smaller communities had a more fully developed sense of the patria chica where they wanted to run their own affairs. Provincial criollos, often under the auspices of the new intendants, had already been meeting to discuss ways to modernize the economy and expand production and trade. They undertook scientific surveys of local resources and adopted some new technologies. Along with these innovations, they could not help but be aware of the notions of freedom and equality espoused not only by the northern European Enlightenment and the French revolution. Even in Spain where the French occupation had undermined centralized authority, a revitalized political vocabulary included terms like liberty and representation. The destabilization

The great central plaza of Mexico City, popularly known as the Zócalo. It is bordered by the cathedral, the vice-regal (now the national) palace, the cabildo quarters, and other public buildings. See also the cover photo for this book.

of hierarchical chains of command in Spain and Mexico made local government officials, including indigenous cabildos, more conscious of the possibilities and pitfalls of political change. Royal officials closely watched their gatherings suspecting that they were conspiratorial. One plot, which included clergymen, military officers, and Indian groups, came to light in Valladolid in 1809. Although the principals were imprisoned for a time, most surfaced in the vanguard of the insurrection that was to follow shortly.

In 1810 important cities of southern Spain fell to French troops, compromising without question the sovereignty of the nation. In that same year it also came to the attention of royal authorities in Mexico City that a conspiracy had formed in Querétaro. Its ringleaders included an aging, dissident priest named Hidalgo. Once again the government dispatched troops to deal with yet another provincial incident.

RECOMMENDED FOR FURTHER STUDY

Archer, Christon, ed. *The Birth of Modern Mexico, 1780–1814*. Wilmington, DE: Scholarly Resources, 2003.

Arrom, Sylvia Marina. *Containing the Poor: The Mexico City Poor House, 1774–1881*. Durham, NC: Duke University Press, 2000.

_____. *The Women of Mexico City, 1790–1857*. Stanford, CA: Stanford University Press, 1985.

Brading, David A. *Church and State in Bourbon Mexico: The Diocese of Michoacán, 1749–1810*. New York: Cambridge University Press, 1994.

_____. *Haciendas and Ranchos in the Mexican Bajío: León, 1700–1860.* New York: Cambridge University Press, 1978.

_____. *The Origins of Mexican Nationalism.* New York: Cambridge University Press, 1985.

_____. *Miners and Merchants in Bourbon Mexico, 1763–1810.* New York: Cambridge University Press, 1971.

Brown, Tracy L. *Pueblo Indians and Spanish Colonial Authority in Eighteenth-Century New Mexico.* Tucson: University of Arizona Press, 2013.

Burkholder, Mark A., and D. S. Chandler. *From Impotence to Authority: The Spanish Crown and the American Audiencias, 1687–1808.* Columbia: University of Missouri Press, 1977.

Cañizares Esguerra, Jorge. *How to Write the History of the New World: Histories, Epistemologies, and Identities in the Eighteenth-Century Atlantic World.* Stanford, CA: Stanford University Press, 2001.

Cooper, Donald B. *Epidemic Disease in Mexico City, 1761–1813.* Austin: University of Texas Press, 1965.

Couturier, Edith B. *The Silver King: The Remarkable Life of the Count of Regla in Colonial Mexico.* Albuquerque: University of New Mexico Press, 2003.

Deeds, Susan M. "Indigenous Rebellions on the Northern Mexican Mission Frontier: From First-Generation to Later Colonial Responses." In *Contested Ground: Comparative Frontiers on the Northern and Southern Edges of the Spanish Empire,* edited by Donna J. Guy and Thomas E. Sheridan, 32–51. Tucson: University of Arizona Press, 1998.

Ducey, Michael T. *A Nation of Villages: Riot and Rebellion in the Mexican Huasteca, 1750–1850.* Tucson: University of Arizona Press, 2004.

Echenberg, Myron. *Humboldt's Mexico: In the Footsteps of the Illustrious German Scientific Traveller.* Montreal-Kingston, CA: McGill-Queen's University Press, 2017.

Gosner, Kevin. *Soldiers of the Virgin. The Moral Economy of a Colonial Maya Rebellion.* Tucson: University of Arizona Press, 1992.

Hamnett, Brian R. *Roots of Insurgency, Mexican Regions, 1750–1824.* New York: Cambridge University Press, 1985.

Humboldt, Alexander von. *Political Essay on the Kingdom of New Spain.* Edited, with an introduction, by Mary Maples Dunn. New York: Alfred A. Knopf, 1972.

Knaut, Andrew L. *The Pueblo Revolt of 1680: Conquest and Resistance in Seventeenth-Century New Mexico.* Norman: University of Oklahoma Press, 1995.

Ladd, Doris. *The Making of a Strike: Mexican Silver Workers' Struggle in Real del Monte, 1788–1775.* Lincoln: University of Nebraska Press, 1988.

_____. *The Mexican Nobility at Independence, 1780–1826.* Austin: University of Texas Press, 1976.

Lafaye, Jacques. *Quetzalcóatl and Guadalupe: The Formation of Mexican National Consciousness, 1531–1813.* Translated by Benjamin Keen, with an introduction by Octavio Paz. Chicago: University of Chicago Press, 1976.

Lindley, Richard B. *Haciendas and Economic Development: Guadalajara, Mexico, at Independence.* Austin: University of Texas Press, 1983.

MacLachlan, Colin M. *Criminal Justice in Eighteenth Century Mexico: A Study of the Tribunal of the Acordada.* Berkeley: University of California Press, 1974.

Mörner, Magnus. *Race Mixture in the History of Latin America.* Boston, MA: Little, Brown & Company, 1967.

Scardaville, Michael C. "Alcohol Abuse and Tavern Reform in Late Colonial Mexico City." *Hispanic American Historical Review* 60/4 (1980): 643–71.

Schroeder, Susan, ed. *Native Resistance and the Pax Colonial in New Spain.* Lincoln: University of Nebraska Press, 1998.

Sheridan, Thomas E., ed. *Empire of Sand: The Seri Indians and the Struggle for Spanish Sonora, 1645–1803.* Tucson: University of Arizona Press, 1999.

Stein, Stanley J., and Barbara H. Stein. *The Colonial Heritage of Latin America: Essays on Economic Dependence in Perspective.* New York: Oxford University Press, 1970.

_____. *Crisis in an Atlantic Empire: Spain and New Spain, 1808–1810*. Baltimore, MD: Johns Hopkins University Press, 2014.

Tutino, John. *From Insurrection to Revolution in Mexico: Social Bases of Agrarian Violence, 1750-1940*. Princeton, NJ: Princeton University Press, 1986.

_____. *Making a New World: Founding Capitalism in the Bajío and Spanish North America*. Durham, NC: Duke University Press, 2011.

Van Young, Eric. "Agrarian Rebellion and Defense of Community: Meaning and Collective Violence in Late Colonial and Independence-Era Mexico." *Journal of Social History* 27/2 (1993): 245–69.

Villella, Peter B. *Indigenous Elites and Creole Identity in Colonial Mexico, 1500–1800*. New York: Cambridge University Press, 2016.

Yetman, David. *Conflict in Colonial Sonora: Indians, Priests, and Settlers*. Albuquerque: University of New Mexico Press, 2012.

CHAPTER 15

THE WARS FOR INDEPENDENCE

HIDALGO AND EARLY SUCCESS

Born in 1753 to a moderately well-to-do criollo family, Miguel Hidalgo y Costilla spent his first 12 years on the Hacienda de San Diego Corralejo in Guanajuato, where his father served the owner as *mayordomo* (resident manager). Encouraged by his father, the boy moved with his older brother, José Joaquín, to Valladolid (today Morelia) and matriculated at the Jesuit Colegio of San Francisco Javier. The brothers had been at their studies only two years when shocking news reached the city: King Charles III of Spain had banished the Jesuits from Spain and all Spanish possessions in the New World. Left without teachers, the boys had to interrupt their schooling, but within a year they had enrolled in the diocesan Colegio of San Nicolás Obispo, also in Valladolid and one of the nineteen colegios and seminaries in Mexico that prepared students for degrees eventually to be awarded by the Royal and Pontifi- cal University in Mexico City. Young Miguel Hidalgo steeped himself in rhetoric, Latin, and theology and found time to study Indian languages. Upon receiving his bachelor's in 1774, he immediately began preparations for the priesthood. The bishop celebrated his sacrament of ordination in the fall of 1778.

Enthusiastic and self-assured, the twenty-eight-year-old priest returned to Valladolid to teach at the Colegio of San Nicolás Obispo, where he eventually became rector. But he was scarcely exemplary from the church's point of view. Before the turn of the century the Holy Office of the Inquisition had been apprised, by rumor and fact, of a curate whose orthodoxy was suspect, who questioned priestly celibacy, who read prohibited books, who indulged in gambling and enjoyed dancing, who challenged the infallibility of the Pope, who doubted the veracity of the virgin birth, who dared to suggest that fornication out of wedlock was not a sin, who referred to the Spanish king as a tyrant, and who had mistresses with whom he fathered several children. Hidalgo was hailed before the Inquisition in 1800, but nothing could be proved.

Hidalgo's future fortunes and misfortunes were cast when, in 1803, he accepted the curacy of the small parish of Dolores, in present-day Guanajuato. Devoting minimal time to the spiritual needs of his parishioners, Father Hidalgo concerned himself primarily with improving their economic potential. He introduced new industries in Dolores: tile making, tanning, carpentry, wool weaving, beekeeping, silk growing, and wine making. He preferred to spend his spare time reading and engaging his fellow criollos in informed debate. A few years after his arrival in Dolores, Hidalgo's path crossed that of Ignacio Allende, a thirty-five-year-old firebrand and a captain in the Queen's Cavalry Regiment in nearby Guanajuato. Allende took the priest into his confidence and introduced him to a coterie of friends among whom were Juan de Aldama, also a military man; Miguel Domínguez, a former corregidor of Querétaro; and his wife, Doña Josefa Ortiz de Domínguez, remembered in Mexican history as *La Corregidora*. The most celebrated female of the independence struggles, Josefa Ortiz de Domínguez was certainly not the only woman who played a role. Many others participated in planning activities and carried messages between rebels, and some were imprisoned for their activities. La Corregidora herself spent several years in jail. And countless women of all classes would provide food and supplies for combatants in the wars to come.

The group had organized a "literary club," as had others in cities throughout New Spain. In their meetings, they discussed ideas coming from Europe, especially those related to improving local economies. The club of Hidalgo and Allende attracted individuals across the Bajío, a region that covers the modern-day states of Querétaro, Guanajuato, and part of Michoacán and San Luis Potosí. Agriculture, mining, and incipient industry had expanded exponentially in the eighteenth century. However, a prolonged drought at the end of the first decade of the nineteenth century had slowed agricultural growth. High inflation had driven up prices since 1780 with no corresponding increase in wages, creating a large oppressed indigenous and casta labor force.

For many progressive thinkers in the Bajío, reform alone would not be sufficient to fix the problems. They began to plot the separation of New Spain from the mother country and set the date of December 8, 1810 for an uprising. Although the conspirators were all admonished to hold their tongues, Marino Galván, a postal clerk, leaked the news to

Miguel Hidalgo y Costilla (1753–1811). One of the most renowned individuals in nineteenth-century Mexican history, Father Hidalgo provided the initial spark for the independence movement.

his superior who, in turn, informed the audiencia in Mexico City. The forewarned Spanish authorities moved on September 13, when they searched the house of Epigmenio González in Querétaro, found bountiful arms and ammunition, and ordered the arrest of the panic-stricken owner. The events of the next few days are known to every Mexican schoolchild, for they are repeated every September 16 amid a wide array of Independence Day celebrations.

Doña Josefa entrusted Ignacio Pérez with the task of carrying the news of the arrest to Ignacio Allende in San Miguel. Not finding him at home, the messenger relayed the news to Juan de Aldama, who immediately set out to inform Father Hidalgo in Dolores. When, about two o'clock on the morning of September 16, he arrived at the priest's house, Aldama found Allende there also. The three realized that orders for their own arrest had probably been issued and decided to strike out for independence at once. Hidalgo rang the church bells, summoning his parishioners to mass earlier than usual that morning. Assembled at the little church in Dolores, the Indians and mestizos, including a group of prisoners released from the local jail, listened to Hidalgo explain their plight and call them to action. The exact words of this most famous of all Mexican speeches are not known or, rather, they are reproduced in almost as many variations as there are historians to reproduce them. But the essential spirit of the message is this:

> My children: a new dispensation comes to us today. Will you receive it? Will you free yourselves? Will you recover the lands stolen 300 years ago from your forefathers by the hated Spaniards? We must act at once. . . . Will you not defend your religion and your rights as true patriots? Long live our Lady of Guadalupe! Death to bad government! Death to the gachupines!

The immediate response to the *Grito de Dolores* was enthusiastic in areas of the Bajío. With Hidalgo at their head, the diverse band of poorly armed Indians and mestizos struck out for San Miguel, picking up hundreds of recruits along the way. When they stopped for a rest about noon at the hamlet of Atotonilco, Hidalgo entered the local church and emerged carrying a banner of the Virgin de Guadalupe. The devotion to the Virgin of Guadalupe as the patron of all New Spain had expanded in the eighteenth century, especially into Indian communities. This emblem may have attracted Indians and poor castas to the revolt, but their economic circumstances were most compelling.

By dusk Hidalgo's band had taken San Miguel without difficulty, for the local militia joined the rebels. The day's dramatic events should have ended with the imprisonment of the local Spanish populace, but as night fell the unpredicted happened. Hidalgo's army, composed primarily of rural Indians but also castas, many of whom were skilled laborers, craftsmen, and muleteers, became a mob. They moved through the streets with their clubs, slings, machetes, bows and arrows, lances, and occasional firearms, pillaging the towns. Hidalgo could not reason with them, and only Ignacio Allende, racing through the streets on horseback and warning prompt retribution, succeeding containing the passions of the crowd. By morning, chaos had begun to subside, but the problem would prove recurrent during the next few months. From San Miguel the rebels moved on Celaya, and after taking the town the mob again subjected the gachupín population to pillage. Celaya was merely a rehearsal for a major encounter at Guanajuato, where the rebel army would be seriously opposed for the first time.

Hidalgo asked the intendant of Guanajuato, Juan Antonio de Riaño, to surrender the city, and he offered full protection to the Spanish citizenry in return. But the news from San Miguel and Celaya had already reached Guanajuato, and Riaño knew that Hidalgo could give no such assurance. He decided to make a stand and congregated the Spanish population in the Alhóndiga de Granaditas, the public granary. Although his people were greatly outnumbered, he believed they could hold out until reinforcements from Mexico City arrived.

Shortly before noon on September 28 Hidalgo began his approach to Guanajuato. He was joined by hundreds of workers from the surrounding silver mines. As the first wave of foot soldiers rushed the improvised fortress, Riaño gave the order to open fire. Hundreds of rebels were cut down by the intendant's artillery. The attackers, led by Juan José Martínez (known affectionately by his nickname El Pípila), then gathered up a bunch of soft pine torches used in the mines and laid them at the foot of the granary's wooden gate. They set fire to them and, as the gate was consumed, a few Indians charged through into the central patio. They were quickly followed by hundreds, perhaps even a thousand. Within the hour most of the refugees were dead. They were stripped, and their naked bodies dragged unceremoniously through the streets to the nearby cemetery of Belén, where they were buried in makeshift graves.

An eyewitness to the events of that day was eighteen-year-old Lucas Alamán, later one of Mexico's most renowned conservative statesmen and historians. In his multivolume history of Mexico he recollected the following:

> This pillage was more merciless than would have been expected of a foreign army. The miserable scene of that sad night was lighted by torches. All that could be heard was the pounding by which doors were opened and the ferocious howls of the rabble when the doors gave way. They dashed in in triumph to rob commercial products, furniture, everyday clothing, and all manner of things. The women fled terrorized to the houses of neighbors, climbing along the roof tops without yet knowing if that afternoon they had lost a father or husband at the granary. . . . The plaza and the streets were littered with broken pieces of furniture and other things robbed from the stores, of liquor spilled after the masses had drunk themselves into a stupor.[1]

It took a day and a half to restore order. The casualty figures were tremendous: over 500 Spaniards and 2,000 rebels, largely Indians, were killed. Hidalgo and Allende now felt strong enough to split their army into two striking forces, and within a month they had captured Zacatecas, San Luis Potosí, and Valladolid. By late October Hidalgo had martialed an army of about eighty thousand marching on Mexico City. The anticipated battle took place on October 30 at the Monte de las Cruces, and there Hidalgo proved that sheer numbers could overcome a small, well-equipped, and disciplined professional army. The Spaniards were forced to retreat back into the city, and as Hidalgo camped on the hills overlooking the capital, he pondered what to do next.

---

1   Lucas Alamán, *Historia de México* Vol. I (Mexico City, Mexico, 1942), 403–4.

A decisive strike at the capital might have ended the Wars for Independence after only a month and a half of fighting. But Hidalgo had taken heavy losses at Las Cruces, he was short on ammunition, and he was uneasy about turning his undisciplined forces loose on Mexico City. Over Allende's objections he decided to order a retreat rather than follow up his victory. Moving northwest toward Guadalajara, many of the rebel troops began to desert. At the same time Spanish forces under General Félix Calleja started to regroup. Guadalajara fell to the insurgents unopposed, but in January 1811 the royalist troops from the south caught up with the rebels. Again Hidalgo and Allende had the numerical superiority, but royal troops under the disciplined General Calleja routed the rebel army.

Hidalgo, Allende, and a number of other leaders, recognizing the futility of trying to regroup their forces, moved northward, hoping to obtain relief in Coahuila and Texas. But their days were numbered. In March 1811, near the scorched desert town of Monclova (Coahuila), they were ambushed by a Spanish detachment. Captured by Governor Manuel Salcedo of Texas, the rebels were marched in chains to Chihuahua, where Allende and the other non-clerical leaders were immediately executed as traitors. Hidalgo, because he was a priest, underwent a trial by the Inquisition. Finding him guilty of heresy and treason, the court defrocked him and turned him over to the secular arm for execution. At dawn on July 31 the firing squad did its job. Hidalgo's corpse was decapitated and his head, fastened to a pole, was displayed on the charred wall of the granary in Guanajuato as an object lesson to potential rebels.

Meanwhile important events were taking place outside of Mexico, where other Spanish American colonies had declared independence. In Spain, the juntas ruling in the name of the king had formed a body called the Cortes de Cádiz to address the needs of governance until Ferdinand VII resumed power. Delegates arrived in Cádiz from all over Spain and from Spanish America, including representatives from Mexico. For the next two years, they worked to produce Spain's first liberal constitution, designed to prevent arbitrary rule, abolish noble privilege, and create a limited monarchy with parliamentary features. The Constitution of 1812 offered representation (although not equal citizenship) to the colonies. The idea appealed to those criollos who did not desire a complete break with the metropolis.

MORELOS AND THE DECLINE OF REBEL FORTUNES

With the death of Hidalgo the rebel leadership was assumed by another parish priest, José María Morelos y Pavón, a mestizo. But by this time sympathy for the cause of independence had waned considerably. Many wealthy criollos had become alarmed at the radical twist the revolution seemed to be taking within Mexico, and still looked to a solution that would conserve ties with Spain. Some criollos favored the elimination of their Spanish rivals but not at the expense of being swept up in some kind of social revolution. They recognized that to the downtrodden Indians and mestizos their white skin, if not their social position, was indistinguishable from that of the gachupines.

When the mantle of insurgent leadership fell to Morelos, he knew full well that he could not count on much criollo support. Unlike his predecessor, he trained a small but effective army that relied primarily on guerrilla tactics to keep the enemy off guard. Dividing his

José María Morelos (1765–1815). With Hidalgo's execution in 1811, Morelos assumed the leadership of the independence movement. Although a strong supporter of Hidalgo, he had very different ideas about how to wage a war and how to constitute a new nation.

attention almost equally between military and political matters, he devised a strategy that called for the encirclement of Mexico City. By the spring of 1813 the circle was completed, isolating the capital from both coasts. Morelos then called for a congress to meet in Chilpancingo (Guerrero) to discuss plans for the nation once the Spaniards were driven out.

Some of the conservative criollos were still unsure of the direction in which Morelos wished to move, but his speech to the delegates at Chilpancingo cleared the air. Morelos invoked the names of the ancient emperors Moctezuma and Cuauhtémoc and implored the delegates to avenge the shameful disgrace of the last three centuries. The congress formally declared independence and agreed upon a series of principles that should be incorporated into a new constitution: sovereignty should reside in the people, and male suffrage should be universal; slavery and all caste systems should be abolished; government monopolies should be abolished and replaced by a 5 percent income tax; all judicial torture should end. Many of these provisions went far beyond those of Spain's Constitution of 1812. The nineteenth-century liberalism of the delegates was tempered only by their insistence that Roman Catholicism should be made the official religion of the new state.

But while the delegates at Chilpancingo engaged in political debate, General Calleja and his Spanish army assumed a new military offensive. In six months' time the Spaniards broke the circle around Mexico City and captured Valladolid, Oaxaca, Cuernavaca, Cuautla, Taxco, and even Chilpancingo itself. The delegates hurriedly packed their bags and moved to the more secure environs of Apatzingán, where they promulgated the constitution they had already largely agreed upon. But what the constitution promised Mexicans on paper the viceroy's army denied them on the field of battle. Meanwhile, in 1814 King Ferdinand VII abolished the 1812 constitution as soon as he was restored to power. In the fall of 1815, Morelos was captured by an enemy detachment and escorted to Mexico City, where he was tried for treason and, like Hidalgo before him, shorn of his religious vestments and executed by a firing squad.

For the next five years the independence movement consisted of little more than sporadic guerrilla fighting. A number of independent bands, inadequately supplied and without any meaningful coordination or even a common vision for the future of Mexico, operated in isolated mountain pockets and the heavily foliaged areas of the coast. The Spanish army was unprepared to conduct an effective counterinsurgency campaign, and the rebels' lack of organization proved to be a strength. Not even the viceroy's newly introduced "flying brigades" (*cuerpos volantes*) could match the mobility of guerrillas conducting hit-and-run warfare. While never able to capture major cities or to turn back the viceregal army, the two most effective independence leaders, Guadalupe Victoria (with two thousand ragged troops in the mountains of Puebla and Veracruz) and Vicente Guerrero (with one thousand men in Oaxaca), seemed themselves invulnerable to defeat. While guerrilla bands of two hundred to three hundred insurgents proliferated and began dominating more and more of the

Territory under Insurgent Control, 1811–13

countryside, the chore of the counterinsurgency army became increasingly difficult, and demoralized troops began to defect. Nevertheless, in 1819 the Spanish viceroy in Mexico City, Juan Ruiz de Apodaca, reported to the Spanish king, Ferdinand VII, that the situation was so well under control that he anticipated no further need for reinforcements.

ITURBIDE AND THE PLAN DE IGUALA

King Ferdinand VII was not concerned only with events in Mexico. He found himself facing insurrection in Central America, the Caribbean, and South America as well. To quell all of these movements, he assembled a powerful fighting force for service in the Americas. In 1820, with these troops facing defeat in many of the colonies, a military revolt in Spain forced the king to restore the Constitution of 1812. When the conservative criollos in New Spain learned that King Ferdinand had accepted the constitution, many for the first time decided to cast their lot with the revolution for independence. Ironically, a conservative colony would thus gain independence from a temporarily liberal mother country.

Of the numerous defections from the cause of Spain to that of an independent Mexico the most significant was that of Agustín de Iturbide. Born in Valladolid of conservative Spanish parents in 1783, Iturbide early displayed an interest in pursuing a military career. He entered the army at the age of fourteen and soon received a royal commission as a lieutenant in the infantry regiment of Valladolid. When Father Hidalgo issued his Grito de Dolores in 1810, Lieutenant Iturbide decided to support the crown in its fight against the rabble that followed the banner of Guadalupe. For almost a decade he fought against the insurgents and on several occasions distinguished himself in the zeal with which he persecuted the enemy.

In the fall of 1820 Viceroy Apodaca invited Iturbide, by then a colonel, to discuss plans for a new offensive against Vicente Guerrero. Iturbide was placed in charge of 2,500 men and left Mexico City for the south in late November. After a few indecisive skirmishes, he asked Guerrero to a meeting during which he proposed to make peace—not war. Iturbide's price for the treason he was contemplating was to dictate the terms of independence. But Guerrero was not easily convinced of either Iturbide's sincerity or his ideas for an independent Mexico. A series of conferences had to be held before the guerrilla warrior and the new convert could issue, on February 24, 1821, their Plan de Iguala.[2] To attract conservative support, it praised the Spanish endeavor in New Spain and held out Spain as the most Catholic, holy, heroic, and magnanimous of nations. But after three hundred years of tutelage it was time for Mexico to strike out on its own. The plan contained twenty-three articles but only three major guarantees: first, the independent Mexican nation would be organized as a constitutional monarchy, and the crown would be offered to King Ferdinand or some other appropriate European prince; second, the Roman Catholic religion would be given a monopoly on the spiritual life of the country, and its clergymen would retain all the rights and privileges they currently enjoyed; and third criollos and peninsulares would be treated equally in the new state while caste distinctions would be abolished. To uphold the promises, a new army,

---

2   In Mexican history revolutionary movements are almost always preceded by a plan that outlines the principles to be embraced. These *pronunciamientos* have been described as part petition and part rebellion, designed to intimidate those in power and attract a wide base of a support.

the Ejército de las Tres Garantías (the Army of the Three Guarantees) would be placed directly under Iturbide's command.

In the Plan de Iguala, Iturbide played his cards with consummate skill. The proposal was imaginative in its conception. Mexicans were weary of a decade of war. The liberal Constitution of Apatzingán had failed to attract sufficient support, and it was clear that to succeed the movement needed help from the conservatives. With liberalism temporarily manifesting itself in the mother country, the timing was perfect. In seeking to reconcile the interests of opposing factions, the plan changed the nature of the fight for independence. Instead of urging death to the gachupines, Iturbide curried their favor. He recognized and capitalized upon the fact that both liberals, who favored the establishment of a republic, and conservatives, who preferred an absolute monarchy, could compromise on this plan as it held out the best hope for independence, something that both groups wanted most.

Within several weeks the broadly based plan began to yield its first dividends as converts began to arrive. Military contingents throughout the country joined the Army of the Three Guarantees, priests urged cooperation from the pulpits, Masonic lodges pledged support, and thousands of drifters again took up the cause. But, most importantly, the community of Spaniards, some fifty thousand strong, found promise in the Plan de Iguala and pledged support. When Guanajuato, Puebla, Durango, Oaxaca, Querétaro, and Zacatecas all fell to the insurgents, Viceroy Apodaca tendered his resignation. His replacement, Juan de O'Donojú, realizing that New Spain was irrevocably lost, signed a treaty that, for the most part, accepted the terms of the Plan de Iguala. The highest-ranking Spanish official in New Spain had thus recognized Mexican independence. But Iturbide, thinking of the future, incorporated into the Treaty of Córdoba one important modification. If no suitable European monarch could be persuaded to accept the Mexican crown, a Mexican congress could choose a Mexican emperor instead. The commander of the Army of the Three Guarantees had begun to feather his own nest.

THE EFFECTS OF THE WARS FOR INDEPENDENCE

Iturbide's triumphal entry into Mexico City in September 1821 marked the end of eleven years of war. The *Gaceta Imperial de México* proclaimed theatrically that not even Rome in its days of grandeur had ever witnessed such an exultant spectacle. Upon receiving gold keys to the city the commander-in-chief explained that they would be used to lock the doors of irreligion, disunion, and despotism and open the gateway to general happiness. But the first door Iturbide opened in Mexico City was that of the great cathedral on the central plaza. Cementing his future relationship with the archbishop, he received communion and listened to a Te Deum offered in his honor.

From the campaigns, Mexico acquired not only its share of heroes and traitors but also a legacy of political violence and economic devastation. The wars exerted an incalculable influence on Mexico's future. The army had converted the dream of independence into reality and was by no means ready to step aside to allow civilians to control the nation's destiny. For a full century the Mexican military would be very much involved in the political processes of government and would bargain with opposing factions for a share of the nation's wealth. The military clique would constitute a ready instrument for unscrupulous politicians to use for their own purposes. More important yet, the basic issues separating different segments of society had not been resolved. Competing groups had cooperated long enough to achieve a common end but, once independence was achieved, the alliance cobbled together by the Plan de Iguala proved transitory. For some the revolution was simply anticolonial in nature and therefore it was over; others wanted its momentum to be carried into the arena of political and economic reform. The internal struggles between liberals and conservatives, between republicans and monarchists, between federalists and centralists, and between anticlericals and proponents of clerical privilege would consume the energies of the neophyte nation for decades and draw many non-elites into their armed conflicts.

If in 1821 it was difficult to predict the instability that was about to ensue, the roots of discord could be traced back into the colonial past for criollos, castas, and indigenous groups. The armies of the independence period consisted of Indians (more than half) and castas (just under a fourth). Although their goals were different from those of the elites, the rural masses had been active in the fighting, in pursuit of materially improving their lives and resolving their local grievances over the preservation of their communities and traditions, culturally mixed as they were by the end of the colonial period. Their participation garnered them little advantage as their concerns were ignored and their privations increased after independence. They could take little solace in the fact that the politically articulate groups in Mexico City demonstrated precious little ability to govern even themselves.

RECOMMENDED FOR FURTHER STUDY

Almaráz, Felix D. *Tragic Cavalier: Governor Manuel Salcedo of Texas, 1808–1813.* Austin: University of Texas Press, 1971.

Anna, Timothy E. *The Fall of Royal Government in Mexico City.* Lincoln: University of Nebraska Press, 1978.

Archer, Christon I. *The Birth of Modern Mexico, 1780–1824.* Wilmington, DE: Scholarly Resources, Inc., 2003.

Benson, Nettie Lee, ed. *Mexico and the Spanish Cortes, 1810–1822.* Austin: University of Texas Press, 1966.

Ducey, Michael T. "Village, Nation, and Constitution: Insurgent Politics in Papantla, Veracruz, 1810–1821." *Hispanic American Historical Review* 79/3 (1999): 463–93.

Fowler, Will. *Forceful Negotiations: The Origins of the Pronunciamiento in Nineteenth-Century Mexico.* Lincoln: University of Nebraska Press, 2011.

Fowler, Will, ed. *Malcontents, Rebels, and Pronunciados: The Politics of Insurrection in Nineteenth-Century Mexico.* Lincoln: University of Nebraska Press, 2012.

Guedea, Virginia. "The Old Colonialism Ends, the New Colonialism Begins." In *The Oxford History of Mexico,* edited by Michael C. Meyer and William H. Beezley, 265–84. New York: Oxford University Press, rev. 2010.

Hamill, Hugh M. "Caudillism and Independence: A Symbiosis?" In *The Independence of Mexico and the Creation of the New Nation,* edited by Jaime E. Rodríguez O., 163–74. Los Angeles, CA: UCLA Latin American Center, 1989.

_____. *The Hidalgo Revolt: Prelude to Mexican Independence.* Gainesville: University of Florida Press, 1966.

Hamnett, Brian R. "Royalist Counterinsurgency and the Continuity of Rebellion: Guanajuato and Michoacán, 1813–20." *Hispanic American Historical Review* 62/1 (1982): 19–48.

Henderson, Timothy J. *The Mexican Wars for Independence.* New York: Hill and Wang, 2009.

Lombardi, John V. *The Political Ideology of Fray Servando Teresa de Mier, Propagandist for Independence.* Cuernavaca, Mexico: Centro Intercultural de Documentación, 1968.

Piccato, Pablo. *The Tyranny of Opinion: Honor in the Construction of the Mexican Public Sphere.* Durham, NC: Duke University Press, 2010.

Robertson, William S. *Iturbide of Mexico.* Durham, NC: Duke University Press, 1952.

Rodríguez O., Jaime E. *"We Are Now the True Spaniards:" Sovereignty, Revolution, Independence and the Emergence of the Federal Republic of Mexico, 1808–1824.* Stanford, CA: Stanford University Press, 2012.

Timmons, Wilbert H. *Morelos: Priest, Soldier, Statesman of Mexico.* El Paso: Texas Western College Press, 1963.

Van Young, Eric. *The Other Rebellion: Popular Violence, Ideology, and the Mexican Struggle for Independence, 1810–1821.* Stanford, CA: Stanford University Press, 2001.

CHAPTER 16

THE FIRST MEXICAN EMPIRE

POMP AND CIRCUMSTANCE

In the best of circumstances nation building is a precarious business, but how does one create a nation out of a newly independent state when the economy is in shambles and the political atmosphere is pervaded by acrimony and mistrust? How does one fashion a set of national contours when ideological fissures and profound regional and ethnic differences tear at the heart of the body politic? These questions obsessed many Latin American leaders in the nineteenth century, but binding nationalisms would be long in coming. For his part, the self-important Iturbide was less concerned with building a nation than with becoming its sovereign.

As provided by the Plan de Iguala, Iturbide named a provisional junta to govern the country. This junta, completely dominated by conservative criollo interests, in turn named him to serve as its presiding officer. The first order of business was to select a five-man regency to exercise executive functions until an emperor could be designated. The junta chose Iturbide as one of the five and awarded him a new military title, Generalísimo de Tierra y Mar (Supreme General of Land and Sea), as well as a salary of one hundred twenty thousand pesos annually.

Meanwhile, an independent congress, also dominated by conservatives, debated Mexico's future. Although a small recalcitrant group tried to muster sympathy for a republic, Iturbide's conservative cohorts controlled the organizational proceedings. While they beat back all attempts at republicanism, they began to waver on a series of economic and military issues. When the congress, though divided, decided to cut back on the size of the Army of the Three Guarantees and decreed that no member of the regency could simultaneously hold military office, Iturbide realized that his ranks were being thinned and that time was no longer on his side. If he failed to act decisively, the crown he wanted so desperately might be denied him.

On the evening of May 18 the *generalísimo* staged a dramatic demonstration in his own behalf. Troops were ordered out of the barracks and into the streets. Firing muskets and rockets into the air and shouting "Viva Agustín I, Emperor of Mexico!" they enticed other soldiers to join them. As the frenzy grew in the downtown business district, thousands of civilians accompanied the mob on its way to Iturbide's residence. Once there, the multitudes demanded

235

that their favorite declare himself emperor at once. Iturbide told friends who were in his home at the time that although he wanted to go out on his balcony and turn them down, he yielded for the sake of the public good.

Despite his feigned deference, the following morning Iturbide appeared personally before the congress and, with his mob shouting in the galleries, the intimidated body named him constitutional emperor of Mexico. In his oath of office he swore before God and the Holy Evangels to uphold and defend the Roman Catholic religion at the exclusion of all others and to enforce all laws and decrees promulgated by the congress that chose him.

With the throne thus occupied, the congress set to work, not on the conspicuous demands of the Mexican nation but on defining proper etiquette and protocol in an obvious attempt to emulate the greatest imperial regime the world had ever known. In June the congress refined the organizational structure of the monarchy, declaring it to be hereditary and assigning titles of nobility to his immediate family. May 19, the day of Iturbide's proclamation, was declared a national holiday, as were his birthday and the birthdays of his children.

The greatest preparations of all were made for the official coronation ceremonies in July. Although several liberal deputies argued that kissing of the hand and bending of the knee were repugnant to the dignity of free peoples, their voices were lost to the monarchist majority. The efforts were all based on a French model, and the congress hired a French baroness who had designed the costumes for Napoleon Bonaparte some twenty-two years before. The congress authorized a new Mexican order, the Knights of Guadalupe, to participate in the coronation. In preparation, jewelry was borrowed, thrones were erected, banners and flags were hung from church towers, and teams of workers were engaged to scour the streets. The citizenry of the capital was being prepared for the most pretentious spectacle ever to occur in Mexico City.

At 8:00 A.M. on Sunday, July 21, 1822, amid the din of artillery salvos and the clamor of several military bands, the imperial cortège worked its way along a carpeted and flower-strewn path to the provisional palace, and the royal family was escorted to the central cathedral by an honor guard recently designated by the congress. At the door the emperor and empress were met by two bishops, who blessed them with holy water and led them to the two thrones placed on the altar. The bishop of Guadalajara then celebrated high mass and consecrated the emperor and empress with sacred oil. With tremendous solemnity the president of the congress placed the crown on Iturbide's head and he, in turn, placed a slightly smaller one on the head of the empress. The bishop then intoned *Vivat Imperator in aeternum*.

While the outer trappings of the empire were pretentious to an absurd degree, they were not entirely without purpose and meaning. Iturbide's understanding of Mexico's past, while by no means profound, was acute enough. He realized that the entire governmental system of the colonial period had been predicated upon loyalty to the king and the crown. Independence obviously undercut the personal loyalty that bound Mexican society together, but the emperor wanted to capitalize upon the time-tested tradition. While he became emperor in name, in fact he became a *caudillo*, a charismatic military leader with a personal following. The congress had given him the legal base he considered vital; the ostentation that engulfed his person helped to reinforce the mystique of his indispensability and to blur the distinctions between the man and the office. Iturbide worked hard to identify the new state with his own person and, for a while, seemed to be succeeding.

Agustín de Iturbide (1783–1824). Changing allegiance from the Spanish to the insurgent cause, Iturbide successfully concluded the fight for independence and had himself named emperor of Mexico.

PROBLEMS FACING THE NEW EMPIRE

The empire was huge. Embracing much of the old viceroyalty of New Spain, it stretched in the north to California and the present-day southwest of the United States, and the south included all of Central America with the exception of Panama. Long subject to what they considered the autocratic rule of Guatemala, Central Americans were divided about whether to unite with the Mexican empire. Iturbide sent in an army of six hundred men to ensure their adhesion to the empire, but the connection remained tenuous.

A more serious problem occurred with the neighbor to the north. The new regime quite naturally wished to secure the official recognition of the United States, an independent republic for nearly fifty years. The cultivation of harmonious relations was deemed vital to the security of Mexico's northern provinces and important for commercial ties. Areas that belonged to Spain in earlier periods, Florida and Louisiana, now belonged to the United States giving it control in the southeast areas bordering the Gulf of Mexico except for Texas which could be threatened by US expansionist tendencies. The Mexican monarch also hoped for a loan of $10 million to help his new government meet its obligations. President James Monroe was reluctant to recognize a monarchy in the Americas.

Iturbide took the lead when he dispatched Manuel Zozaya as minister to Washington. Reception of the Mexican would, in effect, recognize the Mexican regime. With mixed emotions the US president urged the Congress to authorize recognition in December of 1822. Not wishing to impair relations with Mexico from the beginning and feeling the push of those US interests promoting trade, in January 1823 Monroe appointed Joel Poinsett as minister to Mexico, despite the diplomat's serious reservations about the Mexican regime.

But all was not well in Mexico City. The showy imperial façade rested on vulnerable socio-economic foundations. Mexico's colonial economy had depended heavily on silver, but the wars for independence had exacted a high toll on the mines. During the years of internecine strife mine workers left their jobs to join the fight, mine owners and operators were killed, machinery was damaged, and many of the mines were flooded. Without sufficient bullion reaching the mints, coinage slowed. Over $26 million had been minted in 1809; in 1821, less than $6 million. Unemployment was rampant in the mining centers, and the situation was aggravated by jobless soldiers mustered out shortly after the military campaigns ended.

The impact of the wars on Mexico's agricultural output was similar. Both Spanish troops and insurgents destroyed fields, commandeered crops, and killed off cattle and sheep that might have benefited the enemy. Many a hacendado was killed and haciendas burned. Mexico was a rural country at the time of independence, but thousands in Mexico City (population (one hundred fifty-five thousand,) Puebla (sixty thousand), Guadalajara (fifty thousand), and other cities suffered as the price of agricultural products rose steadily in 1822. The average citizen in the city felt the impact of the economic decline, and the government did too as the fiscal system collapsed. In an attempt to make the cause of independence even more popular, the congress lowered many old taxes, such as those on pulque and tobacco, and eliminated others altogether. But commerce and the revenues to be derived stagnated as trade with Spain ended and free trade with new areas faltered in taking up the slack.

To ensure loyalty, soldiers and bureaucrats had to be paid and officers promoted, but the depleted revenues could not begin to cover the extravagant expenses of the imperial regime. Month after month expenses exceeded income. Virtually nobody was willing to invest in the shaky economy or loan money to the government. Available capital had remained largely in the hands of the Spaniards, and most of them began to depart soon after independence. The few moneylenders around proposed interest rates nothing short of exorbitant. In response to the growing crisis, the congress decreed a forced loan on ecclesiastical properties, but this measure was no more than a temporary expedient. Several issues of paper currency, not backed by hard reserves and not trusted by anyone, caused more problems than they solved; as the wheels of the economy ground into ominous stagnation, Mexicans became more and more critical of their new regime.

Criticism was leveled at the emperor from many quarters: from disgruntled veterans who found no employment, from deputies in the congress who really never accommodated themselves to the concept of monarchy, and from a number of courageous journalists who exposed the burlesque aspects of Mexico's empire. Sensitive to criticism, in the summer the emperor suppressed several liberal newspapers that espoused republican ideals and even one conservative one that favored monarchy but argued that the throne should be offered to a European prince. With the newspaper suppressions a group of liberals in the congress, led by Fray Servando Teresa de Mier, an accomplished orator, and Carlos María de Bustamante, began to conspire. Through a government spy who infiltrated congressional circles Iturbide was able to secure an accurate list of his leading enemies and, on August 20, 1822, had them all arrested. The congress protested, and even some of Iturbide's staunchest supporters in the legislative body defended their arrested colleagues. The opposing positions were irreconcilable, and the debates in the fall were heated; their substance was less significant than the fact that they demonstrated a steadily growing majority against the emperor and the imperial concept itself. Even Guadalupe Victoria, Iturbide's erstwhile ally, denounced him as a tyrant. On October 31 Iturbide became the first Mexican chief executive to dissolve the legislative branch of government. The precedent, once established, would be repeated many times before the nineteenth century ran its course.

The reaction in both Mexico City and the provinces was resolute. The antimonarchists found their ranks swelling, and a specific plot crystalized in Veracruz. The self-proclaimed leader was Iturbide's commander in the port city, Antonio López de Santa Anna. Although it is possible that Santa Anna had been schooled in the virtues of republicanism by Carlos María de Bustamante, whom he had met and befriended a few years before, his decision to lead a revolt against the monarchy seems to have had a more fundamental root. As commander of Veracruz, Santa Anna had been assigned the task of driving the last remaining Spanish troops from San Juan de Ulloa, the harbor fortress they still held. But Iturbide believed that Santa Anna had not pursued the enemy forcefully enough. As a result he ordered Santa Anna to Mexico City where he could be closely observed. But Santa Anna would countenance no such move. On December 1, 1822, at the head of some 400 troops, he rode through the streets of Veracruz proclaiming a republic. A few days later he formally launched his revolt under the Plan de Veracruz. Within a month Vicente Guerrero, Nicolás Bravo, and Guadalupe Victoria had joined the movement, enhancing its prestige. Iturbide recognized the seriousness of the problem; it was one thing for deputies in the congress to attack the regime with words and quite another for army officers to attack it with arms and ammunition.

Placing José Antonio Echáverri, the captain general of Veracruz, in charge of the imperial campaigns, Iturbide felt that he had little to fear. Echáverri and Santa Anna had been at each other's throats for months over the most expeditious means for driving the Spaniards out of San Juan de Ulloa. But Echáverri decided to give the emperor a little of his own medicine. Much as Iturbide had made common cause with Vicente Guerrero when dispatched to engage him, Echáverri joined Santa Anna. On February 1, 1823, Echáverri and thirty-three cohorts proclaimed the Plan de Casa Mata. Santa Anna, not having encountered much military success in recent months and realizing that the Plan de Casa Mata was not inconsistent with his own Plan de Veracruz, accepted the new pronunciamiento. Two anti-imperial movements now became one.

One military contingent after another swore allegiance to the Plan de Casa Mata. One province after another fell to the insurgents, and they began marching on Mexico City. They did not have to take the capital by force, however. Realizing that his experiment with monarchy had ended in failure, Iturbide abdicated his throne in the middle of February 1823, some 10 months after coming to office, and accepted a generous pension that would have enabled him to live comfortably. In his resignation address he stated he did not desire to have his name become a pretext for civil war and he made his plans to go into European exile. The rebel army marched into Mexico City unopposed.

AN ASSESSMENT

The first Mexican empire had been a dismal failure. In conception it had merely substituted a new criollo oligarchy for the old gachupín oligarchy and indeed had satisfied many Mexicans hostile to the innovations of nineteenth-century liberalism. The royal household, with all of its gaudy trappings, underscored that little had changed since New Spain won control of its own destiny.

With the advantage of historical hindsight, the revolt, fought under the banner of the Plan de Casa Mata, is laden with irony. The entire antimonarchy fight was made in the name of the congress, which Iturbide had emasculated from the day it accepted his oath of office. One would have thought that at best legislative supremacy, and at worst legislative equality, would have been the political dictum of the nineteenth century. In fact, just the opposite was true. Few practical lessons in nation building derived from the empire. Administrative and legislative experience was still in short supply. The Mexican elite did not yet consider the fact that successful leadership in the wars for independence was by no means synonymous with statesmanship. In the period following the empire Mexico would once again turn to military heroes who had emerged from the campaigns with more than life-sized stature.

But in at least one respect the collapse of the empire marked the beginning of a new day. It brought to power for the first time the criollo middle class, which had early supported the independence movement only to be outflanked by the conservatives after the 1820 liberal revolt in Spain. These criollos were not social revolutionaries in any sense although some nineteenth-century liberal philosophy enabled indigenous communities to adapt its principles to defend their lands and cabildos. While on occasion criollos attacked entrenched interests, their objectives were political, not social. In all innocence they seemed to believe that the docility of the lower classes had no bounds and that the poor would endure their privations forever.

As Mexico prepared to embark upon its second experiment as an independent nation, only one major question had been answered. The monarchists had been so thoroughly discredited that virtually nobody, at least for a while, harbored serious notions about reviving the concept. Mexico would be organized as a republic; the nature of that republic now became the issue at stake. It would provoke violent debate, near anarchy, and finally civil war.

RECOMMENDED FOR FURTHER STUDY

Anna, Timothy E. *Forging Mexico, 1821–1835*. Lincoln: University of Nebraska Press, 1998.

_____. *The Mexican Empire of Iturbide*. Lincoln: University of Nebraska Press, 1990.

Beezley, William H. and Colin MacLachlan. *Mexico's Crucial Century, 1810–1910*. Lincoln: University of Nebraska Press, 2010.

Brading, D. A. *The First America: The Spanish Monarchy, Creole Patriots and the Liberal State, 1492–1866*. New York: Cambridge University Press, 1993.

Henderson, Timothy J. *The Mexican Wars for Independence*. New York: Hill and Wang, 2009.

Lewis, III, William Francis. "Xavier Mina and Fray Servando Mier: Romantic Liberals of the Nineteenth Century." *New Mexico Historical Review* 44/2 (1969): 119–36.

Lombardi, John V. *The Political Ideology of Fray Servando Teresa de Mier, Propagandist for Independence*. Cuernavaca, Mexico: Centro Intercultural de Documentación, 1968.

Poinsett, Joel R. *Notes on Mexico Made in the Autumn of 1822, Accompanied by an Historical Sketch of the Revolution*. New York: Praeger, 1969.

Robertson, William S. *Iturbide of Mexico*. Durham, NC: Duke University Press, 1952.

Seijas, Tatiana, and Jake Frederick. *Spanish Dollars and Sister Republics: The Money That Made Mexico and the United States*. Lanham, MD: Rowman & Littlefield, 2017.

Tenenbaum, Barbara. "Taxation and Tyranny: Public Finances during the Iturbide Regime." In *The Independence of Mexico and the Creation of the New Nation*, edited by Jaime E. Rodríguez O., 201–14. Los Angeles, CA: UCLA Latin American Center, 1989.

Villoro, Luis. "The Ideological Currents of the Epoch of Independence." In *Major Trends in Mexican Philosophy*, edited by Mario de la Cueva, et al., 185–219. Notre Dame, IN: University of Notre Dame Press, 1966.

THE TRIALS OF NATIONHOOD

CHAPTER 17

THE EARLY MEXICAN REPUBLIC

THE CONSTITUTION OF 1824

With the collapse of the empire, a three-man junta governed Mexico provisionally. All three—Nicolás Bravo, Guadalupe Victoria, and Pedro Celestino Negrete—were military men. The precedent of miscasting soldiers as statesmen was now well established. The first order of business was to call elections for delegates to a constitutional congress that would be charged with framing the new charter. The constituent body met for the first time on November 27, 1823, and their focus narrowed to a question that on the surface seemed simple enough: should the new republic be federalist, with more autonomy for the states, or centralist, giving more authority to the central government?

Although there were some exceptions to the general alignment of forces, the centralists found their strength among the clergy, the hacendados, and the army officers, while the federalist firebrands attracted support from those liberal criollos and mestizos who drew on nineteenth-century liberal ideas from French and American revolutions as well as the US Constitution and the liberal Spanish document of 1812. They emphasized the importance of a secular state and equality before the law without ethnic distinction. The chief spokesmen for the federalists were Miguel Ramos Arizpe from Coahuila and Valentín Gómez Farías from Zacatecas. Fray Servando Teresa de Mier and Carlos María de Bustamante championed the centralist cause. When Ramos Arizpe presented the body with a working paper modeled closely after the US constitution, Fray Servando, an iconoclast who once questioned the authenticity of the Virgin of Guadalupe, responded with an eloquent speech. He observed that the experience of the northern neighbor had been entirely different from that of Mexico, and, while a federal system might well be suited to the needs of the United States, it could not work in Mexico for it would weaken the country just when strength from union was required. Speaking of the thirteen colonies to the north, Fray Servando argued:

> They were already separate and independent one from another. They federalized themselves
> in union against the oppression of England; to federalize ourselves, now united, is to divide

ourselves and to bring upon us the very evils they sought to remedy with their federa-tion. . .We are like children barely out of diapers or like slaves who have just unshackled their chains. . . . We might say that nature itself has decreed our centralization.[1]

Fray Servando's arguments, although highly prescient, failed to persuade. Ramos Arizpe and his federalist cohorts also drew upon the lessons of history but interpreted them quite differently. Centralism they equated with despotism. As examples they pointed to the 300 years of colonial rule and the ten months of monarchy, which were also centralistic and authoritarian. They preferred the dispersion of powers inherent in the federal structure and argued that such a system harmonized more closely with Mexico's recently won liberties. A would-be dictator could be thwarted in his nefarious attempts to subject the people only if the states and localities enjoyed a respectable measure of independent power. Arizpe's plea carried the day.

Under the Constitution of 1824 the Estados Unidos Mexicanos were organized as a federal republic composed of nineteen states and four territories. In the separation-of-powers clause delineating governmental authority into the executive, legislative, and ju-dicial branches, the philosophical influence of Montesquieu and the practical influence of the US Constitution of 1787 stand out. The legislature was made bicameral, the upper house designated as the Senate and the lower house as the Chamber of Deputies. Each state was represented by two senators and one deputy for every eighty thousand inhabit-ants. In at least one respect the federal system established in 1824 went beyond its US model and gave the states even greater power than those to the north: both the president and the vice-president were to be elected not by popular vote but by the state legislatures, for a term of four years.

More importantly, however, the autonomy of states in a highly federal system meant that local politics would play a major role in determining the nature of citizenship and political participation, even who could vote. States devised different frameworks to solve local prob-lems. In addition to ideas of equality before the law, European liberalism promoted an end to the power of corporate bodies in favor of privatization, posing a threat to the church and Indian pueblos whose lands were owned by the community as a whole. However, liberal principles did not form a coherent ideology in Mexico but rather were interpreted in diverse ways as forms of popular liberalism. In this milieu, many indigenous communities worked to mold local government and corporatist relationships to fit their idea of liberal citizenship.

While the federalists won on major points of governmental organization, in an impor-tant sense they gave up as much as they gained. The centralists regrouped and scored at least three victories of their own. First and foremost, the Catholic church retained its 300-year mo-nopoly on Mexico's spiritual life. Not surprisingly, many Mexicans saw the church as an in-stitution capable of maintaining order. Moreover, the church held considerable sway among the popular classes, both urban and rural, through its devotional and charitable societies. At the local level, the organizational structures of these societies and parishes ordered daily life and often tended to group people of similar class or occupational status together. Even

---

1 Quoted in *Antología del pensamiento social y político de América Latina* (Washington, DC, 1964), 242–43.

though racial distinctions in Mexico had theoretically been abolished in 1822, indigenous peoples continued to invoke their Indian identity when it served their community interests.

In addition, the president of the country was granted extraordinary powers in times of emergency, powers that could convert him into a dictator while at the same time investing him with the sanction of law. The word *emergency* in the nineteenth century came to be interpreted rather loosely. Finally, the constitution guaranteed members of the clergy and the military their special *fueros*. This time-worn Spanish institution exempted clergymen and military personnel from having to stand trial in civil courts, even if they were charged with the violation of civil law.

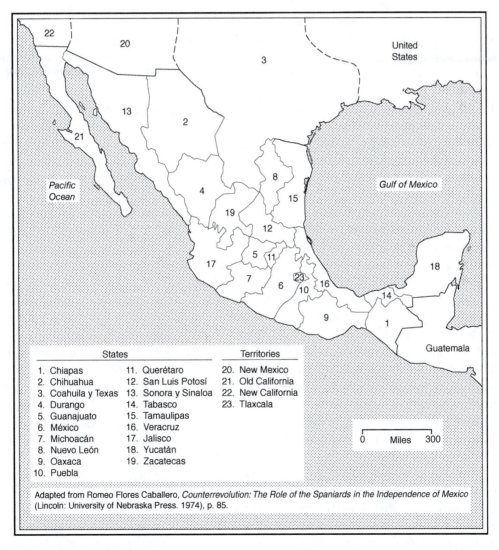

States		Territories
1. Chiapas	11. Querétaro	20. New Mexico
2. Chihuahua	12. San Luis Potosí	21. Old California
3. Coahuila y Texas	13. Sonora y Sinaloa	22. New California
4. Durango	14. Tabasco	23. Tlaxcala
5. Guanajuato	15. Tamaulipas	
6. México	16. Veracruz	
7. Michoacán	17. Jalisco	
8. Nuevo León	18. Yucatán	
9. Oaxaca	19. Zacatecas	
10. Puebla		

Adapted from Romeo Flores Caballero, *Counterrevolution: The Role of the Spaniards in the Independence of Mexico* (Lincoln: University of Nebraska Press. 1974), p. 85.

The Mexican Republic in 1824

THE VICTORIA PRESIDENCY

In Mexico's first presidential election the state legislatures chose as president Guadalupe Victoria and as vice president Nicolás Bravo. The new president, a man of goodwill, was honest and unassuming. He had proven his courage on the battlefield but was not a particularly talented leader. In a mood of compromise he invited several conservatives to serve in the cabinet. They accepted not for purposes of reconciliation but to secure a power base within the government. The president sought to be impartial, but his attempts at fairness degenerated into indecision. Those in whom he placed trust took advantage of him. Unprepared by education or temperament, he proved unable to deal with the immense problems he faced.

The debates of the empire and over the nature of the new republic had bequeathed an intensely political atmosphere, pervaded by mistrust, self-righteousness, and rancor. While exaggerated jealousies magnified trifles, basic ideological cleavages emerged as well and began to manifest themselves in a unique manner. Both of the major political factions identified themselves and their efforts with a branch of freemasonry. The federalists attached themselves to the York Rite Masons (*Yorquinos*) and the centralists to the Scottish Rite (*Escoseses*). The Masonic lodges served as political affiliations for elites, in lieu of a formal political party structure. The upper classes were divided over the type of political system best suited to guarantee order while offering some form of representative government, nor could they agree on which policies would benefit the economy. Nevertheless, they all tended to distrust the masses. Eventually the ideas they espoused in their respective Masonic movements would become the basis for liberal and conservative parties.

One of the more unfortunate incidents to occur during the Victoria presidency was the execution of the former emperor, Agustín de Iturbide. Taking up residence first in Italy and later in England, the exiled monarch heard rumors that the restored Spanish king, Ferdinand VII, was about to undertake a reconquest of Mexico. Early in 1824 he offered his services to the republican government. He had defeated the Spanish army once and was prepared to do battle again in the name of Mexican independence. Congress turned down his good offer and, in fact, passed legislation stipulating that should he dare return to Mexico he would be considered a traitor and would face immediate execution. Impatient and imprudent as ever, Iturbide did not wait for an answer. On May 11, 1824, he left England with his family and retainers for the Mexico. Disembarking at Soto la Marina, north of Tampico, he was soon recognized by the local military commander. The Tamaulipas state legislature met in hurried session and decreed that it must enforce the order of treason handed down by the national congress the month before. On July 19, 1824, standing before a firing squad, Iturbide made a final speech, protesting his innocence and proclaiming his love for the fatherland.

The Victoria administration scored high marks in foreign policy. Not only was Mexico's independence formally recognized by most of Europe, but several treaties of amity and commerce were concluded as well. A treaty with the United States pledged both countries to accept the Sabine River as the eastern boundary of Texas, thus ostensibly settling the boundary question. International problems were addressed more easily than domestic issues.

The new nation's financial situation steadily worsened. Late colonial fiscal policies of the Bourbons had diminished Mexico's capital and monetary reserves, and the early federalist model deprived the national government of sufficient resources and tax authority. Criollos were hard pressed to implement an institutional infrastructure to move the economy forward. Citizens long accustomed to hard specie were reluctant to accept paper money. Domestic commerce, already vulnerable to banditry, burned bridges, and unsafe roads, suffered as a result. The president, not concerned that a large standing army could be a menace to civil liberties, to any hope of future civilian governments, and to a healthy economy, kept over 50,000 men under arms at all times. The new government assumed all national debts from the late colonial period and the monarchy (over 76 million pesos) and sought to support itself by means of import taxes, sales taxes, and new government monopolies. Rampant smuggling largely circumvented import duties; sales taxes were largely avoided by failure to report transactions; and monopolies, after collection expenses, brought in little cash. Not only were the revenues insufficient to pay installments on the debt, but they were unequal to the day-to-day costs of government. Yet the deficit was less significant than the fact that the entire fiscal structure was unsound. The government sought loans from England and received small amounts. These minor infusions of foreign capital did not suffice to stimulate the economy but did mark the first step of Mexican economic dependency.

While efforts to heal the breach between rival factions foundered, the political and economic pressures merged in 1827 and expressed themselves in an armed revolt against President Victoria. The leader of the insurrection was none other than Vice President Nicolás Bravo, who drew upon the Scottish Rite lodges for support. The Yorquinos rallied around the president, and ultimately the revolt was suppressed by Generals Santa Anna and Guerrero. But the precedent of the military coup had been set.

Guadalupe Victoria (1785–1843). Mexico's first president, Victoria found his term disrupted by the internal chaos that came to dominate the country's political life in the first half of the nineteenth century.

DOMESTIC TURMOIL AND A SPANISH INVASION

Passions had not yet subsided when new presidential elections were held in September 1828. The candidate of the liberal faction, Vicente Guerrero, another hero of the wars, was opposed by conservative Manuel Gómez Pedraza, an accomplished scholar who had served in the Victoria cabinet as secretary of war. The election results showed that Gómez Pedraza carried ten of the nineteen state legislatures, but the liberals, feeling little obligation to pay homage to the constitution, charged that he had used his influence with the army to intimidate the legislators. Rather than turn the government over to their enemies, the liberals opted instead for revolution. Once again they found their champion in Antonio López de Santa Anna, but on this occasion the odds were strongly against him. Through persuasion and deception he gradually won others over to the liberal cause. When Juan Alvarez rose up in Acapulco and Lorenzo de Zavala in the environs of Mexico City, the government army had to disperse its forces and the rebels made such headway that the president-elect, already disgusted with partisan abuse, announced that he was giving up the fight. As a result the defeated candidate, Vicente Guerrero, became president and Anastasio Bustamante, a compromise conservative, vice president. Santa Anna, for his efforts, received a division generalship, the highest military rank in the country.

The second president of Mexico is best known for two episodes of his short term. In September 1829, he signed a bill abolishing African slavery, a measure accepted without protest except in Texas, where the institution of slavery had actually been encouraged by previous Mexican legislation. The second event dealt with the expulsion of Spaniards from Mexico, a process that had begun earlier. Many Spaniards had been exempted from the initial laws calling for their exodus, but the congress now decided to enforce the removal of all peninsulares. Word had come that Spain, which had not yet recognized Mexican independence, planned a reconquest of Mexico. The Spanish timing seemed to be excellent. The same day that the congress named Guerrero president it decreed the enforcement of a law, passed under the previous administration, expelling almost all remaining Spaniards from Mexico. The country was rent with factionalism and considerably weakened.

The Spanish expedition of some 3,000 troops left Havana, Cuba (one of the few remaining Spanish possessions in the Americas), in July 1829 under the command of General Isidro Barradas. Landing on the coast of Tamaulipas at the height of summer, the Spaniards were exhausted and demoralized by intense heat, yellow fever, and an acute scarcity of water. To their amazement, however, they found that Tampico had been evacuated in anticipation of a much larger expedition, and they took the forfeited prize.

President Guerrero decided to place government operations in the hands of the man who had ostensibly saved the nation several times, the new division general, Antonio López de Santa Anna. On August 21 Santa Anna attacked Tampico but was repulsed by Barradas's well-entrenched forces. However, the Spaniards had not established any sure line of supply, and Santa Anna opted for a long siege which, he reasoned, would take its toll. As inadequate provisions and yellow fever taxed Spanish resistance, General Barradas decided to surrender. By October most of the Spanish troops were on their way home. The attempted reconquest was Spain's last Mexican hurrah. It touched off a series of reprisals against the few remaining Spaniards in the country, and they began leaving hurriedly.

Santa Anna had saved the nation again. By 1830 few in the country could rival his popularity. Honorific but unremunerative titles began to flow in from all corners of the republic: *Vencedor de Tampico* (Victor of Tampico), *Salvador del País* (Savior of the Country), and *Benemérito de la Patria* (Benefactor of the Fatherland). How his titles and popularity would serve him was not yet clear.

THE FEDERALIST-CENTRALIST STRUGGLE CONTINUES

With the Spanish threat removed, the Mexican liberals and conservatives now resumed their quarrels. When President Guerrero refused to relinquish the extraordinary powers congress gave him to cope with the threat, Vice President Bustamante posed as the champion of constitutionalism. For the second time in Mexico's brief republican history a conservative vice president led an armed revolt against a liberal president. But where Nicolás Bravo had failed, Bustamante, largely because of his influence with the army, succeeded.

With Bustamante in the presidential office, the conservatives took power for the first time since the overthrow of the empire. But their promises would be largely unredeemed. Their support for the church as the vehicle for maintaining control over indigenous people and reducing civil strife was particularly distasteful to liberals who looked to Enlightenment ideas to modernize the country, emphasizing the importance of education. Although the conservatives cut back on the size of the army and renegotiated the English loan, Bustamante was no more able to bring about stability and progress than had his liberal predecessors. And he compounded his shortcomings by giving his fellow Mexicans their first real lessons in military dictatorship.

Grossly intemperate repression targeted Yorquinos. Bustamante suppressed freedom of the press and only those presses upholding the government were allowed to roll. The federal legislature and the judiciary were badgered into acquiescence. Political corruption reached new heights. But the incident that occasioned the greatest public outrage was the capture and execution of the former president, Vicente Guerrero. After his ouster by the Bustamante army, Guerrero gradually made his way to Acapulco, where he accepted passage on the *Colombo*, a ship flying the Italian flag. But Captain Picaluga, a Genoese citizen, had agreed to sell Guerrero to the government for $50,000. As soon as the former president boarded the *Colombo*, he was bound hand and foot and turned over to federal authorities. He was subsequently tried, convicted of treason, and on January 14, 1831, executed.

The execution had a sobering effect as Mexicans began to tally up. Of the five outstanding leaders of the wars of independence, four—Miguel Hidalgo, José María Morelos, Agustín de Iturbide, and now Vicente Guerrero—had died before the firing squad. Only Guadalupe Victoria escaped this fate. The word *traitor* had come to be used too easily and the charge invariably carried the supreme penalty. As a nation, Mexico was unsure of itself. It had struggled since independence. National, state, and local governments dealt with disorder and insolvency. At the local level in the countryside, daily life resonated with traditional agricultural and market cycles, as indigenous communities interpreted notions of liberty within their own frameworks. In cities, indigenous barrios used church institutions to preserve traditions that supported their interests. In general, however, the social structure had not changed in any meaningful way. Executing Vicente Guerrero might have satiated the political vengeance of a few but did nothing to stem devastating epidemics, to repair pitted roads, or to nurture a national healing process. Abolishing the caste system scarcely abolished poverty. Emancipating the slaves did not eliminate malnutrition and illiteracy. It seemed time for a change of direction. Santa Anna marshaled his forces once again, overthrew the Bustamante government, and then returned to his estates in Veracruz.

RECOMMENDED FOR FURTHER STUDY

Archer, Christon I. "Fashioning a New Nation." In *The Oxford History of Mexico*, edited by Michael C. Meyer and William H. Beezley, 285–318. New York: Oxford University Press, rev. 2010.

Arrom, Silvia Marina. "Popular Politics in Mexico City: The Parián Riot, 1828." *Hispanic American Historical Review* 68/2 (1988): 245–68.

Caplan, Karen D. *Indigenous Citizens: Local Liberalism in Early National Oaxaca and Yucatán*. Stanford, CA: Stanford University Press, 2009.

Costeloe, Michael P. *Bonds and Bondholders: British Investors and Mexico's Foreign Debt, 1824–1888*. Westport, CT: Praeger, 2003.

Flores Caballero, Romeo. *Counterrevolution: The Role of the Spaniards in the Independence of Mexico*. Lincoln: University of Nebraska Press, 1974.

Fowler, Will. *Mexico in the Age of Proposals, 1821–1853*. Westport, CT: Greenwood Press, 1998.

Green, Stanley. *The Mexican Republic: The First Decade, 1823–1832*. Pittsburgh, PA: University of Pittsburgh Press, 1987.

Guardino, Peter. *The Time of Liberty: Popular Political Culture in Oaxaca, 1750–1850*. Durham, NC: Duke University Press, 2005.

Hale, Charles A. *Mexican Liberalism in the Age of Mora, 1821–1853*. New Haven, CT: Yale University Press, 1968.

O'Hara, Matthew D. *A Flock Divided: Race, Religion, and Politics in Mexico, 1749–1857*. Durham, NC: Duke University Press, 2010.

Rippy, J. Fred. *Joel R. Poinsett, Versatile American*. Durham, NC: Duke University Press, 1935.

Salvucci, Richard J. *Politics, Markets, and Mexico's "London Debt," 1823–1887*. New York: Cambridge University Press, 2009.

Seijas, Tatiana, and Jake Frederick. *Spanish Dollars and Sister Republics: The Money That Made Mexico and the United States*. Lanham, MD: Rowman & Littlefield, 2017.

Sims, Harold Dana. *The Expulsion of Mexico's Spaniards, 1821–1836*. Pittsburgh, PA: University of Pittsburgh Press, 1990.

Weber, David J. *The Mexican Frontier, 1821–1846: The American Southwest under Mexico*. Albuquerque: University of New Mexico Press, 1982.

CHAPTER 18

SANTA ANNA, THE CENTRALIZED STATE, AND THE WAR WITH THE UNITED STATES

The myths surrounding Antonio López de Santa Anna have made him a caricature that deeply colors our understanding of the 1830s through the mid-1850s in Mexico. He has been depicted as a charismatic but unprincipled leader who epitomizes the nineteenth-century Latin American caudillo—unscrupulous, deceptive, ruthless, profiteering, and opportunistic, with a magetism that attracted loyal and zealous followers. These attributes are in part true, but they are not the whole story. During the period, the presidency changed hands many times, and Santa Anna himself occupied the presidency on several occasions. Even when he was out of the presidency, he exercised powerful influence on the country still struggling to achieve political stability and economic growth. Santa Anna is perhaps best, if not accurately, remembered for Mexico's loss of Texas to secession and other northern territories in the US war with Mexico.

SANTA ANNA: THE CONSUMMATE ARBITER

Antonio López de Santa Anna Pérez de Lebrón was born on February 21, 1794 to a criollo landholding family in Veracruz, where he went to school until he was sixteen and decided to join the royalist army. He supported the crown against the insurgents and won special commendation for his actions until 1821. Then, like many of his criollo comrades, Santa Anna followed Iturbide's lead and switched allegiance.

The highlights of Santa Anna's career in the period immediately following independence have already been touched upon. In 1823, under the banner of the Plan de Casa Mata, he led the republican forces against the empire and contributed in no small way to the overthrow of Iturbide. When Mexico's first vice president, conservative Nicolás Bravo, proclaimed a revolt against President Victoria, Santa Anna took the lead in suppressing the movement and, following the next presidential election, saw to it that the defeated liberal candidate, Vicente Guerrero, was installed in office. In 1829, when Spain tried to bring its former colony back into the fold, it was Santa Anna again who defeated the Spanish forces at Tampico to save the infant republic. In 1832, when the Bustamante dictatorship became intolerable, he overthrew it. On the surface, at least, his career seemed to constitute an unbroken chain of victories in the defense of Mexican liberalism. However, he considered himself and the army to be above politics, dedicated to lending military service to the patria in times of crisis.

Nonetheless, capitalizing on his popularity, liberals urged him to run for president in 1833, and he won by a huge majority. The vice presidency went to Valentín Gómez Farías, a man of intellectual distinction and a politician whose liberal credentials were undisputed. In a move that suggests he truly was not interested in political power, Santa Anna did not take up the post as president. He preferred to return to his hacienda, Manga de Clavo in Veracruz, to oversee the administration of his estates. By all accounts he was a paternalistic hacendado who helped those who worked for him, inspiring their loyalty. In much the same way his populist charisma commanded respect from soldiers. The army was a privileged institution under Santa Anna, but it also came to represent a kind of populist nationalism because its campaigns endeavored to preserve national sovereignty.

Santa Anna's departure left the presidency in the hands of Gómez Farías, who began to sponsor a number of reforms aimed at two entrenched institutions: the army and the church. To curtail the inordinate influence of the army, the reform measures reduced the size of the military and legislated the abolition of the military fueros; army officers would now have to stand trial in civil courts. The clerical reforms were more wide-ranging. Congress advised clergymen to limit their directives and admonitions from the pulpit to spiritual matters. Then, under the prodding of Gómez Farías and his liberal theoreticians José María Luis Mora and Lorenzo de Zavala, congress voted to secularize education. It closed down the University of Mexico with its faculty of priests and declared that all future clerical appointments would be made by the government rather than by the papacy. The mandatory payment of the tithe was declared illegal. In addition, the congress enacted legislation permitting nuns, priests, and lay brothers to forswear their vows. In one final measure the remaining Franciscan missions in northern Mexico were secularized and their funds and property sequestered.

The response from the vested interests was almost predictable. To the rallying cry of *Religión y Fueros*, the church, the army, and other conservative groups banded together and called for the overthrow of the government. Although the conservatives prevailed upon Santa Anna to lead the revolt, he demurred and in the summer of 1833 fought against the insurgents, finally claiming victory in Guanajuato. With a devastating cholera epidemic now in full force, Santa Anna once again returned to Veracruz. However, he warned Gómez Farías to restrain congressional demands that were inciting conservatives to take military action once again.

When that did not happen, Santa Anna decided to intervene believing that only he could control the machinations of conservative elites and clergymen to stir up unrest among the mass of Catholic faithful. In the spring of 1834 with overwhelming popular backing, he resumed the presidency, removed Gómez Farías, closed down congress, and rescinded the reform package. Once again he took up the guise of pacifier and arbiter, seeing himself as the only force capable of preventing a destructive religious war and restoring order to the nation. After achieving this goal, he returned to Manga del Clavo while a new conservative congress enacted legislation, including the abolition of the Constitution of 1824.

General Antonio López de Santa Anna (1794–1876). The dominant figure of the first half of the nineteenth century; Santa Anna actually served in the presidency on many different occasions. A master politician, nobody understood Mexico's political dynamics better.

Whether or not Santa Anna had become a committed centralist, he saw that the federalist constitution had not achieved lasting stability. During another period of his absenteeism, the congress promulgated a new charter. Consisting of seven main parts, it is remembered in Mexico's constitutional evolution as the *Siete Leyes*, or the Constitution of 1836. To ensure centralist organization, the states of the old federal republic were transformed into military departments governed by political bosses handpicked by the president himself. The presidential term was extended from four years to eight, although no president under the constitution would serve that long.

Santa Anna's acquiescence in abolishing the federal republic and replacing it with a centralist state precipitated a series of interrelated events that were to dominate his life and his country for the next twelve years. The switch to centralism was well received by some, as the concept of federalism had already lost much of its appeal, but secessionist attempts occurred in New Mexico and Yucatán. In 1847 after years of unrest Maya campesinos initiated what came to be known as the Caste War of Yucatán. Calling for tax relief and an end to land encroachments, debt peonage, required military service, and threats to community autonomy by the Yucatecan elites, they controlled half of the Yucatecan peninsula by 1848, in a conflict that would continue. But the most serious opposition by far came from the northern province of Texas which, in turn, provoked a disastrous war with the United States.

DISCONTENT IN TEXAS

Throughout the colonial period Texas was one of the northern provinces of New Spain. It was sparsely populated, and the Franciscan missionaries who penetrated the area found the Indian population unreceptive to settlement in missions. At the beginning of the eighteenth century the Texas territory had fewer than three thousand sedentary colonists and, one hundred years later, only seven thousand. Because the Spanish crown wanted to populate and colonize the territory, in 1821, just prior to the winning of Mexican independence, the commandant general in Monterrey granted Moses Austin, an American pioneer, permission to settle some 300 Catholic families in Texas. Austin died, and Mexico became independent before the project could be initiated; but Austin's son, Stephen F. Austin, took up the idea, had the concession confirmed by the new Mexican government, and began the colonization at once. The new agreement authorized Stephen Austin to bring in as many as three hundred families the first year provided that they were of good moral character, would profess the Roman Catholic religion, and agreed to abide by Mexican law. No maximum was set on future immigration into Texas, and, in fact, other concessionaires received similar grants.

A tremendous influx of Americans into Texas ensued. The land was practically free—only ten cents an acre as opposed to $1.25 an acre for inferior land in the United States. Each male colonist over 21 years of age could to purchase 640 acres for himself, 320 acres for his wife, 160 acres for each child and, significantly, an additional 80 acres for each slave that he brought with him. As a further enticement the colonists received a seven-year exemption from the payment of Mexican taxes. By 1827 there were twelve thousand US citizens living in Texas, outnumbering the Mexican population by some five thousand. By 1835 the immigrant population had reached thirty thousand, while the Mexican population had barely passed seventy eight hundred.

The Mexican government originally believed that immigrants from the United States could be integrated into the Mexican community and passed a number of laws to foster this integration. In addition to the requirement that the colonists be Roman Catholic, all official transactions were to be concluded in the Spanish language, no foreigners would be allowed to settle within sixty miles of the national boundary, and foreigners who married Mexican citizens could be eligible for extra land. All governmental efforts to encourage peaceful integration failed, however, as tensions rose between the Mexicans, always more and more in the minority, and the Anglo immigrants. The colonists who came were not, by and large, Roman Catholics; furthermore, a number of them were fugitives from US justice. Political, religious, and cultural conflict did not take long to surface.

One major grievance of the Texans was that the province was appended politically to the state of Coahuila, which had nine times its population. Texans were easily outvoted by the Coahuilans on issues they considered crucial. All appellate courts sat far away in Saltillo, and the time and expense involved in carrying out an appeal completely discouraged the use of the judicial machinery. But the Mexicans had serious grievances as well. A number of filibustering expeditions from the United States, like that of Tennessean James Long, prompted genuine fear that the US government was bent on securing the Texas territory for itself. Although Long's army was subsequently defeated by the Mexicans, clamor in the US Congress and in the American press for changing the boundary or for acquiring much or all of Texas through a new treaty or by stealth excited apprehensions in Mexico City.

As Mexican politicians began to realize that their problems in Texas were getting out of hand, they passed laws to prevent a further weakening of Mexican control. Because slavery was not important anywhere else in the republic, President Guerrero's emancipation proclamation of 1829 clearly targeted Texas. Although manumission was not immediately enforced, it was hoped that the decree itself would make Mexico less attractive to colonists from the US South and would thus arrest future immigration. The colonization law of April 6, 1830, went further by prohibiting all future immigration into Texas from the United States and called for the strengthening of Mexican garrisons, the improvement of economic ties between Texas and the rest of Mexico by the establishment of a new coastal trade, and the encouragement of increased Mexican colonization.

Texans considered these measures repressive, but the last straw for them came with the news from Mexico City that the federal Constitution of 1824 had been annulled. The centralist tendencies of the new regime meant that, instead of having a greater voice in the management of local affairs, the Texans would have no voice at all. As the Texas leaders began to debate their future course of action, they received encouragement for succession, not only from US expansionists who argued theatrically that the Texans should detach themselves from the yoke of dictatorship, but also from a number of Mexican liberals opposed to everything Santa Anna stood for. Among the latter, the most active was Lorenzo de Zavala, a leader of the Constitutional Congress of 1823–24, a founder of the York Rite lodges, and most recently a Mexican minister to France. When Santa Anna invoked extraordinary governmental powers, Zavala advised the Texans that the dictator had forfeited all claims to obedience. The Texans needed little prompting, however; they declared independence, choosing David Burnet as president of the Lone Star Republic and Zavala as vice president.

THE WAR FOR TEXAS INDEPENDENCE

It was time for Santa Anna to take the field again. In the winter of 1835 he moved north at the head of some 6,000 troops. But because of innumerable difficulties during the long trek, not until early March 1836 did he reach the outskirts of San Antonio de Béxar (today San Antonio) and found that the Texans, under the command of William Barrett Travis, had taken refuge in the old Franciscan mission of the Alamo. Among them were such Texas patriots as Davy Crockett and Jim Bowie, as well as Mexicans who opted for independence. The essentials of what happened on March 6 are known to every schoolchild both north and south of the Rio Grande (called the "Río Bravo" in Mexico), though the distortions of nationalism have taken their toll on the history in both countries.

For several days prior to March 6, 1836, Santa Anna had laid siege to the Alamo. The high, stout walls seemed impregnable, and the defenders were not about to surrender to the greatly superior Mexican force. On the late afternoon of March 5 the Texans might have heard a bugle, but most assuredly they did not recognize the sounds coming over the walls as the *degüello*, a battle call used since the time of the Spanish wars against the Moors to signal that the engagement to follow was to be to the death, with no quarter to be shown the enemy. The order had come directly from Santa Anna, and he planned to enforce it.

The next morning the Mexican commander threw waves of soldiers against the adobe fortress. Hundreds were cut down by heavy artillery, but after the first hour the numerical superiority of the attackers began to tell. Several breaches opened in the wall, and the fighting continued inside. The defenders were killed nearly to the last man, including five who were executed as prisoners after the fighting had ended. The high toll on both sides underscored that a peaceful settlement was impossible.

While the battle of the Alamo is famous in the military annals and folklore of the Texas Revolution, a much more significant episode took place several weeks later. General José Urrea engaged a force of Texans under the command of Colonel James W. Fannin at the small town of Goliad. Surrounded and outnumbered, Fannin surrendered in the belief that he and his men would be afforded the recognized rights of prisoners of war. General Urrea wrote to Santa Anna urging clemency for Fannin and the other prisoners, then moved on to another engagement, leaving the Texas prisoners in the charge of Lieutenant Colonel Nicolás de la Portilla. Using the national law of piracy as his authority, Santa Anna sent his reply to Portilla on March 23, stating that the prisoners should be treated as pirates and executed. Nicolás de la Portilla recorded the next two days in his diary as he faced the conflict between his military duty and his moral principles. On March 26, conflicting orders from Urrea and Santa Anna reached him—the latter instructing him to execute all the prisoners immediately.

> What a cruel contrast in these opposite instructions! I spent a restless night.
>
> March 27. At daybreak I decided to carry out the orders of the general-in-chief because I considered them superior. I assembled the whole garrison and ordered the prisoners, who were still sleeping, to be awakened. There were [365]. . . . The prisoners were divided into three groups and each was placed in charge of an adequate guard. . . . I gave instructions to these officers to carry out the orders of the supreme government and the general-in-chief. This was immediately done.[1]

During the month following the battles of the Alamo and Goliad, the Texas army reorganized. Although Santa Anna could take heart from the early military campaigns, and although he had Sam Houston and the Texans on the run, his victories proved to be costly ones. The excesses committed by his troops in both engagements, but especially the execution of the prisoners at Goliad, crystalized opposition to Mexico in the United States and fueled the aspirations of those proponents of Manifest Destiny who believed the United States was destined by providence to expand across the continent. Supplies and volunteers, especially from the Midwest, began to pour into Texas, and by the third week in April Houston caught Santa Anna's troops off guard near the San Jacinto River on April 21. Within half an hour the Mexican army was routed, and Santa Anna himself fled for safety. Two days later he was captured by one of Houston's patrols.

THE LONE STAR REPUBLIC

As a prisoner Santa Anna signed two treaties, one public and one private, with Texas President David Burnet. In the public treaty he agreed that he would not again take up arms against the movement for Texas independence nor would he try to persuade his fellow Mexicans to do so. All hostilities between Mexico and Texas were to cease immediately, and the Mexican army would be withdrawn across the Rio Grande. Prisoners of war in equal numbers would

---

1 Quoted in *The Mexican Side of the Texas Revolution*, trans. and ed. by Carlos E. Castañeda, (Dallas, TX, 1928), 236.

be exchanged. From the Mexican point of view, the secret agreement, later made public, was much more controversial. In return for his own release and transportation to Veracruz, Santa Anna agreed to prepare the Mexican cabinet to receive a peace mission from Texas so that the independence of the Lone Star Republic could be formally recognized.

When he returned to Mexico City, Santa Anna discovered that the treaties had prompted outrage from the intellectual community, the liberals, and many ardent nationalists. On the defensive, he offered the excuse that he had made the promises as an individual and that they were not binding on the government. The legislature responded by enacting a law stipulating that any agreement reached by a Mexican president while held prisoner should be considered null and void. No peace commission from Texas was to be received, and no recognition would be extended.

Texas remained independent as the Lone Star Republic from 1836 to 1845. On the surface it would appear preposterous that without the direct support of the United States, Texas should have been able to retain this independent status in the face of greatly superior Mexican resources and manpower. But Mexico, diverted by other internal problems and political tensions, could not focus solely on Texas. Furthermore, the United States moved quickly to recognize the independence of Texas in March 1837. Although a good deal of sympathy for immediate annexation existed in both Texas and the US Congress, calmer heads prevailed for eight years. Not only did many congressmen believe that annexation would provoke war with Mexico, but the

Santa Anna as a prisoner of Sam Houston. The Mexican victory at the Alamo was offset by Santa Anna's defeat and capture following the battle of San Jacinto.

matter became inexorably entangled in the slavery issue. If Texas entered the Union it would come in as a slave state, and, as a result, annexation was vociferously opposed in New England. In 1844, however, James K. Polk won the presidency on a platform that included annexation. After the election but prior to Polk's inauguration, President John Tyler had an annexation measure introduced as a joint resolution of Congress. It passed both houses in early 1845, setting the stage for a major conflict, and Mexico was clearly being swept into the vortex of war.

THE PRELUDE TO WAR

As soon as the joint resolution annexing Texas passed the US Congress, diplomatic relations ceased and both countries began preparing for war. The Mexican government sought to negotiate a new loan, the proceeds of which would be directed into the war effort if, indeed, the conflict occurred. It also authorized the formation of a new voluntary civilian militia to reinforce regular army units. President Polk ordered army troops into the border region and dispatched naval vessels to the Mexican coast. But he asked the Mexican president, José Joaquín Herrera, to receive a special envoy in Mexico City, and Herrera agreed to receive John Slidell.

The specific issue Slidell was asked to negotiate was a boundary dispute in Texas. Throughout the colonial period the western boundary of Texas had been the Nueces River. The Austin family's grants also recognized the Nueces as the western boundary of Texas. Yet despite thousands of Spanish colonial documents, Mexican documents, and all reliable maps, in December 1836 the congress of the Republic of Texas claimed the Rio Grande as the western boundary. The Texans based their claim on two flimsy grounds. First, during the period of Texas colonization the Mexican government had allowed some US immigrants to settle in the territory between the Nueces and the Rio Grande. It was all Mexico, so it really did not matter. Second, and even more important for the Texas argument, when Santa Anna agreed to withdraw his troops following his stunning defeat at San Jacinto, he ordered them back across the Rio Grande, tacit admission, so the Texans cried, that the western boundary was indeed the Rio Grande. At stake were not merely the one hundred fifty miles between the Nueces and the Rio Grande where they entered the Gulf of Mexico. The Rio Grande meandered not north but northwest, and the Texans claimed it to its source. Thousands and thousands of square miles of territory, indeed, half of New Mexico and Colorado, fell within the claim. When Texas entered the union as the twenty-eighth state, the Polk administration decided to support the Texan pretensions. Albuquerque, Santa Fe, and Taos belonged to the United States as well as San Antonio, Nacogdoches, and Galveston.

The American president wanted still more. Slidell also carried secret instructions to secure California and the rest of New Mexico. Five million dollars was deemed a fair price for the New Mexico territory and $25 million, or even more, for California. But diplomatic secrets had a way of leaking out, even in the middle of the nineteenth century. The Mexican press, learning the true nature of the Slidell mission, appealed to Mexican nationalism; newspapers, circulars, and broadsides threatened rebellion if the president negotiated with the ignominious Yankee pirates. Discussions ended in the midst of fighting between liberals and conservatives.

When Slidell returned to Washington, President Polk held a special cabinet meeting to weigh war feeling. Influential voices, led by Henry Clay, cautioned against war, but the

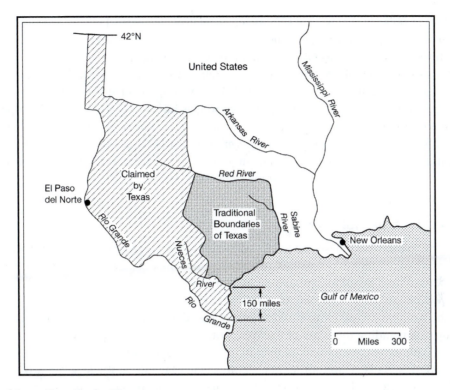

United States–Texas Border Dispute

president had already made up his mind. Nonetheless, Secretary of the Navy George Bancroft and Secretary of State James Buchanan would not vote for a declaration of war unless the United States was attacked by Mexico. By a strange quirk of history, hostilities began that very day. Polk had already ordered General Zachary Taylor into the disputed territory between the Nueces and the Rio Grande. The Mexican commander ordered him to withdraw, but instead Taylor penetrated all the way to the Rio Grande. While the cabinet was meeting, a skirmish broke out between Taylor's dragoons and Mexican cavalry. On the evening of May 9 Taylor reported to Washington that sixteen of his men had been killed or wounded. Polk now had the perfect excuse. He went before the Congress and delivered a provocative war message that bore little resemblance to the truth.

> We have tried every effort at reconciliation. The cup of forbearance had been exhausted even before the recent information from the frontier of the Del Norte. But now, after reiterated menaces, Mexico has passed the boundary of the United States, has invaded our territory, and shed American blood on American soil. She has proclaimed that hostilities exist, and that the two nations are now at war.[2]

---

2   Quoted in Armin Rappaport, ed., *The War with Mexico: Why Did It Happen?* (Chicago, IL, 1964), 6.

Despite objections from the Illinois representative, Abraham Lincoln, the declaration of war was stampeded through Congress. How different things looked from Mexico City: not only had the Americans taken Texas, but they had changed the traditional boundary to double its size. When the Mexicans sought to defend themselves against the additional encroachment, the Yankees cried that Mexico had invaded the United States! Mexico resolved to fiercely resist overt US claims to territory as well as implied assertions of racial superiority. In the still factionalized political milieu, the army overthrew the current president and invited Santa Anna back from his most recent sojourn in Veracruz. The general who had fought the Spanish in 1829, the Texans in 1836, and the French in 1838 would lead his fellow countrymen against the Americans in 1846.

THE COURSE OF THE WAR

Because President Polk, despite a good deal of opposition, moved more decisively than the ephemeral governments in Mexico City, Mexico from the outset was on the defensive. The American strategy called for a three-pronged offensive. The Army of the West would occupy New Mexico and California; the Army of the Center would be sent into northern Mexico; and the Army of Occupation would carry the battle to Mexico City. General Stephen W. Kearny, commanding the Army of the West, got underway first. Leaving Fort Leavenworth, Kansas, with some fifteen hundred men in June of 1846, he began the nine hundred–mile trek toward Santa Fe. Governor Manuel Armijo, not a favorite in the Mexican history textbooks, either accepted a bribe or feared to make a stand. He ordered his three thousand troops to evacuate the town shortly before the Americans arrived on August 19. New Mexico had fallen without the firing of a single shot.

Kearny then divided his army into three. One contingent, under Colonel Sterling Price, continued the occupation of Santa Fe; a second, under Alexander Doniphan, was dispatched directly south to Chihuahua; Kearny himself led the third west to California. California was almost a repeat of New Mexico. By the time Kearny arrived it was already in American hands, having fallen to Naval Commodore John D. Sloat and Colonel John C. Frémont with little opposition from Mexican Californios who believed that the central government had not and could not protect their interests. Doniphan, on the other hand, had to engage the enemy in Chihuahua. The major battle, fought on the outskirts of Chihuahua City, was an artillery duel. Doniphan won the battle, and by February 1847 Chihuahua came under American control. Chihuahuenses were treated to the spectacle of American troops bathing in public fountains, cutting down boulevard shade trees for firewood, and singing "Yankee Doodle" in the main plaza.

The campaign of Zachary Taylor's Army of the Center encountered more difficulty. Taylor's force, some 6,000 strong, moved on Monterrey in August 1846. By September they were in sight of the city but were blocked off by the seven thousand Mexicans soldiers guarding the entrance. Three days of fierce battle took place in the middle of the month. Both sides sustained heavy losses before the Mexican commander sent up the white flag and surrendered the city. By this time Santa Anna had raised an army of about 20,000 men and was training them in San Luis Potosí. The hard march to Saltillo was disastrous. Insufficient

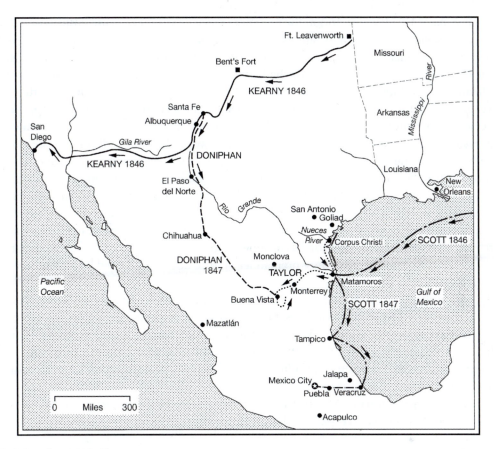

U.S. Invasion, 1846–48

food and water supplies and an unusually harsh winter not only weakened the men but prompted thousands of desertions along the way. Preliminary fighting on February 21 saw Santa Anna force Taylor to pull in his perimeters. The following morning Santa Anna brazenly demanded that Taylor surrender. "Tell Santa Anna to go to Hell," Taylor barked to an aide; but the message actually sent observed proper military niceties and read, "In reply to your note of this date summoning me to surrender my forces at discretion, I beg leave to say that I decline acceding to your request."[3]

The battle of Buena Vista began in earnest later in the day. Santa Anna's assaults on Taylor's well-fortified positions did a good deal of damage, but all were repulsed. Evening found a stalemate. Santa Anna could have attacked again the following morning but instead gathered up a few war trophies—some few flags and three cannon—and carried them back to Mexico City as proof of his victory. In reality, northeast Mexico had been lost to the invaders.

---

3   Quoted in Charles L. Dufour, *The Mexican War: A Compact History, 1846–1848* (New York, NY, 1968), 172.

The major US offensive, and in the end more crucial regarding the pretensions of those Americans who championed the annexation of more Mexican territory, however, was waged by General Winfield Scott's Army of Occupation. As Mexico refused to abandon the fight, the United States resolved to carry the battle to Mexico's heartland and to the capital itself. Making his amphibious landing on March 9, 1847, slightly to the south of the harbor of Veracruz, General Scott and his ten thousand men established their beachhead unopposed. Veracruz, for centuries an object of foreign invasion and attack, was a walled city currently garrisoned by four thousand troops. Scott decided to avoid the fortress of San Juan de Ulloa with its twelve hundred soldiers. By ordering his troops to surround the city and attack from the rear, he not only neutralized the harbor fortress but also cut off the city's source of land supplies and all avenues of exit. Militarily sound, but morally questionable, the plan of attack called for a heavy mortar bombardment of the city that resulted in the deaths of hundreds of innocent civilians. For the next forty-eight hours Scott devastated the city and refused all entreaties of foreign consuls to allow women, children, and other noncombatants to evacuate. He would countenance no manner of truce not accompanied by unconditional surrender.

With military and medical supplies diminished, hundreds of civilian corpses building up in the streets, fires gutting buildings, hospitals destroyed, and the frightening specter of a yellow-fever epidemic mounting, Veracruz surrendered on March 27. Sixty-seven Americans had been killed or wounded, while the toll of Mexican dead within the city numbered between one thousand and fifteen hundred. Civilian deaths outnumbered military casualties almost two to one.

Santa Anna had reached Mexico City when news of the loss of Veracruz arrived. He set out to block General Scott's expected advance on the capital. His troops engaged Scott's force

The US Navy's bombardment of Veracruz resulted in extremely high civilian casualties.

in mid-April and suffered defeat at the mountain pass of Cerro Gordo, some twenty miles east of Jalapa. Santa Anna himself barely escaped capture. He wanted to make one more stand, at Puebla, but the citizenry there refused to cooperate. Scott took the city unopposed. By this time, US newspapers reported not only the devastation, but also accounts of the excesses that has taken place in the northern campaigns. US troops had killed indiscriminately, raped Mexican women, and burned down villages.

Mexico City braced for an imminent attack as the federal district came under martial law and began conscripting a civilian work force to help in the defense preparations. The major preliminary engagements in the capital were fought on the outskirts, where the Americans proved superior in leadership, armament, and tactics. At Churubusco, however, the Mexicans had their finest hour. Fighting bravely, they refused to yield ground to the larger and better-equipped fighting force. Finally intense hand-to-hand combat wore down the Mexicans. On August 20, Santa Anna agreed to negotiate a surrender and used the respite to shore up his defenses within the city itself. When the armistice expired without positive result, Santa Anna was in a position to do battle again.

On the morning of September 7, Scott's cavalry charged Mexican positions at Molina del Rey, and the infantry moved in behind. It was the bloodiest single encounter of the war as the Mexicans suffered over two thousand casualties and the Americans over seven hundred. When the position fell only one fortified site remained in the city—Chapultepec Castle. Located at the crest of a two hundred–foot hill and surrounded by a thick stone wall, the castle was defended by some one thousand troops and the cadets of the military academy. After a furious artillery barrage failed to dislodge the defenders, Scott ordered that the castle be stormed on the morning of September 13. The Mexican land mines failed to explode, and the attackers were able to breach the walls with pickaxes and crowbars. Using scaling ladders, the Americans poured over the top and initiated the bitter hand-to-hand combat. The last defenders were the cadets—the *Niños Héroes*—and because dignity proscribed surrender, many died.

The battle of Chapultepec left the United States nominally in control of Mexico City, but the capital's hostile citizens made life difficult for the victors, carrying out acts of sabotage and rudimentary guerrilla attacks. The anti-war faction in the United States pushed Polk to end the war. He sent Nicholas Tryst with instructions to press for more territory, but the envoy defied his instructions, recognizing that many Americans were skeptical about the benefits of prolonging the conflict that had claimed the lives of thousands of Americans and twice as many Mexicans, including civilians.

THE TREATY OF GUADALUPE HIDALGO AND THE AFTERMATH OF WAR

After a series of difficult negotiations, the treaty ending the war was signed on February 2, 1848, at the village of Guadalupe Hidalgo, just outside of Mexico City. The treaty confirmed US title to Texas and ceded the huge California and New Mexico territories as well. In return Mexico was to retain everything south of the Rio Grande. The United States agreed to make a cash payment of $15 million to the Mexican government and to assume $3.25 million in claims that US citizens had against that government. For a total of $18.25 million—less than one year's budget—Mexico's territory was reduced by half. Because of Mexican insistence, the United

States did obligate itself to protect the property of Mexican citizens who, through no fault of their own, suddenly found themselves residing in the United States. During the next fifty years they would learn that US courts had little interest in enforcing the solemn protections promised by the treaty. Mexicans in New Mexico, Texas, and California who had aided the US armies were rewarded with a persistent onslaught on their lands. Although this did not prevent the growth of vibrant Mexican-American cultural communities throughout the southwest, the aftermath of the war gave rise to a racist anti-immigrant debate that persists to this day.

When the United States signed the Treaty of Guadalupe Hidalgo, it did more than annex half of Mexico. The war and its treaty left a legacy of hostility that would not be easily overcome. While many Mexican intellectuals had not been hesitant to praise the United States, its culture, and its institutions prior to 1846, such commendations became increasingly infrequent in the second half of the nineteenth century. Ironically, from the middle of the sixteenth century, Mexican expeditions had been seeking the Gran Quivira in the north, and finally it was found, at Sutter's Fort, but a few months too late. The gold of California would not make Mexican fortunes or pay its share of Mexico's industrial revolution.

The war reinforced the worst stereotypes that each country held about the other, and these stereotypes in turn contributed to the development of deep-seated prejudices. US historians rationalized, justified, and even commended the decision to wage the war as well as the prosecution of it, on grounds ranging from regenerating a backward people to fulfilling a preordained destiny. The US war with Mexico yielded a virulent Yankeephobia. The fears and hatred of the United States ran deep, and nationalist sentiments were disseminated and popularized in the traditional Mexican *corrido*, the folk song of the common people, as well as in intellectual condemnations of Yankee imperialism. The Niños Héroes came to symbolize all that was best in the Mexican people, especially the young cadet Juan Escutia, who reputedly wrapped himself in the Mexican flag and threw himself over the battlements rather than surrender to the enemy. Every September 13 pilgrimages are made to the monument erected in honor of the boy cadets at the entrance to Chapultepec Park.

The treaty signed at Guadalupe Hidalgo left a stunned Mexico, but the national tragedy did not heal old rifts despite the unifying patriotism of the war. In 1853, Santa Anna once again occupied the presidency and Mexico found itself in difficult economic straits. The president decided that the treasury (and his own office) could be saved only by selling some more of Mexico to the "Colossus of the North." The United States wanted the Mesilla Valley (today southern New Mexico and Arizona) as it offered the best location for building a railroad to newly acquired California. Santa Anna agreed to sell and negotiated what is known in US history as the Gadsden Purchase. For $10 million he alienated thirty thousand square miles of territory but, more importantly, alienated the liberal opposition so thoroughly that they would be rid of him for the last time. The liberal Revolution of Ayutla initiated a movement which mattered more than personalities and politicians who aimed to set the country on a new course.

FURTHER TROUBLES

The United States was not Mexico's only foreign problem, for between the Texas secession and the war with the United States, Mexico became involved in a war with France. During the unremitting series of revolts and counter revolts since independence, the property of foreign nationals often suffered damage. Foreign governments then submitted claims in behalf of their own citizens. Among the numerous French claims were those of a French pastry cook whose delicacies were appropriated and consumed by a group of hungry Mexican soldiers in 1828. In ridicule of the event that followed, Mexican journalists immediately dubbed the episode the "Pastry War."

Conflicting property evaluations, rapid changes in the Mexican government, and the always near-bankrupt state of the Mexican treasury prevented resolution of the French claims for years. In early 1838 the French king, Louis Philippe, demanded payment of $600,000. When Mexico did not comply, Louis Philippe ordered a blockade of the port of Veracruz with a French fleet of twenty-six vessels and over four thousand men. Mexican attempts to negotiate what they believed to be fair compensation ultimately failed, and the government dispatched one thousand men to reinforce the twelve hundred stationed at the venerable, moss-mottled fortress of San Juan de Ulloa in the harbor of Veracruz.

The French initiated their bombardment on the afternoon of November 27, rending a portion of the fortress walls, exploding supplies of ammunition inside, and forcing the Mexican troops to abandon their first line of defense. Proclaiming that honor demanded he take up the challenge once again, Santa Anna offered his services and the Mexican congress declared war on France.

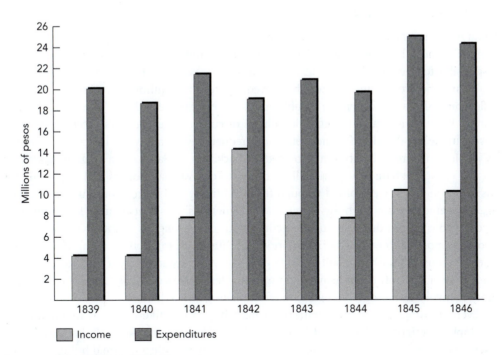

Income and Expenditures, 1839–46

Source: Wilfrid H. Calicott *Church and State in Maxico,*1822–1857 (Durham, N. C., 1926) 160–161.

Santa Anna arrived at Veracruz on December 4; the following morning some three thousand French troops made a landing. In the street fighting that ensued Santa Anna led his troops personally and drove the French back toward the coast. In one of the assaults the Mexican commander had his horse shot out from under him and was severely wounded in the left leg. A few days later it was amputated below the knee. The French, however, had been driven back to their ships and, rather than prolong the venture, they agreed to accept the amount of $600,000, earlier offered by the Mexican government.

The Mexicans could take some heart from having defeated the legions of King Louis Philippe, but there was little time for rejoicing. The liberal-conservative struggle continued unabated. Larger and larger armies (a standing army of 90,000 by 1855) as well as a huge civilian bureaucracy drained the treasury, while industry and commerce stagnated. Successive governments tried every imaginable expedient to replenish the coffers. They recalled old currencies and issued new ones; made forced loans on businesses and on nunneries and other ecclesiastical corporations; obtained voluntary loans from private money lenders called *agiotistas*; confiscated properties; levied new taxes on carriages, coach wheels, all internal trade, and even on dogs, pulque shops, and the gutters of houses; raised old taxes on real estate and imports; and sold lucrative mining concessions to the British. In addition, the government declared a head tax of one and one-half pesos annually on all males between the ages of sixteen and sixty. The average annual government deficit between 1839 and 1846 was 12.7 million pesos.

THE LEGACY OF SANTA ANNA

Santa Anna has the distinction of being the Mexican leader who has inspired the most polemic. For most, he is remembered as a vainglorious and opportunistic despot and traitor, responsible for the loss of half of Mexico's territory. This assessment has elements of truth, but it obscures the circumstances in which he lived. His resort to authoritarianism was, in part, a reflection of the failure of civilian republican rule to foster peace and development in the new nation. Whether federalist or centralist, liberal or conservative, Mexico's elites struggled to govern in the first decades after independence. Frequent revolts and shifts in power, motivated by ideology or personal ambition, provided the backdrop for Santa Anna's path to power.

His economic base in Veracruz allowed him to cultivate supporters and to provide for his troops at times. He profited through flagrant bribery and corruption. But his personal aggrandizement was not wholly materialistic. Evidence shows that he truly saw himself as a courageous patriot dedicated to protecting Mexican sovereignty, as the savior of Mexico, above the political fray. This belief did not keep him from manipulating military and political circumstances when it suited his larger goals. An early supporter of liberal causes, he came to trust that only centralism could impose order in Mexico. He used his growing popularity to invoke extraordinary powers, in effect making him a dictator.

Even allowing for the exaggerations of his critics, a cult-like devotion to Santa Anna developed. Designated "His Most Serene Highness," he arranged for gala balls and banquets to be staged in his honor. Santa Anna's saint's day became a national holiday; friends and favor-seekers brought him gifts. Favored journalists lavished praise on him in eulogistic editorials.

An 1845 lithograph depicting a one-legged Santa Anna standing on Manga de Clavo built on extortions of various kinds.

Perhaps the most bizarre episode of his regime occurred in the fall of 1842. Santa Anna ordered the disinterment of his amputated leg from its quiet repose on his hacienda of Manga de Clavo. The mummified member was transported to Mexico City and, after an impressive procession through the streets of the capital in which the presidential bodyguard, the army, and the cadets from the Chapultepec Military Academy all participated, it was taken to the cemetery of Santa Fe, where it was placed in a specially designed urn and set atop a huge stone pillar. The ceremony was typically Santanesque. Conducted at the site of the shrine, his entire cabinet, the diplomatic corps, and the congress stood in praise as his shattered leg was offered to the fatherland.

In a political atmosphere charged with mistrust, revolts and counter-revolts had become accepted as inevitable concomitants of the social order. In Yucatán's Caste War elites drove Maya rebels into remote areas. Although not all Mayas supported the Caste War while some non-Mayas did, the conflict took on a racial character as Mayas called for an end to ethnic discrimination. Maya leaders historically had made alliances with whites, but when these elites refused, a tenacious group of Maya warriors established a stronghold in today's Quintana Roo. There, they maintained an independent Maya state until the end of the nineteenth century. Drawing on vibrant Maya cultural traditions and a millenarian cult of the Talking Cross, they established a viable agricultural economy and carried on trade with neighboring British Honduras.

Elsewhere in Mexico some material improvements had been recorded, at least in the larger cities. One modernizing official notable for his efforts to rebuild Mexico's economy during Santa Anna's tenure was fiscal conservative Lucas Alamán. Active in trying to boost the mining and textile industries, he also founded Mexico's first development bank, and he served as minister of industry from 1842 to 1846. The textile industry developed rapidly during the 1840s and 1850s but economic retrogression was more noteworthy. Roads were in disrepair, mines were still abandoned, fertile agricultural fields lay vacant, industrialization was a vague hope for the future, foreign trade was largely absent and the national debt was growing.

In the end, the greatest misfortune of the age of Santa Anna was the loss of Texas and the war with the United States, neither of which can be attributed to Santa Anna alone. Mexican elites failed to build a nation with strong institutions and a sound economy. A weak, factionalized nation invited, but certainly did not justify, the aggression by its northern neighbor. Catastrophes wrought by US expansion contributed more to Mexico's impoverishment, its lack of self-esteem, and general demoralization than any other event of the nineteenth century.

RECOMMENDED FOR FURTHER STUDY

Alonzo, Armando. *Tejano Legacy: Rancheros and Settlers in South Texas, 1734–1900*. Albuquerque: University of New Mexico Press, 1998.

Callcott, Wilfrid H. *Church and State in Mexico, 1822–1857*. Durham, NC: Duke University Press, 1926.

Craib, Raymond B. *Cartographic Mexico: A History of State Fixations and Fugitive Landscapes*. Durham, NC: Duke University Press, 2004.

DePalo, William A. *The Mexican National Army, 1822–1852*. College Station: Texas A & M University Press, 1997.

Ducey, Michael T. *A Nation of Villages: Riot and Rebellion in the Mexican Huasteca, 1750–1850*. Tucson: University of Arizona Press, 2004.

Dufour, Charles L. *The Mexican War: A Compact History, 1846–1848*. New York: Hawthorne Books, 1968.

Dumond, Don E. *The Machete and the Cross: Campesino Rebellion in Yucatán*. Lincoln: University of Nebraska Press, 1997.

Fowler, Will. *Santa Anna of Mexico*. Lincoln: University of Nebraska Press, 2009.

_____. *Tornel and Santa Anna: The Writer and the Caudillo, Mexico, 1795–1853*. Westport, CT: Greenwood Press, 2000.

Griswold del Castillo, Richard. *The Treaty of Guadalupe Hidalgo: A Legacy of Conflict*. Norman: University of Oklahoma Press, 1990.

Greenberg, Amy S. *A Wicked War: Polk, Clay, Lincoln, and the 1846 U.S. Invasion of Mexico*. New York: Alfred A. Knopf, 2012.

Guardino, Peter F. *Peasants, Politics, and the Formation of Mexico's National State: Guerrero, 1800–1867*. Stanford, CA: Stanford University Press, 1996.

_____. *The Dead March: A History of the the Mexican-American War*. Cambridge, MA: Harvard University Press, 2017.

Hale, Charles A. "The War with the United States and the Crisis in Mexican Thought." *The Americas* 14/2 (1957): 153–73.

Harris, III, Charles H. *The Sánchez Navarros: A Socioeconomic Study of a Coahuilan Latifundio, 1846–1853*. Chicago: Loyola University Press, 1964.

Henderson, Timothy J. *A Glorious Defeat: Mexico and Its War with the United States*. New York: Hill and Wang, 2007.

Jones, Jr., Oakah L. *Santa Anna*. New York: Twayne Publishers, 1968.

Kendall, George Wilkins. *Dispatches from the Mexican War*. Norman: University of Oklahoma Press, 1999.

Matovina, Timothy M. *The Alamo Remembered: Tejano Accounts and Perspectives.* Austin: University of Texas Press, 1995.

The Mexican Side of the Texas Revolution. Translated and edited by Carlos E. Castañeda. Dallas, TX: P.L. Turner Company, 1928.

Pletcher, David M. *The Diplomacy of Annexation: Texas, Oregon, and the Mexican War.* Columbia: University of Missouri Press, 1973.

Randall, Robert W. *Real del Monte: A British Mining Venture in Mexico.* Austin: University of Texas Press, 1972.

Rappaport, Armin, ed. *The War with Mexico: Why Did It Happen?* Chicago: Rand McNally 1964.

Reed, Nelson. *The Caste War of Yucatán.* Stanford, CA: Stanford University Press, 1964.

Reséndez, Andrés. *Changing National Identities at the Frontier: Texas and New Mexico, 1800–1850.* New York: Cambridge University Press, 2005.

Richmond, Douglas, ed. *Essays on the Mexican War.* College Station: Texas A & M University Press, 1986.

Robinson, Cecil, ed. *The View from Chapultepec: Mexican Writers on the Mexican American War.* Tucson: University of Arizona Press, 1979.

Rugeley, Terry. *Rebellion Now and Forever: Mayas, Hispanics, and Caste War Violence in Yucatán, 1800–1880.* Stanford, CA: Stanford University Press, 2009.

_____. *Yucatán's Maya Peasantry and the Origins of the Caste War.* Austin: University of Texas Press, 1996.

Ruiz, Ramón Eduardo, ed. *The Mexican War: Was It Manifest Destiny?* New York: Holt, Rinehart & Winston, 1963.

Santa Anna, Antonio López de. *The Eagle: The Autobiography of Santa Anna.* Edited by Ann Fears Crawford. Austin, TX: Pemberton Press, 1967.

Santoni, Pedro. *Mexicans at Arms: Puro Federalists and the Politics of War, 1845–1848.* Fort Worth: Texas Christian University Press, 1996.

Seijas, Tatiana, and Jake Frederick. *Spanish Dollars and Sister Republics: The Money That Made Mexico and the United States.* Lanham, MD: Rowman & Littlefield, 2017.

Smith, Justin H. *The War with Mexico.* 2 vols. Gloucester, MA: Peter Smith, 1963.

Stevens, Donald F. *Origins of Instability in Early Republican Mexico.* Durham, NC: Duke University Press, 1991.

Tenenbaum, Barbara. *The Politics of Penury: Debts and Taxes in Mexico, 1821–1856.* Albuquerque: University of New Mexico Press, 1986.

Tijerina, Andrés. *Tejanos in Texas under the Mexican Flag, 1821–1836.* College Station: Texas A & M University Press, 1994.

Valerio Jiménez, Omar S. *River of Hope: Forging Identity and Nation in the Rio Grande Borderlands.* Durham, NC: Duke University Press, 2013.

Vázquez, Josefina. "War and Peace with the United States." In *The Oxford History of Mexico,* edited by Michael C. Meyer and William H. Beezley, 319–48. New York: Oxford University Press, rev. 2010.

CHAPTER 19

SOCIETY AND CULTURE IN THE FIRST HALF OF THE NINETEENTH CENTURY

It is ironic, yet understandable, that historians seeking to learn how a people lived often rely upon the accounts of foreign travelers. That which is commonplace to a local inhabitant is often colorful or unique to a foreigner. The young Frenchman Alexis de Tocqueville related to the citizens of the United States much that they did not know about themselves, and a series of perceptive visitors to Mexico during the first half of the nineteenth century did the same for its people. While their analyses often reflected their own prejudices, their commentaries are invaluable. One has only to disregard their chauvinism and naiveté about the world to read these accounts to gain insights into the past.

POPULATION

The Mexican wars for independence, although small in comparison with other world conflicts, nevertheless took their toll. Accurate casualty figures do not exist, but reliable estimates suggest that a half a million deaths, or about one-twelfth of Mexico's population, is not an exaggeration. The battles left tens of thousands of orphans, widows, disabled, and infirm. The dislocations occasioned by war were not quickly overcome. Impending engagements caused civilians to flee, shopkeepers to close their doors, mothers to pull their children out of school, and those who could afford it to hoard supplies. Many who left a town or city did not return, and families were permanently separated. Several years after the wars ended, visitors to Veracruz reported desolate, grass-grown streets and a generally ruinous appearance. Mexico's rate of population growth, which was rapid prior to 1810, leveled off dramatically for the next twenty years.

Although recovery was slow, change in the prevailing social structure was even slower. Reading the accounts of travelers from the late colonial period and comparing them to accounts in the nineteenth century, one is struck by how little conditions actually changed. To be sure, the gachupines disappeared from the top of the social structure, but the criollos simply stepped into the vacuum. The population grew from 4.5 million in 1800 to over 7.5 million fifty years later, but the social categories of that population remained amazingly static. In spite of the fact that republican government eliminated the racial category *indio* (Indian) from civil jurisprudence (as all Mexicans became citizens and equal under the law), classifying Indians as different continued to dominate nineteenth-century thinking and practice in religious and civil life.

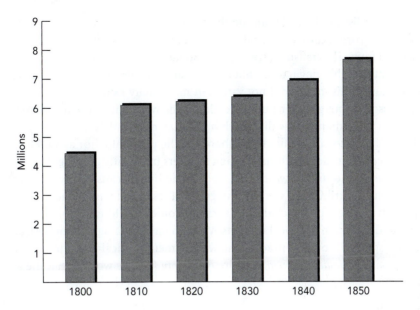

Mexican Population Growth, 1800–50

Source: Howard Cine, *Mexico: Revolution to Evolution, 1940–1960* (New York, 1936), 336.

INDIAN PUEBLOS

Mexico was a rural country in the first half of the nineteenth century. The Indians, making up over a third of the population, lived for the most part in thousands of tiny villages. Although these pueblos varied physically from one climate to another, they presented a uniform cultural pattern. Pueblos were the most tradition-bound unit in Mexican society. In south and central Mexico the huts were made of split reeds covered with thatched roofs. In the north adobe was more common, but in both cases dogs, pigs, and chickens shared the quarters with the family. In 1850 Carl Sartorius, a German natural scientist traveling in Mexico, drew a composite interior from the many Indian dwellings he had seen.

> Inside the hut, upon a floor of earth just as nature formed it, burns day and night the sacred fire of the domestic hearth. Near it, stands the *metate* and *metapile,* a flat and cylindrical stone for crushing the maize, and the earthen pots and dishes, a large water pitcher, a drinking cup and a dipper of gourd shell constitute the whole wealth of the Indian's cottage, a few rude carvings, representing the saints, the decoration. Neither table nor benches cumber the room within, mats of rushes or palm leaves answer for both seat and table. They serve as beds too for their rest at night, and for their final rest in the grave.[1]

Only the larger Indian towns had churches; practically none had schools and Spanish was rarely spoken. Medical care, as it existed, was entrusted to the hands of the local *curandero*. The

---

1   Carl Sartorius, *Mexico about 1850* (Stuttgart, Germany, 1961), 69.

Indian agriculturalist lived largely outside the monetary economy. His own garden provided his daily needs—corn, beans, chile, and, occasionally, in some areas, squash and a few other vegetables and fruits. The craftsman sometimes had money pass through his hands as he could sell his wares at a neighboring market. But he was scarcely better off than the farmer in the next dwelling because, if his money did not vanish in momentary extravagance, he could become prey to the unscrupulous gambler, pulque vendor, or highwayman as he returned to the pueblo.

Women in the Indian village did much more than care for her house. Even when pregnant, she often worked in the field and shared in the physical labor as well as performed all the expected domestic functions. Foreign travelers frequently commented on the heavy loads of firewood the Indian women carried to the hut. Because daily life was difficult, Indian women's contributions were an integral and respected part of the whole apparatus of survival. In a largely patriarchal rural society, women could exert influence as healers, midwives, and selling in the local markets. Women enjoyed a reputation of frugality, and from the village tradition, for practical as well as metaphorical considerations, a phrase was born: *Donde las mujeres comen, las hormigas lloran* (Where women eat, the ants cry).

RURAL TOWNS

The larger rural towns of from one thousand to perhaps thirty-five hundred housed primarily mestizos and Indians who had become more acculturated to the Mexican way of life. Spanish was the language of the street and the home. Market day, sometimes weekly and sometimes biweekly, attracted Indians by the hundreds from the surrounding pueblos to sell their produce. The plazas would be filled with vendors trafficking in cloth, clothing, pottery, cutlery, trinkets, earthenware, and blankets and with Indian women bent over charcoal fires preparing food for passersby. The day's work finished, the evening hours might be given over to gambling, cards, dancing, and perhaps wagering at the local cockfight. The towns generally had one or two *pulquerías* where hours could be idled away sipping the fermented juice of the century plant, the maguey. For those who found the local shop too unclean or the stench too unbearable, itinerant vendors with full jars on their heads made house calls. Invariably, the church was the most prominent architectural structure in the town. Adorned with a respectable number of saints and a few paintings, the gilded altar stood out in crass contrast to the impoverished surroundings.

If life in the rural towns was somewhat easier than in the Indian pueblo, it still left much to be desired. Streets of dirt caused dust in the dry season and awful quagmires during the rains. The schools, in those few towns that had them, featured the crudest of facilities, and the teachers were often only slightly more literate than those who sat at their feet. The one-story houses were constructed of adobe or stone and usually left unpainted. Travelers found no hotels, inns, or public restaurants; they might find lodging for the night in the town hall or in the house of a relatively affluent resident who took pity on them. Joel Poinsett, a man who enjoyed his comforts, expressed dismay at the facilities he found in a small Veracruz town as he was working his way to Mexico City in 1822.

> We supped on our cold provisions, and stretched ourselves out on the landlady's bed, which did not prove a bed of rest. It consisted only of canes laid lengthways, and covered with a blanket. This, and even the smell of raw meat, might have been endured, but we were visited

The village of Chalco, southeast of Mexico City, looked much as it had during the colonial period until the railroad passed through during the second half of the nineteenth century.

> by such swarms of fleas, sancudos, and musquitos [*sic*] that we rejoiced when we saw the light of day beaming through the cane enclosure that constituted the walls of the hut.[2]

The poor males in the towns had one concern that did not trouble those in the Indian village: like their counterparts in the larger cities, they were subject to the dreaded *leva*. A system of forced conscription directed at the uneducated masses (the Indians in the villages were generally excluded simply because they did not speak Spanish), the leva was used by local commanders to fill their military quotas. Troublemakers, vagabonds, and prisoners were taken first. As the demands of the wars for independence, and then the civil wars, continued in the first half of the nineteenth century, tens of thousands of illiterate males were picked up off the streets and pressed into long periods of service without even being allowed to return home to say good-bye to wives, children, and parents.

Both in the Indian village and in the small rural town, inhabitants resisted outside influence in their affairs and defended community land and water rights. Contact with the outside world was limited to the occasional traveler passing through and sometimes the skirmishing various factions in liberal-conservative struggles. Ideologies from the top had little influence except when they might be molded to local purposes.

---

2 Joel R. Poinsett, *Notes on Mexico Made in the Autumn of 1822, Accompanied by an Historical Sketch of the Revolution* (New York, NY, 1969), 23–24.

PROVINCIAL CITIES

One had to visit the larger provincial cities, generally the state capitals, to find evidence of the amenities of wealth and a sense of nationalism. Ranging in population from seven thousand or eight thousand to seventy-one thousand (Puebla in 1852), these cities were well laid out in the classic Spanish pattern. The main streets, paved and well lighted, led into the central plaza surrounded on four sides by the main cathedral, the state or municipal office buildings, and several rows of good shops, generally under a stone arcade. In addition to an impressive selection of native products from many parts of the country, the shops stocked foreign merchandise, and a sizable merchant class thrived. Mexican cities boasted a bullring, a theater, traveling sideshows with tightrope walkers and jugglers, bookstores, and a wide array of public and religious festivals. Unlike in the pueblo or the rural town, many criollos could be found in the better residential areas. A few provincial aristocrats led lives of plenty, but they were exceptions even among the criollo population. A modest number of schools educated only the wealthy. In 1842, for example, about thirteen hundred schools operated in all of Mexico. Total enrollment amounted to only sixty thousand, or less than one percent of the population. Barely a third of the schools were free.

Most of the state capitals grew rapidly in the first half of the nineteenth century. Aguascalientes doubled in population, and Mérida tripled. Veracruz and Guanajuato were almost alone in declining, the former because of constant warfare and heavy bombardments from naval vessels in the harbor and troops on the shore. The latter suffered from the generally depressed character of the surrounding mines. By mid-century Puebla and Guadalajara competed for second place on the nation's population rosters, with Puebla holding a slight lead.

A nineteenth-century woodcut depicting the central plaza of Mérida, Yucatán, about 1850.

MEXICO CITY: THE RICH AND THE POOR

Mexico City comprised a world unto itself, where all of the richest and many of the poorest in the country seemed to congregate. The focal point of the entire nation, it exerted an influence on the country quite out of proportion to its size or its political prominence as the national capital. From a population of 137,000 at the turn of the century, it grew to 160,000 at the time of independence and to 170,000 by 1852. Its wide, relatively clean streets (better lighted than those in New York or Philadelphia) were crowded with expensive imported carriages, a status symbol among the rich. The main cathedral on the central plaza, the *zócalo*, could certainly rival any in Europe. The very bustle of the city set it apart from any other place in the republic. Street urchins hawked newspapers and pamphlets, scribes sitting on the sidewalks penned out messages for the illiterate, gentlemen on horseback paraded their finest mounts, and foreign artists gathered on park benches to sketch Chapultepec Castle or the snow-covered volcanoes of Popocatépetl and Iztaccíhuatl. In addition to numerous primary and secondary schools (again reserved largely for the affluent), Mexico City housed the university, a school of mines, the Art Academy of San Carlos, a well-endowed botanical garden, libraries, museums, and a surprising number of public parks. By the middle of the century a thriving opera was an integral part of the city's cultural life. The literacy rate, for both men and women, rose modestly during the first half of the nineteenth century.

The Mexico City aristocracy, like their counterparts throughout the world, enjoyed their amenities and displayed their wealth conspicuously. Many of the homes were truly luxurious, usually enclosed by high walls for security and privacy. Interior walls boasted fine imported tapestries. Aristocratic women, whether attending the theater, the opera, or even a high mass, displayed a flair for the sometimes revealing clothes designed by their favorite French *modiste*; and the men, while not outdoing their wives in fanciful dress, prided themselves on their ability to duplicate the latest fashions from Paris or London. Marriages among elite families facilitated their accumulation of wealth.

The urban aristocracy, secular and religious, looked good and lived well despite the political chaos that engulfed Mexico after independence.

Describing a ball she attended in 1840, the wife of the Spanish minister to Mexico City noted the female costume:

> One, for example, would have a scarlet satin petticoat, and over it a pink satin robe, trimmed with scarlet ribbons to match. Another, a short rich blue satin dress, beneath which appeared a handsome purple satin petticoat. . . . All had diamonds and pearls . . . I did not see one without earrings, necklace, and broach.[3]

But even middle- and upper-class women joined their poorer sisters in patronizing pawnshops (including the Monte de Piedad, which had been established in the colonial period by the Conde de Regla), where they hocked clothes and utensils for needed cash as part of a flourishing small credit system.

The poorest of the heavily indigent Indian population was concentrated in the Mexico City districts of Santiago Tlatelolco and San Juan Tenochtitlán, but they spilled over into other areas of the capital. When the upper class filed out of the theater or left the opera, they could not fail to see the *léperos*. Described variously in the literature as beggars, vagabonds, panhandlers, riffraff, and outcasts, thousands of them could be seen in the streets of Mexico City every day. Although there were undoubtedly some fakers and reprobates among them, most were genuinely wretched in physical appearance: distressed children with bloated bellies, men and women crippled by war or accident or serious genetic deformities, and men and women of all ages were found pitiably inebriated. Writers and reformers decried the degeneracy of the latter as a threat to the future of the nation.

Not unknown in the colonial period, the léperos became institutionally endemic in the first half of the nineteenth century. No foreign traveler to Mexico City failed to notice them. In 1822, for example, Joel Poinsett callously recorded:

> In front of the churches and in the neighborhood of them we saw an unusual number of beggars, and they openly exposed their disgusting sores and deformities to excite our compassion. I observed one among them wrapped in a large white sheet, who, as soon as he perceived that he had attracted my attention, advanced towards me, and unfolding his covering, disclosed his person perfectly naked and covered from head to heel with ulcers. . . . No city in Italy contains so many miserable beggars, and no town in the world so many blind.[4]

Life for the urban poor who worked rather than begged offered few material rewards. Domestic service, though remuneration was small, was highly sought by both sexes because it generally offered a clean room in which to sleep and food enough to sustain oneself. Professional washerwomen plied their laundering service at public fountains. In the streets the most visible employee was the *cargador*, a direct descendant of the tameme of the colonial period and nothing more than a human beast of burden. In the cities, and between the cities, the sight described by Edward Tayloe, Joel Poinsett's private secretary, described a common sight.

> There are no carts or drays for the transportation of goods, so that everything is carried upon the backs of these poor creatures, who are enabled to carry a load of 300 lbs. by means of

---

3   Fanny Calderón de la Barca, *Life in Mexico: The Letters of Fanny Calderón de la Barca*, ed. Howard T. Fisher and Marion Hall Fisher (Garden City, NY, 1970), 132–33.

4   Poinsett, *Notes on Mexico*, 73.

The cargadores, a legacy of the colonial tamemes, carried everything on their backs.

a leather band or strap, the cargador leaning forward at an angle of about 45°, the burden resting on the back supported by this strap. With so heavy a load they travel great distances, moving in a brisk walk or trot.[5]

But the cargador carrying supplies into the city or delivering on his back an imported French piano had little to complain about in comparison to his counterpart who was drafted from the city to work in the mines. Employed to bring the ore out of the deep shafts and paid by the pound, the cargadores often carried extremely heavy loads on their backs as they worked their way up ladders. Accidents were frequent; the widows might sometimes receive a small share of the last load as compensation.

Indians and mestizos, whether they lived in a small village or in Mexico City, constituted Mexico's labor force: farmers, servants, day laborers, cargadores, vendors, military recruits, craftsmen, and errand boys. Women worked as domestic servants, spinners in the textile mills, food preparers, waitresses, and vendors on the streets and in the marketplaces. They suffered a short, social leash. If they committed no crime but in some way transgressed anticipated norms of female behavior, a magistrate could send them to a *casa de depósito*, a protective institution designed to teach fallen women how to behave. The situation of the male worker could be worse. If accused of a crime, the word of the employer was generally taken and the worker had no recourse. Held in filthy prisons, often without formal charges, the father who stole a loaf of bread was confined a common cell with the convicted murderer, the young boy with the hardened criminal, and the physically challenged with the mentally insane. If Mexican politicians in the first half of the nineteenth century did little to change the fabric of society, it was not because the intelligentsia failed to urge a new course of action. And it was this talented group of Mexican writers, musicians, artists, and scholars that made Mexico City so different from the remainder of the republic.

---

5   Edward Thornton Tayloe, *Mexico, 1825–1828: The Journal and Correspondence of Edward Thornton Tayloe*, ed. C. Harvey Gardiner (Chapel Hill, NC, 1959), 50–51.

INTELLECTUALS AND ARTISTS

The prime literary current in Mexico, as in all of Latin America, in the period following independence was romanticism. Intensely concerned with freedom and individualism, the Mexican romantics, in both prose and poetry, set out to explore the meaning of their newly won independence and to foster a distinctive culture. They turned their backs on Spain and sought to define a new form of national artistic expression. But to understand and convey nascent nationalism they had to understand their Mexico, and thus they began writing with great emotion and sentimentality about the indigenous heritage, the physical environment, the wars of conquest and, of course, the recent movement for independence.

In 1836, young novelists, poets, and dramatists began meeting in the newly formed Academia de San Juan de Letrán, and for the next twenty years the academy midwifed the birth of Mexican national literature. Of the early romantic coterie who met there regularly, only two left indelible impressions on the romantic movement itself: Fernando Calderón (1809–49) and Ignacio Rodrí-guez Galván (1816–42). Calderón, a sometime soldier and liberal politician, experimented with lyric poetry, then turned to drama, both comedy and tragedy. His amusing satirical plays, some with veiled criticism of the Santa Anna dictatorship, were performed on the leading stages of Mexico in the 1840s and 1850s. Rodríguez Galván penned patriotic verse and described the Mexi-can landscape but, most important, lamented the Spanish injustices against the Indian popula-tions. In the process he won his position as Mexico's foremost lyrical poet of the first half of the nineteenth century. His *Profecía de Guatimoc* (1839) has been called the masterpiece of Mexican romanticism, expressing passion, sentimentality, and an anti-Spanish, pro-Indian orientation.

Mexican music, like its literature, rejected its Spanish parentage in the early post-independence years. Nowhere is this more graphically illustrated than in the decision of José Mariano Elízaga (1786–1842), Mexico's most famous composer of the second quarter of the nineteenth century, to drop the title "Don" (signifying the Spanish gentleman) from his name. After independence, the composer informed the Mexican populace that henceforth he preferred to be called simply Citizen Elízaga. By sheer chance he was the piano tutor to Anna María Huarte, who subsequently married Agustín de Iturbide. With the defeat of the Span-ish and the establishment of the empire, Iturbide brought him to Mexico City. His original compositions were all designed for use in the churches, but the liturgy was much too radical for the conservative, Spanish-thinking hierarchy. Citizen Elízaga did encounter success in another venture. In 1824 he founded Mexico's first philharmonic society, and the following year this group initiated Mexico's first national conservatory, the Academia de Música.

The Mexican artistic community strove for a type of new nationalistic expression as well. Scarcely had the new republican government of Guadalupe Victoria been established when Pedro Patiño Ixtolinque, the general director of the Art Academy of San Carlos and Mexico's most famous sculptor, set to work on a monument honoring Father Morelos. An early American visitor to the academy was impressed with its facilities but, displaying a common anti-Catholic bias, also found fault: "Connected with this academy is a disgusting sort of work shop, where gods and saints are manufactured in wood and stone for the churches in town and country."[6] Although the young re-public housed a few artists of unusual talent such as the costumbrista painter José Agustín Arrieta, the three decades following independence were not particularly distinguished years for Mexican art.

---

6   Ibid., 58.

Of all the great Mexican historians of the post-independence years, only one, Lucas Alamán (1792–1853), did not allow an anti-Spanish bias to spoil his historical scholarship; but he was no less partisan than his ideological foes. A criollo aristocrat, a convinced monarchist, and a firsthand witness to the excesses committed by Hidalgo's Indian army in Guanajuato, he came to the defense of the Spanish crown. His five-volume *Historia de México* (1849–52) indicates clearly that he considered Cortés the conveyer of civilization and religion and the founder of the Mexican nation. Spain's imperial system in the New World was benevolent and progressive. The wars for independence, according to Alamán, had to be viewed in two stages. The early stage, that of Father Hidalgo, he censured as an insane attack on property and civilization itself. But the conservative conclusion of the independence movement by Iturbide could be rationalized. The mother country, defying all true Hispanic values, had turned disturbingly liberal with King Ferdinand's acceptance of the Constitution of 1812. The leadership of the independence movement in the colonies actually defended traditionally Hispanic values but in a manner so savage that it set the country on the wrong course.

But Lucas Alamán stands almost alone in the historiography of the 1830s and 1840s. His contemporaries Carlos María de Bustamante, Lorenzo de Zavala, and José María Luis Mora viewed history quite differently—as a struggle against three centuries of Spanish tyranny. The Black Legend, stressing the avarice, inhumanity, and bigotry of the Spaniards, is not difficult to spot. The independence movement was a repudiation of Spain, and the three histories mirroring this rejection contributed in their own way to the cultural disavowal of the Hispanic part of the Mexican spirit. Spain's attempted reconquest in 1829 strongly reinforced this pervasive anti-Hispanism.

Intellectuals and artists began to define Mexico in terms of what it was not, without consensus about what the nation could or should be. But their ideas were taking shape in popular forms like almanacs. Published in the late colonial period to remind people of holy days and print images of important political and religious figures, their content began to change after independence. Not only did they highlight independence heroes and profile other civic leaders, but they also provided bits of everyday information and sections on religion, science, geography, literature, and history. In his almanacs, Fernández de Lizardi introduced illustrations by the engraver José María Torreblanca, who used *El Mono Vano*, "the vain monkey," to mock bad politicians (monkeys were a prevalent image for satirizing all kinds of evils). Other almanacs printed the political predictions of impending upheavals by the fictitious prophet Madre Matiana (a colonial visionary allegedly conducted to hell by the Virgin Mary to witness scenes of God's future wrath). Her "predictions" lasted throughout the century as a platform for debating nationhood, religion, roles of women, and popular culture.

Also contributing to the development of shared popular memories were the figures of the *lotería*, in both the national lottery and a board game that had origins in the colonial period. Lottery cards of personages, places, and objects represented familiar aspects of material and religious culture, sometimes local and sometimes national. In the absence of anything that could be yet defined as national identity, popular images in almanacs and lotería "mocked social pretensions of different stereotypical individuals and promoted pleasurable pride about national geography, monuments, and emblems."[7]

7   William H. Beezley, *Mexican National Identity: Memory, Innuendo, and Popular Culture* (Tucson, 2008), 49.

RECOMMENDED FOR FURTHER STUDY

Arrom, Sylvia Marina. *Containing the Poor: The Mexico City Poor House, 1774–1881*. Durham, NC: Duke University Press, 2000.

_____. *The Women of Mexico City*. Stanford, CA: Stanford University Press, 1985.

Beezley, William H. *Mexican National Identity: Memory, Innuendo, and Popular Culture*. Tucson: University of Arizona Press, 2008.

Brushwood, John S. *Mexico in Its Novel: A Nation's Search for Identity*. Austin: University of Texas Press, 1966.

Calderón de la Barca, Fanny. *Life in Mexico: The Letters of Fanny Calderón de la Barca*. Edited by Howard T. Fisher and Marion Hall Fisher. Garden City, NY: Doubleday, 1970.

Cueva, Marío de la, et al. *Major Trends in Mexican Philosophy*. Translated by A. Robert Caponigri. Notre Dame, IN: University of Notre Dame Press, 1966.

Francois, Marie Eileen. *A Culture of Everyday Credit: Housekeeping, Pawnbroking, and Government in Mexico City, 1750–1920*. Lincoln: University of Nebraska Press, 2006.

Gilmore, N. Ray. "The Condition of the Poor in Mexico, 1834." *Hispanic American Historical Review* 37/2 (1957): 213–26.

González, Deena. *Refusing the Favor: The Spanish-Mexican Women of Santa Fe, 1820–1880*. New York: Oxford University Press, 1999.

Green, Stanley C. *The Mexican Republic: The First Decade, 1823–1832*. Pittsburgh, PA: University of Pittsburgh Press, 1987.

Guardino, Peter. *The Time of Liberty: Popular Political Culture in Oaxaca, 1750–1850*. Durham, NC: Duke University Press, 2005.

Hale, Charles A. *Mexican Liberalism in the Age of Mora, 1821–1853*. New Haven, CT: Yale University Press, 1968.

O'Hara, Matthew D. "*Miserables* and Citizens: Indians, Legal Pluralism, and Religious Practice in Early Republican Mexico." In *Religious Culture in Modern Mexico*, edited by Martin Austin Nesvig, 14–34. Lanham, MD: Rowman & Littlefield, 2007.

Olivera, Ruth R., and Liliane Crete. *Life in Mexico under Santa Anna, 1822–1855*. Norman: University of Oklahoma Press, 1991.

Penyak, Lee M. "Safe Harbors and Compulsory Custody: *Casas de Depósito* in Mexico, 1750–1865." *Hispanic American Historical Review* 79/1 (1999): 83–99.

Poinsett, Joel R. *Notes on Mexico Made in the Autumn of 1822, Accompanied by an Historical Sketch of the Revolution*. New York: Praeger Publishers, 1969.

Ramos, Raúl A. *Beyond the Alamo: Forging Mexican Ethnicity in San Antonio, 1821–1861*. Durham, NC: University of North Carolina Press, 2009.

Sartorius, Carl. *Mexico about 1850*. Stuttgart, Germany: F. A. Brockhaus Komm, 1961.

Shaw, Frederick J. "The Artisan in Mexico City (1824–1853)." In *Labor and Laborers through Mexican History*, edited by Elsa Cecilia Frost, Michael C. Meyer, and Josefina Zoraida Vásquez, 399–418. Mexico City, Mexico and Tucson: El Colegio de México and University of Arizona Press, 1979.

Stevenson, Robert. *Music in Mexico: A Historical Survey*. New York: Thomas Y. Crowell, Co., 1971.

Tayloe, Edward Thornton. *Mexico, 1825–1828: The Journal and Correspondence of Edward Thornton Tayloe*. Edited by C. Harvey Gardiner. Chapel Hill: University of North Carolina Press, 1959.

Ward, Henry G. *Mexico in 1827*. 2 vols. London, UK: Colburn, 1828.

Warren, Richard A. *Vagrants and Citizens: Politics and the Masses in Mexico City from Colony to Republic*. Wilmington, DE: Scholarly Resources, 2001.

Wright Ríos, Edward. *Searching for Madre Matiana: Prophecy and Popular Culture in Modern Mexico*. Albuquerque: University of New Mexico Press, 2014.

LIBERALS AND CONSERVATIVES SEARCH FOR SOMETHING BETTER

CHAPTER 20

THE REFORM AND THE FRENCH INTERVENTION

THE REVOLUTION OF AYUTLA

The Revolution of Ayutla, the armed movement that ousted Santa Anna from power in 1855, brought together some of the most original and creative minds in Mexico. Far from being ivory tower scholars, this group of writers and intellectuals syncretized their own creative work with a spirit of public service, a sense of social consciousness, and a profound desire to see Mexico emerge at last from its long night of political instability and warfare. They sought to reevaluate the Mexican national conscience and redefine national goals. Secularly oriented and antimilitarist, they deeply mistrusted the church hierarchy and had little use for the ambitious, self-serving Mexican army.

Influenced by the European Enlightenment and French philosophy, attorney Melchor Ocampo practiced law, began farming scientifically, cataloged flora and fauna, studied Indian languages, and collected one of the best private libraries in Mexico. He also made the decision to enter politics. In the 1840s and 1850s he served as governor of Michoacán and as a congressman in the national legislature. Shortly after the war with the United States he won acclaim when he became involved in a virtual death struggle with the clergy of Michoacán. The issue—the refusal of a local curate to bury the body of a penniless campesino because the widow could not pay the sacramental fees—became a *cause célèbre*, used effectively by Ocampo to demonstrate the ineptitude and decadence of the ecclesiastical effort.

Other liberals took up the cause of denouncing corruption in both church and state. Among them were Santos Degollado, who also served briefly as governor of Michoacán, and Guillermo Prieto, the son of a Mexico City baker who edited *El Siglo XIX* and popularized the anti-Santa Anna cause. The government persecuted both, forcing them into jail or exile.

But the real leader of the young, socially motivated intellectuals and the personification of Mexican history in the two decades following mid-century was Benito Juárez, a Zapotec

Indian from the state of Oaxaca. Born on March 21, 1806, in the mountain village of San Pablo Guelatao, Juárez was orphaned at the age of three and raised by an uncle. Only a handful of the one hundred fifty villagers knew any Spanish, and Juárez had learned but a few words when, at the age of twelve, he left his adobe home in the Zapotec village and walked forty-one miles to the state capital. An older sister working as a cook in Oaxaca City found employment for the boy in the home of a Franciscan lay brother who was a part-time bookbinder. In return for daily chores in the house and helping in the bindery, the Franciscan paid Juárez's tuition so that he could begin his schooling. At his benefactor's insistence he entered the seminary in Oaxaca but quickly realized that the priesthood was not his calling. He opted instead for the law and worked his way through law school, graduating in 1831.

That year he entered political life on the Oaxaca city council and subsequently served in the state legislature. But he did not abandon his career as a barrister and defended, without fee, groups of poor villagers, challenging the exorbitant rates charged by the clergy for the sacraments or protesting the arbitrary dictates of the local hacendado class. These activities convinced him that only structural alteration of the system could effect the changes he envisioned, and his liberalism strengthened.

When war broke out between Mexico and the United States, Juárez, a delegate in the national congress in Mexico City, was recalled to his home state to serve a term as provisional governor. Later, the defeated and disgraced Santa Anna sought refuge in Oaxaca, but Governor Juárez let him know he was not welcome there. In 1848 Oaxaqueños elected Juárez to a full term as constitutional governor. The Juárez governorship was far from revolutionary, but he did give the state a genuine lesson in energetic, honest, and sound management. Not only did he preside over the construction of fifty new rural schools and encourage female attendance, but he also sought to open the state up to world trade by rehabilitating the abandoned Pacific port of Huatulco. Even more amazing for mid-nineteenth-century Mexico, he reduced the huge state bureaucracy and pushed economic improvements while making regular payments on the state debt.

When Santa Anna returned to power for the last time, he moved to deal with the liberal threat. Juárez was arrested and then exiled to New Orleans. When he arrived in the Louisiana city, he met other Mexicans of his ilk who had taken refuge there. José María Mata and Ponciano Arriaga were active members of a revolutionary clique led by Melchor Ocampo. Juárez joined the exiles in plotting to overthrow the dictatorship when they decided to cast their lot with an old guerrilla chieftain, Juan Alvarez, then leading an antigovernment rebellion in the state of Guerrero. In 1854, the Plan de Ayutla put forth a statement of liberal principles and a long list of grievances against Santa Anna. In Jalisco, Santos Degollado gathered a formidable rebel army around him. Santiago Vidaurri in Nuevo León and Manuel Doblado in Guanajuato pronounced against the dictatorship and joined the Ayutla movement. The exiles in New Orleans helped with arms and ammunition, and in the early summer of 1855 they sent Juárez to Acapulco to join Alvarez as a political aide. With a wide base of support, in August 1853 the liberals forced Santa Anna, whose popularity was at its lowest ebb, to resign and go into exile for the last time.

THE REFORM LAWS

In the new government, Juan Alvarez became provisional president; Ignacio Comonfort, secretary of war; Melchor Ocampo, secretary of the treasury; Miguel Lerdo de Tejada, secretary of development; and Benito Juárez, secretary of justice. The provisional presidency of Alvarez marks the beginning of a period in Mexican history remembered as the Reform. For the first time since the Gómez Farías administration in 1833 the liberals set themselves in earnest to the task of destroying the sustaining structures of the conservative state in order to create a modern, democratic, secular, and capitalist nation.

The first significant piece of legislation to emerge from the Reform bore the name of the secretary of justice. Ley Juárez abolished the military and ecclesiastical *fueros*, the special dispensations exempting soldiers and clerics from having to stand trial in civil courts. Ley Juárez did not, as sometimes contended, abolish all military and ecclesiastical courts; rather, it placed stringent restrictions on their jurisdictions. The ecclesiastical and military courts had competency only in cases involving the alleged transgression of canon or military law. If, on the other hand, a cleric or a soldier were charged with a violation of civil or criminal law, he would be required to stand trial in a state or federal court. Ley Juárez thus became an important milestone in an ongoing battle to secure the concept of equality before the law.

Ley Juárez invoked the fury of the church and conservatives generally. But it also exposed a schism in the ranks of the liberals. The moderates (*moderados*) favored backing down, while the more staunch liberals (*puros*) refused. Before the month was out President Alvarez and most of the cabinet had resigned. The presidency devolved on Ignacio Comonfort, who was more of a compromiser than a firebrand.

In June 1856 President Comonfort's secretary of the treasury, Miguel Lerdo de Tejada, drafted an important new law that the radicals hoped would weaken the church and the

Ignacio Comonfort (1812-63). A bureaucrat of minor importance for most of his life and subsequently a colonel in the militia, Comonfort was thrust into the presidency in 1855 and found himself caught in the endless liberal-conservative struggle.

moderates hoped would increase national revenue. Ley Lerdo prohibited ecclesiastical and civil institutions from owning or administering real property not directly used in day-to-day operations. The Roman Catholic Church could retain its church buildings, monasteries, and seminaries. Local and state units of government would keep their meeting halls, jails, and schools. But both had to divest themselves of other urban and rural property. The massive holdings the church had gradually acquired through the centuries were to be put up for sale at public auction.

Ley Lerdo indicates that neither the puros nor the moderados of the nineteenth century envisioned a social revolution. The liberals wanted to encourage economic entrepreneurship and protect private property. The lands were not to be distributed to the landless campesino but were to be sold. Only the wealthy or at least those in a position secure enough to obtain credit were able to buy. In practice, the enforcement of Ley Lerdo worked to the detriment of the rural masses because it removed the long-standing legal recognition of the Indian communities' rights to own property collectively. The mandate for individual ownership of land meant that many communities could lose their corporate lands (*ejidos*). Ley Lerdo failed to create a new class of small peasant landowners and ultimately abetted the transfer of land to hacendados and some upwardly mobile *rancheros*. In the chaotic years that followed the implementation of Ley Lerdo, the liberal governments did not profit greatly from the break-up and sale of the corporate civil or ecclesiastical properties.

The reformers had not yet finished. In January 1857 President Comonfort signed into law a statute giving the powers of registry to the state, thus depriving the church of an important source of revenue. All births, marriages, adoptions, and deaths were henceforth to be registered by civil functionaries; and cemeteries were placed under the control of a department of hygiene. The church sustained another blow a few months later when the Ley Iglesias prohibited the church from charging high fees for administering the sacraments. The poor were to receive their sacramental blessings at no cost, and those who could afford to pay would be charged modestly.

THE CONSTITUTION OF 1857

The internal tensions provoked by the reform laws were in full evidence when, as provided by the Plan de Ayutla, delegates met to draft a new constitution. Because the conservatives had opposed the Revolution of Ayutla, they were largely unrepresented in the constitutional assembly. Debates took place between moderados and puros.

The federal Constitution of 1857 in many ways was modeled after its ancestor of 1824. The major difference in political structure was provided by an article setting up a unicameral national legislature. For purposes of economy and efficiency, the framers of the document believed that a single house was sufficient, but the main reason for switching from two houses to one was neither of these. It would be better, many believed, to have one strong house, instead of two weak ones, as a legislative bulwark against dictatorship. Mexican history showed as well that a strong national government was mandatory if the country were to escape the perils of exaggerated regionalism. The reform liberals were not nearly so federalist as some have believed.

The Constitution of 1857 represented much more of a liberal victory than its federal predecessor of 1824. The constitution incorporated the Ley Juárez, Ley Lerdo, and Ley Iglesias, and also emphasized individual liberty and the inviolability of property rights. The first 34 articles of the document spelled out in detail equality before the law and freedom of speech, of the press, of petition, of assembly, of the mails, and of education. It further abolished slavery, other compulsory service, and all titles of nobility and guaranteed the rights to carry arms, to have bail, and of habeas corpus.

The articles that prompted the most heated debate touched upon the religious issue. The church hierarchy responded by issuing decree after decree in an attempt to nullify the new constitution. They sought a Catholic republic that protected their interests. Catholics who purchased church property could be threatened with excommunication, along with those who swore allegiance to the objectionable articles of the constitution. Bishop Clemente de Jesús Munguía of Michoacán and Archbishop Lázaro de la Garza of Mexico City specified that the faithful could not accept, among other articles, those which provided for freedom of education, freedom of speech, freedom of the press, freedom of assembly and, of course, Ley Juárez and Ley Lerdo. Pope Pius IX actually backed these positions, declaring the constitution to be null and void.

The strong reaction of the church created a real quandary for Mexicans. If they did not swear allegiance to the constitution, they would be considered traitors to the state; if they did, they would be heretics in the eyes of the church. The dilemma was not merely theoretical, however. Civil servants who refused to take the oath of allegiance to the constitution lost their jobs; soldiers who took it were not treated in Catholic hospitals; if they died, they did not receive the last rites nor were they buried in consecrated ground. Priests who offered the sacraments to communicants who had not forsworn the constitution were suspended. By pitting brother against brother and father against son, the reform laws and the constitution divided Mexican society into two hostile and completely uncompromising camps and led to yet another civil war.

THE WAR OF THE REFORM

The War of the Reform, the civil conflict that engulfed Mexico from 1858 to 1861, represented the culmination of the ideological disputations, the shuffling of constitutions, the church–state controversies, and the minor civil wars that had shattered the peace periodically since independence. The war began, as most Mexican wars, with a new plan, this time the Plan de Tacubaya, proclaimed by conservative general Félix Zuloaga. Emboldened by promises of clerical and military support, Zuloaga promptly dissolved the congress and arrested Benito Juárez, the chief liberal spokesman within the Comonfort government. Recently elected chief justice of the Mexican Supreme Court, Juárez was next in line for the presidency should a vacancy occur in the top office. Finding himself caught between two extremes and not totally comfortable with some of the constitutional provisions, President Comonfort resigned. When the army declared Zuloaga as the new president, Juárez managed to escape north to Querétaro, where his liberal cohorts proclaimed him president. Once again, Mexico plunged into a most passionate and bloody civil war.

The opposing sides in the three-year war defy the simple classification historians have traditionally given. It was not Indians versus whites and rural versus urban. While it is true that the clergy and the army generally supported the Zuloaga government in Mexico City, the Indian masses fell into both camps. The relative autonomy granted under federalism made the liberal cause attractive to indigenous peoples who worked to preserve communal customs. At the same time, the Ley Lerdo could break up their ejido lands, a reason to support conservatives. Recent studies have emphasized another explanation regarding rural indigenous and peasant participation in the nineteenth-century wars. Not isolated from national politics, they participated in ways best suited to preserve their communities. Many found that abstract liberal principals did not guarantee their protection. On the other hand, where the church took a flexible approach to their religiosity, it offered support for community institutions and practices such as cofradías and celebrations that bound people together. As a result a popular, conservative grassroots politics emerged in many areas of the countryside. In Querétaro, for example, the cacique Tomás Mejía led troops for the conservatives. This popular conservatism was not universal in rural areas and others who saw the church as greedy and exploitative threw their lot in with fellow Indian Benito Juárez.

The liberals eventually succeeded in establishing their capital in Veracruz, where they could control the customs receipts and obtain military supplies from the outside world. From there Juárez and his government issued manifestos damning the enemy, enticing support, seeking the recognition of foreign governments, and outlining military strategy. At the same time in Mexico City, the Zuloaga administration declared the reform laws null and void, swore allegiance to the Holy See, took communion in public, and planned military campaigns.

For the first two years of the war the liberals had a hard time holding their own. The conservative army, better trained, equipped, and led, won most of the major engagements and held the most populous states of central Mexico. But when, in the early spring of 1859, General Miguel Miramón attempted to dislodge the liberals from Veracruz, he was beaten back. The fighting throughout the republic was vicious, and noncombatants experienced wanton depredation by overzealous commanders of both armies. The conservatives shot captured prisoners in the name of holy religion, and the liberals did the same in defense of freedom and democratic government, sometimes desecrating churches and executing priests.

The intensity of the military campaigns manifested itself in the political arena as well. The Juárez government issued a series of decrees from Veracruz that made the earlier Reform Laws seem innocuous by comparison. The liberals who had felt short-changed by the constitution would now be satisfied. The decrees made births and marriages civil ceremonies, secularized all cemeteries, outlawed monastic orders,, nationalized all church properties and assets, curtailed the number of official religious holidays, limited religious processions in the streets, and mean-spirited local ordinances even restricted the ringing of church bells. But most importantly, church and state were separated. The reforms tried to rivet together a society in which the church would be indisputably subordinate to the state.

By 1860 the tide of the battle had turned in favor of the liberals. Juárez found two excellent field commanders in Ignacio Zaragoza and Jesús González Ortega, while the enemy unwittingly aided the liberal cause by bickering among themselves. In August, Zaragoza and

González Ortega combined their forces at Silao to hand General Miramón his first serious defeat. The final battle occurred three days before Christmas when González Ortega crushed Miramón's army of eight thousand at the little town of San Miguel Calpulalpan. The newly victorious army, some twenty-five thousand strong, entered Mexico City to a tumultuous welcome on New Year's Day. Juárez arrived ten days later, but victory was no panacea.

DISCONTENT

The desolation left in the wake of the civil conflict showed on the landscape dotted with burned haciendas and mills, potted roads, unrepaired bridges, neglected fields, and sacked

Benito Juárez (1806-72). The presidential terms of Mexico's most noteworthy politician of the mid-nineteenth century were disrupted by civil wars and foreign interventions.

villages. But more importantly, it inscribed the minds and bodies of tens of thousands of exhausted, crippled, and aggrieved Mexicans. Soldiers slowly drifted back home, frequently encountering destruction and no work. Bandits continued to infest the highways. Frustration set in quickly. Only the national government could be expected to smooth the transition, but the tired nation was to have no relief. The liberal victory in 1861 proved to be but a brief respite from the ravages of war. The armies would soon begin marching again, but on this occasion one would wear foreign uniforms.

Although Juárez won the presidential elections held in March 1861, the liberals diverged on many issues, especially on what type of punishment should be meted out to their erstwhile foes. Some favored harsh retribution to make their enemies pay for the ravages they had propagated, but the president opted instead for a more conciliatory policy, to allow opposition in the open forum of the congress. Nonetheless, congressional bickering in his own party, coupled with pressure from the opposition, prompted several cabinet resignations and kept the administration in a constant state of turmoil. On one occasion a congressional vote taken to demand Juárez's resignation lost by a single vote.

TROUBLED FINANCES AND FOREIGN INTERVENTION

In the final analysis, however, economic rather than political difficulties precipitated the next war. Juárez inherited a bankrupt treasury and an army, a corps of civil servants, and a police force that had not been paid. The income from the sale of church property had been considerably less than expected. Commerce stagnated, and most of the customs receipts were already pledged. The nation's woefully inadequate transportation system conveyed merchandise by pack mules, oxen, and human cargadores. Transportation was slow, costly, and inefficient.

In the spring of 1861 the monthly deficit amounted to $400,000, and practically no currency circulated. Worst of all, Mexico's European creditors began clamoring for the repayment of debts, some half a century old. Fully sensitive to the dangers his action might portend, Juárez declared a two-year moratorium on the payment of Mexico's foreign debt. Although he took care to stress that his action did not repudiate but simply suspended payment time of stress, the outcry in Europe was predictable. The large majority of the English, French, and Spanish claims were quite legitimate, for foreign citizens had suffered outrages and losses of life and property.

On October 31, 1861, representatives of Queen Isabella II of Spain, Queen Victoria of Great Britain, and Emperor Napoleon III of France affixed their signatures to the Convention of London. The three nations agreed upon a joint occupation of the Mexican coasts to collect their claims. They envisioned a plan to occupy the customhouse at Veracruz and apply all customs receipts on the debt. Although England and Spain were apparently sincere in the pledge not to seek special advantage in Mexico, France had other designs. French Emperor Napoleon III had embarked upon an aggressive foreign policy in Africa and Indochina and, in a French rendering of manifest destiny, also looked to the Americas as a place where France might implant "civilization" among its Latin cousins. The Mexican imbroglio and overtures from Catholic conservatives presented him with an opportunity to achieve that goal while currying favor with a strong Catholic element in France.

Porfirio Díaz as a young man. Later to serve as president of Mexico for a third of a century, Díaz was catapulted to national fame because of his role in the victory over the French of May 5, 1862.

Some six thousand Spanish troops actually landed in Veracruz first, followed by 700 British marines and two thousand French troops early the next month. As soon as it became obvious that the French harbored notions of conquest, the queens of Spain and Great Britain decided to order their respective troops home.

THE FRENCH INTERVENTION

Within a month after the Spanish and British withdrawal the French army, reinforced with an additional forty-five hundred troops, began to march inland on its war of occupation. Arrogant and overconfident, the invading commander, General Charles Latrille, had already informed his superior in Paris, "We are so superior to the Mexicans in race, organization, morality, and devoted sentiments, that I beg your excellency to inform the Emperor that as the head of 6,000 soldiers I am already master of Mexico."[1] But en route to Mexico City he discovered that Puebla was not going to be an easy prize. President Juárez had assigned the defense of the city to General Ignacio Zaragoza. Encountering unexpected opposition on the morning of May 5, 1862, Latrille attacked recklessly, and within two hours the French had expended half of their ammunition. The French troops, many weakened by the affliction that sometimes smites the foreign visitor to the Mexican countryside, did not acquit

---

1   Quoted in Paul Vanderwood, "Betterment for Whom? The Reform Period: 1855–1875," in *The Oxford History of Mexico*, eds. Michael C. Meyer and William H. Beezley (New York, NY, 2010), 358.

themselves well. General Zaragoza, on the other hand, managed his troops with rare aplomb. In a decisive maneuver, young Brigadier General Porfirio Díaz, commanding the Second Brigade, repelled a determined French assault on Zaragoza's right flank. The dejected invaders retreated to lick their wounds in Orizaba. May 5—Cinco de Mayo—would be added to the national calendar of holidays in honor of the Mexican victory.

Not all Mexicans rejoiced at the news of the French defeat. Not only did many conservative monarchists and just as many church officials succor the recuperating French army but priests used their pulpits to urge their communicants to collaborate with the enemy against the godless government. On August 30, 1862, President Juárez ordered that clerics who excited disrespect for the law would be punished by imprisonment or deportation. He also forbade priests from wearing their vestments or any other distinguishing garment outside of the churches.

Upon hearing of the disaster at Puebla, Napoleon, with a sizable reservoir of manpower to draw upon, ordered some thirty thousand reinforcements. It took fully a year before the French army was prepared to march again. Once more they encountered their heaviest resistance at Puebla, but after a siege of nearly two months, the Mexican defenders under the command of General Jesús González Ortega were forced to turn the city over to the French. President Juárez realized that the fall of Puebla opened the doors to Mexico City. With the support of congress at the end of May, Juárez, his cabinet, and what was left of his army withdrew for San Luis Potosí, and the French army entered the Mexican capital unopposed.

THE NEW GOVERNMENT

Much of Mexico's conservative leadership was less concerned with their country's recent loss of sovereignty than with how the conservatives might profit from the demise of Benito Juárez and his liberal government. On June 16, 1863, the French commander selected a provisional government consisting of thirty-five conservatives. Napoleon III, having conferred with numerous conservative Mexican émigrés, had decided that if a monarchy was good for France, it would be good for Mexico as well. The French ruler chose the Austrian archduke, Ferdinand Maximilian of Hapsburg, to be emperor. In October 1863 a delegation of Mexican conservatives visited Maximilian at Miramar, his magnificent palace on a promontory overlooking the Adriatic near Trieste, and offered him the crown. Maximilian accepted only on the condition that his emperorship be approved by the Mexican people themselves. As strange as his stipulation must have sounded to the conservative monarchists, they agreed to indulge Maximilian in this folly. The plebiscite, held under the auspices of the French army, was a farce; when Maximilian was informed that the Mexican people had voted overwhelmingly in his favor, he accepted the throne.

Before leaving for Mexico, Maximilian entered into an agreement with his benefactor, Napoleon III. The Convention of Miramar pledged the new Mexican emperor to pay all expenses incurred by the French troops during their fight for control of the country. Maximilian also agreed to pay the salaries of the French troops, twenty thousand of whom were to remain in Mexico until the end of 1867, and to assume responsibility for payment of all the claims. In return Napoleon gave Maximilian full command over the French expeditionary force in Mexico. The new emperor, by signing the Convention of Miramar, had tripled Mexico's foreign debt before even setting foot on Mexican soil. But Maximilian was eager to begin a new life in a new world with his wife Charlotte, who would be known in Mexico as Carlota.

THE ARRIVAL OF THE MONARCHS

Ferdinand Maximilian Joseph and Marie Charlotte Amélie Léopoldine arrived in Veracruz aboard the Austrian frigate *Novara* at the end of May 1864. He was thirty-two years old and she only twenty-four when they set out to mount the imperial throne. Descended from Hapsburg and Bourbon royal lines, they were products of European education at its best, schooled in the etiquette of court life, and accustomed to the niceties, proprieties, and extravagances of Viennese aristocratic society. Their first glimpse of Mexico came as a shock as they encountered a sweltering, humid Veracruz where malaria and yellow fever were rampant and sanitation was nonexistent.

Traditionally liberal, the Veracruzanos refused to come out of their whitewashed adobe houses to greet their new monarchs. By the time the small royal party reached the railroad station to begin the tedious journey, Carlota was in tears. As the train wound its way toward Mexico City, the weather cooled and the scenery improved. When the railroad tracks ended, the royal party made the rest of the trip by stage coach. As they neared Mexico City on June 12, they transferred to Maximillian's ornate Viennese carriage and stopped to hear mass at the Basílica de Guadalupe. Maximilian had been advised that it would be wise to curry Indian and church support by paying homage to the Virgin of Guadalupe.

A mass was celebrated for Maximilian and grande dame Carlota when they reached Mexico City after the difficult journey from Veracruz.

Because the national palace was deemed unsuitable, the royal family established their magnificent imperial court at Chapultepec Castle, built originally for the Spanish viceroys at the end of the eighteenth century. But unlike Agustín I, Mexico's first emperor, Maximilian made himself accessible to the people. Once a week he opened the palace to his subjects, and in many small ways he tried hard for acceptance. To acquaint himself with Mexico's problems he toured the provinces and, on occasion, even donned the regional costume and ate the local food. Upon his return he shocked his conservative friends by suggesting that many priests he had met could profit from some basic lessons in Christian charity. Believing that magnanimity would serve him well and win him converts, Maximilian declared a free press and proclaimed a general amnesty for all political prisoners serving terms of less than ten years.

The emperor was pleased with the first few months of his reign, especially when diplomatic recognition began to come in from Europe. In the summer he wrote his younger brother an enthusiastic letter.

> I found the country far better than I expected . . . and the people far more advanced than supposed at home. Our reception was cordial and sincere, free from all pretence and from that nauseating official servility which one very often finds in Europe on such occasions. The country is very beautiful, tropically luxuriant in the coast lands. . . . The so-called entertainments of Europe, such as evening receptions, the gossip of teaparties, etc., etc., of hideous memories, are quite unknown here, and we shall take good care not to introduce them.[2]

INTERNAL DIVISIONS AND EXTERNAL INTERFERENCE

But Maximilian's position was scarcely as idyllic as he imagined. His first serious problem, strangely enough, came from his conservative supporters rather than from the liberals who had been driven out of Mexico City to make room for him. The conservatives, led by Juan Almonte and Archbishop Pelagio Antonio de Labastida, naturally expected that the emperor would immediately set about to suspend the reform laws and return the church properties seized by Benito Juárez. Yet Maximilian's political inclinations tended to the liberal side on the question of the relationship between church and state. Hoping to attract some liberal support to his government, he refused to return church lands. These anti-clerical measures did not persuade liberals whose patriotism demanded overthrow of a monarchy supported by foreign arms and headed by a foreigner. By attempting to find a middle ground between the liberals and the conservatives, Maximilian succeeded only in alienating both.

When Juárez withdrew from Mexico City before the French onslaught, he established his government first in San Luis Potosí and then in Chihuahua. But French troops sent by Marshal François Bazaine pushed his small loyal army north until they found refuge in El Paso del Norte (today Ciudad Juárez) on the US border. Guerrilla warfare conducted throughout the country kept the French army from controlling territory for sustained periods, although French troops won a number of battles. In 1865, Bazaine defeated Porfirio Díaz in Oaxaca

---

2   Quoted in Egon Corti, *Maximilian and Charlotte of Mexico*, vol. 2 (New York, NY, 1928), 431–32.

and temporarily secured that pivotal southern state. In October 1865 Maximilian's French advisers informed him, incorrectly, that Juárez had finally given up the fight and had fled the country, seeking refuge in the United States. Following flawed advice, the emperor issued a controversial and extremely significant decree. The death penalty was made mandatory for all captured Juaristas still bearing arms, to be carried out without appeal within 24 hours of capture. In signing the decree he had not only prompted a war of unparalleled ferocity but, in effect, also signed his own death warrant. Juárez had not abandoned the country and repeatedly promised his supporters that he had no intention of giving up the fight. He realized, however, that he needed substantial help and eventually heeded the advice of his cabinet that he seek it north of the Rio Grande.

The government of Abraham Lincoln had been more than casually interested in France's Mexican venture from the outset. In 1823 President Monroe had intoned his famous doctrine declaring that the American continents were henceforth not to be considered as subjects for future colonization by European powers; any attempt to do so would be viewed as an unfriendly act toward the United States. In the years subsequent to its promulgation the Monroe Doctrine was frequently disregarded by various countries in western Europe but never so blatantly as in 1862 and 1863 when the French intervened. Napoleon III had chosen his time well; six months prior to the signing of the Convention of London the shots fired at Fort Sumter had initiated the Civil War in the United States. Convulsed with severe difficulties, the government in Washington was able to do little but issue a few mild protests. The Union hardly wanted to push France into an alliance with the Confederacy. When it came time to consider recognition of the Mexican empire, however, the Lincoln administration refused. Washington considered the Juárez government in exile to be the legitimate representative of the Mexican people.

As the fortunes of the North improved and those of the Confederacy declined, Juárez embarked upon an all-out campaign to secure assistance from the United States. He charged the head of the Mexican legation in Washington, Matías Romero, a young but forceful diplomat, with the task of securing some implementation of a resolution, passed in 1864 by the US House of Representatives, that condemned the French intervention. At approximately the same time he dispatched an entire team of secret agents to the United States to secure financial and military aid and to begin recruiting American soldiers of fortune. Romero opened discussions with representatives of the Lincoln administration, but progress was impeded by Lincoln's assassination and the necessity of opening a new round of negotiations with the government of Andrew Johnson.

The end of the Civil War brought about a major change in US policy. The North had more than nine hundred thousand men under arms when Lee surrendered to Grant at Appomattox. No longer fearful of offending the French, Secretary of State William Seward began applying pressure to Napoleon III. At the same time the US government, prompted by Romero, closed its eyes to violations of neutrality legislation and allowed Juarista agents to purchase arms and ammunition in California for shipment to west coast Mexican ports under republican control. Juárez's agents were also allowed to pass back and forth across the international line without hindrance from customs officials or border patrols. Some three thousand Union veterans, attracted by good pay and a promised land bonus, joined the

Juarista army. Influenced by these developments as well as a new threat to French security in Europe from Otto von Bismarck, Napoleon made his belated decision to begin withdrawing his foreign legion in November 1866.

The gradual withdrawal of the French troops into early 1867 left Maximilian in an impossible position. To no avail he sent a series of envoys to Paris to convince Napoleon that he should honor the commitment he had made in the Convention of Miramar. Maximilian then toyed with the idea of abdicating his throne, but Carlota appealed to his sense of Hapsburg dignity and convinced him that he must stay on. She had earlier encouraged him to adopt the two-year-old grandson of Agustín de Iturbide as his heir to the throne. The toddler quickly became not only the "last prince of the Mexican empire," but also a pawn in a custody battle. Carlota now traveled to Europe herself, but her appeals to Napoleon and the pope were rejected. Pius IX could not have been happy that Maximilian had taken no steps to restore the church lands in Mexico. A distraught Carlota soon lost her mind.

THE REPUBLICAN VICTORY AND THE AFTERMATH

Spurred on by the fortuitous combination of events in Europe and America, Juárez and his republican army assumed the offensive in the spring of 1866. General Luis Terrazas captured Chihuahua City, while General Mariano Escobedo shattered a strong French column between Matamoros and Monterrey. Before the end of the year the republicans reoccupied much of Mexico. With the French army pulling out of Mexico, the treasury empty, and Carlota sick in Europe, Maximilian reluctantly decided to make one last stand. Mexico's second empire collapsed in the colonial city of Querétaro. Maximilian took command of a few thousand Mexican imperial troops but quickly found himself surrounded by a republican army four times as strong. After nearly one hundred days, Maximilian could no longer withstand the republican siege of Querétaro. Although careful plans had been laid for the emperor's escape, he preferred the solemn dignity of surrender on May 15.

Juárez immediately decided Maximilian's fate; the emperor would be tried by court-martial, and the state would request the death penalty. Despite a rain of pleas for clemency from European monarchs, Latin American presidents, and delegations of tearful, supplicating women, Juárez remained adamant. Thirteen accusations were leveled against Maximilian, including violation of Mexico's sovereignty; but the most important was that he had signed the infamous decree of October 1865 resulting in the death of innumerable Mexican citizens. The chief defense attorneys, Mariano Riva Palacio and Rafael Martínez de la Torre, ardently denied the competence of the court to sit on the case and argued that the leniency shown to Jefferson Davis in the United States after the Civil War should serve as a precedent. The verdict, however, was based more on political considerations than on legal ones. Juárez believed that use of executive clemency, at the end of the War of the Reform, had caused Mexico to pay a terrible price. He wanted to demonstrate to the world that Mexico's existence as an independent nation would not be left to chance or to the goodwill of foreign heads of state. By one vote, the court voted for the death penalty. The final appeal to President Juárez was rejected in the interest of assuring public peace.

A contemporary woodcut depicting the execution of Maximilian and two of his Mexican generals, Tomás Mejía and Miguel Miramón, on the Hill of the Bells outside Querétaro.

On the morning of June 19, after receiving the last sacrament, his executioners led Maximilian to the Hill of the Bells on the outskirts of Querétaro. There they shot him along with several Mexican conservative officers. Édouard Manet's striking images of the execution, painted in the late 1860s, served as powerful criticism of France's ill-fated imperial adventure. As tragic and senseless as the event might have appeared from abroad, fifty thousand Mexicans had just as surely lost their lives fighting the French.

The price of the French Intervention, however, cannot be assessed solely in terms of the lives lost. The attempt to tamper with Mexico's sovereignty had ended in dismal failure, and, as a result, Mexican nationalism and self-esteem began to grow perceptibly for the first time. The United States had helped in a small way, but it had been Mexicans who drove out the French. The republican victory was, at least in part, a vindication of the Constitution of 1857 and the principles it had espoused. The clerical party had been defeated, and although the country had not seen the last of its major church–state struggles, the church and its defenders in the future would seek more modest goals. The conservatives were discredited, at least for the time, because liberalism in the popular mind became identified with moral authority and independence from foreign aggression.

On the other hand, the intervention had left Mexican commerce, industry, and agriculture in a quagmire. Education had suffered immeasurably, and the treasury was still empty. The years without a single, central authority reinforced tendencies toward localism, however patriotic, parts of southern Mexico in Tabasco and Yucatán remained outside of the national fold. A strong nation state had yet to emerge from the political instability and lack of economic growth during much of the nineteenth century.

RECOMMENDED FOR FURTHER STUDY

Anderson, William Marshall. *An American in Maximilian's Mexico, 1865–1866: Diaries of William Marshall Anderson*. Edited by Ramón Eduardo Ruiz. San Marino, CA: Huntington Library, 1959.

Barker, Nancy Nichols. *The French Experience in Mexico, 1821–1861: A History of Constant Misunderstanding*. Chapel Hill: University of North Carolina Press, 1979.

Bazant, Jan. *Alienation of Church Wealth in Mexico: Social and Economic Aspects of the Liberal Revolution, 1856–1857*. New York: Cambridge University Press, 1971.

Berry, Charles R. *The Reform in Oaxaca, 1856–1876: A Microhistory of the Liberal Revolution*. Lincoln: University of Nebraska Press, 1981.

Brittsan, Zachary. *Popular Politics and Rebellion in Mexico: Manuel Lozada and La Reforma, 1855–1876*. Nashville, TN: Vanderbilt University Press, 2015.

Cadenhead, Jr. Ivie E. *Jesús González Ortega and Mexican National Politics*. Fort Worth: Texas Christian University Press, 1972.

Chowning, Margaret. *Wealth and Power in Provincial Mexico: Michoacán from the Late Colony to the Revolution*. Stanford, CA: Stanford University Press, 1999.

Corti, Egon. *Maximilian and Charlotte of Mexico*. 2 vols. New York: Alfred A. Knopf, 1928.

Dabbs, Jack A. *The French Army in Mexico, 1861–1867*. The Hague, Netherlands: Mouton, 1962.

Hamnett, Brian. *Juárez*. London, UK: Longman, 1994.

Ibsen, Kristine. *Maximilian, Mexico, and the Invention of Empire*. Nashville, TN: Vanderbilt University Press, 2010.

Knowlton, Robert J. *Church Property and the Mexican Reform, 1856–1910*. DeKalb: Northern Illinois University Press, 1976.

Mayo, C. M. *The Last Prince of the Mexican Empire*. Cave Creek, AZ: Unbridled Books, 2009.

McNamara, Patrick J. *Sons of the Sierra: Juárez, Díaz, and the People of Ixtlan, Oaxaca, 1855–1920*. Chapel Hill: University of North Carolina Press, 2007.

Miangos y González, Pablo. *The Lawyer of the Church: Bishop Clemente de Jesús Munguía and the Clerical Response to the Mexican Liberal Reforma*. Lincoln: University of Nebraska Press, 2015.

Olliff, Donathon C. *Reforma Mexico and the United States: A Search for Alternatives to Annexation, 1854–1861*. Tuscaloosa: University of Alabama Press, 1983.

Powell, T. G. "Priests and Peasants in Central Mexico: Social Conflict during La Reforma." *Hispanic American Historical Review* 57/2 (1997): 296–313.

Roeder, Ralph. *Juárez and His Mexico*. 2 vols. New York: Viking Press, 1947.

Rugeley, Terry. *The River People in Flood Time: The Civil Wars in Tabasco, Spoilers of Empire*. Stanford, CA: Stanford University Press, 2014.

Scholes, Walter V. *Mexican Politics during the Juárez Regime, 1855–1872*. Columbia: University of Missouri Press, 1957.

Schoonover, Thomas D. *Dollars over Dominion: The Triumph of Liberalism in Mexican–United States Relations, 1861–1867*. Baton Rouge: Louisiana State University Press, 1978.

_____. *Mexican Lobby: Matías Romero in Washington, 1861–1867*. Lexington: University Press of Kentucky, 1986.

Seijas, Tatiana, and Jake Frederick. *Spanish Dollars and Sister Republics: The Money That Made Mexico and the United States*. Lanham, MD: Rowman & Littlefield, 2017.

Sinkin, Richard N. *The Mexican Reform, 1855–1876: A Study in Liberal Nation Building*. Austin, TX: Institute of Latin American Studies, 1979.

Smart, Charles Allen. *Viva Juárez!* London, UK: Eyre and Spottiswoode, 1964.

Smith, Benjamin T. *The Roots of Conservatism in Mexico: Catholicism, Society, and Politics in the Mixteca Baja, 1750–1962.* Albuquerque: University of New Mexico Press, 2012.

Vanderwood, Paul. "Betterment for Whom? The Reform Period: 1855–1875." In *The Oxford History of Mexico*, edited by Michael C. Meyer and William H. Beezley, 349–72. New York: Oxford University Press, rev. 2010.

CHAPTER 21

THE RESTORED REPUBLIC:

NASCENT MODERNIZATION

Modern Mexican history begins with the liberal victory of 1867.[1] In a very real sense the republic became a nation. Concerned with the growth of political democracy in Mexico, Juárez and his republican cohorts would try for a decade to consolidate their victory by implementing the letter and spirit of the Constitution of 1857 and, at the same time, by setting Mexico on the path of modernization. The sailing was far from smooth, but the political process showed signs of maturation. The scars from the recent wars of the reform and the intervention were deep; liberals set out to inaugurate a new era of peace and material progress. Mexicans had to overcome the deeply engrained suspicion that differences of opinion, ideology, and practical politics should inevitably be settled by force rather than by reason. And while all antagonisms did not dissipate during the restoration, bellicosity became less of a reflex action. More important, this nine-year period established the guidelines for the profound changes that would occur in Mexico during the last quarter of the nineteenth century.

JUÁREZ'S THIRD TERM

In marked contrast to Maximilian's entrance into Mexico City in his ornate European carriage in 1864, Juárez entered the capital on July 15, 1867, in a stark black coach. Cheers welled up from the thousands who lined the streets. His reception was triumphant, but although Juárez enjoyed the display of camaraderie and goodwill, he recognized that it was no time to rest on past laurels. He immediately called for presidential elections, announcing himself as a candidate for a third term. Under the circumstances, few knowledgeable politicians believed that a third term was excessive. Most of the first two had been spent on the run with virtually no chance of implementing a progressive program. While preparing himself for the elections, the president undertook an important political reform. In order to manifest

---

1   Daniel Cosío Villegas, ed. *Historia moderna de México*, 9 vols. (Mexico City, Mexico, 1955–72). The first three volumes treat the restored republic.

the primacy of civilian over military rule, he reduced the size of the Mexican army from sixty thousand to twenty thousand men.

In October Juárez won the presidential election and late in the year took office for a third term. He had to face a situation not unlike that which he had encountered in 1861 when he returned to office following the liberal victory in the War of the Reform. The administration had to enunciate a policy toward the conservatives who had supported the French-imposed monarchy. During the fight against the empire, the decrees issued from the Juarista head-quarters concerning French sympathizers had been harsh indeed. The no-nonsense policy was reaffirmed in Querétaro with the trial and execution of Maximilian. But by late 1867 few liberals were still crying for revenge, and it seemed time to adopt a more conciliatory policy. In a gesture of goodwill Juárez set free many political prisoners and reduced the sentences of others.

ECONOMIC AND EDUCATIONAL REFORMS

The new administration wisely directed its energies into two main fields: a revamping of the economy and a restructuring of the educational foundations of the country. Juárez named Matías Romero, who had served his exiled government so effectively in Washington, as sec-retary of the treasury. Romero formulated a plan for economic development that called for the improvement of transportation facilities and the fuller exploitation of natural resources through the attraction of foreign capital. He believed that Mexico's economic future rested largely on the revitalization of the mining industry rather than upon industrialization. The key to increased mineral production required a major revision of Mexico's tax and tariff structure. Despite much congressional opposition, through hard work and thrift Secretary Romero succeeded in bringing some order out of the economic chaos by 1872, but the divi-dends he expected in the form of substantial capital investment would wait for several years.

While tariff and tax revision were important, other factors still discouraged the potential investor. Political instability, minor rebellions, the presence of private armies and groups of bandits for whom lawlessness had become a way of life, all dissuaded foreign capitalists seek-ing lucrative investment fields. Travel on Mexico's roads and shipment of merchandise were precarious. One of the answers was found in a relatively new concept of public security. Prior to the French intervention, Benito Juárez had authorized the establishment of a rural police force, the *rurales*, modeled in some ways on the Spanish *guardia civil*. But jurisdiction over the security guard was divided between two government departments: war and interior. The overlapping and often confusing jurisdictions undermined the effectiveness of the organiza-tion, and it did not amount to much. After the overthrow of the empire, however, Juárez's congress authorized an increased budget for the rurales and, in 1869, placed them under the sole jurisdiction of the Department of Interior. With more adequate funds and with the orga-nizational problem resolved, the rurales began to play a major peace-keeping role. Patrolling the roads, assisting the army, guarding special shipments of bullion and merchandise, and policing local elections, they contributed to the stabilization of life in the countryside.

Without question the most important economic development to occur during the early years of the restoration was the completion of the Mexico City-Veracruz railroad. The enterprise had begun in 1837, and short segments of a couple of kilometers had been completed periodically since that time. But in 1860, when the United States had over thirty thousand miles of track in operation, Mexico had barely 150 miles. The stage between Mexico City and Guadalajara (a distance of some 425 miles) often took more than a week even if it was not mired in the mud or assaulted by bandits. To be sure, construction in the rugged terrain between the Mexican capital and Veracruz on the gulf was an engineering nightmare, for the roadbed had to rise from sea level to over 9,000 feet and had to be built across huge canyons and precipices.

During the period of the empire the concession rights were held by the Imperial Mexican Railway Company, a corporation registered in London. The British engineers who worked for Maximilian made considerable progress in laying portions of the roadbed, but by 1866 the company was almost bankrupt and all work stopped. Upon the restoration of the republic Juárez exempted the company from the forfeiture legislation that applied to all who had supported Maximilian on the condition that construction be resumed. Realizing that the company was broke, Juárez also agreed to pay it an annual subsidy of 560,000 pesos for twenty-five years. The agreement reached by the government and the company produced considerable bombast in the Mexican congress. Among the leading stockholders was Antonio Escandón, a conservative who had been a member of the Mexican delegation that visited Miramar in October 1863. Cries of governmental favoritism to traitors emanated from the congress, but Juárez believed that the railroad was more important than partisan politics and went ahead with his plans.

In an attempt to soothe passions the company was renamed the Ferrocarril Mexicano (Mexican Railroad Company). The British engineers did a noteworthy job of construction, digging endless tunnels and breaching the Barranca de Metlac, a chasm 900 feet across and 375 feet deep. Gradually the company closed the gaps, tied all the rails, and finished the job December 20, 1872. The line was officially inaugurated on January 1 of the following year. Archbishop Pelagio Antonio de Labastida formally blessed the new project at the Buenaventura station in Mexico City. Church endorsement of a liberal government enterprise a decade before would have been unthinkable, but Juárez had been actively mending relations with the church, recognizing that its pervasive cultural influence among the masses fueled popular politics. The successful completion of the railroad whetted the appetite, encouraging other entrepreneurs to contemplate the desirability, indeed the necessity, of constructing other major lines.

Education, too, began to move in a new direction with the restoration of the republic. In the fall of 1867 Juárez appointed a five-man commission to reorganize the entire educational structure of the country. The committee was headed by Gabino Barreda, a medical doctor who had studied in France and become a devotee of the positivist philosophy of Auguste Comte. While positivism would not become the official state doctrine in Mexico for another fifteen years, its roots most definitely can be found in Barreda's educational values. Congress adopted the curriculum recommended by the committee in late 1867, establishing the National Preparatory School to serve as a model; it placed heavy emphasis on arithmetic, the rudiments of physics and chemistry, and practical mechanics in the primary schools and

Spanning the Metlac Ravine was an engineering achievement of major proportions.

further emphasis on mathematics and the natural sciences in the secondary schools. The arts and the humanities, while not entirely ignored, were subordinated to an understanding of the physical world.

More important to Juárez than the curriculum itself was the fact that primary education in Mexico was made free and obligatory for the first time. All towns with a population of over five hundred would have one school for boys and one for girls. Two more schools were to be built for every additional two thousand inhabitants. But, as had been the case in Mexico since the arrival of the Spaniards in 1519, theory and practice, the law and the reality, seldom merged. Universal primary education remained mostly a liberal dream, despite the establishment of some girls' schools.

Juárez and his Secretary of Foreign Relations Sebastián Lerdo de Tejada took special care to cultivate friendly diplomatic relations with Mexico's neighbors and with the powers of Europe, most of which had recognized the empire of Maximilian. In his first address to the congress in 1867 the president acknowledged the sympathy and support of the United States. William Seward's visit to Mexico in 1869 further cemented the relationship, and the two countries agreed to lay claims, accumulated since the Treaty of Guadalupe Hidalgo, before a mixed claims commission. Gradually relations with Europe resumed as well.

DIVISION AMONG THE LIBERALS AND THE DEATH OF JUÁREZ

Juárez's third term was his best, and in the presidential elections of 1871 he decided, against the advice of many friends, to seek a fourth. The one-time pillar of constitutional liberalism had become prey to the nineteenth-century Latin American political myth of indispensability. The election of 1871 was one of the most hotly contested of the nineteenth century as two former supporters ran against him: Porfirio Díaz, who had won his military laurels in the wars against the French, and Sebastián Lerdo de Tejada, the brother of the author of Ley Lerdo. The election occasioned a three-way split in the undisciplined liberal party—Juaristas, Porfiristas, and Lerdistas. Juárez still enjoyed a wide base of popular support and had most of the federal bureaucracy working in his behalf. Lerdo counted on the strong backing of the professional classes and many of the socially prominent and wealthy, while Díaz was supported by some of the military outcasts from the conservative party and many veterans who felt their service had been ignored. Both the Lerdistas and the Porfiristas attacked the concept of continuous reelection as a violation of the republican principles Juárez had always espoused.

When the ballots were counted after the June election, none of the three candidates received the requisite majority of the votes. The choice, according to the Constitution of 1857, thus fell upon the congress. The Juaristas had done well in the congressional elections and dominated that body when it convened in the early fall, eventually securing the election of

A caricature by Santiago Hernández of Juárez and his opposition. Entitled "Little Fingers," it illustrates how the opposition whittled away at Juárez's power.

Juárez. Of the two defeated candidates, Díaz accepted the decision with less grace. On November 8, 1871, he proclaimed himself in revolt against the Juárez regime.

The Plan de la Noria proclaimed that indefinite reelection of the chief executive repudiated the principles of the Revolution of Ayutla and endangered the country's national institutions. No officeholder who exercised national jurisdiction of any kind in the year preceding presidential elections should be eligible to run for that high position. Those who accept the plan, Díaz proclaimed, "will fight for the cause of the people and the people will be the only victors. The Constitution of 1857 will be our banner and less government and more liberty our program."[2] But Díaz's fellow citizens were not yet ready for another armed insurrection, and Díaz was disappointed at the lack of interest his plan generated. While a few local caciques declared for the movement, Díaz had not struck a responsive chord. The army he put in the field was quickly defeated by the federals.

The revolt of La Noria had fallen apart when, on July 19, 1872, Juárez suffered a coronary seizure and died in office. Sebastián Lerdo de Tejada, the chief justice of the Supreme Court, became acting president and scheduled new elections for October. Lerdo enjoyed a reputation for keen intelligence, great oratorical and administrative ability, and unquestionable republican sympathies. He decided to run against Porfirio Díaz in the elections and defeated him easily. Since Díaz's revolution against Juárez had been predicated almost entirely on the principle of no reelection, the caudillo from Oaxaca accepted the outcome.

LERDO'S PRESIDENCY

President Lerdo believed that the foundation of Mexico's future progress rested heavily on the establishment of peace. The material progress he envisioned could not be achieved without order, and order was impossible without firm executive control. The national government had to curb disruptive localism and weaken the army. Mexican liberalism underwent a significant change as it became increasingly elitist and no longer antithetical to centralism and dictatorship. When political disputes occurred in the states or indigenous communities resisted assaults on their autonomy, Lerdo did not hesitate to intervene with federal forces.

Lerdo wisely retained many Juaristas in his government and, in seeking his goals, followed the same general policies that had been formulated by his famous predecessor. He used the rurales to patrol and protect the Mexico City-Veracruz railroad. To foster communications development he let railroad contracts for the construction of a new line north from Mexico City to the US border. A company made up of both Mexican and British investors, the Central Railroad of Mexico, obtained the concession. A US concern, headed by Emile la Sere of New Orleans, received promise of a subsidy of 12,500 pesos for each mile of track it laid down across the Isthmus of Tehuantepec. And, finally, the government encouraged feeder lines to connect with the recently completed Ferrocarril Mexicano and negotiated other contracts for the construction of telegraph lines. Lerdo's goal—to connect all of the state capitals to Mexico City by telegraph—was not reached, but he did add over sixteen hundred miles of telegraph line.

---

2   Quoted in *Historia documental de México*, vol. 2, eds. Ernesto de la Torre Villar, et al. (Mexico City, Mexico, 1964), 361.

Pilgrimages were made to Juárez's tomb in Mexico City long after his death in 1872.

In the field of education Lerdo furthered the efforts of his predecessor. Augmented federal and local funds resulted in a sharp increase in school construction but only a gradual increase in school enrollment. Between 1870 and 1874 the number of schools in Mexico almost doubled, but even in the latter year the 349,000 students represented only one of nineteen school-age children. And years of tradition had established another pattern that was difficult to break; of these only 77,000 were female.

With school construction growing much more rapidly than enrollment, many school seats remained empty. Availability of classroom space was not itself the answer. An available school seat did not mean that a competent teacher would be found or that a poor father would sacrifice the meager supplement to the family income that three or four small children working in the fields, shining shoes, or selling newspapers might provide.

The Lerdo administration made progress in other areas. The government added France to the list of European countries that had restored diplomatic relations. Secretary of the Treasury Romero continued his work on tariff revision and was able to codify his efforts. Lerdo also broke ground on one important political reform. The unicameral national legislature provided by the Constitution of 1857 had been under attack for years. The president proposed that a second house be added, and the legislative branch responded to the request in 1875. A Senate was added to the Chamber of Deputies, bringing the legislature back to the formula that had been first tested in 1824. Lerdo wanted the second, more elite body because he believed that it could be useful to him in his centralization efforts.

Lerdo's administration made progress but he did not emerge from the Mexican presidency unscathed. The enemies mounted, the press assailed him mercilessly, and prominent politicians of both parties spoke out strongly against him. When Lerdo announced that he planned to seek reelection in 1876, Porfirio Díaz perceived that history was finally on his side. In March 1876, five years after his unsuccessful attempt to overthrow Benito Juárez under the Plan de la Noria, Díaz issued the Plan de Tuxtepec, charging that Lerdo had repeatedly violated the sovereignty of the states and the municipalities, sacrificed Mexico's best interests in negotiating the railroad contracts, reduced the right of suffrage to a farce, and squandered public funds. But, most importantly, the plan established no reelection of the president and the governors of the states as the supreme law of the land. Effective suffrage and no reelection were to be the guiding principles of the Mexican political process.

The Revolution of Tuxtepec was decided in one battle as soldiers in a score of states flocked to the new banner. The opposing forces met on November 16 at Tecoac in the state

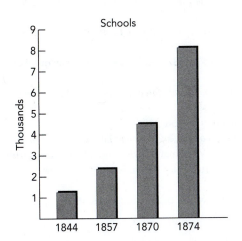
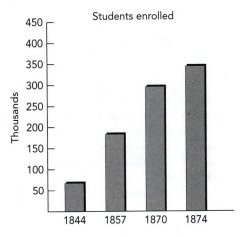

Schools and Student Enrollment, 1844–74

Source: Daniel Cosío Villegas, ed., *Historia moderna de México*, Vol. 3: *La República restaurada, La vida social*, by Luis Gonzálezy González et al. (Mexico, 1957), 643, 692–694.

of Tlaxcala; Díaz, reinforced by cohort Manuel González, carried the day. President Lerdo made his way to Acapulco where a steamer waited to carry him to the United States. Porfirio Díaz occupied Mexico City on November 21, 1876; he would control the country, directly or indirectly, for the next third of a century.

Careful examination of the restored republic reveals it as a critical transition between the demise of the empire and the establishment of the Díaz dictatorship. For the first time in Mexican history the administrations in power seemed to pull the country together rather than to drive it apart. All of the major changes generally attributed to Díaz and his successive cabinets in the last quarter of the nineteenth century and first decade of the twentieth have their base in the years 1867–76: tax and tariff reform; increased public security, especially in the rural areas; recognition of the need to attract foreign capital; the improvement of transportation and communication facilities; the cultivation of better relations abroad; a slightly less antagonistic relationship between church and state; and increased centralism disguised as federalism. Juárez and Lerdo, especially the former, laid the foundations, and Porfirio Díaz would construct the edifice. But modern Mexico did begin in 1867. Díaz's subsequent accomplishments were possible because his two predecessors in the presidential chair had paved the way.

RECOMMENDED FOR FURTHER STUDY

Acuña, Rodolfo F. *Sonoran Strongman: Ignacio Pesqueira and His Times.* Tucson: University of Arizona Press, 1974.

Bazant, Jan. *Alienation of Church Wealth in Mexico: Social and Economic Aspects of the Liberal Revolution, 1856–1875.* New York: Cambridge University Press, 1971.

Caplan, Karen D. *Indigenous Citizens: Local Liberalism in Early National Oaxaca and Yucatán.* Stanford, CA: Stanford University Press, 2009.

Chassen-López, Francie. *From Liberal to Revolutionary Oaxaca: The View from the South, Mexico, 1867–1911.* University Park: Pennsylvania State University Press, 2004.

Glick, Edward B. *Straddling the Isthmus of Tehuantepec.* Gainesville: University Press of Florida, 1959.

Knapp, Frank A. *The Life of Sebastián Lerdo de Tejada: A Study of Influence and Obscurity.* Austin: University of Texas Press, 1951.

Mallon, Florencia E. *Peasant and Nation: The Making of Postcolonial Mexico and Peru.* Berkeley: University of California Press, 1995.

Scholes, Walter V. *Mexican Politics during the Juárez Regime, 1855–1872.* Columbia: University of Missouri Press, 1957.

Sinkin, Richard N. *The Mexican Reform, 1855–1876: A Study in Liberal Nation Building.* Austin, TX: Institute of Latin American Studies, 1979.

Smart, Charles Allen. *Viva Juárez!* London, UK: Eyre and Spottiswoode, 1964.

Thomson, Guy P. C., with David G. LaFrance. *Patriotism, Politics, and Popular Liberalism in Nineteenth-Century Mexico: Juan Francisco Lucas and the Puebla Sierra.* Wilmington, DE: Scholarly Resources, 1999.

Vanderwood, Paul. "Genesis of the Rurales: Mexico's Early Struggle for Public Security." *Hispanic American Historical Review* 50/2 (1970): 323–44.

Weeks, Charles A. *The Juárez Myth in Mexico.* Tuscaloosa: University of Alabama Press, 1987.

CHAPTER 22

SOCIETY AND CULTURE IN THE MIDDLE OF THE NINETEENTH CENTURY

RURAL LIFE

Mexico remained overwhelmingly rural in the 1850s, 1860s, and 1870s, and life for the average citizen changed little. Those who resided in the Indian pueblo or the mestizo village lived much like their parents or their grandparents. In terms of earning power, standard of living, diet, life expectancy, and education, the life of rural Mexicans during the empire and the restored republic closely mirrored the past. In many cases, however, communities did engage with national changes, often through a popular politics oriented toward molding the new to fit the old.

The gap separating brown and white Mexico, poor and rich Mexico, was not bridged in the middle of the century. It might even have grown more pronounced. Writer Francisco Pimentel described the dichotomy of Mexican worlds in 1865:

> The white is the proprietor; the Indian the worker. The white is rich; the Indian poor and miserable. The descendants of the Spaniards have within their reach all of the knowledge of the century and all of the scientific discoveries; the Indian is completely unaware of it. The white dresses like a Parisian fashion plate and uses the richest of fabrics; the Indian runs around almost naked. The white lives in the cities in magnificent houses; the Indian is isolated in the country, his house a miserable hut. They are two different peoples in the same land; but worse, to a degree they are enemies.[1]

Foreign travelers to Mexico found the main roads slightly improved over a generation earlier, but most others were still an abomination. Scarcely a visitor to the country failed to note the banditry that plagued the highways. The wife of Prince Salm-Salm, one of Maximilian's confidants, described the anxieties of passengers of the stagecoach from Veracruz to Mexico City:

---

1 Quoted in Luis González y González, et al., *Historia moderna de México*, vol. 3: *La república restaurada, La vida social*, ed. Daniel Cosío Villegas (Mexico City, Mexico, 1957), 151.

It occurs very frequently that the diligence is attacked and plundered by robbers, and many horrible adventures of that kind are recorded, furnishing the passengers not very reassuring matter for conversation, and keeping them in a continual excitement. . . . The coachman does not even attempt to escape or resist; it is his policy to remain neutral, for if he acted otherwise it would not only be in vain, but cost him his life—a bullet from behind some bush would end his career on the next journey. . . .[2]

Overnight lodging in the larger towns, while generally not elegant, had improved since the early post-independence years. But accommodations were still lacking in rural areas. William Marshall Anderson, a U.S. citizen who visited Mexico during the empire, found in one southern village "no shelter nor place to rest but a miserable grass covered shanty, no bigger or better than my sheep pen." As he moved north the architecture changed but not the amenities. "Unplastered stone walls and a dirt floor constitute the comfort and elegance of our accommodation."[3]

By the 1850s and 1860s rural Mexicans were certainly long accustomed to violent depredations including theft and rape. French troops reportedly comported themselves even worse than their American predecessors of 1846–48. Already active in popular politics that sought to strengthen their communities, indigenous and mixed-race campesinos began to express proto-nationalist sentiments. In Oaxaca and other areas, some communities developed new collective identities that mixed elements of popular liberalism or conservatism, folk Catholicism, traditional customs and communal rights, and the acceptance of new ideas about property and commercial agriculture.

The social consequences of war did not end with the expulsion of the French. When President Juárez cut back on the size of the Mexican army, tens of thousands of former soldiers faced an uncertain future. Not a few of them formed bands and took out their frustrations on rural villages or hacienda complexes. The newspapers of the period were filled with stories of brigandage and plunder that the newly formed rurales could only contain in part.

POPULATION AND SOCIAL PROBLEMS

As might be expected during a period of foreign war and domestic turmoil, the population of Mexico grew slowly during the middle of the nineteenth century. Some of the state capitals even lost inhabitants, and northern Mexico still supported a scanty population. From a figure of 7,860,000 in 1856, the census countered only 8,743,000 Mexicans in 1874. The slow rate of growth cannot be attributed to a low birth rate. To the contrary, the birth rate remained consistent overall, but war casualties and a high infant mortality rate kept the population down.

---

2   Princess Felix Salm-Salm, *Ten Years of My Life*, vol. 1 (London, UK, 1876), 183–85.
3   William Marshall Anderson, *An American in Maximilian's Mexico, 1865–1866: The Diaries of William Marshall Anderson*, ed. Ramón Eduardo Ruiz (San Marino, CA, 1959), 15, 80.

Saltillo, the capital of Coahuila, hardly grew at all in the 1860s and 1870s, but it was one of the more charming provincial capitals of the north.

Policymakers during both the empire and the restored republic wished to open up new lands, and some even spoke of the need to encourage the development of a new class of independent farmers by encouraging European immigration. New legislation in the 1850s and 1860s sought to do this while averting the earlier disastrous experience in Texas. Nonetheless, religious intolerance, political instability, and much administrative mismanagement all mitigated against a successful program. The three thousand immigrants from western Europe, the United States, and China who began to arrive annually during the restoration did not even offset the emigration of Mexicans to the United States. In 1876 only about twenty-five thousand people in Mexico were foreign-born and almost all resided in the larger cities.

Mexico City's population grew to two hundred thousand during the restored republic, and the capital experienced some remarkable physical transformations. Without question the most notable was the construction of an impressive new thoroughfare that connected Chapultepec Castle to the heart of the city. The project initiated under Maximilian, who had named it the Calzada de la Emperatriz in honor of Carlota, did not reach completion until the period of the restored republic. Benito Juárez changed the name, most appropriately, to the Paseo de la Reforma, still today an impressive boulevard.

Growth and change in Mexico City also accelerated social problems. Prostitution had long been accepted as a necessary evil in Mexico, but when the women of the street began openly soliciting clients at the entrance to the main cathedral and the hundreds of smaller churches, a public uproar followed. Those who called for moral reform pointed to the burgeoning rate of venereal disease and the perversion of the young and innocent. As the nineteenth century progressed, public discourse shifted to emphasize the moral and physical health of the nation. Its advocates increasingly connected childbirth and reproduction with

The turbulence of the French Intervention and the restoration made it inevitable that soldiers would be found congregating in Mexico City.

the nation. The mother-child bond was essential to the healthy political and religious re-production of the state. New laws aimed to increase regulation of medical care and prostitu-tion. Legislation also targeted alcoholism and vagrancy deemed to lead to degeneracy. More oversight governed drinking places, calling for separation between elite and popular spaces.

The Roman Catholic Church had always made alms giving a virtue, and by the middle of the nineteenth century mendicancy had become a prominent feature of larger towns and cities, with beggars numbering in the thousands in Mexico City. Men and women pleading for assistance—the disabled, the blind, alcoholics, even abandoned children—were found everywhere in the capital. When ignored on the streets or in the churches, they moved from door to door in both residential and business zones. Government attempts to curb mendi-cancy included the establishment of new charitable institutions and hospitals for the poor, but these efforts accomplished little. Nevertheless, some Catholic lay organizations like the Ladies of Charity of St. Vincent de Paul, established in 1863, did attain more success in their efforts to assist the poor through welfare programs and schools. These activities provided an outlet for religious social sensibilities among those, especially women, who defied anticleri-cal reforms. These groups represented an emerging social Catholicism that would expand services to the needy.

THE THREE CLASSES

The lot of the urban working class at midcentury was only slightly better than that of the un-employed. Job security was nonexistent, the worker being completely subject to the whims of the employer. While the industrial revolution had scarcely touched Mexico, the capital did have its share of factories producing textiles, soap, cigarettes, flour, and alcoholic beverages. The thousands working in these small industries enjoyed but few protective laws. Legislation regulating child labor, safety precautions, and other working conditions was scant; and officials seldom enforced those laws on the books. Slightly better off were people who worked for themselves, the tens of thousands of street vendors each with a distinctive call, hawking tortillas, sweet bread, fruit, flowers, water, ice, candy, pottery, straw baskets, tamales, pulque, roasted corn, milk, ice cream, rosaries, crucifixes, pictures of the Virgin of Guadalupe, and an endless variety of other goods. But their diet was grossly deficient and their life expectancy short; most were illiterate and lived in primitive housing on the outskirts of Mexico City.

For the illiterate city dweller or the recent immigrant from the countryside, domestic service provided an opportunity to work. As a generation earlier, the maids, gardeners, doorkeepers, valets, stable masters, chambermaids, and nannies did relatively well. They received up to fifteen pesos a month without food, or four pesos with room and board. But they were at least assured a clean room in which to live and, despite long hours, tolerable working conditions in a relatively safe residential district of the capital.

The still tiny middle class—composed of shopkeepers, merchants, small independent entrepreneurs, professional men, government officials, and other white-collar workers— lived comfortably but without amenities. The houses (often rooms above their stores) were small but adequately furnished with locally made products. Tiles or straw mats covered the floor; rugs were unusual. Because of a grossly inadequate water supply system, few smaller homes had private baths. Public bathing facilities were scarce and inconvenient enough that neither daily nor weekly bathing was common; the trade in cheap perfumes and colognes prospered.

The district of Tacubaya, at the western end of the city contained most of the palatial residences of the wealthy families. A genuine showplace, an English visitor in the 1860s described it as a district where "all the men with heavy purses build villas and country houses,

Growing from a poor Indian community to the most fashionable suburb of Mexico City, by 1850 Tacubaya often housed Mexican presidents, cabinet ministers, bishops, and all of the wealthiest residents of the capital, both Mexican and foreign. At midcentury its population stood at five thousand, but vacationers swelled the count to sixty-five hundred during the summer months.

to which they retire in the summer months. . . . It is really a very pretty place."[4] Students or professors from the Art Academy of San Carlos frequently decorated the façades of the houses. Elegant patios, marble staircases, carved doors, crystal chandeliers, gold candelabra, imported pianos and carpets, rosewood furniture, and old Spanish paintings could be found in every aristocratic home. Most also had private chapels with the patron saints of the family's members represented. The real marks of distinction, however, were the resplendent private baths, decorated with imported French fixtures. Many of these aristocratic homes required twenty or twenty-five servants to keep them going. Some of the affluent required fewer but hired more in unabashed ostentation.

Women who visited Mexico in the 1860s and 1870s often commented upon the general ignorance of the ladies of the genteel aristocracy they found there. One wonders just how much the ladies of Europe knew about Mexican women of any class. Most daughters of upper and middle class families went to school or received tutoring. The vast majority of women had little access to the educational system.

SOCIAL AMUSEMENTS AND CULTURAL ACHIEVEMENTS

Some everyday diversions cut across class lines. Members of the lower, middle, and upper strata could be seen enjoying the promenades around the Alameda, the great central park in the downtown business district, which was equipped with hydrogen gas lamps in 1873. Everyone enjoyed the free concerts staged in the bandstands of the public parks, and all partook of secular or religious fiestas. Public fairs and touring circuses from Europe or the United States also attracted all elements of society, as did games of dice played outdoors. But the greatest social leveler of all was the bullfight, a spectacle where the cabinet minister could converse with his shoeshine boy and the aristocrat from Tacubaya could debate the awarding of ears and tails with his gardener.

The bullfight was introduced in Mexico in the early sixteenth century and quickly became a cultural institution. The main ring used in Mexico City in the middle of the century was the Plaza del Paseo Nuevo. Built in 1851 at a cost of almost one hundred thousand pesos, it seated ten thousand and filled to capacity each time a fight was held. To be sure, the more affluent sat in the shade and the masses in the sun, the rich drank cognac and the poor pulque; but they all saw the same show. Toreros Bernardo Gaviño, Pablo Mendoza, and Ignacio Gadea were the rage of the era. But not all of the performances demonstrated skill and, after one particularly bad fight in 1867 during which several horses were killed and blood filled the ring, the press began a concerted campaign for abolition of the sport. Emphasizing the brutality of the spectacle, the opponents succeeded in having the congress pass legislation outlawing bullfighting in the Federal District. Despite the outcry from the owners of the bullrings, the raisers of fighting stock, the performers, and the thousands of fans bullfighting ceased until 1874 when a new ring was dedicated in Tlalnepantla, just outside the Federal District. The placards announcing the Sunday spectacles were plastered all over the walls of the capital.

---

4   J. F. Elton, *With the French in Mexico* (London, UK, 1867), 37–38.

A Sunday bullfight at the Plaza de Toros de San Pablo, near Mexico City.

The arts did not necessarily mirror popular culture but they tended toward more social awareness in the mid-nineteenth century. Focused neither in the complete rejection of the Spanish past nor in profound social transformation, intellectuals did advocate a path for mexicanidad, instilling pride in the nation through the establishment of a new, stronger, secular, more developed, and progressive Mexico.

In literature the romantic novel was not superseded but did assume a distinctly new flavor. The new novel, while no less moralistic than the old, took an instructive tone. To a generation that had witnessed many civil wars and two foreign wars, the cultural orientation was historical, and the historical novel lent itself perfectly to the goals of the new intelligentsia. Armies, and especially foreign ones, marching through poor native villages, raping and looting on their way, provided an abundance of subject matter for historical novelists like Juan A. Mateos, Ireneo Paz, and Vicente Riva Palacio. These writers evoked compassion in the reader not because the Indians and mestizos were poor but because they were Mexican and subject to abuse.

The literary giant of the period was Ignacio Manuel Altamirano (1834–95). Born to Indian parents in Tixtla, Guerrero, he went to school first in the pueblo and later in Mexico City; but his education was interrupted by the wars of the reform and the French Intervention. Elected to congress in 1861 he voiced radical opinions. After the expulsion of the French he edited several literary journals and then turned his attention to the novel, a literary form he believed should be didactic. In 1869 and 1871 he published two widely acclaimed short novels, *Clemencia* and *La Navidad en las montañas* (translated as *Christmas in the Mountains*). Set in Guadalajara during the French Intervention, *Clemencia* propounded the ideal of patriotism through the characterization of an officer in the republican army. More profound in social content, *La Navidad en las montañas* attacked forced conscription (the leva), urged the development of a new educational system, and denounced the clergy for its failure to meet the real needs of Mexicans. At the same time, Altamirano believed the church had a role to play in alleviating rural poverty. The importance of cultivating social Christianity and progressive roles for priests was also addressed in Juan Díaz Covarrubias's 1858 novel *Gil Gómez, el insurgente*.

As emperor, Maximilian underwrote the production costs of an opera by Melesio Morales, Mexico's foremost midcentury composer, but not even the fine arts could escape the intense partiality of the age. The old Art Academy of San Carlos, subsequently changed to the National Academy, was redesignated the Imperial Academy by Maximilian. Dedicated Juarista liberals in the academy could not serve Maximilian in good conscience, and many resigned their posts. After the French were expelled, the academy became the National School of Fine Arts. Music of social awareness followed on the heels of Maximilian's defeat with Aniceto Ortega's two most famous marches, both completed in 1867, that celebrated the defeat of the invader. They were appropriately entitled *Marcha Zaragoza* and *Marcha Republicana*.

Two key figures dominated Mexican art in the 1850s, 1860s, and 1870s: Pelegrín Clavé (1810–80) and Juan Cordero (1824–84). Clavé, a Spaniard by birth, taught at the academy for almost twenty years. He was a portrait painter of the first class; his fine depiction of Benito Juárez, hanging today in the Chapultepec Museum of History. Cordero, much like the historical novelists of the period, infused his painting with historical and philosophical themes that taught a message. In 1874 he completed a mural in the main staircase of the National Preparatory School entitled *Triumph and Study over Ignorance and Sloth*. It depicted Mexican progress in terms of science, industry, and commerce. This trilogy,

Gabino Barreda (1818–81). Barreda, who founded the National Preparatory School in 1867, also introduced Mexico to the positivism of Auguste Comte and in the process provided the philosophical underpinnings for Mexican *cientificismo*. In good positivist fashion, the curriculum he introduced at the school subordinated the arts to the sciences.

he believed, would destroy ignorance and greed. A more scientific visual culture can also be seen in the maps and atlases of Antonio García Cubas, who combined older cartographic methods with new technologies to illustrate precise geographical coordinates. His *Carta general de la República Mexicana*, drawn in 1857, was the first published map of the Mexican nation-state. The innovations in visual culture also reflected the emergence of the positivist creed in Mexico, expounded by Gabino Barreda, the director of the National Preparatory School.

Nowhere is the midcentury culture of a new Mexico better illustrated than in the field of philosophy, and seldom can the beginning of a philosophical movement be so accurately pinpointed as Mexican positivism. On September 16, 1867, in an Independence Day celebration in Guanajuato, Gabino Barreda delivered an eloquent speech subsequently known as the "Civic Oration." As a student of Auguste Comte, Barreda had read and observed widely. He interpreted Mexican history as a struggle between a negative spirit (represented most recently by the alliance of the conservative and the French) and a positivist spirit (embodied by the liberal republican forces). The combative phase of the struggle had ended with the execution of Maximilian, and the country was now prepared to embark upon the constructive phase. Barreda was optimistic. Mexico's material regeneration could be achieved through the most prudent application of scientific knowledge and the scientific method. He ended his speech by coining a new slogan for the new Mexico: "Liberty, Order, and Progress." Within a short time, however, Mexican liberals would sense that liberty was not an equal partner in the positivist trinity. It would be sacrificed, almost meticulously, to order and progress. The liberal party would split asunder over the positivist issue, and the moderates, who placed their faith in order and progress, would gain the upper hand. Championing a gradualist approach to positivist dogma, they would be the harbingers of Mexican modernity.

RECOMMENDED FOR FURTHER STUDY

Altamirano, Ignacio Manuel. *Christmas in the Mountains*. Translated by Harvey L. Johnson. Gainesville: University Press of Florida, 1961.

Anderson, William Marshall. *An American in Maximilian's Mexico, 1865–1866: The Diaries of William Marshall Anderson*. Edited by Ramón Eduardo Ruiz. San Marino, CA: Huntington Library Publications, 1959.

Arrom, Silvia Marina. *Containing the Poor: The Mexico City Poor House, 1774–1881*. Durham, NC: Duke University Press, 2001.

Brushwood, John S. *Mexico in Its Novel: A Nation's Search for Identity*. Austin: University of Texas Press, 1966.

Carrera, Magali M. *Traveling from New Spain to Mexico: Mexican Mapping Practices of the Nineteenth Century*. Durham, NC: Duke University Press, 2011.

Elton, J. F. *With the French in Mexico*. London, UK: Chapman & Hall, 1867.

Jaffary, Nora E. *Reproduction and Its Discontents in Mexico: Childbirth and Conception from 1750 to 1905*. Chapel Hill: University of North Carolina Press, 2015.

Hale, Charles A. *The Transformation of Liberalism in Late Nineteenth-Century Mexico*. Princeton, NJ: Princeton University Press, 1989.

McCrea, Heather. *Diseased Relations: Epidemics, Public Health, and State Building in Yucatán, Mexico, 1847–1924*. Albuquerque: University of New Mexico Press, 2011.

Nesvig, Martin A., ed., *Religious Culture in Modern Mexico*. Lanham, MD: Rowman & Littlefield, 2007.

Pedelty, Mark. *Musical Ritual in Mexico City: From the Aztec to NAFTA*. Austin: University of Texas Press, 2004.

Rugeley, Terry. *Of Wonders and Wise Men: Religion and Popular Cultures in Southeast Mexico, 1800–1876.* Austin: University of Texas Press, 2001.

Salm-Salm, Princess Felix. *Ten Years of My Life.* 2 vols. London, UK: Richard Bentley & Son, 1876.

Stevenson, Robert. *Music in Mexico: A Historical Survey.* New York: Thomas Y. Crowell, Co., 1971.

Toner, Deborah. *Alcohol and Nationhood in Nineteenth Century Mexico.* Lincoln: University of Nebraska Press, 2015.

Wasserman, Mark. *Everyday Life and Politics in Nineteenth-Century Mexico.* Albuquerque: University of New Mexico Press, 2000.

Wilson, Robert A. *Mexico: Its Peasants and Its Priests.* New York: Harper & Brothers, 1856.

Zea, Leopoldo. *The Latin American Mind.* Translated by James H. Abbott and Lowell Dunham. Norman: University of Oklahoma Press, 1963.

_____. *Positivism in Mexico.* Translated by Josephine H. Schulte. Austin: University of Texas Press, 1974.

THE MODERNIZATION OF MEXICO

Distinguished for its strength, dynamism, and creativity, the Mexican art endeavor has long commanded world attention and acclaim. Centuries before that first colossal encounter between the European and American worlds, ancient Mexican architects were designing massive pyramids and laying out imposing cities, replete with temples, palaces, plazas, and ball courts. As these structures integrated the supernatural, transformed the physical landscape, and altered the surrounding skyline, talented artists and master sculptors were summoned to decorate the walls with paintings, fill the niches with statues, and inspire the masses. In the process they left their indelible aesthetic touch in the form of murals and sculptured figures fashioned with equal skill from materials as dissimilar as soft clay and hard stone.

The sixteenth century witnessed not only Spain's physical conquest but an artistic invasion as well. New forms and new styles resting on an absolutely different ethic came to dominate creative output. For three full centuries Spanish colonial art and architecture proved a faithful handmaiden to a distinctive Hispanic culture. Just as in the mother country, colonial art and architecture came to the service of the Roman Catholic religion. The most extravagant exemplars of colonial architecture are found in the countless churches and cathedrals that adorned city plazas and dotted the Mexican countryside from the rain forests of the south to the deserts of the far north. Few colonial structures could compete with them in either quality or scale. In the sixteenth and early seventeenth centuries, it was the awe-inspiring but austere classic style that dominated church architecture, giving way in the later seventeenth century to the baroque with its easily recognizable sculptured facades and proliferation of ornamentation, and ultimately yielding to an elaborate extension of the baroque known as Churrigueresque.

Although New Spain's viceregal and ecclesiastical authorities sat for portraits, most painting examined religious themes. Baroque painting of the seventeenth century featured the lives of saints and a militant, triumphant church, first on altarpieces and then in enormous freestanding canvases. Cristóbal de Villalpando (ca. 1649–1714) excelled in this genre with commissioned works of brilliant pictorial vitality in the cathedrals of Mexico City and Puebla. His painting of Mexico City's plaza mayor near the turn of the eighteenth century (the cover image for this book) departs from religious expression to portray the enormous square with its cathedral (left) and the viceregal palace (top), exposing the damage to its façade from the 1692 revolt. The painting depicts bustling commercial activity in the plebeian Baratillo market stalls (center) and the upscale Parián with imported merchandise from Asia (below). Over a thousand figures embody novohispanos of all social, ethnic and occupational groups including clerics, soldiers, men on horseback, children, indigenous women selling pulque and food, buyers, and beggars. The juxtaposition of the viceroy in his carriage and the Indian tameme lugging a heavy bundle through the gathering of wealthy women and men in their finery (bottom) conveys stark class difference. Yet Villalpando's ordering of space reveals no conflict in this detailed panorama of daily intermingling.

Colonial sculpture differed from its pre-Columbian predecessor as it was regularly carved from wood embellished with polychrome. The devotional statuary (called santos or bultos), in concert with the religious paintings, clearly served the purposes of Spain's evangelical mission and most often found its permanent home in the magnificent churches and convents of the viceroyalty. Another expression, unique to Mexico, is the category of casta paintings that depicted the offspring of a multitude of racial mixtures.

With Mexico's independence from Spain at the beginning of the nineteenth century, art assumed a distinctly secular tone for the first time. Although a number of independence heroes were captured with oil on canvas, a changing nineteenth-century artistic imagination gradually expanded to embrace a much larger and diverse Mexican universe. No longer preoccupied with religious expression, a new genre known as costumbrista interpreted everyday life and customs, documenting the intrinsic vitality of an urban street scene or the elation of a local fiesta. The costumbristas shared the stage with Mexico's nineteenth-century landscape artists, best exemplified by José María Velasco. These painters found their inspiration in the majesty of a towering volcano, or the freshness of a river flowing bank to bank. Attentive always to the subtleties of light and color, the landscape painters detailed panoramic images of Mexico's incredibly rich and varied topography. As the country moved hesitantly from the incessant chaos of the early nineteenth century to become a more stable and modern polity, the artistic community participated in the important transition to modernity. The artists of the late nineteenth century made it their task to reach an international audience in the effort to offset the negative Mexican image too often held by influential foreign nationals.

It was with Mexico's twentieth-century social revolution that the rich artistic heritage of the centuries culminated in a muralist renaissance. Beginning in the 1920s and 1930s the revolutionary muralists, enjoying generous government patronage, brought their genius to the walls of public buildings where they could interpret and disseminate the lessons of Mexico's revolutionary ideal. Flanked by a coterie of gifted artistic compatriots, the three giants of the movement were Diego Rivera, José Clemente Orozco, and David Alfaro Siqueiros. While Orozco attended Mexico's well-known San Carlos Academy, Rivera and Siqueiros studied painting in Europe.

A quintessential expression of the art of social protest, the Mexican muralists accentuated the grandeur of Mexico's Indian past, criticized the excesses of the conquest, and found ample opportunity to censure corruption or betrayal of revolutionary ideals. While emphasizing content over form, their technique was superb. Even today art critics look in vain to find a more momentous example of public art in the twentieth century, for it changed the way Mexicans looked at themselves and how the outside world viewed Mexico. Yet other Mexican artists, like Rufino Tamayo, who earned international acclaim, broke tradition with the muralists and turned to more universal representations.

The north courtyard of the palace in the magnificent city of Palenque dates from the seventh century A.D. Maya architects designed it not only to be aesthetically pleasing but to withstand the ravages of time.

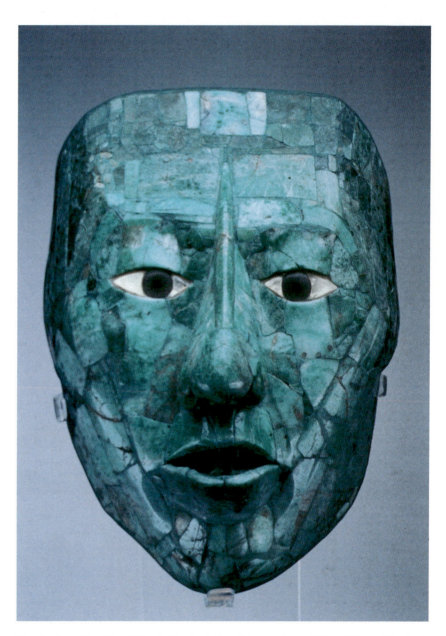

The death mask of Pacal. Hanab Pacal ruled at Palenque from 615 to 683 A.D. His death mask, fashioned improbably of jade mosaic, was found in Palenque's Temple of Inscriptions and today is included in the rich collection of the National Museum of Anthropology.

Anthropomorphic female figurine from Nayarit, Classic Period. Prior to the conquest many indigenous peoples of western Mexico buried the dead, accompanied by decorative offerings, in underground tombs. Finely polished and then protected with lacquer, this beautiful ceramic work of a female giving birth was uncovered in one of these *tumbas de tiro* in central western Mexico.

Cacaxtla Mural. Flourishing from around 700 A.D. to 950 A.D., the fortified city of Cacaxtla in what is now Tlaxcala encapsulates much of the depth and diversity of pre-Columbian architecture, painting, and statuary. The mural pictured here portrays a figure adorned in eagle regalia and standing on the omnipresent religious symbol of ancient Mexico, the feathered serpent.

Cathedral of Oaxaca. Located on Oaxaca City's main plaza (the zócalo) the cathedral's massive fortified walls and twin bell towers are reminiscent of sixteenth-century churches, but the facade with its exquisitely carved figures and bas-relief columns clearly identify it as baroque. Utilizing local limestone of a greenish yellow tone, construction began in the sixteenth century but took over a century to complete.

One of Mexico's most unique churches, Santa María de Tonantzintla in the state of Puebla, features the extensive use of ceramic tile. Completed in the eighteenth century, the simple beauty and symmetry of the tiled exterior stands in stark contrast to the interior, which encompasses a veritable explosion of the Mexican Churrigueresque.

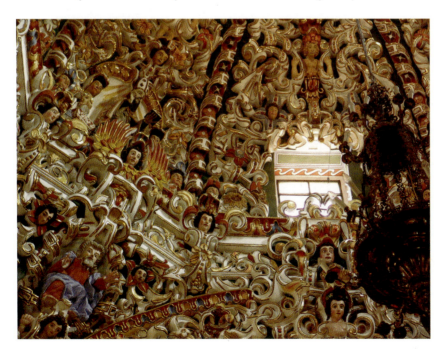

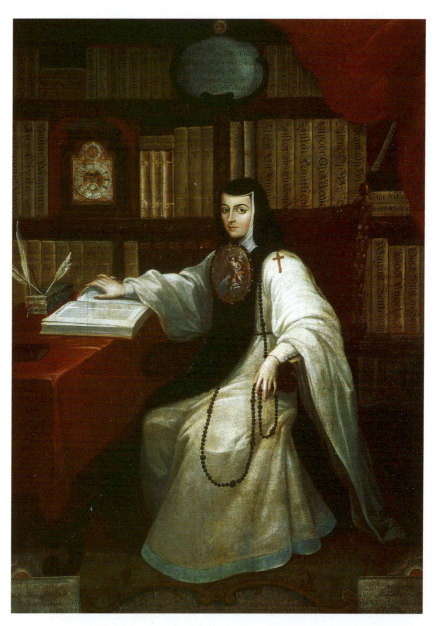

Portrait of Sor Juana Inés de la Cruz. Miguel Cabrera (1695–1768), the most prolific and distinguished Mexican artist of the colonial period, devoted much of his distinguished career to producing works to adorn church altars and sacristies; but he also left this stunning portrait of the most renowned lady of the colonial church, Sor Juana Inés de la Cruz.

De Chino cambujo y d'India ; Loba

Casta painting by Miguel Cabrera *De chino cambujo y d'India, Loba*, 1763. Late in his career Cabrera moved beyond religious art to test his considerable talent in *casta* painting. This unique genre, with no European model upon which to build, captured the centrality of mestizaje to Mexican colonial life by depicting parents of different races with beautiful children showing unmistakable indebtedness to both.

José Agustín Arrieta, *La Sorpresa*, 1850. Born in Puebla and trained in Mexico City, Arrieta delighted in street and market scenes. This oil on canvas open air market is one of his most famous and now has its home in the National Museum of History.

(Opposite page, bottom) Luis Coto, *La Colegiata de Guadalupe*, 1859. Landscape painter Luis Coto found a way to contrast the old traditional Mexico and the new modern Mexico. On the northern edge of Mexico City at Tepeyac Hill, where the Virgin appeared to Juan Diego in 1531, he painted the seventeenth-century Guadalupe Collegiate Church behind a new locomotive pulling carriages.

Salvador Murillo, *El Puente de Chiquihuite*, 1875. In an area of Mexico long remembered for its oxcarts and mule trains, landscape painter Murillo found the modernization symbolism of a long bridge and steam engine pulling a train too much to resist in this oil on canvas painted at the end of the Restored Republic.

José María Velasco, *The Valley of Mexico from the Cerro de Tepeyac*, 1894. Combining minute foreground detail and a broad panoramic vision, Velasco was Mexico's master nineteenth-century landscape artist. Here, the towering twin volcanoes of Popocatépetl and Iztaccíhuatl dominate the skyline of the high valley of Mexico.

Diego Rivera from *Día de los Muertos*, 1923–24. Decorating the Court of the Fiestas at Mexico's Ministry of Education, Rivera's Day of the Dead mural celebrates the unique festival with raucous music and drinking. No kings, no viceroys, no bishops, no presidents or generals are to be found but rather a coterie of everyday Mexicans of different colors, different social classes, dead and alive, brought together by culture and tradition and joined in solidarity.

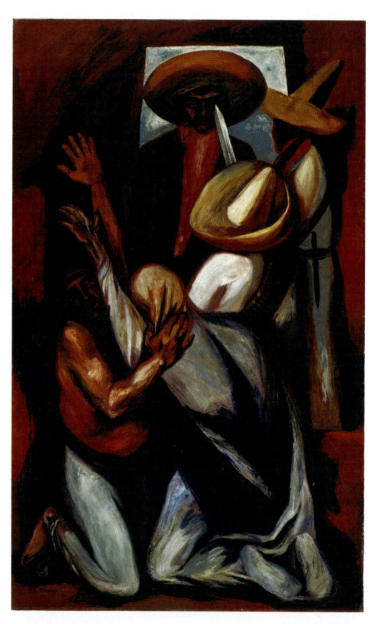

José Clemente Orozco, *Zapata*, 1930. Orozco's Zapata, arguably his most celebrated work, was painted eleven years after the assassination of the famous Mexican revolutionary. Silhouetted in a doorway, a pensive and charismatic Zapata and two of his soldiers witness the utter despair of two peones.

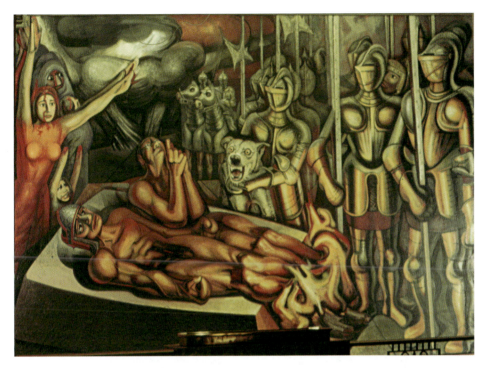

David Alfaro Siqueiros from the *Tormento de Cuauhtémoc*, 1951. The imagery of this mural in Mexico City's Place of Fine Arts is so powerful and intense that it leaves little doubt about Siqueiros's understanding of what happened to Aztec chieftain Cuauhtémoc while a captive of the Spaniards during the conquest.

Diego Rivera, *Paisaje Zapatista*, 1915. Rivera symbolically evoked the power of the peasant revolution in this painting that predated Orozco's rendering of Zapata. The abstract landscape illustrates the influence of cubism as Rivera applied it to unmistakably Mexican material culture.

Rufino Tamayo, *Dos Figuras en Rojo*, 1973. Distancing himself from the muralists, the Oaxacan painter Tamayo abstained from using art as a political statement and drew on Mexican folk art and pre-Columbian motifs to produce works rich in color and texture that became more abstract over time. Here, we see a man and a woman rendered ambiguously in both their interior and exterior forms.

CHAPTER 23

THE PORFIRIATO
Order and Progress

Porfirio Díaz directed the course of the Mexican nation for a third of a century during a fascinating and vital period of the entire western world. Innovation characterized the era—in technology, political and economic systems, social values, and artistic expression. Otto von Bismarck transformed the German states into a nation. William Gladstone introduced England to a new kind of liberalism. The leading powers of Europe partitioned Africa unto themselves. The United States emerged as a world power, and Spain lost Cuba, Puerto Rico, and the Philippines—the last remnants of its once-glorious empire. Russia experienced a revolution that, though abortive, presaged things to come in 1917. Pope Leo XIII enunciated *Rerum Novarum*, proclaiming that employees should be treated more as men than as tools. Thomas Hardy and Thomas Mann revolutionized the world of fiction, while Renoir and Monet did the same for art. But even in a world of profound change, Porfirio Díaz's Mexico must be considered remarkable.

MEXICO IN 1876

When Díaz assumed control of Mexico in 1876, except in a few of the larger cities, the country had scarcely been touched by the scientific, technological, and industrial revolutions of the nineteenth century. While much of western Europe and the United States had been transformed in the last fifty years, Mexico had languished, less out of inertia than because of the intermittent political chaos and economic losses.

Although the period of the restoration had pointed Mexico in a new direction, plans for change had only been partially implemented. In 1876 Díaz inherited an empty treasury, a long list of foreign debts, and a huge bureaucratic corps whose salaries were in arrears. Mexico's credit rating abroad was abominable, and its politics had become somewhat of a joke in Europe. The value of Mexican imports consistently exceeded the value of exports, presenting a serious balance-of-payments problem and making it virtually impossible to secure sorely needed infusions of foreign capital. The Mexican affluent, knowing the precarious nature of the political process, would not invest their own resources to any large degree. Because of

321

graft, ineptitude, and mismanagement, public services languished. The mail, if it arrived at all, came inexcusably late.

Mining had never really recovered from the chaotic days of the wars for independence. A small number of mines operated inefficiently without benefit of technological improvements, and no coordinated efforts at new geological exploration had been undertaken. The economic situation of agriculture was much the same. Modern reapers and threshers and newly developed chemical fertilizers remained oddities. Practically nothing had been done to improve the breeding of stock animals.

When Díaz came to the presidency the iron horse had just started to compete with the oxcart, the mule train, and the coach. Telegraph construction had barely begun. The dock facilities on both coasts were in sad disrepair, and many of the most important harbors were silted with sand. Veracruz was so unsafe for shipping that some favored abandoning it altogether. The rurales had not yet been able to contain banditry and rural violence. A tremendously high infant mortality rate testified to the lack of modern sanitation and health facilities even as the last quarter of the nineteenth century began. Yellow fever plagued the tropical areas of the Gulf coast, particularly in the immediate environs of Veracruz.

Mexico City had a special health problem. Situated in a broad valley, it was surrounded by mountains and a series of lakes, almost all of which were at a higher elevation than the city. Heavy rains invariably brought flooding. In addition to extensive property damage (floods often caused adobe walls to crumble), the waters then stagnated in low-lying areas for weeks and months. Gastrointestinal and typhus disease frequently followed on the heels of a serious flood. Projects to provide an adequate drainage system for the city had been proposed since the early colonial period. The height of the surrounding mountains, however, thwarted proposals for a foolproof system of drainage canals and dikes, and the projects initiated from time to time could not produce lasting results.

ORDER AND PROGRESS UNDER DÍAZ

If progress were to displace stagnation, Díaz believed it would be necessary first to change Mexico's image drastically and to remove the stigma popularly associated with Mexican politics. Only if the potential investors from the United States and Europe became convinced that stability was supplanting turbulence could they be expected to offer their dollars and pounds sterling, for profit, to quickly vitalize the manufacturing, mining, and agricultural sectors of the Mexican economy. The task, then, as Díaz perceived it, was first to establish the rule of law. He was fully prepared to accept the positivist dictum of order and progress, in that order.

Díaz acceded to power with acknowledged liberal credentials and personal integrity. Born to a family of modest means in the city of Oaxaca in 1830, he tried studying first for the priesthood and then for the law. But he eventually opted for a career in the army. Joining the Oaxaca National Guard in 1856, he fought under the liberal banner during the War of the Reform. With the liberal victory promotions came with startling rapidity, and by the time of his history-making defeat of the French in Puebla on May 5, 1862, he was a thirty-two-year-old brigadier general. During the period of the empire he won additional military fame championing the cause of liberal republicanism as a guerrilla fighter against the French army. Not even his abortive revolt of La Noria against Benito Juárez or his successful revolt of Tuxtepec against Lerdo de Tejada, both fought in defense of the liberal principle of no re-election, tarnished his liberal reputation.

During his first term, which lasted until 1880, Díaz faced a number of insurrections. Agrarian rebellions protesting seizure of village lands flared in many states, but not all the revolts had agrarian roots. Some were prompted by Díaz's failure to reward supporters or by his heavy-handed appointments at the state level. But the most serious were a number of revolts launched along the US border in support of exiled president Lerdo de Tejada. These military movements not only threatened the success of Díaz's pacification program but also damaged his efforts to cultivate more friendly relations with his northern neighbor. He did not hesitate to meet force with force. Rebel leaders not shot down on the field of battle were disposed of shortly after their capture. Characteristic of Díaz's attitude toward those who would disrupt the national peace was his reaction to a revolt in Veracruz during his first year in office. When Governor Luis Mier y Terán asked for instructions concerning captured rebels in that state, Díaz reportedly telegraphed him, *Mátalos en caliente* (Kill them on the spot). Such lessons were not lost on potential revolutionaries elsewhere. Less tranquil than often portrayed in the post-1880 period, violent disruptions gradually abated. Yet violence did shatter peace as often as in the past. Over 800 corpsmen had been added to the rurales to curb brigandage. Order beckoned, along with progress.

Within a couple of years of his assumption of the presidency Díaz had been recognized by most of western Europe and Latin America, but the United States held out pending the satisfactory resolution of several outstanding problems. To overcome one obstacle, Díaz in 1876 agreed to terms that would satisfy US claimants over damages to their properties in Mexico. The Hayes administration had one further grievance. Groups of Mexican bandits and Indians occasionally crossed the border, attacked settlements in the United States, and drove herds of cattle back into Mexico. The Mexican government, in the name of national sovereignty, refused to grant permission to US forces to cross over into Mexico in pursuit. In the summer of 1877 border depredations brought the two nations almost to the brink of war. While Díaz would not permit American troops to enter Mexican territory, at this crucial junction, he dispatched additional troops of his own to the border region to prevent further encroachments. Tensions gradually subsided, and President Hayes authorized recognition of the Díaz regime in the spring of 1877.

During his first administration Díaz also began to put Mexico's economic house in order. As a symbolic gesture he reduced his own salary and then ordered similar reductions for other government employees. Thousands of useless bureaucrats were eliminated from the rolls altogether. In addition, the administration attacked a problem endemic since the colonial period—smuggling. To stem the annual loss of hundreds of thousands of dollars in import and export duties along the US border and in Mexico's leading ports, Díaz decreed heavy sentences for individuals and companies trafficking in smuggled goods. To stimulate legal commerce with the United States the Mexican government opened three new consulates along the Texas border, at Rio Grande City, Laredo, and Eagle Pass.

As Díaz's first term drew to a close, several states urged that the no reelection law be amended so that Díaz could be eligible to serve another term. But Díaz preferred the law as it was; it provided that neither the president nor the state governors were eligible for immediate reelection but could serve again after the lapse of an intervening term. He dutifully retired from office. By voluntarily stepping aside Díaz could give further substance to the growing conviction abroad that Mexico had begun to mature politically. As the term ended, Díaz threw his support behind 47-year-old Manuel González, an imposing military man who had rendered yeoman service in the fight against Lerdo and who currently served as secretary of war. González won the election with a large majority.

THE GONZÁLEZ PRESIDENCY

The González presidency generated controversy. The new president wanted to follow the patterns established by Díaz and, in fact, even brought his predecessor into the government for a short time as head of the Department of Development. Revenues increased, but so did expenditures as the administration plunged headlong into further development. Modernization was expensive. Railroad construction continued, but the US companies required large subsidies from the government—as high as $9,500 for each kilometer of track laid. The government also fostered new steamship lines and established the first cable service in the country. But González had overextended spending and found himself without sufficient funds to meet government obligations.

Stories of graft and corruption began filling the press, and political pamphlets denouncing the regime circulated on the streets of Mexico City. They charged the president and his cabinet with a variety of personal and public improprieties, including negotiating illegal contracts and receiving rebates, selling government properties to administration favorites for practically nothing, stealing from the treasury at a fantastic rate, and sexual misconduct. The public turned against the president.

Some of these charges may have been exaggerated, but González had directed legal changes that allowed for the government to appropriate lands it deemed were not being used. These newly public lands could be sold to private investors. Not surprisingly, bribery and misappropriation of indigenous lands ensued. González should be given credit for encouraging the developmental process that had begun timidly with the restoration of the republic. His efforts to stimulate railway construction and to make lands available for the expansion of commercial agriculture established a base from which Porfirio Díaz could readily implement his modernization program.

THE RETURN OF DÍAZ

Díaz used his four years out of office to build a new political machine. He served for a brief time in the González cabinet and for slightly over a year in the governorship of his native state of Oaxaca. His understanding of local Oaxacan politics served to condition his thinking about the means to deal with rural villagers in pursuing his goals. Although he was not adverse to using force, he realized the efficacy of negotiating across interest groups to strike a balance that would further elite interests without gratuitous violence. He also inserted himself more firmly into elite circles through marriage. His first wife, Delfina Ortega, had died in 1880; the following year he married Carmen Romero Rubio, the daughter of Manuel Romero Rubio, a Lerdista statesman and cabinet member. She was eighteen; Díaz had just celebrated his fifty-first birthday. When they traveled to the United States on their honeymoon as Mexico's representatives to the New Orleans World's Fair, newspapermen often mistook her for his daughter. The well-bred, sensitive, and perfectly-prepared-to-be-a-first-lady Señora Díaz began to educate her husband in the social graces, and within a couple of years Díaz was much more the polished gentleman when he ran for the presidency in 1884. In September Díaz swept to victory. From this time forward he would not feel the need to step out of office after completing each term and would remain in the presidency continuously until 1911. The conditions that greeted him in 1884 were a far cry from those of 1876.

FOUNDATIONS OF MODERNIZATION

Returning with renewed vigor, Porfirio Díaz had a plan for consolidating his political position and stabilizing the country. Mexico entered a period of sustained economic growth the likes of which it had never before experienced. As Mexico entered the modern age, steam, water, and electric power began to replace animal and human muscle. A number of new hydraulic- and hydroelectric-generating stations were built as the modernization process tied itself to the new machines it supported. The telephone arrived amid amazement and wonder in the 1880s. The Department of Communications and Public Works supervised and coordinated the installation of the wireless telegraph and submarine cables. A hundred miles of electric tramway connected the heart of Mexico City to the suburbs.

A major breakthrough in health and sanitation occurred when Díaz hired the British firm of S. Pearson and Son, Ltd., to bring modern technology to the drainage problem of Mexico City. For 16 million pesos the English engineers and contractors, with the experience of the Blackwell Tunnel under the Thames and the East River Tunnel in New York behind them, successfully completed a thirty-mile canal and a six-mile tunnel that relieved the Mexican capital of the threat of constant flooding and resultant property damage and disease. At approximately the same time the face of the country transformed to bolster the nation's own self-respect and its image abroad. A public building spree changed the contours of boulevards, parks, and public buildings. Monuments and statues were dedicated to the world's leading statesmen, intellectuals, and military figures. A new penitentiary costing 2.5 million pesos opened in 1900 and a 3-million-peso post office in 1907. A new asylum for the insane, a new municipal palace, and a new Department of Foreign Relations were dedicated prior to the centennial celebrations of 1910. The white marble National Theater, however, missed the centennial target date, and the heavy structure began to sink into the spongy subsoil of Mexico City before it could be finished. Each time a new project was completed, the government staged an elaborate, formal dedication to which foreign diplomats, dignitaries, and businessmen received special presidential invitations. Their impressions of Mexico, relayed to colleagues back home, would help effect the change of image.

Mexico's own adaptation of positivism provided the philosophical underpinning of the regime. The *científicos*, as those who followed in the footsteps of Gabino Barreda came to be known, were not all orthodox Comteans. Some blended Comte with John Stuart Mill, and others added a large dose of Herbert Spencer. Many científicos harbored a profound disdain for the rural illiterate masses, whom they blamed for Mexico's failure to progress after independence. The idea that Mexico's future lay solely with criollo elites would only be reinforced as the processes of modernization widened the gulf between wealthy, forward-looking capitalists and poor laborers, believed to be mired in tradition and in need of firm control.

The president and his científico advisers realized first of all that they needed to undertake a series of structural reforms to place Mexico's economic house in order, and they were fortunate to find an economic genius in their midst. José Ives Limantour, soon renowned in European financial circles, was the son of a French émigré. A man of many talents, he was a scholar, an accomplished jurist, and a dedicated linguist. First as subsecretary and then secretary of the treasury, he applied the best positivist thought of the day to the reorganization of the country's finances which offered a fertile field for his talents. For Limantour, Mexico's future depended upon its economic regeneration. Gradually, during the 1880s and 1890s Secretary Limantour lowered or eliminated the duties on many imports and permitted special tariff exemptions for economically depressed areas of the country. He also negotiated a series of loans at favorable rates of interest.

As significant as any of the individual reforms was Limantour's decision to overhaul the nation's administrative machinery so that the reforms could be properly implemented. While it would be foolhardy to suggest that all graft and corruption were eliminated, Limantour did improve the situation markedly, at least at the lower echelons of government. The dividends were startling. In 1890 Mexico paid the last installment of the debt to the United States, growing out of the mixed claims settlement. Four years later Mexico not only had balanced its budget for the first time in history but actually showed revenues running slightly ahead of expenditures. This economic surplus allowed Díaz to reward his followers and

José Limantour (1854–1935). An advocate of positivism, Limantour, as secretary of the treasury, brought order and reason to Porfirian finances. Able and attentive to detail, he was the epitome of the Porfirian statesman who would reinvent Mexican society.

build political and social networks among Mexican elites who supported him. When he left office in 1911 the treasury had about 70 million pesos in cash reserves. Beyond all expectations, he had succeeded in reassuring the outside world that Mexico had not only turned the corner but also deserved international dignity and respect.

The image abroad did change. As Limantour applied his skills to the reorganization of the treasury and the country met its foreign obligations on a regular basis, Mexico opened diplomatic relations with all of Europe and signed new treaties of friendship, commerce, and navigation with Great Britain, France, Norway, Ecuador, and Japan. For the first time Mexico began to participate actively in international conferences. Limantour's friend and proponent of Mexican liberalism, Emilio Rabasa, served as a diplomat and enjoyed a distinguished career as a politician and constitutional lawyer. Foreign heads of state lavished their praise on the Díaz regime, by the late 1880s and early 1890s, bestowing medals and decorations on the president.

THE RAILROAD BOOM

Díaz was fully prepared to take advantage of the good economic indicators and the new reputation he had so assiduously cultivated. His government embarked upon a multifaceted program to modernize the transportation and mining sectors of the economy. To accomplish this he turned to foreign investment and technology in the 1880s. The Mexican Central Railroad Company, backed by a group of Boston investors, received the concession

Porfirio Díaz (1830–1915). As soldier, rebel, statesman, and president, Díaz compelled respect and dominated his country as no previous figure in the nineteenth century.

to construct the major line north from Mexico City to El Paso, Texas. Work began from both terminal points, and the 1,224-mile project was completed in an amazingly short four-year period. The Central was soon flanked by two other new lines to its east and west. In 1888 the Mexican National Railroad Company, originally chartered under the laws of Colorado but subsequently purchased by a group of French and English entrepreneurs, successfully completed a new narrow-gauge line between Mexico City and Laredo, Texas, a distance of eight hundred miles and the shortest route from the Mexican capital to the US border. Shortly after the turn of the century it was converted to standard gauge. Finally the Sonora Railroad Company, headed by Thomas Nickerson, built the line between Guaymas, on the Pacific Ocean, and Nogales, Arizona. By 1890 the total trackage of these three major companies approached two thousand miles.

Efforts to connect the country from east to west did not proceed so smoothly. After earlier attempts to build a line across the Isthmus of Tehuantepec languished, in 1894 Chandos S. Stanhope completed a line, but the construction work and terminal facilities were grossly inadequate. Díaz then turned o S. Pearson and Son, Ltd., the famous British concern. Sir Weetman Dickinson Pearson drove an especially hard bargain, and the completed line proved to be one of the most costly in Mexican history. In 1907 trains ran regularly between Puerto México on the Gulf coast and Salina Cruz on the Pacific. With the Panama Canal already under construction, the Tehuantepec Railroad would soon be rendered obsolete.

Numerous lesser lines were undertaken in the 1880s and 1890s. A line in the south connected Mexico City with Guatemala, and short feeder lines linked most of the state capitals with the major trunks running between Mexico City and the US border. By the end of the

The arrival of the daily train triggered a burst of activity in hundreds of Mexican towns. This scene was captured by American photographer Sumner W. Matteson in the station of Amecameca in 1907.

Díaz regime railroads interlaced the entire country; from about four hundred miles of track in 1876, Mexico in 1911 could boast fifteen thousand. Approximately 80 percent of the capital outlay came from the United States. In 1908, however, under the constant prodding of Limantour, the Díaz government purchased the controlling interest in the major lines.

These achievements did not come easily. Mexico's lack of requisite managerial skills and an overall developmental culture meant that years passed before the railroads were smooth-running operations; but ultimately they would contribute to the tremendous economic transformation of the country. As the cities were linked to the outlying areas, raw materials could be shipped to industries and finished goods distributed to a greatly expanded domestic market. As products could be quickly transported to population centers and the leading ports, new agricultural lands, specializing in commercial agriculture, were opened, and land values increased as campesinos were dispossessed of their lands.[1] Mexico's textile industry, for example, relied primarily upon imported cotton at the beginning of the Díaz period; but with the opening of new lands in the north, near the railroad lines, cotton production by 1910 not only doubled but made the country almost self-sufficient. When the railroad arrived in Morelos the sugar planters began importing new machinery and setting up new mills to expand production. The larger market for locally produced products drove the costs down and, at least theoretically, widened the base of consumer use. Communities isolated by geography and centuries of tradition gradually came into greater contact with one another.

Nothing symbolized the Porfirian modernization program more graphically than the railroads. The discourse of development as expressed by writers, artists, and politicians found its center in the railroads, emblematic of material progress and technological advances. They also engendered notions of modern citizenry and national identity. At the same time, this powerful engine of modernity invited criticism of the costs and dislocations it wrought on laborers and campesinos.

THE REVIVAL OF MINING

The railroads offered a means to many ends, not least among them the revival of Mexico's potentially wealthy mining industry. The railroads, of course, provided the only practical and economical means of transporting massive shipments of ore. Equally important, the Díaz-controlled legislature passed a new mining code in 1884. In order to appeal to the foreign investor the code made no mention of traditional Hispanic jurisprudence reserving ownership of the subsoil for the nation. Further, the proprietor of the surface was explicitly granted ownership of all bituminous and other mineral fuels. Several years after enactment of the mining code, the government revised mining tax laws, exempting certain minerals altogether and lowering the tax rates on others. US and European investors recognized the potential for great profits and entered Mexico in increasing numbers in the 1880s and 1890s.

---

1 One perceptive analysis of some fifty-five agrarian protests during the early Porfiriato indicates that over more than 90 percent occurred at a distance of less than forty kilometers from a new or projected railroad line. See John Coatsworth, "Railroads, Landholding, and Agrarian Protest in the Early Porfiriato," *Hispanic American Historical Review* 54/1 (1974): 55–57

The new miners introduced modern machinery and new processes of extracting the metal from the ore, producing a radical transformation of the entire industry.

Between 1880 and 1890 foreigners initiated three large mining developments in Mexico: Sierra Mojada in Coahuila; Batopilas in Chihuahua; and El Boleo in Santa Rosalía, Baja California. Within a few years the Sierra Mojada region yielded a thousand tons of silver and lead per week, and Batopilas had made a fortune for its owners. El Boleo, under French and German ownership, proved to be one of the richest copper mining areas in North America.

The introduction of the cyanide process, which made it profitable to extract metal from ores containing only a few ounces of metal to the ton, revolutionized the mining of gold and silver. Largely because of new explorations and the adoption of modern mining techniques, the value of gold production rose from about 1.5 million pesos in 1877 to over 40 million pesos in 1908. Silver production followed a similar pattern, rising from 24.8 million pesos in 1877 to over 85 million pesos in 1908.

Some of the foreign investment came in the form of huge conglomerates. The Guggenheim interests, for example, spread out over much of Mexico and entered numerous interrelated mining activities. They owned the American Smelting and Refining Company, based in Monterrey but with large plants in Chihuahua, Durango, and San Luis Potosí. Daniel Guggenheim and his six brothers owned or controlled the Aguascalientes Metal Company, the

Colonel William Greene's town of Cananea, Sonora, was the hub of Mexico's copper production and a symbol of the foreign domination of the country's natural resources.

Guggenheim Exploration Company, and the Mexican Exploration Company. In addition, the Guggenheims acquired many already proven mines, such as the Tecolote silver mines and the Esperanza gold mine, as well as new mines in Durango, Chihuahua, Coahuila, and Zacatecas. By 1902 Guggenheim investments in northern Mexico totaled some $12 million.

Other foreign investors came to Mexico with practically nothing and built multimillion-dollar businesses. Perhaps the best example is Colonel William Greene, the copper king of Sonora. In 1898 Greene obtained an option on a Sonoran copper mine for forty-seven thousand pesos from the widow of Ignacio Pesqueira, a former governor of the state. Greene sold stocks for his mining venture on Wall Street, and within a few years his Cananea Consolidated Copper Company became one of the largest copper companies in the world, operating eight large smelting furnaces and employing thirty-five hundred men. With some of the profits Greene became a lumber factor and a rancher; one of his ranches grazed some 40,000 head of cattle. The employment opportunities offered by mining and agricultural enterprises located near the Mexico-US border gave rise to the increased mobility of laborers as they crossed back and forth.

OIL FIELDS AND OTHER INDUSTRIAL ENTERPRISES

American and British investors engaged in a spirited competition for the exploitation of Mexico's oil. The first wells were sunk in areas where surface seepages clearly indicated the presence of petroleum reserves, but after the turn of the century systematic geological exploration began in earnest. The American interests were led by Edward L. Doheny, an American who had successfully developed oil fields in California; he now purchased over six hundred thousand acres of potentially rich oil lands around Tampico and Tuxpan. Within a short time his Mexican Petroleum Company brought forth Mexico's first commercially feasible gusher, El Ebano.

The British answer to Doheny was Sir Weetman Dickinson Pearson, who had worked on the drainage of Mexico City, the modernization of the Veracruz harbor, the reconstruction of the Tehuantepec Railroad, and the building of the terminal facilities at Puerto México and Salina Cruz. Enjoying cordial relations with Díaz, Pearson eventually obtained drilling concessions in Veracruz, San Luis Potosí, Tamaulipas, and Tabasco. Progress came slowly at first to Pearson's El Aguila Company, but a dramatic hit brought forth the Potrero del Llano, number 4, a gusher that, when successfully capped, produced more than 100 million barrels in eight years. Doheny's Mexican Petroleum Company and Pearson's El Aguila Company, whose board of directors included Porfirio Díaz, Jr., dominated the petroleum industry in the early twentieth century and within a few years made Mexico one of the largest petroleum producers in the world.

It would be an exaggeration to suggest that Mexico experienced a profound industrial revolution during the Díaz years, but the industrial process did make itself felt. In 1902 the industrial census listed fifty-five hundred manufacturing industries. The volume of manufactured goods doubled during the Porfiriato. The process began in Monterrey, Nuevo León, where, in addition to the huge Guggenheim interests, other American, French, German, and British investors backed industrial enterprises. Attracted by excellent transportation facilities and by the progressive policies of Governor Bernardo Reyes, which included tax exemptions for industries, foreign and domestic capital funneled into Mexico's first important steel firm, the Compañía Fundidora de Fierro y Acero de Monterrey. Within a few years the company produced pig iron, steel rails, beams, and bars; and by 1911 it put out over sixty thousand tons of steel annually. Monterrey was soon dubbed the Pittsburgh of Mexico.

In 1890 José Schneider, a Mexican of German extraction, founded the Cervecería Cuauhtémoc which quickly became the largest and most important brewery in the country. Among its products was Carta Blanca, the number-one selling beer in Mexico. By 1900 it produced bottles for its products, other kinds of glassware, bottle caps, and packing cartons for both local use and national consumption.

Other industrial concerns based in Monterrey constructed new cement, textile, cigarette, cigar, soap, brick, and furniture factories, as well as flour mills and a large bottled-water plant. Capital investment in the city grew steadily throughout the Díaz regime but most dramatically during the first decade of the new century, when it rose from under 30 million to over 55 million pesos. Smaller fledgling textile and paper mills, cement factories, leather works, and soap, shoe, explosives, and tile manufacturers located themselves in other areas of the country; but by 1910 Monterrey was without question the industrial capital of Mexico.

The improvement of harbor and dock facilities during the Porfiriato opened Mexico up to world commerce on a grander scale than ever before. Millions of pesos spent on Veracruz transformed it markedly, although Tampico, located at the mouth of the Panuco River, rivaled its status as chief port. After US engineers supervised the dredging of the harbor and the modernizing of dock facilities, this northern city grew rapidly as a business and commercial center and challenged Veracruz in volume handled. Similar improvements were made in the harbors of Mazatlán, Manzanillo, Puerto México, and Salina Cruz. By the turn of the century the number of serviceable ports had increased to ten on the Gulf coast and fourteen on the Pacific side. Partially because of the improvements in port facilities and partially because of Limantour's reforms in the tariff structure, Mexico's foreign trade (exports and imports) increased from about 50 million pesos in 1876 to nearly 488 million pesos in 1910.

Although many of the trappings of traditional society still persisted, the Mexico of the first decade of the twentieth century was a far cry from that of 1876. Improved public services and modern transportation and communication facilities crisscrossed the country, opening it to new ideas and influences. The economy boomed, and dynamism permeated the atmosphere. Technology in general and mechanization in particular made tremendous strides. Foreign travelers for the first time marveled more than they criticized, for peace and growth allowed them the luxury of contemplating the many natural beauties Mexico had to offer. Mexico's foreign credit rating became firmly established throughout the world. But perhaps the most important product of the modernization process was that Mexicans, especially urban Mexicans, began to view themselves differently. A new consumer culture started to alter urban lifestyles. Self-confidence replaced the stigma occasioned by the decades of internecine strife. For a third of a decade Mexicans saw no major civil wars, no major liberal-conservative struggles, and no major church-state controversies. Mexico was assuming its rightful position in the twentieth-century world. Few yet questioned the costs the transformation had exacted because the material dividends seemed so self-evident. But the price paid was great, and the rapid modernization contained seeds of self-destruction.

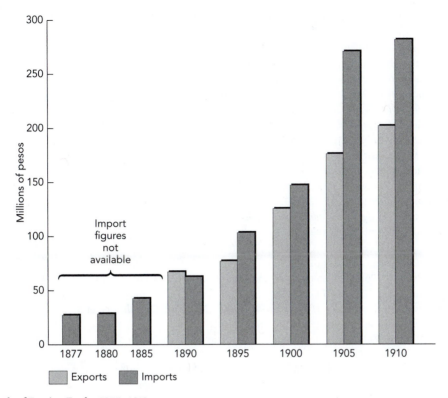

Growth of Foreign Trade, 1877–1910

Source: Estadisticas Económicas del Porfiriato: Comercio Exterior de México, 1877–1911 (Mexico, 1960).

RECOMMENDED FOR FURTHER STUDY

Beatty, Edward. *Institutions and Investment: The Political Basis of Industrialization in Mexico before 1911*. Stanford, CA: Stanford University Press, 2001.

Beezley, William H., and Colin MacLachlan. *Mexico's Crucial Century, 1810–1910*. Lincoln: University of Nebraska Press, 2010.

Benjamin, Thomas, and William McNellie, eds. *Other Mexicos: Essays on Regional Mexican History, 1876–1911*. Albuquerque: University of New Mexico Press, 1984.

Bernstein, Marvin D. *The Mexican Mining Industry, 1890–1950: A Study of the Interaction of Politics, Economics, and Technology*. Albany: State University of New York Press, 1964.

Boortz, Jeffrey L., and Stephen Haber, eds. *The Mexican Economy, 1870–1930: Essays in the Economic History of Institutions, Revolution, and Growth*. Stanford, CA: Stanford University Press, 2002.

Buchenau, Jürgen. *Tools of Progress: A German Merchant Family in Mexico City,1865-Present*. Albuquerque: University of New Mexico Press, 2004.

Buffington, Robert M., and William E. French. "The Culture of Modernity." In *The Oxford History of Mexico*, edited by Michael C. Meyer and William H. Beezley, 373–405. New York: Oxford University Press, rev. 2010.

Coatsworth, John. "Railroads, Landholding, and Agrarian Protest in the Early Porfiriato." *Hispanic American Historical Review* 54/1 (1974): 48–71.

Coerver, Donald. *The Porfirian Interregnum: The Presidency of Manuel González of Mexico, 1880–1884*. Fort Worth: Texas Christian University Press, 1979.

Ficker, Sandra Kuntz. "Economic Backwardness and Firm Strategy: An American Railroad Corporation in Nineteenth-Century Mexico." *Hispanic American Historical Review* 80/2 (2000): 267–98.

Frazer, Chris. *Bandit Nation: A History of Outlaws and Cultural Struggle in Mexico, 1810–1920*. Lincoln: University of Nebraska Press, 2006.

Garner, Paul. *British Lions and Mexican Eagles: Business, Politics, and Empire in the Career of Weetman Pearson in Mexico, 1889–1919*. Stanford, CA: Stanford University Press, 2011.

_____. *Porfirio Díaz: Profiles in Power*. Harlow, UK: Longman, 2001.

Hale, Charles A. *Emilio Rabasa and the Survival of Porfirian Liberalism: The Man, His Career, and His Ideas, 1856–1930*. Stanford, CA: Stanford University Press, 2008.

Hart, John Mason. *Empire and Revolution: The Americans in Mexico since the Civil War*. Berkeley: University of California Press, 2002.

Hibeno, Barbara. "Cervecería Cuauhtémoc: A Case Study of Technological and Industrial Development." *Mexican Studies* 8/1 (1992): 123–43.

Kroeber, Clifton, B. *Man, Land and Water: Mexico's Farmland Irrigation Policies, 1885–1911*. Berkeley: University of California Press, 1984.

Matthews, Michael. *The Civilizing Machine; A Cultural History of Mexican Railroads, 1876–1910*. Lincoln: University of Nebraska Press, 2014.

Meyers, William K. "Politics, Vested Rights, and Economic Growth in Porfirian Mexico." *Hispanic American Historical Review* 57/3 (1977): 425–54.

Mora-Torres, Juan. *The Making of the Mexican Border: The State, Capitalism, and Society in Nuevo León, 1848–1911*. Austin: University of Texas Press, 2001.

Pletcher, David M. *Rails, Mines, and Progress: Seven American Promoters in Mexico, 1867–1911*. Ithaca, NY: Cornell University Press, 1958.

Razo, Armando. *Social Foundations of Limited Dictatorship: Networks and Private Protection during Mexico's Early Industrialization*. Stanford, CA: Stanford University Press, 2008.

Schell, Jr., William. *Integral Outsiders: The American Colony in Mexico City, 1876–1911*. Wilmington, DE: Scholarly Resources, 2001.

Tinker Salas, Miguel. "Sonora: The Making of a Border Society, 1880–1910." *Journal of the Southwest* 34/4 (1992): 429–56.

Tischendorf, Alfred. *Great Britain and Mexico in the Era of Porfirio Díaz*. Durham, NC: Duke University Press, 1961.

Topik, Steven C. "The Emergence of Finance Capital in Mexico." In *Five Centuries of Mexican History*, Vol. II, edited by Virginia Guedea and Jaime E. Rodríguez, 227–42. Mexico City, Mexico and Irvine: Instituto Mora and University of California Irvine, 1992.

Trillo, Mauricio Tenorio. "1910 Mexico City: Space and Nation in the City of the Centenario." *Journal of Latin American Studies* 28/1 (1996): 75–105.

Wasserman, Mark. *Capitalists, Caciques and Revolution: The Native Elite and Foreign Enterprises in Chihuahua Mexico, 1854–1911*. Chapel Hill: University of North Carolina Press, 1984.

_____. *Pesos and Politics: Business Elites, Foreigners, and Government in Mexico, 1854–1940*. Stanford, CA: Stanford University Press, 2015.

Weiner, Richard. *Race, Nation, and Market: Economic Changes in Porfirian Mexico*. Tucson: University of Arizona Press, 2004.

Wells, Allen. *Yucatan's Gilded Age: Haciendas, Henequen and International Harvester*. Albuquerque: University of New Mexico Press, 1985.

CHAPTER 24

THE COSTS OF MODERNIZATION

DICTATORSHIP BY FORCE

Modernization came to Mexico during the Díaz regime not simply as the result of positivist theory and careful economic planning. The peace that made it all possible was in part attributable to brute force, but also to Díaz's ability to create networks of political and social power that discouraged opposition. Díaz maintained himself in power from 1876 to 1911 by a combination of adroit political maneuvering, intimidation, and, whenever necessary, callous use of the federal army and the rurales. He was the consummate bully.

Throughout the thirty-four years the dictator maintained the sham of democracy. The government held elections periodically at the local, state, and national levels; but they were invariably manipulated in favor of those candidates from local family oligarchies who held official favor. The press throughout the epoch was tightly censored; journalists who dared to oppose the regime on any substantive matter found themselves in jail or exile, while recalcitrant editors found their newspapers closed down. Filomeno Mata, the editor of the *Diario del Hogar*, suffered imprisonment over thirty times for his anti-reelectionist campaigns. While a few persistent critics were killed, the large majority of journalists opted to self-censor their criticisms.

The dictator played political opponents against one another or bought them off. He regularly shifted potentially ambitious generals or regimental commanders from one military zone to another to assure that they would be unable to cultivate a power base. State governors were invited to assume the same position in other states or to become congressmen, cabinet secretaries, or diplomats to remove their influence at home. Not even members of the Díaz family were immune. When the dictator's nephew, Félix Díaz, decided to run for the governorship of Oaxaca against Don Porfirio's wishes, he shortly found himself on a ship bound for Chile, where he took up a diplomatic post. Most influential Mexicans cooperated with the regime in order to receive political favors and lucrative economic concessions. Díaz himself never accumulated a personal fortune, but many of his civilian and military supporters in high positions had ample opportunity for graft. The científico advisers, for example, always seemed to know in advance the route of a new boulevard or railroad line; the property could thus be bought up at a low price and sold back to the government for a profit.

When Díaz needed to use force it was provided by the army and the rurales. He recognized the need for professionalizing the army and, although he did not invite foreign military missions into the country, he did send military observers to West Point and to the French officer's school at St. Cyr. The recently reorganized Colegio Militar de Chapultepec provided formal instruction for the officer corps and made use of the most current European training manuals. By the turn of the century about half of the active officers (but few of the generals) were graduates of the Chapultepec academy. The cadets, resplendent in snappy uniforms, were highlighted at the frequent military parades during which Díaz took the opportunity to display the latest armament obtained from France or Germany. Such spectacles masked Díaz's failure to provide education for the rank-and-file and imbue them with moral virtue and patriotic zeal. Usually conscripted by force, their behavior frequently mimicked that of the bandits or criminals they were supposed to suppress. Agents of order were crucial to the modernizing project, but they enjoyed little of its benefits and a reputation of ill repute.

The rurales, Díaz's praetorian guard, also constituted an important enforcement tool for the *Pax Porfiriana*. The dictator strengthened the corps considerably, not simply to curtail brigandage in the rural areas but to serve as a counterpoise to the army itself. By the end of the regime the strength of the rurales had been increased to over twenty-seven hundred men. While the force was not large, the dictator used it to good advantage. In addition to its

To reinforce the desired image, the rurales were always featured during military parades. Sumner Matteson photographed this salute to President Díaz on May 5, 1907.

original patrolling functions, Díaz had rural corpsmen guard ore shipments from the mines, support local police forces, escort prisoners, enforce unpopular court decisions, and guard public payrolls and buildings. Research has shown that the rurales were neither as harsh nor as efficient as conventionally thought, but Díaz used their exaggerated reputation for cruelty and excess. The myth served his purposes well, for the rurales were feared by brigands, marauders, political opponents, and recalcitrant villagers. When trouble flared it was often more prudent to send in the nearest corps than to allow a distinguished federal general the chance to enhance his reputation.

Díaz used the military not only to force compliance with the dictates of Mexico City but to administer the country as well. By the mid-1880s it was not unusual for military officers, most often generals of unquestionable loyalty, to dominate the state governorships and to be well represented among the three hundred *jefes políticos* (local political bosses). In 1900, although relative peace had already been achieved, Díaz was still spending almost one-fourth of the total budget on the military establishment. He believed it was worth it because the modernization process was so intertwined with his concept of enforced peace.

Díaz's científico advisers have been labeled racist for their conscientious denigration of the Indian population. But the generalization has certain flaws, for it presupposes a monolithic philosophical framework within the científico community. José Limantour was less a follower of Comte than of Darwin. He adapted notions of natural selection and survival of the fittest to Mexican reality as he understood it and emerged from his introspection calling for an aristocratic elite to reorder society. He expected little or no help from the Indian population. Francisco Bulnes, a prolific historian and apologist for científico rule,

The federal artillery corps, well trained and well equipped, was the pride of the Díaz army.

was more openly racist. Five million (white) Argentines, he argued, were worth more than 14 million Mexicans. He characterized the Mexican Indian as sullenly intractable and hopelessly inferior, not because of innate corruption of his genes but because his grossly deficient diet sapped his mental, moral, and physical vitality. Less biologically oriented was Justo Sierra, the most famous científico of all. Cofounder of the conservative newspaper *La Libertad*, author of *Evolución política del pueblo mexicano*, secretary of education during part of the Porfiriato, and first rector of the national university, Sierra argued forcefully that social and cultural forces, not biological ones, had shaped the Indian's inferior position. And unlike Limantour and Bulnes, Sierra asserted the Indian's educability. But the schools built during the Porfiriato, even when the Department of Education was in Justo Sierra's hands, existed primarily in the cities, not in the rural areas where they might serve the Indian and mestizo population. At the end of the Porfiriato Mexico still had 2 million Indians speaking no Spanish. They had been left aside.

THE HACENDADOS

Mexico greeted the twentieth century still a predominantly rural country, and the rural peasantry bore most of the costs of modernization. The payment was exacted in fear of the rurales, intimidation by local hacendados, constant badgering by jefes políticos and municipal officials, exploitation by foreign entrepreneurs, and, most important, seizure of private and communal lands by government-supported land sharks.

Haciendas dotted the rural areas along with indigenous and mixed villages. The number of large landholdings, more predominant in the north where livestock raising suited the environment, had increased in the nineteenth century. Railroad construction began to push land values up, but exaggerated land concentration proliferated after the enactment a new land law in 1883. This law, designed to encourage foreign colonization of rural Mexico, authorized land companies to survey public lands for the purpose of subdivision and settlement. For their efforts the companies received up to one-third of the land surveyed and the privilege of purchasing the remaining two-thirds at bargain prices. If the private owners or traditional ejidos could not prove ownership through legal title, their land was considered public and subject to denunciation by the companies.

The process that ensued was predictable. Few rural Mexicans in the north could prove legal title. All they knew for sure was that they had lived and worked the same plot for their entire lives, and their parents and grandparents had done the same. Their boundary line ran from a certain tree to a certain stream to the crest of a hill. The central and southern Indians and campesinos who could produce documents, some dating back to the colonial period, were convinced by the speculators and their lawyers that the papers had not been properly signed, notarized, stamped, or registered. Not even those communal ejidos that could produce titles of indisputable legality were immune. The Constitution of 1857 with its reform laws was once again applied to the detriment of the ejidos, and with greater vigor than ever before.

Within five years after the land law became operative, land companies had obtained possession of over 68 million acres of rural land and by 1894 one-fifth of the total land mass of Mexico. Not yet completely satisfied, the companies received a favorable modification of the law in 1894, and by the early twentieth century most of the villages in rural Mexico had lost their ejidos and some 134 million acres of the best land had passed into the hands of a few hundred fantastically wealthy families. Over one-half of all rural Mexicans lived and worked on the haciendas by 1910.

The Mexican census of 1910 listed 8,245 haciendas in the republic, but a few landlords, often tied together by a marriage network of family elites, individually owned ten, fifteen, or even twenty of them. Though varied in size, haciendas of forty to fifty thousand acres were not at all uncommon. Fifteen of the richest Mexican hacendados owned haciendas totaling more than three hundred thousand acres each. The state of Chihuahua affords a classic example of how the hacienda system operated and brought wealth and prestige to one extended family. Throughout the Díaz regime the fortunes of that north central Mexican state were guided by the Terrazas-Creel clan. Don Luis Terrazas, the founder of the dynasty, had served as governor prior to the French intervention and fought with Juárez against the French in the 1860s. His land acquisitions began shortly thereafter, when he obtained the estate of Don Pablo Martínez del Río, a French sympathizer. In the 1870s, 1880s, and 1890s, in and out of the gubernatorial chair, he acquired additional haciendas, profiting immensely from the land laws of the Díaz government. By the early twentieth century Terrazas owned some fifty haciendas and smaller ranches totaling a fantastic 7 million acres. Don Luis was the largest hacendado in Mexico and perhaps in all of Latin America; his holdings were eight times the size of the legendary King Ranch in Texas. He owned five hundred thousand head of cattle, two hundred twenty-five thousand sheep, twenty-five thousand horses, five thousand mules, and some of the best fighting bulls in the western hemisphere. Encinillas, northwest of Chihuahua City, was the largest of his haciendas, extending to some 1,300,000 acres and employing some two thousand campesinos. San Miguel de Babícora contained over eight hundred fifty thousand acres, while San Luis and Hormigas were over seven hundred thousand acres each.

The wealth and power of the Terrazas family cannot be judged in terms of landholding and its related activities alone. Don Luis also owned textile mills, granaries, railroads, telephone companies, candle factories, sugar mills, meatpacking plants, and several Chihuahua mines. Each of his twelve children married well. Daughter Angela Terrazas married her first cousin, Enrique Creel, the son of an American consul in Chihuahua and a man of wealth, erudition, and prestige. Enrique Creel served several times in the state governorship and was Mexico's secretary of foreign relations in 1910–11. Creel's own haciendas totaled more than 1,700,000 acres. One of the founders and directors of the Banco Minero de Chihuahua, he was a partner, furthermore, in many of his father-in-law's enterprises and directed or owned iron and steel mills, breweries, granaries, and a coal company. Two of Luis Terrazas's sons Alberto and Juan each had haciendas totaling over six hundred thousand acres, while his son-in-law Federico Sisniega held some two hundred sixty thousand acres and was a director of the Banco Nacional de Chihuahua.

It is virtually impossible to calculate the extent of either the fortune or the power wielded by the Terrazas-Creel clan. Luis Terrazas himself probably did not know how much he owned. He surely did know, however, that the value of rural land in Chihuahua rose from about $.30 per acre in 1879 to about $9.88 per acre in 1908. Had he been able to liquidate only his personal, nonurban landholdings on the eve of the Mexican revolution, he would have carried over $69 million to the bank.

One can be certain that little of major importance occurred in Chihuahua without the approval of patriarch Don Luis Terrazas. During the Díaz regime members of the extended family sat for a total of sixty-six terms in the state legislature and twenty-two terms in the national congress. Because residency requirements were loosely defined, Enrique Creel and Juan Terrazas became national senators from other Mexican states. Municipal and regional officialdom bore either the Terrazas-Creel names or their stamp of approval.

A handful of powerful sugar families dominating the state of Morelos—the García Pimentels, the Amors, the Torre y Miers, and a few others—had to increase production by expanding into new lands to be able to fund the purchase of expensive new machinery. As no public lands were available, they completely encircled small ranches and even villages, thereby choking off infusions of economic lifeblood. Some towns stagnated, while others vanished from the map altogether. The town fathers of Cuautla could not even find sufficient land for a new cemetery and were reduced to burying children in a neighboring village.

The circumstances through which land was privatized throughout Mexico were complex and varied. Although outsiders appropriated much communal land, not all communities shared land in an egalitarian fashion, and internal conflicts frequently played into the hands of hacendados and merchants. For example, in the vanilla-producing lands of Papantla in Veracruz, wealthier Totonac Indians benefited from state privatization schemes to the detriment of other, less affluent members of their communities, who rebelled against them and were repressed. In other cases, Indian communities that developed ideologies of popular liberalism or conservatism to successfully defend their autonomy and lands earlier in the nineteenth century, found their claims increasingly denied. In the Huasteca area of San Luis Potosí, campesinos found allies in the clergy and developed strategies that mixed anarchist and socialist ideas with traditional communal values, to oppose privatization. Their resistance led to the Huastecan Peasant War, 1879–84, which was eventually suppressed by the federal army.

THE CAMPESINOS

The millions of rural Mexicans who found themselves in dying villages or subsisting as campesinos on the nation's haciendas were worse off financially than their rural ancestors a century before. The average daily wage for an agricultural worker remained almost steady throughout the nineteenth century—about thirty-five centavos. But in the same one hundred-year period the price of corn and chile more than doubled, and beans cost six times more in 1910 than in 1800. In terms of purchasing power correlated with the price of corn or cheap cloth, the Mexican campesino during the Díaz regime was twelve times poorer than the US farm laborer.

Working conditions varied considerably from region to region and even from hacienda to hacienda, but they were generally poor. Campesinos often availed themselves of the talents of a scribe to spell out their gamut of complaints. While it was not uncommon for the campesino to be allotted a couple of furrows to plant a little corn and chile and on occasion to receive a small ration of food from the hacienda, he worked from sunrise to sunset, often seven days a week, raising crops or tending cattle. Sometimes he was allowed to cut firewood free; on other occasions he paid for the right. The scant wages he received most often were not paid in currency but in certificates or metal discs redeemable only at the local *tienda de raya*, an all-purpose company store located on the hacienda complex. Credit was extended liberally, but the prices, set by the hacendado or the mayordomo (overseer), were invariably several times higher than those in a nearby village. For the hacendado the situation was ideal. The taxes on his land were negligible; his labor was, in effect, free, for all the wages that went out came back to him through the tienda de raya with a handsome profit. The campesino found himself in a state of perpetual debt, and by law he was bound to remain on the hacienda so long as he owed a single centavo. Debts could be passed on to the children. Should an occasional obdurate campesino escape, except in situations of labor shortage, he had scarcely any place to go. Many states had laws making it illegal to hire an indebted campesino.

The bookkeeping procedures in the tienda de raya always seemed to work to the disadvantage of the illiterate campesino. Goods charged against his account were more expensive than they would have been had he been able to pay cash. And other items were often debited to his account. Charges for a marriage ceremony or a funeral often exceeded the monthly wage. Management added fines for real or imagined crimes on the hacienda, in addition to forced contributions for fiestas and interest on previous debts

Stories of corporal punishment of the campesino (petty theft could bring two hundred lashes) and sexual violation of the young women on the haciendas abound. Conditions on the henequen haciendas of Yucatán may have been the worst in the republic. While the rebellious Mayas of the Cross in the eastern Yucatán peninsula maintained a more autonomous but politically fragmented existence, the henequen hacendados worked their Maya campesinos like slaves. Many of the campesinos in Yucatán were deportees from other parts of Mexico (some were Yaqui Indians from Sonora who violently and continuously resisted the expropriation of their lands, and others were convicted criminals) forced to work in chains, while flogging was not uncommon. Little evidence exists to show that such horrific physical maltreatment was widespread throughout Mexico. However, campesino families were everywhere subject to the personal whims of the hacendado or the mayordomo, and hacienda records and correspondence to local, state, and even national officials reveal that complaints targeted intolerable working conditions, and dishonest record keeping in the tienda de raya.

The record of these complaints offers ample evidence that campesinos did not acquiesce to exploitative conditions without protest and that they were sometimes able to negotiate better terms. In the surrounding villages, Indians and campesinos employed a range of tactics to preserve varying levels of autonomy and slow the privatization of their lands. In some cases, they made deals with political and economic elites to produce crops for commercial market; in others, they used legal maneuvers and forms of petty resistance to evade compliance with official dictates. The early Díaz administration showed more inclination to negotiate these strategies, but by 1900 a more entrenched authoritarian regime had become less responsive to local cultures and, in fact, worked to reinvent community traditions to serve modernization. Yet these effects did not eradicate a developing campesino consciousness in many areas of Mexico.

The dichotomies of nineteenth-century Mexican life, especially those of wealth and poverty, stood out prominently on the hacienda. The main hacienda house was sumptuous, externally and internally. But the hacendado would seldom spend more than a few months a year there. Most often he had other haciendas and inevitably businesses to manage in the cities, and then he had to visit his children in their fine European or US boarding schools. The hacienda provided, in addition to its income, a summer vacation home, a change of pace, and social status. Extended families could be comfortably accommodated, and young boys, donned in charro costume and mounted on carefully bred and well-groomed horses, could fancy themselves country squires. Birthdays, saints' days, and feast days were reason enough to move the family from the state capital to the hacienda for an outing; on special occasions, like an eighteenth birthday or a wedding, entire train cars could be reserved to carry guests, musicians, local dignitaries, and domestics.

Life for the campesinos who worked for the hacendado presents a starkly different picture. Because mayordomos administered "justice" on the hacienda, the campesino had no genuine judicial rights or legal recourse. If a mayordomo overreacted in punishment of some real or imagined offense, he was accountable to nobody. Within a mile of the grand hacienda house, campesinos lived in miserable, one-room, floorless, windowless adobe shacks.

For a couple of centavos the rural, illiterate Mexicans could hire a scribe to scratch out a few lines to a relative or friend.

Water had to be carried in daily, often from long distances. Where they had been allotted individual plots, campesinos could only attend to them after sunset, when the important work of the day had been completed. Twice a day a few minutes would be set aside to consume some tortillas wrapped around beans and chile, washed down with a few gulps of black coffee or pulque. Protein in the form of meat, fish, or fowl, even on the cattle haciendas, was a luxury reserved for a few special occasions during the year. Infant mortality on many haciendas exceeded 25 percent.

Local fiestas on haciendas and in nearby villages provided diversions. An amateur bull-fight could be staged in the hacienda corral, and resident aficionados would try their hand with a half-grown fighting bull that somehow looked bigger as it got closer. Gatherings of friends might feature singing, dancing and especially corridos that narrated misfortunes, popularized bandits, or satirized elites. When accompanied by mezcal or pulque these entertainments could erupt in violence and injuries.

Porfirio Díaz had developed his country at the expense of his countrymen. The great material benefits of the age of modernization seldom filtered down to the people. Their lives were not in the least changed because the new National Theater was built in Mexico City or because José Limantour was able to borrow money in London or Paris at 4 percent. In fact, for the masses at the bottom the cost of modernization had been too great. Moreover, even many who had benefitted from economic expansion became increasingly frustrated by its exclusionary character.

In 1907, photographer Sumner Matteson was surprised to find burros, horses, mules, and people sharing quarters in this pulque hacienda, where the stench of animals was rivaled only by the stench of fermenting pulque.

RECOMMENDED FOR FURTHER STUDY

Anderson, Rodney D. *Outcasts in Their Own Land: Mexican Industrial Workers, 1906–1911*. DeKalb: Northern Illinois University Press, 1976.

Flandrau, Charles M. *Viva Mexico!* Urbana: University of Illinois Press, 1964.

Hart, Paul. *Bitter Harvest: The Social Transformation of Morelos, Mexico, and the Origins of the Zapatista Revolution 1840–1910*. Albuquerque: University of New Mexico Press, 2006.

Holden, Robert H. *Mexico and the Survey of Public Lands: The Management of Modernization, 1876–1911*. Dekalb: Northern Illinois University Press, 1994.

Hu-Dehart, Evelyn. *Yaqui Resistance and Survival: The Struggle for Land and Autonomy, 1821–1910*. Madison: University of Wisconsin Press, 1984.

Katz, Friedrich. "Labor Conditions on Haciendas in Porfirian Mexico: Some Trends and Tendencies." *Hispanic American Historical Review* 54/1 (1974): 1–47.

Kouri, Emilio. *A Pueblo Divided: Business, Property, and Community in Papantla, Mexico*. Stanford, CA: Stanford University Press, 2004.

Meyers, William K. *Forge of Progress, Crucible of Revolt: The Origins of the Mexican Revolution in La Comarca Lagunera, 1880–1911*. Albuquerque: University of New Mexico Press, 1994.

Neufeld, Stephen B. *The Blood Contingent and the Military in the Making of Modern Mexico, 1876–1911*. Albuquerque: University of New Mexico Press, 2017.

Newman, Elizabeth T. *Biography of a Hacienda: Work and Revolution in Rural Mexico*. Tucson: University of Arizona Press, 2014.

Raat, William D. "Ideas and Society in Don Porfirio's Mexico." *The Americas* 30/1 (1973): 32–53.

Ruiz, Ramón. *The People of Sonora and the Yankee Capitalists*. Tucson: University of Arizona Press, 1988.

Saka, Mark Saad. *For God and Revolution: Priest, Peasant, and Agrarian Socialism in the Mexican Huasteca*. Albuquerque: University of New Mexico Press, 2013.

Snodgrass, Michael. *Deference and Defiance in Monterrey: Workers, Paternalism, and Revolution in Mexico, 1890–1950*. New York: Cambridge University Press, 2003.

Vanderwood, Paul. *Disorder and Progress: Bandits, Police and Mexican Development*. Wilmington, DE: Scholarly Resources, rev. 1992.

_____. *The Power of God Against the Guns of Government: Religious Upheaval in Mexico at the Turn of the Nineteenth Century*. Stanford, CA: Stanford University Press, 1998.

Walker, David W. "Homegrown Revolution: The Hacienda Santa Catalina del Alamo y Anexas and Agrarian Protest in Eastern Durango, Mexico, 1897–1913." *Hispanic American Historical Review* 72/2 (1992): 239–73.

_____. "Porfirian Labor Politics: Working Class Organizations in Mexico City and Porfirio Díaz." *The Americas* 37/3 (1981): 257–90.

Washbrook, Sarah. *Producing Modernity in Mexico: Labour, Race, and the State in Chiapas, 1876–1914*. New York: Oxford University Press, 2012.

Wasserman, Mark. "The Social Origins of the 1910 Revolution in Chihuahua." *Latin American Research Review* 15/1 (1980): 15–38.

Wells, Allen. "Family Elites in a Boom-and-Bust Economy: The Molinas and Peóns of Porfirian Yucatán." *Hispanic American Historical Review* 62/2 (1982): 224–53.

Wells, Allen, and Gilbert M. Joseph. *Summer of Discontent, Seasons of Upheaval: Elite Politics and Rural Insurgency in Yucatán, 1876–1915*. Stanford, CA: Stanford University Press, 1997.

Womack, Jr., John. *Zapata and the Mexican Revolution*. New York: Alfred A. Knopf, 1968.

Young, Elliott. *Catarino Garza's Revolution on the Texas-Mexico Border*. Durham, NC: Duke University Press, 2004.

CHAPTER 25

SOCIETY AND CULTURE DURING THE PORFIRIATO

The changes in Mexican society and culture during the Porfiriato paralleled those in the political and economic realms. Most noteworthy perhaps was the fact that a middle class began to grow and view Mexico differently. For the first time Mexico had shown its potential and had begun to catch up with a rapidly changing world. The nation's achievements in technology and culture went on display around the globe at world fairs and expositions in Europe and the United States.

POPULATION

The stability of the Porfiriato resulted in Mexico's first period of prolonged population growth. In the absence of war and its social dislocations and with modest gains recorded in health and sanitation, the population grew from 8,743,000 in 1874 to 15,160,000 in 1910. From 1810 to 1874 the average annual population growth had been about 43,000, but during the Díaz era population increased at an average of 180,000 per year. Mexico City and the state capitals grew even more rapidly than the population at large, increasing some 88.5 percent during the epoch. From a population of 200,000 in 1874, Mexico City in 1910 was home to 471,066 Mexicans.

Railroad development, mining activities, and port improvements caused a number of tiny villages to burgeon into towns and cities. Torreón, at the intersection of the Mexican Central Railroad and the International Railroad (running from Eagle Pass, Texas, to Durango), jumped from fewer than 2,000 inhabitants in 1876 to over 43,000 in 1910; Sabinas, Coahuila, from 788 to 14,555; and Nuevo Laredo from 1,283 to almost 9,000. The two port terminuses of the Tehuantepec Railroad recorded similar gains. Puerto México had only 267 inhabitants in 1884 but reached 6,616 by 1910, while Salina Cruz grew from 738 in 1900 to almost 6,000 total some ten years later. Colonel Greene's copper town of Cananea hardly existed at the beginning of the Porfiriato. From a population of about 100 in 1876, it catapulted to almost 15,000 in 1910.

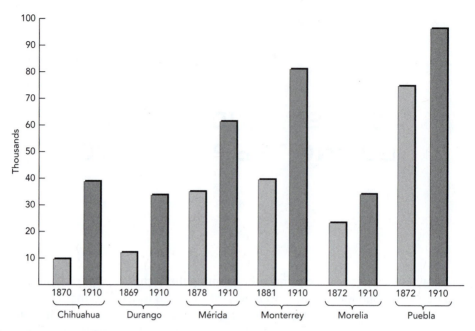

Population of Selected Mexican Cities during the Porfiriato

Source: Keith A. Davies, "Tendencias demográficas urbanas durante el siglo xix en México," *Historia Mexicana* 21 (1972): 481–524: John Barrett, *Mexico: A General Sketch* (Washington, D.C., 1911), 53.

URBAN IMPROVMENTS

The rapid growth of towns and cities throughout the republic was accompanied by an obvious dynamism in society. Travelers marveled at the amount of construction going on everywhere. In the Oaxacan capital (known as the Emerald City), officials and elites developed tourism, sports, and leisure activities; used urban planning and architecture to beautify and socially order the city; and implemented reforms in sanitation and social hygiene. The Catholic church supported Porfirian modernization and moral reform in Oaxaca City, illustrating how the Díaz regime's efforts to court the church had paid off. And in many areas the church revitalized its hold over indigenous peoples and women through new devotional associations and practices.

By 1910 all the state capitals had electricity and most had tramways. Weekly newspapers became dailies, potable water systems and sewage systems were extended, hospitals were constructed, and new hotels sprang up to cater to the increasing tourist trade. Even small, out-of-the-way towns improved their facilities. The transportation system in Mexico City was excellent, with first-, second-, and third-class streetcars and cabs carrying passengers throughout the city. Streetcars sometimes baffled the uninitiated. One caught the eye of an Irish visitor during the late Porfiriato.

> A curious feature of the streets is the electric tramway hearse. Frequently one sees a funeral consisting of a number of cars on the rails; first comes an open one like a long low truck with a black catafalque covering, under which reposes the coffin and the wreaths; the next

may be another piled up with wreaths and crosses, and then follows car after car with the mourners. This of course stops all the tramway traffic for the time being.[1]

Another sign of progress could be seen in the fire prevention program put in place in Mexico City during the last half of the nineteenth century. Engineers applied new technologies and experts trained fire-fighting brigades. Regulations enforced new zoning and construction laws as officials oversaw the removal of wooden sidewalks. A fire insurance program developed along with new medical treatments for burn victims.

A most dramatic change occurred in the field of law and order. Scarcely a traveler in the late nineteenth century failed to comment upon the relative absence of obvious crime and political upheaval. New criminal codes were enacted as lower-class behavior became increasingly associated with criminality. Municipal authorities endeavored to clean up the streets by removing street peddlers, beggars, prostitutes, and homeless people from the public eye. Reformers advocated the building of modem prisons, hospitals, orphanages, and trade schools.

The changing face of urban Mexico was accompanied by a not-too-subtle modification of the value structure. Porfirio Díaz recoiled at English and US suggestions that the time-honored tradition of the Mexican bullfight amounted to nothing more than a cruel and barbarous spectacle. It was the epitome of a clash of values. The phenomenon has been perfectly captured by historian William Beezley, who wrote that while most Mexicans saw "the ballet of cape and animal," foreigners "saw only blood and sand." Díaz ultimately placed a higher premium on international respect than on preserving this part of Mexico's Hispanic heritage and, although he later reversed himself, during his first administration prohibited bullfighting in the Federal District, Zacatecas, and Veracruz, areas where tourists would be most likely to witness the Sunday event. An American import soon offered itself as a substitute. Abner Doubleday's baseball made its Mexican debut in the 1880s and had caught on beyond anyone's expectations by the turn of the century. Not a few Mexican traditionalists lamented the exchange of the bat, the ball, and the baggy pants for the cape, the sword, and the suit of lights.[2]

GENDER AND CLASS

The Porfiriato also witnessed changes in the roles of women as a select few began to enter professions hitherto regarded as the sole preserve of men. The medical school in Mexico City graduated its first female doctor in 1887, and by the turn of the century others had followed. In the 1890s and early 1900s women began to make significant inroads into dentistry, law, pharmacy, higher education, and journalism. A new commercial school for women was inaugurated in 1903, and shortly thereafter its classes were filled. More women entered the ranks of factory workers. In this changing gender milieu, Porfirian authorities turned their attention to the need to control women's public conduct. In the eyes of reformers, female workers who interacted with others on the street were corrupting influences and not far from

1 Mary Barton, *Impressions of Mexico with Brush and Pen* (London, UK, 1911), 45–46.
2 These themes are developed in William H. Beezley, *Judas at the Jockey Club and Other Episodes of Porfirian Mexico* (Lincoln, NE, 1987), 13–25.

prostitutes in terms of morality. Female heads of households rejected these suspicions and asserted their rights to support their families, as well as their rights to possess honor.

Many rural migrants to Mexico City of course did not find industrial jobs, and women in particular often worked as live-in maids while their children ended up in orphanages where they could be adopted to provide personal services to the middle and upper classes. Although the higher social strata conceived of their own children as needing nurture and protection, they did not have the same view of family life for the poor.

Women also left the confines of home more frequently to participate in charitable activities. Interestingly, the liberal anticlerical laws of the Reforma had provided new opportunities for Catholic women who now joined church-sanctioned lay associations and became more active participants in public society. In one extraordinary instance, far from the nation's capital in the state of Oaxaca, a woman achieved high economic and political status. Juana Catarina Romero defied patriarchal norms as she progressed from her early origins as a poor mestiza cigarette vendor to become a powerful *cacica* (political leader) and economic entrepreneur in Tehuantepec. Juana Cata used her wits and her contacts, including Porfirio Díaz, to educate herself; develop economic pursuits in textiles, commercial agriculture, and sugar refining; and support philanthropic endeavors in education, cultural activities, and public health.

The burgeoning of consumer culture during the Porfiriato also drew women to Mexico City's central district to shop in the new department stores that appeared in the late nineteenth century: Puerto de Liverpool and Palacio de Hierro. These French-inspired retail stores took their

Life for the peon on the hacienda was bad; living in a city slum was even worse. But nowhere was it more difficult than in the mines.

place alongside the modern buildings that were changing the physical landscape of the capital. They made ample use of newspaper advertising and catalogs to attract shoppers, both female and male, from the emerging middle class, known as the *gente decente* (decent class). Their culture of consumption, rather than wealth, helped to define their identities as modern citizens.

French influence also manifested itself in the tobacco company El Buen Tono, founded by Ernesto Pugibet. The manufacture of cheap, machine-rolled cigarettes exploded as advertising appealed to Mexican men of different classes. One gimmick employed an elegantly dressed fellow, Electric Man; as he walked the streets his coat lit up with electric lights announcing a particular brand of cigarettes. Varying price levels targeted class distinctions among the broad base of consumers and modern marketing techniques contributed to the formation of collective identities based on the brand they chose. Pugibet also built model housing for his employees, a far cry from the wretched conditions of most urban workers.

For most Mexicans, improvements would have to wait. Old problems persisted. There was certainly more crime and alcoholism than foreign visitors saw in the tourist zones of the cities. The léperos and cargadores continued to attract their attention. Although most visitors were not aware of the working conditions in the factories throughout the republic, the plight of the urban laborer had changed little, but there were many more of them, including women. A few employers initiated modest reform early in the twentieth century. The Cervecería Cuauhtémoc in Monterrey, a Mexican-owned and Mexican-managed enterprise, was the first major industrial concern to adopt the nine-hour day. Few other Mexican industries, however, and practically none owned by foreigners, followed suit. Even at the end of the Porfiriato the workweek for the large majority of urban laborers was seven days and the workday eleven or even twelve hours. Pensions were almost unknown, as was compensation for accidents suffered on the job.

The diet of the lower classes—day laborers, rank-and-file soldiers, beggars, domestics, street vendors, and the unemployed—remained barely adequate. Corn, beans, chile, and pulque still constituted the staples; meat was almost totally absent. The grossly deficient diet and unsanitary living conditions made the masses susceptible to a wide array of debilitating diseases, and the large majority passed their entire lives without a single visit to a qualified doctor. Life expectancy remained constant—about thirty years. Infant mortality remained unacceptably high, averaging 30 percent for most of the Porfiriato. A Protestant missionary in Díaz's Mexico recalled his impressions.

> I used to ask, "How many of you, fathers and mothers, have children in heaven?" Usually all hands would promptly go up, while the replies came, *"Tengo cinco." "Tengo ocho."* . . . Deplorable ignorance as to proper sanitary conditions in the home and the care of children is responsible for a large proportion of this death harvest among the little ones. Children's diseases, as measles and scarlet fever, carry multitudes away.[3]

The lower-class barrios of Mexico City—La Merced, La Palma, and Nonoalco—had no indoor plumbing and only one public bathhouse per fifteen thousand people. Garbage collection was sporadic at best. Only the completion of Mexico City's drainage canal registered

---

3   Alden Buell Case, *Thirty Years with the Mexicans: In Peace and Revolution* (New York, NY, 1917), 61–62.

Modernization occurred at the expense of the poor, in both urban and rural settings.

a positive impact on the lower-class neighborhoods as the masses at least escaped the ravages of seasonal flooding.

Consumption of pulque and other alcoholic beverages among the lower classes did not increase during the Porfiriato, but the public and private outcry against alcohol did. Because officials unempirically linked alcoholism to robberies, sex crimes, child abandonment, and mendicancy, morality campaigns took form throughout the country. The Catholic press initiated a journalistic campaign, and state and local governments enacted legislation to curtail the use of alcoholic beverages. But limiting the hours of pulquerías and restricting new openings seemed to do little good, so laws tried to make these spaces as uncomfortable as possible—no windows, no chairs, no music, and, most important, no women. Sensational crime stories became best sellers for newspapers and served as morality tales to encourage proper behavior, but also to draw the line between "virtuous" elites and the "degenerate and deviant" poor, who were considered most likely to become serial killers, rapists, and thieves. In response a penny press emerged to satirize such negative portrayals of working-class men and their masculinity. Using vernacular street talk, the penny press expressed the demand for working-class citizenship and contributed to the formation of working-class consciousness.

José Guadalupe Posada (1852–1913), Mexico's most famous printmaker, parodies a fashionable lady during the Porfiriato.

At the same time, the middle class was expanding as the earning power of skilled artisans, government bureaucrats, scribes, clergymen, low-ranking army officers, and professional men had increased modestly. The booming economy made it possible for many a small businessman and neighborhood merchant to move his family from the drab room above the store or from his parents' residence into a larger and more comfortable apartment or house. The extension of water and sewage facilities provided many the luxury of indoor plumbing for the first time in their lives. The middle-class diet included meat and soup several times a week.

With middle-class status, creating the proper impression became important. It was not unusual for the monthly wage or monthly profit to be idled away on a single night of entertainment for friends. While the middle-class wife was beginning to break out of the home, she generally resigned herself to her husband's marital infidelity and prerogatives as head of the family. Laws still protected the moral order of families and a gender order that favored males. Studies of courtship and marriage promises across rural landscapes reveal a literate culture of passionate love-letter writing. Such letters turned up in judicial cases in which young women sought, often futilely, to hold letter writers faithful to their promises of marriage. One study examines how hearts, eyes, and souls constitute a kind of "sentimental anatomy" in these passionate letters.[4]

---

4   William E. French, *The Heart in a Glass Jar: Love Letters, Bodies, and the Law in Mexico*. (Lincoln, 2015).

Families taught middle-class children to make class distinctions based upon outward appearances. If a well-dressed person appeared at the door, they were expected to report to their parents *Allí está un señor*; but if the caller was dressed poorly, the proper announcement was *Allí está un hombre*.[5] Although only recently sprung from the lower class themselves, many members of the middle class assumed a moral superiority over the downtrodden.

While the poor lived in deteriorating conditions and a new, small middle class emerged in the cities, the rich became more convinced than ever that civilization itself rested upon the pillar of private property. The pinnacle of social acceptance during the Porfiriato was to be invited, for monthly dues of seven hundred pesos, to enjoy the amenities of the Jockey Club in Mexico City. Located in the Casa de Azulejos, the most opulent mansion in the capital, one could enjoy a sumptuous dinner there, spend an hour at the baccarat table, and hope to see cabinet ministers, governors, military zone commanders, or perhaps even Don Porfirio and Doña Carmen themselves.

One measure of aristocratic success was to see how French one could become in taste and manners. The advantages of a French education and a French governess for aristocratic children were beyond debate. Beautiful Spanish colonial furniture was stored away, and modern French furniture adorned the houses. When Mexican composer Gustavo E. Campa wrote an opera based on the life of Nezahualcoyótl, "the Poet King of Texcoco," he entitled it not *El Rey Poeta* but *Le Roi Pòete* and prepared the libretto in French. Membership in the Sociedad Filarmónica y Dramática Francesa assured one of brushing elbows with the most Frenchified members of Mexican society at a concert or a ball. The Paseo de la Reforma was redecorated to look like the Champs Elysées, while architectural design aped *fin-de-siècle* Paris. When Mexican millionaire Antonio Escandón donated a statue of Columbus to adorn the fashionable avenue, he commissioned the Parisian sculptor Charles Cordier to do the work. Having no notion of the revolution that would soon engulf Mexico, the aristocracy blissfully celebrated Bastille Day, July 14, with almost as much enthusiasm as their own independence day.

French cuisine reigned supreme in the capital. The best and most expensive restaurants were the Fonda de Recamier and the Maison Doreé. Between the Consommé Brunoise Royale and the Tournedos au Cèpes, one could sip imported French wine and listen to the orchestra play "Bon Aimée," "Amoureuse," "Rendezvous," or some other tune everyone knew to be *à la mode*. For the athletic there was also membership in the French Polo Club and for the more sedate a season ticket to the French comic opera. Those who had pretensions to both music and athletics adopted the cancan, a French import that took Mexico by storm in the 1880s.

CULTURAL AND INTELLECTUAL LIFE

Literary expression during the Porfiriato found nineteenth-century romanticism yielding first to realism and almost simultaneously to modernism. The realists of the period hoped that the enforced stability of the Porfiriato would encourage the development of the arts. Not a socially conscious group, the realists viewed the poor not as oppressed but rather as lazy and shiftless.

---

5   Jesús Silva Herzog, *Una vida en la vida de México* (Mexico City, 1972), 9.

José López Portillo y Rojas (1850–1923) typified the realist genre. Born to a prominent Guadalajara family, he studied law and traveled widely in Europe, imbibing the French spirit, before dedicating himself to literature. In his novel *Nieves* (1887) López Portillo recognized that an occasional hacendado might brutalize a campesino, but he found no fault with the system that conditioned the relationship or anything reprehensible in a society that tolerated it. His solution was a simplistic one. It was all a matter of volition. The poor of Mexico simply had no desire to improve themselves.

The modernist writers of the Porfiriato showed themselves to be stylistically innovative and concerned with refinements in the language. Projecting a new kind of imagery, the modernists favored a symbolic revolt not against Porfirian society but against nineteenth-century culture. The best and most versatile of the modernist fiction writers was Amado Nervo (1870–1919). At the turn of the century he moved to Paris—for Mexicans a cultural mecca—where he met the founder of the Latin American modernist movement, the Nicaraguan poet Rubén Darío. Before his literary career ended, Nervo had written more than 30 volumes—novels, poetry, short stories, plays, essays, and criticism. The theme of his first novel, *El bachiller* (1895), was sensational and even horrifying. A young priest, tempted by physical love, castrates himself to avoid seduction. In this and other works Nervo showed himself a perceptive amateur psychologist. His insight into the motivations of the protagonists he created and his appreciation of the conflicts between the material and the spiritual captivated his readers.

The Art Academy of San Carlos continued to dominate the artistic community, but it was poorly supported by the government. The future giants of Mexican art—Diego Rivera and José Clemente Orozco—studied at the academy and began perfecting the techniques that would win them world acclaim two decades hence. While teachers placed heavy emphasis upon copying European models, a few of the students began to break with tradition and experiment with Mexican themes.

Díaz and his científico advisers, in art as in so many other areas, continued to show preference for all things foreign. To celebrate the centennial of Mexico's independence, the government constructed a new building to house a Spanish art display and provided a subvention of 35,000 pesos for the show. When the Mexican artists at the academy protested that they wanted to put on a national art show to coincide with the celebrations, they received little assistance from the government. Those who saw their exhibition probably understood why the regime chose not to support it. It was youthful, exuberant, and iconoclastic in both technique and theme. Gerardo Murillo, who changed his name to Dr. Atl, a Náhuatl word meaning "water," had experimented with wax, resin, and oil to depict scandalous bacchanals, while other young artists developed Indianist themes. Many of Mexico's most promising artists exhibited there for the first time, departing from staid European models. Slums and brothels decorated canvases, and somber Indian faces depicted the stark reality of Mexican life. This was not the impression of the stable, conservative, white, progressive Mexico that Díaz wanted portrayed.

In either case, the images being projected from the national stage had little connection to how people were entertaining themselves at the local level at popular performances of religious and civic themes. These celebrations certainly embodied aspects of local and regional culture, but over the nineteenth century they acquired a more national character in their representations of patriotic figures as well as political and ethnic stereotypes. An important popular source for learning about the outside world (other regional cultures and the life of the big city) could be found in the itinerant puppet theater that enjoyed increasing popularity after independence. Puppeteers traveled throughout Mexico, introducing marionettes who used regional and rural twists to elucidate features of Mexican history, culture, and civic duty through humor and irony. One of the most popular was Vale Coyote, whose bag of tricks showed the popular classes how to survive in the world of their "betters." Puppet performances and popular fiestas blended local and national elements, encouraging people to think about how they defined themselves in relation to other Mexicans.[6]

In another new development, state and local officials began to place bandstands in community plazas where musical groups, that had accompanied military forces earlier, performed at patriotic and religious celebrations. Implicitly, their mission was to instill civic virtue and nationalistic pride. The tradition became firmly established in Oaxaca where bands offered recreational Sunday matinees, playing romantic and heroic melodies along with regional tunes.

While a sense of collective national identity was evolving for the masses, Mexican scholars were examining how the nation had developed from pre-Columbian times. Some turned to organizing prehispanic artifacts that had been collected in various institutions since the late colonial period. A national Mexican museum had been established in 1825 to house collections related to history, archaeology, and natural history. In 1906, Secretary of Public Education Justo Sierra relocated the natural history materials; the other collections became part of the renamed National Museum of Archaeology, History, and Ethnography. Professional archaeology in Mexico was in its infancy, as most nineteenth-century forays into antiquity had been undertaken by foreigners who appropriated artifacts for their home museums. The Porfirian government took steps to protect this patrimony and assert control over ancient ruins, initiating the reconstruction of Teotihuacan. Symbolically connecting the present to advanced civilizations and empires of antiquity (imitating other nations who looked to their Greek and Roman pasts) served to enhance Mexican prestige in the world. To be sure, this project had nothing to do with contemporary Indians viewed as a vulgar liability that needed to be hidden from visiting foreign dignitaries.

Perhaps the greatest historian of the epoch was Joaquín García Icazbalceta (1825–94), who collected and edited several monumental series of colonial documents and prepared a bibliography of the sixteenth century—*Bibliografía mexicana del siglo XVI*—listing and annotating all of the books published in Mexico between 1539 and 1600. But his most distinguished work was a four-volume biography of the first bishop and archbishop of Mexico, Fray Juan de Zumárraga.

Justo Sierra (1848–1912) set himself to the task of attempting a new interpretive synthesis of Mexican history. The result would occupy a unique niche in Mexican historiography.

---

6   William H. Beezley, *Mexican National Identity: Memory, Innuendo, and Popular Culture* (Tucson, AZ, 2008), 98–145.

México: Su evolución social was published at the turn of the century and shows Sierra as an eclectic. Unlike the historians who preceded him, Sierra, from a new perspective, could view Mexican history with optimism. The chaotic and unseemly events of the early nineteenth century had been, for him, necessary steps in the progress of humankind. In Sierra's analysis of his contemporary Mexico, even Díaz did not emerge completely unscathed. While Sierra could not overlook the authoritarianism of the regime, on balance he found it to be simply a step in Mexico's evolutionary process toward liberty.

During the three and one-half decades of peace and economic growth a younger generation of liberal intellectuals gradually emerged. As they began to expose some of the obvious shortcomings of the regime, many experienced harsh retribution. Despite harassment, intimidation, and incarceration, these young intellectuals were not easily dissuaded from their goals and contributed in no small way to the outbreak of revolutionary activity in Mexico in 1910.

RECOMMENDED FOR FURTHER STUDY

Agostini, Claudia. *Monuments of Progress: Modernization and Public Health in Mexico City, 1876–1910*. Calgary: University of Calgary Press, 2003.

Alexander, Anna Rose. *City on Fire: Technology, Social Change, and Hazards of Progress in Mexico City, 1860–1912*. Pittsburgh, PA: Pittsburgh University Press, 2016.

Barrett, John. *Mexico: A General Sketch*. Washington, DC: Pan American Union, 1911.

Barton, Mary. *Impressions of Mexico with Brush and Pen*. London, UK: Methuen, 1911.

Beezley, William H. *Judas at the Jockey Club and Other Episodes of Porfirian Mexico*. Lincoln: University of Nebraska Press, 1987.

_____. *Mexican National Identity: Memory, Innuendo, and Popular Culture*. Tucson: University of Arizona Press, 2008.

Blum, Ann S. *Domestic Economies: Family, Work, and Welfare in Mexico City, 1884–1943*. Lincoln: University of Nebraska Press, 2009.

Brushwood, John S. *Mexico in Its Novel: A Nation's Search for Identity*. Austin: University of Texas Press, 1966.

Bueno, Christina. *The Pursuit of Ruin: Archaeology, History, and the Making of Modern Mexico*. Albuquerque: University of New Mexico Press, 2016.

Buffington, Robert. *A Sentimental Education for the Working Man: The Mexico City Penny Press, 1900–1910*. Durham, NC: Duke University Press, 2015.

Buffington, Robert, and Pablo Piccato, eds. *True Stories of Crime in Modern Mexico*. Albuquerque: University of New Mexico Press, 2009.

Bunker, Steven B. *Creating Mexican Consumer Culture in the Age of Porfirio Díaz, 1876–1911*. Albuquerque: University of New Mexico Press, 2012.

Case, Alden Buell. *Thirty Years with the Mexicans: In Peace and Revolution*. New York: Flemming H. Revel Company, 1917.

Charlot, Jean. *The Mexican Mural Renaissance, 1920–1925*. New Haven, CT: Yale University Press, 1967.

Chassen-López, Francie R. "A Patron of Progress: Juana Catarina Romero, the Nineteenth-Century Cacica of Tehuantepec." *Hispanic American Historical Review*, 88/3 (2008), 393–426.

Díaz, María Elena. "The Satiric Penny Press for Workers in Mexico, 1900–1910: A Case Study in the Politicisation of Popular Culture." *Journal of Latin American Studies*, 22/3 (1990), 497–526.

Esposito, Matthew D. *Funerals, Festivals, and Cultural Politics in Porfirian Mexico*. Albuquerque: University of New Mexico Press, 2010.

Fowler-Salamini, Heather, and Mary Kay Vaughan, eds. *Women of the Mexican Countryside, 1850–1990: Creating Spaces, Shaping Transition*. Tucson: University of Arizona Press, 1994.

French, William E. *The Heart in a Glass Jar: Love Letters, Bodies, and the Law in Mexico*. Lincoln: University of Nebraska Press, 2015.

_____. *A Peaceful and Working People: Manners, Morals, and Class Formation in Northern Mexico*. Albuquerque: University of New Mexico Press, 1996.

Garza, James A. *The Imagined Underworld: Sex, Crime, and Vice in Porfirian Mexico City*. Lincoln: University of Nebraska Press, 2008.

Hale, Charles A. *The Transformation of Liberalism in Late Nineteenth-Century Mexico*. Princeton, NJ: Princeton University Press, 1989.

Heath, Charles V. *The Inevitable Bandstand: The State Band of Oaxaca and the Politics of Sound*. Lincoln: University of Nebraska Press, 2015.

Neufeld, Stephen and Michael Matthews, eds. *Mexico in Verse: A History of Music, Rhyme, and Power*. Tucson: University of Arizona, 2015.

Overmyer-Velázquez, Mark. *Visions of the Emerald City: Modernity, Tradition, and the Formation of Porfirian Oaxaca, Mexico*. Durham, NC: Duke University Press, 2006.

Piccato, Pablo. *City of Suspects: Crime in Mexico City, 1900–1931*. Durham, NC: Duke University Press, 2001.

Pilcher, Jeffrey M. *The Sausage Rebellion: Public Health, Private Enterprise and Meat in Mexico City, 1890–1917*. Albuquerque: University of New Mexico Press, 2006.

Porter, Susie S. *Working Women in Mexico City: Public Discourse and Material Conditions, 1879–1931*. Tucson: University of Arizona Press, 2003.

Sierra, Justo. *The Political Evolution of the Mexican People*. Translated by Charles Ramsdell. Austin: University of Texas Press, 1969.

Sloan, Kathryn A. *Runaway Daughters: Seduction, Elopement, and Honor in Nineteenth-Century Mexico*. Albuquerque: University of New Mexico Press, 2008.

Tenorio Trillo, Mauricio. *Mexico at the World's Fairs: Crafting a Modern Nation*. Berkeley: University of California Press, 1996.

Tyler, Ron, ed. *Posada's Mexico*. Washington, DC: Library of Congress, 1979.

Vaughan, Mary Kay. *The State, Education and Social Class in Mexico, 1880–1928*. DeKalb: Northern Illinois University Press, 1982.

Wasserman, Mark. *Everyday Life and Politics in Nineteenth-Century Mexico: Men, Women and War*. Albuquerque: University of New Mexico Press, 2000.

Widdifield, Stacie G. *The Embodiment of the National in Late Nineteenth Century Mexican Painting*. Tucson: University of Arizona Press, 1995.

Wood, Andrew G. *Revolution in the Street: Women, Workers, and Urban Protest in Veracruz, 1870–1927*. Wilmington, DE: Scholarly Resources, 2001.

Wright-Rios, Edward. *Revolutions in Mexican Catholicism: Reform and Revelation in Oaxaca, 1887–1934*. Durham, NC: Duke University Press, 2009.

THE REVOLUTION OF 1910

CHAPTER 26

MADERO AND THE LIBERAL INDICTMENT OF THE PORFIRIATO

THE LIBERAL LEADERSHIP

The opening of the twentieth century found Mexico a far different place from what it had been only twenty-five years earlier. It would be sheer folly to gainsay the tremendous material benefits that had accrued in the industrial, commercial, and mining fields. At the same time, it is easily argued that the successes of modernization created the environment for discontent and that, in the revolutionary aftermath, the economic achievements of the Porfiriato were ignored for decades. Porfirian capitalism shunned the masses and scarcely began to create a broad base of consumers; the economic surplus generated by the dynamic economy had been largely appropriated by the few. A system that perpetuated itself for the sake of order and economic progress, and atrophied in the process, became less and less palatable to an increasing number of young, socially aware Mexicans. The federal Constitution of 1857, with its theoretical guarantees, had been violated incessantly. Elections at all levels of government were a farce. The administration of justice in rural Mexico was a euphemism for the capricious whims of the local jefe político. Freedom of the press did not exist, and the restrictions of the Reform limiting the participatory role of the clergy were not enforced. To those who were concerned with the longevity of the regime, Don Porfirio became "Don Perpetuo," while those more concerned with the brutality dubbed him "Porfiriopoxtli." The científicos continued to be loyal apologists for the dictatorship, but a younger generation of intellectual activists, embracing a new faith and unwilling to be intimidated by the arrogance of the científicos, began to question the dictatorship.

One of the first to speak out for reform was Wistano Luis Orozco, a jurist from Guadalajara who addressed social, not political, issues. In 1895 he wrote a volume criticizing the Díaz land laws and the land companies that profited from them. Arguing that the concentration of landownership was detrimental to both the rural peasantry and the progress of agriculture, he called for the government to break up and sell all public lands and begin buying up some of the huge haciendas for the same purpose. Not propagandizing for revolution, he believed the reforms he envisioned could be effected from within the administration. In San Luis Potosí,

Camilo Arriaga, a mining engineer by profession, rejected the positivist doctrine and by the turn of the century counted himself in the small anti-Díaz camp. A typical nineteenth-century liberal, Arriaga moved into the opposition fold because of Díaz's *modus vivendi* with the Roman Catholic Church. In late 1900 he called for the organization of liberal clubs throughout Mexico and summoned a national liberal convention to meet in San Luis Potosí in 1901.

The least timid members of the liberal movement in the early twentieth century were the Flores Magón brothers—Jesús, Ricardo, and Enrique. In August of 1900 the brothers began publication of *Regeneración*, a Mexico City weekly. Not yet ready to preach the injustice of private land ownership, through its columns they supported the nascent liberal movement in San Luis Potosí and decried the excesses of Porfirismo. But when they attacked a local jefe político in Oaxaca in the columns of *Regeneración*, the brothers were arrested in the late spring of 1901 and confined to Belén prison for a year. Their arrest served to invigorate the liberal movement as freedom of the press and suppression of the jefes políticos became new causes the liberals could add to their militant anticlericalism. By the time the Flores Magón brothers were released Camilo Arriaga had been arrested, as had other leaders of the liberal cause. The brothers renewed their attacks, in the columns of *El Hijo de Ahuizote*. Two more arrests convinced them to leave Mexico in 1904 and revitalize their attack on the Díaz regime from exile in the United States.

From San Antonio, Texas, the Flores Magón brothers and Arriaga, who joined them shortly, began soliciting funds from liberals to reinstitute *Regeneración*. Former subscribers and liberal clubs throughout Mexico made small contributions, and an unexpected benefactor was found in Francisco I. Madero, son of a wealthy Coahuila hacendado. The first issue of the newly revived tabloid came off the press in the fall of 1904. The *Regeneración* published from San Antonio took a more militant and belligerent tone attacking Díaz and proposing

Cartoon from *El Hijo de Ahuizote* titled "The Governors Praying for Díaz Support."

The great grandson of Enrique Flores Magón has revived the original location of where the protest publication was published. Today, the Casa de El Hijo de Ahuizote, which houses part of the Flores Magón archive, serves as a cultural center in Mexico City.

Photo of the modern façade of the Casa de El Hijo de Ahuizote.

more radical changes. In reaction, Díaz authorized an assassination attempt on the Flores Magón brothers; it failed, but prompted the liberals in exile to move away from the border to St. Louis, Missouri where they resumed publication of *Regeneración* in 1905 and organized a revolutionary junta. Local St. Louis authorities soon arrested the Flores Magón brothers, charging them with violating US neutrality laws. Although they were released, Ricardo's subsequent activities in other parts of the United States landed him in jail several times, and he died in Fort Leavenworth, Kansas, in 1922.

In the summer of 1906 the junta in St. Louis published its Liberal Plan. Part of it rehashed of nineteenth-century liberal concerns, calling for freedom of speech, freedom of the press, suppression of the jefes políticos, the complete secularization of education, and the nationalization of all church property. But the Liberal Plan of 1906 heralded a new age of liberalism. Socially oriented measures included the abolition of the death penalty (except for treason), educational reform in favor of the poor, and prison reform emphasizing rehabilitation rather than punishment. More revolutionary yet was the call for a nationwide eight-hour workday and a six-day workweek, the abolition of the tienda de raya, the payment of all workers in legal tender, and the prohibition of child labor. The plan did not overlook the rural areas of Mexico, advocating a state takeover of all uncultivated lands to be redistributed to those who would work them. To enable the small farmer to take advantage of this move, an agricultural credit bank would be established to provide low-interest loans. And, finally, special emphasis would be placed on restoring the ejido lands seized illegally from the Indian communities.

Treatment of the Mexican liberal party. A print by José Guadalupe Posada.

The discontent over the political abuses of the Díaz dictatorship had been gradually transmuted into a new gospel of social reform. Articulated by middle-class reformers, the new rhetoric resonated not only with the urban working class that had expanded with modernization but also with the popular liberalism that had evolved in rural villages after the defeat of the French. Even Porfirio Diaz had used indigenous and campesino aspirations for "liberty" and autonomy to build his own base of support. His later indifference to community traditions and "folk" liberalism had not made them disappear, however, and local cultures still harbored the hybrid civil and religious belief systems that could nurture defiance to alien impositions. How the new social thought would mesh with traditional values was not yet apparent, but copies of *Regeneración* smuggled into Mexico were being read by the reform-minded middle classes and labor organizers.

LABOR UNREST

On June 1, 1906, the Mexican workers at Colonel William Greene's Cananea Consolidated Copper Company went out on strike. Young socialist activists in Cananea, Sonora—Manuel Diéguez, Estéban Calderón, and Francisco Ibarra—had been in correspondence with the exiles, had formed an affiliate liberal club in Cananea, and had agitated the workers, distributing copies of *Regeneración*. The grievances of the miners at Cananea were manifold. The company paid less than their US counterparts for performing the same jobs and consigned qualified Mexican laborers to undesirable posts, while staffing the technical and managerial positions with US personnel. The workers elected a delegation to negotiate these matters, and salary and hours, with management. When Colonel Greene refused to arbitrate, the activists decided to stop all company operations.

The violence began in the company lumberyard. Disgruntled but unarmed workers attempted to force their way through a locked gate, and the resident manager ordered high-pressure water hoses turned on them. When the gate finally buckled and the workers swarmed into the yard, they were greeted with several volleys of rifle fire. During the chaos of the next hour several dozen Mexicans and two US managers were slain. The remaining workers retreated, leaving the lumberyard in flames. In this explosive atmosphere, Colonel Greene informed Governor Rafael Izábal of the danger and telephoned friends across the border in Arizona to raise a volunteer force in his behalf. When the governor was apprised that the rurales could not arrive until late the next day, he gave permission for 275 Arizona Rangers to cross the border to patrol the streets of Cananea. To veil the violation of Mexico's neutrality, Izábal did not allow the Rangers to enter the country as a force. They crossed over individually and were subsequently sworn in as Mexican volunteers.

The situation in Cananea was still tense when the American force arrived, together with Governor Izábal. While no major military engagements ensued, the Rangers and the workers did exchange fire on several occasions, and deaths resulted on both sides. Late in the day a detachment of rurales arrived under the command of Colonel Emilio Kosterlitzky. "Justice" was quick for those workers Kosterlitzky considered ringleaders: he rounded them up and hanged them from trees. The workers, threatened with induction into the army, returned to their jobs. Nonetheless, the strike focused attention on the Díaz policy of protecting

Mothers, wives, sisters, and daughters supported the miners' demands by demonstrating in Cananea.

foreigners at the expense of Mexicans. US troops had been allowed to cross into Mexican territory and kill Mexicans to guard the interests of an American mining magnate.

The discontent of the miners at Cananea proved not to be an isolated phenomenon. Liberal leaders among textile workers in Veracruz organized the Gran Círculo de Obreros Libres and began seeking affiliate clubs in neighboring states. The last six months of 1906 witnessed the most intense labor conflict of the entire Porfiriato, with several textile strikes. The major showdown occurred in January 1907 in the Río Blanco textile mills near Orizaba. Working conditions there were nothing short of horrendous, with a common workday of twelve hours, grossly inadequate wages, and a policy requiring workers to pay for the normal depreciation of the machinery they used. Children of eight and nine years of age performed physically demanding work. All strikes and affiliation with the Gran Círculo were illegal. The abuses seemed so patent that the workers agreed to lay their complaints directly before President Díaz for his arbitration. The dictator heard the complaints, but then supported the textile owners on almost every count. On Sunday, January 6, the workers held a mass meeting and decided to strike the following day.

The trouble set in at the grocery counter of the tienda de raya. Several wives of striking workers were refused credit for food. Insults led to pushing and shoving, then fisticuffs, and finally shooting. The enraged strikers put the tienda de raya to flame, and the local jefe político ordered in the rurales and the federal troops who fired point-blank into the crowd and killed several women and children along with numerous workers. By the end of the confrontation, the dead numbered more than one hundred.

Again, law and order reigned at the expense of personal liberty and social justice. Furthermore, Díaz's resort to brutal repression took place at a time when real wages were falling and natural and other disasters had resulted in food shortages. The Mexican silver peso lost value as major nations switched to a gold standard and the export economy suffered from its close ties to the US economy during the financial panic of 1907.

HEIGHTENED POLITICAL ACTIVITY

Despite the liberal indictment and the suppression of the nascent labor movement, most Mexican politicians believed that change could be effected through the political process. Díaz reinforced this position in early 1908 when he granted an interview to the US journalist James Creelman.

> No matter what my friends and supporters say, I retire when my presidential term of office ends, and I shall not serve again. I shall be eighty years old then. I have waited patiently for the day when the people of the Mexican Republic should be prepared to choose and change their government at every election without danger of armed revolution and without injury to the national credit or interference with the national progress. I believe that day has come. I welcome an opposition party in the Mexican Republic.[1]

Díaz's bombshell that he did not plan to seek reelection in the upcoming presidential elections of 1910 ushered in a rash of political activity and intellectual ferment. The Yucatecan sociologist Andrés Molina Enríquez, a positivist but not a Porfirista, published *Los grandes problemas nacionales* (*The Great National Problems*). A brilliant analysis of contemporary Mexican society, the work called for a penetrating program of reform, especially in the rural areas. Molina Enríquez feared that agrarian discontent could be manipulated by radicals or anarchists if reforms were not undertaken.

A still more influential book, *La sucesión presidencial en 1910* (*The Presidential Succession in 1910*), came from the pen of Francisco I. Madero. Unlike Molina Enríquez, Madero held that Mexico's problems were primarily political in nature, deriving from military dictatorship. He urged Mexicans to take Díaz at his word and to form an opposition party, an anti-reelectionist party dedicated to the principles of effective suffrage and no reelection. Madero's book affirmed that the desired change could be effected through the ballot box and, together with the Creelman interview, it set into motion the political forces that would ultimately lead to the conflagration in the fall of 1910.

Within the administration itself various factions began to vie for the mantle of succession. The followers of General Bernardo Reyes, the capable and energetic former governor of Nuevo León and secretary of war, pushed their hero as a logical successor to Díaz. Other científicos, led by José Limantour, supported the current government of Díaz and Ramón Corral, his vice president and a former governor of Sonora, and it was not long before Reyes was sent off to Europe with a contrived assignment that was tantamount to political exile.

---

1   Quoted in Frederick Starr, *Mexico and the United States: A Story of Revolution, Intervention and War* (Chicago, IL, 1914), 253.

MADERO AND THE ANTI-REELECTIONIST CAUSE

The political opposition to Díaz in the 1910 presidential elections would come, at any rate, from outside the official party as Francisco I. Madero dedicated himself to the anti-reelectionist cause. Born in Coahuila in 1873 to a family of wealth and prestige, young Madero received the best education that money could provide. The family had garnered a fortune in mining, land speculation, cattle, and banking; Madero's father was happy to send his teenage son to Paris and then to Berkeley, California, for proper grooming. Upon his return to Coahuila, Madero assumed the administration of several family haciendas. He not only observed the gross social inequities firsthand but took time to ponder the pathetic written complaints that detailed stories of physical abuse by mayordomos and tales of poverty that left children without shelter or food, of sickness without the possibility of medical care, of military conscription as a means of punishment, and of incarceration without the formalities of law. Realizing that his family haciendas were simply a microcosm of rural Mexico, Madero became convinced that the only solution was democracy. Though Madero had initially contributed to the cause of the Flores Magón brothers, he became estranged from them as they grew more radical.

To foment anti-reelectionism and test the political winds, Madero toured Mexico in the last half of 1909. During the summer and early fall he made public appearances throughout the country to build a revolutionary network. In the winter, Madero, his close confidants, and his wife continued their political tours to Querétaro, Guadalajara, Manzanillo, Mazatlán, and the northern states of Sonora and Chihuahua. Exploiting resentment over a generational gap, Madero offered himself as an energetic, capable, and articulate young leader in stark contrast to a tiring and decrepit regime—not a member of Díaz's cabinet was under sixty, and many of the state governors were in their seventies. Especially well received in Chihuahua, Madero held several meetings with Abraham González, an ardent foe of the dictatorship and president of the Centro Anti-reeleccionista Benito Juárez.

Anti-reelectionists held their convention in April 1910 with broad geographical representation. The 120 delegates in attendance, following the lead of Abraham González and his Chihuahua colleagues, officially nominated Madero for the presidency. The convention chose as his running mate Dr. Francisco Vásquez Gómez, a distinguished physician but a lukewarm liberal at best.

The philosophy of the anti-reelectionist party came out gradually during the campaign that carried the candidate to twenty-two of the twenty-seven Mexican states. Mexican presidents, Madero argued, should serve only a single term, focusing not on the next election but on the next generation. Political reform, predicated upon free and honest elections, was basic to the entire program. Social benefits might then accrue, but democracy was the one imperative. During a campaign speech in San Luis Potosí, Madero was interrupted by a question voiced from the audience asking why he did not break up his own haciendas. Madero's answer epitomized his philosophy. The Mexican people, he responded, did not want bread; they wanted liberty. Not long thereafter, the Díaz administration began arresting anti-reelectionist leaders, including Madero himself.

On election day, June 21, 1910, with Madero in prison in San Luis Potosí and thousands of his anti-reelectionist colleagues in jails throughout the republic, Díaz and Ramón Corral declared an overwhelming victory for still another term. His family arranged for Madero's release on bail with the proviso that he confine himself to the city of San Luis Potosí. He remained in the city for several months, but in early October, he managed to board a north-bound train in disguise and escaped to the United States.

THE LAST HURRAH

Soon after the election Díaz began preparations for his final extravaganza. In September he would celebrate his eightieth birthday and Mexico the 100th anniversary of its declaration of independence. Pageants and commemoration celebrated the Díaz regime. The government unveiled a soaring column capped by a gold angel on the Paseo de la Reforma in honor of the independence movement along with an equally impressive monument to the Niños Héroes at the entrance to Chapultepec Park. Distinguished guests from abroad had their expenses paid to partake of the festivities at gala balls in their honor where imported French champagne flowed like water. Flags waved everywhere, parades crowded the streets, fireworks lit up the night skies, and *mariachis* (folk musicians) strolled the downtown avenues. Foreign governments took part as well. The American colony sent Díaz and the Mexican people a statue of its own independence hero, George Washington, and the Italians—not to be outdone—sent one of Giuseppe Garibaldi. The Third French Republic returned the keys to the city of Mexico that had been ingloriously sequestered by the army of Napoleon III a half-century before. King Alfonso XIII demonstrated the lasting fraternity of the Spanish people by returning the uniform of José María Morelos.

The lavish displays of civic virtue demanded that beggars be pushed off of the streets of the capital city so that the guests would receive the proper impressions of a prosperous Mexico. The cost of the celebrations exceeded the entire educational budget for the year 1910. While the champagne flowed for a few, tens of thousands suffered from malnutrition. While visitors rode in shiny new motorcars on well-paved streets in the center of the city, mud and filth engulfed barrios of the working poor and unemployed. In September 1910 Mexico appeared to many to be enjoying its finest hour. A mask for the millions living in poverty, this showy façade would be short-lived.

THE PLAN DE SAN LUIS POTOSÍ

For years Francisco Madero had resisted the prodding of liberals who exhorted that Díaz must be overthrown by force. But when he escaped from San Luis Potosí and made his way north to the sanctuary of the US border, he realized that it was no longer possible to unseat the dictator by constitutional means. In the middle of October 1910, he began drafting a revolutionary plan in San Antonio, Texas. To avoid any possible international complications with the United States, he dated the plan October 5, his last day on Mexican soil, and called it the Plan de San Luis Potosí.

Aquiles Serdán and his family in Puebla. A print by Fernando Castro Pacheco.

Peoples, in their constant efforts for the triumph of the ideals of liberty and justice, find it necessary at certain historical moments to make the greatest sacrifices. Our beloved fatherland has reached one of those moments.

. . . this violent and illegal system can no longer exist. . . . I declare the last election illegal and accordingly the republic, being without rulers, I assume the provisional presidency of the republic until the people designate their rulers pursuant to the law. . . .

I have designated Sunday, the 20th day of next November, for all the towns in the republic to rise in arms after 6 o'clock P.M.[2]

The Plan de San Luis Potosí, like *La sucesión presidencial en 1910* before it, reflected primarily political concerns with a few vague and ill conceived references to Mexico's social maladies. Yet the boldness of the statement and the self-confidence it projected struck a responsive chord. The leaders who had previously worked for the anti-reelectionist party began preparing for November 20. The revolution actually began two days prematurely in the town of Puebla. There the local liberal leader, Aquiles Serdán, had stored arms and ammunition in his home. An informant notified the police, and Serdán and his family became the first martyrs of the new cause. Madero himself crossed over into Mexico on the evening of November 19, but, when his expected rebel army failed to rendezvous, he crossed back into the United States without firing a shot. It was not yet clear that the masses would rally to the cry of *¡Viva la Revolución!*

---

2   The text of the plan can be found in Isidro Fabela, ed., *Documentos históricos de la revolución mexicana*, vol. 6 (Mexico City, Mexico, 1960–73), 69–76.

The Mexican guerrilla at the beginning of the revolution would soon be immortalized in legend and song.

THE RISE OF REBEL ARMIES AND THE RESIGNATION OF DÍAZ

Local corridos record the names of the many who took up arms everywhere on the stipulated day. But nowhere did the sparks fly as in Chihuahua. Town after town responded on November 20 and 21. Among them, Toribio Ortega marched on Cuchillo Parado, Guillermo Baca on Hidalgo del Parral, Pancho Villa on San Andrés, and Pascual Orozco on San Isidro and Miñaca.

The rebel forces did not constitute armies, but neither were they merely campesino mobs. They included rank-and-file campesinos, servants, shopkeepers, mechanics, beggars, miners, federal army deserters, lawyers, US soldiers of fortune including African Americans, young and old, bandits and idealists, students and teachers, engineers and day laborers, the bored and the overworked, the aggrieved and the adventuresome. Some were attracted by commitment to the cause and some by the promise of spoils; some joined impulsively and others with careful forethought. Some preferred Flores Magón radicalism and some Madero liberalism; many had heard of neither. Even among the politically astute some viewed the November movement as a fight against hacendados, others decided to offer their lives to oppose local jefes políticos, while still others saw the revolution as a chance to recapture Mexico from the foreign capitalists. But they all shared the conviction that Díaz symbolizedf all of Mexico's ills and that any change would be better. Thus, they were willing to strap cartridge belts on their chests; find, buy, or steal rifles somewhere; and become *guerrilleros*. Indifferently armed, without uniforms, with no notion of military discipline, the disparate rebel bands lived off the land and attacked local authorities and small federal outposts in tiny pueblos. They enjoyed a dormant but fortuitous asset—the cooperation of much of rural Mexico. Madero's communications network began to inform him that his recent efforts had not been in vain.

The Díaz regime dispatched army units and corps of rurales on scattered missions in Mexico's ten military zones, and slowly they began to curtail the spread of the rebellion. Only in Chihuahua did Madero's movement continue to grow. The military leadership there had devolved upon Pascual Orozco, Jr., a tall, gaunt mule skinner whose business had suffered because he did not enjoy the favor of the Terrazas-Creel machine. Working with Abraham González, the leader of the anti-reelectionists in the state, Orozco began recruitment in the Guerrero district. González supplied some modest funds and a few weapons. By November 20, Orozco had attracted about 40 men to the cause. During the next two weeks, striking rapidly from the almost inaccessible *sierras* of western Chihuahua, he garnered more victories. Pancho Villa, José de la Luz Blanco, and other local leaders placed themselves under his command; and the Orozco army increased twentyfold. On January 2, 1911, the Chihuahua rebels ambushed and almost totally destroyed a large federal convoy sent to pursue them. Now cocksure, Orozco stripped the dead soldiers of their uniforms, wrapped up the articles of clothing, and sent them to Don Porfirio with a graphically descriptive taunt: *Ahí te van las hojas; mándame más tamales* (Here are the wrappers; send me some more tamales).

Soon the insurrection began to bear fruit in Sonora, Coahuila, Sinaloa, Veracruz, Zacatecas, Puebla, Guerrero, and Morelos. In Baja California the Flores Magón brothers and their followers had the government on the run. Picking their own ground and their own time of battle, small rebel contingents throughout the country kept the uncoordinated and poorly supplied federals constantly off balance. The rebels, on the other hand, moved in smaller units, lived off the land, and generally enjoyed the sympathy and cooperation of the local populace. They found it easier to smuggle in ammunition from the United States than federal commanders did to requisition it from Mexico City.

In the late spring of 1911 Orozco and Villa convinced Madero (who had no military expertise) that the northern rebels should expend all their energy on capturing Ciudad Juárez, the border city across the Rio Grande from El Paso, Texas. By early May, with the most seasoned rebel troops congregated on the outskirts of the city and ready to attack, Madero suddenly changed his mind. Fearing that stray rebel shells might fall on El Paso and thus occasion US intervention, he ordered a retreat which was promptly ignored by Orozco. Thousands of El Paso residents climbed to their rooftops to watch the proceedings and cheer on their favorites. On the morning of May 10, the rebels' superior numbers and fire power overcame the federal resistance. Low on ammunition and completely encircled by the enemy, General Juan Navarro decided to surrender and hoisted a white flag over the federal barracks.

Madero did not know whether to be grateful, angry, or embarrassed. Against his order Orozco had handed him an important city, an official port of entry from the United States, and a provisional capital. When a few days later the provisional president named his cabinet, Orozco's name was curiously absent. A showdown took place on May 13 during a meeting of the new provisional government. Revolvers in hand to emphasize their point, Orozco and Villa burst into the room with a series of demands that highlighted their frustrations with Madero's failure to reward his rebel followers and appoint men who would more forcefully advance their goals.

The battle of Ciudad Juárez (May 1911) proved to be the decisive engagement for control of the north.

Momentarily defused, the confrontation had significance that no one present could have foreseen. Though only five months old, the revolutionary coalition was already falling apart. The military's challenge to the civilian leadership would be repeated regularly for the next chaotic decade. But more important yet, the affair portended an age of bitter factionalism that exacerbated personal rivalries, turned Mexican against Mexican, extended the war, exacted a tremendously high toll of life, and increased the pain and anguish for hundreds of thousands.

Meanwhile, rebels throughout the country took heart and redoubled their efforts, taking control of town after town. Business fell victim to the trauma of uncertainty, and the press became increasingly outspoken in criticism of the regime. Federal troops began deserting to the revolution *en masse*. Díaz reluctantly agreed to dispatch a team of negotiators to meet with Madero and his staff. The Treaty of Ciudad Juárez provided that Díaz and Vice President Corral would resign before the month was out. Francisco León de la Barra, the secretary of foreign relations and an experienced diplomat, would assume the interim presidency until new elections could be held. Don Porfirio signed his resignation and submitted it to the congress on May 25, 1911. On his way to Veracruz and ultimate exile, Porfirio Díaz reputedly told Victoriano Huerta, the commander of his military escort, "Madero has unleashed a tiger. Now let's see if he can control it." The remark, both prophetic and reflective of Díaz's keen perception of his fellow countrymen, augured ominous consequences.

Díaz had indeed been overthrown, but the revolution had scarcely triumphed. It had barely yet begun. The conviviality and jubilee of the next few days soon gave way to acrimonious debate as Mexicans began to ask themselves what, exactly, they had won. Their

The revolutionary leadership following the capture of Ciudad Juárez. The coalition would soon fall apart.

answers, of course, were predicated upon what had motivated them to join the movement at the outset. As the dictator sailed away into European exile, the one bond that had held them together vanished from sight.

THE INTERIM PRESIDENCY AND DIVISION WITHIN THE REBEL RANKS

The interim presidency of León de la Barra (May to November 1911), whose cabinet included many Porfiristas, alienated many of Madero's radical supporters, including the Flores Magón brothers. Emiliano Zapata in Morelos adopted a cautious wait-and-see attitude. Orozco in Chihuahua still bristled from his recent encounter with Madero. Unaware that the rumblings within his ranks were serious, in early June, Madero left the north for Mexico City. His seven hundred–mile journey by train was truly triumphant as thousands of enthusiastic admirers greeted him at large and small stations along the way. His reception in the capital was no less spectacular, as recorded by Edith O'Shaughnessy, the wife of the US chargé d'affaires in the Mexico City embassy.

> There was a great noise of *vivas*, mingling with shouts of all kinds, tramping of feet, and blowing of motor horns. I could just get a glimpse of a pale, dark-bearded man bowing to the right and left. . . . People came from far and near, in all sorts of conveyances or on foot, just to see him, to hear his voice, even to touch his garments for help and healing. . . .[3]

Among those there to greet Madero and talk to him was the most famous revolutionary of all—Emiliano Zapata. Like Orozco in the north, Zapata had never been a campesino. His family had passed on a little land to him, and he supplemented his modest income as a muleteer, a horse trainer, and a stable master. Elected in 1909 to local office, Zapata represented the villagers of Anenecuilco, Morelos, who had managed to hold onto their lands as independent campesinos. Eager to help them avoid the fate of campesinos, Zapata decided

---

3   Edith O'Shaughnessy, *Diplomatic Days* (New York, NY, 1917), 53.

Emiliano Zapata (1879–1919). Although Zapata played only a minor role in the fight again Díaz, his stature as a revolutionary grew steadily until his assassination in 1919.

to link his predominantly agrarian cause with the larger rebel movement and began recruiting an insurgent army.

His military contributions to the overthrow of the Díaz dictatorship were minor, but he had scored several victories over the federal forces by the time Díaz submitted his resignation in May 1911. Now, Zapata wanted to talk to Madero about the one matter that concerned him most—the land problem in Morelos. To Zapata the overthrow of Díaz had genuine meaning only if land were immediately restored to the pueblos. In a dramatic encounter Zapata, with a large sombrero on his head and his carbine in his hand, gestured to the gold watch Madero sported on his vest and then made his point.

> Look, Señor Madero, if I, taking advantage of being armed, steal your watch and keep it, and then we meet again sometime and you are armed, wouldn't you have the right to demand that I return it?
>
> Of course, General, and you would also have the right to ask that I pay you for the use I had of it.
>
> Well, this is exactly what has happened to us in Morelos where some of the hacendados have forcibly taken over the village lands. My soldiers, the armed peasants, demand that I tell you respectfully that they want their lands returned immediately.[4]

---

4   Quoted in Gildardo Magaña, *Emiliano Zapata y el agrarismo en México*, vol. 1 (Mexico City, Mexico, 1934–52), 160.

With characteristic caution Madero made no immediate commitment, but when he traveled to Morelos shortly thereafter, he insisted that Zapata demobilize his army as a prerequisite to reducing tensions in the state. Zapata detected something absurd in the request. The revolutionaries had won; yet while the federal army remained intact, the victorious rebels were asked to disband. To show good faith the southern rebel reluctantly agreed. His acquiescence was for naught as interim President León de la Barra sent federal troops into the state to enforce the demobilization order. Madero was furious, but the tenuous peace had already been shattered. With the state of Morelos again in revolt by August, Madero, perhaps through no fault of his own, could add Zapata's name to his growing list of enemies.

The campaign for the 1911 presidential elections took place in a tense political atmosphere. Madero's party met in Mexico City in August and nominated him by acclamation. But the vice presidential pick divided the convention. Madero decided to dump his 1910 running mate, Francisco Vásquez Gómez, in favor of a Yucatecan lawyer and journalist, José María Pino Suárez. The convention gave Madero his choice, but Vásquez Gómez and his followers would never reconcile themselves to their sudden political demise. The opposition candidate around whom many of the old regime could rally, albeit without enthusiasm, was General Bernardo Reyes. By early fall the election was in full swing and the debate heated. In the aftermath of a physical attack by Madero supporters on Reyes at a Mexico City rally, and Reyes, perhaps realizing that his campaign stood little chance of victory anyway, withdrew from the race and went into a self-imposed exile in San Antonio, Texas. Another powerful enemy was on the list.

The election took place without further incident on October 1, 1911. Only minor candidates opposed Madero, and he swept to an overwhelming victory. Madero's faith in democracy would soon be put to the test and, while his faith would remain unshaken, democracy would fall victim to the rancor and passion of the day.

DISAPPOINTING REFORMS

Bursting with optimistic idealism, Madero approached his presidential challenge with all the fresh enthusiasm of the novice, and his first priority was to restore order. Madero the president, unlike Madero the revolutionary, found himself quickly besieged with demands from all sides. Only when established in the presidential office did he begin to realize fully that the revolution had profoundly different meanings to different groups of Mexicans. The spurious alliance began to break up irretrievably. Of the disparate elements he had previously counted in his ranks, those of nineteenth-century liberal persuasion, interested in political reform and the growth of democracy, supported him while both the aristocratic elite he displaced and the social revolutionaries he embraced became increasingly hostile. The press began to assail him mercilessly but, in the best democratic tradition, he gave it full rein and stoically accepted the barbed criticism and cruel satires.

Although he could defy anyone to show him where he had ever promised sweeping reform, he did, nevertheless, embark upon a meager and imperfect program to restructure the prevailing social order. Though unwilling to accede to Zapata's urgent demand that land be immediately restored to the villages, the president appointed the National Agrarian

Francisco I. Madero (1873–1913). President of Mexico in the crucial period following the overthrow of Díaz, Madero had a faith in democracy that proved ill-suited to the political realities of the day.

Commission, under the chairmanship of his conservative cousin Rafael Hernández, to study the land question. Hernández urged that the government begin purchasing a few private estates for subdivision and sale to the small farmer. But only 10 million pesos were allocated to the project, and the hacendados demanded such high prices for the land that even this modest plan was soon abandoned in favor of restoring some ejido lands that had been seized illegally during the late Porfiriato. The burden of proof, however, fell on the villages, and few village leaders could overcome the bewildering legal arguments thrown in their faces by the hacendados' lawyers. A handful of cases were settled in favor of the villages, but progress on the agrarian question was meager.

In the area of labor reform, late in 1912 the congress authorized the formation of the Department of Labor but placed it, too, under the jurisdiction of conservative Hernández with a paltry budget of forty-six thousand pesos. After a convention with government officials in Mexico City, a group of textile factory owners promised to initiate a ten-hour day; but in practice the working schedules did not change. Nonetheless, labor organizers no longer felt so intimidated. Encouraged by the possibilities of revolutionary change, a group of radicals under the leadership of Juan Francisco Moncaleano, a Spanish anarchist, founded the

Casa del Obrero Mundial. Not properly a union, the Casa served as a place where labor leaders could meet, exchange views, and, through their official newspaper, *Luz*, disseminate propaganda favorable to the cause. Madero caught between business interests and labor demands feared labor strikes and, although no labor massacres on the scale of Cananea and Río Blanco were recorded, government troops and local police authorities dispersed striking workers on a number of occasions. Hernández interpreted the strikes as inspired by agitators rather than intolerable conditions and had Moncaleano expelled from the country. However, strikes continued, and labor unrest began to disrupt the Mexican economy once again.

In the field of education the social reformers were again disappointed. Although Madero had promised to broaden the educational base during the presidential campaign, the annual budget for 1911–12 allocated only 7.8 percent for educational programs, as opposed to 7.2 percent during the last year of the Porfiriato. The new president did manage to build some fifty new schools and to initiate a modest program of school lunches for the underprivileged. His education program failed to deliver a dramatic increase in expenditures or a project for revising the científico curriculum.

In sum, the liberals of the twentieth-century stripe felt swindled by Madero as the administration failed at both the national and state levels. The disappointed began to realize that reform would proceed at a slow and gradual pace. Meanwhile another more menacing factor diverted Madero's attention and energies. A series of revolts broke out against him before he even had a chance to make himself comfortable in the presidential chair. The revolution's lack of ideological cohesion had begun to exact a terrible toll and in the process imperiled the administration itself.

RECOMMENDED FOR FURTHER STUDY

Albro, Ward S. *To Die on Your Feet: The Life, Times and Writings of Práxedis G. Guerrero*. Fort Worth: Texas Christian University Press, 1996.

Beezley, William H. *Insurgent Governor: Abraham González and the Mexican Revolution in Chihuahua*. Lincoln: University of Nebraska Press, 1973.

Beezley, William H., and Colin MacLachlan. *Mexicans in Revolution, 1910–1946*. Lincoln: University of Nebraska Press, 2009.

Bell, Edward I. *The Political Shame of Mexico*. New York: McBride, Nast, 1914.

Blaisdell, Lowell L. *The Desert Revolution: Baja California, 1911*. Madison: University of Wisconsin Press, 1962.

Cockcroft, James D. *Intellectual Precursors of the Mexican Revolution, 1900–1913*. Austin: University of Texas Press, 1968.

Creelman, James. *Díaz: Master of Mexico*. New York: D. Appleton and Company, 1916.

Cumberland, Charles C. *Mexican Revolution: Genesis under Madero*. Austin: University of Texas Press, 1952.

Guzmán, Martín Luis. *Memoirs of Pancho Villa*. Translated by Virgina H. Taylor. Austin: University of Texas Press, 1965.

Gonzales, Michael J. *The Mexican Revolution, 1910–1940*. Albuquerque: University of New Mexico Press, 2002.

Harris III, Charles H., and Louis R. Sadler. *The Secret War in El Paso: Mexican Revolutionary Intrigue, 1906–1922*. Albuquerque: University of New Mexico Press, 2009.

Hart, John M. "The Mexican Revolution of 1910–1920." In *The Oxford History of Mexico*, edited by Michael C. Meyer and William H. Beezley, 409–37. New York: Oxford University Press, 2010.

_____. *Revolutionary Mexico: The Coming and Process of the Mexican Revolution*. Berkeley: University of California Press, 1987.

Henderson, Peter V. N. *Félix Díaz, the Porfirians, and the Mexican Revolution*. Lincoln: University of Nebraska Press, 1981.

_____. *In the Absence of Don Porfirio. Francisco León de la Barra and the Mexican Revolution*. Wilmington, DE: Scholarly Resources, 1999.

Horne, Gerald. *Black and Brown: African Americans and the Mexican Revolution, 1910–1920*. New York: New York University Press, 2005.

Joseph, Gilbert M., and Daniel Nugent, eds. *Everyday Forms of State Formation and Negotiations of Rule in Modern Mexico*. Durham, NC: Duke University Press, 1994.

Knight, Alan. *The Mexican Revolution*. Vol. 1: *Porfirians, Liberals and Peasants*. New York: Cambridge University Press, 1986.

La France, David G. *Revolution in Mexico's Heartland: Politics, War, and State Building in Puebla, 1913–1920*. Wilmington, DE: Scholarly Resources, 2003.

MacLachlan, Colin M. *Anarchism and the Mexican Revolution*. Berkeley: University of California Press, 1991.

Meyer, Michael C. *Huerta: A Political Portrait*. Lincoln: University of Nebraska Press, 1972.

_____. *Mexican Rebel: Pascual Orozco and the Mexican Revolution, 1910–1915*. Lincoln: University of Nebraska Press, 1967.

O'Shaughnessy, Edith. *Diplomatic Days*. New York: Harper and Brothers Publishers, 1917.

Raat, William D. "The Diplomacy of Suppression: *Los Revoltosos*, Mexico and the United States, 1906–1911." *Hispanic American Historical Review* 56/4 (1976): 529–60.

Ross, Stanley R. *Francisco I. Madero, Apostle of Mexican Democracy*. New York: Columbia University Press, 1955.

Shadle, Stanley F. *Andrés Molina Enríquez: Mexican Land Reformer of the Revolutionary Era*. Tucson: University of Arizona Press, 1994.

Sherman, John W. "Revolution on Trial: The 1909 Tombstone Proceedings against Ricardo Flores Magón, Antonio Villarreal and Librado Rivera." *Journal of Arizona History* 32/2 (1991): 173–94.

Starr, Frederick. *Mexico and the United States: A Story of Revolution, Intervention and War*. Chicago, IL: The Bible House, 1914.

Truett, Samuel. *Fugitive Landscapes: The Forgotten History of the U.S.-Mexico Borderlands*. New Haven, CT: Yale University Press, 2006.

Turner, John Kenneth. *Barbarous Mexico*. Austin: University of Texas Press, 1969.

Wasserman, Mark. *The Mexican Revolution: A Brief History with Documents*. Boston, MA: Bedford/St. Martin's, 2012.

Wolfskill, George and Douglas W. Richard, eds. *Essays on the Mexican Revolution: Revisionist Views of the Leaders*. Austin: University of Texas Press, 1979.

Womack, Jr., John. *Zapata and the Mexican Revolution*. New York: Alfred A. Knopf, 1968.

CHAPTER 27

REVOLTS AND DICTATORSHIP OBSTRUCT THE DEMOCRATIC OVERTURE

REVOLTS AGAINST THE NEW GOVERNMENT

Emiliano Zapata was the first to pronounce against the new regime. In November 1911 the Zapatistas promulgated their famous Plan de Ayala, in which Zapata's goals were further developed and articulated by Otilio Montaño, a schoolteacher from Ayala. After withdrawing recognition of Madero and recognizing Chihuahuan Pascual Orozco as titular head of the rebellion, the plan spelled out its program of agrarian reform.

> The lands, woods, and water that the landlords, científicos, or bosses have usurped . . . will be immediately restored to the villages or citizens who hold the corresponding titles to them. . . . The usurpers who believe they have a right to those properties may present their claims to special courts that will be established on the triumph of the Revolution. Because the great majority of Mexicans own nothing more than the land they walk on, and are unable to improve their social condition in any way . . . because lands, woods, and water are monopolized in a few hands . . . one-third of these properties will be expropriated, with prior indemnification, so that the villages and citizens of Mexico may obtain ejidos, townsites, and fields.[1]

The armed conflict began immediately and quickly spread from Morelos to the neighboring states of Guerrero, Tlaxcala, Puebla, Mexico, and even into the Federal District. Madero's federal commanders could not contain the spread of the rebellion, as the Zapatista army continued to grow. By early 1912 Zapata had disrupted railroad and telegraph service and taken over a number of towns; he had repeatedly defeated the federals and had the government on the run.

At approximately the same time General Bernardo Reyes launched a second movement in the north in December 1911. Madero's fear that General Reyes still enjoyed a wide base of support among the army proved unfounded as few northern Mexicans wanted a return

---

1   The entire plan is quoted in Jesús Silva Herzog, *Breve historia de la revolución mexicana* vol. 1 (Mexico City, Mexico, 1962), 240–46.

to the past. Realizing that his sluggish revolution was not garnering sufficient support, on Christmas Day Reyes surrendered to a detachment of rurales. The commander of Mexico's third military zone, General Jerónimo Treviño, sent him first to prison in Monterrey and then had him transferred to the Prisión Militar de Santiago Tlaltelolco in Mexico City to await trial for treason.

At the end of the year a third revolt broke out against Madero in Chihuahua. Emilio Vásquez Gómez, believing that he and his brother Francisco had been unfairly treated in the last elections, launched his movement calling for Madero's ouster from office. At the end of January Madero was shocked to learn that the Vasquistas had captured Ciudad Juárez. The president knew full well the significance of this border city where his own revolt had triumphed. Realizing the popularity that Pascual Orozco enjoyed in the north, Madero commissioned the Chihuahua commander to take charge of the government campaigns. For the rank and file of the Vásquez Gómez army Orozco—not Madero—had been responsible for the overthrow of Díaz. Orozco had recruited the troops and led them in battle. He was the symbol of Chihuahua manhood and living proof that a poor, indifferently educated northerner could humble a professional army trained in the big city. The Vasquistas, not wishing to fight Orozco, agreed to meet with him. In the simple, folksy idiom of the north, Orozco made an impassioned speech calling for national unity and persuaded the rebel army to lay down arms without firing another shot.

A few months later the most serious antigovernment movement broke out in the north, by the same man who had just called for national unity and saved Madero from the Vasquista offensive. Pascual Orozco drew on a mixed base of rebel support, including many who called for social change. It also enjoyed the conservative financial support of the Terrazas clique in Chihuahua, who believed they could control the movement once it triumphed.

The Plan Orozquista, dated March 25, 1912, was the most comprehensive call for reform yet voiced from Mexican soil. It caustically attacked Madero for failing to abide by his own principles as set forth in the Plan de San Luis Potosí, citing state and local government corruption, nepotism, and favoritism. Not only had Madero's cousin, Rafael Hernández, been awarded the critical cabinet position of secretary of development but his uncle, Ernesto Madero, had been made secretary of the treasury; a relative by marriage, José González Salas, served as secretary of war; brother Gustavo Madero and four other members of the family were in the congress; brother Raúl Madero received a series of government-supported military assignments; another relative was on the Supreme Court; two were in the postal service; and yet another was an undersecretary in the cabinet. Government army uniforms came from cotton cloth manufactured in Madero mills, while ammunition was purchased from cousin José Aguilar's munitions plant in Monterrey.

The Plan Orozquista embraced social reform, drawing its inspiration from the Liberal Plan of 1906. It called for a ten-hour workday, restrictions on child labor, improved working conditions, higher wages, and the immediate suppression of the tiendas de raya. Anticipating the surge of economic nationalism that would sweep over Mexico in the next two decades, it proposed the immediate nationalization of the railroads. Agrarian reform also figured prominently. Persons who had resided on their land for twenty years were to be given title to it, while all lands illegally seized from the peasantry were to be returned. All lands owned by the government were to be distributed, and, most important, land owned by the hacendados, but not regularly cultivated, would be expropriated.

With alarming speed Orozco amassed a large army—some eight thousand strong—and began marching south to Mexico City. Capturing federally held towns along the way the rebels prepared themselves for a major showdown. The anticipated battle occurred at Rellano, close to the Chihuahua–Durango border. Madero's secretary of war, José González Salas, opted to command the government forces personally, only to be humiliated by Orozco's untrained rebels. As the federals retreated in disarray, González Salas, fearful of public rebuke, committed suicide. With panic growing in Mexico City, Madero named Victoriano Huerta to head a new government offensive which he launched in late May 1912. By sheer chance the artillery duel once again occurred on the fields of Rellano, but with different results on this occasion. Not only was Huerta a better field commander than his predecessor, but the Orozquistas were handicapped by lack of ammunition. Huerta pushed them back to the north and in the process temporarily saved the teetering Madero government.

Madero had no time for rejoicing for in early October 1912 a fifth serious rebellion broke out against him. This time Félix Díaz, the nephew of Don Porfirio, called an army together in Veracruz. Clearly counterrevolutionary in orientation, the Felicista movement comprised many disgruntled supporters of the former dictator. Félix Díaz appealed to the army and suggested that Madero had trampled on its honor by passing over many competent career officers and placing self-made revolutionary generals in charge of key garrisons. Only the troops stationed in Veracruz came to Díaz's support; other army units isolated the rebels in Veracruz, forcing them to surrender. A hastily conceived court-martial found Díaz guilty of treason and sentenced him to death, but a compassionate Madero commuted the sentence to imprisonment. Díaz was taken under arms to the capital and placed in the Federal District penitentiary. Madero's generosity was in no way reciprocated. Within two months Félix Díaz in one Mexico City prison had established contact with Bernardo Reyes in another, and the two were plotting to overthrow the government. This sixth rebellion would succeed, and Madero would lose not only his office but, a victim of his own ideals, his life as well.

THE OVERTHROW OF MADERO

Planned for several months, the military coup that began in Mexico City on February 9, 1913, drastically altered the course of the Mexican revolution. The capital had thus far been spared the ravages of the war that had engulfed much of the nation since November 1910. Now Mexico City residents would be given practical instruction in the full destructive significance of civil war. Early in the morning of February 9, General Manuel Mondragón, supported by several artillery regiments and military cadets, released Bernardo Reyes and Félix Díaz from their respective prisons and marched on the National Palace. Reyes, sporting a fancy military uniform and mounted on a white horse, led the charge and was felled by one of the first machine gun blasts. The rebel leadership then devolved on Félix Díaz. When loyal government troops repulsed the assault on the National Palace, Díaz led his troops westward across the city and installed his army in the Ciudadela, an old and well-fortified army arsenal. Madero, disregarding the advice of several confidants, named General Victoriano Huerta to command his troops. It proved to be a momentous decision.

For the next ten days—the Decena Trágica—Mexico City became a labyrinth of barricades, improvised fortifications, and trenches. Artillery fire exchanged between the rebels in the Ciudadela and the government troops in the National Palace destroyed buildings and set fires. As commercial establishments closed their doors for the duration, consumer goods became scarce and people panicked. Downtown streets were strewn with burning cars, runaway horses, and abandoned artillery pieces. Live electric wires dangled precariously from their poles. Looters broke store windows and carried off wares with complete impunity. On one occasion an artillery barrage opened a breach in the wall of the Belén prison and hundreds of inmates scurried through the opening to freedom. A few surveyed the chaos outside and decided to remain.

With neither side able to gain a clear military advantage, civilian casualties mounted into the thousands and bodies began to bloat in the streets. Foreign residents sought the sanctuary of embassies, but not all made it in time. Most traffic came to a halt as only ambulances, military vehicles, and diplomatic automobiles, identified by special flags, moved on the streets. On February 17, after nine days of constant fighting, Madero summoned Huerta and asked when the fighting could be expected to cease. Huerta assured him that peace would be restored to the beleaguered city the following day. The residents of the capital were awakened early on the morning of February 18 by the sounds of artillery and machine gun fire, just as they had been for the previous nine days. But in the afternoon the clamor of war stopped. Huerta had decided to change sides. He withdrew recognition of the federal government and dispatched General Aureliano Blanquet to the National Palace to arrest the president. Blanquet encountered Madero in one of the patios and, with revolver in hand, proclaimed, "You are my prisoner, Mr. President." Madero retorted, "You are a traitor." But Blanquet simply reaffirmed, "You are my prisoner."[2] Within a half-hour Vice President Pino Suárez, Madero's brother Gustavo, and most of the cabinet had been arrested as well.

The agreement according to which Huerta joined the rebels is known as the Pact of the Embassy because the final negotiations were conducted under the aegis of the American ambassador in Mexico City, Henry Lane Wilson. A typical diplomat of the age of dollar diplomacy, Wilson saw his role as protector of US business interests. Throughout the Madero presidency he had meddled shamelessly in Mexico's internal affairs, and during the Decena Trágica he played an active part in charting the course of events. The German ambassador to Mexico, Admiral Paul von Hintz, recorded the daily events of the 1912–1914 period, along with the activities of Wilson and other schemers. On one occasion, in concert with the British, German, and Spanish ministers, the American ambassador even demanded Madero's resignation, alleging as his reason the tremendous damage to foreign property in Mexico City. After being rebuffed by the Mexican president, Wilson changed his tactics and worked actively to bring Huerta and Díaz to an accord. On the evening of February 18 the two generals met with Wilson at the American embassy and hammered out the pact that justified the coup and made Victoriano Huerta provisional president.

---

2   Quoted in Michael C. Meyer, *Huerta: A Political Portrait* (Lincoln, NE, 1972), 57.

A federal machine gun nest awaits the rebel advance.

In the city of Mexico, at nine-thirty in the evening on February 18, 1913, General Félix Díaz and Victoriano Huerta met in conference. . . . General Huerta stated that because of the un-bearable situation created by the government of Mr. Madero, he had, in order to prevent the further shedding of blood and to safeguard national unity, placed the said Madero, several members of his cabinet, and various other persons under arrest. . . . General Díaz stated that his only reason for raising the standard of revolt was a desire on his part to protect the national welfare, and in that light he was ready to make any sacrifice that would prove beneficial to the country. . . . From this time forward the former chief executive is not to be recognized. The elements represented by Generals Díaz and Huerta are united in opposing all efforts to restore him to power. . . . Generals Díaz and Huerta will do all in their power to enable the latter to assume . . . the provisional presidency.[3]

Wishing to cloak his assumption of power in some semblance of legality, Huerta first secured the official resignations of Madero and Pino Suárez and then convened a special evening session of the congress. The resignations were accepted by the legislative body with only five dissenting votes, and the presidency legally passed to the next in line, Secretary of Foreign Relations Pedro Lascuráin. Sworn into office at 10:24 P.M., Lascuráin immediately appointed General Huerta as secretary of interior and at 11:20 P.M. submitted his own resignation. The Constitution of 1857 provided that in the absence of a president, a vice-president, and a secretary of foreign relations, the office passed to the secretary of interior. Huerta, clad in a

---

3   The Pact of the Embassy has been translated and included in its entirety in ibid., 235–36.

formal black tuxedo, was sworn into office shortly before midnight. Madero-style democracy had ended in derision as Mexico had its third president in one day.

Another political charade followed soon after. On the evening of February 21, 1913, Francisco Madero and José María Pino Suárez were transferred from the National Palace, where they had been held prisoners since the day of their arrest, to the Federal District penitentiary. The capital city newspapers the following day blared an improbable tale. A group of Madero's supporters attacked the convoy escorting the prisoners, attempted to free them, and during the ensuing melee both the former president and vice president were killed. Virtually no one believed this official version, but few Mexicans knew what really happened. Madero and Pino Suárez had been taken to the penitentiary under the guard of Francisco Cárdenas, a major in the rurales. When the convoy reached the prison, Cárdenas ordered the captives out of the cars and, by prearranged signal, the spotlights high on the wall were turned off. The hapless men were then shot point-blank. To this day, no one has been able to ascertain who ordered the assassinations, although suspicion fell on Huerta.

HUERTA

Victoriano Huerta was born of a Huichol Indian mother and a mestizo father in a small Jalisco village. Attending a poor local school run by the parish priest, he learned to read and write and showed some natural talent for science and mathematics. As a teenager he served as an aide to a career general who used his influence in Mexico City to have Huerta accepted at the National Military Academy. Despite his mediocre educational background, he did well as a cadet and received his commission in 1876 as a second lieutenant assigned to the army corps of engineers.

Huerta's prerevolutionary career coincided almost exactly with the Díaz dictatorship, and he became an effective agent of Don Porfirio's system of enforced peace. During the thirty-four-year Porfiriato, Huerta fought in the north against the Yaqui, in the south against the Maya, and in the central part of the country against other Mexicans unhappy with the autocratic regime. Encountering much success on the field of battle, he rose rapidly in the ranks and by the turn of the century became a brigadier-general. National prominence and some notoriety engulfed him for the first time in the summer of 1911 when interim President León de la Barra dispatched him to Morelos to enforce the demobilization of the Zapatista troops.

When Bernardo Reyes and Félix Díaz planned the military coup of February 1913, their emissaries approached Huerta and solicited his support. He refused the invitation, however, not out of loyalty to the Madero administration but rather because he wanted the leadership for himself. When Bernardo Reyes died during the first major encounter, the situation changed. Huerta dallied for a week and, having determined that he would be able to control Félix Díaz, made his decision to change sides. Within a few days federal generals and state governors began to pledge support for the new regime. A group of talented statesmen and intellectuals accepted cabinet portfolios. Sanitation workers started to scour the bloodstained streets of the capital and to attack a 10-day backlog of garbage. Red Cross units tried to identify hundreds of decaying corpses, and electricians repaired wires dangling dangerously from their poles. Restoring order, however, did not proceed well everywhere.

REBELLION AND MILITARIZATION

The first genuinely ominous sign came from the northeast where Coahuila governor Venustiano Carranza, an ardent Madero supporter, announced his decision not to recognize the new regime. Carranza issued a circular telegram to other state governors exhorting them to follow his good example. Within a few weeks he found support in Chihuahua and Sonora. Pancho Villa assumed military leadership of the anti-Huerta movement in Chihuahua, while Alvaro Obregón, a man of considerable military talent, took charge of the antigovernment operations in neighboring Sonora. The alliance of the northern revolutionaries, and their formal pronouncement of defection, was sealed in late March when representatives from the three states affixed their signatures to the Plan de Guadalupe. After withdrawing recognition of the Huerta government, the plan named Venustiano Carranza as "First Chief" of the Constitutionalist Army and provided that he, or someone designated by him, would occupy the interim presidency upon Huerta's defeat. An exclusively political document, the plan embodied no program of social reform.

In southern Mexico Huerta encountered an implacable enemy of a different sort. Emiliano Zapata angrily rejected Huerta's invitation to pledge support of the government. In fact, the southern rebel arrested and subsequently executed the federal peace commissioners sent to garner his allegiance. Zapata, declared himself in rebellion because he saw no hope that the federal government under Huerta would begin to restore the village lands in Morelos. Not trusting the Constitutionalist dedication to agrarian reform either, Zapata never allied himself with the anti-Huerta movement in the north. But by forcing the government to divert some of its war effort from the north to the south, Zapata placed additional military pressure on the new regime.

Facing rebellion in the north and in Morelos, Huerta announced brazenly to the congress that he would reestablish peace with the federal army of fifty thousand troops, at any cost. Nonetheless, in March and April the Constitutionalists scored impressive victories in Sonora and Chihuahua, while in the south Emiliano Zapata had done the same. The psychology of the civil war changed drastically in May when First Chief Carranza, in a singularly intemperate decree, announced that federal soldiers who fell into rebel hands would be executed summarily. Huerta responded that he would militarize Mexico to the teeth.

Factories and stores not related to the war effort were required to close on Sundays so that civilian employees could be given military training. Railroads left civilian passengers and freight standing in the stations so that military personnel and hardware could be shipped to where it was needed. The National Arms Factory, the National Artillery Workshops, and the National Power Factory received new equipment to increase their productive capacities. Scarcely a week passed without a showy military parade or public display of the latest military equipment, along with Huerta sporting his favorite dress uniforms replete with ribbons covering the left side of his jacket and medals draped from his neck. In the late summer of 1913 school after school found its governing regulations changed to provide for the mandatory wearing of military uniforms. Training in the military arts and sciences was added to the curricula. Most importantly, the president decreed constant increases in the size of the federal army—from fifty thousand to one hundred thousand to two hundred thousand and finally to a two hundred fifty thousand, or about twelve times the number of troops available to Porfirio Díaz when the revolution broke out.

Modern technology is brought to warfare. In one of the first military uses of aircraft, Huerta employed eighty-horsepower planes similar to these in reconnaissance and bombing raids against the Villistas in the north.

When small pay increases failed to attract enlistees in large numbers, Huerta fell back on a time-honored tradition—the leva, a system of forced conscription directed exclusively at the indigent masses. Thousands of them were picked up off the streets of the barrios in the large cities and from the surrounding countryside and sent into the field. The crowds emerging from a bullfight or staggering out of a cantina closing its doors for the night were favorite targets, as were criminals in jail for minor offenses. Not surprisingly, the leva caused a steady decline in the quality of the federal army. The lack of adequate training meant no *esprit de corps*, no discipline, and tremendously high desertion rates. In the fall of 1913, entire units of new recruits to turned themselves and their equipment over to the enemy without firing a single shot.

The civil war took a tremendous toll in1913 and 1914. The population of a village could double to triple overnight as a large military unit moved in to camp. Because there was no advance notice, a week's stay could deplete stores of food, supplies, and other basic necessities, thus aggravating the obscenities of war. When the troops withdrew, they left villages on the verge of starvation. The receipts a local merchant might receive as the troops emptied his store were scarcely worth the paper they were hastily scrawled on.

With his military position deteriorating, Huerta became increasingly impetuous, egotistical, and dictatorial. Recognizing the potential value of a controlled press, Huerta initiated an extensive policy of censorship, removing, exiling, and jailing editors who adopted hostile attitudes. A vast network of secret agents and spies reported on the activities of real and potential enemies, and by the fall of 1913 the jail cells in Mexico City and many of the state capitals bulged with political prisoners. The most reprehensible facet of the Huerta dictatorship was its unbridled use of political assassination. After the senseless slaying of Madero and Pino Suárez, the regime targeted Maderista governor Abraham González and many army officers, congressmen, professional men, and petty bureaucrats who manifested their discontent.

In the most celebrated case of all, Senator Belisario Domínguez from Chiapas, an outspoken critic of the regime, ignored the good counsel of friends in the senate, and asked for the floor to read a prepared statement.

> Peace, cost what it may, Mr. Victoriano Huerta had said. Fellow Senators, have you studied the terrible meaning of those words . . . ? The national assembly has the duty of deposing Mr. Victoriano Huerta from the presidency. He is the one against whom our brothers in the north protest with so much reason. . . . You will tell me, gentlemen, that the attempt

is dangerous; for Mr. Victoriano Huerta is a bloody and ferocious soldier who assassinates without hesitation anyone who is an obstacle to his wishes; this does not matter gentlemen! The country exacts from you the fulfillment of a duty, even with risk, indeed the assurance, that you are to lose your lives.[4]

Two weeks later Belisario Domínguez died from an assassin's bullet. The morally outraged senate passed a resolution requesting full information from the president and resolving to remain in permanent session. Two days later Huerta responded by dissolving both houses of the legislature and arresting the majority of the congressmen.

ECONOMIC PROBLEMS AND FOREIGN RELATIONS

The war Huerta was fighting against the Constitutionalists in the north and the Zapatistas in the south could not be supported by an empty treasury. By relying on the leva to fill the ranks of the federal army, Huerta depleted the work force in both the cities and the countryside. With no pickers, cotton rotted in the fields, coffee beans fell off the trees, and sugarcane remained unharvested on the large plantations. Mines closed operations; cattlemen in the north lost thousands of head to the rebels; and fruit growers, realizing their perishable products were extremely vulnerable to transportation delays, cut back production. As food and manufactured goods became scarce, a black market began to flourish in the larger cities, and the entire economic structure of the country suffered. In response, the government expediently issued paper money without adequate hard reserves to back it up. The new paper issue depreciated almost as soon as it rolled off the press. Not to be outdone, the Constitutionalists and the Zapatistas issued their own currency, as did a number of states and large mining and industrial concerns. Late in 1913 at least twenty-five different kinds of paper currency circulated, making it impossible to ascertain fluctuating exchange rates. Counterfeiters had a field day while bankers and tax collectors became paralyzed.

In addition to his military and economic problems, Huerta faced one other dilemma. The United States not only refused to recognize his regime but adopted a frankly hostile attitude toward him. Woodrow Wilson came to the US presidency almost simultaneously with Victoriano Huerta's rise to power. While the American ambassador to Mexico, Henry Lane Wilson, urged recognition, President Wilson and his newly appointed secretary of state, William Jennings Bryan, both with an abiding faith in the concept of the democratic state, refused. To the White House, Huerta, who came to power by forcefully ejecting the previous regime, represented all that was wrong with Latin America. Unprepared by temperament or training to understand the complexities of the Mexican revolution, President Wilson decided to apply his own standards of political ethics to the situation.

Demonstrating little faith in the reports received from Ambassador Wilson, the president and the secretary of state decided to dispatch special agents to Mexico to report on the nature of the growing conflict. They first sent William Bayard Hale. Speaking no Spanish, Hale relied heavily on the US business community for his information, but he managed

---

4   Quoted in Ibid., 137–38.

Together with several other kinds of scrip, this twenty-peso note from Chihuahua state was used by the Constitutionalists in late 1913 and early 1914.

interviews with several high-level Mexican officials as well. Although most informants favored early recognition of the regime, Hale capitulated to President Wilson's sense of moral rectitude, characterizing Huerta as "an ape-like man, of almost pure Indian blood. He may be said to subsist on alcohol. Drunk or only half drunk (he is never sober) he never loses a certain shrewdness."[5] By playing into President Wilson's moral diplomacy, Hale sealed the fate of Ambassador Wilson who was recalled and replaced by John Lind, a former governor of Minnesota and a longtime friend of Secretary Bryan.

If there was ever any hope for a reconciliation between the United States and Mexico in the late summer and fall of 1913, Lind's reports to Washington eliminated it. Speaking no more Spanish than Hale and being even less conversant with Mexican politics, his dispatches were haughty, bellicose, inaccurate, and often laden with anti-Catholic and anti-Indian slurs. His characterization of the Mexican cabinet ("a worse pack of wolves never infested any community") reveals more about Lind than about Huerta's advisers. Given President Wilson's insistence that Huerta had to go, there were only two genuine avenues open: Wilson could intervene militarily in Mexico, or he could intervene indirectly by channeling US aid to the Constitutionalists in the north. He chose the second alternative first, and, when that did not work, he opted for military intervention.

DOMESTIC REFORMS

Amazingly, despite the military, economic, and diplomatic pressures the regime faced, Huerta and his advisers found some time for domestic programs. The enemies of the dictatorship labeled them counterrevolutionary, an attempt to reincarnate the age of Díaz. But examination of the regime's social programs reveals that they were anything but that. While Porfirio Díaz had never allocated over 7.2 percent of his budget for education and Madero had raised the percentage slightly to 7.8 percent, Huerta projected a 9.9 percent

---

5   Quoted in Larry D. Hill, *Emissaries to a Revolution: Woodrow Wilson's Executive Agents in Mexico* (Baton Rouge, LA, 1973), 31.

allocation for educational services. Still inadequate, Huerta did manage the construction of one hundred thirty-one new rural schools with seats for some ten thousand new students. Secretary of Education Nemesio García Naranjo initiated a new curriculum at the National Preparatory School. Breaking sharply with the positivist tradition of Gabino Barreda, García Naranjo made more room for the study of literature, history, and philosophy. He did not abandon the sciences but argued persuasively that the other branches of learning should not be sacrificed to them. By creating a reasonable balance between the arts and the sciences, the secretary struck an important first blow at the científico philosophy of education.

The anticientífico posture of the regime manifested itself in Indian policy as well. Administration spokesman Jorge Vera Estañol early championed *indigenismo* arguing that national unity was impossible when millions of Indians were estranged from the rest of the population by language, customs, diet, and life expectancy. He advocated, without sufficient funding, a rural education program intended to bring the Indian into the mainstream of national life.

The regime initiated a modest agrarian reform program by distributing free seed to anyone who asked for it and by expanding the activities of the agricultural school in Mexico City. Of greater practical significance Huerta authorized the restoration of 78 ejidos to the Yaqui and Mayo Indians of Sonora. He instructed Eduardo Tamariz, Mexico's secretary of agriculture, to begin studying the problem of land redistribution. Tamariz could find nothing in the Constitution of 1857 that authorized the expropriation of land, so he found his solution in the taxation provisions of the constitution. If taxes were increased on the large haciendas, the land would be less valuable for speculative purposes and hacendados would have to consider sale. Without congressional authorization, Huerta went ahead on his own and decreed an increase in land taxes.

In the areas of labor, church policy, and foreign relations the Huerta regime also departed from the models of the Porfiriato. Not a social revolution, Huerta's programs were not counterrevolutionary either, according to Huerta's principal biographer, Michael Meyer. While it is true that Huerta's abuse of political power can justifiably be likened to Don Porfirio's authoritarianism, nevertheless, in the larger social sense both Huerta and his advisers recognized that the days of Díaz had passed

US INTERVENTION AND THE FALL OF HUERTA

By the spring of 1914 Huerta, losing his wars on both the military and the economic fronts, faced a steadily deteriorating relationship with the United States. Early in 1914 President Wilson beefed up the American fleet stationed off Mexican waters. In April a seemingly insignificant event augured the most serious US-Mexico dispute since the war of the mid-nineteenth century. Captain Ralph T. Earle of the USS Dolphin, stationed off the coast of Tampico, ordered a small landing party to go ashore, ostensibly for supplies. Still in government hands, Tampico had been attacked by Constitutionalists several days before and the federal forces awaited a more concerted assault. When US sailors wandered into a restricted dock area, the government ordered their arrest on the spot.

Within an hour orders came for the sailors' release, accompanied by an official apology. But Rear Admiral Henry T. Mayo, commander of the naval forces off Tampico, considered the apology insufficient and demanded more. Since the boat carrying the sailors to shore allegedly flew the American flag, Mayo insisted that the Mexican government hoist the American flag at some prominent place on shore and present a twenty-one-gun salute to it. President Wilson considered the demands reasonable and prepared himself to make the incident a *casus belli* should Huerta not publicly recant in exactly the manner prescribed. Huerta's secretary of foreign relations insisted that the small landing craft had not carried the flag but agreed to the salute on the condition that the United States return the salute to the Mexican flag. The White House considered the rejoinder impertinent, for both President Wilson and Secretary of State Bryan realized that a US salute to the Mexican flag could be considered tantamount to recognizing the Huerta regime.

With neither side knowing exactly what to do next, the stalemate broke when the US consul in Veracruz wired Washington that a German ship, the Ypiranga, would arrive in that port on April 21 with a large shipment of arms for Huerta. President Wilson gave immediate orders for a naval occupation of Veracruz. The marines took the city but Mexican casualties mounted into the hundreds, including many noncombatants of both sexes. An indignant public outcry arose from Mexico City. Congressmen denounced the United States, and mobs looted American-owned businesses, tore down the statue of George Washington, and threatened tourists. Mexican newspapers urged retaliation against the "Pigs of Yanquilandia." In Monterrey the US flag was ripped from the consulate and burned on the spot. But in the capital, the Stars and Stripes flag was tied to the tail of a donkey and used to sweep clean the streets of the central plaza.

President Wilson's attempt to rid Mexico of a dictator almost backfired. Venustiano Carranza and the majority of his Constitutionalists, the supposed beneficiaries of the Veracruz intervention, expressed their strong disapproval of the blatant violation of Mexican sovereignty. Huerta, however, could not capitalize upon their displeasure, and his call for all Mexicans to lay aside internal differences and present a united front went unheeded. Even the initial indignation expressed in Mexico City soon dissipated as the US troops, despite rumors to the contrary, did not march on Mexico City as they had in 1847.

As Huerta called in his troops to make a show of force against the Americans, the Constitutionalists in the north and the Zapatistas in the south quickly moved into the military vacuums. By the early summer, with Pancho Villa's capture of Zacatecas, Huerta's military position had become untenable. The continued occupation of Veracruz meant that revenues from the customhouse were stopped before they reached the federal treasury. Recognizing that the diplomatic, economic, and military pressures had all conspired to his disadvantage, Huerta resigned on July 8, 1914. In his statement of resignation he placed the prime responsibility for what had happened to Mexico on the Puritan who resided in the White House.

Woodrow Wilson bears much of the responsibility for Huerta's overthrow. He meddled shamelessly in Mexico's internal affairs and, without the semblance of a threat to US security, shed innocent Mexican blood to effectuate the foreign policy objectives he deemed opportune. Nonetheless, Wilson cannot be held accountable for the larger calamity that had struck the Mexican nation. Not all Mexico's domestic ills were orphans of US bullets as Mexicans had not yet agreed on the meaning of their revolution. Francisco Madero's well-meaning but ineffectual experiment with democracy had failed when he had urged caution and moderation on the burning social issues of the day. Huerta's dictatorship failed as well. While he was not unwilling to give the social reformers the chance to institute change, many Mexicans could no longer bring themselves to accommodate another brutal dictatorship

US Navy "bluejackets" engage Mexican defenders at Veracruz in April 1914.

that exalted order at the expense of liberty. The number of options still open were gradually being reduced, but the better day had not yet dawned.

RECOMMENDED FOR FURTHER STUDY

Blaisdell, Lowell L. "Henry Lane Wilson and the Overthrow of Madero." *Southwestern Social Science Quarterly* 43/2 (1962): 126–35.

Buchenau, Jürgen, and William Beezley, eds. *State Governors in the Mexican Revolution, 1910–1952: Portraits in Conflict, Courage, and Corruption.* Lanham, MD: Rowman & Littlefield, 2009.

Calvert, Peter. *The Mexican Revolution, 1910–1914: The Diplomacy of the Anglo-American Conflict.* New York: Cambridge University Press, 1968.

Cumberland, Charles C. *Mexican Revolution: The Constitutionalist Years.* Austin: University of Texas Press, 1972.

Grieb, Kenneth J. *The United States and Huerta.* Lincoln: University of Nebraska Press, 1969.

Harris III, Charles H., and Louis R. Sadler. *The Texas Rangers and the Mexican Revolution.* Albuquerque: University of New Mexico Press, 2004.

Hill, Larry D. *Emissaries to a Revolution: Woodrow Wilson's Executive Agents in Mexico.* Baton Rouge: Louisiana State University Press, 1973.

Katz, Friedrich. *The Life and Times of Pancho Villa.* Stanford, CA: Stanford University Press, 1998.

Knight, Alan. *The Mexican Revolution.* Vol. 2: *Counter Revolution and Reconstruction.* New York: Cambridge University Press, 1986.

Meyer, Michael C. "The Arms of the *Ypiranga.*" *Hispanic American Historical Review* 50/3 (1970): 543–56.

_____. *Huerta: A Political Portrait.* Lincoln: University of Nebraska Press, 1972.

Quirk, Robert E. *An Affair of Honor: Woodrow Wilson and the Occupation of Veracruz.* New York: Norton, 1967.

Schuler, Freidrich E., ed. *Murder and Counterrevolution in Mexico: The Eyewitness Account of German Ambassador Paul von Hintze, 1912–1914.* Lincoln: University of Nebraska Press, 2015.

Vanderwood, Paul J. "The Picture Postcard as Historical Evidence: Veracruz: 1914." *The Americas* 45/2 (1988): 201–26.

Wilson, Henry Lane. *Diplomatic Episodes in Mexico, Belgium, and Chile.* Garden City, NY: Doubleday Page, 1927.

CHAPTER 28

THE ILLUSORY QUEST FOR A BETTER WAY

THE CONVENTION OF AGUASCALIENTES AND NEAR ANARCHY

The years following Victoriano Huerta's ouster count as the most chaotic in Mexican revolutionary history as the quarrels among erstwhile allies began. In 1914 First Chief Venustiano Carranza allowed that a convention should be held to bring revolutionary factions together and to determine who should be the provisional president of Mexico until national elections could be scheduled. The Constitutionalist leadership selected the town of Aguascalientes in neutral territory to host the convention and extended invitations to all the important revolutionary groups, the number of delegates apportioned according to how many troops had been deployed in the recent anti-Huerta campaigns.

The military delegates, in a wide array of uniforms and most carrying rifles with full cartridge belts, began to arrive in Aguascalientes in early October. At one of the early sessions Alvaro Obregón, the first chief's official spokesman, presented the convention with a Mexican flag inscribed with the words, "Military Convention of Aguascalientes." Each delegate placed his signature on the flag and swore allegiance to this assembly. The impressive display of confraternity did not last for long, however. When the Zapatista delegation arrived, a few days late, its leader, Paulino Martínez, asked to speak. In a deliberate affront to Carranza and Obregón, he recognized Villa and Zapata as the genuine leaders of the revolution and argued that "effective suffrage and no-reelection" had no meaning for the vast majority of Mexicans. The revolution had been fought for land and liberty. The speech presaged a serious schism in the convention between Villistas and Zapatistas, on the one hand, and Carrancistas and Obregonistas, on the other. Rather than sectarian squabbles, the debates reflected fundamental differences on the direction the revolution should take.

The vice chair of the Zapatista delegation, Antonio Díaz Soto y Gama, spoke next. A thirty-year-old socialist and a polished orator, he delineated future lines of combat.

I come here not to attack anyone but to evoke patriotism and to stimulate shame. I come to excite the honor of all of the delegates to this assembly. . . . Perhaps it is necessary to invoke respectable symbols [gesturing to the Convention flag], but I fear that the essence of patriotism does not lie in the symbols, which are, after all, quite similar to the farces of the church. . . . I believe that our word of honor is more valuable than all of the signatures stamped on this flag. In the last analysis this flag represents nothing more than the triumph of the clerical reaction championed by Iturbide. I will never sign this flag. . . . That which we called Independence was not independence for the Indian, but independence for the criollo, for the heirs of the conquerors who continue infamously to abuse and cheat the oppressed Indian.[1]

Soto y Gama's speech provoked continuous interruptions from supporters and foes. Some of the delegates even pointed pistols in his direction. The acrimony occasioned by the impassioned speech foretold the basic division between supporters of the politically oriented plans of San Luis Potosí and Guadalupe and the agrarian Plan de Ayala.

When, against Carranza's wishes, the convention chose Eulalio Gutiérrez as provisional president of Mexico, the first chief, disavowed the action and, from Mexico City, ordered his followers to withdraw. Some, including Alvaro Obregón, obeyed, while others made common cause with the Zapatistas and Villistas. As Villa's troops marched on the capital to install Gutiérrez in the presidency, civil war again loomed large. Carranza withdrew his Constitutionalist government to Veracruz. The US government had agreed to pull out its troops just in time for Carranza to make the gulf port his provisional capital.

MULTIPLE CIVIL WARS

In early December 1914 Carranza's two principal antagonists, Pancho Villa, "the Centaur of the North," and Emiliano Zapata, "the Attila of the South," staged a dramatic meeting at Xochimilco on the outskirts of Mexico City. While their followers had knotted the bonds of intellectual camaraderie at the convention, the two leaders had never before met. The historian Robert Quirk has recreated the encounter from eyewitness accounts.

Villa and Zapata were a study in contrasts. Villa was tall and robust, weighing at least 180 pounds, with a florid complexion. He wore a tropical helmet after the English style. . . . Zapata, in his physiognomy, was much more the Indian of the two. His skin was very dark, and in comparison with Villa's his face was thin with high cheek bones. He wore an immense sombrero, which at times hid his eyes. . . .

The conference began haltingly . . . both were men of action and verbal intercourse left them uneasy. . . . But then the conversation touched on Venustiano Carranza and suddenly, like tinder, burst aflame. They poured out in a torrent of volubility their mutual hatred for the First Chief. Villa pronounced his opinion of the middle class revolutionaries who followed Carranza: "Those are men who have always slept on soft pillows. How could they

---

1   Quoted in Isidro Fabela, ed., *Documentos históricos de la revolución mexicana*, vol. 23 (Mexico City, Mexico, 1960-73), 181-82.

Pancho Villa (*left*) and Emiliano Zapata (*right*) meet in Mexico City. The camaraderie was more apparent than real.

ever be friends of the people, who have spent their whole lives in nothing but suffering?" Zapata concurred: "On the contrary, they have always been the scourge of the people. . . . Those *cabrones!* As soon as they see a little chance, well, they want to take advantage of it and line their own pockets! Well, to hell with them!"[2]

These two great popular heroes of the revolution could not have been more different in terms of temperament. Zapata was reserved and cautious but resolute, steadfast, and fair in carrying out his promises, while the more physically dominant and intemperate Villa embodied a frontier code of fearlessness, honor, violence, and vengeance in pursuing his objectives. Yet each man instinctively projected confidence, empathy, and commitment to the aspirations of his followers in ways that inspired the fiercest loyalty. Zapata more single-mindedly pursued agrarian reform, and Villa represented a broader spectrum of social groups and interests. While both shared a profound disdain for Carranza, their alliance produced no military cooperation against Carranza. The early months of 1915 saw the Mexican Revolution degenerating into unmitigated anarchy. Civil wars ravaged many states. Civilian casualties mounted as atrocities were committed on all sides.

---

2   Robert E. Quirk, *The Mexican Revolution, 1914-1915: The Convention of Aguascalientes* (New York, NY, 1963), 135-38.

    With his own conventionist coalition falling apart as well, provisional President Gutiér-
rez abandoned Mexico City and Obregón took the capital unopposed. Gutiérrez established
a new government in Nuevo León; Carranza, claiming national executive control as first
chief, continued to govern from Veracruz; the Zapatistas supported Roque González Garza as
president, while Pancho Villa ruled from Chihuahua. None of the governments recognized
the paper money, coinage, or legal contracts of the others.

    The muddied political waters cleared somewhat in the most famous military engagement
of the revolution—the battle of Celaya—in April 1915. While Pancho Villa prepared to put
his slightly tarnished record of military victories on the line, Alvaro Obregón had immersed
himself in the battle reports from war-torn Europe. He had learned how to blunt a concerted
cavalry charge by encircling carefully laid out defensive positions with rolls of barbed wire. In
early April, when Villa attacked with a force estimated at twenty-five thousand men, Obregón
had planned his defenses with consummate skill. Villa launched a furious cavalry charge,
Obregón's well-placed artillery and machine guns began cutting the attackers to pieces. Villa
was forced to retreat but in the middle of the month tried again to dislodge Obregón's forces.
The second Villista offensive suffered even greater disaster. Villa threw his cavalry against
the barbed-wire entrenchments only to see wave after wave massacred. When it all ended,
thousands of bodies were strewn across the fields of Celaya and impaled on the barbed wire.
Obregón's official report listed over four thousand Villistas dead, five thousand wounded,
and six thousand taken prisoner. He calculated his own losses at 138 dead and 227 wounded.

Pancho Villa (1878-1923). Never an "armchair general," Villa often led his troops into battle. His famous Division of the North, numbering some fifty thousand men, was the largest revolutionary force ever amassed in
America.

The battle of Celaya did not immediately destroy Villa's capacity to make war, but it did presage his ultimate defeat. By the summer and fall of 1915 First Chief Carranza had gained the upper hand as both the Villistas in the north and the Zapatistas in the south found themselves increasingly isolated and without national support. From the United States, President Wilson threw official support behind the Constitutionalists. He extended diplomatic recognition to the Carranza regime in October infuriating Pancho Villa, who had courted the United States for years. Determined not to turn the other cheek, he began to take his vengeance on private US civilians.

The first serious incident occurred at Santa Isabel (today General Trías), Chihuahua. On January 9, 1916, at El Paso, Texas, a group of US mining engineers and technicians from the Cusi Mining Company boarded a train for Mexico. Assured of a safe conduct from the Constitutionalists, they set out to reopen the Cusihuiriachic silver mine. At the hamlet of Santa Isabel, a band of Villistas stopped the train and boarded the car carrying the Americans. The attackers dragged them off and murdered fifteen on the spot.

An even more controversial incident occurred exactly two months later. Early in the morning of March 9, 1916, Villa dispatched 485 men across the border from Palomas, Chihuahua, and attacked the dreary, sun-baked adobe town of Columbus, New Mexico, where Villa had been buying guns and ammunition. Apparently his retailers had not delivered the last shipment paid for by Villistas. Villa's motive has been much debated by historians; certainly retaliation for the arms swindle is the simple answer. But others have seen it as an attempt to expose Carranza as having sold out to the United States in return for diplomatic recognition. If the incident prompted a US invasion and Carranza did nothing, he could be revealed as having forfeited Mexican sovereignty.

One of the first shots stopped the large clock in the railroad station at 4:11 A.M. For the next two hours the Villistas terrorized the town's four hundred inhabitants. Shouting *¡Viva Villa!* and *¡Muerte a los Gringos!*, they shot, burned, and looted. Troopers from the US Thirteenth Cavalry succeeded in driving them off by daybreak, but eighteen Americans had been killed, many were wounded, and the town was burned beyond recognition.

Immediate clamor for US intervention first came from Senator Albert Bacon Fall of New Mexico who called for a five hundred thousand men to occupy all of Mexico. President Wilson rebuffed the request, but dispatched a small punitive expedition under the command of General John J. Pershing, an army man who years before had chased the Apache chief, Geronimo, through the same northern Mexican desert. It took a week for Pershing to organize his expedition, and that was more than enough time for Villa to cover his tracks. Approximately six thousand US army troops wandered hot and thirsty through the rough terrain in a futile effort to locate their prey. Little, if any, help could be expected from the rural Mexicans, and as the Americans entered small pueblos they were often greeted with shouts of *¡Viva Mexico, Viva Villa!* As the expedition cut south into Mexico, First Chief Carranza ordered Pershing to withdraw. Not yet ready to admit defeat, Pershing engaged a group of Carrancista troops ordered to forestall his southward thrust. When hostilities began he received orders to withdraw gradually to the north, but the expedition did not leave Mexico until January 1917. By that time the United States had spent $130 million in its unsuccessful attempt to catch and punish the Columbus raiders.

General Pershing's cavalry expedition into northern Mexico may have hardened his troops for the upcoming war in Europe, but his effort to capture Pancho Villa was in vain.

THE CONSTITUTION OF 1917

The failure of the Pershing punitive expedition notwithstanding, Villa got progressively weaker and Carranza gradually consolidated his position in Mexico City. The first chief's advisers convinced him that the time had come to give some institutional basis to the revolution that had engulfed the nation for almost six years. In an attempt to legitimize the revolution he reluctantly agreed to convoke a congress to meet in Querétaro for the purpose of drawing up a new constitution. Remembering how he had lost control of the Convention of Aguascalientes, he vowed not to repeat the error in Querétaro. No individual or group who had opposed the Constitutionalist movement would be eligible to participate; thus, no Huertistas, Villistas, or Zapatistas were included among the delegates when the first session convened in November 1916. First Chief Carranza quickly learned that the Constitutionalists themselves were scarcely in ideological agreement.

The delegates at Querétaro represented a new breed of Mexican politician and, in a sense, constituted a new social elite. Unlike the Convention of Aguascalientes, military men constituted only 30 percent of the delegates. Over half had university educations and professional titles. The large majority were young and middle class; because they had been denied meaningful participation during the Porfiriato, many were politically ambitious.

With every intention of controlling the proceedings, Carranza submitted to the Querétaro Congress a draft of a new constitution that differed little from the Constitution of 1857, although it contained a series of sections strengthening executive control.

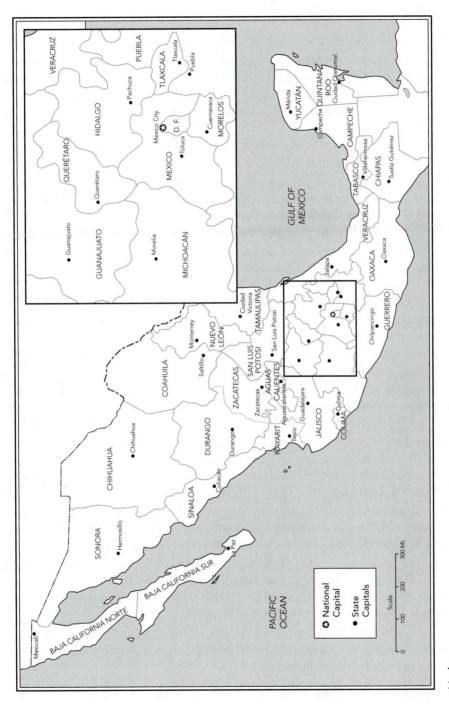

Mexico

It occasioned an inevitable split in the congress between those moderates who supported Carranza and the radicals (called "Jacobins" by their opponents) who desired rapid social reform.

The debates in Querétaro, focusing on everything from temperance to prison reform, were acrimonious. After the first few votes had been taken, it was clear that the radicals held the majority. Led by thirty-two-year-old Francisco Múgica, they succeeded in pushing through a number of anticlerical provisions and three extremely significant articles that came to embody the fundamental orientation the revolution was to assume in the 1920s and 1930s.

Intense anticlericalism surpassed that of the liberal-conservative struggles during the nineteenth century. In addition to the old arguments, article after article limited the powers of the church. Provisions declared marriage a civil ceremony; made priests ordinary citizens, denied special legal status; banned public worship outside the confines of the church; allowed state legislatures to determine the maximum number of priests within state boundaries; required all priests in Mexico to be native-born; prohibited clergymen from forming political parties; and mandated government approval for new church buildings. The anticlerical tenor of the Querétaro congress also surfaced in one of the three most important articles.

Múgica's committee on education drafted Article 3, and his proposal touched off passionate exchanges on the floor of the congress. Few took umbrage at the principle that primary education should be free and obligatory in the Mexican republic, but Múgica and his radical also demanded that education should be secular. The lessons of history convinced Múgica that the church was the implacable enemy of the Mexican people and an unrepentantly anti-democratic institution. Despite concerted opposition from Félix Palavicini and other Carranza supporters in the congress, when the final vote was taken, Francisco Múgica's Article 3 passed by a margin of almost two to one. With the radicals' dominance well established, two other major issues were resolved in their favor. The ensuing disputations on land and labor left no doubt that a new age of liberalism had dawned.

Article 27 addressed Mexico's endemic land problem and can be considered a direct outgrowth of Díaz's alienation of Mexico's subsoil rights and his policy of allowing land companies to appropriate traditionally communal lands. Even with the Zapatistas absent, Article 27 required that lands seized illegally from the peasantry during the Porfiriato be restored and provision be made for those communities that could not prove legal title. Equally important, the private ownership of land was no longer considered to be an absolute right but rather something of a privilege. If land did not serve a useful social function, it could be appropriated by the state: "The nation shall at all times have the right to impose on private property such limitations as the public interest may demand, as well as the right to regulate the utilization of natural resources . . . in order to conserve them and to ensure a more equitable distribution of public wealth." A special section of Article 27 deeply disturbed foreign nationals who owned property in Mexico.

Only Mexicans by birth or naturalization have the right to acquire ownership of lands, waters . . . or to obtain concessions for the exploitation of mines or waters. The state may grant the same right to foreigners, provided that they agree before the Department of Foreign Relations to consider themselves as nationals in respect to such property, and bind themselves not to invoke the protection of their government.[3]

The last, precedent-breaking article treated the labor question and sought to provide a reasonable balance between labor and management. Article 123 provided for an eight-hour workday, a six-day workweek, a minimum wage, and equal pay for equal work regardless of sex or nationality. Most importantly, it gave both labor and capital the right to organize for the defense of their respective interests and allowed workers the right to bargain collectively and go on strike.

Not nearly as radical as many contemporary observers found it, the Constitution of 1917 soundly repudiated nineteenth-century laissez-faire liberalism. Although ideologically indebted to the Liberal Plan of 1906, the Plan Orozquista, and the Plan de Ayala, it was more reformist than revolutionary. Even so, Carranza accepted it with great reluctance.

THE CARRANZA PRESIDENCY, 1917-1920

Carranza handily won the special elections that were held in March 1917. On May 1st he assumed the reins of a country far from pacified and economically distressed. The banking structure had been shattered, in part because of the general chaos but also as a direct result of the worthless paper money that had inundated the commercial markets. Mining suffered enormous losses, with gold production declining some 80 percent between 1910 and 1916 and silver and copper production falling off 65 percent during the same period. Industrial production fell off as well, and wages were depressed. The communication and transportation networks barely functioned. Agricultural shortages pushed food prices up, and the inflation took a terrible toll on poor urbanites trying to live in a monetary economy.

Carranza had little intention of enforcing the Constitution of 1917, and he believed the revolution to be over. In fact, it had scarcely begun. Under Article 27 Carranza distributed only 450,000 acres of land, a paltry sum when one considers that many individual hacendados had more than this and Luis Terrazas alone owned in excess of 7 million acres. The land Carranza did distribute had been taken away from his political enemies—this was neither the spirit nor the intent of Article 27.

The record of the administration on labor was no better. Even before the new constitution was enacted, Carranza used his army to put down a strike of workers in Veracruz protesting payment of wages in worthless paper currency. When railroad workers declared a strike in 1916, Carranza found it treasonous and arrested the leaders. Nonetheless, labor continued to organize and in 1918, Luis Morones founded the first nationwide union, the Confederación Regional Obrera Mexicana (CROM). Earlier in the decade many workers demonstrated that they did not need the federal government as their advocate; for example, cotton textile workers in Puebla and Veracruz did not hesitate to challenge their bosses on

---

3   Quoted in *Diario de los debates del Congreso Constituyente, 1916-1917* vol. II (Mexico City, Mexico, 1960), 1098.

Venustiano Carranza (1859-1920). The first chief of the Constitutional Army assumed the presidency in 1917 but, despite revolutionary rhetoric, moved slowly on the issues of social reform. His timidity on these central issues ultimately cost him popular support.

issues of wages and hours of work. They organized powerful unions that shaped the implementation of state labor codes with comprehensive protections for labor. Women also participated as labor activists in Nuevo León and Tamaulipas.

World War I complicated Carranza's presidency. He hoped that the United States would enter the conflagration early, thus distracting Washington from intervening in Mexican affairs. But Mexico's own position had to be carefully defined. Would the country follow other Latin American nations in breaking diplomatic relations with Germany? While many prominent Mexicans urged this course of action, others argued with understandable passion that the United States had invaded Mexico on numerous occasions.

As Carranza considered the situation, on January 19, 1917, Germany's ambassador presented him with the "Zimmerman telegram," sent by the German foreign secretary, Arthur Zimmerman. The cable was intercepted and decoded by the British, and then passed on to the United States and eventually to the press, publishing it on March 1st. In this note Zimmerman proposed that if Mexico would formally ally with Germany, on the successful conclusion of the war Mexico would receive the territory in Texas, New Mexico, and Arizona that it had lost in the mid-nineteenth century. The intent was to forestall US entry into the war by creating a diversionary front on the US southern border. Mexico's complicated relations with Germany, Japan, and the United States during this period have been analyzed carefully by the historian Friedrich Katz, who concluded that Carranza, although not averse to worrying the United States about a possible Mexican alliance with Germany, rejected the Zimmerman proposal in April. Mexico maintained formal neutrality throughout the war.

While the European conflict disquieted Mexico and resulted in some economic dislocation, the slow pace of the reform program can be attributed in large measure to Carranza. Of all the disillusioned groups of revolutionaries in Mexico, the Zapatistas were most dismayed.

The president sent thousands of federal troops into Morelos under trusted General Pablo González. Conducting a competent campaign, González took a number of Zapatista towns, but the guerrilla chieftain himself eluded capture. During the relentless fighting in Morelos—perhaps the most terrible of the entire revolution—the government charged thousands of innocent civilians with aiding Zapatistas and executed them. Entire towns were burned, crops methodically destroyed, and cattle stolen. The Zapatistas responded in kind and on one occasion blew up a Mexico City-Cuernavaca train, killing some four hundred passengers, mostly civilians.

In March 1919 Zapata directed an open letter to Carranza. A passionate statement, it helps to explain why Zapata had fought every Mexican head of state for a full decade. Zapata addressed the letter not to the president whom he did not recognize, nor to the politician whom he did not trust, but to Citizen Carranza.

> As the citizen I am, as a man with a right to think and speak aloud, as a peasant fully aware of the needs of the humble people, as a revolutionary and a leader of great numbers . . . I address myself to you Citizen Carranza. . . . From the time your mind first generated the idea of revolution . . . and you conceived the idea of naming yourself Chief . . . you turned the struggle to your own advantage and that of your friends who helped you rise and then shared the booty—riches, honors, businesses, banquets, sumptuous feasts, bacchanals, orgies. . . .
>
> It never occurred to you that the Revolution was fought for the benefit of the great masses, for the legions of the oppressed whom you motivated by your harangues. It was a magnificent pretext and a brilliant recourse for you to oppress and deceive. . . .
>
> In the agrarian matter you have given or rented our haciendas to your favorites. The old landholdings . . . have been taken over by new landlords . . . and the people mocked in their hopes.
>
> EMILIANO ZAPATA[4]

Carranza finally chose deception to end his problem with Zapata. With help from General Pablo González, he formulated a daring plot to kill the unbending revolutionary. Colonel Jesús Guajardo, one of González's subordinates in the Morelos campaigns, wrote to Zapata that he wanted to mutiny and to turn himself, some five hundred men, and all of their arms and ammunition over to the Zapatistas. Zapata demanded proof of Guarjardo's sincerity, for tricks had been played in the past, and asked that several former Zapatistas, who had previously defected to the federal cause, be tried by court-martial and executed. Colonel Guajardo agreed and carried out the order. Zapata began to be convinced when he heard from his own network of spies that Guajardo had captured the town of Jonacatepec in the name of the Zapatistas. He then agreed to meet the defecting federal officer, on April 10, 1919, at the Hacienda de Chinameca in his home territory. With only a few men accompanying him, Zapata rode into the hacienda in the early afternoon. A young eyewitness later described what happened.

---

4   Quoted in Isidro Fabela, ed., *Documentos históricos de la revolución mexicana*, vol. 23 (Mexico City, Mexico, 1960-73), 305-10.

Ten of us followed him just as he ordered. The rest of the people stayed [outside the walls] under the trees, confidently resting in the shade with their carbines stacked. Having formed ranks, [Guajardo's] guard looked ready to do him honors. Three times the bugle sounded the honor call; and as the last note died away, as the General in Chief reached the threshold of the door . . . at point blank, without giving him time even to draw his pistols, the soldiers who were presenting arms fired two volleys, and our unforgettable General Zapata fell never to rise again.[5]

Rid of his most implacable adversary, Carranza would also die by the bullet. In 1920, when the president attempted to name his own successor, Alvaro Obregón allied himself with fellow Sonorans Adolfo de la Huerta and Plutarco Elías Calles and declared himself in revolt. Under a new revolutionary banner, the Plan de Agua Prieta, an army of northerners began marching on Mexico City. In May, Carranza fled the capital and, on his way into exile, was assassinated by one of his own guards in the village of Tlaxcalantongo.

The Carranza presidency confronted an economy in shambles and a country still politically factionalized. Although most scholars credit him with building a victorious revolutionary coalition and mounting a vigorous defense of Mexican sovereignty against the United States, they also characterize him as a ruthless opportunist with little empathy for the social goals or the populist politics of the revolution. Carranza's sympathies lay with the middle classes. Unable to prevent the enactment of the progressive articles of the Constitution of 1917 in the areas of educational, labor, and land reform, during his presidency he undermined them at every turn. He reduced the federal budget for education, tried to crush labor union organization, and shunned land reform except to use it to punish his enemies (for example, in confiscating lands from his political rivals in Coahuila, the Madero family). Against his intransigence, his shrewd Sonoran enemies drew the strength and insight that would bring them to power and assure them a popular base of support.

ÁLVARO OBREGÓN, 1920-1924

With the election of Álvaro Obregón to a four-year presidential term in 1920, Mexican politicians set to work on implementing the constitution that had been drafted and promulgated at Querétaro in 1917. The war-torn country was closer to peace than it had been for a decade. Zapata had been killed, and, just a few weeks before Obregón assumed the high office, even the indomitable Pancho Villa had accepted a peace offering from the federal government—the hacienda of Canutillo in Durango. The rigorous defender of the poor swallowed his pride to settle down or perhaps to bide his time before the next tempest.

With the support of fellow Sonorans de la Huerta and Calles (together the three became known as the Sonoran triangle or dynasty), in the ministries of finance and interior, Obregón immediately turned his attention to the pressing problems of national reconstruction.

---

5   Quoted in John Womack, Jr., *Zapata and the Mexican Revolution* (New York, NY, 1968), 326.

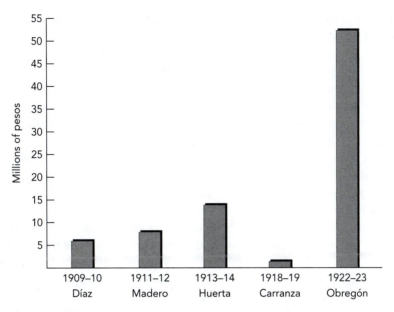

Federal Expenditures for Education

Source: Celerino Cano, "Análisis de la Acción Educativa," in *Mexico, 50 Años de Revolución*, vol. 4: *La Cultura* (Mexico, 1962), 36.

Álvaro Obregón (1880-1928). President of Mexico from 1920 to 1924, Obregón is shown here recovering from the amputation of his right arm following the battle of Santa Rosa (1915).

A powerful and persuasive orator, he enjoyed a wide base of popular support. Far from radical, he did embrace social reform. Unfortunately, the beginning of his administration coincided with the post–World War I economic slump, resulting in widespread hunger and privation. Prices of gold, silver, copper, zinc, henequen, and cattle were depressed. Unemployment was rampant in these industries, and the government's foreign exchange from these products fell off drastically. Only the price and demand for oil remained stable, and by 1921 Mexico was producing 193 million barrels, making it the world's third largest producer of petroleum. Oil reserves, even with an inadequate taxation structure, sustained the administration and enabled the president to embark upon a modest implementation of the Constitution of 1917.

Beginning with Article 3 Obregón named José Vasconcelos, one of Mexico's most illustrious men of letters, to be secretary of education. Educated in Mexico City, Vasconcelos received his law degree at the age of twenty-three. Late in the Porfiriato his antipositivist views led him to join the Ateneo de la Juventud, and he shortly distinguished himself as one of the most brilliant minds in Mexico. An enthusiastic supporter of Francisco Madero, he became a Constitutionalist at the time of Huerta's coup. Vasconcelos briefly served as rector of the National University and then accepted the portfolio of education.

Vasconcelos championed a broad spectrum of educational endeavors and became the patron of the rural school. With dramatically increased federal funds placed at his disposal, he sent dedicated teachers into hundreds of hamlets with a basic curriculum: reading, writing, arithmetic, geography, and Mexican history. Vasconcelos strove to inspire the teachers with a deep sense of national mission in the midst of intellectual debate over how to craft a cultural nationalism that would bring together so many diverse peoples, languages, traditions, and isolated areas. Some of the villages were a two- or three-days' ride by horseback from the nearest railroad station, most lacked electricity, and few amenities of the comfortable life were to be found. In addition, the new teachers were not always welcomed with open arms. They often encountered deep hostility from villagers who did not want to change their traditional ways wholesale; this was especially true in indigenous communities that had remained more isolated. Urban revolutionaries had little understanding of the embeddedness of popular Catholicism in the glue that held communities together.

Vasconcelos's plan did not aspire to segregate the Indians but through education to incorporate them into the mainstream of mestizo society. This initiative did not mean an erasure of the ancient past and folklore, but rather to bring them to the service of the state in creating a hegemonic culture capable of unifying the nation. While the past would be praised and symbolized artistically, the contemporary Indian would disappear. Vasconcelos's early, rather utopian (if not racist) thinking envisioned a future *raza cósmica*, a hybrid race, that would unite humanity. In his memoirs he described the process as follows:

> I also set up auxiliary and provisional departments, to supervise teachers who would follow closely the methods of the Catholic missionaries of the Colony among Indians who still

do not know Spanish. . . . Deliberately, I insisted that the Indian Department should have no other purpose than to prepare the native to enter the common school by giving him the fundamental tools in Spanish, since I proposed to go contrary to the North American Protestant practice of approaching the problem of teaching the native as something special and separate from the rest of the population.[6]

Vasconcelos oversaw the construction of over one thousand rural schools between 1920 and 1924, more than had been constructed during the previous fifty years. To support the new endeavor, he began a program of public libraries. Almost two thousand libraries had been established by 1924, most of them stocked with books designed to reinforce the humanist tradition of Mexico's new intelligentsia. Government presses printed millions of primary readers for both the schools and the libraries. A library set for a typical rural school consisted of about fifty books packed in special crates that could be transported on muleback.

Vasconcelos believed in the utility of informal education as well and employed some of Mexico's leading artists—Diego Rivera, José Clemente Orozco, and David Alfaro Siqueiros—to begin ornamenting the walls of public buildings with murals. Designed for the people rather than for the art critics, the murals embodied largely anthropological and historical themes that sought to instruct the literate and illiterate alike in the truths that Mexico's leaders wished to inculcate. However, Vasconcelos became increasingly critical of the polemical, Marxist nature of the often massive wall paintings in government buildings.

Article 3 of the constitution had stipulated, of course, that education should be secular and free, but President Obregón found it impossible to eliminate all church schools because the state had neither the funds nor the teachers to educate all the children in Mexico. Forced to allow Catholic school with some restrictions, Obregón encouraged the work of Protestant missionaries in Mexico. He openly endorsed the work of the YMCA (Asociación Cristiana de Jóvenes) and even supported its activities with state funds. The church naturally opposed this new development but, with a few exceptions, open hostilities were avoided. Few realized in the early 1920s that church–state relations were undergoing a lull before a terrible storm.

Obregón's labor policy favored Luis Morones and the newly formed Confederación Regional Obrera Mexicana (CROM). Because labor development had been so long stifled at the national level, Obregón leaned in the opposite direction to support CROM's leader, Luis Morones who worked to establish a balance between labor and capital rather than attack the structure of the capitalist system. These modest goals produced a mutually supportive relationship between the government and CROM. In turn, for labor support, the administration financed the CROM's national labor conventions and provided free railroad passes for anyone who wished to attend. Blessed with not only government benevolence but also an increasingly emboldened working class, membership in the union rose steadily from 50,000 in 1920 to an estimated 1.2 million in 1924.

Other developing unions did not fare so well, however. Two radical labor groups, the Communist Federation of the Mexican Proletariat and the anarchist-led Industrial Workers

---

6   José Vasconcelos, *A Mexican Ulysses: An Autobiography*, trans. William Rex Crawford (Bloomington, IN, 1963), 152.

of the World, tried unsuccessfully to gain a foothold in the labor movement. Obregón expelled a number of foreign labor leaders from the country and declared strikes of the radical unions illegal. He was equally obdurate with the conservative Roman Catholic union movement. Many Mexican labor leaders, however, had expected more support from Obregón. When asked to intervene in labor's behalf, the president time after time responded that the issue in dispute should be resolved at the state or local level. In states with progressive governors and militant workers, labor did not fare too badly. The federal government had limited power.

On the matter of agrarian reform Obregón again showed himself as a compromiser. He was aware that the Mexican economy, for better or for worse, was still tied to the hacienda system and that a rapid redistribution of land would result in reduced agricultural productivity. The rural population would produce enough to feed itself but not enough to feed the nonagrarian sector of the society. Even though he recognized the abject poverty of many rural areas, he decided not to declare all-out war on the hacendados of the republic. By the time his term expired in 1924, he had distributed only 3 million acres to 624 villages, primarily in areas where the government had strong political enemies. The land went to the communal ejidos rather than outright to individuals, but the number of villagers directly benefiting numbered one hundred thirty thousand. The radical agrarianists, such as Antonio Díaz Soto y Gama, believed that the president's agrarian logic was faulty. Luis Terrazas alone still owned as much land as the total distributed by the administration. Obregón had failed to strike while the agrarian iron was hot. Although he had distributed nine times the amount of land reallocated by distributed by Carranza, seven years after the adoption of the constitution, Article 27 had not yet benefited the majority of rural Mexicans.

Why had Obregón not moved faster in the agrarian field? His reservations were confirmed in part by the agrarian situation in Michoacán, where radical governor Francisco Múgica attempted to forge alliances with campesinos by arming them and encouraging their attempts to occupy ejido lands. His agrarian and anticlerical policies produced chaos when he ran afoul of local politics and patronage networks, resulting in his removal by Obregón. In explaining his more moderate course, the president declared before congress, "We must not destroy the big estates before creating the small one. . . . I am of the opinion that we must act cautiously."[7] Furthermore, in his attempt to reestablish political stability he faced the specter of possible US intervention to protect the interests of its citizens owning property in Mexico. The fears were not idle ones, as US troops had been in Mexico twice since the revolution began, once in Veracruz and two years later in the north in the futile attempt to capture Pancho Villa.

RELATIONS WITH THE UNITED STATES

Obregón's presidential term coincided with the Republican administration of Warren G. Harding in the United States. Supported by big business, Harding had won the presidency by a landslide and sought to encourage private enterprise, both at home and abroad. Of all

---

7   Quoted in Eyler N. Simpson, *The Ejido: Mexico's Way Out* (Chapel Hill, NC, 1937), 87-88.

the corporate enterprises that dominated the Republican convention of 1920, none rivaled the oil interests of Harry F. Sinclair, Edward L. Doheny, and Jake Hammon. Within a couple of years the extent of petroleum influence in Harding's administration would be exposed to the world in the Teapot Dome scandal.

For several years, through powerful lobby groups such as the National Association for the Protection of American Rights in Mexico and the Oil Producer's Association, under the chairmanship of Edward Doheny, American businessmen had been urging the US government to become more active in the defense of their Mexican interests. Often working through Secretary of Interior Albert Bacon Fall (later arrested in the Teapot Dome scandal), they presented their case to the American president. Their Mexican oil properties, they contended, were about to be seized out from under them by Article 27 and, accordingly, the United States should not recognize the Obregón regime. When Secretary Fall wrote, "So long as I have anything to do with the Mexican question, no government of Mexico will be recognized, with my consent, which does not first enter into a written agreement promising to protect American citizens and their property rights in Mexico,"[8] President Harding was willing to be persuaded. The United States did not recognize Obregón during the first three years of his administration.

Although Obregón needed the oil revenues, he could not buckle under US pressure; it would have been political suicide. The apparent impasse was averted by the Mexican Supreme Court. When, in September 1921, the Texas Company challenged the retroactive application of Article 27 in the Mexican courts, the Supreme Court handed down a decision propounding the doctrine of "positive acts." The oil lands could not be seized under Article 27 if the company in question had performed some "positive act" (such as erecting drilling equipment) to remove oil from the soil prior to May 1, 1917, the date on which the constitution went into effect. If the company had not engaged in such a "positive act" prior to May 1, 1917, or if the concession had been granted after that date, Article 27 could be invoked at the pleasure of the state. Commissioners from both countries met in the summer of 1923 on Bucareli Street in Mexico City at the interior ministry. Under the terms of the agreements they reached, the Mexican government in essence agreed to uphold the doctrine of "positive acts" in its future relations with all the oil companies, and the Harding administration promised, in return, to extend diplomatic recognition. In addition, the two countries agreed to establish a mixed claims commission to adjudicate the claims US citizens had brought against Mexico for damages suffered during the revolution.

POLITICAL TENSIONS AND REBELLION

At about the same time that the commissioners of the two countries formulated the Bucareli agreements, an extraordinary event occurred in Parral, Chihuahua. The retired General Pancho Villa had just traveled from Canutillo to the little village of Río Florido to participate in the christening of an old comrade's baby son. After the ceremony Villa went on to Parral, where he spent the night before returning to his famous hacienda. Early the following

---

8   Quoted in John W. F. Dulles, *Yesterday in Mexico: A Chronicle of the Revolution, 1919-1936* (Austin, 1961), 159.

morning, surrounded by his bodyguards, he began the return trip to Canutillo. As his Dodge touring car turned onto Calle Gabino Barreda, eight men armed with repeating rifles burst out of a corner house and peppered the automobile. Within seconds Villa and several of his companions were dead.

Responsibility for assassinations in Mexico has never been an easy fix. Some contemporaries considered the murder to have been a personal affair in which a group of aggrieved citizens took vengeance for prior Villista depredations. But most believed that the murder was politically motivated, as Mexican politics had begun to heat up once again during the summer of 1923 and Villa had threatened to come out of retirement.

The assassination of Villa tended to exacerbate an already tense political atmosphere. The nationalists were unhappy with the Bucareli agreements. Obregón, they contended, had truckled to the American oilmen and their White House representatives. The time was approaching when a decision had to be made concerning the presidential succession of 1924, and Obregón chose to support his fellow Sonoran and secretary of interior, Plutarco Elías Calles. This choice touched off political violence.

The revolt that began in Mexico in late 1923 combined the antagonisms of various interest groups. Many conservatives, including a number of wealthy hacendados and Catholic leaders, feared that Plutarco Calles was too radical. They were joined by military men, disgruntled at Obregón's reduction of the federal army. But the rebellion was not simply an alliance of conservatives as many ardent nationalists, unhappy with the Bucareli agreements, pledged their support of the new movement, as did a number of labor leaders who had not been included within the ranks of the CROM. The opposition coalesced around that other leading figure from Sonora, Adolfo de la Huerta.

Despite the wide base of opposition, Obregón had his own sources of strength. Those unions under CROM control supported him unabashedly, as did a number of campesino organizations. Although some key army garrisons went over to the rebel side, many significant ones remained loyal to the government. But, most importantly, the recent diplomatic recognition by the United States provided Obregón's government not only with moral support but also an ample supply of war matériel. The fighting itself lasted only a few months; but it was a grueling episode for those who thought the days of violence had passed, and the toll of lives was tremendous. Some seven thousand Mexicans died before the rebels of de la Huerta admitted their defeat.

As he neared the end of his term, Álvaro Obregón had at great cost asserted the dominance of the national government. Yet for many, the pace of social reform had been too slow. Obregón's cautious pragmatism had promoted some of the revolutionary goals, but not a few intellectuals, politicians, and journalists criticized the gradual nature of the process to implement the changes promised in the Constitution of 1917. Now they waited to see if Plutarco Elías Calles would be any different.

RECOMMENDED FOR FURTHER STUDY

Bortz, Jeffrey. *Revolution within the Revolution: Cotton Textile Workers and the Mexican Labor Regime, 1910-1923*. Stanford, CA: Stanford University Press, 2008.

Braddy, Haldeen. *Pershing's Mission in Mexico*. El Paso: Texas Western College Press, 1966.

Brunk, Samuel. *Emiliano Zapata: Revolution and Betrayal in Mexico*. Albuquerque: University of New Mexico Press, 1995.

Clark, Marjorie. *Organized Labor in Mexico*. Chapel Hill: University of North Carolina Press, 1934.

Clendenen, Clarence C. *The United States and Pancho Villa: A Study in Unconventional Diplomacy*. Ithaca, NY: Cornell University Press, 1961.

Coerver, Don M., and Linda B. Hall. *Texas and the Mexican Revolution: A Study in State and National Border Policy, 1910-1920*. San Antonio, TX: Trinity University Press, 1984.

Dulles, John W. F. *Yesterday in Mexico: A Chronicle of the Revolution, 1919-1936*. Austin: University of Texas Press, 1961.

Gilderhus, Mark T. *Diplomacy and Revolution: U.S.-Mexican Relations under Wilson and Carranza*. Tucson: University of Arizona Press, 1977.

Haddox, John H. *Vasconcelos of Mexico*. Austin: University of Texas Press, 1967.

Hall, Linda B. *Alvaro Obregón: Power and Revolution in Mexico, 1911-1920*. College Station: Texas A&M University Press, 1981.

_____. *Oil, Banks, and Politics: The United States and Postrevolutionary Mexico, 1917-1924*. Austin: University of Texas Press, 1995.

Harris, Charles H., and Louis R. Sadler. *The Great Call-Up: The Guard, the Border, and the Mexican Revolution*. Norman: University of Oklahoma Press, 2015.

Hart, John M. *Revolutionary Mexico: The Coming and Process of the Mexican Revolution*. Berkeley: University of California Press, 1987.

Henderson, Timothy J. *The Worm in the Wheat: Rosalie Evans and Agrarian Struggle in the Puebla-Tlaxcala Valley of Mexico, 1906-1927*. Durham, NC: Duke University Press, 1998.

Hernández, Sonia. *Working Women into the Borderlands*. College Station: Texas A&M Press, 2014.

James, Timothy M. *Mexico's Supreme Court: Between Liberal Individual and Revolutionary Social Rights, 1861–1934*. Albuquerque: University of New Mexico Press, 2013.

Katz, Friedrich. *The Life and Times of Pancho Villa*. Stanford, CA: Stanford University Press, 1998.

_____. *The Secret War in Mexico: Europe, the United States and the Mexican Revolution*. Chicago, IL: University of Chicago Press, 1981.

Lear, John. *Workers, Neighbors, and Citizens: The Revolution in Mexico City*. Lincoln: University of Nebraska Press, 2001.

Lieuwen, Edwin. *Mexican Militarism: The Political Rise and Fall of the Revolutionary Army*. Albuquerque: University of New Mexico Press, 1968.

Martínez, Oscar J. *Fragments of the Mexican Revolution: Personal Accounts from the Border*. Albuquerque: University of New Mexico Press, 1983.

Niemeyer, Jr., E. V. *Revolution at Querétaro: The Mexican Constitutional Convention of 1916-1917*. Austin: University of Texas Press, 1974.

Pastzor, Suzanne B. *The Spirit of Hidalgo: The Mexican Revolution in Coahuila*. Calgary, Canada: University of Calgary Press, 2002.

Quirk, Robert E. *The Mexican Revolution, 1914-1915: The Convention of Aguascalientes*. New York: Citadel Press, 1963.

Richmond, Douglas W. *Venustiano Carranza's Nationalist Struggle, 1893-1920*. Lincoln: University of Nebraska Press, 1984.

Santiago, Myrna J. *The Ecology of Oil: Environment, Labor, and the Mexican Revolution, 1900-1938*. New York: Cambridge University Press, 2006.

Schell, Patience A. *Church and State Education in Revolutionary Mexico City*. Tucson: University of Arizona Press, 2003.

Schuler, Friedrich. *Secret Wars and Secret Policies in the Americas, 1842-1929*. Albuquerque: University of New Mexico Press, 2011.

Simpson, Eyler N. *The Ejido: Mexico's Way Out*. Chapel Hill: University of North Carolina Press, 1937.

Vasconcelos, José. *A Mexican Ulysses: An Autobiography.* Translated by William Rex Crawford. Bloomington: Indiana University Press, 1963.

Welsome, Eileen. *The General and the Jaguar: Pershing's Hunt for Pancho Villa.* Lincoln: University of Nebraska Press, 2007.

Wilkie, James W. *The Mexican Revolution: Federal Expenditure and Social Change since 1910.* Berkeley: University of California Press, 1967.

Womack, Jr., John. *Zapata and the Mexican Revolution.* New York: Alfred A. Knopf, 1968.

CHAPTER 29

SOCIETY AND CULTURE DURING THE REVOLUTIONARY YEARS

THE IMPACT OF THE REVOLUTION ON THE MASSES

The rapid changes in the presidential chair, the heated debates in Aguascalientes and Querétaro, and the redounding phrases of the Constitution of 1917 had less significance for the Mexican masses than the violence of the first revolutionary decade that most dominated their lives. For every prominent death—Francisco Madero, José María Pino Suárez, Pascual Orozco, Emiliano Zapata, or Venustiano Carranza—one hundred thousand nameless Mexicans also died. By any standard the loss of life was tremendous. Although accurate statistics were not recorded, moderate estimates calculate that between 1.5 and 2 million lost their lives in those terrible ten years. In a country with a population of roughly 15 million in 1910, few families did not directly feel the pain as one in every eight Mexicans was killed. Even Mexico's high birthrate could not offset the carnage of war. The census takers in 1920 counted almost a million fewer Mexicans than they had found only a decade before.

Some marching armies had been equipped with small medical teams, and Pancho Villa even fitted out a medical train on which battlefield operations could be performed. But medical care was generally so primitive that within a week after a major engagement deaths of wounded often doubled or tripled losses sustained immediately on the battlefield. And in more cases than one, both federals and rebels, enemy prisoners were executed rather than cared for and fed. Civilian deaths rose into the hundreds of thousands as a result of indiscriminate artillery bombardments and, in some cases, the macabre policy of placing noncombatants before firing squads in pursuit of some imperfectly conceived political or military goal.

It is axiomatic that war elicits not only the worst but often psychotic behavior in otherwise normal human beings. In Mexico, the cumulative stress of exhaustion and constant exposure to death produced atrocities during the first decade of the revolution and, on occasion, led to behavior that can only be termed sadistic. The rape and inhumanity visited upon civilians by soldiers became legendary in the folklore of the revolution. One could pass off stories of mutilated prisoners hanged from trees or telephone posts as exaggerations had not scores of eager photographers captured hundreds of horrifying scenes for posterity. Bodies with hands or legs or genitals cut off were a grotesque caricature of a movement originally motivated by the highest ideals.

Execution without benefit of trial was common during the violent decade of 1910–20. Bodies were left hanging for weeks as object lessons.

Fratricidal horrors so outrageous and so cataclysmic exacted burning resentment and fear in the civilian population. An approaching unit invariably meant trouble for poor, rural Mexicans. The best that could be hoped for was a small band demanding a meal. But often the demands were more outrageous the war did not lend itself to decency or compassion. In northern Mexico tens of thousands of rural Mexicans joined their middle class and wealthy counterparts in seeking the security of the United States. On a single day in October 1913 some eight thousand refugees crossed the border from Piedras Negras, Coahuila, to Eagle Pass, Texas. While the vast majority left the country with the idea of returning once the situation stabilized, most remained in the United States where many contributed to invigorating Catholicism in the southwest. In central and southern Mexico there was virtually no place to run, and the civilian population had no choice but to keep their heads low and resign themselves to the worst. Two months spent clearing a field and planting crops under a burning sun could be wiped out in five minutes as an army of five hundred horsemen galloped through the carefully tilled rows of corn and beans. Then they might stop at the one-room hut and confiscate the one milch cow and four turkeys that held out some promise for a slightly less redundant diet in the six months to follow. The documentary evidence from the period suggests forcefully that the excesses of war cannot be attributed simply to one side or another. Both federals and rebels were guilty.

What was the impact of the early revolution on people's lives? We can learn much from the thousands of images captured not only by myth-making photographers like Agustín Víctor Casasola and Manuel Ramos, but by the scores of others including many women, that illustrate the human price of warfare. Other depictions jump from the pages of Luis

González's perceptive and beautifully written account of the Michoacán village of San José de Gracia (population about 1,200 in 1910). By 1913, when violence engulfed the region for the first time,

> Don Gregorio Pulido had given up taking local products to Mexico City, for bands of revolutionaries made the roads unsafe for travel. The San José area began to return to the old practice of consuming its own products. Trade declined. . . . . . From 1913 on, increased poverty was the rule. . . . Everything in San José shifted into reverse. The revolution did no favors for the town or the surrounding *rancherías*. . . . Parties of rebels often came to visit their friends in San José, either to rescue the girls from virginity, or to feast happily on the delicious local cheeses and meats, or to add the fine horses of the region to their own. . . . They summoned all the rich residents and told them how much money in gold coin each was to contribute to the cause. In view of the rifles, no one protested.[1]

The feared "armies" did not look much like armies. Standard uniforms were unheard of among the rebels, and weapons consisted of whatever could be found or appropriated. Sometimes makeshift insignias identified rank but gave slight clue as to group affiliation. Anonymity served rebel commanders well as it left them unconcerned with the niceties of accountability, but it caused problems for the rural campesino wanting to respond correctly to the question, "Are you a Huertista, a Villista, or a Carrancista?"

For Mexican women, the lived experience of the revolution brought changes, both unwelcomed and appreciated, to their daily routines. With husbands, fathers, and sons serving somewhere in the ranks, they were subjected to the terror and indignity of wanton assault. But many did not mope or simply stay home to become the target of rape. Freeing themselves from the eternal task of grinding corn, thousands joined the revolution and served the rebel armies in the capacity of spies and arms smugglers. So active were the women in smuggling ammunition across the border in Ciudad Juárez that the US Customs Bureau had to employ teams of female agents to search the undergarments of suspicious, heavy-looking women returning from shopping sprees in El Paso.

A noteworthy role assumed by women was that of *soldadera*. The soldaderas were more than camp followers. They provided feminine companionship, to be sure, but because neither the federal army nor the rebel armies provided commissary service, they foraged for food, cooked, washed and, in the absence of more competent medical service, nursed the wounded and buried the dead. Both sides depended upon them, and in 1912 a federal battalion actually threatened mutiny when the secretary of war ordered that the women could not be taken along on a certain maneuver. The order was rescinded. Not infrequently, the soldaderas actually served in the ranks, sometimes with a baby slung in a *rebozo* or a young child clinging to their skirts. Women holding officer ranks were not uncommon in the rebel armies.

The soldadera endured the hardships of the campaign without special consideration. While the men were generally mounted, the women most often walked, carrying bedding, pots and pans, food, firearms, ammunition, and children. Often the men would gallop on ahead, engage the enemy in battle, and then rest. By the time the women caught up, they were

---

1   Luis González, *San José de Gracia: Mexican Village in Transition* (Austin, TX, 1974), 124–25.

ready to move again, and the soldadera would simply trudge on. Losing her special "Juan" in battle, she had little choice but to take another, to prepare his favorite meal and share his bed. Not a few gave birth in makeshift military camps and some even on the field of battle.

The hard life of the soldadera was a relative thing. A fascinating oral history of a Yaqui woman from Sonora who was deported to Yucatán, cut her hands raw on the henequen plants, and saw her babies die from lack of adequate care reveals that she did better as a soldadera. She later recalled that "her personal misery decreased by impressive leaps and

Among the disparate revolutionary contingents in Mexico, the Yaqui Indians of Sonora figured prominently in the campaigns of the northwest.

bounds. . . . At no point during the next several years did she view her life as anything but a tremendous improvement after Yucatán."[2] In another twist on the powerful appeal of a military vocation for women who wished to enjoy the satisfaction of becoming fully masculine, Amelia Robles changed her gender to become Zapatista colonel Amelio Robles and later received a veteran's pension for service to the revolution.[3]

In contrast to such behaviors, public displays of chivalry persisted. One traveler to Mexico City in 1918 was especially amused by the sign he found posted in the streetcar:

GENTLEMEN: When you see a lady standing on her feet you will not find it possible to remain sitting with tranquility. Your education will forbid you to do so.

GENERAL MANAGER OF THE RAILWAYS[4]

In an oblique and unintended way the revolution contributed to the emancipation of the Mexican woman. As the shortage of adult males in the cities contracted the labor supply, women began to make some inroads into the labor force. At first their contributions consisted of the simplest type of work in stores and factories, but once escaped from the confines of the house they would not be persuaded easily to return. In Yucatán, Governor Salvador Alvarado encouraged advances in women's rights, and in 1916 he sponsored the Congreso Femenino in Mérida, Yucatán. But even his support still defined women in terms of their roles as wives, mothers, and educators and limited their full membership in public life. So while it can be argued that the revolution opened up social spaces for women, it was in the feminine role as educators/nurturers that women most readily found work in promoting literacy, welfare, hygiene, and temperance. Similarly, female factory workers learned that they would best be served by framing their demands for justice in wages and other benefits in part by linking them to their roles as homemakers and family members.

The revolution, to be sure, had different meanings to different Mexicans during those years of greatest violence. But a most recurrent theme was the fear of the leva, the institution that snatched away the male population for service in the military. Edith O'Shaughnessy, the wife of the US chargé in Mexico City, described the leva in her memoirs.

I was startled as I watched the faces of some conscripts marching to the station today. On so many was impressed something desperate and despairing. They have a fear of . . . eternal separation from their loved ones. They often have to be tied in the transport wagons. There is no system about conscription here—the press gang takes any likely looking person. Fathers of families, only sons of widows, as well as the unattached, are enrolled, besides women to cook and grind in the powder mills.[5]

Foreigners also suffered, because the revolution was in part a reaction against Díaz's coddling of foreign interests, and not a few revolutionaries took out their wrath on the

2   Jane H. Kelly, "Preliminary Life History of Josefa (Chepa) Alvarez" (mimeographed, 1970), 16.

3   Gabriela Cano, "Unconcealable Realities of Desire: Amelio Robles's (Transgender) Masculinity in the Mexican Revolution," in *Sex in Revolution: Gender, Politics, and Power in Modern Mexico*, ed. Jocelyn Olcott, et al. (Durham, NC, 2006), 35–56.

4   Quoted in P. Harvey Middleton, *Industrial Mexico: 1919 Facts and Figures* (New York, NY, 1919), 6.

5   Edith O'Shaughnessy, *A Diplomat's Wife in Mexico* (New York, NY, 1916), 58.

Armies had to be fed, and the task of grinding corn for the daily supply of tortillas continued as it had for centuries.

A familiar sight between 1910 and 1920, the *soldaderas* experienced both the excitement and privations of life on the military campaign.

foreign community. Cast in the role of exploiters, foreign oilmen and miners were forced to pay not only taxes to the government but tribute to various groups of rebels and bribes to local bandits. But other frugal and industrious foreigners, without the slightest claim to exploitation, suffered racist terror. After a battle for control of Torreón in 1911, more than two hundred peaceful Chinese residents were murdered simply because they were Chinese. A few years later Villistas expelled Spanish citizens from Torreón and confiscated their property. Colonies of US Mormons in Chihuahua and Sonora, after being terrorized repeatedly, packed up those belongings they could carry and left their adopted home. Some ramifications of the revolution on the US side of the border were horrific for Mexican Americans living there. The anonymous Plan de San Diego of 1915 called on Mexicans to reconquer the southwest that had been lost in 1848 and kill all the Anglo men. Although few ethnic Mexicans living in Texas had anything to do with the plan, perhaps authored by Carrancistas, Texas Rangers and vigilantes used it as an excuse to launch a campaign of racial terrorism, which killed thousands of Mexicans and confiscated their properties.

City dwellers, too, experienced the ravishments of war. Almost all of the larger cities in the country hosted battles at some time between 1910 and 1920, and some witnessed three or four devastating engagements. The sight of burning buildings, the sound of wailing ambulances, and the nausea of mass burials brought home in tangible terms the most immediate meaning of the revolution. Starvation reached major proportions in Mexico City, Guadalajara, and Puebla. The construction boom of the Porfiriato ended shortly after the outbreak of

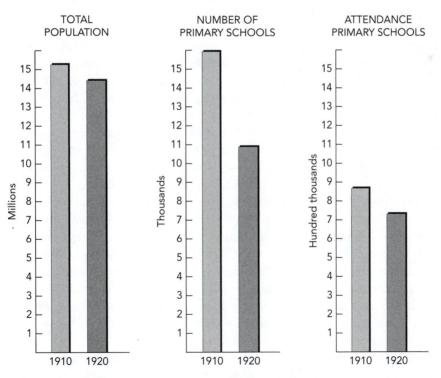

The Violence Takes a Toll

hostilities. While a few unfinished public projects reached completion, for the most part those workmen who could be spared from the ranks toiled to clear debris, repaired damaged structures, knocked down gutted buildings, and tried to put the railroad lines back in operation.

The early revolution took a terrible toll in education. Hundreds of schools were destroyed and hundreds of others abandoned. In the Federal District alone the number of primary schools in operation declined from 332 in 1910 to 270 in 1920. The story repeated itself in city after city, town after town. Total primary school attendance in the country declined from eight hundred eighty thousand to seven hundred forty thousand in the same ten-year period.

CULTURAL CREATIVITY

Warfare, however, did not extinguish creative spirit in Mexico. What is striking is how the turmoil of war and the collapse of old institutions engendered both social change and cultural creativity. As we have seen, gender roles experienced transformations from the Porfiriato through the early revolution. New public spaces opened for women not only in jobs and consumer culture, but also in artistic endeavors. The life of Esperanza Iris offers a window onto significant changes for women forged in the artistic world. She began her career as an actress during the late Porfiriato as part of a theater tradition dating back to the late colonial period that grew rapidly in the wake of waves of rural migrants arriving in Mexico City in the late nineteenth century. Moreover, theater-going provided opportunities for women as spectators to partake of the public life of the city, albeit in spaces segregated by class: elite audiences enjoyed the large, posh theaters of the area west of the Zócalo (main plaza), while the lower-classes were entertained in the *carpas* (tents), cantinas, and on the streets to the north and east of the main plaza. Esperanza Iris rose through the popular venues to become one of the divas of her generation, leveraging her popularity to open her own theater in 1918.

The Teatro Esperanza Iris (today it is called the Theater of the City), in the well-heeled western zone on Donceles street, was her crowning glory as an actress and brought new cultural influences from Europe to the capital city. The Bataclán was a dance revue, initially performed at the Teatro Iris by a troupe of Parisian women in 1925, that introduced the curvilinear Deco body and the concept of the New Woman to a Mexico emerging from the ravages of the violent phase of the revolution. The New Woman was strong, opinionated, sexual, and most of all visible in public spaces, providing an opening for the redefinition of gender norms in a Mexican context that would flourish in the 1930s.

The early revolution spawned creativity in a multiplicity of cultural arenas. During the last year of the Porfiriato a group of young thinkers had banded together to form the Ateneo de la Juventud. Among its charter members was a small group that would come to dominate early revolutionary thought: Antonio Caso, Alfonso Reyes, José Vasconcelos, and Martín Luis Guzmán. Meeting fortnightly, the members of the Ateneo began to formulate a philosophical assault on materialism in general and on positivism in particular. Impressed with Immanuel Kant and Arthur Schopenhauer, but most especially with Henri Bergson's masterpiece *L'Evolution créatrice* (1907), they lashed out against the científicos and launched a movement for ideological and educational reform.

By 1912 the members of the Ateneo began to give some practical application to their antipositivist posture. Interested in moving into areas that Díaz had ignored, in December

1912 they founded a "people's university," the Universidad Popular Mexicana, and took their message to the factories and shops in Mexico's leading population centers. Mexico's future happiness, they preached, did not depend upon commercial or industrial growth but rather upon social progress. The Universidad Popular Mexicana did not offer degrees; rather, it tried to bring humanistic knowledge to those who would not otherwise receive it. Stressing lessons in citizenship and patriotism as well as practical instruction in hygiene and stenography, the *ateneístas* who constituted the faculty not only lectured but sponsored weekend tours to art galleries, museums, and historical and archaeological sites. They all served without pay.

The winds of change shook the literary and artistic communities as well. A new age in the Mexican novel was born in 1915 when Mariano Azuela (1873–1952) wrote *Los de abajo* (translated as *The Underdogs*). A classic in twentieth-century Mexican literature, *Los de abajo* chronicles the life of Demetrio Macías to probe the meaning of the revolution. Historical novels were not new in Mexico, but Azuela added new ingredients, relating the story not in the sophisticated dialogue of the French school but in the colloquial language of the Mexican masses. Avoiding the intrusion of secondary plots, Azuela tells the story of real revolutionaries, not those who intellectualized the movement and coined its resounding phrases. Demetrio Macías is caught up in the struggle without really knowing why, yet when confronted with complex decisions, is able to make proper choices with amazing spontaneity. Luis Cervantes, a middle-class federal deserter, joins Macías's guerrilla band and tries to articulate the revolutionary goals for him, but the uneducated Macías recognizes the shallowness and hypocrisy of Cervantes's explanations and the inherent opportunism in his actions.

The day-to-day dehumanizing realities of the revolution abound in the novel—pillage, looting, burning, destruction, theft, and general debauchery. Illustrative of the passion the revolution evoked is Azuela's description of the battlefield after a struggle for control of Zacatecas: "The three hundred-foot slope was literally covered with dead, their hair matted, their clothes clotted with grime and blood. A host of ragged women, vultures of prey, ranged over the tepid bodies of the dead, stripping one man bare, despoiling another, robbing from a third his dearest possessions."[6] The novel ends where it began—at the Canyon of Juchipila. Demetrio Macías, by this time a general, is killed where he first ambushed a federal convoy. The circle has been completed, and nothing has really changed. After all the suffering and killing, the revolution seems to be back where it began. While social programs have been shunted aside and forgotten, the revolution has become almost self-perpetuating—it just goes on and on. Shortly before he dies Demetrio's wife asks him why he must continue fighting. He answers by tossing a rock over a precipice and responding with a beautifully appropriate metaphor: *Mira esa piedra cómo ya no se para* (Look at that rock—it just keeps rolling).

The harsh realities of the revolution provided fodder for witty corridos that spread news about the fighting, praising and lampooning heroes and villains on both sides of the struggle. Perhaps the most famous of these is an early version of *La cucaracha*. The chorus goes like this:

---

6   Mariano Azuela, *The Underdogs*, trans. E. Munguía (New York, NY, 1963), 80–81.

La cucaracha, la cucaracha	The cockroach, the cockroach
Ya no puede caminar	Now she cannot walk
Porque no tiene	Because she hasn't
Porque le falta	Because she's missing
Marijuana que fumar.	Marijuana to smoke.

And in one of its many verses:

Todos se pelean la silla	It's a battle to the top
Que les deja mucha plata.	To get the spoils of war.
En el norte Pancho Villa	In the north, it's Pancho Villa
Y en el sur ¡Viva Zapata!	In the south, ¡Viva Zapata!

At the same time, musical styles were changing to reflect Mexican traditions. Manuel Ponce (1882–1948), a talented young pianist and composer from Zacatecas introduced a new nativist movement. Ponce decried that Mexican salons in 1910 should welcome only foreign music. He urged the acceptance of the native folk tradition and created classical music based on popular Mexican tunes. In an essay he attacked the stodgy salons.

> Their doors remained resolutely closed to the *canción mexicana* until at last revolutionary cannon in the north announced the imminent destruction of the old order. . . . Amid the smoke and blood of battle were born the stirring revolutionary songs soon to be carried throughout the length and breadth of the land. *Adelita*, *Valentina*, and *La Cucaracha* were typical revolutionary songs soon popularized throughout the republic. Nationalism captured music at last. Old songs, almost forgotten, but truly reflecting the national spirit, were revived, and new melodies for new corridos were composed. Singers traveling about through the republic spread far and wide the new nationalistic song; everywhere the idea gained impetus that the republic should have its own musical art faithfully mirroring its own soul.[7]

Ponce was a major contributor to the movement he described. In 1912 and 1913 he composed his *canciones mexicanas*, including the famous *Estrellita*. And at approximately the same time he was training the individual destined to become the most illustrious name in twentieth-century Mexican music—Carlos Chávez.

Of all the intellectual and artistic groups in the country, Mexican painters showed themselves to be most restless. Having already embarrassed the Díaz regime at the centennial celebrations of 1910, these recalcitrant artists continued to scandalize staid society during the first decade of the revolution. When neither interim President León de la Barra nor Francisco Madero agreed to remove the Porfirian director of the Art Academy of San Carlos, the artists took matters into their own hands. Not only did they go out on strike demanding the resignation of the director but on one occasion they pelted the poor soul with rotten tomatoes. The desired change came with Victoriano Huerta, who named Alfredo Ramos Martínez, an impressionist, as director. Ramos Martínez reformed the curriculum, deemphasizing the stifling classroom training in copying and formal portrait work that strived for photographic precision. Instead he encouraged the students to venture out into their Mexican world and paint what they saw and what they felt.

---

7 Quoted in Robert Stevenson, *Music in Mexico: A Historical Survey* (New York, NY, 1971), 233–34.

When the Constitutionalists came in, Ramos Martínez went out but his innovative ideas were not to be overturned. The new director, Dr. Atl (Gerardo Murillo), was even less conventional than his predecessor. Politically a loyal Carrancista but artistically a free spirit, Dr. Atl wanted to convert the academy into a popular workshop for the development of "spiritually authentic" arts and crafts independent from Western traditions.

The second decade of the twentieth century was still an experimental period for the Mexican artist. Diego Rivera spent most of his time in France and Spain, dabbling with some success in cubism. David Alfaro Siqueiros abandoned the brush for the gun and served in the Carrancista army for several years, storing up penetrating impressions of camp life, battles, and death, all of which he would later recreate. José Clemente Orozco spent much of his time painting posters and sketching biting political cartoons and caricatures for Carrancista newspapers. In different ways these three giants of twentieth-century Mexican art were preparing themselves for an artistic renaissance and the most important development in Latin American painting—the muralist movement of the 1920s and 1930s.

SOCIAL CHANGE

Even during the chaos of violence, certain unstructured social change occurred in Mexico. Internal migrations took place, northerners and southerners came into more frequent contact with one another, and distinct regional language patterns began to yield to a more homogeneous national tongue. Increased travel, even that occasioned by the leva, provided a broader conception and a deeper appreciation of Mexico. Greater physical mobility brought about by the war tended to increase mestizaje and began to incorporate previously isolated zones. Thousands of Mexicans escaped obscurity and rose to positions of tremendous power in the various armies. Even though they did not always exercise their newfound influence with moderation, for them the revolution was an agent of social change.

By 1920 a new kind of revolutionary nationalism had begun to emerge. The dead heroes had become martyrs to a young generation of Mexicans who did not always realize that their favorite protagonists had been killed fighting one another. The heroes loomed larger in death than in life, and their errors of judgment and human frailties could be overlooked. Madero became a symbol of democracy, Orozco and Villa of Mexican manhood, Carranza of law and justice, and Zapata of land for the humble. The newly developing revolutionary nationalism had its antiheroes as well: Porfirio Díaz, who had caused the holocaust, and Victoriano Huerta, the very incarnation of treachery and deceit.

In concrete terms, life for the great majority did not improve in the early years after the revolution. In fact, because of the violence, it deteriorated in many ways. But the base of power in the republic had shifted into new hands, and the country seemed to be on the threshold of better times.

RECOMMENDED FOR FURTHER STUDY

Alonso, Ana María. *Thread of Blood: Colonialism, Revolution, and Gender on Mexico's Northern Frontier.* Tucson: University of Arizona Press, 1995.

Azuela, Mariano. *The Underdogs.* Translated by E. Munguía. New York: New American Library, 1963.

Baldwin, Deborah J. *Protestants and the Mexican Revolution: Missionaries, Ministers and Social Change.* Champaign: University of Illinois Press, 1990.

Brunk, Samuel. *The Posthumous Career of Emiliano Zapata: Myth, Memory and Mexico's Twentieth Century.* Austin: University of Texas Press, 2008.

Brushwood, John S. *Mexico in Its Novel: A Nation's Search for Identity.* Austin: University of Texas Press, 1966.

Buffington, Robert M. *Criminal and Citizen in Modern Mexico.* Lincoln: University of Nebraska Press, 2000.

Cano, Gabriela. "Unconcealable Realities of Desire: Amelio Robles's (Transgender) Masculinity in the Mexican Revolution." In *Sex in Revolution: Gender, Politics, and Power in Modern Mexico,* edited by Jocelyn Olcott, et al. Durham, NC: Duke University Press, 2006.

Chang, Jason Oliver. *Chino: Anti-Chinese Racism in Mexico, 1880–1940.* Champaign: University of Illinois Press, 2017.

Chao Romero, Robert. *The Chinese in Mexico, 1882–1940.* Tucson: University of Arizona Press, 2010.

Charlot, Jean. *The Mexican Mural Renaissance, 1920–1925.* New Haven, CT: Yale University Press, 1967.

Ettinger, Patrick W. *Imaginary Lines: Border Enforcement and the Origins of Undocumented Migration, 1882–1930.* Austin: University of Texas Press, 2009.

González, Luis. *San José de Gracia: Mexican Village in Transition.* Austin: University of Texas Press, 1974.

Guzmán, Martín Luis. *The Eagle and the Serpent.* Translated by Harriet de Onís. Gloucester, MA: Peter Smith Publisher, 1969.

Harris, III, Charles H., and Louis R. Sadler. *The Plan de San Diego: Tejano Rebellion, Mexican Intrigue.* Lincoln: University of Nebraska Press, 2013.

_____. *The Texas Rangers and the Mexican Revolution: The Bloodiest Decade.* Albuquerque: University of New Mexico Press, 2004.

López, Rick. *Crafting Mexico: Intellectuals, Artisans, and the State after the Revolution.* Durham, NC: Duke University Press, 2010.

Macías, Anna. "Women and the Mexican Revolution, 1910–1920." *The Americas* 37/1 (1980): 53–82.

Madrid, Alejandro L. *Sounds of the Modern Nation: Music, Culture and Ideas in Post-Revolutionary Mexico.* Philadelphia, PA: Temple University Press, 2008.

Martínez, Anne M. *Catholic Borderlands: Mapping Catholicism onto American Empire, 1905–1935.* Lincoln: University of Nebraska Press, 2014.

Mraz, John. *Photographing the Mexican Revolution: Commitments, Testimonies, Icons.* Austin: University of Texas Press, 2012.

Middleton, P. Harvey. *Industrial Mexico: 1919 Facts and Figures.* New York,: Dodd, Mead and Company, 1919.

O'Shaughnessy, Edith. *A Diplomat's Wife in Mexico.* New York: Harper and Brothers, 1916.

Poniatowska, Elena. *Las Soldaderas: Women of the Mexican Revolution.* El Paso, TX: Cinco Puntos Press, 2006.

Robe, Stanley L. *Azuela and the Mexican Underdogs.* Berkeley: University of California Press, 1979.

Romanell, Patrick. *Making of the Mexican Mind.* Lincoln: University of Nebraska Press, 1952.

Rutherford, John. *Mexican Society during the Revolution: A Literary Approach.* New York: Clarendon Press, 1971.

Salas, Elizabeth. *Soldaderas in the Mexican Military: Myth and History.* Austin: University of Texas Press, 1990.

Simmons, Merle E. *The Mexican Corrido as a Source for Interpretive Study of Modern Mexico (1870–1950).* Bloomington: Indiana University Press, 1957.

Sluis, Ageeth. *Deco Body, Deco City: Female Spectacle and Modernity in Mexico City, 1900–1939.* Lincoln: University of Nebraska Press, 2016.

Smith, Stephanie J. *Gender and the Mexican Revolution: Yucatan Women and the Realities of Patriarchy.* Chapel Hill: University of North Carolina Press, 2009.

Smith, Stephanie J., and Patience A. Schell, eds. *The Women's Revolution in Mexico, 1910–1953.* Lanham, MD: Rowman & Littlefield, 2007.

Sommers, Joseph. *After the Storm: Landmarks of the Modern Mexican Novel.* Albuquerque: University of New Mexico Press, 1968.

Stevenson, Robert. *Music in Mexico: A Historical Survey.* New York: Thomas Y. Crowell, Co., 1971.

THE REVOLUTIONARY AFTERMATH

CHAPTER 30

CALLES: SUPREME CHIEF OF AN INSTITUTIONALIZED REVOLUTION

JEFE MÁXIMO, 1924-34

For a full decade beginning in 1924 Mexico found itself in the firm grip of General Plutarco Elías Calles. Born in Guaymas, Sonora, in 1877 to a family whose fortune had declined, Calles attended normal school in Hermosillo, did quite well in the classroom, and upon graduation, became a primary school teacher in the public school system. His political career began with the revolution, and he served in a number of minor political and military capacities before becoming provisional governor of his home state in 1917. His loyal support of Obregón over a ten-year period won for him official endorsement for the presidency in 1924 and, with labor and agrarian support, he carried the election easily.

CALLES'S DOMESTIC PROGRAM

Conservative elements in Mexico were far from elated by the election that year, for Calles enjoyed a radical reputation. Landowners, both domestic and foreign, feared loss of property; industrialists anticipated higher wages for their workers; and church leaders recognized the new president as a confirmed anticleric. Calles soon let it be known that his domestic policy would not be characterized by the compromise and caution so typical of his predecessor. He not only was willing to ride the swelling tide of social revolution but sincerely believed, at least at the outset, that its course was inevitable. The most strong-willed president since Díaz, Calles had an abiding faith in his own political instinct. Outspoken but often eloquent in public oratory, Calles was not tormented by scruple when treating with his enemies. As the years passed he became more intent on controlling revolutionary factions and relied heavily on the army to dispatch government foes. Political prisoners began filling the jails, and an alarming number "committed suicide."

Calles inherited a more sound financial situation than had Obregón, and he built upon it by establishing the Banco de México, implementing tax reforms, reducing the public debt, and introducing infrastructural projects in road building and rural electrification. To build popular support, he made gestures to campesinos and workers. He more than doubled the amount of land that Obregón had distributed; the vast majority of these 8 million acres went to communal ejidos. To further productivity, the administration initiated a series of irrigation projects, established new agricultural schools, and began to extend agricultural credit to the small farmer. Some of these reforms benefited Zapatistas in Morelos, and even the Maya campesinos of the Caste War were finally lured into the national family as the last of the rebellious villages accepted land titles from the government.

Calles' labor policy continued to favor Luis Morones and the Confederación Regional Obrera Mexicana (CROM), as a means of expanding political support; in fact, Morones was brought into the cabinet as secretary of labor and quickly became the president's most intimate confidant. Other highly placed CROM officials served in the congress and in the state legislatures and even held state governorships. CROM brought hundreds of independent unions under its umbrella, and organized hundreds of new unions. By 1928 CROM membership had reached 1.8 million, and the parent organization had affiliates in most of the states. The influence of the CROM became pervasive and its support of the government unabashed. The confederation even prevented printers from typesetting anti-Calles publications. The president returned the favors by supporting the CROM against employers and, more important, against other unions, in particular, Communist unions. Communist recruitment in Mexico, supported by the publications *El Machete* and *El Libertador* made little headway during the revolutionary years, and Calles suppressed a strike by Communist railway workers in 1926. Wages rose by about 30 percent. But by 1928 many sincere labor leaders had begun to worry about Morones. He had become a wealthy man, and most believed that his diamond rings, new automobiles, and vast holdings in urban real estate had been acquired with union funds and through various extortion schemes.

In the area of education Calles had inherited a positive foundation for nation building from Obregón and Vasconcelos. In 1924 there were approximately one thousand federally supported rural schools in operation. Calles and his able secretaries of education, José Manuel Puig Casauranc and Moisés Sáenz, continued the emphasis on rural education and added two thousand rural schools. To facilitate the acculturation of the Indian, they placed heavy emphasis on the teaching of Spanish and increased efforts to promote popular nationalism, sometimes perceived as assaults on local autonomy and custom. The muralist movement continued to flourish, serving as an educational tool for the non-literate masses intended to teach Mexican history and promote political consciousness.

The government built a health and sanitation program almost from scratch. When the revolution broke out in 1910, sanitation conditions in Mexico were hardly better than they had been during the colonial period. The newly organized Department of Public Health superintended the establishment of a sanitary code designed to ensure cleaner markets and purer public milk supplies. For the first time in Mexican history, the government undertook major vaccination campaigns and in 1926 alone inoculated over 5 million Mexicans against smallpox. The Calles administration also began regular inspections of bakeries, butcher shops, dairies, cantinas, and barber shops closing down those establishments that did not meet prescribed sanitary standards and fining their owners.

A prosperous Luis Morones came to dominate the Mexican labor movement under President Calles. At one time considered a possible successor to Calles, charges of corruption put an end to his political ambitions.

RELATIONS WITH THE UNITED STATES

Relations with the United States still centered around oil. The Bucareli agreements notwithstanding, US Ambassador James Sheffield sought further assurances that foreign property interests would be protected. When Calles refused to go beyond the earlier promises, Sheffield started to bombard the US State Department with red-scare dispatches. The coincidence of the Mexican and Bolshevik revolutions troubled US observers, who tended to equate the two despite the fact that no direct connection existed between them. Nonetheless, Sheffield gradually convinced his superior, Secretary of State Frank B. Kellogg, that a Bolshevik plot was about to divest US citizens of their just property rights. In the summer of 1925 Secretary Kellogg made a remarkable statement to the press.

> The Government of Mexico is now on trial before the world. We have the greatest interest in the stability, prosperity, and independence of Mexico. . . . But we cannot countenance violation of her obligations and failure to protect American citizens.[1]

In a terse rejoinder the Mexican president declared that his government was well aware of its international obligations, but he rejected outright the inherent threat to Mexico's sovereignty in the secretary's pronouncement. He would never allow any nation to create in Mexico a privileged position for its nationals. To indicate that he would countenance no tampering with Mexico's sovereignty, Calles directed the legislature to enact a new petroleum law in December 1925. The legislation required all oil companies to apply to the government for a confirmation of their concessions. To determine whether or not to grant the confirmations, Mexico would apply the doctrine of "positive acts," as had been provided under the terms of the Bucareli agreements, but the concessions would be granted only for a period of fifty years. As Calles began to enforce the new petroleum law, relations between Mexico City and Washington almost reached the breaking point.

---

1   Quoted in David Bryn-Jones, *Frank B. Kellogg: A Biography* (New York, NY, 1937), 176.

In 1927 President Calvin Coolidge replaced Ambassador Sheffield in Mexico City with an old friend from Amherst College, Dwight Morrow, a partner in the famous financial firm of J. P. Morgan. Mexicans were, of course, convinced that the United States had sent yet another representative of Wall Street to press the case for the oil companies. But Morrow turned out to be a pleasant surprise. His first formal address in Mexico City presaged a more harmonious diplomatic atmosphere: "It is my earnest hope," he advised his Mexican audience, "that we shall not fail to adjust outstanding questions with that dignity and mutual respect which should mark the international relations of two sovereign and independent states."[2]

From the outset Morrow demonstrated a genuine interest in everything Mexican. He and his family lived in a Mexican-style house and shopped in the open marketplaces, marveling at native pottery and textiles. The ambassador visited the rural areas, taking special interest in new schools and irrigation projects and inquiring generally about the progress of the social revolution. He even began to study Spanish—not common for US ambassadors in the 1920s—and invited Charles Lindbergh to Mexico on a goodwill tour. In an unusually informal relationship, the president and the ambassador began having breakfast together and, in this relaxed atmosphere, they set to work on the sticky diplomatic problems besetting the two countries.

When the oil controversy first came up, Morrow did not warn that Mexico was on trial before the world; rather, in soft, diplomatic language he told Calles that he believed the issue should be settled in the Mexican courts and expected no special consideration for US citizens. Calles was impressed and quite possibly used his influence to see that the courts rendered a compromise decision. The Supreme Court ultimately held that the oil companies did have to apply for new concessions from the government, that the doctrine of "positive acts" would apply, but that the new permits would not expire at the end of fifty years. For the first time Washington had formally recognized Mexico's full legal sovereignty, even when the interests of US citizens were involved.

THE CRISTERO REBELLION AND THE ASSASSINATION OF OBREGÓN

Calles's most serious problem turned out to be not with the United States but rather with the Roman Catholic Church. Much more anticlerical than Obregón, who had turned his back on the anticlerical articles of the constitution, Calles decided to enforce them. Anticlericalism had diverse promoters, ranging from radicals who saw the church as the main architect of backwardness and lack of progress for the masses to moderates who hoped to reform the church or harness its moral authority to revolutionary ends. Both positions could be found among teachers and functionaries of the ministry of public education. The tensions building through the early 1920s between the church and the government escalated after an interview given to the press by the archbishop of Mexico, José Mora y del Río, in February 1926. Reacting to the implementation of anticlerical provisions in a number of states, the archbishop argued that Roman Catholics could not in conscience accept the constitution. Calles used

---

2   Quoted in David C. Bailey, *Viva Cristo Rey: The Cristero Rebellion and the Church-State Conflict in Mexico* (Austin, TX, 1974), 176.

this declaration to strike with both fists. He first disbanded religious processions, then began deporting foreign priests and nuns and closing church schools, monasteries, and convents. He also decreed that all Mexican priests had to register with civil authorities. The response of the church was both unique and unexpected. On July 31, 1926, the archbishop declared a strike, and on the following day, for the first time since the arrival of the Spaniards four centuries earlier, no masses were celebrated in Mexico.

The strike lasted for three full years; babies went unbaptized and the old died without receiving the last rites. Not a peaceful strike, Calles became more intemperate, gross, and even obscene in his denunciations of the clergy and the pope. Catholic leaders in Michoacán, Guanajuato, Puebla, Oaxaca, Zacatecas, Nayarit, and especially in the backcountry of Jalisco began organizing the masses to resist the godless government in Mexico City. To the cry of *¡Viva Cristo Rey!* Anacleto González Flores, René Capistrán Garza, and Enrique Gorostieta led bands of Cristeros against government outposts. Sordid excesses took place on both sides, and the motivations of combatants were not linked solely to religion but also to perceived violations of local autonomy and agrarian struggles. The Catholic guerrillas burned down the new government schools, murdered teachers, and covered their bodies with crude banners marked *VCR*. In April 1927 the Cristeros dynamited a Mexico City–Guadalajara train, killing more than one hundred innocent civilians. Not to be outdone, the government troops tried to kill a priest for every dead teacher, encouraged children to throw rocks through stained glass windows, looted churches, and took great pleasure in converting them into stables. Cristeros, or suspected Cristeros, were shot perversely without benefit of trial, some swearing to the last moment that an enemy had painted *¡Viva Cristo Rey!* on their houses. The military superiority of the federal army gradually wore down the Cristeros, but when Calles's presidential term expired in 1928, the rebellion was not yet completely suffocated. The conflict provoked the exodus of many Catholics to the United States where they raised money and generated propaganda to support the Cristeros. At the same time they came to constitute a significant bloc of US Catholics, especially in the Southwest.

The presidential election of 1928 and its immediate aftermath shocked the nation. The Constitution of 1917 had recently been amended to provide for a six-year presidential term and, with Alvaro Obregón specifically in mind, the possibility of reelection if it were not immediate. As the electoral process began to unfold, Calles threw his support behind the former president, no doubt thinking that Obregón would return the favor in 1934. Two opposition candidates also entered the fray: General Francisco Serrano, a former secretary of war, and General Arnulfo Gómez, a capable military man who had performed yeoman service in quelling the de la Huerta rebellion of 1923. Both candidates concentrated their efforts on Obregón and attacked the principle of reelectionism, but when they decided the election of 1928 was not going to be fair, they rebelled against the government. Within two months both opposition candidates had been captured and executed.

Obregón's victory brought no relief, however, for he never assumed office. On the afternoon of July 17, 1928, he attended a garden banquet in Mexico City's plush district of San Angel, along with many dignitaries who joined the new administration. While the guests dined, a 26-year-old artist, José de León Toral, sketched caricatures of those sitting at the head table. After showing some of his better drawings to several guests, he moved toward the head table to show the president his work. As soon as Obregón nodded his approval, Toral took a pistol from his pocket and fired five shots into the president-elect's head. Some of the irate guests beat young Toral almost beyond recognition. Several officials intent on investigating the assassination stopped the hysterical mob. Toral refused to answer any questions, even under torture. Only the threat of harm to his family elicited the desired information. In subsequent weeks, a story of church-state conflict unfolded.

Toral's deeply religious sentiments had led him into mysticism when the Cristero Rebellion broke out. A few months prior to the assassination he had been introduced to a nun, Sister Concepción Acevedo de la Llata, remembered in Mexican history simply as Madre Conchita. When the church declared its strike she offered spiritual consolation to the faithful in her own home. Toral and the young zealots who met regularly at Madre Conchita's house became increasingly militant as the rebellion grew more outrageous. They began manufacturing bombs and even discussed plans for killing Obregón. Finally Toral was chosen, or assumed responsibility, for implementing a mission they all considered to be divinely inspired. To make sure everything went as planned Toral began target practice in early July with a pistol borrowed from one of Madre Conchita's friends. Shortly after his confession, Madre Conchita and a number of others were arrested as well.

With historical roots going back centuries, anticlericalism assumed gigantic proportions in the late 1920s and 1930s. Among the ardent advocates were women, long thought to be the "pious" gender.

The trial, conducted in November, offered a great public spectacle, the most sensational judicial inquiry since the trial of Maximilian. In a gesture of unparalleled magnanimity Obregón's widow asked the court to show Toral mercy, but the state was in no mood to turn the other cheek. The prosecuting attorney and the attorney general who testified in behalf of the state were warmly applauded by the gallery. On the other hand, the defense attorney, Demetrio Sodi, was heckled, disparaged, and shouted down with cries of "Death to the Assassin!" and "Death to the Prostitute Concha!" Jurors, fearful for their lives, came to the courtroom armed with pistols. Taunts of mockery and threats of lynching interrupted the proceedings, as did promises of reprisals to the jurors should they vote to acquit. The crowd became so agitated during the summation by Attorney Sodi that he was unable to conclude his defense. The jury did not deliberate long. Toral's act, after all, had been witnessed by many; he implicated Madre Conchita during his testimony, and her denials were unconvincing. Toral got the death sentence, and Madre Conchita, because Mexican law forbade the execution of women, received a prison sentence of twenty years.

THE MAXIMATO AND THE SHIFT TO THE RIGHT

Obregón's assassination created a political vacuum, and only Calles commanded sufficient respect to fill it. He decided not to assume the presidential office himself but would control the nation's destiny as the power behind the scenes. The congress, charged with choosing an interim president until new elections could be held, selected Calles's man, Emilio Portes Gil, a lawyer and former governor of Tamaulipas. Portes Gil proved to be the first of three puppets to fill out Obregón's term, but Calles, as "the Supreme Chief" (*Jefe Máximo*), clearly called the shots. By the time the election of 1929 occurred, Calles had united revolutionary factions and many caciques in a new, widely based political party, the Partido Nacional Revolucionario (PNR). Under his direction, the PNR began to fashion a grand myth that celebrated a revolutionary family headed by the supreme "father." The official party would change its name on several occasions, but its attempts to control the Mexican political process would remain intact for the next 70 years.

When the special election occurred, Calles and his newly organized PNR nominated Pascual Ortiz Rubio for the presidency. The opposition candidate, running under the rubric of the National Anti-Reelectionist party, was the more experienced and much better-known José Vasconcelos. Vasconcelos directed his campaign against the Jefe Máximo rather than against Ortiz Rubio, arguing that a vote for Ortiz Rubio amounted to a vote for Calles. When the government announced the results, Ortiz Rubio was declared the winner by the unbelievable margin of 1,948,848 to 110,979. He served only two years. Shortly after he attempted to oppose Calles on several policy decisions, he picked up a morning newspaper to read that he had resigned. On this occasion the Jefe Máximo picked General Abelardo Rodríguez, a man who had profited from his political position in Baja California, where he invested in several casinos.

Despite the musical chairs played in the presidential office, the years 1928–34 boasted accomplishments. Calles initiated the professionalization and depoliticization of the Mexican army, a process completed under the puppets. Giving the military a major voice within the PNR reduced the threat of anti-government insurrections and smoothed the way for cutting military expenses. Equally important to political well-being and stability was the resolution of the Cristero Rebellion. Ambassador Morrow played a major but unofficial role in the reconciliation as he arranged a series of meetings between Calles, Portes Gil, and Father John Burke, a prominent Catholic leader in the United States. In early June 1929 Father Burke convinced the Mexican leaders that they should allow several exiled bishops to return to the country to participate in the negotiations. By late June a compromise had been hammered out. The church agreed that priests would have to register with the government and that religious instruction would not be offered in their schools. The government declared publicly that it had no intention of destroying the integrity of the church and even allowed that religious instruction would not be prohibited within the confines of the churches themselves. As a result, the hierarchy ordered the Cristeros to lay down their arms and the priests to resume religious services. The resolution of the church–state controversy at this level did not heal the ruptures that the Cristero wars had exposed in so many local conflicts, where popular Catholicisms constituted a crucial element of local identity. Popular religiosity in myriad forms would continue to shape politics and national identity in ways that cannot always be defined as anti-modern or anti-state.

For most of the Maximato, the revolution shifted to the right as the economy stagnated and the pace of social reform slowed, in part because of the onset of the Great Depression. Adding to growing unemployment in Mexico, five hundred thousand Mexicans and Mexican Americans were repatriated by the US government. Oil and metal exports lost markets, industries were paralyzed, and even government workers were fired. As federal revenues dropped by 25 percent and wages declined, many politicians made accommodations with landowners and businessmen. Others enriched themselves by dipping into the treasury; these new "millionaire socialists" sent capital out of the country and bought luxury homes, for example, in the vacation resort of Cuernavaca along what became known as the "Street of Forty Thieves." Land redistribution slowed to a snail's pace, and in at least one case was even reversed. The Terrazas family had been forced to sell most of its huge landholdings during the Obregón presidency but now was allowed to buy them back. The labor movement was abandoned as the government withdrew its support of the CROM and increasingly suppressed strikes. Luis Morones surely had profited at the public trough, but workers paid for his excesses.

The Great Depression had contributed to slowing the pace of social reform, but it cannot explain the extent to which corruption and political repression had pervaded the revolutionary leadership.

> This period [1928–34] . . . is most perplexing. If it were possible to discover what had taken hold of the leadership of Mexico in those debased and clouded years, it would illumine much of Mexican history. Here was a group of new men, most of whom had come from the ranks of the Revolution and had risked their lives in a hundred battles for the redemption of the people from poverty and serfdom. . . . and yet, at the first opportunity, each fell an easy victim to pelf [ill-gotten money] and power. . . .[3]

Revolutionary principles seemed to have been totally discredited, but the last two years of the Maximato saw glimmers of political redemption as the PNR began to articulate

---

3   Frank Tannenbaum, *Mexico: The Struggle for Peace and Bread* (New York, NY, 1956), 69-70.

new reform programs for workers and campesinos. In his study of Calles, Jürgen Buchenau has argued that Abelardo Rodríguez was not simply another puppet of the Jefe Máximo. Calles's declining health and popularity had rendered him less active, with the result that Rodríguez's administration saw the revival of populist trends in the educational, agrarian, and labor sectors, even before the social revolution found its greatest protagonist in 1934.

RECOMMENDED FOR FURTHER STUDY

Bailey, David C. *Viva Cristo Rey: The Cristero Rebellion and the Church-State Conflict in Mexico*. Austin: University of Texas Press, 1974.

Bernstein, Marvin D. *The Mexican Mining Industry, 1890-1950: A Study of the Interaction of Politics, Economics, and Technology*. Albany: State University of New York Press, 1964.

Bortz, Jeffrey. "The Genesis of the Mexican Labor Relations System: Federal Labor Policy and the Textile Industry, 1925–1940." *The Americas* 52/1 (1995): 43-70.

Boyer, Christopher R. *Becoming Campesinos: Politics, Identity, and Agrarian Struggle in Postrevolutionary Michoacán, 1920-1935*. Stanford, CA: Stanford University Press, 2003.

Brewster, Keith. *Militarism, Ethnicity, and Politics in the Sierra Norte de Puebla, 1917-1930*. Tucson: University of Arizona Press, 2003.

Bryn-Jones, David. *Frank B. Kellogg: A Biography*. New York: G. P. Putnam's Sons, 1937.

Buchenau, Jürgen. *Plutarco Elías Calles and the Mexican Revolution*. Lanham, MD: Rowman & Littlefield, 2007.

Butler, Matthew. *Popular Piety and Political Identity in Mexico's Cristero Rebellion, 1927-1929*. New York Oxford University Press, 2004.

Carr, Barry. "The Mexican Communist Party and Agrarian Mobilization in the Laguna, 1920-1945: A Worker-Peasant Alliance?" *Hispanic American Historical Review* 67/3 (1987): 371-404.

Dawson, Alexander S. *Indian and Nation in Revolutionary Mexico*. Tucson: University of Arizona Press, 2004.

Dulles, John W. F. *Yesterday in Mexico: A Chronicle of the Revolution, 1919-1936*. Austin: University of Texas Press, 1961.

Fallaw, Ben. *Religion and State Formation in Postrevolutionary Mexico*. Durham, NC: Duke University Press, 2013.

Gauss, Susan M. *Made in Mexico: Regions, Nation, and the State in the Rise of Mexican Industrialism, 1920s-1940s*. College Station: Pennsylvania State University Press, 2010.

Lieuwen, Edwin. *Mexican Militarism: The Political Rise and Fall of the Revolutionary Army*. Albuquerque: University of New Mexico Press, 1968.

Marak, Andrae M. *From Many, One: Indians, Peasants, Borders, and Education in Callista Mexico, 1924-1935*. Calgary, Canada: University of Calgary Press, 2009.

Martinez, Anne M. *Catholic Borderlands: Mapping Catholicism onto American Empire, 1905-1935*. Lincoln: University of Nebraska Press, 2014.

Meyer, Jean. *The Cristero Rebellion: The Mexican People between Church and State, 1926-1929*. New York: Cambridge University Press, 2008.

Purnell, Jennie. *Popular Movements and State Formation: The Agraristas and Cristeros of Michoacán*. Durham, NC: Duke University Press, 1999.

Quirk, Robert E. *The Mexican Revolution and the Catholic Church, 1910-1929*. Bloomington: Indiana University Press, 1973.

Simpson, Eyler N. *The Ejido: Mexico's Way Out*. Chapel Hill: University of North Carolina Press, 1937.

Spenser, Daniela. *The Impossible Triangle: Mexico, Soviet Russia, and the United States in the 1920s*. Durham, NC: Duke University Press, 1999.

_____. *Stumbling Its Way Through Mexico: The Early Years of the Communist International.* Translated by Peter Gellert. Tuscaloosa: The University of Alabama Press, 2011.

Suárez-Potts, William J. *The Making of Law: The Supreme Court and Labor Legislation in Mexico, 1875-1931.* Stanford, CA: Stanford University Press, 2012.

Tannenbaum, Frank. *Mexico: The Struggle for Peace and Bread.* New York: Alfred A. Knopf, 1956.

Tuck, Jim. *The Holy War in Los Altos: A Regional Analysis of Mexico's Cristero Rebellion.* Tucson: University of Arizona Press, 1982.

Wasserman, Mark. "Strategies for Survival of the Porfirian Elite in Revolutionary Mexico: Chihuahua during the 1920s." *Hispanic American Historical Review* 67/1 (·1987): 87-107.

Young, Julie G. *Mexican Exodus: Emigrants, Exiles, and Refugees of the Cristero War.* New York: Oxford University Press, 2015.

CHAPTER 31

CÁRDENAS AND THE ESSENCE OF THE REVOLUTION

CÁRDENAS

The many Mexicans impatient with the progress of the revolution in 1934 could take heart from the election of Lázaro Cárdenas to the presidency in that year. His revolutionary career was typical of many who worked their way rapidly through the military ranks, ultimately reaching the grade of brigadier general by the end of the first violent decade. But Cárdenas was a civilian at heart. Not an imposing figure physically, he claimed attention as a pensive, methodical man of principle and deep conviction. He had that special charismatic quality of evoking passionate enthusiasm among many and strong dislike among some. And he was no run-of-the-mill politician. Supporting first Obregón and then Calles, be became, in the 1920s, a dominant force in his home state of Michoacán. Cárdenas's objectives were genuinely radical, but he would face serious opposition from powerful interests in implementing lasting social reforms.

Cárdenas' governorship in Michoacán from 1928 to 1932 offered Mexicans a preview of what they might expect. The governor allowed himself to be confronted by the people and listened more than he spoke. He actually made important policy decisions, not on the advice of his confidants but on the direct information received from the public. During years when the national government shirked its educational responsibilities, Cárdenas opened one hundred new rural schools in Michoacán, inspected many classrooms personally, and made sure that the teachers received their salaries on time. He also encouraged the growth of labor and campesino organizations and even managed a modest redistribution of land at the state level. Throughout it all he continued to live modestly.

As the presidential elections of 1934 approached, Calles decided to throw his support behind Cárdenas, fully believing that the forty-year-old governor would follow his dictates. With the official endorsement of the Jefe Máximo, Cárdenas carried the 1933 Partido Nacional Revolucionario (PNR) convention and easily won the presidency in July 1934. Immediately he broke with tradition as he cut his own salary in half and refused to move into the presidential mansion in Chapultepec. Instead, he kept his own modest home. Cárdenas had observed the six-year-old Maximato with some discomfort and once in office determined that he was going to free himself of Calles's domination, revitalize the revolution, and carry it back to the left. Aware that Calles's control over the puppets had rested heavily on army support, the new chief executive assiduously began to cultivate promising junior officers. Not only did he raise salaries and benefits, but he also supported internal reforms within the military designed to educate and impose the idea of revolutionary citizenship on lower-class recruits. The attempt to institutionalize the army in the service of revolutionary engagement had mixed results. Although the army did not become a completely reliable ideological ally, by 1935 Cárdenas became confident enough to remove Calles supporters from the cabinet and other high governmental and military posts. When Calles discovered that he could not manipulate this president, he spoke out vociferously against the administration. In the spring of 1936 Cárdenas ordered the arrest of Calles and a few of his close supporters and sent them into exile in the United States.

Throughout his administration, Cárdenas relied on shifting and heterogeneous coalitions of ideological and opportunistic supporters at national and regional levels, but he also encountered subtle although tenacious resistance from business, church, and landowning interests that stymied reforms and forced him to make deals with local caciques and tactical converts from Callismo. He avoided militant confrontations except in the case of San Luis Potosí's powerful caudillo Saturino Cedillo. As Cedillo became more and more disaffected by and outspoken against Cárdenas's agrarian and oil policies, the president forced his hand; Cedillo withdrew recognition of the government and declared himself in open rebellion. Although the caudillo had strong agrarian backing and the financial support of conservative interests, both domestic and foreign, Cárdenas's army remained loyal and quelled the rebellion within a matter of months.

Cárdenas continued to manifest populist tendencies and did his utmost to keep close contact with the public. While cabinet secretaries and foreign dignitaries fidgeted fretfully in the presidential waiting room, Cárdenas would receive delegaion of workers or campesinos and patiently listen to their problems. A contemporary observer recounted that one morning the president's secretary laid before him a list of urgent matters and a telegram.

> The list said: Bank reserves dangerously low. "Tell the Treasurer," said Cárdenas. Agricultural production falling. "Tell the Minister of Agriculture." Railroads bankrupt. "Tell the Minister of Communications." Serious message from Washington. "Tell Foreign Affairs." Then he opened the telegram which read: My corn dried, my burro died, my sow was stolen, my baby is sick. Signed, Pedro Juan, village of Huitzlipituzco. "Order the presidential train at once," said Cárdenas. "I am leaving for Huitzlipituzco."[1]

The story is undoubtedly apocryphal; yet that it circulated in a sophisticated capital indicates the reputation the president enjoyed. More deeply committed to social reform than any previous Mexican head of state, Cárdenas worked to achieve his goals by building popular support through mass mobilizations of campesinos and workers in sometimes tenuous alliances.

---

1   Quoted in Anita Brenner, *The Wind That Swept Mexico: The History of the Mexican Revolution, 1910–1942* (Austin, TX, 1971), 91.

DOMESTIC REFORMS

Agrarian reform more than anything else dominated the administration's concern during the first few years just as agriculture continued to be the main pillar of the economy. Since the initiation of the land redistribution program some 26 million acres of land had been parceled out, but the figure appeared more impressive on paper than in Mexico's rural zones. Millions of Mexican campesinos still owned no land at all and felt cheated by two decades of revolutionary rhetoric. Cárdenas early made up his mind to fulfill twenty years of promises. By the time his term expired he had distributed 49 million acres, about twice as much as all his predecessors combined. By 1940 approximately one-third of the Mexican population had received land under the agrarian reform program and about half of Mexico's arable land was held by twenty thousand ejidos. Large cattle haciendas on arid or semiarid land remained relatively untouched by the redistribution program. Although Terrazas lands were confiscated early, many were later returned.

The vast majority of the land distributed did not go to individuals or even heads of households but rather to the communal ejidos or collectives. The land was held in common by the communities, sometimes to be reapportioned to individuals for their use and sometimes to be worked by the community as a whole. The largest and most important of the ejidos dating from the Cárdenas redistribution was the huge Laguna cotton ejido, some 8 million acres on the Coahuila–Durango border. The 30,000 families that worked the Laguna collective cooperatively engaged primarily in the cultivation of long-staple cotton but also grew large amounts of wheat, alfalfa, and maize for commercial sale. Most of the families also held small individual plots on which they grew their own subsistence crops. But the Laguna experiment consisted of much more than the mere redistribution of land. Government-supported schools were established, social services in the area were extended, and a modern ejido hospital was built in Torreón, in the center of the Laguna operation. Modernized technologies and attempts to conserve water achieved mixed results at Laguna. Paradoxically, in the long run, the management of water undermined redistribution and culminated in contaminating water and favoring developers. Although the Laguna ejido was the biggest single cooperative land venture initiated by Cárdenas, other large ejidos were established in Yucatán, Baja California, Sonora, Chiapas, and Michoacán. These ventures required large-scale financing, and for this reason the administration founded the Banco de Crédito Ejidal. During the Cárdenas years this agrarian bank made loans available to some thirty-five hundred ejidos.

The ejido was no economic or social panacea, however. A rapid population growth in rural Mexico tended to offset early increases in production, and the Banco de Crédito Ejidal did not possess sufficient capital to meet the continually growing demands. In addition, much favoritism and some corruption circumscribed the distribution of ejido loans. The production of many ejidos, even Laguna, which received adequate loans from the agrarian bank, declined. Cotton production fell by almost nine thousand tons from 1936 to 1938, and henequen production on the new Yucatecan ejidos dropped by forty-five thousand tons during the same period.

Was the ejido program then a failure? The economists answered yes, but Cárdenas had embarked upon the ejido program to meet a social need. Critics harshly denounced cooperative agriculture, but they could not deny the fact that Cárdenas' dedication to agrarian

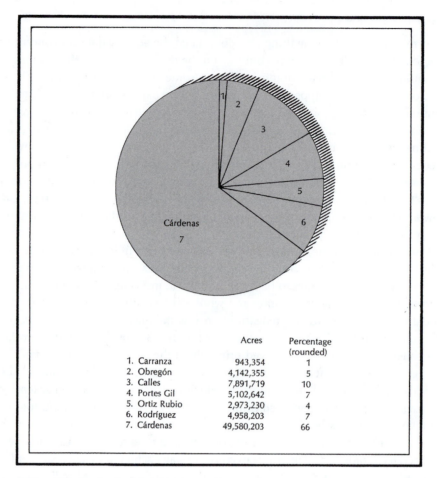

	Acres	Percentage (rounded)
1. Carranza	943,354	1
2. Obregón	4,142,355	5
3. Calles	7,891,719	10
4. Portes Gil	5,102,642	7
5. Ortiz Rubio	2,973,230	4
6. Rodríguez	4,958,203	7
7. Cárdenas	49,580,203	66

Percentage of Land Distribution by Administration, 1915–40

reform diminished the power of the traditional hacienda complex in many parts of Mexico. Millions of campesinos benefitted from land apportionments although sometimes insufficiently. The type of servitude that had bound hacendado and campesinos for centuries was broken by 1940. Life in rural Mexico scarcely became idyllic as a result. Per capita income, infant mortality, and indeed life expectancy lagged behind that of the cities; but the gap in the quality of life between rural and urban Mexico began to decrease for the first time. The government organized campesino leagues into the National Campesino Confederation (CNS) making it the base of agrarian support in the official party. Cárdenas's land reform program fared best in areas that sustained large campesino mobilizations, especially in cases where indigenous and mestizo campesinos had resisted land takeovers aggressively. In other local situations, for example Yucatán and Puebla, landowners both Mexican and foreign, worked with local officials to derail changes.

Land reform was the clarion call of the revolution, not only in the distribution of ejidal property but also in the management of the *montes*, wilderness or forestlands. Montes were communal properties, dating back to the colonial period, on which campesinos lived and felled timber for charcoal production and wood for building supplies. Conflict over how best to administer them came to a head in the 1930s as campesinos and politicians vied for control of the forests, both arguing that their position was for the good of the nation. Lázaro Cárdenas, as part of his larger commitment to land reform, elevated the Department of Forests, Game, and Fisheries to a cabinet post. Under the direction of Miguel Ángel Quevedo, the department took on an ambitious program of forestry management, education programs, and the development of national parks and protected areas for the conservation of flora and fauna. Scientists and forestry officials attempted to organize cooperatives of campesinos to make better use of the economic potential of their forest lands while also encouraging the use of conservation techniques to preserve the forests. This was often met with skepticism by campesinos who feared that their rights to the land would be usurped. Some of the national parks flourished while others encountered class and cultural resistance from developers and local communities.

The relationship between the Cárdenas administration and the church was mixed. The president was an anticleric; during his campaign, in the state of Tabasco, he declared "Man should not put his hope in the supernatural. Every moment spent on one's knees is a moment stolen from humanity."[2] When the PNR met in 1933 to nominate Cárdenas for the presidency, it adopted a platform that, among other things, called for the teaching of socialist doctrine in the primary and secondary schools. A new curriculum had previously been developed by the secretary of education, Narciso Bassols, one that incorporated sexual education. Vociferous opposition from the church succeeded in getting the government to back down somewhat on sex education but not on socialist ideals. No full-scale Cristero-like revolt erupted, but smaller, local militant Catholic movements were active in thwarting implementation of parts of the reform program. At the same time, the activities of Catholic lay organizations gathered new steam in the area of socioeconomic welfare. Catholic women, in particular, expanded their efforts to improve conditions for women and children, with an emphasis on Catholic education and moral reform of families.

Cárdenas significantly increased federal expenditures for education and although more Mexicans learned to read and write, population growth outpaced the educational budget, foiling the attempt to decrease the overall illiteracy rate. The president believed that a socialist education program would serve to foment cultural nation building and to modernize rural society. Beyond the basic curriculum, teachers were expected to help organize people in the countryside in campesino leagues or trade unions and to offer practical training. Scientific approaches to farming, for example, could provide material benefits. Women received instruction to promote public health and raise their children as part of the revolutionary family. The government also promoted Women's Leagues for Social Struggle to encourage civic and secular activism designed to create a multiethnic, multicultural nationalism based on the promise of social justice and development. Civic patriotic fiestas competed with traditional religious celebrations. In response, indigenous and campesino communities, often

---

2   Quoted in Albert L. Michaels, "The Modification of the Anti-Clerical Nationalism of the Mexican Revolution by General Lázaro Cárdenas and Its Relationship to the Church-State Detente in Mexico," *The Americas* 26 (1969): 37.

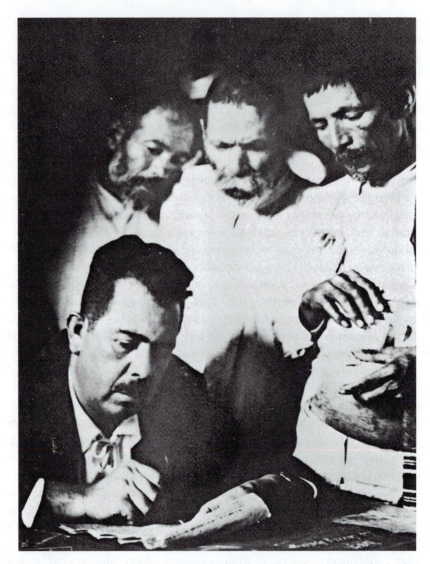

Distributing more land than all of his predecessors combined, Cárdenas here assigns a land title to a group of peasants.

with the backing of the church, resisted changes that threatened their local identities. At the same time, they selectively appropriated new ideas and practices and engaged in interactions with other social groups. To varying degrees, communities participated in shaping multicultural nationalism.

While the church fought to foster social conservatism in patriarchal families, the state worked to promote stable, healthy, and productive working families in a modern industrial economy. Mexican law had begun to conceptualize childhood and adolescence as life stages in need of nurture. The traditional gendered view that fathers worked to support the family while full-time mothers guarded the moral education of their children had never worked for most of the population. Debates on the role of the family resulted in legislation to curb child labor and modernize adoption laws.

In this milieu, children came to play an important role in the development of national identity. Long used to represent the symbolic hope of the nation in moral reform campaigns, in general children were to be seen, not heard. But, under revolutionary reforms, they came to occupy center stage, in what one historian has called the child-centered society of 1920s and 1930s Mexico. Not merely symbols of the new nation, they emerged as citizens in their own rights. While they might not have been old enough to exercise the responsibilities of citizenship bestowed on adults, they could participate in the building of the nation-state through the many state-sponsored campaigns of cultural nationalism. They became civic beings rather than minor family members. Drawing inspiration from international and national conferences on the child, the government directed more spending to children's rights and education.

Beginning with the leadership of José Vasconcelos in the Ministry of Education under Calles, art became a particular focus of children's education. As the muralist movement was central to defining the national esthetic, art education, beginning at the elementary level, taught students across Mexico to draw and paint using revolutionary symbols and history as the basis of the instruction. The children's magazine *Pulgarcito* published the art work of students and functioned as a pedagogical tool. Intended to serve all Mexican children, the magazine paid lip service to indigenismo while focusing primarily on urban society. Subsequent efforts to create cultural consciousness and involve children in nation building included puppet theater, radio programming, and peer literacy initiatives.

To strengthen labor mobilization President Cárdenas chose a new vehicle. Annoyed at the deep-seated corruption that had beset organized labor under Luis Morones, the president supported Vicente Lombardo Toledano, a one-time CROM lieutenant, in his effort to form a new national union. More intellectually oriented than Luis Morones, Lombardo Toledano embraced the Marxist ideas of class struggle and aspired to unite all Mexican workers in a trade union powerful enough to ensure their fight for collective bargaining and improved standards of living. Lombardo Toledano succeeded in joining together some three thousand unions and six hundred thousand workers to form what became in 1936 the Confederation of Mexican Workers (CTM). The CTM made Lombardo Toledano its secretary-general, and although Cárdenas did not give the secretary-general a government position, he pledged to support his efforts although he forcefully opposed Toledano's efforts to integrate campesino organizations in the CTM. Within two years the membership had passed one million. Lombardo Toledano went on to organize the Latin American Confederation of Workers and to participate in anti-fascist popular front movements.

The CTM in its capacity as spokesman for Mexican workers engaged in many different activities. It sponsored health and sanitation projects and organized a series of sports and recreational programs. Most important, the union addressed the inequitable wage structure of the country. A survey in 1930 had estimated that the minimum daily wage on which a head of household might adequately support his family was four pesos and revealed, at the same time, that the average minimum wage in Mexico was one peso, six centavos. As

Lombardo Toledano sought to rectify the wage structure in the country, he found himself blocked at every step by both Mexican and foreign management. Only by concerted effort did the CTM finally succeed in having a new minimum wage of three pesos, fifty centavos adopted on a nationwide basis.

NATIONALIZATION OF OIL COMPANIES

Without question Cárdenas' most dramatic encounter during his six-year presidential term was the oil controversy with the United States, a matter that had ostensibly been resolved by his predecessors. The dispute began, innocently enough, as a conflict between labor and management within the petroleum industry. In 1936 Mexican workers struck for higher wages and better working conditions. While the oil workers were paid quite well in comparison to other Mexican laborers, the oil companies were extracting huge profits from the country and refused to negotiate seriously with union representatives. Worse yet, company policies more often than not demeaned the Mexican worker. To many, little had changed since the miners struck Colonel Greene's Cananea Consolidated Copper Company in 1906. As the strike in the oil industry began to weaken the Mexican economy, President Cárdenas ordered that the dispute be settled by an industrial arbitration board. The board examined the records of the companies and the living conditions of the workers and issued a decision ordering an increase in wages by one-third and an improved pension and welfare system. The companies, claiming that the order meant an increase in operating costs of over $7 million, appealed the decision to the Mexican Supreme Court, which ultimately upheld the original decision of the arbitration board. When the foreign-owned companies refused to obey the Supreme Court decision in its entirety, President Cárdenas held that they had flagrantly defied the sovereignty of the Mexican state and on March 18, 1938, signed a decree nationalizing the holdings of seventeen oil companies that became the foundation of Petróleos Mexicanos (PEMEX).

The nationalization decree became an immediate *cause célèbre*. Cárdenas received congratulatory telegrams from many other Latin American heads of state. Beginning in the Maximato, Mexico had endeavored to cultivate better relations with other Latin American countries that sometimes viewed Mexico (and not just the United States) as meddling in their affairs. In 1930, Genaro Estrada, the foreign minister, established a major principle of Mexico's foreign policy. The Estrada Doctrine proclaimed the right to self-determination of all nations and argued against the intervention of foreign governments in sovereign nations. These principles were widely embraced throughout Latin America and allowed Latin American countries to challenge the United States in Pan-American and Inter-American conferences. Cárdenas's Foreign Minister Eduardo Hay continued to espouse non-interventionism while he fomented cultural diplomacy across the Americas and the world through cultural exchanges of art, music, and sports.

Nationalism also evoked the patriotism of the vast majority of Mexicans. In anticipation of the compensation Mexico would have to pay for the expropriation, Mexicans lined up to offer donations: school children offered their lunch money and women their jewels. Even Cuauhtémoc Cárdenas, the young son of the president, offered the contents of his piggy bank to the cause. A few days after the decree was signed, a huge celebration was held in Mexico City to honor the bold move for economic independence.

Cárdenas was reassured by the support he garnered, for he realized that the reaction would be quite different in the United States. Many US newspapers expressed outrage, and not a few politicians called for intervention to head off a Communist conspiracy on the very borders of the United States. But there would be no intervention on this occasion, as Franklin D. Roosevelt had come to the US presidency enunciating a new "Good Neighbor" policy of nonintervention in Latin America, and he was sympathetic to Cárdenas' social reform program which resonated with his own New Deal. His ambassador to Mexico, Josephus Daniels, did his utmost to ensure that the oil companies negotiated in good faith. The compensation issue was fraught with difficulty as the companies, led by Standard Oil of New Jersey, bombarded the US public with articles and pamphlets vilifying Cárdenas and labeling the expropriation as common theft. The negotiations over compensation paralleled and perhaps benefited from those involving Mexican expropriations of land from US owners that took place between 1927 and 1940. The diplomatic struggles in these cases, for example, over properties of the Colorado Land Company in Baja California and others in the Yaqui valley of Sonora, established guidelines used in the oil dispute. Eventually the rural lands received compensation to the tune of just over $20 million dollars, but Mexico also got some benefits in capital investments that followed. While the companies claimed the value of their expropriated properties to be in the neighborhood of $200 million (and the British companies claimed an additional $250 million), Cárdenas countered that, since the original investment had been recovered several times and since the subsoil belonged to the Mexican nation, a just figure for the American companies was $10 million. Ultimately a mixed claims commission agreed upon a figure of almost $24 million, plus 3 percent interest effective from the day of expropriation.

A CHANGE IN ORIENTATION

Shortly after the expropriation Cárdenas decided to alter the structure of the PNR which Calles had created in 1929. Realizing that Mexico was embarking upon difficult economic times, the president wanted an even more broadly based national party and for that reason established the Partido Revolucionario Mexicano (PRM), on a corporatist model that provided the umbrella for various sectors of society: military, labor, agrarian, and popular. The party, and Cárdenas as its supreme leader, aspired to be the ultimate arbiter of social conflicts. As the official party was all-inclusive, it should encounter little opposition in state or national elections. It used patriotic holidays and the media to inculcate the idea that it represented the interests of all deserving Mexicans, who would enjoy solidarity and benefits of membership in the revolutionary family.

Nonetheless, the federal government was not all powerful; it functioned through shifting alliances with social sectors and regional power brokers to advance policies of economic nationalism and expand programs to incorporate marginalized groups. Powerful opposition from the church, industrialists (especially the Monterrey Group), landowners, and provincial elites had at various times and in different places, blocked or blunted policies considered too radical and antithetical to their interests. Eventually many of these interests would join the Partido de Acción Nacional (PAN), founded in 1939 to oppose anti-clericalism.

Mexico's "Women's Workers' Army" supports the Cárdenas oil expropriation decree during the May Day celebration in 1938.

International anti-fascism at first hindered the PAN's growth, as the Mexican government moved to accept Spanish refugees fleeing from Francisco Franco's fascist regime and to eliminate Falangist pro-Nazi groups in Mexico. Cárdenas not only accepted thousands of Spanish exiles, but also gave asylum to the Russian revolutionary Leon Trotsky.

In 1938 the leftist revolution began to lose some of its thrust and, in retrospect, the oil expropriations climaxed the socialist and nationalist orientation of Cárdenas' program. The president's last two years were characterized by economic difficulty. PEMEX, inheriting antiquated machinery and a lack of trained technicians got off to a shaky start. The situation worsened when Cárdenas learned that he could not buy spare parts for equipment in the

United States. As oil revenues declined, the national debt rose and rampant inflation set in. Between 1935 and 1940 food prices alone rose by a staggering 49.39 percent.

The reform program was expensive, and cuts had to be made somewhere. Educational initiatives decelerated, and land redistribution slowed markedly after 1938 as Cárdenas implemented agrarian reform primarily to garner political support. At the same time, he became more and more sensitive to labor agitation and strikes. And even as US oil interests had lost out in Mexico in a climate of economic nationalism, other US companies increased their investments in Mexican mining, tourism, and industry, a harbinger of things to come after 1940. In evaluating the Cardenista presidency, historian Alan Knight has argued persuasively:

> . . . Cardenismo was, in terms of its objectives, a genuinely radical movement, which promised substantial change . . . it also embodied substantial populist support. . . . [Yet] precisely because of its radicalism, it faced severe resistance not only of an overt kind, but also of a more surreptitious, covert, and successful kind, which led it to fudge, compromise, and retreat on several issues; and that, in consequence, its practical accomplishments were limited and even these which were attained during 1934–40 ran the risk of being subverted in later years by more conservative administrations. None of this, perhaps, is very new or surprising. But the implication of the argument . . . is that Cárdenas—as a vehicle for radical reform— was less powerful, less speedy, and less capable of following its proposed route across a hostile terrain than is often supposed; that, in other words, it was more jalopy than juggernaut.[3]

In 1939 the recently formed PRM met to choose its presidential candidate. It was expected that Cárdenas would throw his support to his longtime political ally Francisco Múgica, but instead the president, believing it was time to change the orientation of the revolution, supported his secretary of war, Manuel Avila Camacho, scion of a powerful landowning family in Puebla. Cárdenas' support assured Avila Camacho of the nomination. Conservatives rallied behind the PAN candidate, Juan Andreu Almazán, a wealthy Catholic landowner, but Avila Camacho easily won the election.

THE ADMINISTRATION OF AVILA CAMACHO, 1940–46

The Mexican citizenry knew little about Avila Camacho prior to the 1940 presidential campaign; in fact, he was nicknamed "the Unknown Soldier." Avila Camacho had joined the revolution in 1914 and gradually worked his way up through the military ranks. His reputation in the army was one of a compromiser rather than a forceful leader. During the course of the campaign, when asked about his feelings toward the church, he answered with the words, *Soy creyente* (I am a believer). The candid response presaged things to come. It meant specifically that anticlericalism was not going to be a focus of his administration, but more generally it meant that neither would the implementation of Articles 3, 27, and 123 be considered the touchstone of social progress. With the war in Europe threatening the Mexican economy, the leaders of the Partido Revolucionario Mexicano (PRM), like Avila Camacho, felt it was time to change direction.

---

3   Alan Knight, "Cardenismo: Juggernaut or Jalopy?" *Journal of Latin American Studies* 1 (1994), 79.

Because the president was determined to embark upon new programs, he began to phase out some of the old. Land redistribution did not stop entirely, but the pace certainly slowed. Whereas Cárdenas had distributed over 49 million acres, Avila Camacho parceled out fewer than 12 million. In addition, because he favored small, private ownership, emphasis was no longer placed on distribution to the ejido but rather to the heads of individual families.

Avila Camacho's educational program also reflected a change of direction, placing heightened emphasis on private initiative. Under the slogan "Each one teach one," the president and his secretary of education, Jaime Torres Bodet, had the congress enact a law exhorting each literate Mexican to instruct one or more illiterates in the fundamentals of reading and writing. The program began amid great fanfare with the president, his cabinet secretaries, and much of the federal and state bureaucracy setting aside an hour each day to give practical reading instruction. Soon, however, the original enthusiasm lagged, and the program slacked off. Obviously, private initiative was not going to achieve what neither church nor state had been able to accomplish over centuries—the elimination of illiteracy. Although the government did not wholly abandon its revolutionary ideology, neither did it persecute the Catholic church as Mexicans became more adept at reconciling their religious beliefs with a secularizing society. Women had taken more active roles in Catholic lay organizations, and new religious inclinations such as Pentecostalism took root. Hybrid, homegrown spiritual movements fused religion with patriotic ideology. At the same time, Catholic charitable activities had slowed, putting more pressure on government social programs.

The president replaced Marxist labor leader Vicente Lombardo Toledano with the more conservative Fidel Velásquez. Lombardo Toledano's departing speech was caustic and indicated his anger at the recent turn of events that suggested the victory of the bourgeoisie over the working class. The press, for some time having portrayed Lombardo Toledano as inordinately egotistical, pointed out that he had used the word *I* (Yo in Spanish) sixty-four times in the farewell address and took the occasion to dub him "the Yo-yo Champion."

Under Velásquez's leadership, government support of the Confederación de Trabajadores de México (CTM) was held to a minimum. Rejecting what he judged to be Marxist domination of the confederation, Velásquez supported moderate elements within the union. Although the new labor leader promoted small increases in wages, they did not keep pace with the rapidly growing inflation that engulfed the Mexican economy. All areas of the country were hit, but especially Mexico City. The entire philosophy of the union movement changed. Velásquez did not even protest vigorously when the administration enacted measures limiting the use of strikes. Displeased with the new leadership, in 1942 workers from the textile and building trades industries withdrew from the CTM, signaling that labor would not completely acquiesce to state control. The most important potential benefit to accrue to the workingman was the creation of a social security agency, the Instituto Mexicano de Seguro Social (IMSS), in 1943; but the initial coverage was so limited that only a small percentage of the workers fell under the program at this time. When Avila Camacho left office fewer than 250,000 workers participated.

WORLD WAR II

World War II broke out in Europe while Lázaro Cárdenas was in the last year of his term, and the president left it to his successor to define Mexico's position. After the Russo-German nonaggression pact of 1939, both the Mexican left led by Lombardo Toledano and Múgica, and the right, led by Almazán, adopted a pro-German position. But when in the summer of 1941 Hitler broke his promises and ordered the German army toward Moscow and Leningrad, the Mexican left could no longer support the Axis cause. President Avila Camacho enunciated an unmistakably pro-Allied course of action, and only a few Mexican fascists and neo-fascists failed to support him. One day after the Japanese attack on Pearl Harbor, Mexico broke diplomatic relations with the Axis powers.

Most Mexicans were satisfied that breaking diplomatic relations was sufficient and that the ultimate step of declaring war was unnecessary. The United States and Mexico appointed members to a joint defense board, and Avila Camacho deported German, Italian, and Japanese diplomats from Mexico. In March 1942, when the president participated in the opening of the new Benjamin Franklin Library in Mexico City, he pointed to the stark cultural contrast between free societies that valued books and the Nazis who burned them. But Mexico would not have entered the war had not Germany forced its hand. On the night of May 14 a German submarine operating in the Caribbean torpedoed and sank the *Potrero de Llano*, a Mexican tanker that was fully lighted and properly identified. On May 24 a second Mexican tanker, the *Faja de Oro*, was torpedoed. Thereupon the president went before the congress and announced that, although Mexico had tried to avoid war, the country could

May Day demonstrators destroy a Nazi flag in front of a German-owned electric company.

no longer accept dishonor passively. He asked for and, without serious debate, received his declaration of war. Furthermore, as wartime propaganda shows, Mexico's involvement provided an opportunity for the government to deemphasize revolutionary ideology in favor of democratic idealism and to discourage opposition. Wartime cooperation with the United States went a long way to repair ties in the previously strained relationship between the two neighbors.

On September 16, 1942, on the 132nd anniversary of the Grito de Dolores, an amazing and unprecedented display of camaraderie occurred on the balcony of the National Palace. Six former presidents—Adolfo de la Huerta, Plutarco Elías Calles (invited to return from the United States), Emilio Portes Gil, Pascual Ortiz Rubio, Abelardo Rodríguez, and Lázaro Cárdenas—linked arms with Avila Camacho to indicate that past antagonisms had been forgotten and that Mexico was fully united in time of war.

Secretary of Interior Miguel Alemán was charged with eliminating subversive activity within the national boundaries. Once a stiff espionage act passed the congress, he began seizing German, Italian, and Japanese properties including banks, drug firms, hardware stores, and coffee plantations to prevent them from being used as bases of propaganda or espionage. Intelligence and national security were delegated to the military, a move that allayed officers' dissatisfaction with cuts to the armed forces budget. The ideal of a professionalized, apolitical military gave way to a relationship in which an ethos of deference to civilian government did not always eliminate military influence on the state. Alemán's secret service rooted out several Gestapo agents and other spies operating clandestine

Mexican nurses march in support of the war effort.

radio stations and relaying instructions to German submarines in the Atlantic. Japanese immigrants to Mexico (who had been arriving as laborers since the late nineteenth century), were spared some of the horrors of the mass incarceration that occurred in the United States. However, over one hundred thousand were forced into internment camps and lost their property as well as their individual liberty. They encountered marked hostility in northern Mexico where anti-Asian prejudices had been responsible for attacks on Chinese immigrants earlier in the century. In some southern states where Japanese Mexicans had been integrated into communities, their neighbors defended them. But many, not only first generation, were detained for periods and then released while others were deported.

Mexico's valuable oil fields and munitions factories were placed under strict military control. Some modernization of the Mexican army occurred as it received military supplies through the Lend-Lease p Velás rogram of the United States. The Avila Camacho administration also moved to provide a small military contingent for service with the Allies. The members of the joint defense board decided that Air Force Squadron 201 should be prepared for duty in the Far East. Approximately 300 Mexican aviators and support personnel received their training in the United States and were assigned to the Fifth Air Corps in the Philippines. Using the P47 Thunderbolt as its operating aircraft, Squadron 201 participated in bombing and strafing raids in the Philippines and Formosa in early 1945, and some Mexicans lost their lives. After the war the squadron received commendations from General Douglas MacArthur and a hero's welcome upon return to Mexico.

More important than token military support, Mexico provided strategic war materials for the Allied war effort. Zinc, copper, lead, mercury, graphite, and cadmium flowed into US war plants and were transformed into military products. The increased demand for these raw materials could have caused prices to soar, but the Mexican government instituted price controls as further testimony to its cooperation.

The most unique, and ultimately the most controversial, contribution to the war effort was the mutual decision made by Avila Camacho and Franklin D. Roosevelt to allow Mexican laborers (*braceros*) to serve as agricultural workers in the United States. The draft in the United States had depleted the workforce, and Mexicans picked up the slack as they began to harvest major crops. The terms of the carefully spelled out agreement authorized workers to receive free transportation to and from their homes, forbade them from displacing US workers or to be used to suppress wages, set minimum wages at 46 cents an hour (later raised to 57 cents), and authorized Mexican labor officials to make periodic inspections to certify that the rules were being enforced. By the spring of 1943, despite the opposition of organized labor in the United States, the program expanded to include nonagricultural labor as well. When the war ended, approximately three hundred thousand Mexicans had worked in twenty-five different states, some as far north as Minnesota and Wisconsin. Problems arose in the program, for the regulations were not always enforced and the workers encountered deep-seated prejudices in the United States. Yet braceros often built networks of solidarity internally and sought transnational support, among other strategies that allowed them to define their own racial and behavioral norms.

With thousands of men working as braceros in the United States, Mexican women were called upon to serve the country by working in industry, in the fields, and at home.

INDUSTRIALIZATION

Although it would be an exaggeration to suggest that its support during World War II materially influenced the outcome, nevertheless Mexico made a more substantial contribution than any other Latin American country. Moreover, the war was of singular importance for Mexico's internal development. It marked improved relations with the United States and an acceleration of the country's economic development even as agricultural production declined.

Wartime shortages in the United States and Europe deprived Mexico of its normal sources of imported manufactured goods and convinced even the doubters of the need for industrialization. The goal was not simply to meet the demands of the domestic market but to produce a surplus of manufactured goods for export to other Latin American countries. Even during the last years of the Cárdenas administration, Mexican social scientists had begun to argue the absurdity of dividing the same pie into smaller and smaller pieces. To provide a better life for the vast majority of the people, it was imperative that the country's economic base be expanded through a major program of industrialization. The program not only would provide additional employment for a rapidly growing population but also, through increased productivity, generate wealth and improve the standard of living for the masses.

To foster industrial expansion the Avila Camacho administration established the Nacional Financiera, a government-owned bank created primarily to provide loans to industry but also to oversee the industrial process. In each year of the administration the favorable loans of the Nacional Financiera increased dramatically, reaching a total of 286.8 million pesos by 1945.

In addition, other incentives, such as tax exemptions and tariff protection, persuaded potential investors to take acceptable risks. With the CTM in the hands of Fidel Velásquez, he readily pledged his support to the new industrialists. Native Mexican capital began to pour into new industrial pursuits but, because the program was such an ambitious one, in 1944 the congress passed legislation allowing foreign participation in industrialization with the proviso that Mexican capital own the controlling stock in any mixed corporation. Some US investors jumped at the opportunity. The Export–Import Bank in the United States also extended credits.

The new and often young industrialists took it upon themselves to educate Mexican politicians, and indeed the public, in the virtues of industrial growth. In 1942 they founded the Cámara Nacional de la Industria de Transformación to develop an industrial consciousness in the country and to convince policymakers that without industrialization the masses were doomed to perpetual privation. During the Avila Camacho years industrialization dominated the front pages of newspapers. The Cámara became an effective propaganda agency and lobby, arguing that what was good for industry was good for the nation. Its initial goal was to foster those industries that relied on Mexican raw materials, for example, cereal processing, edible oil from agricultural products, sugar, alcohol, and the manufacture of fibers and chemicals. The ultimate goal was to export manufactured goods.

The industrial push gathered momentum throughout the war years as a wide range of old industries were expanded and new ones initiated. The textile, food-processing, chemical, beer, and cement industries grew rapidly. Pig iron production increased from 99,200 metric

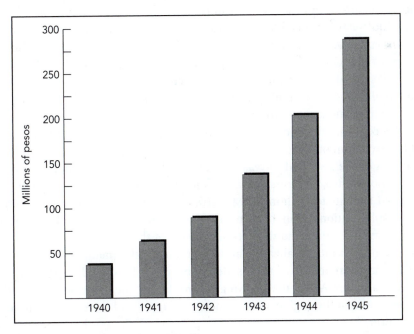

Industrial Loans of the Nacional Financiera, 1940–45

Source: Sanford A. Mosk, *Industrial Revolution in Mexico* (Berkeley, 1950), 238.

tons in 1930 to 240,300 in 1946, and during the same period steel nearly doubled from 142,200 metric tons to 257,900. Electrical capacity rose by 20 percent, and the industrial proletariat grew steadily in size.

As predicted, industrialization generated new wealth. The national income almost tripled, from 6.4 billion pesos in 1940 to 18.6 billion in 1945. Per capita income jumped from 325 pesos the year Avila Camacho was inaugurated to 838 pesos during his last year in office. As social critics quickly pointed out, however, increased per capita income for a growing middle class did not necessarily mean a more equitable distribution of wealth or increased earning power for the poor. Furthermore, tax exemptions for investors were part of a more general weakness in the tax structure, which produced insufficient revenue.

The post-Cárdenas period had moved away from social justice economics. The agrarian revolution languished. Productivity on most of the ejidos had not lived up to expectations, and government planners decided not to experiment further with communal agriculture. This certainly did nothing to alleviate social unrest in rural areas. The agrarian movement led by Rubén Jaramillo in Morelos attracted supporters, but its efforts were increasingly met by government repression.

For almost a decade the official party had gradually opened up. By 1946 it was no longer dominated by intellectuals, agrarian reformers, and ardent defenders of the labor movement. It now represented the business and industrial communities as well as economists and technicians. To symbolize the change without giving up the revolutionary myth, in 1946 the party decided to change its name to the Partido Revolucionario Institucional/Party of the Institutionalized Revolution (PRI). The party was organized on a corporatist structure of interest groups: campesinos, urban labor, and a more amorphous sector of middle-class organizations. For a still relatively weak federal government to rule through this single party, its leaders undertook frequent negotiations and crafted shifting alliances not only with the constituent groups on a national level, but also with local, regional, and state officials and interests. Although the old caudillismo had disappeared, state leaders like Puebla governor Maximino Ávila Camacho (brother of the president) could still exert influence on national decision making. The authoritarian tendencies of local leaders could inhibit the implementation of national policies, but they could also be used to carry them out.

The power of the state had increased under Cárdenas, but it did not become a Leviathan that subordinated the popular classes and civil society. Agrarian and labor reforms had delivered benefits to millions of Mexico's campesinos and workers, explaining why Cárdenas is still a national icon. In terms of economic nationalism, Cárdenas nationalized the oil industry and completed the nationalization of the railways. His policies had provided an opening for industrialization and economic development, promoting a capitalist bourgeoisie that even benefitted from state intervention. This trend continued vigorously under Avila Camacho. Again, in Alan Knight's words: ". . . the jalopy was hijacked by new drivers; they returned the engine, took on new passengers and then drove it in quite a different direction."[4]

---

4   Ibid., 107.

RECOMMENDED FOR FURTHER STUDY

Albarrán, Elena Jackson. *Seen and Heard in Mexico: Children and Revolutionary Cultural Nationalism*. Lincoln: University of Nebraska Press, 2014.

Ashby, Joe C. *Organized Labor and the Mexican Revolution under Cárdenas*. Chapel Hill: University of North Carolina Press, 1967.

Bantjes, Adrian. *As If Jesus Walked on Earth: Cardenismo, Sonora, and the Mexican Revolution*. Wilmington, DE: Scholarly Resources, 1998.

Becker, Marjorie. *Setting the Virgin on Fire: Lázaro Cárdenas, Michoacán Peasants, and the Redemption of the Mexican Revolution*. Berkeley: University of California Press, 1996.

Benjamin, Thomas. "Rebuilding the Nation." In *The Oxford History of Mexico*, edited by Michael C. Meyer and William H. Beezley, 438–470. New York: Oxford University Press, rev. 2010.

Blum, Ann S. *Domestic Economies: Family, Work, and Welfare in Mexico City, 1884–1943*. Lincoln: University of Nebraska Press, 2009.

Boyer, Christopher, ed. *A Land Between Waters: Environmental Histories of Modern Mexico*. Tucson: University of Arizona Press, 2012.

_____. *Political Landscapes: Forests, Conservation, and Community in Mexico*. Durham, NC: Duke University Press, 2015.

Brenner, Anita. *The Wind That Swept Mexico: The History of the Mexican Revolution, 1910–1942*. Austin: University of Texas Press, 1971.

Castro, Justin J. *Radio in Revolution: Wireless Technology and State Power in Mexico, 1897–1939*. Lincoln: University of Nebraska Press, 2017.

Chew, Selfa. *Uprooting Community: Japanese Mexicans, World War II, and the U.S.-Mexico Borderlands*. Tucson: University of Arizona Press, 2015.

Cline, Howard. *Mexico: Revolution to Evolution, 1940–1960*. New York: Oxford University Press, 1963.

Cronon, E. David. *Josephus Daniels in Mexico*. Madison: University of Wisconsin Press, 1942.

Dwyer, John J. *The Agrarian Dispute: The Expropriation of American-Owned Rural Land in Postrevolutionary Mexico*. Durham, NC: Duke University Press, 2008.

Fallaw, Ben. *Cárdenas Compromised: The Failure of Reform in Post-revolutionary Yucatán*. Durham, NC: Duke University Press, 2001.

Fallaw, Ben, and Terry Rugeley, eds. *Forced Marches, Soldiers and Military Caciques in Modern Mexico*. Tucson: University of Arizona Press, 2012.

García, Jerry. *Looking Like the Enemy: Japanese Mexicans, the Mexican State, and US Hegemony, 1897–1945*. Tucson: University of Arizona Press, 2014.

Jayne, Catherine E. *Oil, War and Anglo-American Relations: American and British Reactions to Mexico's Expropriation of Foreign Oil Properties, 1937–1941*. Westport, CT: Greenwood Press, 2001.

Jones, Halbert. *The War Has Brought Peace to Mexico: World War II and the Consolidation of the Post-Revolutionary State*. Albuquerque: University of New Mexico Press, 2014.

Joseph, Gilbert M., and Jürgen Buchenau. *Mexico's Once and Future Revolution: Social Upheaval and the Challenge of Rule since the Late Nineteenth Century*. Durham, NC: Duke University Press, 2013.

Kiddle, Amelia M. *Mexico's Relations with Latin America during the Cárdenas Era*. Albuquerque: University of New Mexico Press, 2016.

Kiddle, Amelia M., and María L. O. Muñoz, eds. *Populism in Twentieth Century Mexico: The Presidencies of Lázaro Cárdenas and Luis Echeverría*. Tucson: University of Arizona Press, 2010.

Knight, Alan. "Cardenismo: Juggernaut or Jalopy?" *Journal of Latin American Studies* 26/1 (1994): 73–107.

Loza, Mireya. *Defiant Braceros: How Migrant Workers Fought for Racial, Sexual, and Political Freedom*. Chapel Hill: University of North Carolina Press, 2016.

Millon, Robert P. *Mexican Marxist: Vicente Lombardo Toledano*. Chapel Hill: University of North Carolina Press, 1966.

Moreno, Julio. *Yankee Don't Go Home: Mexican Nationalism, American Business Culture, and the Shaping of Modern Mexico, 1920–1950*. Chapel Hill: University of North Carolina Press, 2003.

Mosk, Sanford A. *Industrial Revolution in Mexico*. Berkeley: University of California Press, 1950.

Navarro, Aaron. *Political Intelligence and the Creation of Modern Mexico, 1938–1954*. University Park: Pennsylvania State University Press, 2010.

Olcott, Jocelyn. *Revolutionary Women in Postrevolutionary Mexico*. Durham, NC: Duke University Press, 2005.

Paz, Maria Emilia. *Strategy, Security, and Spies: Mexico and the U.S. as Allies in World War II*. University Park: Pennsylvania State University Press, 1997.

Rankin, Monica. *¡Mexico, la patria! Propaganda and Production during World War II*. Lincoln: University of Nebraska Press, 2009.

Rath, Thomas. *Myths of Demilitarization in Post-Revolutionary Mexico, 1920–1960*. Chapel Hill: University of North Carolina Press, 2013.

Santiago, Myrna J. *The Ecology of Oil: Environment, Labor, and the Mexican Revolution, 1910–1938*. New York: Cambridge University Press, 2006.

Schuler, Friedrich E. *Mexico between Hitler and Roosevelt: Mexican Foreign Relations in the Age of Lázaro Cárdenas, 1934–1940*. Albuquerque: University of New Mexico Press, 1998.

Sherman, John W. *The Mexican Right: The End of Revolutionary Reform, 1920–1940*. Westport, CT: Praeger, 1997.

Wakild, Emily. *Revolutionary Parks: Conservatism, Social Justice, and Mexico's National Parks, 1910–1940*. Tucson: University of Arizona Press, 2011.

Weyl, Nathaniel, and Sylvia Weyl. *The Reconquest of Mexico: The Years of Lázaro Cárdenas*. New York: Oxford University Press, 1939.

Wilkie, James W. *The Mexican Revolution: Federal Expenditure and Social Change since 1910*. Berkeley: University of California Press, 1967.

Wolfe, Mikael D. *Watering the Revolution: An Environmental and Technological History of Agrarian Reform in Mexico*. Durham, NC: Duke University Press, 2017.

CHAPTER 32

SOCIETY AND CULTURE IN THE POSTREVOLUTIONARY PERIOD

DAILY LIFE IN COUNTRYSIDE AND CITY

Between 1920 and 1940 the lives of average Mexicans changed more rapidly than they had in any previous twenty-year period. The population decline of the decade of violence stopped and, with the greater political stability of the 1920s and 1930s, the number of people began to climb rapidly. When Obregón came to office in 1920 the total population of the country was slightly over 14 million, but when Cárdenas turned over the presidency to his successor twenty years later the total had almost reached 20 million. Mexico was not yet an urban country although the percentage of population living in communities with fewer than twenty-five hundred people had slipped from about 70 percent in 1920 to some 65 percent in 1940. By then cultural anthropologists found fewer Indians who spoke a native tongue exclusively.

The new *ejidatario* in rural Mexico, unlike his campesino forefather, was no longer bound to the hacienda. He could travel as freely as his pocketbook allowed. It was no longer necessary to purchase daily necessities in the tienda de raya, but if he did shop in the ejido store, he would likely find prices somewhat lower than those in the nearby community. The old mayordomos, of course, were gone, and in most cases ejido officials were elected by the ejidatarios themselves.

Thousands of families who had fled their villages in search of security during the early revolution returned to find many things transformed. Hard-surface roads began to supplant bumpy dirt pathways, and buses rolled over them with more or less regularity. Bicycles began to push burros off the highways. Tractors challenged the ox-drawn plow. Gasoline engines, rather than mules or horses, turned the mills that ground the corn, and gasoline pumps drew the water from nearby streams. Electricity arrived even in some small towns.

The anthropologist George M. Foster recorded some of the major changes in Tzintzuntzan, Michoacán, in the 1930s.

The first major cultural impact of modern times occurred . . . in the spring of 1931. General Lázaro Cárdenas, then Governor of Michoacán, sent a Cultural Mission consisting of teachers who specialized in plastic arts, social work, music, home economics, physical education, and "small industries," and a nurse-midwife and an agricultural engineer. . . . Most villagers were reluctant to cooperate, to help find living quarters, and to aid staff members and rural teachers. . . . In spite of such difficulties, however, the Mission had a big effect. A number of the more progressive families agreed to whitewash their houses, to improve the appearance of the village, and the present plaza, then a barren wasteland with a few houses, was cleaned up, sidewalks were marked out, flowering jacaranda trees were planted, a fountain . . . was built . . . and place was cleared for a bandstand. At the end of the first month there was an open house exposition of arts, crafts, sports, and civic betterments, to which General Cárdenas came as guest of honor. . . . Electricity was brought in from Pátzcuaro in 1938 and running water . . . was installed about the same time. . . . In 1939 for the first time village children had ready access to the full six years of primary schooling.[1]

The rural school in the 1920s and 1930s became a focal point of village life. Economic and social activity centered on programs initiated by the rural teachers as the ministry of education tried to instill revolutionary nationalism. Schools challenged, although not always successfully, the domination of the church over cultural life. Regional responses to new impositions varied as they provoked both dialogue and conflict between communities and outsiders. Professional medical specialists gradually entered the countryside. Although some villagers regarded them with suspicion, the outsiders frequently exchanged knowledge with local healers and midwives. Life expectancy improved and the infant mortality rate dropped from 222 deaths per thousand in 1920 to 125 twenty years later. But by no means did all of the essentials of the good life come to rural Mexico between 1920 and 1940. Poverty continued to be the single most pervasive characteristic of rural life.

City life became more pleasant, at least for some, as the amenities of technology became increasingly commonplace. Mexico's first commercial radio station began transmission in 1923, and scores huddled around each neighbor lucky enough to own or have access to a receiver. Two years later the department of education established its own radio station and began beaming educational broadcasts to primary schools recently equipped with receivers. *Radionovelas*, broadcasts of sporting events, and constant streams of music helped relieve the tedium of daily life. The federal government initiated a new radio program in 1937 called *La Hora Nacional*, intended to integrate listeners into the national mainstream through programs on Mexican culture, folklore, art, and music. Popular music flourished on the radio, in dance halls like the Salón México, and in films with the rhythms and lyrics of *mariachi* and *ranchera* music; even Afro-Caribbean introductions like the *danzón* and the *bolero* became part of the canon of musical nationalism. Popular composer and lyricist Agustín Lara has been called the "minstrel of the national soul;" his boleros evoked forbidden sensual pleasures and emotional intimacy. Despite the misogynist lyrics, his romanticizing of male sexuality appealed to women of all classes in urban areas.

---

1   George M. Foster, *Tzintzuntzan: Mexican Peasants in a Changing World* (Boston, MA, 1967), 26–29.

As Mexico left the era of the silent film and moved into the age of sound, Fernando de Fuentes's *Allá en el Rancho Grande* awoke world interest in the Mexican cinema.

Another revolution in popular culture occurred in film. By the mid-1930s the commercial cinema had begun to challenge the bullfight for preeminence in entertainment. Hollywood films dominated, but the Mexican film industry received support under Cárdenas to promote mexicanidad. The most interesting films relayed patriotic content depicting the glories of the revolution, like Ezequiel Carrasco's *Viva México* (1934) and Luis Lezama's *El Cementerio de los Aguilas* (1938). But the greatest commercial success was Fernando de Fuentes's musical *Allá en el Rancho Grande* (1936), starring Tito Guízar and Esther Fernández. The extraordinary box office profits of this film led to a cinematographic genre of folk films, soon to be dominated by two towering figures of popular culture, Jorge Negrete and Pedro Infante. The melodramatic tropes of Golden Age cinema promoted an idealized Mexico and sought to draw mass spectators to share laughter and tears.

Without question, the internal combustion engine most changed the lifestyle of the urban areas. The motor car had arrived in Mexico shortly before the outbreak of hostilities in 1910, but, because of the tremendous dislocations of that first revolutionary decade, it did not begin to transform Mexican life until after 1920. By 1925, fifty-three thousand motor vehicles were digesting 35 million gallons of gasoline annually; 15 years later the number of vehicles had tripled and gasoline consumption had quadrupled. In the early 1920s the motor vehicle was still a prestige symbol, carrying a select few to and from their offices or their families on an occasional weekend outing. Later in the decade motor car racing became popular, and often left a toll of people killed or injured. But by the 1930s, with a tremendous increase in the number of trucks and buses, the internal combustion engine had transformed commercial life as well as disrupted staid social patterns. Automobiles, trucks, and buses required an expanded highway network; and Mexican engineers and day laborers completed several thousand miles of new, hard-surface roads. Road building acquainted Mexicans with places beyond the bounds of the patria chica, promoted tourism, revitalized local economies, and facilitated industrial development.

The growth of Mexico City was nothing short of spectacular. The high national rate of population growth, coupled with an internal migration from rural to urban areas, gave Mexico City, with nearly 1.8 million people in 1940, an increase of more than a million in only two decades. The dramatic growth yielded its share of social problems as neither the job market nor the school system could absorb the tremendous influx. The medical infrastructure and public health initiatives were sorely tested as well, as syphilis reached epidemic proportions in the national metropolis in the 1920s and the government sought to control prostitution. Those fleeing to the capital in search of a better life often than not encountered disappointment. Rapid growth in other cities also caused difficulties for tens of thousands of recent arrivals. While Mexicans laughed with derision at the prohibition experiment in the United States, alcoholic consumption rose sufficiently in Mexico in the 1920s to cause alarm in the medical and scientific communities and to occasion anti-alcohol campaigns.

Demographic growth gave rise to another, more salutary change. Revolutionary governments, particularly in the 1930s, began to shape Mexico City to reflect the new ideological landscape that was neither colonial nor Porfirian. A particular kind of Mexican modern style developed in the capital city that merged international Deco with an idealized vision of an indigenous rural past, both imagined through women's bodies—the hypermodern, streamlined flapper or the voluptuous, exoticized native. The hybridity of Mexican Deco, in the way it could adapt or reshape the cultural past, undergirded its nationalistic character. Revolutionaries inherited the task of completing the Palace of Fine Arts (Palacio de Bellas Artes), begun in the Porfiriato to celebrate the centenary of Mexican independence, but not finished. Mexican architects complemented the imposing neoclassical exterior with a stunning Deco interior, and the building was inaugurated in 1934. Deco architecture dominated the 1920s development of the Condesa neighborhood and its centerpiece, the Parque México in central Mexico City, known today for its *fresa* (yuppie) nightlife and upscale apartments.

While the national theater and an upscale neighborhood were designed for elites, urban development projects also targeted the working classes, especially the many women who migrated to the capital after the war. Markets served as spaces of independence where women could sell their wares, bargain for the best price, and contribute to the vitality of the city. The traditional outdoor markets which represented an idealized indigenous past could be reborn in permanent indoor markets, subject to sanitary regulations. In 1934, for example, the Abelardo Rodríguez Market opened its doors. Built within the exterior walls of a convent near the Zócalo, the functional Deco interior housed a theater, day-care center, and a school for the children of the many women who worked there. Murals on interior walls, depicting a peaceful countryside, assured patrons of the benefits won by the revolutionaries. To this day, the market is a bustling space of commerce in the busy Centro Histórico, surrounded by an informal economy that persists despite the many attempts to quash it.

Aspects of life were changing for Mexican women as we now know from recent rich scholarship on women and gender relations in the period from 1920 to 1940. The revolution did not bring radical transformations for women, but it did accelerate a process begun earlier by economic modernization in opening up more social spaces for them outside the home. The revolution could be said to have modernized patriarchy as it redefined gender roles under a paternalistic umbrella. For men, this meant reining in a masculinity based

Palacio de Bellas Artes after its renovation for the bicentennial.

on violence to create a self-disciplined, hard-working "revolutionary" man. For women, it opened up more jobs in education and social services in roles that conformed to the idealized feminine state of motherhood with its implied self-denial and nurturing instincts. These mostly urban middle-class women could teach children and poor mothers how to become modern citizens.

When women's public aspirations went further than participating in the areas of education and moral reform—for example, when they tried to assert equality in the workplace, justice in wages or rents, or the right to vote—the revolutionary state was not so accommodating. For the most part, union bosses were able to keep women in the least skilled factory jobs, ejidatarios were male, and politicians worked to limit female suffrage. Images of the "new" woman (primarily white and middle-class) in newspapers, advertising, and film promoted domesticity, marriage, and motherhood. More negative stereotypes presented women (especially poor indígenas) as abused and victimized—in need of education and moral reform. The "chica moderna," with bobbed hair, ready-to-wear dress, and stiletto shoes, was still a controversial figure who threatened gender norms. Workplaces were still construed as fraught with sexual danger.

The façade of the Abelardo Rodríguez public market near the Zócalo.

Nonetheless, more and more women entered the worlds of business, education, government service, and medicine. Between 1920 and 1924 only 223 Mexican women received university degrees; ten years later the figure had doubled. By 1930 women participated more actively in civic work than at any previous time, and hundreds of thousands had successfully rebelled against family-arranged marriages. In some areas, women became powerful voices in labor organizing. This was the case of female coffee sorters in Córdoba, Veracruz, where women successfully balanced activism with work and family life to advocate for their rights. Often, in order to gain traction, activist women couched their quest for citizenship in the discourse of motherhood and family. This strategy along with the revolutionary paternalism of men, including President Cárdenas, helped women get the right to vote in a number of Mexican states, but full female suffrage would have to wait until the 1950s.

While Mexicans were struggling to establish a new identity, immigration from the Middle East and Asia challenged the limits of the ideal of mestizaje and questioned the definition of what it meant to be Mexican. In the nineteenth century, Arab immigrants began to arrive during the Porfiriato and came in increasingly numbers as the Ottoman empire fell. Initially using Mexico as a stopover on the way to the United States, eventually Mexico became a destination of choice for many Middle East immigrants who styled themselves as Lebanese, rather than use the terms Turks or Arabs that acquired racist overtones in the Mexican context. Overall the community thrived, establishing Arab-language schools, publications, and organizations; today the Mexican-Lebanese Cultural Institute estimates that there are eight hundred thousand Mexicans of Middle Eastern descent. As time went on, their children identified as Mexican, but their influence is still felt in Mexico today with figures like Salma Hayek and Carlos Slim who proudly proclaim their Middle Eastern heritage. More importantly, the *taco al pastor*, meat marinated in a spicy red sauce served with pineapple, onion, and cilantro, is an adaptation of *schwarma* brought to Mexico City in the 1930s.

The history of Chinese and Japanese migration to Mexico dates to the colonial period, as many crossed the Pacific with the Manila galleons, some against their will. In the nineteenth century, a new kind of immigration began with large numbers of Chinese who came as laborers. They constituted a significant part of the labor force that built many of the railroads running north to connect Mexico to markets in the United States. In the northern borderlands, many Chinese immigrants settled, despite vociferous and sometimes violent racism directed toward them by Mexicans. Mexicali, which to this day boasts a large Chinese-Mexican population, attracted agricultural workers and merchants who became an important part of building the agricultural base of the region.

Most Chinese immigrants in the early twentieth century were male; they sought to settle permanently and many married Mexican spouses despite a law that stripped these women of their Mexican citizenship. While the law was generally ignored, there were instances when the state acted and expelled families; recent research has looked at the Mexican-Chinese communities who resided in Hong Kong and Macau until they were repatriated to Mexico in 1960. Early Japanese immigrants went to Chiapas to work on coffee plantations; most settled in the borderlands and became part of what it means to be Mexican in northwest Mexico and the US southwest. Sushi Saga in Tucson, Arizona is owned by a Japanese-Mexican family that migrated from Sonora. The menu boasts traditional Japanese sushi and Mexican tacos with fusion rolls named after cities in Sonora.

CULTURAL NATIONALISM IN THE ARTS

Mexican culture during the period 1920–40 came to the service of the revolution. The artistic, literary, and scholarly communities, with an abiding faith in the new thrust of Mexican life, supported revolutionary ideals by contributing their unique talents to awakening consciousness in the new social order. The aim was to fashion a national citizen and promote national solidarity among diverse sectors of the Mexican population. The process is nowhere better illustrated than in the cultural achievements of Mexico's most famous painters.

The restlessness of Mexico's artistic community had been apparent during the late Porfiriato and the first revolutionary decade, but Mexican art came into its own and won world acclaim after 1920. Secretary of Education José Vasconcelos commissioned leading artists to fill the walls of public buildings with didactic murals, and Mexico's artistic renaissance combined European training and indigenous motifs in the service of the revolution. Art was no longer directed to the privileged few who could afford to buy a canvas; it was for the public. If Mexico was not yet able to provide a classroom and a seat for every child in the country, some measure of popular education could be provided by a muralist movement carried out on a scale grander than any the world had yet known.

David Alfaro Siqueiros, *Head of an Indian*.

A detail from Rufino Tamayo's *Allegories of Music and Song* (1933).

Juan O'Gorman, *Enemies of the Mexican People*.

Coordinating his efforts with the artists' union, the Syndicate of Technical Workers, Painters, and Sculptors, Vasconcelos instructed the artist simply to paint Mexican subjects. To be sure, youthful enthusiasm carried some astray; but giants such as Jean Charlot, Rufino Tamayo, Juan O'Gorman, David Alfaro Siqueiros, Fernando Leal, and Roberto Montenegro emerged in the process as well. In particular, two muralists began to dominate the movement. That they are highlighted in these pages is not to diminish the magnitude of outstanding works by the numerous talented artists and architects of the period. As John Lear illustrates, many other artists' collectives flourished as they interacted with labor organizations to place the proletariat at the center of their work. They played a fundamental role in creating a new national identity that blended influences of nationalism and internationalism.

During the 1920s and 1930s, Diego Rivera (1885–1957) became the most renowned artist in the western hemisphere and one of the most imposing artists of the twentieth century. A man of boundless talent and energy, he used the Indian as his basic motif. Rivera's realistic murals did not invite freedom of interpretation as he depicted humanistic messages for the illiterate masses on the walls of the Agricultural School in Chapingo, the Cortés Palace in Cuernavaca, the National Preparatory School, the Department of Education, and the National Palace in Mexico City. The Spaniard during the colonial period and his criollo offspring during the nineteenth century had enslaved the Indian and had kept him in abject poverty. It was now time to integrate the Indian into the mainstream of society just as Rivera was incorporating him into the mainstream of his murals. Although Rivera emphasized content over form, he was without rival in technique. His symmetry was near perfect, but his

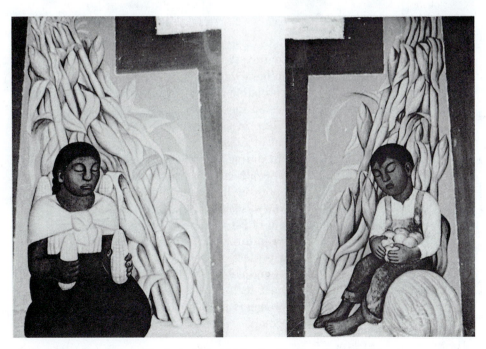

Details from Diego Rivera's mural in the Agricultural School at Chapingo (1926–1927).

genius emerged even more clearly in his use of line and color. He invariably depicted Indians in soft, gentle lines, with earthen red and brown tones, while the oppressors, white foreigners and white Mexicans, were portrayed in sharp lines and harsh colors.

Rivera's greatest masterpiece was composed at the Agricultural School in Chapingo. With esthetic originality and flamboyance, Rivera spelled out his appreciation of the new revolutionary ideology. Not only did his frescoes display the virtues of land redistribution, but they offered lessons of sociopolitical reality. On one wall he portrayed bad government—the campesinos betrayed by false politicians, fat capitalists, and mercenary priests. But the opposite wall was one of revolutionary hope—a scene of agricultural cultivation, a rich harvest, and a liberated peasantry. Nude female figures, and his own pregnant wife, represented the bounty of a productive earth. Just in case the humanist agrarian message might be lost, he painted over the main stairway of the building, "Here it is taught to exploit the land, not man."

Diego Rivera's *The Billionaires* (1928), a mural in the Department of Education, satirizes international capitalism.

Diego *Rivera's Awaiting the Harvest* (1923), a fresco in the Court of Labor, Department of Education.

Only slightly less famous than Rivera, but no less a genius, was José Clemente Orozco (1883–1949). As the violent decade passed, Orozco abandoned his career as a biting political caricaturist for mural art. Less a realist than Rivera, Orozco could be more forceful, expressive, and passionate. He was willing to experiment with new techniques as well as themes. His brutal and distorted Christs, grotesque depictions of God, and nude Madonnas pilloried all religious piety and brought forth a storm of protest. While angry crowds mutilated some of his frescoes, Vasconcelos did not interfere with Orozco's freedom of expression although the secretary was becoming increasingly anti-Marxist, even pro-fascist. Orozco's scenes of violence during the revolution bring to mind Francisco Goya's *Horrors of War*, and he might well have had the Spanish master in mind when he conceived them.

Orozco had his tender moments too. During the 1920s, when he could see the first hesitant steps of social progress, some of his murals portray hope. His famous fresco *Cortés and Malinche* shows two nude and carnal figures sitting over the figure of the old, prostrate Mexico and represents the process of mestizaje, the biological and spiritual origin of the Mexican people. But in the 1930s, even as the pace of social reform began to accelerate, Orozco became increasingly disillusioned with the progress being made. After spending several years in the United States, he went back to his native Jalisco, and in the Instituto Cabañas in Guadalajara he decided to return to the theme of the conquest. The new Cortés he portrayed was a powerful, violent conqueror in full armor and with sword in hand. The only hope held out is that the spirit whispering in Cortés's ear might convince him to use his power and technology for good rather than for evil.

Also nationalistic, but less public, in her painting was Frida Kahlo (1907–54). Her marriage at the age of twenty to Diego Rivera gave her access to the intellectual avant-garde, but she easily earned recognition on her own as a painter who drew on the tradition of Mexican religious folk art to self-referentially portray human suffering. Her struggle to understand national identity in post-revolutionary Mexico and her battle to overcome debilitating physical impairments are stunningly depicted in the bloody and fragmented bodies of her subjects and her self-portraits. Kahlo also encouraged her students to represent everyday life by painting objects of popular folk art. The ways in which her own production embraced mestizaje and rejected traditional conceptions of gender (and especially of the self-abnegating Virgin Mary) became more fully appreciated in the late 20th century, both in Mexico and abroad.

The painters were not alone in transforming a national art into a nationalistic one. The literary community contributed as well with its novels of the revolution. Two of the best came from the pen of Martín Luis Guzmán (1887–1976), who published *El águila y la serpiente* (translated as *The Eagle and the Serpent*) in 1928 and *La sombra del caudillo* (*The Shadow of the Leader*) the following year. The first constitutes a novelized personal memoir of the young Guzmán, who left the comfortable life of a university student to join the revolution and found himself a Villista. Captivated by Villa's personality, yet always afraid of his violence, Guzmán sketched the Centaur of the North most vividly in his discussion of revolutionary justice.

> This man wouldn't exist if his pistol didn't exist. . . . It isn't merely an instrument of action with him; it's a fundamental part of his being, the axis of his work and his amusement, the

José Clemente Orozco's *Modern Migration of the Spirit* (1933), from the fresco *Quetzalcóatl and the Aspirations of Mankind,* was painted at Dartmouth College.

constant expression of his most intimate self, his soul given outward form. Between the fleshy curve of his index finger and the rigid curve of the trigger there exists the relation that comes from the contact of one being with another. When he fires, it isn't the pistol that shoots, it's the man himself. Out of his very heart comes the ball as it leaves the sinister barrel. The man and the pistol are the same thing.[2]

Villa did not turn out to be the ideal man Guzmán had hoped for. The intellectual simply could not communicate with the people's hero and ultimately took his leave. Guzmán never abandoned his revolutionary faith, but he began to wonder whether the goals could be attained without all the violence.

Guzmán's disenchantment with the politics of the revolution became even more evident in *La sombra del caudillo,* a novel inspired by the presidential election of 1928, which

2   Martín Luis Guzmán, *The Eagle and the Serpent,* trans. Harriet de Onís (Garden City, NY, 1965), 210.

José Clemente Orozco's fresco *Cortés and Malinche.*

saw opposition candidates Francisco Serrano and Arnulfo Gómez both dead by election day. Mexico's most powerful novel decrying dictatorship, *La sombra del caudillo* is written with truculence and righteous indignation. But even here Guzmán does not give up on the revolution. To the contrary, he directed passionate condemnation against Calles for having betrayed the ideals of the movement.

In a less cynical vein, Nellie Campobello (1900–1986) used short narrative portraits in *Cartucho* (1931) to portray the violence of the revolution but at the same time to honor the people who sacrificed their lives for it. *Cartucho* is especially significant because it is the only testimonial depiction by a woman to have been published in the immediate aftermath of the revolution. In this work and in *Las manos de mamá* (1937), translated as *My Mother's Hands*, Campobello also highlights the changes provoked by the revolution for women and indigenous peoples in the Mexican north of Pancho Villa.

The Indianist novel of the revolution reached its apex in 1935 with Gregorio López y Fuentes's *El Indio.* Without naming a single character or place, López y Fuentes is able to portray the Indian, not as the noble savage, but as a man beset with social problems that society can help to overcome. The plot is not intricate as the author was more interested in atmosphere. He admirably succeeded not only in illustrating the wide chasm between Indian and white society but also in making intelligible the deepest suspicions of whites harbored in the Indian community. López y Fuentes received Mexico's first National Prize for Literature for this perceptive model.

The cultural nationalism focusing on the Indian was carried into the arena of music by Carlos Chávez (1899–1978). After studying in Europe and the United States, in his late twenties Chávez returned to Mexico to become director of the National Conservatory of Music and to begin a brilliant career as a conductor, pianist, musical scholar, and composer. His *Sinfonía India* (1935) and *Xochipili-Macuilxochitl* (1940) were scored for pre-Columbian instruments, but realizing that not all performing orchestras would be able to acquire such esoteric accouterments as strings of deer hooves, he made provision for modern substitutes. But both rhythmically and melodically the compositions were inspired by Mexico's indigenous heritage, as well as other vernacular music and dance. Chávez was fully integrated into overall efforts to promote cultural nationalism; he affiliated the conservatory with the Ministry of Public Education and collaborated on many projects with other intellectuals, artists, and academics, even some of whom, like Aaron Copland, he met in the United States and lured to visit Mexico. He sponsored Silvestre Revueltas as the conductor of the conservatory orchestra, and encouraged his research into vernacular music. Revueltas composed orchestral music and film scores, including the suite for the film *Redes* (1936), on which he collaborated with American photographer Paul Strand. A movie of social realism, the film focuses on the battles of a poor Veracruz fishing community with big business and corrupt bosses. The magnificent score beautifully evokes the aura of realism and inspires empathy for the downtrodden villagers. The message of social injustice is startlingly rendered.

Also keenly interested in issues of social justice were the anthropologists who studied indigenous communities. They aspired to cultural nationalism but in a way that diverged from Vasconcelos' ideas about assimilation. Vasconcelos was interested in accumulating a record of cultural diversity as part of the nation's patrimony but not in preserving discrete Indian cultures and values. With the publication in 1922 of Manuel Gamio's highly important three-volume *La población del valle de Teotihuacán*, Mexican archaeologists, ethnologists, and social anthropologists began to take a new look not only at antiquities but at contemporary Indian problems as well. Rejecting theories of racial inferiority and the anti-Indian posture of many nineteenth-century intellectuals, they set out to depict the glories of the Indian past, to restore Indian arts and crafts, and in general to revitalize contemporary Indian cultures. Their efforts to valorize indigenous cultures (known as *indigenismo*) were greatly facilitated in 1936 when the government established the Departamento Autónomo de Asuntos Indígenas and three years later the Instituto Nacional de Antropología e Historia. No great historical work emerged from the period in the proliferation of biographies to venerate or disparage the many revolutionary leaders. Porfirio Díaz, of course was demonized.

Despite the mediocre record of Mexican historians from 1920 to 1940, the country's overall cultural production was remarkable during those two decades. The revolutionary state supported the movement for cultural nationalism through the patronage of popular arts, mural painting, music, radio, and film; by renaming streets and other places for revolutionary heroes and events; and through educational programs that tried to assimilate indigenous peoples and secularize local cultures. The degree to which these wide-ranging efforts succeeded in fomenting nation building and shared popular memories varied, but they did contribute to the formulation of one powerful and dynamic vision of Mexican national identity. This revolutionary identity had not obliterated forms of Catholic nationalism, but it captured the Mexican spirit and yielded a sense of national confidence and pride for many. The artistic outpouring of the 1920s and 1930s was unequaled in Latin America.

RECOMMENDED FOR FURTHER STUDY

Alfaro-Velcamp, Teresa. *So far from Allah, So close to Mexico: Middle Eastern Immigrants in Modern Mexico.* Austin: University of Texas Press, 2007.

Benjamin, Thomas. *La Revolución: Mexico's Great Revolution as Memory, Myth, and History.* Austin: University of Texas Press, 2000.

Bliss, Katherine. *Compromised Positions: Prostitution, Public Health and Gender Politics in Revolutionary Mexico City.* University Park: Pennsylvania State University Press, 2001.

Brushwood, John S. *Mexico in Its Novel: A Nation's Search for Identity.* Austin: University of Texas Press, 1966.

Buffington, Robert M. *Criminal and Citizen in Modern Mexico.* Lincoln: University of Nebraska Press, 2000.

Campobello, Nellie. *Cartucho and My Mother's Hands.* Translated by Doris Meyer and Irene Matthews. Austin: University of Texas Press, 1988.

Chang, Jason Oliver. "Racial Alterity in the Mestizo Nation." *Journal of Asian American Studies* 14/3 (October 2011): 331–359.

Charlot, Jean. *The Mexican Mural Renaissance, 1920–1925.* New Haven, CT: Yale University Press, 1967.

Chew, Selfa. *Uprooting Community: Japanese Mexicans, World War II, and the U.S.-Mexico Borderlands.* Tucson: University of Arizona Press, 2015.

Coffey, Mary K. *How a Revolutionary Art Became Official Culture: Murals, Museums, and the Mexican State.* Durham, NC: Duke University Press, 2012.

Craven, David. *Diego Rivera as Epic Modernist.* New York: G. K. Hall and Co., 1997.

Delpar, Helen. *The Enormous Vogue of Things Mexican: Cultural Relations between the United States and Mexico, 1920–1935.* Tuscaloosa: University of Alabama Press, 1992.

_____. "Mexican Culture, 1920–45." In *The Oxford History of Mexico*, edited by Michael C. Meyer and William H. Beezley, 508–33. New York: Oxford University Press, rev. 2010.

Folgarait, Leonard. *Mural Painting and Social Revolution in Mexico, 1920–1940: Art of the New Order.* New York: Cambridge University Press, 1998.

_____. *So Far from Heaven: David Alfaro Siqueiros' The March of Humanity and Mexican Revolutionary Politics.* New York: Cambridge University Press, 1987.

Foster, George M. *Tzintzuntzan: Mexican Peasants in a Changing World.* Boston, MA: Little, Brown and Company, 1967.

Fowler-Salamini, Heather. *Working Women, Entrepreneurs, and the Mexican Revolution: The Coffee Culture of Córdoba, Veracruz.* Lincoln: University of Nebraska Press, 2013.

González, Fredy. "Chinese Dragon and Eagle of Anáhuac: The Local, National, and International Implications of the Ensenada Anti-Chinese Campaign of 1934." *Western Historical Quarterly* 44/1 (Spring 2013): 49–68.

Guzmán, Martín Luis. *The Eagle and the Serpent.* Translated by Harriet de Onís. Garden City, NY: Doubleday, 1965.

Hayes, Joy Elizabeth. *Radio Nation: Communication, Popular Culture and Nationalism in Mexico, 1920–1950.* Tucson: University of Arizona Press, 2000.

Hershfield, Joanne. *Imagining La Chica Moderna: Women, Nation, and Visual Culture in Mexico, 1917–1936.* Durham, NC: Duke University Press, 2008.

Hershfield, Joanne, and David R. Maciel, eds. *Mexico's Cinema: A Century of Film and Filmmakers.* Wilmington, DE: Scholarly Resources, 1999.

Hu-Dehart, Evelyn. "Racism and Anti-Chinese Persecution in Mexico." *Amerasia Journal* 9/2 (1982), 1–28.

_____. "Voluntary Associations in a Predominantly Male Immigrant Community: The Chinese on the Northern Mexican Frontier, 1880–1930." In *Voluntary Organizations in the Chinese Diaspora.* Edited by Khun Eng Kuah and Evelyn Hu-DeHart, 141–168. Hong Kong: Hong Kong University Press, 2006.

Indych-López, Anna. *Muralism without Walls: Rivera, Orozco, and Siqueiros in the United States, 1927–1940.* Pittsburgh, PA: University of Pittsburgh Press, 2009.

Krippner, James, ed. *Paul Strand in Mexico*. New York and Mexico City, Mexico: Aperture/Fundación Televisa, 2010.

Lahr-Vivaz, Elena. *Mexican Melodrama: Film and Nation from the Golden Age to the New Wave*. Tucson: University of Arizona Press, 2016.

Lear, John. *Picturing the Proletariat: Artists and Labor in Revolutionary Mexico, 1908–1940*. Austin: University of Texas Press, 2017.

López, Rick. *Crafting Mexico: Intellectuals, Artisans, and the State after the Revolution*. Durham, NC: Duke University Press, 2010.

López y Fuentes, Gregorio. *El Indio*. New York: Ungar, 1961.

Macías-González, Víctor M., and Anne Rubenstein, eds. *Masculinity and Sexuality in Modern Mexico*. Albuquerque: University of New Mexico Press, 2012.

Mora, Carl J. *Mexican Cinema: Reflections of a Society, 1896–1980*. Berkeley: University of California Press, 1982.

Olcott, Jocelyn, Mary Kay Vaughan, and Gabriela Cano, eds. *Sex in Revolution: Gender, Politics, and Power in Modern Mexico*. Durham, NC: Duke University Press, 2006.

Reed, Alma. *Orozco*. New York: Oxford University Press, 1956.

Schiavone Camacho, Julia Maria. *Chinese Mexicans: Transpacific Migration and the Search for a Homeland, 1910–1960*. Chapel Hill: University of North Carolina Press, 2012.

Sluis, Ageeth. *Deco Body, Deco City: Female Spectacle and Modernity in Mexico City, 1900–1939*. Lincoln: University of Nebraska Press, 2016.

Turner, Frederick C. *The Dynamic of Mexican Nationalism*. Chapel Hill: University of North Carolina Press, 1968.

Vaughan, Mary Kay. *Cultural Politics in Revolution: Teachers, Peasants, and Schools in Mexico, 1930–1940*. Tucson: University of Arizona Press, 1996.

Vaughan, Mary Kay, and Steven E. Lewis, eds. *The Eagle and the Virgin: Nation and Cultural Revolution in Mexico, 1920–1940*. Durham, NC: Duke University Press, 2006.

Wolfe, Bertram D. *The Fabulous Life of Diego Rivera*. New York: Stein and Day, 1969.

Wood, Andrew Grant. *Agustín Lara: A Cultural Biography*. New York: Oxford University Press, 2014.

DEVELOPMENT AND DISSENT UNDER A ONE-PARTY SYSTEM

CHAPTER 33

FROM REVOLUTION TO EVOLUTION

MIGUEL ALEMÁN, 1946–52

In January 1946, the official party for the first time endorsed a civilian, Miguel Alemán, as its presidential candidate. Alemán's administration represented a change in postrevolutionary leadership. The new generation of cosmopolitan civilian officials did not come from a military background but rather from the educated middle class. These technocrats (professionals with specialized skills and advanced education), many of whom had attended the same preparatory school and the National University, led the campaign to make Mexico a modern industrialized state, advancing the "Mexican miracle" of the postwar years.

The new president reduced the military's share of the budget to less than 10 percent of the total for the first time in the twentieth century, and the generals accepted the decision, in part because of the military's new role in intelligence services. Over the years the military share of the budget was gradually reduced from 70 percent in 1917 to 7 percent in 1952. More successfully than its Latin American neighbors, Mexico curbed the problems of rampant militarism although the army remained a powerful ally of the government.

With a healthy dollar reserve turned over to him by his predecessor, Alemán launched an impressive number of public works projects designed both to provide jobs for a steadily growing labor force and to meet a series of crucial developmental needs. Most important was the construction of dams to control flooding, increase arable land acreage, and supply ample power for the modernization impulse. The Morelos Dam on the Colorado River near Mexicali worked agricultural wonders in the northwest as some seven hundred thousand arid acres were reclaimed and converted into a rich truck-farming zone. In the northeast, in cooperation with the US government, work commenced on the Falcón Dam in the lower Rio Grande Valley. Completed in 1953, the year after Alemán left office, the Falcón project yielded substantial agricultural benefits as well. The major project in the south was the harnessing of the Papaloapan River in the states of Puebla, Veracruz, and Oaxaca. Not only were tens of thousands of acres added to the agricultural base of the nation, but a series of hydroelectric stations contributed to the tripling of Mexico's electrical output capacity by 1952.

Other large-scale public works centered on improving the communications network. In addition to modernizing the railway system, Alemán completed Mexico's segment of the Pan-American Highway. This all-weather road made possible automobile travel between the United States and Guatemala. Of equal importance commercially was the completion of the Isthmian Highway, which connected Puerto México and Salina Cruz across Tehuantepec. To cater to the tourist traffic, an increasingly important source of foreign exchange, Alemán ordered the construction of a four-lane superhighway between the capital and the Pacific resort town of Acapulco, soon to become a playground for the world's rich. In total, paved roads increased from about 2,500 miles in 1946 to over ten thousand by 1952.

Postwar Mexico was prosperous and booming for a growing middle class. Hundreds of small factories, not only in Mexico City but in Monterrey, Guadalajara, Puebla, and San Luis

The main library at the National University of Mexico, University City.

Potosí, took advantage of the cheap and abundant source of electric power and began to transform the economy and the face of the nation. Low taxes and high rates of profit encouraged both Mexican and foreign capital to continue investing in the industrial sector of the economy. Petróleos Mexicanos (PEMEX) expanded its activities; new pipelines and refineries, coupled with accelerated drilling, made it possible for the state-owned corporation to double its production between 1946 and 1952.

The most impressive construction project of all was the new University City built to house the National University of Mexico. Dedicated in 1952, the campus of three square miles stood out as one of the most modern in the world, boasting unparalleled architectural and artistic achievements. The plans were conceived by leading artists such as Juan O'Gorman (1905–82), the buildings designed by talented architects such as Félix Candela, and the walls adorned with anthropological and historical murals by Rivera and Siqueiros. Alemán considered the university a monument to his own presidency, and the first thing visitors encountered when entering the campus in the 1960s was a huge statue of Alemán himself.

Relations between the United States and Mexico strengthened considerably in the Cold War period. Accepting an invitation from President Truman, Alemán became the first Mexican head of state to visit Washington. Truman also called upon the Mexican president in Mexico City in 1947 and delighted his hosts by placing a wreath at the monument of the Niños Héroes, the boy cadets who had fallen fighting US troops 100 years before.

A mural by José Chávez Morado at the Faculty of Science Building, University City.

Both congresses voted to return all trophies of war sequestered in the middle of the nineteenth century. The outward manifestations of goodwill had practical effects as well. The United States was able to count on Mexican support in the cold war, and loans from the Export–Import Bank flowed into Mexico at an accelerated pace. Trade relations became more interdependent than ever before. National agencies and state governments promoted tourism; in 1952 alone US travelers left hundreds of millions of dollars in the country. The porous border between the two nations also facilitated the illegal entry of narcotics into the United States. Not a new issue, bootlegging and smuggling had been common since the nineteenth century and intensified after the revolution and included female traffickers. The most famous, Lola la Chata, dealt marijuana, heroin, and morphine from the 1930s to the 1950s until her final arrest in 1957. During much of her career she received protection from government officials and police, a problem that would only intensify over time.

To some, Mexico seemed a model of health and prosperity. But behind the showy façade Alemán had created, serious problems had begun to sap the vitality of the institutionalized revolution. Mexico's tax structure, the most regressive in Latin America, could not provide sufficient funds for education. As an example, the library at the new University City, while a marvel to gaze at, was embarrassingly short of books. Row after row of empty shelves symbolized the building spree that failed to cope with basic issues and emphasized form over content. Worse still, as new primary and secondary schools were built throughout the country, teachers' salaries were so paltry that it was almost impossible to staff them with qualified

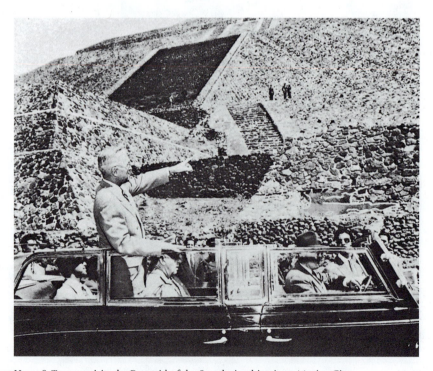

President Harry S. Truman visits the Pyramid of the Sun during his trip to Mexico City.

professionals. School attendance remained low. Of the 6 million schoolchildren in the age bracket six to fourteen, fewer than 2.25 million attended classes on a regular basis. Despite the emphasis successive administrations since 1920 had placed on rural education, the 1950 census revealed that only 5 percent of rural children finished the sixth grade.

Corruption beset the administration and many new millionaires emerged between 1946 and 1952. Alemán had built a reputation as something of a playboy in Hollywood who engaged in dalliances with actresses, and then went on to amass a huge fortune as president. The displays of sprawling mansions, yachts, and airplanes, paid for with bribes, demonstrated that venality had sabotaged any remnants of an already stagnant reform program for urban workers and the rural poor. Politicians built their new homes in older fashionable districts like Tabubaya and in the new suburbs of Las Lomas de Chapultepec. Among the most scandalous and venal politicians was Maximino Ávila Camacho, brother of the former president. As governor of Puebla and then as a cabinet minister he became even more wealthy. The contracts he divvied out for telecommunications and road building earned kickbacks of at least 15 percent. According to his archenemy Lombardo Toledano, Maximino ". . . boasts of twenty houses in the Chapultapec hills, twenty automobiles, and half a million pesos worth of fine, pure-blooded, Arabian horses; he affirms in a loud voice that he has two hundred silk suits with two hundred pairs of shoes."[1] Attendees compared his lavish parties with Roman orgies. Greed and hedonism had become the order of the day.

During World War II, the Mexican government appropriated, from Allied and German propaganda efforts within the country, the necessary skills to improve media technology. This led to the diminishing influence of newspapers and radio programs produced directly by the PRI as it handed out contracts to new media outlets in return for their loyal support. The precedent set the course for the growth of privatized Mexican media empires such as Emilio Azcárraga's Televisa that monopolize television even today.

While PRI politicians continued to mouth revolutionary euphemisms, the industry-driven economy widened socioeconomic inequalities. The labor movement was not crushed, but it was intimidated. When in April 1950 Secretary of the Treasury Ramón Beteta exhorted the increasingly powerful industrialists of Monterrey to keep their costs down so that Mexican industry could become competitive, in effect he invited them to keep wages depressed. When petroleum workers struck, the government dispatched troops to patrol the fields and sacked 50 union leaders. Despite John Maynard Keynes's revolution in economic theory, the Mexican worker was not yet to be confused with a consumer. Real wages had fallen after 1939 and did not get back to the level of that year until 1968.

THE PRESIDENCY OF RUIZ CORTINES, 1952–58

When PRI officials met to choose Alemán's successor, many believed it crucial to rekindle confidence in the integrity of the party. In order to repudiate the rampant corruption of the Alemán administration, they selected sixty-one-year-old Adolfo Ruiz Cortines, whose

---

1 Quoted in Stephen R. Niblo, *Mexico in the 1940s: Modernity, Politics, and Corruption*, (Wilmington, DE, 1999), 283.

personal honesty and devotion to service were impeccable. During his governorship of Ve-racruz and tenure as secretary of interior under Alemán he had garnered a reputation for party loyalty, efficiency, and integrity. With official party support he defeated his leading opponent, Miguel Henríquez Guzmán, by a margin of almost five to one.

Ideologically much akin to his predecessor, the hard-working but unspectacular president did not disappoint those who had urged a cleansing of bureaucratic corruption. He announced in his inaugural speech that he would demand strict honesty and ordered all public officials to make public their financial holdings. During the next several years he fired a number of notorious grafters, but these measures hardly ended corruption. In an even more significant political reform he pushed through the congress legislation fully enfranchising the Mexican woman in 1953. This long overdue measure culminated years of active campaigning by women's organizations throughout the country.

The Mexican economy remained dynamic during the Ruiz Cortines years as industry continued to receive government support and, in turn, established an entire series of new records for production. A devaluation of the peso in 1953 (to a rate of 12.50 to the dollar) helped stabilize the economy and prompt new foreign investment.US capital, encouraged by the healthy economic indicators, poured into the country unhesitatingly, and US visitors in the larger cities saw familiar signs advertising General Motors, Dow Chemicals, Pepsi-Cola, Coca-Cola, Colgate, Goodyear, John Deere, Ford, Proctor and Gamble, Sears Roebuck, and other corporate giants that would not have dared to invest their stockholders' dollars in Mexico twenty years earlier. The new, mixed economy seemed to be working.

Believing that Alemán had overtaxed the idea of public works, the new Mexican president did not initiate many grandiose construction schemes, but he did see hundreds of his predecessor's projects through to completion. Whereas Alemán had built huge dams, Ruiz Cortines sponsored smaller projects; whereas Alemán had built superhighways, Ruiz Cortines paved two-lane roads to help farmers get their products to a suitable market.

For the first time since its foundation in 1943, the IMSS expanded its coverage sufficiently to constitute an agency of genuine social importance and one that emphasized the paternalism of state hegemony. Appointed by Ruiz Cortines as director, Antonio Ortiz Mena not only obtained increased funding but moved the services into the countryside for the first time. The number of IMSS-sponsored clinics rose from 42 to 226 and hospitals from 19 to 105. Public health improved but services were unequally distributed. Rural services did not yet approximate urban ones, but a beginning was at least made as about one hundred thousand rural persons received some kind of social security coverage for the first time. The basic issue of low wages persisted. Although salaries did rise by an average of 5 percent a year in the period from 1952 to 1958, many workers lost their increases to inflation, which rose annually at a rate of 7.3 percent. Unionized workers in the steel industry had job security, but suffered under corrupt union bosses. In general, social workers and welfare advocates emphasized changes in daily practices and diet to improve nutrition and working-class living standards. They tried to enlist wives and mothers to encourage new habits of work and saving. These efforts could not overcome the basic problem of low salaries and had the effect of reinforcing family hierarchy and paternalism.

Throughout his term of office Ruiz Cortines found himself caught up in a situation over which he had no direct control. Mexico's population was growing at a rate that began to alarm not only social scientists but also his political advisers. When Lázaro Cárdenas came to power the population of the country was only about 16 million. But by 1958 it had doubled to more than 32 million. The population explosion was compounded by a con-comitant trend toward urbanization. While the national growth rate had reached 3.1 percent a year by 1955 (as opposed to 1.9 percent from 1930 to 1940), the growth rate of the major cities approached 7 percent a year. The Federal District jumped from 3 million in 1952 to an amazing 4.5 million only six years later.

Large-scale commercial agriculture expanded with the benefit of "green-revolution" tech-nologies such as fertilizers, hybrid seeds, and insecticides, resulting in cheaper grain prices that put small producers out of work. Drawn by unemployment and the lure of industry, hundreds of thousands of rural Mexicans flocked to the cities in hope of a better life, but few found it. The industrial revolution required skilled, not unskilled, labor. The need for more jobs, schools, health services, sewage disposal plants, streets, and houses in the cities was now taxing even the extraordinary postwar prosperity. Although by 1958, 1.5 million Mexicans earned their living from industry, the laboring force grew faster than industry could provide jobs. At precisely the time when the apparent thrust of the country was di-rected toward modernization, Ruiz Cortines found it necessary to order the use of hand labor rather than machinery on public works just to keep the new workforce occupied. Many poor women from the countryside took exploitative jobs as domestic servants, while other unemployed Mexicans tried to survive in a growing informal economy, selling handicrafts and cheap goods on the streets.

Ruiz Cortines considered himself a custodian of the revolution as he announced repeat-edly that he had full faith in revolutionary institutions. But surely his policies would have repulsed the heroes of the 1910 movement. The postwar generation of Mexican politicians had redefined priorities. The burdens of industrial development again fell most heavily on those who were least able to bear them. By the 1950s, the modernizing authoritarian system of politics had been set in place. The one-party state did not abandon the use of force but increasingly relied on cooptation, offering incentives, and an adulatory media to impose hegemony. The "soft" authoritarianism of the state would persist throughout the century, abetted by a weak judicial system that discouraged punishment for political crimes commit-ted by professional *pistoleros* (gunmen).

Mexican radicals were alienated by the new trends, especially by the government's in-creasing repression of popular protests from campesinos and workers, as well as by election rigging. Discontented students, especially at the working-class Instituto Politécnico Nacional, began to organize protests in 1956. In rural areas, the military sided with politicians and landowners to put down resistance. More violence erupted in Morelos when the Jaramillista agrarians launched a revolt against the government in 1953. Zapatistas and other rural peoples who had fought in the revolution continued to constitute an ardent base of sup-port for the PRI despite having suffered economically from modernization policies. The PRI had succeeded in manipulating the collective memories of rural communities to perpetuate the image of Cárdenas as a revolutionary populist who had their interests at heart. The PRI governments used negotiation, some compromise, and force to quell campesino mobiliza-tions in an attempt to uphold order in areas of glaring economic inequalities. When efforts by the Jaramillista leadership to form new campesino organizations and raise awareness of injustices met with repression, these dissidents rebelled and were eventually crushed. As the PRI institutionalized its authoritarianism in rural areas, it had the effect of creating counter-hegemonic heroes and martyrs.

In another manifestation of discontent with the anti-revolutionary drift, the Mexican anthropologist Eulalia Guzmán claimed to have found the bones of Cuauhtémoc in a small Guerrero town in 1949. Her effort to counter the veneration of the remains of the conqueror Cortés, buried in a Mexico City church, and to promote Mexico's indigenous heritage, was revealed as a hoax, but it symbolized the ongoing struggle over Mexican identity. Was Mexico the nation of exploiters or of the virtuous Indians depicted by Diego Rivera?

The official party, the PRI, had pre-empted the political life of the country. Party nomina-tion was tantamount to election at national and state levels, but municipal elections were more often contested. Though the party itself was broadly based and incorporated many seg-ments of society, its domination of the political process produced nothing less than a con-tradiction in terms—a one-party democracy in which the leaders operated through regional power brokers and frequently renegotiated alliances and redistributed patronage.

As Mexico's distinguished political critic and respected scholar, Daniel Cosío Villegas, pointed out in a brilliant analysis of what was happening to the Mexican revolution, the shifts of the last decades had produced uneven effects despite economic growth.

> Strictly speaking the only problem of great magnitude is the rate at which the population in-crease may very well strain the country's physical, human and economic resources, and that if energetic measures are not taken, it may present a very serious problem. . . . The political situation is decidedly less satisfactory. . . . The election [of the president, governors, and local authorities] is far from popular, being decided by personalist forces that rarely or never represent the genuine interests of large human groups. The economic and political power of the president of the Republic is almost all-embracing and . . . it is impossible for one man to know the special needs of each city or town and which person or persons are most suitable to resolve them.[2]

Ruiz Cortines's last message to the congress was atypical of Mexican politicians of the twentieth century. The social imperfections of the system troubled him more than the deficiencies of one-party rule or corruption. The Mexican masses, the outgoing president conceded, had not benefited from the revolutionary process as much as he had antici-pated. Illness, ignorance, and poverty had not been overcome. The desired balance be-tween economic development and social justice had tipped in favor of the former. The pace of the social movement had slowed and, since 1940, had almost ground to a halt. Perhaps a moderate shift to the left could mute government critics and reinstill some faith in revolutionary ideals.

---

2   Daniel Cosío Villegas, *Change in Latin America: The Mexican and Cuban Revolutions* (Lincoln, NE, 1961), 30–33.

RECOMMENDED FOR FURTHER STUDY

Berger, Dina. *The Development of Mexico's Tourism Industry: Pyramids by Day, Martinis by Night*. New York: Palgrave MacMillan, 2006.

Berger, Dina, and Andrew Grant Wood, eds. *Holiday in Mexico: Critical Reflections on Tourism and Tourist Encounters*. Durham, NC: Duke University Press, 2010.

Brandenburg, Frank. *The Making of Modern Mexico*. Englewood Cliffs, NJ: Prentice Hall, 1964.

Carey, Elaine. *Women Drug Traffickers: Mules, Bosses, and Organized Crime*. Albuquerque: University of New Mexico Press, 2014.

Cohen, Deborah. *Braceros, Migrants, Citizens, and Transnational Subjects in the Postwar United States*. Chapel Hill: University of North Carolina Press, 2011.

Cosío Villegas, Daniel. *Change in Latin America: The Mexican and Cuban Revolutions*. Lincoln: University of Nebraska Press, 1961.

Dormady, Jason. *Primitive Revolution: Restorationist Religion and the Idea of the Mexican Revolution, 1940–1968*. Albuquerque: University of New Mexico Press, 2011.

Gillingham, Paul. *Cuauhtémoc's Bones: Forging National Identity in Modern Mexico*. Albuquerque: University of New Mexico Press, 2011.

Gillingham, Paul, and Benjamin T. Smith, eds. *Dictablanda: Politics, Work, and Culture in Mexico, 1938–1968*. Durham, NC: Duke University Press, 2014.

López-Alonso, Moramay. *Measuring Up: A History of Living Standards in Mexico, 1850–1950*. Stanford, CA: Stanford University Press, 2012.

McCormick, Gladys I. *The Logic of Compromise in Mexico: How the Countryside Was Key to the Emergence of Authoritarianism*. Chapel Hill: University of North Carolina Press, 2016.

Middlebrook, Kevin J. *The Paradox of Revolution: Labor, the State and Authoritarianism in Mexico*. Baltimore, MD: Johns Hopkins University Press, 1995.

Mosk, Sanford A. *Industrial Revolution in Mexico*. Berkeley: University of California Press, 1950.

Newcomer, Daniel. *Reconciling Modernity: Urban State Formation in 1940s León, Mexico*. Lincoln: University of Nebraska Press, 2004.

Niblo, Stephen R. *Mexico in the 1940s: Modernity, Politics, and Corruption*. Wilmington, DE: Scholarly Resources, 1999.

Padilla, Tanalís. *Rural Resistance in the Land of Zapata: The Jaramillista Movement and the Myth of the Pax Priista, 1940–1962*. Durham, NC: Duke University Press, 2008.

Quintana, Alejandro. *Maximino Ávila Camacho and the One-Party State: The Taming of Caudillismo and Caciquisimo in Post-Revolutionary Mexico*. Lanham, MD: Rowman & Littlefield, 2010.

Ross, Stanley R., ed. *Is the Mexican Revolution Dead?* New York: Alfred A. Knopf, 1966.

Schiavone Camacho, Julia Maria. *Chinese Mexicans: Transpacific Migration and the Search for a Homeland, 1910–1960*. Chapel Hill: University of North Carolina Press, 2012.

Schuler, Friederich. "Mexico and the Outside World." In *The Oxford History of Mexico*, edited by Michael C. Meyer and William H. Beezley, 471–507. New York: Oxford University Press, rev. 2010.

Scott, Robert E. *Mexican Government in Transition*. Urbana: University of Illinois Press, 1959.

Smith, Benjamin T. *Pistoleros and Popular Movements: The Politics of State Formation in Postrevolutionary Oaxaca*. Lincoln: University of Nebraska Press, 2009.

Tannenbaum, Frank. *Mexico: The Struggle for Peace and Bread*. New York: Alfred A. Knopf, 1956.

CHAPTER 34

THE LULL AND THE STORM

ADOLFO LÓPEZ MATEOS, 1958–64

The presidency of Adolfo López Mateos temporarily stayed growing criticism of the Partido Revolucionario Institucional (PRI) and social discontent, but disaffection would erupt and then smolder in the next decade. The PRI nominee, López Mateos, the well-educated son of a small-town dentist, won the presidency in 1958 with about 90 percent of the total vote. His conservative, proclerical Partido de Acción Nacional (PAN) rival, Luis H. Alvarez, did not fulfill the hopes of his party in capitalizing on the fully enfranchised Mexican women's vote, thought to be influenced by the church. The women's vote increased the total ballots cast but scarcely changed the official party's margin of victory.

President López Mateos presented a stark contrast to his sixty-seven-year-old predecessor. Only forty-seven at the time of his election, he was dynamic, energetic, and personally attractive. Having served as secretary of labor during the Ruiz Cortines administration, he had won a reputation as a liberal for his management of labor disputes; only a few of the thirteen thousand cases he handled degenerated into strikes. He enjoyed the backing of Lázaro Cárdenas and seemed to be just the right man at the right time. More intellectually oriented than presidents of recent vintage, he indicated during the campaign that he planned to nudge the country back in the direction of social reforms. Hundreds of thousands of young Mexicans, disheartened with growing social inequality since the Second World War, identified with López Mateos, much as the youth of the United States would, a few years later, identify with President John F. Kennedy.

Shortly after his inauguration the new president was asked to comment on his political philosophy and he answered with the words, "I am left within the Constitution." Mexican Communists, and other radicals whom he judged to be left of the constitution, were not treated with kid gloves. López Mateos removed Communist leadership from the teachers and railroad unions and imprisoned Mexico's internationally known muralist and Communist David Alfaro Siqueiros on charges of "social dissolution," an amorphous kind of sedition. But just as local and foreign businessmen and industrialists sat back and relaxed, thinking that they had an unexpected friend in the presidential chair, López Mateos also began to demonstrate that he intended to depart from the overwhelming influence of his predecessors' conservative, business-oriented policies.

Land redistribution, almost abandoned in favor of commercial agricultural development, was stepped up once again, on both an individual and a collective basis. During his six-year term López Mateos parceled out some 30 million acres, more than any president except Lázaro Cárdenas. He also cleared and opened up new agricultural lands in extreme southern Mexico. State intervention in the economy accelerated from 1958 to 1964 as the administration purchased controlling stock in a number of foreign industries. In 1962, for example, the government gained control of the US and Canadian electric companies and, not being able to divine a future in which energy would become a luxury, authorized huge, wasteful electric signs proudly announcing *La electricidad es nuestra* (The electricity is ours). At about the same time the government also purchased the motion picture industry, the production and distribution of which had been largely under US domination. The president pledged to keep the price of tickets low so that all people could avail themselves of this medium of entertainment. Social welfare projects, most notably medical care and old age pensions expanded, as did the Instituto Mexicano de Seguro Social (IMSS) program for rural Mexico. By 1964 public health campaigns had significantly reduced tuberculosis and polio rates, while malaria was almost completely eliminated.

Even after the emphasis on agrarian reform programs, life for workers on the maguey plantations of Yucatán remained difficult.

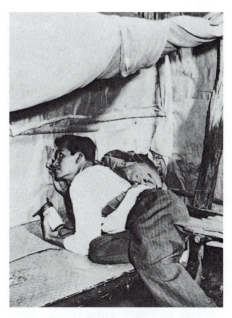

A major campaign to eradicate malaria in 1962 and 1963 yielded positive results.

Curious villages inspect the newly completed sewer system in the state of Chiapas.

Like his predecessors, López Mateos continued to skirt the issue of birth control. Despite a maternal mortality rate 10 percent higher than that of the United States; as many as one million Mexican babies were born in 1962 and almost 1.5 million in 1963. But he did recognize the tremendous dislocations occasioned by rapid urbanization and initiated modest steps to accommodate the dramatically increasing population. For the first time in history the government entered the housing business on a large scale. Low-cost housing projects were initiated in the major industrial cities, many of which had become encircled with shanty towns of indescribable misery and poverty. One of the largest housing developments in Mexico City covered some 10 million square feet of a former slum, housed one hundred thousand persons, and contained 13 schools, four clinics, and several nurseries. The rents were modest: $6.00 a month for a one-bedroom apartment and $16.00 a month for a three-bedroom unit. To complement public housing, the president also developed an incentive program designed to encourage industry to stay away from the greater Mexico City environs. In 1960, on the fiftieth anniversary of the revolution, Mexico's urban population surpassed its rural population for the first time.

López Mateos's labor supporters reacted with shock in 1959 when the president used federal troops to put down a major railroad strike. Arguing that the strike threatened to paralyze the country, he arrested a number of leaders, including Demetrio Vallejo, the head of the union. During the twentieth century, railroad workers had built a strong industrial union. As the PRI moved to exert control by placing compliant bosses in union affiliates, leftist reformers organized against them and called for walkouts. The first two strikes, with

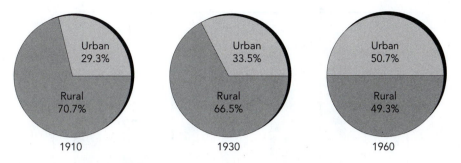

Urban–Rural Population Distribution

Source: *Mexico, 1966: Facts, Figures and Trends* (Mexico, Banco Nacional, 1968), 32.

substantial participation of female railway workers, achieved an increase in wages and medical benefits. Grassroots pressures ignited the third strike, prompting government reprisals. Cold War politics had contributed to labeling labor activism as subversive or Communist.

To blunt the criticism of his labor suppression, López Mateos decided to implement an almost forgotten article of the Constitution of 1917 that called for labor to share in the profits with management. In 1962 a special commission, the Comisión Nacional para el Reparto de Utilidades, was convoked to implement the profit-sharing plan. The formula agreed upon was complicated, dependent upon the amount of capital investment and the size of the labor force within each industry. But by 1964 many Mexican laborers earned an extra 5 to 10 percent a year under the profit-sharing law.

The educational policy of the López Mateos administration renewed the emphasis on the rural school. By 1963 education had become the largest single item in the Mexican budget, and the educational doubled the amount that allocated for national defense. While the rate of illiteracy in Mexico had been cut from some 77 percent in 1910 to less than 38 percent in 1960, the population explosion in a real sense had nullified the results. In absolute numbers there were more illiterates in 1960 (13,200,000) than there had been at the time of the Plan de San Luis Potosí (11,658,000).

To attack illiteracy, the president and his secretary of education, Jaime Torres Bodet, who had also served under Avila Camacho, launched a two-pronged assault. Through an ingenious system of prefabricated schools costing only $4,800 per unit, the number of rural classrooms increased rapidly. The government furnished the building materials and the technical assistance, and individual communities provided land and the actual labor. In this way villages received a genuine stake in the educational process. López Mateos also decided to initiate a system of free and compulsory textbooks. On this program he encountered opposition. Although a number of leading scholars participated in the preparation of the books, they tended to reflect revolutionary myths. The Roman Catholic Church took umbrage at the treatment afforded many of its efforts throughout Mexican history. The National Union of Parents Association, a conservative organization supported by the PAN and a number of leading clerics, led demonstrations against the books, insisting that their imposition on a mandatory basis constituted a totalitarian act designed to standardize thought in

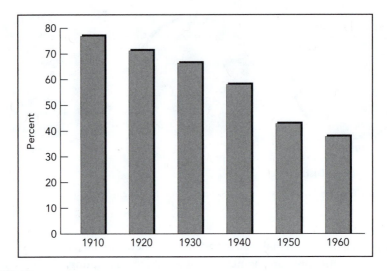

Illiteracy, 1910–60

Source: James W. Wilkie, *The Mexican Revolution: Federal Expenditure and Social Change since 1910* (Berkeley, 1967), 208.

In an attempt to reduce illiteracy, López Mateos revived the idea of adult reading classes.

the Mexican republic. At the same time radical leftists opposed the textbooks because they exalted revolutionary accomplishments and overlooked the shortcomings. López Mateos was not intimidated, and the books were adopted throughout the country over the protests.

In 1964, the president inaugurated the new National Museum of Anthropology, an architectural marvel designed by Pedro Ramírez Vázquez, to house the country's rich archaeological and ethnographic heritage. In the enormous structure, exhibition halls ringed by gardens with outdoor exhibits surround a courtyard. This patio boasts a huge pond and a vast square concrete umbrella supported by a single pillar that emits an artificial waterfall. A stunning monument to Mexico's indigenous cultures, it became Mexico's most visited museum. In the 1960s, in addition to Ramírez Vázquez other great Mexican architects including Rafael Mijeres, Félix Candela, and Mario Pani collaborated with the official party to create spaces and public art that attempted to define mexicanidad and shape people's behavior. They designed space at the National University and for the Olympic games.

If Mexico's rate of economic growth under López Mateos did not quite keep pace with that under Miguel Alemán and Adolfo Ruiz Cortines, the economy remained strong. British and French capital poured into the new petrochemical division of Petróleos Mexicanos (PEMEX). Private initiative constructed luxury hotels, and tourists came in droves to Acapulco and the newly developed resort town of Puerto Vallarta, leaving behind millions of dollars for government programs. By 1964 Mexico was self-sufficient in iron, steel, and oil. Local capital no longer felt the need to seek investment fields elsewhere and, indeed, purchased controlling stock in the Mexican telephone network. And in 1963 Mexican bonds were sold on US and European markets for the first time since the Díaz regime. Nonetheless, sustained economic growth continued to be unequally distributed.

THE FOREIGN POLICY OF THE LÓPEZ MATEOS ADMINISTRATION

Mexico's foreign policy from 1958 to 1964 paralleled the administration's efforts to achieve a balance between its revolutionary legacy and its place in the modernizing world. Coming to the presidency only a few months before Fidel Castro's July 26 revolution ousted rightest Cuban dictator Fulgencio Batista, López Mateos occupied himself with defining the Mexican position on the most crucial Latin American issue of the postwar period. Publicly he opted for a policy of total nonintervention in Cuba's internal affairs. Arguing the national sovereignty and juridical equality of all states, Mexico refused to condemn the Castro regime, voted against Cuba's expulsion from the Organization of American States, and remained the only country in the Western Hemisphere to retain air service and diplomatic relations with Cuba. The public stance served to appease the Mexican left and demonstrate independence from the United States, while the government secretly aided US efforts to undermine the Cuban regime through its intelligence agents and diplomatic personnel. When French president Charles de Gaulle visited Mexico City in the spring of 1964 and received the honor of being the first foreign head of state ever to speak from the presidential balcony overlooking the Plaza de la Constitución (Zócalo), the two leaders congratulated one another on escaping the tutelage of the superpowers. Mexico's independent foreign posture was a theme relayed in a series of trips that López Mateos and his close associates made to Yugoslavia, Poland, Indonesia, India, Canada, and a number of African countries.

By his own reckoning, López Mateos's greatest diplomatic victory concerned the final resolution of a century-old boundary dispute with the United States—the Chamizal controversy. At the end of the war with the United States the boundary had been set at the Rio Grande. But because of the sandy texture of the soil, especially in the area of El Paso, the river periodically shifted its bed. In 1864 it moved suddenly to the south, leaving some six hundred acres of Mexican territory north of the river in the state of Texas. Mexico, of course, claimed that this land, the Chamizal, was part of the national domain, but various arbitration commissions had been unable to reach an accord suitable to the US government. When President John F. Kennedy visited Mexico City in 1962, he was informed that the Chamizal continued to be a reminder of *Yanqui* imperialism and ordered the US ambassador, Thomas Mann, to enter into new negotiations with the Mexican government for its final resolution. In the summer of 1963 the United States agreed to return the disputed territory to Mexico, to reimburse the El Paso residents for their lost property, and to share the costs of building a new international bridge and a concrete-lined channel to eliminate possible future disputes.

An assassin's bullet took John Kennedy's life before he could sign the agreement, but his successor, Lyndon Johnson, met López Mateos at the Chamizal in September 1964 and formalized the arrangement. Once again, through adroit diplomacy the Mexican president had retained the goodwill of the United States and pleased Mexican nationalists.

MOUNTING CRITICISM OF THE ONE-PARTY SYSTEM

Criticism of the PRI's monopoly on government continued to build during the López Mateos administration. His election in 1958 with 90 percent of the total vote marked 30 consecutive years of rule by the official party. The party not only had won every contest for the presidency but also had captured all of the senatorial and gubernatorial races. The PRI had succeeded in identifying itself with the revolution, and the revolution was practically synonymous with the state. The PRI's colors—red, white, and green—were identical to those on the national flag; these colors animated its symbol on the ballot so that even illiterates could not miss the connection between the party and the nation. In addition, the PRI was able to mobilize bountiful resources to get its message across and to buy votes.

By the early 1960s an increasingly sophisticated electorate began to question the bossism, favoritism, and corruption that had beset the PRI officialdom. A party without any genuine opposition was accountable to nobody. A party that could embrace the leftist policies of Cárdenas and the business-oriented policies of Alemán was ideologically bankrupt. How could it be expected to embark upon a meaningful redistribution of wealth designed to close the still gigantic gap between rich and poor? Alienation was broadly based, but teachers, in particular, mobilized and protested, calling for democracy and social justice. Groups of university students and normal school students sympathetic to the Cuban revolution held demonstrations calling for the latter. Pablo González Casanova, a distinguished Mexican social scientist, argued in his perceptive *Democracy in Mexico*: "Democracy exists to the extent that the people share the income, culture, and power; anything else is democratic folklore or rhetoric."[1]

López Mateos responded by sponsoring an amendment to the constitution that altered the electoral procedures in the Chamber of Deputies. To broaden the opposition in the lower house of the legislature, his amendment provided that any party winning 2.5 percent of the national vote was entitled to five congressmen whether or not the candidates actually

---

1   Pablo González Casanova, *Democracy in Mexico* (New York, NY, 1970), 194.

won their respective races. For every additional .5 percent of the vote these parties would receive an additional congressman, up to a total of 20, each of whom would occupy a new seat, not replace an elected congressman. Because of the new law the PAN received twenty congressional seats in the 1964 elections and the Partido Popular Socialista (PPS), ten seats. The electoral revision was a step in the right direction, but it did not end the debate on the shortcomings of Mexican democracy.

THE COMING STORM

López Mateos is the most fondly remembered president of the post-war era. Like his contemporary in the United States, John F. Kennedy, part of his appeal undoubtedly lies in his style and charisma. But when the occasion demanded it, he exerted forceful leadership. At the same time he was no doctrinaire and appreciated the value of compromise. Yielding to appeals and petitions, he made it a point to pardon muralist Siqueiros at the end of his term. Almost as soon as he left office he suffered a severe stroke and lay in a coma for six years until his death in 1970. He was eulogized as a nationalist who defended Mexican interests in the world community and a humane statesman who appreciated the concerns of the powerless masses at home. Yet new tensions lay just below the surface.

Mexico was not alone in the tumultuous world of the 1960s. Modernization in general, and communications technology in particular, interlaced nations and dramatically shrank the globe. Word of Martin Luther King's assassination reached Angola only minutes after it reached Atlanta, and Robert Kennedy's assassination was known in São Paulo almost as soon as it was known in San Francisco. By the end of the 1960s the entire literate world knew that the United States had dropped a greater tonnage of bombs on Vietnam than the total dropped on all fronts during World War II. Massive marches for peace, for civil rights, and for the right of agricultural workers to organize were reported on the front pages of the world's press.

Mexicans in their living rooms, watching the evening news, saw the destruction of the black ghetto in Washington, the burning of Watts, and riots in Tokyo, Prague, and Berlin; they saw Parisian students pelting police on the Boulevard St. Michel and the senseless killing of students at Kent State University. While the late 1960s did not witness any worldwide conspiracy of the young a youthful commonality of interest transcended national borders. The international pantheon of heroes, with a few national adaptations, included Che Guevara, Ho Chi Minh, Malcolm X, and Mao Zedong. Mexico was soon treated once again to the spectacle of violence.

DÍAZ ORDAZ AND POLITICAL DISCONTENT, 1964–70

When the PRI leadership chose Gustavo Díaz Ordaz as the presidential candidate for 1964, it badly misread the temper of the times. Díaz Ordaz had served as secretary of interior in the López Mateos cabinet and was tinged with policy decisions that reform-minded groups could not stomach. It had been he who applied the laws of "social dissolution" against David Alfaro Siqueiros and other radicals. Born in Puebla, Díaz Ordaz was reputed to be the most conservative official party candidate of the twentieth century. But after winning the election by the customary official party margin, he pledged to carry out the policies initiated by his predecessor.

The electoral reform law that provided for minority representation in the lower house was interpreted to allow the seating of several minority parties in addition to the PAN—the Partido Popular Socialista (PPS) and, although it did not quite reach 2.5 percent of the vote, the Partido Auténtico de la Revolución Mexicana (PARM). But the PAN, the only genuine opposition party, received an unfavorable ruling in the congressional elections. The congressional seats they actually won from PRI candidates would now be subtracted from the total of twenty they were allowed under the constitutional amendment. The decision represented rejection of a democratizing tendency, and the trend continued with the sad and disappointing case of Carlos Madrazo.

Shortly after coming to office, President Díaz Ordaz appointed Madrazo, a reform-minded liberal, to be president of the PRI. Championing a series of far-reaching innovations designed to promote internal democratization of the party, increase rank-and-file participation, reduce the vast power of local and state bosses, and bring more women into the organization, he ran headlong into the vested interests. In the spring of 1965, when Madrazo introduced new reforms designed to regularize nomination procedures at the local level, the state political machines rose up in rebellion and convinced Díaz Ordaz to fire him. Then, when PAN candidates won the mayoralties of Tijuana and Mexicali in Baja California Norte, the government annulled the elections because of "irregularities." Opposition leaders charged that the PRI was stealing elections with total impunity.

An earlier manifestation of Díaz Ordaz's refusal to tolerate dissent had occurred in 1964 when a physicians' strike began in Mexico City. Although doctors, nurses, and other medical personnel in the state-run hospitals began their movement calling for salary increases, improved working conditions, and educational opportunities, government intransigence led them to expand their demands to larger issues of social justice for underprivileged Mexicans. The doctors eventually accused the government of crass negligence that promoted hunger and death. Díaz Ordaz had his intelligence agents infiltrate the movement and in January 1965 suppressed it with riot police and the firing of many medical workers.

THE OLYMPIC GAMES AND TLATELOLCO

Discontent with the official party spread. Campus after campus exploded with strikes and violence as local university issues merged with national political unrest. A massive strike at the National University in the spring of 1966 resulted in the resignation of the rector. Federal troops were dispatched to restore order on university campuses in Michoacán and Sonora. A major showdown was about to ensue and the students picked their time carefully. Mexico was planning its greatest extravaganza since the centennial celebrations of 1910.

The International Olympic Committee accepted Mexico's bid to host the summer games in 1968, making it the first Latin American and developing country to have this "honor." Athletes, trainers, representatives of the press, and hundreds of thousands of visitors from the entire world would descend on Mexico and subject it to scrutiny. Construction of athletic facilities, hotels, housing projects, tourist facilities, and a new modern subway system preceded the games. Despite budgetary uncertainty, construction workers on round-the-clock shifts finished the major installations on time. To add a unique flavor to the international sports spectacular, the government scheduled a simultaneous cultural Olympics, featuring international art exhibitions, book displays, lectures, concerts, and plays. Administration spolesmen fended off early charges from critics that the costs were exorbitant for a country such as Mexico, arguing that not only would the visitors leave behind tens of millions of dollars but the facilities themselves would be put to good use later. Mexican elites saw the occasion as an opportunity to highlight the country's prosperity and assert Mexican leadership in the Third World, while attempting at the same time to efface "Indian" traits that they believed made Mexico appear backwards to outsiders.

The trouble began almost innocently in July 1968 with a fight between the students of two Mexico City schools, a college preparatory school and a nearby vocational school. The principal of the high school called for police help, and the mayor of the Federal District, General Alfonso Corona del Rosal, erred badly in sending out the *granaderos*, a despised paramilitary riot force. The granaderos stopped the intramural fight but in the process politicized a large portion of the student population in Mexico City. A few days later, as leftist students gathered to celebrate the July 26 anniversary of the Cuban Revolution, they met the granaderos again, and on this occasion a full-scale street riot ensued. But nobody had yet been killed.

In August 1968 as city workers put the finishing touches on the various construction projects, tensions between the students and the government reached the breaking point. Huge demonstrations took place the campuses of the National University and the National Polytechnic Institute, and a National Student Strike Committee formed. A list of demands framed in the language of civil liberties accentuated tensions; students insisted that all political prisoners be released, that the chief of police be fired, that the granaderos be disbanded, and that the law of "social dissolution" be repealed. Secretary of Interior Luis Echeverría agreed to enter into private discussions with the student leadership, but when the students demanded that the dialogue be broadcast publicly on radio and television, negotiations broke down. On August 27 the National Student Strike Committee brought together in the Zócalo an estimated 500,000 people, the largest organized antigovernment demonstration in Mexican history. The rally lasted well into the night, and when the government moved tanks and armored cars into the downtown area, violence and the first verified student death ensued.

Under pressure and with the Olympic games fast approaching, Díaz Ordaz took a hard line. Refusing to address student concerns, he stepped up security. In the middle of September, with the capital bedecked with Olympic flags and signs of welcome and the students occupying the campus of the National University, Díaz Ordaz ordered ten thousand army troops, in full battle dress, to seize the campus. Some five hundred demonstrators were thrown into jail, and the new rector of the university, Javier Barros Sierra, resigned in protest of the army occupation of his campus. For two weeks, bands of disgruntled students and other demonstrators not associated with the university roamed Mexico City streets, periodically seizing and burning buses, barricading streets, and pillaging. The climax came on October 2, 1968, at a place that will not be forgotten in Mexican history—Tlatelolco (the site of the ancient Aztec marketplace).

Strike organizers called for still another outdoor rally at the Plaza de las Tres Culturas in the district of Tlatelolco in order to criticize the government for its failure to comply with their earlier demands. The rally was not large by recent standards, perhaps only 5,000, including many women, children, and innocent spectators who lived nearby. The speeches were emotional, but the demonstration was peaceful. At about 6:30 P.M., army and police units arrived in tanks and armored vehicles. When the demonstrators failed to disband as ordered, the granaderos moved in and began to disperse them with billy clubs and tear gas. The government's version of what happened, carried the next day in the Mexican press, claimed that terrorists in nearby apartment buildings began firing on the police. Others insisted that the police opened fire first and that only then did snipers (probably from the government's Olympic Battallion) in the buildings begin to shoot.

At any rate, when the army units uncovered their high-caliber machine guns and other automatic weapons, thousands of innocent people were caught in the crossfire. Helicopters dropped flares into the crowds and the troops, opting not to err on the side of safety, sprayed indiscriminately from short range. Official government statistics admitted first eight, then

The Plaza de las Tres Culturas, a tourist attraction for thousands, became a battleground for hundreds in October 1968. Courtesy of James W. Wilkie.

Gold medalist Tommie Smith and bronze medalist John Carlos give a Black Power salute at the 1968 Olympics in Mexico City.

eighteen, and finally forty-three deaths; but few knowledgeable Mexicans accepted mortality figures under three or four hundred and some have charged that the number was well over a thousand. Ambulances wailed through the night as hospitals and clinics filled beyond capacity with the wounded and dying. By the next morning, Mexico City jails held over two thousand new prisoners. One has only to recall the trauma that engulfed the United States after Kent State, a tragedy of much lesser proportion, to appreciate the anger and despair that Mexicans felt as the story was gradually pieced together over the next few days. But shock quickly gave way to recriminations as Carlos Madrazo attributed the killings to police brutality. The decision had been a political one, and it greatly altered public perception of the country's leadership. In turn, as long as the PRI held power, the government blocked any official investigation of the tragedy.

The Olympic Games themselves went off without violent protests from Mexicans although black athletes from the United States raised their fists in symbolic support of the Black Power movement.[2] In 1968, activists served notice across the world—most famously in Prague, Chicago, and Mexico City—that they would fight against racial, socioeconomic, and political injustices.

In Mexico, Tlatelolco represented an explosion that followed thirty years during which the PRI had steadily increased its repressive apparatus. Reflections on the massacre filled the

---

2 In his 2008 autobiography *Silent Gesture*, gold-medal winner Tommie Smith claimed the protest was a "human rights" salute. Tommie Smith with David Steele, *Silent Gesture: The Autobiography of Tommie Smith* (Philadelphia, PA, 2007), 100.

pages of journalistic accounts and novels. Some activists who believed in peaceful protest to promote change now, armed with Marxist-Leninist and New Left ideals, turned to violence as they organized urban and campesino guerrilla units to carry out bombings and other terrorist acts. The student movement failed to engender wide, popular support for democracy and served to generate support for the government's hard line. The PRI's legitimacy was being eroded, but its demise was not yet near.

The aftermath of Tlatelolco overshadowed other aspects of the Díaz Ordaz presidency. Federal expenditure for education reached over 26 percent of the total budget, one of the highest rates in the entire world. Urban renewal projects in the northern border cities catered to the tourist trade, and tourists left record amounts of money in Ciudad Juárez, Tijuana, Nogales, Piedras Negras, and Matamoros. Mexico launched the Border Industrialization Program in 1964 to encourage border development and job growth. Plants called *maquiladoras* were established along the border to assemble goods from materials imported from the United States; finished products were then sent back across the border. Thousands of Mexican workers, predominantly women, found jobs, but they worked for abysmal pay in environmentally poor conditions. In another economic trend, the Green Revolution, while increasing deforestation and other ecological damage, had boosted Mexican agricultural production in corn, beans, and wheat since the late 1950s, primarily on the lands of private commercial producers. Government subsidies for consumers of corn and beans made production less profitable for the large growers, many of whom turned to livestock raising and exporting beef. Others began to produce exportable fruits. This meant that by 1970 Mexico was forced to import staple foods. The economy continued to grow but showed signs of stress toward the end of Díaz Ordaz's term, with creeping inflation and a negative trade balance.

Mexico took the lead in international conferences, securing pledges that Latin America should be declared a nuclear-free zone. Under other circumstances, Díaz Ordaz might have been remembered for these accomplishments but, just as the administration of Richard M. Nixon will be remembered less for finally extricating the United States from Vietnam than for the shame of Watergate, the names of Díaz Ordaz and his successor will always be associated with the unpardonable tragedy at Tlatelolco.

RECOMMENDED FOR FURTHER STUDY

Alegre, Robert. *Railroad Radicals in Cold War Mexico: Gender, Class, and Memory*. Lincoln: University of Nebraska Press, 2014.

Aviña, Alexander. *Specters of Revolution: Peasant Guerrillas in the Cold War Mexican Countryside*. New York: Oxford University Press 2014.

Brewster, Claire, and Keith Brewster. *Sport and Spectacle in Post-Revolutionary Mexico*. New York: Routledge, 2010.

Carey, Elaine. *Plaza of Sacrifices: Gender, Power, and Terror in 1968 Mexico*. Albuquerque: University of New Mexico Press, 2005.

Castañeda, Luis M. *Spectacular Mexico: Design, Propaganda, and the 1968 Olympics*. Minneapolis: University of Minnesota Press, 2014.

Eckstein, Susan. *The Poverty of Revolution: The State and the Urban Poor in Mexico*. Princeton, NJ: Princeton University Press, 1977.

González Casanova, Pablo. *Democracy in Mexico*. New York: Oxford University Press, 1970.

Grindle, Merilee S. *Bureaucrats, Politicians, and Peasants in Mexico: A Case Study in Public Policy*. Berkeley: University of California Press, 1977.

Hundley, Norris, Jr. *Dividing the Waters: A Century of Controversy between the United States and Mexico*. Berkeley: University of California Press, 1966.

Iber, Patrick. *Neither Peace nor Freedom: The Cultural Cold War in Latin America*. Cambridge, MA: Harvard University Press, 2015.

Joseph, Gilbert M., and Daniela Spenser, eds. *In from the Cold: Latin America's New Encounter with the Cold War*. Durham, NC: Duke University Press, 2008.

Keller, Renata. *Mexico's Cold War: Cuba, the United States, and the Legacy of the Mexican Revolution*. New York: Cambridge University Press, 2015.

Kurlansky, Mark. *1968: The Year That Rocked The World*. New York: Random House Paperbacks, 2005.

Liss, Sheldon. *A Century of Disagreement: The Chamizal Conflict, 1864–1964*. Washington, DC: University Press of Washington, DC, 1965.

Lomnitz, Larissa Adler. *Networks and Marginality: Life in a Mexican Shantytown*. New York: Academic Press, 1977.

Muñoz, María L.O. *Stand Up and Fight: Participatory Indigenismo, Populism, and Mobilization in Mexico, 1970–1984*. Tucson: University of Arizona Press, 2016.

Paz, Octavio. *The Other Mexico: Critique of the Pyramid*. New York: Grove Press, 1972.

Pensado, Jaime M. *Rebel Mexico: Student Unrest and Authoritarian Political Culture during the Long Sixties*. Stanford, CA: Stanford University Press, 2013.

Poniatowska, Elena. *Massacre in Mexico*. New York: Viking Press, 1975.

Ross, Stanley, ed. *Views across the Border*. Albuquerque: University of New Mexico Press, 1978

Smith, Tommie, with David Steele. *Silent Gesture: The Autobiography of Tommie Smith*. Philadelphia, PA: Temple University Press, 2007.

Soto Laveaga, Gabriela, and Claudia Agostini. "Science and Public Health." In *A Companion to Mexican History and Culture*, edited by William H. Beezley, 561–74. Hoboken, NJ: Wiley-Blackwell, 2011.

Wilkie, James W. *The Mexican Revolution: Federal Expenditure and Social Change since 1910*. Berkeley: University of California Press, 1967.

Williams, Edward J. *The Rebirth of the Mexican Petroleum Industry*. Lexington, MA: Heath, 1979.

CHAPTER 35

FAILURES OF DEVELOPMENT
IN THE ONE-PARTY STATE

LUIS ECHEVERRÍA, 1970–76

The political atmosphere had not returned to normal when Mexico held its 1970 presidential election. PRI candidate Luis Echeverría had been secretary of interior during the recent Olympic trouble, and the Mexican left held him largely responsible for the government's overreaction. With a reputation for inflexibility and intolerance, he scarcely seemed the man to foster an atmosphere of national consensus. Echeverría decided to campaign vigorously, yet he failed to capture public imagination.

During the first year of his term, President Echeverría showed himself as a man of boundless energy; he put in long hours and demanded the same of those who surrounded him. He nurtured himself on face-to-face dialogue with farmers in dusty villages and workers in urban factories. Cultivating a populist image, he quickly began to counter his reputation by ostensibly moving to the center and then to the left. He would sidestep regional and corporate power groups to directly address the needs of Mexico's marginalized peoples. To the chagrin of the conservative business community, he began renewing initiatives in rural Mexico and even announced that perhaps industrialization had to slow down. A major emphasis was placed on extending the rural road system and rural electrification. Caught in the worldwide inflation of the early 1970s, he tried to minimize its impact on the poor by ordering rigid price controls of basic commodities; at the same time, luxury items were hit with a new tax of 10 percent, and a 15 percent surtax was added to all bills in first-class restaurants and night clubs. Echeverría even moderated his earlier lack of concern for family planning and halfway through his administration gave a cautious endorsement to birth control. Although Echeverría surprised his critics most when he released the majority of Mexico's student prisoners from the Lecumberri prison in early 1971, he confirmed their perception of him when he ordered a paramilitary group called Los Halcones to brutally repress a student demonstration on Corpus Christi Day in June 1971, leaving twenty-five dead and many others injured.

Violence wrought more violence as a series of bank robberies in the fall were traced to revolutionaries of the Movimiento Armado Revolucionario (MAR). Other robberies and political kidnappings followed: Jaime Castrejón, rector of the University of Guerrero, and Julio Hirschfield, director of the nation's airports, both fell into rebel hands. Terrance Leonhardy, US consul general in Guadalajara, was kidnapped, as were the British honorary consul, Anthony Duncan Williams; Fernando Aranguren, a wealthy Guadalajara business-man; and Nadine Chaval, the daughter of the Belgian ambassador. A wealthy Monterrey industrialist, Eugenio Garza Sada, was killed during a kidnapping attempt; and a train car-rying tourists was assaulted in southern Sonora, resulting in the deaths of four travelers. In the summer of 1974, President Echeverría's father-in-law, Guadalupe Zuno Hernández, a former governor of Jalisco, was captured and held for ransom by a group calling themselves the Fuerzas Revolucionarias Armadas del Pueblo (FRAP).

In the mountains of Guerrero, the roots of the guerrilla movements were deep. Campesino protests had long been suppressed by local caciques and later by federal military counter-insurgency campaigns orchestrated by the PRI. In the wake of campesino massacres in the 1960s, campesinos took up arms in guerrilla movements to fight for control of their agricul-tural production as well as democracy and social justice. The state terror that had spawned these movements lashed out in greater fury as rebels robbed banks and kidnapped wealthy elites for ransom to finance their movement. Campesinos carried out successive land inva-sions. After the first head of the guerrilla movement, Genaro Vásquez, was killed in 1972, Lucio Cabañas, a former schoolteacher, assumed the leadership. He took inspiration not from Marxist revolutionaries, but from Emiliano Zapata. The eyes of the nation focused on Cabañas when guerrillas under his command kidnapped Guerrero senator Rubén Figueroa, at the time a candidate for governor. Ten thousand army troops were dispatched to Guerrero to capture the guerrillas, but it took them over a year to do the job. In 1974, Cabañas and twenty-seven of his men were killed in gun battles with the army. The government then waged a campaign of excessive violence, using torture and murder to eliminate not only sus-pected subversives, but all protest. That the state of Guerrero suffered more than any other from coercion by state and federal powers would continue to be borne out, culminating most horrendously in 2014.

As pressures continued to build against the authoritarian PRI, Echeverría attempted to deflect criticism. He brought more young people into important positions in the govern-ment than any previous head of state. Laws lowered the voting age to eighteen and reduced the age for holding congressional office. Other administration programs should have been well received by youth. Mexico granted diplomatic asylum to Hortensia Allende, widow of the murdered Chilean president, and accepted other Chilean political refugees.

In 1972 the administration nationalized the tobacco and telephone industries. Echever-ría's foreign travels opened new avenues of trade and, by extension, sought to lessen de-pendence upon the United States. He also sought to stimulate a Mexican pharmaceutical industry through a program that supported the production of *barbasco*, a wild yam cultivated by campesino farmers in Oaxaca and used in making steroid hormones for birth control. This initiative had the potential to benefit the farmers, research scientists, and health care though the results were mixed as the endeavor played out in the face of competing interests, including transnational corporations that gained exclusive controls. Forest management in

Mexico had come under the direction of the PRI through corporations (*paraestatales*) in which the government was the primary shareholder. Both corruption and mismanagement hindered the efforts to conserve or develop resources, and benefits rarely redounded to rural communities. In 1972, Echeverría launched a deforestation program, intended to clear over fifteen hundred square miles for commercial agriculture, especially oriented to produce beef for national and international markets. Mexico would continue to destroy woodlands and other natural resources for development projects, often promising rural communities a share, but depriving them of any control—and thus access to resources and markets. Rural campesino associations and environmentalists rarely succeeded in opposing these projects.

In the end, Echeverría's initiatives did little to curtail the alienation that had set in across all sectors of Mexican society. To be sure, part of the problem could be attributed to the inflation rate, which topped 20 percent in both 1973 and 1974. But to ascribe the alienation simply to the rate of inflation or even to the gradual demise of Mexico's postwar economic miracle would be to miss the point. In at least one sense some of the revolution's successes, rather than its shortcomings, contributed to the growing tensions in Mexican society as rising expectations engendered by economic and social changes were not met.

By the late 1960s and early 1970s, the young, sophisticated generation of Mexican students had absorbed an incredible amount of revolutionary rhetoric. A typical Sunday outing in Mexico City could include a car or taxi ride by the Monument to the Revolution and then on to Avenida 20 de Noviembre, where the bookstores carried posters not of Sophia Loren and the Beatles but of Emiliano Zapata and Pancho Villa. Then, on Avenida Francisco I. Madero the walls would be plastered with billboards propagandizing the PRI. And on Sunday every radio station in the country was required by law to carry "La Hora Nacional," the programming dinosaur created in the 1930s to help foster a national consciousness, but now dedicated to emitting blatant pro-government propaganda. It combined musical and cultural presentations with three- to four-minute orations on themes such as "The Pride of Being Mexican," "One Must Defend the Revolution," and "The March of Revolutionary Progress."

In a move to promote the culture of indigenismo, if not the self-determination of Mexico's indigenous population, in 1975 the government organized the First National Congress of Indigenous Peoples. Actually a government initiative to showcase the organization of an indigenous social movement in Mexico, the congress provided a platform for representatives of the 3.5 million people who self-identified as belonging to an Indian group in the 1970 census, about 10 percent of the total population. They succeeded in at least airing their demands for self-determination and more local autonomy. Eventually, the creation of the Coordinadora Nacional de Pueblos Indígenas (CNPI) served as a vehicle for actual indigenous engagement with the government on Indian policies and demands for greater self-determination although it suffered from internal dissension.

Another powerful tool for winning hearts and minds had been growing since the 1950s. Televisa emerged as the most powerful media conglomeration not only in Mexico, but in all of Latin America. Its television programs, seen by more than 25 million viewers, promoted modernity, consumer values, and, most of the time, the PRI. Nonetheless Mexicans, not only students and intellectuals but also growing numbers of the Mexican middle classes, were not easily taken in as they considered the social and economic realities of their country.

Luis Echeverría (b. 1922). The most active president since Cárdenas, Echeverría was interested primarily in foreign policy, but his energies were directed to the country's serious economic woes.

The 1970s found Mexico suffering a large balance of payments deficit. The rate of industrial growth had been impressive, but it had rested on the foundation of government protection. Mexican industry was not cost-effective and not generally competitive in world markets. It was unable to turn the balance of payments tide. The government frantically printed and borrowed more money. With imports outstripping exports by almost $3.5 billion in 1975 alone, Echeverría, currying the global south for support in a bid for the secretary-generalship of the United Nations, ordered his ambassador in the world organization to cast two votes equating Zionism and racism. Since he had earlier made a speech comparing Yasser Arafat to Benito Juárez, the result should not have surprised him. In early 1976 Jewish groups in the United States organized a tourist boycott of Mexico. Empty resort hotels dramatically testified that a substantial proportion of Mexico's tourist industry of $2.5 billion had been curtailed. Other factors, such as shortages of electric power, steel, and transportation facilities, contributed to a decline in the rate of economic growth. Echeverría had repeatedly lectured his citizenry on the need for democratization in Mexico and the value of a free press. As the economic situation deteriorated, however, he found himself attacked on all sides. When criticism from Mexico's largest daily newspaper, *Excélsior*, became too severe, the administration removed its editor, Julio Scherer García. By the summer of 1976, rumors were rampant that for the first time in 22 years Mexico would have to devalue the peso. The president's repeated assurances to the contrary did not prevent the flight of huge amounts of pesos as wealthy Mexicans exchanged their currency for dollars and investment in the United States and Europe. Capital flight in 1976 alone might have topped $6 billion. Mexican pundits quickly coined a new pejorative to deride their unpatriotic countrymen. *Sacadólares* (dollar extractors) would enter the day-to-day parlance.

The decision to devalue came in September, and the peso fell from 12.50 to 20.50 to the dollar, a 60 percent devaluation. Once the initial shock subsided, Mexicans accepted the devaluation stoically as they were assured that the resultant reduction of imports and growth of exports would combine to shore up the economy. But Mexican policy makers had not allowed the peso to float long enough to reach its true level. A month later a second devaluation of an additional 40 percent was announced in Mexico City. Psychologically, the second was more painful than the first, for it pointed up financial mismanagement of major proportions. Emblematic of rampant government corruption, Echererría managed to leave office an extraordinarily wealthy man.

With the country still in shock, a serious old problem surfaced once again. Thousands of landless Sonora campesinos moved onto privately owned lands in the rich Yaqui Valley and seized several hundred thousand acres from some eight hundred owners. Although the land seizures were being adjudicated in the Mexican Supreme Court, Echeverría, with not two weeks remaining in his presidential term, took matters into his own hands. He declared the seizures legal and gave the campesinos two hundred fifty thousand acres for communal development. The uproar could have been expected; Mexican industrialists and businessmen joined the former landowners in a huge protest strike. Using populist tactics, Echeverría tried to paper over the failure of the PRI to reform the political system and cover up his own repressive tactics.

The twelve years encompassed by the Díaz Ordaz and Echeverría administrations, 1964–76, highlighted troubles in Mexico's post–World War II experience. Since the entrenchment of the institutional revolution in the early 1940s, Mexican confidence had been bolstered repeatedly by the country's political stability and remarkable economic success. Mexico seemingly had separated itself from the systemic problems of its neighbors to the south. But by 1975 and 1976, it was obvious to Mexicans and foreigners alike that the political system and economic structure had proved themselves to be quite fragile. This fragility would be severely tested in the years to come.

JOSÉ LÓPEZ PORTILLO, 1976–82

On December 1, 1976, José López Portillo, the presidential candidate of the Partido Revolucionario Institucional (PRI), replaced Luis Echeverría in the Mexican presidency. While a few Mexicans evidenced optimism on that inauguration day, the vast majority found little cause for celebration, given the economic crisis and an anachronistic political system.

Prior to the famous Arab oil embargo in the early 1970s, the world gave too little attention to energy, conservation, or the influence of petroleum and petroleum by-products on inflation and power politics. By the late 1970s and early 1980s these issues dominated the national and international press. In some circles it became archaic to speak of the First, Second, and Third worlds. It seemed more appropriate to categorize nations as oil producers and oil consumers and to formulate new conceptualizations of dependency and interdependency.

The large petroleum discoveries made in southeastern Mexico (primarily in the states of Tabasco and Chiapas and offshore in the Gulf of Mexico) antedated the inauguration of López Portillo, but their extent and influence grew markedly during his administration and came to overshadow everything else. In 1980, López Portillo verified that proven reserves topped 60 billion barrels, while probable reserves approached 200 billion.

From the outset, López Portillo followed a policy of gradual, not dramatic, daily increase in oil production, resisting pressures from the United States to move faster. The economic infrastructure was not prepared to digest suddenly huge infusions of foreign capital without negative side effects. More importantly, it then seemed obvious that the price of petroleum in the future was not going to decline. Oil production grew from about eight hundred thousand barrels per day in 1976 to 2.3 million barrels a day in 1980. In 1981 Mexico became the world's fourth largest producer. The tripling of production during the administration did not reveal the whole story of how petroleum influenced the Mexican economy. For two reasons, Mexico's earning of petrodollars rose much more rapidly than the increased production figures would seem to suggest. First, a large percentage of the increase was destined for the international, not the domestic, market. Even more important was the steadily spiraling price of a barrel of crude. During the same period that production tripled, earnings from petroleum sales increased twelvefold, from $500 million in 1976 to about $6 billion in 1980. Prospects for a healthy and dynamic economy never looked better.

Mexican petroleum wealth had an incalculable impact on how the country viewed itself and how it related to others in the international community. In an energy-hungry world, petroleum production carried unusual international prestige. Mexico's new oil muscle was flexed repeatedly in its relations with the United States. In a dramatic but symbolic gesture, López Portillo was one of the first Latin American heads of state to announce that his country could not support the Carter administration's boycott of the Moscow Olympics. When the United States and Mexico could not agree on the price of natural gas, the Mexican president brazenly decided to burn off excess gas rather than sell to the United States at a figure judged to be inequitable. Subsequently, the new administration of Ronald Reagan quickly learned that outward manifestations of friendship and goodwill would not change Mexico's foreign policy, which supported the Sandinista Revolution in Nicaragua. In 1981 Mexico joined France in a declaration recognizing rebel guerrillas in El Salvador as a representative political force. These incidents were less a new hostility than a reflection of the new petroleum equation in United States-Mexico relations.

Only the most naïve considered petroleum a panacea for Mexico's sundry social and economic problems, but few realized the dangers that petro-dependency portended for the future. The first indications of trouble were faint and subtle. By the late 1970s, López Portillo was faced with an unemployment rate of almost 25 percent and an underemployment rate of nearly 50 percent of the country's workforce. Petroleum was a capital-intensive, not a labor-intensive, industry. With continuing increased production it could absorb perhaps 150,000 new workers each year, but by 1980, 800,000 Mexicans were entering the job market annually. Jobs would have to be created in other sectors of the economy.

Industry maintained healthy growth during the López Portillo administration but agricultural production of grains, which had been insufficient for at least a decade, fell further behind with the increase in population. Fearful that the newly found petrodollars could all be expended on food imports, in March 1980 the president announced the formation of Sistema Alimentario Mexicano (SAM), the Mexican Food System. SAM's goals called for agricultural growth of 4 percent a year and self-sufficiency in basic grains by 1985. A few months after SAM was proclaimed, the World Bank approved a loan of $325 million, the

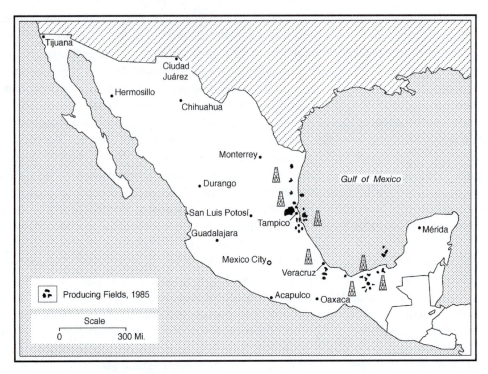

Mexican Oil Zones (Including Off-shore)

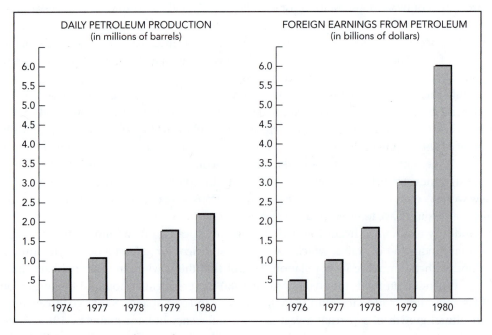

Growth of the Mexican Petroleum Industry

Between 1980 and 1982, Presidents José López Portillo and Ronald Reagan met on four occasions. The public cordiality of the visits notwithstanding, the two countries found it difficult to agree on important issues such as undocumented workers and the revolutionary turmoil in Central America.

largest loan that agency had ever made, to help implement the program. Increased agricultural production not only promised to improve the standard of living in rural areas but, by eliminating the need for huge food imports, would greatly ameliorate Mexico's unfavorable balance of trade. The goals were sound, but the success rate fell short of spectacular, as the implementation of the plan was plagued by mismanagement and inefficiency. Several years after López Portillo left office, Mexico still imported about 10 million tons of food annually, and the crisis in the agricultural sector spurred increased immigration to the cities. Mexico's 1980 census did reveal one promising trend. In the early postwar years, the percentage of illiterates in Mexico constantly declined, but because of the population explosion, the absolute number of illiterates rose. After 1970, however, Mexico experienced not only a decline in the percentage of illiterates from 28 percent to 17.1 percent by 1980 but also a drop of 1.5 million in the absolute number of illiterates. The education efforts of all the postwar administrations had finally made some headway.

THE ECONOMIC SLIDE BEGINS

López Portillo led Mexico on an unparalleled spending spree. Government construction, public works, social welfare projects, and government subsidies of consumer goods all meant an increased government participation in the economy. The number of state-owned enterprises quadrupled during the Echeverría and López Portillo administrations. Although national income was insufficient to cover the costs, Mexico's vast petroleum reserves made the international banking community willing, indeed eager, to extend large loans. Understandably, the interest rates were appallingly high and repayment would burden subsequent administrations. Mexico's massive deficit spending ressted on the supposition that continuing rises in the price of oil would allow the country to generate new wealth and repay its foreign obligations. But contrary to all expectations, petroleum prices did not rise. Because of the world oil glut of the early 1980s, they began to decline.

In 1982, during the last year of his administration, López Portillo found himself in a position even worse than that of Luis Echeverría in 1976. The Mexican rate of inflation greatly exceeded that in the United States, and the peso was again overvalued in relation to the dollar. As Mexican businessmen lost confidence in the economy, they began investing abroad and opening new bank accounts in the United States. To stop the monetary flight, in February the president ordered the Central Bank to stop buying and selling dollars and to allow the peso to find its true worth. Within a few days, it had lost one-third of its former value as it slipped from twenty-six to thirty-seven pesos to the dollar, and by summer of 1982 had sunk to one hundred pesos, marking the peso's lowest value ever. Concomitant price increases and tight currency controls created near panic in both business and government circles. It was only the tip of the iceberg.

In the last analysis, López Portillo applied the brakes too late, after he had first tried to squander Mexico into prosperity. The oil miracle had become the oil nightmare, and the president came under severe fire for mishandling the economy and demonstrating a lack of judgment and leadership. His response was unanticipated as he accused the country's private banks of looting, greed, and disloyalty for participating in the frenzied flight of Mexican capital in the amount of $22 billion. He had found a perfect scapegoat. In September 1982, without first soliciting any advice from his cabinet, the president dramatically nationalized fifty-nine of the country's banks. The nationalization of the banks did not prove to be an economic elixir. Many of them were in bad financial shape and assuming their burden was like putting chains on the national economy. The presidential action proved only that clear thinking seldom accompanies clenched fists.

As López Portillo's administration came to an end, Mexicans were incensed to learn that the president, despite his pious incantations about others, had taken care of himself. Failing to keep one eye on history, he had constructed four large mansions for himself and his family on prime land. The López Portillo compound was dubbed "Dog Hill," a sarcastic reminder of the president's earlier remarks that he would defend the peso "like a dog." As he departed Mexico for an extended vacation in Europe, he left behind Mexico's worst economic crisis of the twentieth century.

RECOMMENDED FOR FURTHER STUDY

Aviña, Alexander. *Specters of Revolution: Peasant Guerillas in the Cold War Mexican Countryside*. New York: Oxford University Press 2014.

Bailey, John. *Governing Mexico: The Statecraft of Crisis Management*. New York: St. Martin's Press, 1988.

Boyer, Christopher R. *Political Landscapes: Forests, Conservation, and Community in Mexico*. Durham, NC: Duke University Press, 2015.

Brannon, Jeffrey, and Eric N. Baklanoff. *Agrarian Reform and Public Enterprise in Mexico: The Political Economy of Yucatán's Henequen Industry.* Tuscaloosa: University of Alabama Press, 1987.

Camp, Roderic Ai. *Mexico's Mandarins: Crafting a Power Elite for the 21st Century.* Berkeley: University of California Press, 2002.

_____. *Oxford Handbook of Mexican Politics.* New York: Oxford University Press, 2011.

_____. "The Time of the Technocrats and Deconstruction of the Revolution." In *The Oxford History of Mexico,* edited by Michael C. Meyer and William H. Beezley, 569–97. New York: Oxford University Press, rev. 2010.

Centeno, Miguel A. *Democracy within Reason: Technocratic Revolution in Mexico,* 2nd ed. University Park: Pennsylvania State University Press, 1997.

Domínguez, Jorge I., ed. *Mexico's Political Economy: Challenges at Home and Abroad.* Beverly Hills, CA: Sage, 1982.

González de Bustamante, Celeste. *"Muy buenas noches:" Mexico, Television and the Cold War.* Lincoln: University of Nebraska Press, 2012.

Grayson, George W. *Mexico: From Corporatism to Pluralism?* New York: Harcourt Brace, 1998.

Hellman, Judith Adler. *Mexico in Crisis.* New York: Holmes and Meier, 1983.

Kiddle, Amelia, and María L. O. Muñoz, eds. *Populism in Twentieth Century Mexico: The Presidencies of Lázaro Cárdenas and Luis Echeverría.* Tucson: University of Arizona Press, 2010.

Levy, Daniel, and Gabriel Székely. *Mexico: Paradoxes of Stability and Change.* Boulder, CO: Westview Press, 1983.

Martínez, Oscar J. *Troublesome Border.* Tucson: University of Arizona Press, 1988.

Muñoz, María L.O. *Stand Up and Fight: Participatory Indigenismo, Populism, and Mobilization in Mexico, 1970–1984.* Tucson: University of Arizona Press, 2016.

Ochoa, Enrique. *Feeding Mexico: The Political Uses of Food since 1910.* Wilmington, DE: Scholarly Resources, 2000.

Riding, Alan. *Distant Neighbors: Portrait of the Mexicans.* New York: Alfred A. Knopf, 1985.

Roxborough, Ian. *Unions and Politics in Mexico: The Case of the Automobile Industry.* New York: Cambridge University Press, 2009.

Schmidt, Samuel. *The Deterioration of the Mexican Presidency.* Tucson: University of Arizona Press, 1991.

Shapira, Yoram. *Mexican Foreign Policy under Echeverría.* Beverly Hills, CA: Sage, 1978.

Sherman, John W. "The Mexican 'Miracle' and Its Collapse." In *The Oxford History of Mexico,* edited by Michael C. Meyer and William H. Beezley, 537–68. New York: Oxford University Press, rev. 2010.

Soto Laveaga, Gabriela. *Jungle Laboratories: Mexican Peasants, National Projects, and the Making of the Pill.* Durham, NC: University of North Carolina Press, 2009.

Teichman, Judith A. *Policy-making in Mexico: From Boom to Crisis.* Boston, MA: Allen & Unwin Book Publishers, 1988.

Velasco, J.A. *Impacts of Mexican Oil Policy on Economic and Political Development.* Lexington, MA: Lexington Books, 1983.

Walker, Louise. *Waking from the Dream: The Mexican Middle Classes after 1968.* Stanford, CA: Stanford University Press, 2013.

CHAPTER 36

SOCIETY AND CULTURE
A NEW INTERNATIONALISM

In the period after World War II, Mexico became more fully integrated into the international community than ever before. The country's charter membership in the United Nations at the close of the world conflict symbolized an end to the exclusive concern for parochial matters and a more profound interest in great world issues. Mexican presidents traveled widely, carrying Mexico's message to Europe, Africa, Asia, and South America. They were determined to begin exerting leadership in the developing world. This new world outlook effected a basic change in self-image. Many perceived that the problems faced by the nation—rapid population growth, urbanization with its attendant social dislocations, persistent poverty, serious pollution, and ecological imbalance—were not only Mexican but global. Through science, technology, and economy the world had become increasingly interdependent, and solutions to these problems were scarcely possible within the confines of the national boundaries. Yet globalization of the world's economies posed new dilemmas for Mexico.

POPULATION

The social and cultural changes of the postwar years were every bit as dramatic as those that had characterized the Porfiriato. The population growth was nothing short of fantastic, doubling in the twenty-three-year period between 1940 and 1963 and continuing to burgeon in geometric proportion. At the end of World War II, the population of the country numbered some 22 million; by 1980 it had grown to more than 80 million.

As Mexico's birth rate proliferated after the revolution, advocates of population control had their ups and downs in the postwar period. They were crushed by the 1968 papal encyclical banning all methods of artificial contraception because they recognized the truth in the bad quip that the rich get richer and the poor get children. During the presidential campaign of 1970, Luis Echeverría, the father of eight, announced that Mexico did not need to limit family size. In that same year, some six hundred thousand Mexican women underwent illegal abortions and thirty-two thousand of them died. In 1972, in the face of incontrovertible evidence, the

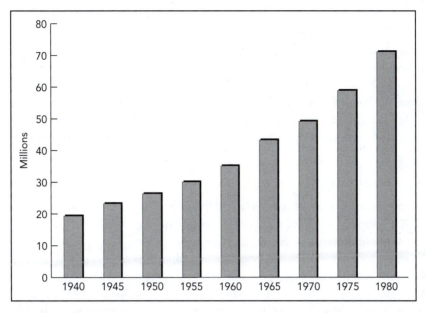

Mexican Population Growth, 1940–1980

Council of Mexican Bishops performed a remarkable *volte-face* and issued a pastoral letter declaring that Mexican couples should in good conscience make responsible decisions about the size of their families. The president agreed, and government-sponsored clinics began making birth control information available to those who requested it. The program began in a small way; the sell was very soft, but by 1980 López Portillo had earmarked over 500 million pesos annually for the family planning program and some dividends had been recorded. A population growth rate that had hovered between 3.2 and 3.4 percent during the 1970s began to drop, and demographers were cautiously optimistic that the birth rate would continue to decline.

With women having fewer children, more entered the workforce. They also became more active in pushing for their rights. The movement for women's rights had built up steam during the postwar years, with the full enfranchisement of women in 1955 just the

Posters such as this, with an unmistakable message, became increasingly common in Mexican cities in the 1970s and 1980s. If conservative Catholics were offended by the modest invitation to consider birth control, they were surely shocked in 1997 when billboards in Mexico City brazenly urged Mexicans to enlist condoms in the war against AIDS.

La familia pequeña vive mejor
decida la suya . . .
(The small family lives better
decide on yours . . .)

The Two-Child Family

beginning. More important was the feminist victory scored in 1974. While the equal rights amendment languished in the United States, President Echeverría sent a bill to the congress asking that Mexican men give women their full stake in society. The law that passed promised in theory women equal job opportunities, salaries, and legal standing. Beginning in the 1970s, the feminist movement began seriously to challenge laws and social practices denigrating the role of women. For the first time in its ninety-nine years, the prestigious Mexican Academy of the Language admitted a woman, Dr. María del Carmen Millán. Shortly thereafter Griselda Alvarez Ponce de León became governor of the state of Colima.

LEISURE AND SPORT

Mass communication, and most especially television, changed not only patterns of leisure but the information level of the urban citizenry. By the mid-1960s, Mexican television was no longer the sole preserve of the middle and upper classes. Television antennas sprouted from the most decaying of urban slums and attested to the vastness of the audience. Television sets proliferated in the next several decades and came to outnumber refrigerators and showers in Mexican households. In the summer of 1969, millions of Mexicans watched in amazement as Neil Armstrong took his first tentative steps on the surface of the moon. Since the 1960s, more and more people had access to a television set, even if it had belonged to a relative or neighbor, making soap operas (*telenovelas*), musicals, and traditional sporting events viewing staples. Another source of entertainment was found in *historietas* (comic books) directed to adults as well as children, which could be enjoyed even by those whose reading ability was minimal. Often assuming the role of moral mentor, some were steeped in history, others in romance, and still others in family tragedy. Capturing the full spectrum of life's delights, disappointments, and ironies, their appeal was extensive.

Sports constituted another major source of entertainment. *Fútbol* (soccer) has been at the top of the list for most of the twentieth century, whether it is being played on homegrown fields or in the stadiums around the country. Formal organization in soccer leagues and teams lagged until the 1940s when the sport became professionalized. The two most popular teams, Club América in Mexico City and the Guadalajara Chivas, developed a friendly national rivalry over the years. When Mexico's largest stadium, the Estadio Azteca, opened in 1966 with a seating capacity of over eighty-seven thousand, it became the home for América and also for the Mexican national team, called the Tricolor because it sports the three colors of the Mexican flag: green, red, and white. A few years after the Azteca opened, Mexico hosted the FIFA World Cup in 1970. Located at an altitude of seventy-two hundred feet, the stadium poses a serious challenge to teams unaccustomed to the relative lack of oxygen.

Other sports, boosted by television coverage, grew in popularity after World War II and helped to integrate Mexico into the modern world. Mexico professionalized boxing and several of its athletes achieved international standing by the 1970s. Baseball, which had been introduced in the nineteenth century, struggled to develop and sustain leagues in Mexico, but many of its players realized success in US major league baseball. Fernando Valenzuela from Sonora, one of the best pitchers of the 1980s, played for the Los Angeles Dodgers and won the Rookie of the Year award in 1981. Some 100 Mexicans play in the major leagues today.

A minor sporting attraction of the 1930s became an enthralling spectacle in the postwar period. The Mexican variant of professional wrestling, *lucha libre*, fascinated hundreds of thousands. Unlike its American counterpart, almost all of the participants wore masks, enhancing the aura of inscrutability. But even with concealed faces, it was nearly impossible to confuse good and evil in these carefully choreographed physical melodramas. Heroes (the *técnicos*) were pitted against villains (the *rudos*) in a metaphor of life's constant struggles. Like any classic melodrama, the emotions of the audience were shamelessly manipulated as a series of behemoth scoundrels visited indignities on an equal number of long-suffering heroes. Taunting the crowd with endless gimmicks, the *rudos* evoked profound passions, while the *técnicos* inevitably emerged larger than life. It was no accident that the most beloved *luchadores* of the post-World War II period adopted monikers linked to the church. Young and old alike could applaud the heroics of El Angel Blanco or the icon El Santo, while excoriating the outrageous and cheating tactics of the vicious Médico Asesino or the bully Cavernario Galindo. But no match commanded more attention than the 1955 epic when, in virtue triumphant, El Santo unmasked and shamed the Sombra Vengadora.

A celebrity of gigantic proportion, El Santo commanded admiration and awe as much for his wholesome image as for his prowess in the ring.

Civic fiestas, with their colorful parades and musical performances, offered another distraction for Mexicans throughout the country on national holidays, for example on September 16 with the Grito de Dolores celebrating Mexican independence from Spain. Historical commemoration ceremonies honored Benito Juárez and Emiliano Zapata in order to reinforce the myths of revolutionary nationalism. Even more numerous were the processions, pilgrimages, and fiestas marking the Catholic religious holidays that reemerged after the 1930s when the church made accommodations with the government. Mexican Catholicism came in many packages, ranging from its socially progressive organizations that emerged after Vatican II to the right-wing branches like Opus Dei and the Legionaries of Christ, making it attractive to a broad range of the faithful in urban and rural areas.

In Mexico City, museums, with free admission on Sundays, combined leisure and learning. The monumental Museum of Anthropology offered a splendid display of Mexico's indigenous history and accomplishments. Covering twenty acres within Chapultepec Park, the museum houses salons displaying artifacts from particular regions and cultures, including those of Teotihuacan, the Olmecs, Toltecs, Mixtecs, Zapotecs, Aztecs, and Mayas. One of the highlights is the Aztec calendar, a twelve-foot, twenty-five-ton, carved basalt slab from the fifteenth century. It numbers among the many treasures discovered under the Zócalo and other areas during the construction of the first subway line.

An architectural and anthropological achievement of gigantic proportions, the new Museum of Anthropology in Mexico City (above and on opposite page) became a prime tourist attraction in the 1970s.

In the 1940s, the National Institute of Anthropology and History (INAH) began to undertake the colossal task of cataloguing and protecting well over 300,000 monuments and sites considered part of Mexico's prehispanic and historical patrimony. Over time, INAH's professional staff has developed hundreds of archaeological sites and museums open to the public throughout the country. From 1978 to 1982, under the direction of anthropologist Eduardo Matos Moctezuma, INAH stepped up efforts to excavate the Templo Mayor (the main temple of the Aztecs). The Museum of the Templo Mayor opened several years later to display the findings, including the magnificent monolithic disk from the fifteenth century depicting a shattered Coyolxauhqui, the sister of

Huitzilopochtli. The recovery of the past, rather than an anachronistic endeavor, became emblematic of Mexico's technological modernity.

Nowhere was this connection more ironically displayed than in the planning for Mexico City's subway system. When work began in 1967, Mexico City's metro signaled

One of the most modern subways in the world, the Mexico City system was running to capacity and beyond within a few months of its completion. In 1990, more than five million Mexico City passengers were using the eighty-seven miles of the metro's double tracks every day. Plans to add an additional thirty-seven miles of track were canceled because of financial exigencies.

a dramatic modernization of the cityscape. Making room for the metro entailed removing some familiar aspects of the urban landscape and introducing residents to the new spaces of the network's underground tunnels and stations. Planners adopted a pictographic system to integrate the metro with pre-Columbian, colonial, and contemporary features, as well as the use of color to distinguish different lines. They designed icons to identify each metro station, connecting it with an existing historical, urban architectural, or other relational feature. For example, the sign for Balderas station is a cannon on display in the nearby library above ground, while the stop at the huge Merced market is represented by a crate of apples. Chapultepec in nahuatl means hill of the grasshopper endowing that station with its image of a leaping insect. For those who could not read, the symbols were manageable even though some required a stretch to make the connection with the place.

FILM AND MUSIC

In the "golden age" of Mexican filmmaking from 1935 to the late 1950s, Mexicans eagerly watched their leading actors and idols, Pedro Infante, Jorge Negrete, María Félix, and the stunningly beautiful Dolores del Río (who also had a successful Hollywood career), in

Dolores del Río dances with Fred Astaire in the 1933 Hollywood film *Flying Down to Rio*.

dramatic roles. Films with budgets subsidized by Hollywood, largely in the style of melo-drama, entertained Mexican audiences while inculcating important lessons about mexicani-dad, gender norms, and surviving in the growing cities.

Much of the early post-revolutionary filmmaking aimed at building a unified vision of the nation that obscured differences of class and ideology while reinforcing patriarchy and gender roles. The 1946 film *Enamorada* depicts the revolutionary education of an upper-class woman as she learns to put the needs of the nation above her own, a reflec-tion of the fear that if women were given the right to vote they would not support the party, thus postponing women's suffrage until the 50s. Films like *María Candelaría* (1943) and *Río Escondido* (1947) both spin narratives about young women, one indigenous, the other mestiza, in which their lives are sacrificed for the greater good. Moreover, both films use rural Mexico to define a particular mexicanidad that reflects an indigenous ideal rather than the reality of Indians' contemporary lives. In the construction of mexicanidad, as filmmakers sought to project a cohesive national identity, women's lives were used as narrative devices to warn moviegoers of danger if they did not move forward with the revolutionary state.

While films of the Golden Age reflected the need to define a coherent national iden-tity, they also served to teach moviegoers how to navigate an increasingly urban society. Carlos Monsivais wrote: "In the neighborhood cinemas one acquires basic skills that help to orient one in the city . . . the pleasure of joining the community. . . . During

María Candelaria, directed by Emilio Fernández, was the first Latin American film to win the top prize at the Cannes Film Festival in 1946. *Opposite page:* Del Río as the tragic María Candelaria.

the period 1920–1960 cinemas multiply and are the center of . . . 'neighborhood identity. . . .'"[1] *Nosotros los pobres* (1947), which Monsivais described as the "apex of Mexican melodrama," presents a web of intrigue, deception, and thievery, reflecting the perceived ills of modern life in the capital city, while an innocent young woman falls into prostitution in *Aventurera* (1950), finally redeeming herself and ending the film happily married.

As the Golden Age of Mexican cinema waned in the late 1950s, some of these lessons were presented in less dramatic, funnier movies. Cantinflas (Mariano Moreno) began his career in the *carpa* (tent) theaters of the capital and rose to be one of the most famous comedians in Latin America through the 1940s. In the 1950s, he emerged as an international movie star featured in *Around the World in Eighty Days* as Jean Passepartout, valet to David Niven's Phileas Fogg. In his films on Mexico, actually produced at Columbia Studios in Hollywood, he navigated the perils of urban life in films like *El bolero de Raquel* (1957), *El analfabeto* (1961), and *El padrecito* (1963). By the mid-1960s, Mexican disillusionment with politics extended to cinema, where audiences became less willing to entertain melodramatic films with strict lessons about identity, women's roles, or the ills of urban life. Moreover, Hollywood invested less in Mexican cinema as television came to replace movie theaters for many.

---

1 Quoted in Elena Lahr-Vivaz, *Mexican Melodrama: Film and Nation from the Golden Age to the New Wave* (Tucson, AZ, 2016), 17.

Cantinflas.

The Americanization of popular culture that increasingly pervaded Mexico after World War II prompted criticism not only from postrevolutionary governments but also from many Mexican intellectuals. But in a world tied ever closer together by the wonders of technological change and mass media, cultural insularity was neither practical nor attractive to most. These changes did not mean that all Mexican culture became derivative as many forms of peculiarly Mexican counterculture evolved in novels, comic books, telenovelas, films, and cabaret performances that offered sharp political satire and social criticism.

However, one foreign import, rock music, began to compete seriously with traditional Mexican music forms in the 1960s and by the 1970s had become dominant among the young. Rock bands slowly began to replace the trios and mariachi bands as Mexican youth's music of choice. After the 1969 Woodstock festival, Mexicans produced the Avándaro Music Festival in the Valle de Bravo outside Mexico City in 1971, attracting over 200,000 *rockeros*. The performance included the Who's rock opera *Tommy* with a live band, legendary rock accordionist Carlos Steward, and several actors, as well as Armando Nava and Los Dug Dugs performing "Let's Make It Now." Throughout the day and evening, barbed criticisms of government repression and foul language erupted from the audience, prompting the shut-off of a radio station broadcast. Some of the performers were subsequently hounded by the government, forcing them underground.

The spectacle midwifed a new Latin rock genre known as *la nueva onda* and touched off a new national debate. While purists viewed *rocanrol* as crassly imitative of the worst in US hippie culture and the government saw it as subversive, others credited it as a significant break with the cultural forms preferred by Mexico's institutional revolution. In its wake, groups such as Los Hitters and Los Johnny Jets enjoyed fleeting fame as well as a measure

Cantinflas made his international debut in the film *Around the World in Eighty Days.*

of financial success. For those who liked hard rock, few could compete with the Dug Dugs. The 2012 film, *Gimme the Power*, features the band Molotov and offers a history of this musical evolution, along with government attempts to censor it.

LITERATURE, ART, AND SCHOLARSHIP

Mexico became a country of vibrant intellectual ferment in the half-century following World War II. Mexico City was clearly the cultural capital of the country and by 1985 could boast twenty daily newspapers and two hundred fifty periodicals. The television and film industries were based in the capital, as were the most outstanding art galleries and museums. The cosmopolitan city served as the crucible for Mexico's literary genius. Many famous writers emerged throughout the postwar period, as new literary journals and magazines of social protest provided the grist for healthy cultural debate.

The postwar years saw the demise of both indigenismo and the novel of the revolution as Mexican writers began their quest for the universal. While nobody could question the mexicanidad of Octavio Paz (1914–98), his writing revealed greater concern for ecumenical matters than for the heroes and apostates of the great revolution. Born in Mexico City four years after the revolution broke out, he was, by the 1950s, one of the most profound and prolific members of the new intelligentsia. As with many of the great intellects of the postwar period, it was often difficult to pinpoint where his philosophy ended and his literature began. In essays, in drama, and, above all, in poetry, he sought to link the Mexican experience with that of all humanity through the common denominators of suffering and tragedy. His most penetrating work, *El laberinto de la soledad* (translated as *The Labyrinth of Solitude, 1950*), is a psychological study of the Mexican character but was conceived in the United States, where Paz was able to observe Mexicans in a foreign milieu. Solitude for Paz was a condition that Mexicans had to comprehend through their history to understand themselves:

> Solitude—the feeling and knowledge that one is alone, alienated from the world and oneself—is not an exclusively Mexican characteristic. All men, at some moment in their lives, feel themselves to be alone. And they are. To live is to be separated from what we were in order to approach what we are going to be in the mysterious future. Solitude is the profoundest fact of the human condition.[2]

In the chapter "Sons of La Malinche." Paz's inquiry into the Mexican psyche presents a brilliant analysis of variations on the verb *chingar*, perhaps the most versatile of Mexican words, in its multiple meanings that range from failure to victim to violated.

Paz's criticism of the revolution was far from mundane. In a work he called *Posdata* (1970) and published in English under the title *The Other Mexico: Critique of the Pyramid*, he decried the intellectual paucity of the literary enterprise in Mexico, especially the failure of the intelligentsia to relate the Mexican experience to the larger world. His career culminated in 1990 when he won the Nobel Prize for Literature; eight years later, at the time of his death, he was remembered by many as the greatest twentieth-century poet and essayist of the Spanish-speaking world.

While Octavio Paz broke out of the mold many considered properly Mexican, Juan José Arreola (1918–2001) in a number of works turned his back on Mexican themes. Four years younger than Paz, Arreola developed a sharp, biting satire of the bourgeois values of postwar Mexican society. Culturally indebted to Bertolt Brecht and Albert Camus, he was sarcastic, irreverent, hyperbolic, humorous to the point of cruelty, and blatantly sexist. Arreola jabbed mercilessly at the pomposity and deceptions of his world. In one notably wicked short story, he invented a plastic woman and advertised her as would befit the merchandising practices of the new Mexico.

> Wherever the presence of woman is difficult, onerous, or prejudicial, whether in the bachelor's bedroom or in the concentration camp, the use of Plastisex is highly recommended. . . . We will furnish you with the woman you have dreamed about all your life: she is manipulated by automatic controls and is made of synthetic materials that reproduce at will the most superficial or subtle characteristics of feminine beauty.

---

2   Octavio Paz, *The Labyrinth of Solitude: Life and Thought in Mexico*, trans. Lysander Kemp (New York, NY, 1961), 195.

Our Venuses are guaranteed to give perfect service for ten years—the average time
any wife lasts—except in cases where they are subjected to abnormal sadistic practices. . . .
Though submissive, the Plastisex is extremely vigorous, since she is equipped with an electric motor of one-half horse power. . . . Nude, she is simply unexcelled; pubescent or not, in
the flower of youth, or with autumn's ripe opulence, according to the particular coloring of
each race or mixture of races.[3]

Perhaps the most creative of the postwar writers was novelist Carlos Fuentes
(1928–2012). Born in 1928 to a middle-class family, Fuentes took a law degree at the National University and then studied international law at Geneva. His most famous novel,
La región mas transparente (*Where the Air Is Clear*), published in 1958, is a cynical story
of disillusionment with the revolution. But it is scarcely a novel of the revolution in the
classic sense. While those familiar with the outlines of Mexican history in the twentieth
century might find it easier than others to comprehend, more than anything else it is a
Marxist critique of human nature and a creative condemnation of capitalism. The names
and the places are clearly Mexican, but the major themes—the abuses of power, the self-
serving opportunism of the bourgeoisie, the pointless existence of the *nouveau riche*, and
the tendency of the new society to accept all things foreign—clearly have an applicability
transcending Mexico.

Fuentes went on to become one of the most admired writers in the Spanish-speaking
world. He was a catalyst, along with others like Gabriel García Márquez and Mario Vargas
Llosa, of the Latin American literature boom of the 1960s and 70s. Politically engaged in
promoting social justice and human rights, he withdrew his support for the Cuban revolution when it became too authoritarian. Appointed Mexican ambassador to France in 1975,
he resigned in protest two years later when former president Gustavo Díaz Ordaz, who had
sent troops to fire on student protestors in 1968, was named ambassador to Spain. His
novels, short stories, plays, and essays are known for their cultural, political, and historical
insights about Mexico, as well as their exploration of universal themes of love, death, and
memory. When Fuentes died suddenly in 2012, the Mexican nation mourned the loss of a
public figure who commanded authority when he voiced their disappointments and dreams.
Fellow writer and political commentator Federico Reyes Héroles eulogized his friend as the
soul of the people:

"Alexis de Tocqueville used to say that the strength of a nation resides in the force of its
memories and the power of its dreams. But a nation's memory, and its dreams, have to be
embodied in words. Only through words can we know ourselves, share, and exist in both
the individual and in the collective. But a word does not fall from a tree like a delicious fruit.
Words need engineers to set the foundation, architects to invent the form; and, perhaps the
most difficult to find, words need a soul that can feel both for itself and for others."[4]

Many of Carlos Fuentes' works have been translated into English, as well as other languages, and a number earned national and international prizes. Often mentioned as a

---

3   Juan José Arreola, *Confabulario and Other Inventions*, trans. George D. Shade (Austin, TX, 1974), 134–39.
4   *Reforma*, May 17, 2012, 25.

candidate for the Nobel Prize in Literature, Fuentes never obtained it. The writer had his critics in Mexico; both Octavio Paz and well-known contemporary historian Enrique Krauze saw him as out of touch with the country, but many Mexicans regretted that he had been overlooked for the most coveted award in literature.

Critiques of Mexican identity proliferated during the 1950s, 1960s, and 1970s, exposing the failure of the revolution to incorporate diverse ethnic groups and classes in a national project. Caciquismo, corruption, and moral decay pervade Juan Rulfo's *Pedro Páramo* (1955). Several novels by Rosario Castellanos set in Chiapas, including *Oficio de tinieblas* (1962), and *Los recuerdos del porvenir* (1963) by Elena Garro (the wife of Octavio Paz), continued to depict themes of violence and ethnic injustice in rural Mexico but with the added dimension of gender oppression.

Perhaps, as Mary Kay Vaughan has suggested, we should look beyond the literary giants to understand the 60s generation by examining the political, social, and artistic influences of the postwar period on an individual life. In her revealing portrait of a young painter, she explores several formative processes that Pepe Zúñiga shared with the "rebellious" or creative youth of his era. One was the mid-century emphasis on children's welfare through health campaigns, churches, schools, textbooks, sports and especially radio shows, that fostered an ethos of work and responsibility but also an appreciation for amusement and popular culture. In addition, national and transnational mass media, cinema, music, and art exposed youth to a new cosmopolitanism in a period of economic growth and cultural dynamism. Pepe grew up in a family that migrated from Oaxaca to Mexico City aspiring to achieve middle-class mobility, but his growing humanist sensibility along with a longing for self-expression led him to reject a traditional vocation and choose to study art at the La Esmeralda painting school, founded in 1942 by Rivera, Kahlo, and others. His experiences there led him to forums of criticism in theater, museums, and art. He increasingly questioned his own identity and the anti-democratic nature of the state. Freeing himself from restrictive social conventions after a time studying in Paris (an experience that other students enjoyed in the many cross-cultural exchanges of the period), he found his own artistic voice. Vaughan evocatively paints Pepe Zúñiga as emblematic of the 60s rebels who advocated political and cultural democratization.[5]

The tragedy of Tlatelolco catalyzed a protracted national debate and spawned its own impressive body of literature in the 1970s. Unified only in its recognition that the slaughter left scars that would never wholly heal, Tlatelolco literature found expression in the essay, poetry, short story, and novel. Octavio Paz and Carlos Fuentes dominated the outpouring of perceptive political essays searching for accountability. Other searching or partially fictionalized responses are epitomized by Carlos Monsiváis's *Días de guardar* (1970), Arturo Azuela's *Manifestación de silencios* (1979), Elena Poniatowska's *La noche de Tlatelolco* (1971), Luis Spota's *La plaza* (1977), Gonzalo Martre's *Los símbolos transparentes* (1978), and Fernando del Paso's *Palinuro de México* (1977). No matter what the specific genre, the body of literature itself testified eloquently to the fact that the Mexican intelligentsia insisted that such an untoward episode should be neither repeated nor forgotten. When Poniatowska was awarded the Xavier Villarrutia Literary Prize for *La noche de Tlatelolco*, she would not accept it, insisting that the only persons worthy of a prize were

---

5   Mary Kay Vaughan, *Portrait of a Young Painter: Pepe Zúñiga and Mexico City's Rebel Generation* (Durham, NC, 2015).

those who had given their lives at the Plaza de las Tres Culturas that fateful October evening in 1968. Tlatelolco, in essence, became not only a backdrop, not only a focus of literary discourse, but a major point of departure for much of the Mexican literature published in the period following the infamous events of 1968. The cultural outpouring combined with political pressure to force the government to declare October 2, 1998, a national day of mourning and to order flags flown at half staff. The modest concession took thirty years.

Shortly thereafter, in the presidency of Vicente Fox, the attorney general's office made an effort to bring to justice the officials responsible for killing dissidents at Tlatelolco and in its aftermath. Secret security files were opened up, leading to revelations about the roles of key players, including former president Luis Echeverría, who allegedly ordered paramilitaries known as the Falcons (Los Halcones) to attack student marchers in Mexico City in 1971. At least twenty-five protesters were killed. Government prosecutor Ignacio Carrillo Prieto charged Echeverría with genocide (defined as systematic crimes against the lives of members of any national group); but for many, including the Mexican Supreme Court, this tactic was too much of a stretch, and they lamented that the Fox government had not called for the establishment of a truth commission to pursue the matter. Nonetheless, throughout 2004 and 2005, the Mexican public read the lurid details of state-sponsored violence. In June 2006, Echeverría was arrested and charged with crimes related to the 1968 and 1971 killings, but a judge ruled that Mexico's statute of limitations prevented his prosecution.

Political corruption, along with social and environmental concerns, began to displace national identity as the most frequent motif in Mexican narratives of the late 20th century, as evidenced in José Emilio Pacheco's *Morirás lejos* (1967) and *Las batallas en el desierto* (1981). The voices of women and gays also emerged more openly in works like Angeles Mastretta's *Arráncame la vida* (1985) Guadalupe Loaeza's *Las niñas bien* (1987), and Luis Zapata's *El vampiro de la colonia Roma* (1979).

Mexican art in the postwar period also rejected—in fact, rebelled violently against—the nationalistic indigenismo. Mexican art and photography had been summoned to the service of the revolution in constructing a vision of national identity that bound the people to the vision of the leaders as a unified whole. But the patriarchal revolutionary family fell into disfavor. Moving away from mythical allegories depicting cloud-covered volcanoes, pyramids, and indigenous people in picturesque clothing, photographers like Tina Modotti, Manuel Alvarez Bravo, Lola Alvarez Bravo, and Graciela Iturbide began to portray Mexico as Mexicans making themselves through struggle. Modern visual culture was essential to both the invention of and resistance to a revolutionary hegemonic order.

Although Mexican painters of the 1950s and 1960s never achieved the fame of the great revolutionary muralists, some of the new experiments with abstract expressionism, drip painting, and even op art were exciting to some and completely bewildering to others. Remedios Varo was born in Spain but realized the greatest part of her surrealist painting in Mexico during the 1950s. Most of her characters appear mystical and solitary, people and cats with almond-shaped eyes, traveling in cosmically propelled vehicles through a world of magic and imagination. Among the *avant-garde* was José Luis Cuevas (1934–2017), who epitomized the rejection of traditional muralism when he stated that what he wanted for his country's art was "broad highways leading to the rest of the world rather than narrow trails connecting one adobe village to another."[6] Many of his contemporaries agreed, and the new generation, including Olga Costa, Jesús Reyes, Pedro Coronel, and Carrillo Gil, executed paintings that could have been conceived anywhere in the western world. They did not believe it necessary to capture the spirit of an idealized revolution, to reaffirm their mexicanidad, or to instruct the masses. But it was Juan Soriano who depicted the movement best, and in 1957 a distinguished jury of artists at the Salón de la Plástica Mexicana gave him the first prize ever awarded to Mexican abstract painting. Soriano later articulated his views on the new Mexican art to Elena Poniatowska in a celebrated interview.

> Siqueiros limits himself to one country—Mexico. And to one political idea. I'm interested in ideas that are much broader. . . . Siqueiros . . . wants to create a strongly nationalistic art. And I believe that his art is excellent because it expresses him. But I want, and have always wanted to be universal. . . . Those murals are only tourist bait. They're the same kind of thing as those gigantic posters of the travel agencies: *Visit Mexico*. Furthermore those murals reveal nothing. They're a chronicle and not a poetic creation. Diego Rivera created a completely bureaucratic art. He made himself a propagandist of the victorious revolution. . . . I reproach him for having completely prostituted the pictorial language, reducing it to little more than a caricature, vulgarizing it. Because, don't you see, the caricature is a creation of the bourgeoisie. . . . I'm not concerned with my nationality. I can assure you I don't carry it like a chip on my shoulder, nor do I have to remind myself daily that I'm a Mexican.[7]

Another celebrated artist, Rufino Tamayo, did not completely abandon native motifs but rendered them abstractly with surrealist influences (see his painting *Dos figuras en rojo* in the color insert section of this book). In 1981, he founded the Museo Tamayo Arte Contemporáneo, which houses his modern art collection. The Museo Rufino Tamayo in his birthplace of Oaxaca holds his extensive pre-Columbian collection.

To the amusement of some and to the shock of others, Mexican painting turned iconoclastic in the 1970s and 1980s, first reinterpreting Mexican popular culture motifs within a more personal than national context. Later postmodern tendencies fused past and present styles in often unconventional and innovative ways and media, including installation art. Artistic impiety was epitomized by the sacrilegious work of Rolando de la Rosa. His 1988 art exhibit featured the face of Marilyn Monroe superimposed on the image of the Virgin of Guadalupe and the face of actor Pedro Infante similarly substituted for that of Christ in his rendition of the Last Supper. A generation or two earlier this type of mocking materialism would have occasioned major outcries, but most viewers simply shrugged their shoulders.

Historical scholarship had not fared well in the two decades prior to World War II, for historians often found it impossible to reconcile their faith in the revolution with documentary evidence available to them. But in the postwar years historical scholarship came of age. Between 1940 and 1951, three important institutions—El Colegio de México, the Escuela Nacional de Antropología e Historia, and the Instituto de Historia of the National University—were founded and devoted major effort to improving historical training. Reacting

---

6   José Luis Cuevas, "The Cactus Curtain," *Evergreen Review* 2 (1959): 120.
7   Quoted in Elena Poniatowska, "Interview with Juan Soriano," *Evergreen Review* 2 (1959): 144–49.

against the blatant partisanship of the prorevolutionary school that had emerged in the 1920s and 1930s, the new generation of historians was much more concerned with methodology, archival research, careful bibliographical preparation, and documentary publication. The preparation of excellent regional histories and microhistories got a boost as the century progressed by the opening of many new scholarly institutions in all of the Mexican states.

One of the most remarkable historical endeavors undertaken in Mexico in the postwar era was the project of Daniel Cosío Villegas. In the late 1940s, he began work on an ambitious, multivolume history of modern Mexico. Twenty-five years later the ninth and final volume appeared, and the project had received acclaim as one of the most innovative Latin American historical enterprises of the twentieth century. The *Historia moderna de México* covers the years from the restoration of the republic in 1867 to the outbreak of the revolution, with separate volumes treating the political, economic, social, and international aspects of the period. Cosío planned the project with extreme care, founding in 1950 the Seminar on Modern Mexican History at El Colegio de México. This workshop brought together talented researchers who, under Cosío's direction, prepared extensive bibliographies; compiled statistical data; searched out the major manuscripts, printed documentation, and newspapers; and cooperated in the production of the finished volumes. Based on scientific research, the main thesis that connected the work attributed the birth of modern Mexico to the restored republic rather than to the Porfiriato or the revolution.

In the period from 1940 to 1982, Mexico's identity as a modernizing and internationally connected nation underwent chaotic shifts from the Mexican economic "miracle" to the brutality of the state and its aftermath. The student challenge to patrimonial authoritarianism was answered by the tragedy of Tlatelolco, effectively obliterating the government myths of an imagined harmonious national community and a contented revolutionary family. While state-controlled radio and television strengthened their national monopoly on the commercial fabrication of culture, artistic performances and production, along with transnational mass media and foreign influences, refashioned the official story. Debates over cultural authenticity could not overshadow the creative efforts by Mexicans to understand and transform their lives.

RECOMMENDED FOR FURTHER STUDY

Arreola, Juan José. *Confabulario and Other Inventions.* Translated by George D. Shade. Austin: University of Texas Press, 1974.

Benjamin, Thomas. *La Revolución: Mexico's Great Revolution as Memory, Myth, and History.* Austin: University of Texas Press, 2000.

Brushwood, John S. *Mexico in Its Novel: A Nation's Search for Identity.* Austin: University of Texas Press, 1966.

de Beer, Gabriella. *Contemporary Mexican Women Writers: Five Voices.* Austin: University of Texas Press, 1996.

Cuevas, José Luis, "The Cactus Curtain." Special issue, "Eye of Mexico," *Evergreen Review* 2/7 (1959): 11–20.

Eagan, Linda. *Carlos Monsiváis: Culture and Chronicle in Contemporary Mexico.* Tucson: University of Arizona Press, 2001.

Flaherty, George. *Hotel Mexico: Dwelling on the '68 Movement.* Berkeley: University of California Press, 2016

Florescano, Enrique. *National Narratives in Mexico: A History.* Norman: University of Oklahoma Press, 2006.

Fuentes, Carlos. *The Death of Artemio Cruz.* Translated by Sam Hileman. New York: Noonday Press, 1966.

_____. *Where the Air Is Clear.* Translated by Sam Hileman. New York: Ivan Obolensky, 1960.

Goldman, Shifra M. *Contemporary Mexican Painting in a Time of Change.* Austin: University of Texas Press, 1981.

Gutiérrez, Natividad. *Nationalist Myths and Ethnic Identities: Indigenous Intellectuals and the Mexican State*. Lincoln: University of Nebraska Press, 1999.

Hale, Charles A. "The Liberal Impulse: Daniel Cosío Villegas and the *Historia moderna de México*." *Hispanic American Historical Review* 54/3 (1974): 479–98.

Hall, Linda B. *Dolores del Rio: Beauty in Light and Shade*. Stanford, CA: Stanford University Press, 2013.

Irwin, Robert McKee. *Mexican Masculinities*. Minneapolis: University of Minnesota Press, 2003.

Jorgensen, Beth E. *The Writings of Elena Poniatowska: Emerging Dialogues*. Austin: University of Texas Press, 1994.

Joseph, Gilbert M., Anne Rubenstein, and Eric Zolov, eds. *Fragments of a Golden Age: The Politics of Culture in Mexico since 1940*. Durham, NC: Duke University Press, 2001.

Lahr-Vivaz, Elena. *Mexican Melodrama: Film and Nation from the Golden Age to the New Wave*. Tucson: University of Arizona Press, 2016.

Lerner, Jesse. *The Maya of Modernism: Art, Architecture, and Film*. Albuquerque: University of New Mexico Press, 2011.

Levi, Heather. *The World of Lucha Libre*. Durham, N.C.: Duke University Press, 2008.

Lewis, Oscar. *The Children of Sánchez: Autobiography of a Mexican Family*. New York: Vintage Books, 1961.

Lipp, Solomon. *Leopoldo Zea: From Mexicanidad to a Philosophy of History*. Waterloo, ON, Canada: Wilfrid Laurier University Press, 1980.

Lomnitz-Adler, Claudio. *Deep Mexico, Silent Mexico: An Anthropology of Nationalism*. Minneapolis: University of Minnesota Press, 2001.

Lorey, David E. *The University System and Economic Development in Mexico since 1929*. Stanford, CA: Stanford University Press, 1993.

Mraz, John. *Looking for Mexico: Modern Visual Culture and National Identity*. Durham, NC: Duke University Press, 2009.

Paz, Octavio. *The Labyrinth of Solitude: Life and Thought in Mexico*. Translated by Lysander Kemp. New York: Grove Press, 1961.

_____. *The Other Mexico: Critique of the Pyramid*. New York: Grove Press, 1972.

Pescador, Juan Javier. *Crossing Borders with the Santo Niño de Atocha*. Albuquerque: University of New Mexico Press, 2009.

Pilcher, Jeffrey. *Cantinflas and the Chaos of Mexican Modernity*. Wilmington, DE: Scholarly Resources, 2001.

Poniatowska, Elena. "Interview with Juan Soriano." Special issue, "Eye of Mexico," *Evergreen Review* 2/7 (1959): 141–152

Rubenstein, Anne. *Bad Language, Naked Ladies, and Other Threats to the Nation: A Political History of Comic Books in Mexico*. Durham, NC: Duke University Press, 1998.

_____. "Mass Media and Popular Culture in the Postrevolutionary Era." In *The Oxford History of Mexico*, edited by Michael C. Meyer and William H. Beezley, 598–633. New York: Oxford University Press, rev. 2010.

Sheppard, Randal. *A Persistent Revolution: History, Nationalism, and Politics in Mexico since 1968*. Albuquerque: University of New Mexico Press, 2016.

Steele, Cynthia. *Politics, Gender and the Mexican Novel, 1968–1988: Beyond the Pyramid*. Austin: University of Texas Press, 1992.

Taylor, Kathy. *The New Narrative of Mexico: Sub-versions of History in Mexican Fiction*. Lewisburg, PA: Bucknell University Press, 1994.

Vanderwood, Paul J. *Juan Soldado: Rapist, Murderer, Martyr, Saint*. Durham, NC: Duke University Press, 2004.

Vaughan, Mary Kay. *Portrait of a Young Painter: Pepe Zúñiga and Mexico City's Rebel Generation*. Durham, NC: Duke University Press, 2016.

Wilkie, James W., Michael C. Meyer, and Edna Monzón de Wilkie, eds. *Contemporary Mexico: Papers of the IV Congress of Mexican History*. Berkeley: University of California Press, 1976.

Young, Dolly J. "Mexican Literary Reactions to Tlatelolco, 1968." *Latin American Research Review* 20/2 (1985): 71–85.

Zolov, Eric. *Refried Elvis: The Rise of the Mexican Counterculture*. Berkeley: University of California Press. 1999.

CRISIS AND CHANGE IN AN ERA OF GLOBALIZATION

CHAPTER 37

THE NEO-LIBERAL STATE: A PATH TO DEMOCRACY?

MIGUEL DE LA MADRID: FROM CRISIS TO CRISIS, 1982–88

When forty-seven-year-old Miguel de la Madrid was told that he had won the Mexican presidency, he reportedly quipped to a friend, "Fraud, fraud!" If he did utter those words, one could scarcely have blamed him. He faced the sobering prospect of inheriting the leadership of a country beset with economic problems so serious that they threatened to disrupt the social order. The ensuing months would set the country on a new path.

Educated at the National University of Mexico and subsequently at Harvard University, Miguel de la Madrid's rise to his country's highest office was nothing short of meteoric. Despite his relative youth, his formal education and previous experience in public administration prepared him better for the tasks that lay ahead than most of his twentieth-century predecessors. He had campaigned on a firm pledge of moral renovation, a promise to eliminate the corruption so endemic in the Mexican public sector. During his first year in office, revelations of corruption during the administration of López Portillo were carried in the front pages of the press almost on a daily basis. Although President de la Madrid did not prosecute his predecessor, he did strike out against other high-ranking government officials. In one spectacular case, Jorge Díaz Serrano, the former director of Petróleos Mexicanos (PEMEX), was indicted for embezzlement of $43 million. Díaz Serrano was convicted and sentenced to a ten-year jail term.

Even more outrageous were the alleged crimes of Arturo Durazo, Mexico City's chief of police and a friend of López Portillo since childhood. "El Negro Durazo" was charged with fifty murders, trafficking in drugs, and extortion of superlative proportions. His luxurious residence in the coastal resort of Zihuatanejo was nicknamed "The Parthenon," to which it bore some resemblance. His palatial home near Mexico City came complete with its own discotheque, modeled after New York City's famous Studio 54. Weekend guests, flown to the $2.5 million estate in police helicopters, marveled at Durazo's string of race horses, nineteen collector's automobiles, casino, gymnasium, and cellar of vintage wines. Not even the most shrewd businessmen, they opined, could have accumulated this kind of fortune on a government salary of $65 per week. But Durazo escaped prosecution by fleeing the country prior to the order for his arrest; after legal delays, he was finally extradited in 1986 and subsequently convicted. The victories in the two cases were largely symbolic as Mexicans knew that the battle against governmental malfeasance had scarcely been won. The country's comptroller general synopsized the issue perfectly when he stated that Mexican corruption was like garbage: it had to be removed daily.

An equally persistent dilemma was the country's deepening economic crisis. The peso began to slip against the dollar in 1984 and then began a veritable plunge on the free market. Many stood in disbelief as it plummeted from 150 to 200 and then to 380 to the dollar during the summer of 1985, but the bottom had not been reached. By autumn 1986, currency houses and money brokers along the United States-Mexico border were exchanging the peso at an incredible 800 to 1. The year 1987 was even more catastrophic for the peso. When the year opened it took 950 pesos to purchase a dollar, but by December the exchange rate was an incredible 2,300 to 1. The relationship between the two countries' currencies was so out of kilter in the summer of 1987 that a US tourist could ride the Mexico City metro over two thousand times for one dollar or make ten thousand calls on a pay phone for the same amount.

Mexico's foreign debt under Miguel de la Madrid grew in geometric proportion. Although the president succeeded in arranging a rescheduling of payments on the debt, the pressure on him was tremendous. Political parties, campesino groups, and labor unions of the left, following the lead of Cuba's Fidel Castro, urged him to repudiate the debt or at a minimum to declare a unilateral moratorium on repayment. De la Madrid agreed that the interest rates being paid on Mexico's debt were excessive, but realized the necessity of rekindling some

Elected in July 1982, Miguel de la Madrid succeeded López Portillo as president. He recognized that he would face difficult times but could not have predicted that the country was on the verge of economic collapse.

degree of confidence in the world's banking community and financial markets. He opted for economic austerity, not repudiation.

Responding to pressures from the International Monetary Fund, de la Madrid not only curtailed many new projects but also announced sweeping cuts in social spending, reductions in federal subsidies for foodstuffs and rents, the sale of inefficient and unprofitable state-owned enterprises, and a freeze on federal employment. Using the considerable influence of the presidential office, he did his best to limit the size of wage increases in the labor force and he eliminated thousands of federal jobs. The economic reforms began a process that would subsequently burgeon under the rubric of neoliberalism, the economic and political philosophy stressing trade liberalization, privatization of state-owned enterprises, reductions in social service spending, and economic deregulation. Under de la Madrid, Mexico joined the General Agreement on Tariffs and Trade and sold off some seven hundred companies, owned or partially owned by the government.

As the country struggled economically, suddenly tragedy struck during the morning rush hour on September 19, 1985, as Mexico City paid the price of sitting at the juncture of three of the earth's tectonic plates. An earthquake registering in excess of 8 on the Richter Scale devastated the capital, leaving as many as ten thousand dead, many more injured, and damage estimated at $4 billion. Several hundred buildings collapsed and thousands were damaged, leaving multitudes of people homeless, without food or water. When the de la Madrid administration responded at a snail's pace, Mexican citizens organized grassroots organizations to dig themselves out of the disaster. International relief arrived, after initial hesitancy on the part of the government to receive it. Nonetheless, many analysts believe that the earthquake served as a catalyst for the emergence of an embryonic civil society in Mexico. A plethora of groups began to advocate for democratic reforms to the bankrupt

In late 1987 when it took eleven thousand five hundred twenty-centavo pieces to buy one US dollar, Mexicans simply refused to carry the hefty coin. Enterprising owners of hardware stores in Sonora devised an imaginative solution. Not concerned about defacing national currency, they drilled holes in the middle of the coins and found brisk business in the good-quality washers.

Damage in Mexico City was extensive, and the clean-up task monumental, after the earthquake of September 19, 1985.

political system, women's and indigenous rights, affordable housing, and environmental protections. Although most of these organizations and alliances did not sustain themselves vigorously over time, civil society continued to organize at subsequent moments of crisis.

The last years of the de la Madrid administration saw Mexico slip deeper and deeper into the economic morass. In addition to the collapse of the peso, inflation soared to unprecedented heights. Official inflation rates, released by Mexico's Central Bank, reported 63.7 percent in 1985, 105.7 percent in 1986, and 159 percent in 1987. The person on the street swore that the actual figures were even higher. Increases in the cost of gasoline, corn, wheat, and electricity led the assault on the consumer price index, but no product or service emerged unscathed. The only thing that matched the rapid rise in prices was the rapid growth of the foreign debt. When de la Madrid left office in December 1988, the Mexican government owed foreigners a whopping $105 billion in outstanding debts.

UNITED STATES-MEXICO RELATIONS

Two major problems defying easy solution dominated United States-Mexico relations in the 1970s and 1980s. Both of them concerned movement across the common border, and both of them had national significance that transcended the international line that divides the two countries.

Since the 1950s, the United States-Mexico border region has witnessed one of the most profound demographic shifts in world history not conditioned by either war or epidemic disease. The result of a high birthrate and massive northern migration in Mexico and the equally telling Sunbelt phenomenon in the United States, the population soared on both sides of the border. In 1940, only about 16 million persons occupied the four US and six Mexican states that share the international line. At the beginning of 1990, the estimated population of the same ten states had risen to over 60 million. The dramatic swell has not only dominated day-to-day human relations of the region but also drives international relations as well. The border between the countries is permeable, and not only to people. Disease, polluted water, contaminated air, and drugs, to cite but a few examples, refuse to respect the artificial line drawn by nineteenth-century politicians to ratify the work of nineteenth-century generals.

Of the major problems growing out of a common international boundary, the most protracted centers on the undocumented worker. Beginning in the 1970s unemployment, underemployment, persistent poverty, and the undeniable lure of the United States prompted hundreds of thousands of Mexican workers to cross the border illegally into the United States each year in pursuit of gainful employment. The number of undocumented workers in the United States continued to grow throughout the 1980s.

The undocumented worker phenomenon became an emotionally charged topic that precipitated much national and international debate. Everyone agreed that the United States had the right to enforce its immigration laws and to regulate entries into the country. But there was no consensus on precisely what should be done and how. US anti-immigrant groups argued that Mexicans were a drain on US social services and that they took jobs away from Americans by working for such low wages. A broad range of labor organizations in the

United States began calling for tighter controls, while an equally broad spectrum of employers, in both rural and urban areas, favored the maintenance of the status quo.

A solution of sorts was reached in 1986 when the US Congress passed the Immigration Reform and Control Act (the Simpson-Rodino Act). The main features of the legislation provided for a tighter enforcement of immigration policy, sanctions against those who knowingly employed undocumented workers, and an amnesty for those workers who could establish continued residence in the United States since 1982. But Simpson-Rodino did not solve the undocumented worker problem because it addressed only those factors that pulled the Mexican workers toward the United States, ignoring those that pushed them out of Mexico. The undocumented continued to come, as there was no shortage of US employers willing to offer work despite threatened sanctions. The fundamental problems remained. In 1989, Jorge Bustamante, Mexico's leading border specialist, reported that earnings sent back to Mexico by undocumented workers totaled $1.25 billion annually, making this source of income the country's third largest source of foreign exchange.

The second problem that plagued the generally good relations between Washington, DC and Mexico City, and that contributed to a politically charged atmosphere, was the unremitting flow of drugs across the United States-Mexico border. The smuggling of contraband between the two countries certainly was nothing new. Arms and ammunition, automobiles, trucks, agricultural equipment, household items, and scores of other products had long evaded the eyes, regulations, and taxing authority of the customs agents. What made the problem so volatile in the late 1980s was the especially insidious nature of the illegal cargo. The international drug traffic, both sides agreed, not only left its legacy of abuse and dependence but also fostered an entire host of parasitic crimes, especially in the border region. Authorities from the two countries, however, agreed on little else. The public was soon treated to the most bizarre misapplication of the theories of the Scottish economist Adam Smith: US officials found the problem to be simply one of supply, while their Mexican counterparts more accurately retorted that it was simply one of demand.

Following the murder of US Drug Enforcement Administrative agent Enrique Camarena near Guadalajara, in 1986 and 1987 the US Congress held formal hearings on terrorism and drugs. These hearings prompted the most intemperate statements on Mexico's alleged lack of cooperation on the drug issue despite indications to the contrary from the US ambassador in Mexico City. By 1988, Mexico-bashing had become a favorite pastime of those who could think of no other reasons for the US failure to win its much publicized war on drugs. In that year, the US Senate failed to certify Mexico for economic assistance because it was not doing enough to intercept the flow of drugs before they crossed the border.

As Mexico was about to enter the last decade of the twentieth century, a steadily increasing number of its citizens had become disillusioned with pervasive corruption and with politics as usual. Nongovernmental organizations that coalesced after the disastrous earthquake had introduced new actors into the political stage calling for electoral and social reforms. At the same time, the shift to neoliberalism in the age of globalization had not reduced poverty and social inequities. Some PRI activists began to call for major change even if they were unsure where the path might lead. Together with fellow Mexicans of the opposition parties they would have an answer sooner than anticipated.

THE ELECTIONS OF 1988 AND OVERTURES TO DEMOCRATIZATION

The 1980s were a decade of democratization or redemocratization throughout much of Latin America. In most of the region, this phenomenon meant replacing military dictatorships with civilian governments chosen in an open or a relatively open electoral process. In Mexico, democratization was something different. The army had ceased to call the political shots in Mexican politics decades earlier. Democratization in Mexico meant opening up the political system, recognizing that it had systemic weaknesses, and making it more responsive to the Mexican citizenry. The process was far from innocuous, for it meant that the influential political bosses in the country would have to share their power with others.

Not new to the 1980s, because of Mexico's unique twentieth-century experience, one political party had gained almost absolute electoral dominance. This official party, under different names, had won every election for president and every election for the thirty-one governorships since 1929. If an occasional member of an opposition party could be found occupying a seat in the national congress, it was most likely because Mexico's electoral law permitted the seating of a limited number of defeated candidates based on the percentage of votes cast for their respective parties in the last election. For most, presidential elections meant little more than a meaningless ritual.

As the official party became synonymous with the government, and thus commanded huge resources as well as incredible patronage, elections became a farce. In Mexico's one-party democracy, citizens, for all practical purposes, were denied the element of choice. The most influential television news program in the country, Televisa's *Twenty-Four Hours*, hosted for almost three decades by newscaster Jacobo Zabludovsky, largely supported the Partido Revolucionario Institucional (PRI) and the government. Similarly, much of the print press

Jacobo Zabludovsky was Mexico's lead newscaster for almost 30 years. He died in Mexico City in 2015.

exhibited little independence. *Excélsior*, a newspaper that had been founded with the revolution in 1917, gradually lost public confidence for its timid approach to government criticism, even when official scandals begged for full disclosure. Government control of the media was most often achieved informally through bribes and threats, but some independent newspapers emerged, including *La Jornada*, founded in 1984 by Carlos Payán.

In the 1980s, several opposition parties (conservative in the north and leftist in the south), capitalizing on increasing dissatisfaction with the performance of the official party, began to score some modest victories in state and local elections. With some regularity, the official party overturned the electoral results and had its own candidates installed in office. In this process, the PRI increasingly lost legitimacy. Even more significant were the proliferating civil society groups—nongovernmental organizations that had turned away from the Mexican state, especially after the 1985 earthquake, to deal with a host of political and social issues. The growing challenges to the system were clearly evident in the presidential elections of 1988.

The Partido de Acción Nacional (PAN) and its presidential candidate, Manuel Clouthier, a millionaire industrialist, articulated the conservative position. Clouthier ran on a platform calling for a closer relationship with the United States, a more limited role for the government in the economy, a more vigorous private sector and, of course, an end to electoral fraud by the PRI. The leftist opposition came from Cuauhtémoc Cárdenas, the son of former president Lázaro Cárdenas and a previous PRI governor of Michoacán. Cárdenas, who had harbored presidential ambitions for some time, broke with the official party over the issue of how presidential candidates were chosen as well as the question of the extent to which Mexico would have to adhere to neoliberal economics. He ran on the ticket of the Corriente Democrática, a coalition that temporarily united a broad spectrum of leftist parties. Cárdenas agreed with Clouthier on one platform plank—the need to bring an end to the PRI's electoral fraud—but differed sharply on other issues. He called for greater independence from the United States and a move away from the PRI's neoliberal policies.

The PRI candidate, Carlos Salinas de Gortari, epitomized the successful technocrat. He had earned a doctorate in economics from Harvard University and in the de la Madrid cabinet was secretary of planning and budget. For the first time in recent memory, the press gave extensive coverage to the opposition. Election day surprised even the most astute political observers. The election was close enough for all three candidates to claim victory. Salinas ultimately was declared the winner in an election most probably stolen from Cárdenas, who appeared to be leading the vote count. A sudden computer crash stopped the vote tallying for several days. When the result was announced, Salinas was declared the winner by a narrow margin. The political stock of PRI had fallen so precipitously that Salinas barely received a majority of the votes cast. The notion of a credible opposition was no longer a whimsical delusion.

The democratizing process continued during the gubernatorial elections of 1989. In an electoral result that shocked everyone, PAN candidate Ernesto Ruffo won the governorship of Baja California Norte. In the first test of his pledge to fair elections, President Salinas accepted the outcome. More change followed. In 1991 blatant electoral fraud cost PRI candidates two additional governorships in the states of Guanajuato and San Luis Potosí.

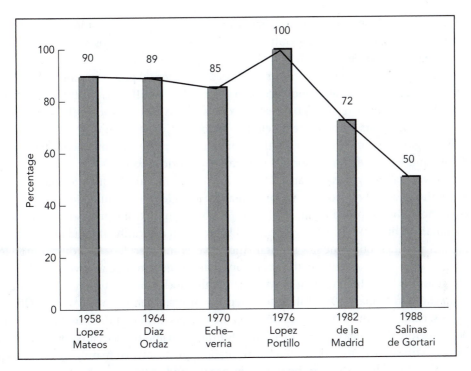

Mexican Presidential Elections, 1958–88: PRI Candidates' Percentage of Votes

The Chihuahua governorship fell to PAN candidate Francisco Barrios, the former mayor of Ciudad Juárez in 1992. The president even endorsed a series of political reforms long called for by his political opposition. These included regulation of party finances, limits on campaign expenditures, and greater access to news outlets by opposition parties. Mexican political culture had begun a metamorphosis that would culminate in startling fashion in 2000.

SALINAS AND NEOLIBERALISM

The political education of Carlos Salinas de Gortari, like that of many recently elected heads of state throughout the world, was grounded in a new vocabulary of neoliberal reform. The Berlin Wall collapsed, as did the communist experiment in Eastern Europe. The Soviet Union and Yugoslavia fell apart just as East and West Germany fell together. Fear of nuclear apocalypse no longer dominated political discourse. And most surprising of all, formerly socialist countries began to embrace what had previously been considered the capitalist demon. With Mexico's economic position so deteriorated, President Salinas decided that it was time for Mexico, too, to begin marching to a new cadence.

Neoliberal policies, already underway, became the bedrock of the Salinas administration. Fundamentally an antisocialist doctrine, neo-liberalism championed the free market by placing stringent limits on government regulation of economic forces. It enshrined competition, favored free trade as the natural response to the new global economy, and argued that corporations should be given greater independence. Government subsidies for food and transportation should be severely restricted, and trade unions should be more modest in their demands. In short, neoliberalism represented an unambiguous rejection of the solutions Mexico had tested since 1917.

Salinas began to exorcise the ghosts of Mexico's anticlerical past. The process culminated in the president's memorable audience with Pope John Paul II and, in 1992, with the restoration of diplomatic relations between Mexico and the Vatican. Those relations had been severed for 130 years. Then came amendments to the Constitution of 1917 that legalized public religious celebrations, allowed the church to own property again, permitted religious schools, and welcomed foreign priests to preach on Mexican soil.

Nor were labor rights sacrosanct. During his second month in office, Salinas struck out against the powerful oil workers' union and arrested its leader, Joaquín Hernández Galicia, better known by his pseudonym, La Quina. To labor's outrage, the president answered that La Quina and his two leading associates had been arrested because of fraud and corruption in union activities, but some saw the dramatic move as an object lesson to other union leaders who might demand more on the wage front than the government was willing to concede. A few months later the president moved against the dock workers' union in Veracruz. Not yet finished, in January 1992 Salinas ordered the arrest of labor leader Agapito González Cavazos, charging him with tax evasion. It seemed no accident that this arrest occurred only one day before González Cavazos's Union of Journeymen and Industrial Workers was scheduled to go on strike against thirty-three maquiladora plants owned mainly by US interests.

Early in the administration the president began mild criticism of the ejido system, the sacred cow of agrarian reformers since the early 1920s. In one speech he had the temerity to call the ejidos unproductive and ultimately concluded that they had been a failure. They no longer represented the hope of a prosperous future for the nation's campesinos; rather, they were the cause of rural poverty. They explained why Mexico in the 1990s was not self-sufficient in food production and why rural income was only one-third that of the remainder of the country.

Land redistribution, for Salinas, was a bankrupt solution to a problem with roots in Mexico's ancient past. Its importance as a mechanism to bring social justice to impoverished campesinos had long been overshadowed by lack of agricultural productivity. New laws, unthinkable just a decade earlier, followed quickly. Challenging the sacrosanctity of Article 27 of the Constitution of 1917, they provided for the private ownership of lands formerly owned by the ejidos. Not only did campesinos get title to their land, but for the first time in the twentieth century, they could trade it, mortgage it, rent it, or even sell it.

All the changes were predicated on a neoliberal reassessment of the proper role of government in addressing society's ills. As Mexico looked toward the twenty-first century, it was clear that the state would exercise a more constricted role than it had in the past. Salinas attributed much of Mexico's economic dilemma to an exaggerated statism, which had seen the government move into the private sector and acquire ownership and control of over one thousand private companies. These the president began to privatize. By early 1992, over 85 percent of them had been sold back to the private sector. Among the economic giants quickly purchased by consortia of private investors were BANAMEX (Banco Nacional de México) and BANCOMER (Banco de Comercio), Mexico's two largest banks, and TELMEX

(Teléfonos de México), the country's only telephone company. The latter was bought by Carlos Slim Helú, the son of Lebanese immigrants, initiating his climb to become Mexico's and eventually one of the world's wealthiest men. Other investors grabbed up government steel companies, hotels, sugar refineries, steel mills, and mines. Only a few government concerns such as Petróleos Mexicanos (PEMEX), considered crucial to national security, were excluded from divestiture proceedings.

The shift to a free market economy enabled Salinas to lower Mexican inflation to a tolerable 10 percent by 1993 and to reduce Mexico's foreign debt by some $25 billion. But it also served another purpose as an integral part of a calculated policy to foster a closer relationship with the United States. From the outset Salinas believed that Mexico's economic malaise could best be addressed by the successful conclusion of the North American Free Trade Agreement (NAFTA) with the United States and Canada. Salinas and his supporters argued that the agreement would herald more capital investment and as a result more well-paying jobs for Mexicans and a more powerful voice for Mexico in international diplomacy. Ultimately this position carried the day. Aware that Europe would formally enter into its own common market on January 1, 1993, President Salinas, President George H. W. Bush, and Canadian Prime Minister Brian Mulroney believed that only a new, large, combined North American market would be competitive. The three signed NAFTA just as Salinas reached the midpoint of his presidential term and shortly before President Bush turned over the White House to Bill Clinton. By the fall of 1993, free trade had become the centerpiece of the Salinas administration. Nevertheless, opposition from labor unions and environmentalists in the United States made passage by the US Congress a challenge, but NAFTA did pass in November 1993.

To soften the impact of neoliberal restructuring, the Salinas administration implemented anti-poverty programs. PRONASOL (National Solidarity Program, 1989) awarded funding to communities for local projects, for example, to supply clean drinking water or pave roads, as long as they paid some of the cost or contributed labor. Corruption and manipulation of these funds for political ends meant that only about half of them actually reached their intended destinations. PROCAMPO (1993) offered direct subsidies to farmers in an effort to counter the same kinds of payments long enjoyed by US farmers. These programs did not succeed in stemming widespread social discontent, as the country was shocked to learn on the day NAFTA was due to go into effect.

On January 1, 1994, a serious antigovernment rebellion broke out in the southern state of Chiapas. The rebels demanded agrarian and educational reforms as well as respect for indigenous rights. Led by a charismatic commander who called himself simply Sub-Comandante Marcos, a Maya Indian army, the Ejército Zapatista de Liberación Nacional (EZLN), attacked army outposts and captured several towns including San Cristóbal de las Casas, the second largest city in the state. President Salinas sent army troops, rocket-equipped aircraft, and helicopter gun ships to engage the rebels; but ultimately negotiations conducted under the auspices of Bishop Samuel Ruiz—not military might—restored a tenuous peace. The rebellion focused national attention on an ethnic group and a region of the country unfulfilled by the promises of the revolution. Subsequently in 1997, paramilitary troops massacred forty-five people in the town of Acteal, mostly women and children, demonstrating that local landowners had no problem ignoring the peace accords and would continue to repress those demanding social justice and indigenous autonomy.

A still greater shock to the Mexican body politic and to the country's self-image occurred in March 1994. The attractive and energetic PRI candidate for president, Luis Donaldo Colosio, campaigning on a platform to make his party more responsive to the people, was assassinated during a campaign appearance in the border city of Tijuana. Conspiracy theories, reminiscent of those in the United States following on the heels of the assassination of John F. Kennedy thirty years earlier, surfaced everywhere: in the press, in television commentaries, in the classrooms, and in coffee shop conversation. While the evidence suggested that a single, perhaps deranged, gunman, Mario Aburto Martínez, fired the shots, many

Sub-Comandante Marcos, leader of the Chiapas rebellion in early 1994, is wearing the mask that was the emblem of the rebels. Symbolically the masks represented the faceless indigenous populations of Mexico, but in a more practical sense they afforded the protections of anonymity.

believed that his actions were part of a wider, politically motivated plot hatched either by the PRI old guard or "dinosaurs" who opposed reforms within the party, or by Salinas himself. A second political assassination a few months later was equally disquieting but initially commanded less attention. José Francisco Ruiz Massieu, the second highest ranking official in the PRI and majority leader-elect in the senate, was shot to death outside a Mexico City hotel. The murdered politician's brother, Mario Ruiz Massieu, served as Mexico's deputy attorney general, and President Salinas placed him in charge of the investigation. Ultimately it would be this killing, not the Colosio assassination, that would carry public scandal to new heights in the months and years ahead.

TRYING TO KEEP ON COURSE

To replace Colosio, the PRI chose Ernesto Zedillo, a career public official and like his predecessor an economist educated in the Ivy League. His campaign speeches signaled that he too would promote neo-liberal policies. A rising tide, he suggested, lifts all boats, a concept not comforting to those without a boat. The election was close. The conservative PAN candidate ran a better race than expected but the left, now organized in the Partido Revolucionario Democrático (PRD), earned only 17 percent of the vote; Cuauhtémoc Cárdenas was unable to capitalize on his 1988 popularity. Ernesto Zedillo came out ahead but for the second time in a row the winner of the presidential sweepstakes barely garnered 50 percent of the popular vote. Rather than evidence of general public acclaim, the narrow victory suggested that voters were looking for stability in the uncertain climate of economic difficulties, political assassinations, and the insecurity provoked by the Chiapas uprising.

Zedillo's first months in office coincided with a series of new pressures on the Mexican economy that saw the peso once again begin to slide rapidly against the dollar. It lost 46 percent of its value between December 1994 and January 1995 and continued to fall for the next two months. At the same time the Mexican *bolsa* (the stock market) collapsed in brisk trading. Businesses closed down and banks began foreclosing on urban and rural properties. Even the state-owned bus company, called Route 101, went into bankruptcy. Inflation, under control for several years, began to rise once again. Interest rates soared, reaching a usurious 100 percent in some areas, and hundreds of thousands lost jobs. Once again, Mexico implemented austerity measures.

Seeking to cast blame elsewhere, President Zedillo uncovered another mariner's metaphor. He claimed that his administration had inherited a leaking boat from his predecessor. A truculent Salinas fired back with his own broadside, charging the new administration with gross mismanagement of the economy. The broad panorama of economic pressures combined with the continuing insurgency in Chiapas had eroded investor confidence. A tainted PRI gubernatorial "victory" in the state of Chiapas continued to subvert the appeal of Mexico's brand of democracy and reminded its citizens of the still desperate need for political reform.

Realizing the international implications of another Mexican economic collapse, US President Bill Clinton urged a $40 billion loan to rescue the Mexican peso. Political pressures in the United States prompted a reduction to $20 billion, but once extended that sizable loan guarantee, coupled with a series of difficult and unpopular economic reforms, slowed further devaluations of the peso and helped Zedillo place his country on a stabilization path. The vast majority of those who lost their jobs during the economic crisis found new ones as inflation was reduced and the peso stabilized. In 1997 Mexico recorded a 7 percent rate of economic growth. Zedillo opened Mexico's natural gas sector to private investment and created a private pension system. His program to alleviate poverty by providing cash payments to families in exchange for regular school attendance, health clinic visits, and nutritional support achieved some successful and was emulated in subsequent administrations under the title *Oportunidades*. The president also scored one additional victory, even though it proved short-lived. By the late fall of 1995, utilizing a skillful combination of diplomacy and military force, he persuaded the rebels in Chiapas to lay down their arms and work for political solutions to their genuine grievances. Unfortunately, negotiations subsequently stalled.

In another political arena, the government accepted PAN victories in several gubernatorial races. The conservative opposition captured the governorship of Guanajuato and a second consecutive governorship in Baja California Norte. Faced with the reality that the PRI monopoly was ending, the president worked hard to convince his fellow Mexicans of his commitment to true democracy and the rule of law. Not initially successful in this daunting task, nor in tallying notable breakthroughs in Mexico's long war against the country's drug lords, he first tried reorganizing special police units designed to carry out the battle and then created a new federal police force to do the same. However, the vast sums of money available to the traffickers enabled them to infiltrate police organizations, bribe high officials, and carry out their nefarious activities almost with impunity.

In many ways Zedillo's biggest problem, the one that most eroded confidence in the system and rendered consensus impossible, was a public scandal that made even the most confirmed Mexican skeptic blush and turn away in disbelief.

THE TALE OF FOUR BROTHERS

The news of intrigue, corruption, big money, narcopolitics, and murder that began to surface in February 1995 resulted in the arrest of the former president's brother, Raúl Salinas de Gortari. Charged with masterminding and paying $300,000 for the murder of José Francisco Ruiz Massieu in September 1994, he was sent to the high-security Almoloya prison to await trial.

As the melodrama was pieced together, the Mexican public learned that Ruiz Massieu was the former brother-in-law of Carlos and Raúl Salinas de Gortari, having been married to their sister Adriana. Could it be that the president's brother ordered the assassination of their former brother-in-law? Carlos Salinas protested his brother's innocence, claimed that the arrest of his brother was unjustified, and even staged a short hunger strike to drive home his point. Few Mexicans found solace in the ex-president's protestations, especially when they learned that the first official he had placed in charge of the investigation, Mario Ruiz Massieu, the slain politician's brother, had not pursued the investigation vigorously and perhaps even directed a cover-up. In March 1995 Ruiz Massieu fled to the United States, and although he successfully resisted extradition to Mexico, investigations revealed he had accumulated millions of dollars during his term of office, with the proceeds coming largely from Mexican drug lords. Ruiz Massieu committed suicide in his New Jersey apartment in September 1999.

The detailed investigation into the activities of Raúl Salinas alleged even greater misconduct. In addition to the charge of murder, investigators uncovered evidence of his direct links to both the Gulf coast and Pacific coast drug cartels. He also allegedly accepted huge payments for arranging private access to the president. His corrupt activities earned him the sobriquet Señor Diez Porciento (Mr. Ten Percent), the usual "commission" he charged for facilitating the receipt of lucrative government contracts. President Salinas's massive privatization of profitable government-owned companies provided his brother with the opportunity to amass a fortune amounting to hundreds of millions of dollars deposited in 48 different bank accounts.

The embarrassed former president felt the heat from the beginning and withdrew his name from consideration for the directorship of the World Trade Organization, a prestigious international position that most assuredly would have been his. In March 1995, he went into self-imposed exile, living for short periods in the United States and Canada before taking up a longer residence in Ireland. Political cartoonists in both Mexico and the United States had a field day, and dolls depicting the former president, bald, big-eared, and in striped prison clothes, were sold by outdoor vendors on almost every street corner of the capital. T-shirts showing him waving good-bye to Mexico with his middle finger extended could not be manufactured quickly enough to meet the eager demand. From the Zócalo to the Zona Rosa street performers lampooned the former president, his presidency, the press that had supported him, and the sycophants who had surrounded him.

Eventually, in the "trial of the century" of January 1999, Raúl Salinas was found guilty as charged and given fifty years in prison. His conviction did not bring closure to the political speculation about the tawdry episode, especially when an appeals court later reduced the

After capturing the mayoralty of Mexico City, Cuauhtémoc Cárdenas is mobbed by his supporters on election night. Those supporters who anticipated that the triumph presaged a future presidential victory would be disappointed.

sentence to 27.5 years on a technicality. Mexicans could not rid themselves of the perception that Carlos Salinas must have been implicated in some way.

Citizens had their first opportunity to register their collective displeasure in the summer of 1997. Congressional elections and six gubernatorial contests were scheduled for July 6. In addition, for the first time in history, Mexico City residents could vote for their mayor, heretofore an appointive office. Two open governorships, in the central state of Querétaro and the northern industrial state of Nuevo León, fell to opposition candidates, but that was merely the tip of the iceberg. Cuauhtémoc Cárdenas, twice defeated as a left of center presidential candidate running on the PRD ticket, won the mayoral election of Mexico City. Even more startling, the PRI lost its congressional majority for the first time in seven decades. If there was a new mandate, it came from neither the left nor the right. The vote was for change. While the liberal PRD scored strongly in the capital election, the conservative PAN won the two opposition governorships and a majority of the opposition congressional seats—an unequivocal rejection of the official party concept. Mexicans stood up to be counted and they said to the dominant party, "Enough!"

When political cartoonists in the United States grew weary of lampooning Whitewater scandals, the fund-raising imbroglios by both Democrats and Republicans, and alleged sexual improprieties in the Oval Office, they found tempting targets in Mexico.

RECOMMENDED FOR FURTHER STUDY

Anderson, Joan B., and James Gerber. *Fifty Years of Change on the U.S.-Mexico Border: Growth, Development, and Quality of Life*. Austin: University of Texas Press, 2007.

Babb, Sarah. *Managing Mexico: Economists from Nationalism to Neoliberalism*. Princeton, NJ: Princeton University Press, 2001.

Camp, Roderic Ai. *Crossing Swords: Politics and Religion in Mexico*. New York: Oxford University Press, 1997.

Castañeda, Jorge G. *The Mexican Shock: Its Meaning for the United States*. New York: New Press, 1995.

Collier, George A. *Basta: Land and the Zapatista Rebellion in Chiapas*. Oakland, CA: Institute for Food and Development Policy, 1994.

Cornelius, Wayne A., and David Myhre, eds. *The Transformation of Rural Mexico: Reforming the Ejido Sector*. San Diego, CA: Center for U.S.-Mexican Studies, 1998.

Delano, Alexandra. *Mexico and Its Diaspora in the United States: Policies of Emigration Since 1848*. New York: Cambridge University Press, 2011.

Foweraker, Joe, and Ann L. Craig, eds. *Popular Movements and Political Change in Mexico*. Boulder, CO: Lynne Rienner, 1990.

Fuentes, Carlos. *A New Time for Mexico*. New York: Farrar, Straus and Giroux, 1996.

Gallagher, Kevin P. *Free Trade and the Environment: Mexico, NAFTA, and Beyond*. Stanford, CA: Stanford University Press, 2004.

Ganster, Paul, and David E. Lorey. *The U.S.-Mexican Border into the Twenty-First Century*. 2nd ed. Lanham, MD: Rowman & Littlefield, 2008.

Harvey, Neil. *The Chiapas Rebellion: The Struggle for Land and Democracy*. Durham, NC: Duke University Press, 1998.

Henck, Nick. *Subcommander Marcos: The Man and the Mask*. Durham, NC: Duke University Press, 2007.

Higgins, Nicholas P. *Understanding the Chiapas Rebellion: Modernist Visions and the Invisible Indian*. Austin: University of Texas Press, 2004.

LaBotz, Dan. *Democracy in Mexico: Peasant Rebellion and Political Reform*. Boston, MA: South End Press, 1995.

Mattiace, Shannan L. *To See with Two Eyes: Peasant Activism and Indian Autonomy in Chiapas, Mexico*. Albuquerque: University of New Mexico Press, 2003.

Meyer, Lorenzo. "The Second Coming of Mexican Liberalism: A Comparative Perspective." In *Cycles of Conflict, Centuries of Change*, edited by Elisa Servín, et al., 271–303. Durham, NC: Duke University Press, 2007.

Middlebrook, Kevin, ed. *Dilemmas of Political Change in Mexico*. San Diego, CA: UCSD Center for Mexican Studies, 2004.

Moksnes, Heidi. *Maya Exodus: Indigenous Struggle for Citizenship in Chiapas*. Norman: University of Oklahoma Press, 2012.

Morris, Stephen D. *Political Reformism in Mexico: An Overview of Contemporary Mexican Politics*. Boulder, CO: Lynn Rienner, 1995.

Needler, Martin. *Mexican Politics: The Containment of Conflict*. Westport, CT: Praeger, 1995.

Purcell, Susan Kaufman, and Luis Rubio, eds. *Mexico under Zedillo*. Boulder, CO: Lynne Rienner, 1998.

Schultz, Donald E., and Edward J. Williams, eds. *Mexico Faces the 21st Century*. New York: Praeger, 1995.

Stephen, Lynn. *Zapata Lives! Histories and Cultural Politics in Southern Mexico*. Berkeley: University of California Press, 2002.

Williams, Heather. *Social Movements and Economic Transition: Markets and Distributive Conflict in Mexico*. New York: Cambridge University Press, 2001.

Womack, John. *Rebellion in Chiapas*. New York: New Press, 1999.

CHAPTER 38

THE CHALLENGES OF DEMOCRATIZATION

THE ELECTIONS OF 2000

As a result of the PRI debacle, Mexico's first presidential election in the new millennium defied Mexican political memory. President Zedillo kept his pledge to place Mexico on a true democratic course, and he ultimately paved the way for the defeat of his own party. Attention focused not on lackluster Francisco Labastida, the candidate of the PRI, or on Cuauhtémoc Cárdenas, the mayor of the Federal District and head of the PRD ticket, but on the flamboyant Vicente Fox, running as the candidate of the conservative PAN. Fox, a prosperous rancher, former chief executive of Coca-Cola de México, and popular governor of the state of Guanajuato, ran an outstanding campaign. Often appearing at political events wearing cowboy boots and an open shirt, the physically imposing six-foot-four Fox clearly sought to break out of the stuffy mold carefully fashioned by generations of official party candidates. His special chemistry with fellow Mexicans would ultimately pay huge political dividends. Fox also benefited from another source of support. Over the previous several years, the Catholic church had become increasingly active alongside civic groups arguing the need for democratic reforms, thus strengthening its position as a legitimate moral voice in the heated atmosphere of political corruption. Middle-class Mexicans who once would have shied away from the proclerical PAN were no longer so put off by its ties to the church.

Throughout much of the campaign political pollsters had Fox and Labastida in a dead heat, with Cuauhtémoc Cárdenas running a distant third. In a nationally televised April presidential debate Fox hit hard on seventy years of PRI incompetence, false promises, and corruption; polls showed he won the debate in a landslide. From that time forward a Fox presidential victory was no longer unthinkable.

In the months ahead Labastida's talk of a "new PRI" seemed more and more a contradiction of terms as he was incapable of divorcing himself from the unpopular policies, major scandals, and minor shenanigans of his predecessors. Mexicans went to the polls in record numbers on July 2, 2000, and handed the heretofore invincible PRI a stunning defeat. Those anticipating charges of fraud, electoral intimidation, denial of access to ballots, or unfair counting of the vote in an attempt to overturn the results would have to await the US presidential election between George W. Bush and Al Gore three months later. The Mexican presidential election of 2000 was relatively clean and, unlike in the United States, the country would not have to endure months of electoral uncertainty.

In his finest hour, President Ernesto Zedillo addressed the nation, acknowledging the Fox victory and pledging a smooth transition. For the first time in seventy-one years Mexico's president would not represent the PRI, and the revolutionary myth-making manipulated by the official party would come to an end. Most historians agree that social reform provisions of the Constitution of 1917 were implemented, intermittently and in varying intensity, until 1940. These advances beg the question of whether social progress would have occurred without the revolution. As progress waned, in order to garner support, government rhetoric invoked patriotic revolutionary nationalism in memory, myth, and invention as a hegemonic tool long after the 1930s to garner support. Most Mexicans viewed it as a sham long before Salinas jettisoned the façade in 1988. As the twenty-first century dawned, the reality that social priorities had languished in favor of economic development could not be denied. Furthermore, authoritarian political corruption and mismanagement had contributed to widening the gap between rich and poor and to denying social justice for all Mexicans. While jubilant mobs crowded the streets, the stilted distribution of wealth manifested itself in the millions of illiterate; low wages and high unemployment; inadequate housing; and insufficient medical care, especially in the rural areas. The industrial and vehicular smog of the Federal District choked the Mexican capital and threatened health problems of major consequences. One Mexico City suburb, Ciudad Nezahualcóyotl, with a population of more than 3 million, rivaled the largest slums in the world. Children scavenged in huge garbage dumps, where the stench of despair hung in the air. In the rural areas, a million campesinos still worked plots too small to sustain themselves and their families. Well over half of all Mexicans had no access to running water in their places of

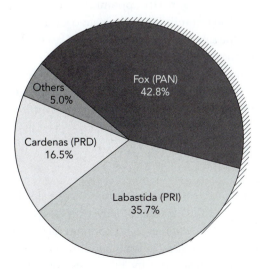

The 2000 Mexican Presidential Election

residence. Real income declined in the 1980s and 1990s as inflation consistently outran rises in the minimum wage. Poverty and malnutrition persisted despite increases in caloric intake, a decline in infant mortality, and a rise in life expectancy. It was small consolation that for some, opportunities for education and upward mobility had expanded, and more people had access to higher education.

Inauguration day, December 1, 2000, found Mexicans basking in democratic legitimacy for the first time in seven decades; and many were optimistic that the transition to democracy would be accompanied by economic prosperity and social justice, just as Fox had pledged. On that memorable day the president-elect conducted a bit of unofficial business prior to receiving the oath of office and donning the red, white, and green presidential sash. He visited the Basilica of Guadalupe and joined thousands of other worshippers in paying homage to Mexico's famous patroness. This symbolic act may have annoyed some secularists, but it was more emblematic of a state and a church having learned to live with each other despite their disagreements on social issues.

Vicente Fox's PAN had moved from the conservative, Catholic party of its origins. Fox's early actions showed how the PAN had shifted toward the center of the political spectrum. Rumors that the new president might further limit already strict abortion rights or privatize PEMEX proved to be unfounded. He refused to endorse the archbishop of Mexico's anti-abortion homily, which argued that even in the case of rape women must accept the mysterious designs of God. Although personally opposed to abortion, the president countered that he would not introduce any new legislation to change Mexico's abortion laws. Similarly, when President George W. Bush suggested that US capitalists might want to invest in Mexican petroleum, Fox rejected the idea politely. The nationalization of the oil industry by Lázaro Cárdenas in 1938 was memorialized every year and still considered an epic event in Mexico's twentieth-century experience. PEMEX, which accounted for about a third of all government revenues, was not yet for sale to foreign investors.

In another move to show that his administration would try to play the political middle, Fox appointed cabinet members from the left and the right. His appointment of Carlos Abascal—a staunch conservative, pro-industrialist, and Catholic heir to a Cristero family—as secretary of labor was a concession to the right. At the same time he named Jorge Castañeda, a leftist intellectual and long-time critic of US relations with Mexico, as secretary of foreign relations. His appointment to Mexico's top diplomatic post made it possible for Fox, at least in the short run, to counter arguments that he might be too pro-American in his foreign policy, even as he sought to enhance the new market-driven economy and to attract further US investment.

THE FOX SEXENIO: A LOST OPPORTUNITY?

The optimism that accompanied Mexico's transition to democracy in electoral terms slowly eroded over the course of the Fox presidency because of his failure to deliver on campaign promises, especially those related to economic reform. Some of these shortcomings can be attributed to his own management style as well as ineptness at statecraft and building coalitions in a situation where his own party did not have a legislative majority. But it was not all his fault. The opposition to Fox was split between two ideologically divergent parties. Policy gridlock became evident early as the PRI and PRD sabotaged a number of his initiatives to reform the tax structure and the energy sector. Political ineffectiveness became even more pronounced when the PRI was the major winner in the congressional elections of 2003. Furthermore, the PRI still controlled a majority of state and local governments as well as union and campesino corporations, not to mention its ties with de facto powers in the media and business. Not only did the tensions between the executive and the legislative branches fester and occasionally flare over the next few years, but the PAN and the administration itself were wracked with internal friction. Because of his attempts to build coalitions, Fox frequently found himself at odds with his own party. And early investigations into irregularities in his campaign contributions from a group called Los Amigos de Fox, accused of illegally funneling money from US donors, made Mexicans question the president's commitment to fighting corruption.

Abruptly in January 2003, Jorge Castañeda resigned from the cabinet after having been frustrated in his attempts to improve relations with the United States and to reach an accord that would ensure fairer treatment for Mexican migrant laborers. Ironically, given his earlier support for the Cuban Revolution, he had also unsettled Mexico's close relationship with US nemesis Fidel Castro. Castañeda was accused of pressuring Castro to make an early exit from a March 2002 United Nations summit on financing for development held in Monterrey, Mexico, in order to please the US delegation and President Bush. He also publicly criticized Cuba for human rights violations and arranged for President Fox to meet with Cuban dissidents on a visit to the island nation. Fox replaced Castañeda with his secretary of economy, Luis Ernesto Derbez; and other cabinet shuffles and dismissals of high-level officials followed in 2003. In May 2004, Fox scolded Energy Secretary Felipe Calderón for appearing to launch a rival presidential bid, prompting Calderón to leave the government.

The controversies stirring the most gossip about the Fox administration had to do with "Martita." Fox married his former spokesperson, Marta Sahagún, exactly a year after taking office. Like Hillary Clinton in the United States, the outspoken "Martita" stepped beyond the bounds of activities considered appropriate for a presidential wife. In a move perhaps more reminiscent of Argentina's Eva Perón than Hillary Clinton, she created her own philanthropic foundation, Vamos México, and collected millions from the country's wealthy for projects destined to help the less privileged. Rumors about her political aspirations to succeed her husband as president circulated wildly in the press and made her the object of much derision in political cartoons and rock songs. In 2004, speculation came to an end after Vamos México was accused of siphoning off funds from the National Lottery. Fox's own chief of staff resigned, alleging that the first lady's political ambitions were out of control and that Fox was acting like the autocrats who preceded him. Even though the president finally intervened and announced they would both go home at the end of his term, Marta Sahagún continued to be a lightning rod. After being criticized for having spent too much public money on her wardrobe, the well-heeled first lady donated her favorite outfits to charity.

Fox promised to boost Mexico's annual economic growth to 7 percent. Gridlock and mini-scandals helped subvert this effort, as did a slowdown in the world economy at the beginning of his presidency. Annual economic growth was closer to 1 percent than 7, and certainly less than the 5 percent registered annually between 1996 and 2000. The president's proposal to implement a value-added tax on food, medicine, schoolbooks, and educational fees cost him the support of middle and lower sectors and certainly provided fodder for the opposition parties, who charged him with ignoring the less privileged. And, in fact, the inequities in income distribution grew as the lower and middle sectors slipped while the top monopolized modest economic growth.

Fox skirted the political problem of privatizing PEMEX, even though it was the most highly taxed and indebted oil company in the world and unable to meet all of Mexico's natural gas and petrochemical needs; but he did push through reforms that allowed for some private investment in electricity. Although export growth expanded modestly, in 2003 China replaced Mexico as the third largest exporter of goods to the United States. The president's pledges to boost employment also encountered difficulties as jobs in the maquiladoras (also known as *maquilas*) and the Mexican manufacturing industry declined or remained stable.

In the area of social services, Mexico was constrained by lending agencies but, even with slightly higher social spending per capita under the Oportunidades program, the Fox administration made few advances in human capital investment that might ultimately boost productivity—in the areas of education, health, and job training. For many Mexicans, Fox's campaign promises to battle the stubborn causes of persistent poverty rang hollow as the income gap widened. Attempts to orient the school curriculum toward science and technology ran into trouble when it looked as if the curricular innovations would displace an emphasis on Mexico's pre-Columbian past, the "pride" of the nation.

The contemporary predicaments of indigenous people were certainly nothing to boast about. Mexico's native populations, especially those in the south, counted among the most impoverished groups in the nation. High infant mortality rates, low life expectancy, malnutrition, and elevated rates of illiteracy pervaded Indian communities. But complicating their escape from privation was the fact that they also had been victims of systematic racial discrimination for five centuries. Government programs designed to assist had to be ever mindful of cultural traditions and value systems now more than ever out of step with neoliberal plans for economic growth. In an effort to address the Indian problem throughout the country, Fox named Xochitl Gálvez, an Otomí Indian and highly successful technical consultant, to head the Office of Indian Affairs. The resources at her command were small, however, and the subsequent dismantling of the National Indigenous Institute signaled that the administration would put its efforts into integrating Indian cultures rather than bolstering communal traditions and solidarity. This direction was also evident in the unfolding of the Chiapas situation.

The Zapatistas had continued to attract national and international support for their aims via the Internet, which transmitted the goals of the revolutionary indigenous committees that formed in local communities. Articulated in their own voices and by spokesperson Marcos's poetic communiqués, these included rights to land, work, housing, food, health care, and education, as well as local autonomy, democracy, justice, and peace. The cyber connection with the outside world had kept the revolt alive and discouraged the government from taking heavy-handed measures to repress it. During his campaign, Fox had boldly asserted that he would be able to resolve the Zapatista problem in fifteen minutes. To be sure, his first efforts in freeing Zapatista prisoners from Mexican jails and reducing the military presence in Chiapas indicated that he was sincere in his commitment to find a constructive solution. He also sent to congress legislation proposed by the Zapatistas themselves to give indigenous peoples more control over their traditional lands and natural resources. To garner support for the legislation, the Zapatistas undertook a march from Chiapas to Mexico City in February and March 2001. They wore their marquee masks but, as previously agreed, left their arms at home. Indigenous Zapatista leaders and Sub-Comandante Marcos, by this time revealed to be former university professor Rafael Guillén, addressed a rally of thousands at the Zócalo, demanding the "people who are the color of the earth" no longer be Mexico's forgotten masses.

They wanted to lay their grievances before congress, but many PRI and PAN congressmen opposed giving them an official forum. After the president pressured legislators to change their stance, Zapatista leaders, with their spokesperson Marcos conspicuously absent, appeared on March 28 before a two-hour joint session of congress that was nationally televised. Their chief spokesperson was a Maya Indian woman, Comandante Esther. She enthralled the viewing audience as she argued fervently and persuasively for the passage of an Indian rights bill. The impact of her impassioned plea on congress was more difficult to determine as many Panistas and hard-liners from the PRI boycotted the session. Ultimately an Indian rights bill passed congress and was incorporated into the constitution, but it was a greatly watered-down version of Zapatista goals. From their stronghold in Chiapas, the rebel leaders decried its failure to include the crucial measures that would give Indians the tools to revive their communities and promote their economic well-being. The Zapatista movement remained alive but marginalized throughout the Fox administration.

Another popular protest arose in May 2006 when teachers in Oaxaca went on strike demanding better pay as well as programs to help poor schoolchildren. They were supported by a grassroots organization called the Popular Assembly of the Peoples of Oaxaca (APPO), which sponsored a number of massive protest marches against the government. The unpopular PRI governor, Ulíses Ruiz, refused to heed their demands and in June sent police to remove the protesters from their encampment in the center of Oaxaca City, provoking a confrontation in which many people were injured and several killed. As the struggle persisted with more repressive measures by Ruiz, many Mexicans demanded his resignation. In October the Mexican Senate approved a resolution calling upon the governor to step down to help restore law and order; he refused. The situation laid bare the conundrum of a weak central power; had the PRI still held the presidency, the governor would have been out in an instant. Nor could civil society fill the power gap. Eventually the teachers ended the strike; but the state government continued to quash peaceful protest. The impasse had further repercussions in discouraging the tourist economy, a key source of income for one of Mexico's most impoverished states. It also pointed up one of the most serious obstacles to Mexican democracy: a weak system of the rule of law. In most states, governors appoint prosecutors and judges, making it difficult to bring corrupt or oppressive officials to justice. Fox had supported efforts to reform the judicial system, but much remained to be done.

In reality, President Fox never galloped shoulder to shoulder with Sub-Comandante Marcos, but he did create a political track which made possible the Zapatistas' slow trot into Mexico City in March 2000.

MEXICO AND THE UNITED STATES IN THE AGE OF TERRORISM

On September 11, 2001, Vicente Fox and millions of his fellow Mexicans stood mesmerized before television sets watching the horrific terrorist attack on the Twin Towers of the World Trade Center in New York City and the Pentagon in Washington, D.C. With Mexico's northern neighbor no longer impervious to terrorist assault, the Mexican president was offered his first opportunity to give tangible meaning to the friendship he had openly professed since the day of his inauguration. Visibly moved, his response was quick and unambiguous.

His government expressed condolences, pledged solidarity, and categorically rejected all forms of terrorism. In the days ahead he began actively cooperating with the United States to strengthen border surveillance and bolster security at the American Embassy in Mexico.

To be sure, a few spokespersons for the Mexican left found in the unspeakable tragedy an opportunity to berate US foreign policy even while huge plumes of smoke still billowed from collapsed buildings and thousands were unaccounted for and presumed dead. But the vast majority of Mexican citizens rejected outright the notion that the United States somehow got what it deserved. Dozens of Mexicans were among the foreign nationals from seventy-eight countries buried under the rubble at what came to be called Ground Zero. Mexicans were less concerned with the nationality of the victims than with simple respect for the sanctity of human life.

Whatever Fox's sentiments may have been about supporting the ensuing war, polls showed that over 70 percent of the Mexican population opposed an action seen as another manifestation of US imperialism and a thinly veiled attempt by the Bush administration to manage crucial Mideast oil reserves. As the United States pressured Mexico to support its position, the Fox administration assented to the demands of thousands of Mexican protesters, and Mexican diplomats joined Chile, their hemispheric neighbor on the UN Security Council, in objecting to the use of military force. Moral solidarity in the face of terrorism was one thing; abandoning diplomacy for military might, and even greed, was another. Mexico, it seems, had not lost its commitment to an independent foreign policy. Fox, however, was not prepared to support former national security advisor and the current Mexican ambassador to the United Nations Adolfo Aguilar Zinser, an important political ally in his contest for the presidency. When the ambassador gave a speech in which he accused the United States of arrogantly regarding Mexico as its "backyard," Fox recalled and dismissed him.

In the final analysis, the September 11 tragedy and the subsequent war in Iraq adversely affected Mexico's relations with the United States. Antiterrorism measures and concerns about the security of US borders put a damper on the immigration reforms contemplated by the two presidents. When President George W. Bush hosted his Mexican counterpart at the White House less than a week before the terrorist attacks, he called Mexico "our most important foreign relation." Yet Mexico quickly faded into the background (if not the backyard), and the Fox administration's inability to achieve US commitments to immigration reform was seen as another example of failed expectations and unfulfilled promises. Nonetheless, Fox did not ignore the migrant issue as previous Mexican presidents had. The president spoke out publicly for migrants' rights, and Mexico established new consulates and programs in the United States to aid them. During his administration, migrant earnings sent back to Mexico, remittances, became Mexico's second most important source of foreign exchange after oil. Western Union developed programs to help workers convey these remittances and worked with federal, state, and local officials in Mexico to implement economic development projects across local communities in Zacatecas and four other Mexican states.

With estimates of illegal Mexican immigrants in the United States at more than ten million, the immigration problem presented enormous complexities. Undocumented Mexicans lived in every state, and the population burgeoned in the interior southeast and the western mountain states, where the cost of living was lower. Opponents issued the familiar charges against them; among the most vociferous were racists in vigilante groups like the Minutemen Project formed on the Arizona border to detain illegal migrants and get them deported. Many other observers countered that Mexican labor was vital to many US businesses. In 2005, the service sector (especially hotels and restaurants) employed about a third of illegal immigrants, followed by the construction industry, food processing, and farming. Furthermore, the average family income of undocumented families was about 40 percent below that of legal immigrants. Enforcement of immigration laws was lax, prompting renewed calls for sanctions against employers and a physical fence stretching along the 2,000-mile border. At the same time, the living conditions of migrants were often substandard, if not abominable, and they faced hazardous work situations and racist retaliation.

The availability of jobs in both the informal and formal economies, which perpetually seek to cut costs, undoubtedly feeds illegal immigration. Experts argue that the situation depicted in the film *A Day without a Mexican*, which comically highlights how the economy and law enforcement would come to a standstill in California bereft of its Mexican population, is exaggerated. But pro-immigration advocates also believe that with cheap labor no longer available, prices would rise for food, child care, and household maintenance. Businesses would have to pay higher wages, and some would be forced to shut down. With illegal immigrants producing over $900 billion a year in goods and services, 9 percent of the overall US economy, it was difficult to see how the immigration issue would be resolved in the foreseeable future.

Realistic solutions have been complicated by the fact that undocumented worker mythologies are nurtured by vested-interest groups. Contrary to popular opinion, undocumented workers do not constitute an overwhelming drain on social services. The best evidence is that most of them have federal and state taxes deducted from their wages but do not reap the benefits of the tax system for fear of being detected and reported to immigration authorities; a good number actually file tax returns. Equally evident is the myth that a great many displace US workers and in a major way contribute to unemployment north of the international boundary. Undoubtedly, some US workers have been displaced, but a large majority of the undocumented fill positions that would remain vacant at wage levels falling below minimum scale.

Dangers to the migrants themselves are another problem, as revealed in the countless human tragedies that occur each year. Crossing the border illegally immediately converts a law-abiding citizen into a fugitive from justice with no protection from the varied forms of human exploitation. The Mexicans, called *coyotes*, who contract with individual workers for surreptitious entry and transportation to a job often maintain supportive ties with migrants, but some have been known to collect their fees and deliver their human cargo to US immigration authorities. US employers have been known to set up two-week pay periods and, after receiving thirteen days of labor from an entire work force, call in the border patrol, thus relieving themselves of the need to meet the payroll. Vigilantes have sometimes physically brutalized job seekers.

Unintended tragedies also abound as many undocumented workers have died in the scorching heat of desert border crossings. This problem became more pronounced as the Bush administration stepped up border security in the San Diego and El Paso areas, driving much of the illegal traffic into the Arizona desert. When deaths approached as many as five hundred per year, humanitarian groups like No Más Muertes organized in Arizona to place water along the routes traveled by migrants. Anti-immigrant anger in the United States escalated in 2005 and 2006. By that time the Border Patrol had more than tripled in number of agents since 1990. Rejecting a proposal by President Bush to give guest worker visas to illegal immigrants who came to the United States before February 2004, the US House of Representatives passed a draconian bill at the end of 2005 that criminalized illegal entry and stipulated severe punishments for employers who hired undocumented workers. The Senate did not follow suit, but Congress did pass the Secure Fence Act the next fall, providing funding to fence 700 miles of the border. Mexicans and other Latinos did not accept these callous actions quietly. In the spring of 2006, thousands of them organized protest marches in Los Angeles and other large US cities. Local radio talk show hosts and Catholic churches were instrumental in encouraging these efforts.

In another arena of cross-border tensions, the Fox administration made aggressive efforts to combat drug trafficking, perpetually abetted by federal, state, and local officials and police since the 1980s. During his administration, Fox jailed more top cartel leaders than any previous president, arrested nearly fifty thousand people on drug charges, destroyed numerous clandestine landing strips, and eradicated thousands of poppy and marijuana fields. But the administration's efforts were thwarted not only by escapes of cartel leaders from prison but by the seeming ease with which they could run cocaine operations from their jail cells. The arrests of drug lords had the effect of prompting bloody battles between rival cartels, while the supply of drugs to the United States and to growing numbers of Mexican consumers did not diminish. Joaquín Guzmán (El Chapo), head of the Sinaloa cartel, escaped from a maximum-security prison shortly after Fox took office. Osiel Cárdenas continued to protect the Gulf cartel's millions of dollars of interests after his incarceration by bribing officials and police in northern Mexico.

In the war between the two cartels, kidnapping and deaths escalated, taking the lives of more than one hundred soldiers and federal drug agents throughout Mexico. An all-out gang war erupted on the streets of Nuevo Laredo in 2005, resulting in the bloody executions of scores of people, including the police chief who had pledged to rid the force of police corrupted by drug money or intimidated by threats. Meanwhile, the murders of several hundred young women in Ciudad Juárez over the previous decade, widely thought to be connected to police involved in protecting the drug industry, were not investigated forcefully. While drug lords liberally spent money for social services in their home communities, grisly crimes took the lives of innocent citizens as well as members of organized crime. Although Fox put Nuevo Laredo under federal control, the government seemed to lack resources to forcefully combat the drug problem. The president compared the explosion of killings to the Al Capone era of the 1920s in the United States and noted that it takes years to get rid of organized crime in an industry worth billions of dollars.

DILEMMAS OF DEMOCRATIZATION

Inadequate efforts to fight the drug trade only contributed to Fox's declining popularity. Nor was the "lame duck president" immune to criticism for intemperate remarks. Mexicans had been used to his shoot-from-the-hip speaking style since Fox's days on the campaign trail. But he shocked many when he stated to a meeting of Texas businessmen in May 2005 that Mexican immigrants in the United States were doing jobs that not even blacks wanted. In November, at the Summit of the Americas in Argentina, he traded insults with South American presidents and a war of words between Fox and Venezuelan populist president, Hugo Chávez, resulted in the recalling of both countries' ambassadors.

A more damaging embarrassment to the administration occurred earlier in 2005. Even though the Fox administration had a strong record of supporting free and fair elections throughout Mexico, the president could not distance himself from the machinations of the PRI and the PAN to discredit the PRD mayor of Mexico City, Andrés Manuel López Obrador, known by his initials as AMLO. The left-leaning mayor had garnered enormous popularity in the Federal District for maintaining fiscal stability while conducting urban renewal and providing needed social services to the poor and the elderly. As PRI and PAN congressmen saw their parties' hopes for the presidency in 2006 erode, they conspired to have the federal government indict AMLO on a trumped-up charge. He was accused of approving a city project to widen a road to a public hospital on a small piece of land acquired by his predecessor but whose ownership was in litigation. This highly transparent manipulation was designed to nip AMLO's presidential aspirations in the bud. Since the Mexican constitution prevents anyone under indictment from running for the presidency, AMLO's political opponents planned to have him waiting out the elections in jail.

Their efforts were foiled by the Mexican people, who saw the charges as a throwback to "politics as usual." In April 2005, just after the congressional vote to strip AMLO of the judicial immunity he enjoyed as mayor, an estimated three hundred thousand outraged citizens staged a protest in the Zócalo. The entire incident had the effect of discrediting the PAN and the PRI, while boosting support for AMLO. To prevent chaos and further damage to his own party, Fox dissuaded the attorney general's office from prosecuting the mayor. As 2005 drew to a close, the presidential election campaign was in full swing, with PRD candidate AMLO leading the polls by a small margin. He was followed by the PRI candidate Roberto Madrazo who, despite being tainted by political corruption himself, had won the nomination in a contentious internal party struggle, and Felipe Calderón from the PAN.

The balance sheet on Mexico's momentous political shift after 2000 has yet to be determined by history, but early analyses were not charitable as many characterized the Fox presidency as a "lost sexenio" and an opportunity squandered. In the political realm, the first opposition government in seventy years did score some successes in supporting electoral democracy, and Fox promoted measures to strengthen the judiciary and the rule of law, as well as the independence of the federal electoral commission. He also provided the impetus for a law in 2003 that made all federal executive branch agencies more transparent. The transparency law constituted a significant step in the direction of creating a democracy in which political appointees and government agencies could be held accountable for their actions. Not surprisingly, the law was not vigorously enforced. In addition, because Mexico's constitution does not allow for reelection, elected officials feel little pressure to be accountable to their constituencies. In defense of Fox, some argued that electoral democracy takes time to mature, but Mexico's ingrained political culture seemed hardly to have suffered even a lump as authoritarian practices and clientelistic relationships persisted in all three major parties.

THE 2006 ELECTIONS AND THE PRESIDENCY OF FELIPE CALDERÓN

As it turned out, even the most imaginative Mexican minds did not anticipate the results of the 2006 presidential election, held on July 2. Although the PRD's AMLO had run significantly ahead in the polls during the early months of the year, the PAN's Felipe Calderón narrowed the lead as the election drew near, while Roberto Madrazo of the PRI slipped far behind, illustrating that his party's mid-term congressional gains did not yet presage a dramatic revival of the historically dominant party. More importantly, the election demonstrated that the political transformation of 2000 was not an anomaly.

The leading contenders seemed to represent opposite poles on the political spectrum. AMLO, who hailed from humble origins in Tabasco, had risen through the party ranks of the PRI before becoming a key figure in the newly formed PRD. Building upon his record as Mexico City mayor, he campaigned in a coalition of the PRD and several minor parties called Por el Bién de Todos (For the Good of All). Following leadership trends in Brazil, Argentina, Chile, and Uruguay, he criticized neoliberal policies that had left many people behind despite general economic growth, vowing instead to work to provide health care and education for the poor, as well as initiate needed infrastructural changes. His support was strongest in Mexico City and in the more indigenous areas of Mexico. The Harvard-educated Calderón, son of a PAN founder from the state of Michoacán, advocated the continuation of neoliberal policies as a means to develop human capital through a competitive economy that would create more jobs and to overhaul the energy and tax sectors. Rallying support from more middle-class voters outside the capital, especially in the north, he endeavored to show himself as independent from the lame duck Fox.

The campaign heated up as the candidates traded insults, with Calderón contending that AMLO's performance as mayor demonstrated that he was irresponsible and that his promises to the poor smacked of a messianic complex (while also suggesting that AMLO looked a lot like Hugo Chávez of Venezuela). Calderón's support surged in the polls after the first national televised presidential debate, in which AMLO declined to participate. Many analysts believed that this was a mistake; whether true or not, AMLO had clearly underestimated his rival, and he delayed in mounting a more forceful critique of Calderón's record and the PAN's negative attack ads. Especially damaging was the allegation that AMLO was "*un peligro para México*" (a danger to Mexico).

On July 2, over 41 million Mexicans (60 percent of eligible voters) went to the polls. At first, the results were too close to call; but on July 6, the Federal Electoral Commission declared Calderón the winner, by less than a percentage point of the vote. Chaos threatened as AMLO's supporters took to the streets to cry fraud. AMLO urged his followers to undertake a campaign of civil disobedience. PRD supporters turned out in the hundreds of thousands to protest in Mexico City's Zócalo, charging that big money and crooked politics had skewed the result and that there was fraud in the tallying of votes (an accusation refuted by international election observers). They also criticized the Federal Electoral Commission for not imposing sanctions on the PAN for overspending and other violations of campaign rules.

Following legal procedures, the coalition For the Good of All then presented formal complaints before the Federal Electoral Court (Tribunal Electoral del Poder Judicial de la Federación—TEPJF) that charged irregularities in specific voting districts and violations of

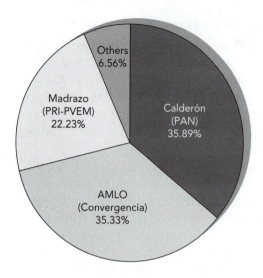

Presidential Election, 2006

rules that regulated campaign ads and prohibited direct presidential influence in the elections. To the public, AMLO addressed his call for a total recount of votes.

Meanwhile, Calderón claimed victory and formed a transition team. Although the PAN garnered more seats than any other party coalition in both the Chamber of Deputies and the Senate, it did not win an absolute majority. In the Chamber of Deputies, the PRI's votes would be necessary to give either side a majority.

While the country awaited a decision from the electoral tribunal (by law, the court of last appeal), thousands of PRD supporters set up camps along the main thoroughfare of the Paseo de la Reforma and in the Zócalo to mount a systematic protest with daily rallies. When it became apparent that the TEPJF would recount ballots in only a tenth of the voting precincts, AMLO intensified his attacks on Mexico's flawed institutional structures and called for a "national democratic convention" to produce a new governing charter that would provide political, economic, and social justice for all Mexicans. On September 1, with the congressional buildings surrounded by military and police barricades, PRD deputies and senators took over the floor of the congressional session hall and prevented the president from delivering his last annual message in person.

On September 5, the court delivered a verdict, declaring Felipe Calderón Hinojosa the president-elect of Mexico. The final count gave him a margin of 233,831 votes (just above a half of a percentage point) over AMLO. The unanimous judicial decision recognized minor voting irregularities and censured President Fox and the businessmen's council for improper conduct in the campaign, but ruled that none of these violations was sufficient to prevent the free exercise of the vote.

Although the Calderón presidency began in a highly charged and polarized atmosphere, the former federal deputy came to office with more political savvy about how to work with the congress than any previous president. He was actually aided in this endeavor by AMLO's refusal to recognize his victory, which created deep ruptures within the leftist coalition and initially retarded the active participation of the PRD in congress. As a result, the PRI, which had earned the least number of congressional seats, moved quickly to fill the vacuum and take over important leadership positions in congressional committees. As AMLO continued to proclaim himself the "legitimate" president, he lost support in his own party and earned the disapproval of more than 70 percent of the Mexican public.

Calderón had campaigned on free market principles as the ultimate solution for dealing with poverty, but after tens of thousands of Mexicans tested his resolve in the early months of his administration by protesting rising food prices, he supported a price cap for tortillas, that most basic staple. The price of tortillas had risen 40 percent in just three months, in contrast to a 4 percent increase in the minimum wage (still less than $5 a day). In other early initiatives, Calderón raised the wages of the armed forces and police to lessen the lure of bribery for these underpaid officers. At the same time, he capped the salaries of high-level civil servants. Some Mexicans observed that his administration was not interested in or effective at regulating the disproportionate profits made by Mexican billionaire Carlos Slim Helú, whose company Telmex provided 80 percent of Mexico's telephone land lines and charged among the highest fees in the world. Slim and his family corporation also dominated the Mexican market for mobile telephones and broadband connections, owned Mexico's Sanborns chain, and had investments in a variety of other infrastructural sectors. In 2008, they invested in the *New York Times* and Saks, Inc. Their wealth was estimated to be the equivalent of 7 percent of Mexico's annual economic output; Slim's rank among the world's billionaires, according to *Forbes Magazine*, fluctuated between the first and third positions. Slim's near monopolies were not an isolated phenomenon; other private companies dominated their markets, for example, in cement (CEMEX) and television (Televisa).

Carlos Slim Helú.

During his campaign, Calderón had pledged to implement judicial and energy reform; his success in getting measures passed in these two areas involved political trade-offs between the left and the right. According to most analysts of the impediments to Mexican democracy, the lack of a political structure and a culture that respects the rule of law is the greatest problem. Many argued that Mexico was becoming more democratic in terms of electoral competition and freedom of expression in the media, but comprehensive judicial reforms were necessary to prosecute crimes resulting from flagrant abuses of power. Public support for such reforms were buttressed by the unresolved situation in Oaxaca, where Governor Ulíses Ruiz continued to exercise heavy-handed power with impunity, and by other high-profile cases in which state and local officials sheltered criminals and flagrantly ignored laws that protected freedom of speech and social activism in areas like environmental justice, municipal autonomy, and women's rights.

It has been estimated that in Mexico as many as 75 percent of crimes are not reported because of lack of trust in the authorities; when they are reported, more than 90 percent are never resolved or punished. On the other hand, it is not unusual for one to be convicted without any evidence, an abuse starkly portrayed in the prize-winning documentary *Presunto Culpable (Presumed Guilty)*, which was released in 2009 but did not get wide circulation in Mexico until 2011. The dysfunctional justice system breeds impunity and does little to stop narcoviolence. Mexico's constitution embraces the concept of *amparo*, literally a writ of protection that allows for an individual to file an injunction claiming a violation of her/his constitutional guarantees. Intended to protect an individual against abuses of power, the miscarriage of justice, or human rights abuses, in practice amparo has long favored elites and more recently criminals in avoiding prosecution.

Beyond judicial abuse, corruption is a fact of life in Mexico ranging from petty to corporate levels. Some estimates hold that Mexican households spend several billion dollars a year on bribes, often to obtain services that should be free. According to the World Bank, entrenched corruption costs Mexico 9 percent of its trillion-dollar GDP each year. The corrupt corporate culture that requires payoffs is not a novelty in Mexico, but its excesses were revealed to the world in a 2012 investigation by the *New York Times* into how Wal-Mart had taken over much of the Mexican retail sales market. It turned out that Wal-Mart de México was not the passive victim of a corrupt culture that insisted on bribes as the cost of doing business, but rather an aggressive competitor that repeatedly offered payoffs totaling some $25 million to subvert the law and circumvent regulatory safeguards. The company obtained permits for at least 19 stores across Mexico in areas where construction was strictly prohibited, some in environmentally fragile areas and others that infringed on archaeological zones. Despite the evidence, Mexico's federal anticorruption agency virtually absolved Mexican officials and Wal-Mart.

An important step in the direction of reform was achieved in July 2008 when President Calderón signed a constitutional amendment that requires prosecutors and defense lawyers to argue their cases in court and discontinues the practice of judges making decisions based on written statements from lawyers. The changes entail major retraining and restructuring of the court system and will take years to implement. The amendment also reinforces the rights of defendants by affirming the presumption of innocence.

In April 2008, President Calderón introduced his proposal for energy reform, unleashing a flood of debate on its merits. Few people doubted that the oil issue needed to be addressed as Mexico's reserves had been declining since the mid-1980s and were not expected to last more than 10 years; furthermore, the administration of PEMEX was seen as grossly inefficient. Because oil revenues funded about 40 percent of the federal government budget, reforms were urgently needed. After months of hearings, public consultations with citizens, and a takeover of congress by opponents that was orchestrated by AMLO, the three main parties came together to pass a version of the original proposal in seven bills.

The changes gave PEMEX greater autonomy and budgetary control, as well as the right to contract with private firms, but only in exploration and production activities; even in these cases one-quarter of contracted work had to be done by domestic providers. Outside participation in transportation, storage, and refining was still prohibited, reflecting the lingering vestige of economic nationalism that provoked the most debate. Mexican control of its most valuable economic resource continued to be a hot political issue. Other reforms widened the ministry of energy's power to plan and regulate oil and gas and promoted projects for sustainable and renewable energy.

Other economic and social reforms contemplated by the Calderón administration were stymied by the world economic downturn in 2008, when Mexico's close ties to the United States became a greater liability. Manufacturing began to decline, exports decreased, and Mexico experienced huge job losses in urban areas. The rural economy of corn producers continued to decline as food imports increased by 26 percent in 2008, contributing to about half of Mexico's growing trade deficit. The peso had lost nearly a quarter of its value by the end of 2008, and Secretary of the Treasury Agustín Carstens predicted zero economic growth for 2009. The prophecy turned out to be true when, in 2009, the economy shrank by 6 percent. It began to recover in 2010, finally achieving gains of over 3 percent in annual GDP growth rates by the end of Calderón's term.

Internal crises in Mexico further slowed recovery. In 2009, Mexico experienced an influenza epidemic that threatened to become a world pandemic. Quickly dubbed "swine flu," it is formally known as the H1N1 virus, a subvirus of influenza A that in the past was extremely virulent—for example, in the 1918 influenza pandemic which killed millions of people worldwide. Although scientists could not pinpoint the specific geographical origin of the outbreak, the first cases were apparently reported in the state of Veracruz in February. When the virus was first identified in the United States as having a mixture of pig, bird, and human strains, it had already crossed the border. Although the epidemic spread around the world beginning in April (reaching over 70 countries by early June), the World Health Organization monitored the situation day by day and only officially categorized it as a global pandemic on June 11, 2009, with the caveat that the decision reflected the global spread of the disease and not an increase in its severity, which differed little from ordinary influenza outbreaks.

After Mexico experienced a relatively high number of deaths from the epidemic, primarily because the cases were not identified as H1N1 until April and therefore not treated with any flu vaccine, the Mexican government quickly put aggressive public health measures in place in April and May. Officials closed down government operations, schools, museums, libraries, and many private businesses like restaurants and bars. Public celebrations and church services were also canceled. The metropolis of Mexico City eerily resembled a ghost town; those people who ventured out onto the streets wore protective masks. Although panic was largely avoided in Mexico as the epidemic evolved with less severe results and the United States resisted the calls of some to close the border, other countries took more drastic measures—for example, in China authorities quarantined all Mexicans who arrived in the country, forcing the Mexican government to charter a plane to fetch them home. And fears of catching the flu prompted many prospective tourists to cancel their flights and hotel reservations for Mexico; by summer tourism had declined by 40 percent, a significant loss since tourism accounted for 30 percent of Mexico's foreign exchange.

Taking into consideration this crisis and the 2008 recession, the economy performed reasonably well when compared to other nations. A competitive currency, foreign capital investment, and durable goods exported to the United States helped Mexico weather the storm, although the Cálderon government failed to achieve structural reforms in the economy, directed at creating jobs and alleviating poverty. In the final analysis, however, Felipe Cálderon will not be remembered for his neoliberal economic legacy as it was completely overshadowed by his failed strategy in the fight against organized crime and drug cartels.

RECOMMENDED FOR FURTHER STUDY

Bobrow-Strain, Aaron. *Intimate Enemies: Landowners, Power, and Violence in Chiapas.* Durham, NC: Duke University Press, 2007.

Call, Wendy. *No Word for Welcome: The Mexican Village Faces the Global Economy.* Lincoln: University of Nebraska Press, 2011.

Camp, Roderic Ai. *The Metamorphosis of Leadership in a Democratic Mexico.* New York: Oxford University Press, 2010.

_____. *Mexico: What Everyone Needs to Know.* New York: Oxford University Press, 2011.

_____. *Politics in Mexico: The Democratic Consolidation.* 5th ed. New York: Oxford University Press, 2007.

Campos, Isaac. *Home Grown: Marijuana and the Origins of Mexico's War on Drugs.* Chapel Hill: University of North Carolina Press, 2012.

Castañeda, Jorge G. *Ex Mex: From Migrants to Immigrants.* New York: New Press, 2007.

Castañeda, Jorge G., and Robert A. Pastor. *Limits to Friendship: The United States and Mexico.* New York: Alfred A. Knopf, 1988.

Driver, Alice. *More or Less Dead: Femicide, Haunting, and the Ethics of Representation.* Tucson: University of Arizona Press, 2015.

Eisenstadt, Todd. *Politics, Identity, and Mexico's Indigenous Rights Movements.* New York: Cambridge University Press, 2011.

Eiss, Paul. *In the Name of El Pueblo: Place, Community, and the Politics of History in Yucatán.* Durham, NC: Duke University Press, 2010.

García-Gorena, Velma. *Mothers and the Mexican Antinuclear Power Movement.* Tucson: University of Arizona Press, 1999.

Haber, Stephen, et al. *Mexico since 1980.* New York: Cambridge University Press, 2008.

James, Timothy M. *Mexico's Supreme Court: Between Liberal Individual and Revolutionary Social Rights, 1861–1934.* Albuquerque: University of New Mexico Press, 2013.

Levy, Daniel, and Kathleen Bruhn. *Mexico: The Struggle for Democratic Development.* 2d ed. Berkeley: University of California Press, 2006.

Lyon, Sarah. *Coffee and Community: Maya Farmers and Fair-Trade Markets*. Boulder: University Press of Colorado, 2010.

Pansters, Wil, ed. *Violence, Coercion, and State-Making in Twentieth-Century Mexico: The Other Half of the Centaur*. Stanford, CA: Stanford University Press, 2012.

Reynolds, Clark W., and Robert K. McCleery. "The Political Economy of Immigration Law: Impact of Simpson-Rodino on the United States and Mexico." *Journal of Economic Perspectives* 2/3 (1988): 117–31.

Rubio, Luis, and Susan Kaufman Purcell. *Mexico under Fox*. Boulder, CO: Lynne Reinner, 2004.

Sabet, Daniel M. *Police Reform in Mexico City: Informal Politics and the Challenge of Institutional Change*. Stanford, CA: Stanford University Press, 2012.

CHAPTER 39

PROBLEMS AND PROMISE

THE SPECTER OF THE BORDER

A bloody drug war defined Calderón's presidency. It was not new, harking back decades to the birth of Mexican drug cartels. In the twentieth century, PRI governments had essentially offered the cartels protection as long as they did not disrupt the peace in Mexico and concentrated their efforts on shipping narcotics to the United States and Canada rather than stimulating a consumer market within Mexico's borders. The Mexican state closed its eyes to the involvement of federal, state, and local politicians and police who could be bought off by the drug traffickers.

Intensifying efforts begun by Vicente Fox, Felipe Calderón decided to declare all-out war on the Mexican drug cartels that had broken the unwritten agreement and were expanding their markets in Mexico as well as in the United States, to the tune of $15 to $25 billion (around 10 percent of Mexican GDP) in annual profits. In the decade since the end of the twentieth century global consumption of both marijuana and cocaine had more than doubled, while that of opiates had tripled. El Chapo had outlived his enemies and expanded the operations of the Sinaloa cartel; while it was the largest, competition from others intensified. The profits in cocaine alone could triple in value from the time of purchase in Colombia to its wholesale value in the United States; retail sales could triple the price once again. Methamphetamines also began to be manufactured on a large scale in Mexico, first with legal and then illegal imports of chemicals from China.

President Calderón, working with US agencies (including the Drug Enforcement Administration, the Bureau of Alcohol, Tobacco, Firearms and Explosives, the CIA, and the FBI), devised a strategy to go after the cartel leaders, to confiscate money, weapons, and drugs, but his major innovation was to mobilize the army and the navy to combat the traffickers, in order to bypass the problem of official and police involvement in protecting the trade. This effort worried many Mexicans concerned about the abuse of power by the military, but more alarmingly it unleashed a wave of violence among the cartels in which substitutes for the murdered and imprisoned leaders vied for turf. Narcotraffickers themselves were the initial targets of increasingly vicious murders, in which victims were decapitated among other brutalities. But innocent victims increasingly got caught in the crossfire. Narcoviolence expanded at the street level. By the end of Calderón's presidency as many as sixty thousand people had died and one hundred thousand had disappeared. Among the casualties were politicians, especially mayors who refused to be bought off, and journalists who investigated and reported the trade, often targeted by governors who were involved in the trade themselves.

Government attempts to smash the drug trade spurred a major fight between the Gulf and Sinaloa cartels for control of northeast Mexico, and narco enclaves became even more entrenched in Sinaloa, the Sierra Madre Occidental, and the lowlands in Michoacán and Guerrero. The worst violence took place in Chihuahua (especially in Ciudad Juárez), Nuevo León, Coahuila, and Durango. The Zetas, former army commandos, originally hired as assassins by the Gulf cartel, split off and formed their own organization dedicated not only to drug smuggling but also extortion, kidnapping, and human trafficking. When casino owners in Monterrey refused to pay for protection in 2011, the Zetas set fire to the building, killing fifty-two people, including elderly women who were playing bingo. The cartels found new ways to transport drugs beyond hiding them in the billions of dollars of goods crossing the border. They bought planes and dug underground tunnels that stretched under the border from Mexico into Arizona and California. A growing arsenal of arms was easily purchased in the United States, where gun controls were lax or nonexistent. Bribing Mexican officials was old hat (even Mexico's drug czar was revealed to be on the take in 2008), but now American border patrol guards could also be bought.

The cartels doled out bribes to federal, state, and municipal authorities. Entire police forces and prison security guards were on the payroll in many places. The drug business means jobs and investment: cartel leaders spread their largesse to communities, building public works, schools, and clinics. They gave money to the church. These self-made men are celebrated in narco corridos and on narco blogs as machos and Robin Hoods. The latter comparison misses the mark since the cartel leaders don't rob the rich to pay the poor—drug lords even "invest" in big business.

As violence escalated, citizens' groups formed to protect their neighborhoods and communities. In Cuernavaca, the torture and murder of the son of Mexican poet Javier Sicilia in March 2011 prompted his father to found the Movement for Peace with Justice and Dignity. He organized caravans to tour the country and the United States to bring attention to the plight of victims' families, who were largely ignored by the government. The movement blamed Calderón's strategy for the worsening violence, charging that Mexico was on the brink of social and moral collapse. The president met with victims and apologized for their losses, but he refused to back down on the deployment of the military (also accused of murder and rape in the morass of violence).

The elephant in the room, of course, is the United States—the source of about 35 million drug users and an untold stockpile of arms. Acknowledging this problem, Secretary of State Hillary Clinton and President Barack Obama visited Mexico in 2009 to meet with officials. They were also troubled by the fact that Mexican drugs are funneled through distribution centers across US cities like Atlanta to move cocaine, marijuana, and cash. The Mérida Initiative, already approved by the US Congress, was providing financial and military assistance to Mexico's efforts to thwart the drug trade. Obama promised more cooperation at the border and in April named a border czar to oversee US activities to end the cartel violence (and to reduce the flow of illegal immigration). But there was no change in the basic strategy to stem the drug trade, which continued unabated throughout the rest of Calderón's administration, overshadowing other problems and initiatives. The weakness of the Mexican state was palpable; it had no monopoly on violence, and the absence of a strong state, the prevalence of corruption, and US market demand for drugs as well as the supply of weapons coalesced in an intractable problem.

The other unsolved conundrum that linked Mexico and the United States was of even longer standing. Illegal migration (including a growing number of women migrants) had been on the rise at the time of Calderón's election. NAFTA had become an important stimulant because imports of cheap US commodities put local Mexican farmers out of business and encouraged migration; remittances from across the border could crucially underpin community survival. But a combination of new border surveillance techniques, the construction of the seven hundred-mile fence, and the economic downturn in the United States began to stem migration in August 2007; by the next year migration from the south had dropped by 25 percent. Still, several million undocumented immigrants remained in the United States, working primarily in service industries (over 50 percent) and in construction and manufacturing (38 percent). However, the setbacks in the housing and service sectors in the United States also meant a decline in employment opportunities for resident migrants and precipitated a drop in remittances of nearly 4 percent in 2008, the first decline since Mexico began tracking money flows in 1995.

The migrant stream slowed substantially by 2010, when fewer than one hundred thousand border-crossers stayed in the United States, the lowest number since the 1950s. Evidence suggests that by this time the Mexican economy was providing more employment and educational opportunities in Mexico itself, where the birth rate had dropped. Drug violence on the border posed another deterrent to migration, along with higher prices being charged by coyotes. The border wall in Arizona and an expanded pool of border agents presented greater risks.

The economic slide and the growing volume of drug smuggling stimulated anti-immigrant sentiment in parts of the United States. The conflation of undocumented immigration with terrorism and drug trafficking reached hysterical proportions in some areas. In Arizona, the radically conservative, if not racist, governor and legislature pushed through Senate Bill 1070 in 2010, the strictest anti-immigrant legislation in recent history. The Arizona law required that state law enforcement officers attempt to determine an individual's immigration status during a lawful stop, detention, or arrest when there was reasonable suspicion that an individual was an illegal immigrant. It imposed penalties on those sheltering, hiring, and transporting unregistered aliens. Critics of the legislation saw it as encouraging racial profiling and staged protests demanding its repeal. Cities and convention organizers across the country called for boycotts of Arizona. But there was considerable support for tougher immigration laws nationwide in view of the failure of the federal government to take up immigration reform after it stalled in the wake of 9/11. Other states enacted laws similar to SB1070. Legal challenges over the constitutionality of the Arizona law and its compliance with civil rights protections delayed its implementation, and eventually the US Supreme Court struck down some of its provisions while upholding the statute that required immigration status checks during law enforcement stops.

The border wall and surveillance cameras stretch endlessly across the landscape of southern Arizona, disrupting the exchange of people, plants, and animals.

Although these legal battles did not move the US Congress to take action on immigration, another event did cause some of its members to rethink their stance on the Latino population. In the 2012 federal elections, Democratic Party candidates, including President Barack Obama, defeated a substantial number of Republican contenders who ran on anti-immigrant platforms. The Latino vote (10 percent of the electorate) turned out to be a crucial factor, as Latinos/Hispanics voted overwhelmingly (71 percent) in favor of Obama. Prior to the election, by executive order, the president had halted the deportation of as many as a million illegal immigrants who were brought to the United States as children. Republicans had repeatedly blocked passage of the Dream Act, which would have provided residency and a path to citizenship for immigrant children who arrived in the United States as minors, graduated from US high schools, and lived in the country continuously for at least five years prior to the bill's enactment.

The Democrats' appeal to immigrant and minority communities alarmed Republicans who had supported mass deportations of Mexicans. Hispanics are the fastest-growing minority in the United States, estimated to grow to 132 million strong by 2050, making up 30 percent of the country's population. For this reason, Republican Party leaders began to talk about reaching out to this constituency, although they did not appear ready to consider comprehensive immigration reform, leaving the issue unresolved. Barack Obama continued to support enforcement of the border, deporting millions of new arrivals, despite the recognition by many Americans that Mexican immigrants contributed more to the United States than they took from it.

THE PRI REBORN IN THE 2012 ELECTIONS

The midterm Mexican congressional elections in 2009 favored the PRI, a reflection of Calderón's unpopularity over the drug war and a splintered PRD. The PRI was intent on a comeback in 2012, and the party leaders had found their golden candidate in Enrique Peña Nieto. First groomed to become the governor of the state of Mexico in 2005 at the age of 39, the physically attractive and youthful politician had served in several state government positions before being elected governor. As governor, Peña Nieto had succeeded in carrying out some of his promises to improve public transportation, build clinics, and expand the state's tax base. However, he ran into trouble when he sent police to crush those who opposed an expansion of Mexico City's airport into the municipality of San Salvador Atenco in 2006, unleashing more civil unrest. The violent detention and imprisonment of protestors provoked calls from Amnesty International and others to free innocent prisoners, punish excessive police force including rape, and reduce excessive sentences. Peña Nieto was also criticized for the high rate of femicides in the state of Mexico, and the sudden death of his wife in 2006 provoked more concern. He remarried in 2010, this time to well-known television soap opera actress Angela Rivera. In 2011, he became the official PRI candidate for the presidency. Many Mexicans believed he was tutored by old party stalwarts, including Carlos Salinas de Gortari.

The 2012 presidential campaign featured candidates from the three main parties plus one from the New Alliance Party who ran to build the constituency of the powerful teacher's union leader, Esther Elba Gordillo. She had dominated educational policy in Mexico for years, despite attempts to reform a flawed system that rewarded loyalty over merit. The PAN tapped Josefina Vázquez Mota, the first woman to run on the ticket of a major political party. She had served in the Calderón administration but did not have the support of the party's leadership; she campaigned on the slogan "Josefina Diferente" to distance herself from the current administration. As a result of federal electoral laws, women had come to hold a quarter of congressional seats, but only 6 percent of the country's mayors were female. Political analysts attribute this low number to a patriarchal culture and a lack of transparency in the political process.

The PRD had mended some of its cracks but the left was still divided. After the popular PRD mayor of Mexico City, Marcelo Ebrard, withdrew his candidacy, the party selected Andrés Manuel López Obrador. As the campaign got underway, AMLO, whose candidacy suffered from memories of the aftermath of the 2006 elections, and Vázquez Mota were running far behind Peña Nieto, who garnered a huge share of press and television coverage. Rumor had it that PAN leaders had made a pact to support the PRI candidate. Supporters of the PAN and PRD candidates staged rally after rally, targeting Peña Nieto's record as governor and poking fun at mistakes he had made in campaign speeches and interviews, suggesting that he was ill prepared, poorly educated, and out of touch with Mexico's problems. Nonetheless, it looked as though he would steamroll into the presidency—that is, until the Internet threw him a curve.

In May before the July 2012 elections, Peña Nieto held a campaign event at the Universidad Iberoamericana, a private institution originally founded by Jesuits and whose students were mostly middle class. Jesuit influence regarding social justice had resulted in political resistance from the students on several occasions in the twentieth century. When he responded unsatisfactorily to students' questions about the Atenco problem, they began to heckle him. Pursued by students, he fled the campus but could not duck the student protest movement that followed. Begun by 131 students, it became known as the Yo Soy 132 (I am the 132nd) as students from more than a dozen universities in Mexico City and others in the states joined. Rallies, organized on Facebook and Twitter, took place weekly and summoned large crowds. Students demanded democratization of the media (that had overwhelmingly favored Peña Nieto, apparently selling news coverage to the PRI) to guarantee the right to information and freedom of expression. As a group the students did not support any particular candidate, but AMLO's numbers began to rise in the polls. The movement called for reforms to create secular, free, scientific, pluricultural, democratic, humanist, popular, critical, and quality education, as well as health care for all. The students wanted a truly participatory democracy and the removal of the army from public security. Yo Soy 132 spurred optimism among students and others that civil society could bring pressure to change the political system; some called it the "Mexican Spring," placing it in the context of recent protest movements in the Middle East and North Africa. The movement certainly raised consciousness about the media monopolies, articulated broad public concern about human rights and the way the drug wars were being waged, and offered support to those who wanted to modernize and democratize the educational system.

The elections were held on July 1, 2012, with 63 percent of registered voters turning out to cast their ballots. Peña Nieto won the presidency with 39.1 percent of the vote, followed by López Obrador (32.43 percent) and Vázquez Mota (26.04 percent). López Obrador lost by a much narrower margin than predicted, an illustration of media bias and the public awareness generated by Yo Soy 132 regarding lack of transparency and democracy. AMLO

The 2012 student protesters used the internet, Facebook, and Twitter to organize their rallies where they wore t-shirts and carried signs bearing the logo "Yo Soy 132."

contested the results, charging that the Mexican media had treated his candidacy with inequality in relation to Peña Nieto. He presented considerable evidence of the means used to buy votes for the PRI (most notoriously the distribution of supermarket debit cards as gifts). The federal electoral court not only dismissed these allegations but actually ruled that AMLO had surpassed campaign limits on spending, proving to many that the Federal Electoral Institute had been compromised by legislative changes to its party membership. Protest rallies continued through inauguration day on December 1, 2012. On a another note, with the election of Miguel Angel Mancera as mayor who garnered 63 percent of the vote, the PRD retained control of Mexico City, an endorsement of its leadership in promoting improved public transportation, environmental initiatives to reduce pollution, beautification of the cityscape, crime prevention, and sexual equality.

Meanwhile the new senators and deputies took their seats on September 1, 2012, with the PRI in the majority (about 32 percent in both houses), followed by the PAN with just over a quarter and the PRD just under a fifth. Minor parties claimed the remaining seats and were expected to be an important factor in making alliances with the three major entities. Three important developments followed. In November, the congress passed a labor reform bill that weakened the power of the unions (although it did not include measures to improve their transparency and accountability) by allowing for subcontracting, employment trial periods, and hourly wages for temporary hires. The second event was the signing of the Pacto por México—an informal agreement in which the major parties agreed to promote reforms in the judicial system, national security, the education system, and the energy and business sectors, with an emphasis on increasing competition within the latter two. It was signed by all three party leaders, although the PRD representative stated that his support did not reflect all sectors of his party. Many PRD members, including López Obrador, had already formed a new party called MORENA (Movement for National Regeneration) to reinvigorate the left.

The third major legislative development occurred on February 25, 2013, when the president signed into law a sweeping educational reform that called for a system of uniform standards for teacher hiring and promotion based on merit (for years teaching positions in some states could be bought or inherited), as well as the first census ever of Mexican schools,

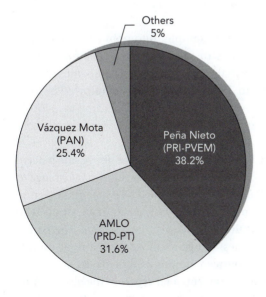

Presidential Election, 2012

teachers, and students. The law also extended the school day and implemented changes intended to boost the quality of education and graduation rates. The congress thus theoretically fulfilled one of the planks of the Pact for Mexico, pitting itself against the powerful teachers' union of 1.5 million members. The union, headed by Elba Esther Gordillo for more than twenty years, had just reelected her to another term in October 2012. On February 27, authorities arrested her and charged her with embezzling over one hundred fifty million dollars from union funds. Mexicans were surprised by the arrest but not by the charges of corruption. In exchange for union support, political leaders (both PRI and PAN) had looked the other way for years while Gordillo had purchased an airplane, bought a luxurious home on Coronado Island in the United States, deposited money in Swiss bank accounts, undergone a series of face lifts, and racked up an enormous credit card debt at Nieman-Marcus. A 2012 documentary, *De panzazo (Barely Passing)*, had excoriated the educational system, and the need for reform was widely recognized. The removal of "La Maestra," or *The Teacher*, signaled to many that the new government was serious about change, but others saw it as an old tactic of the PRI to enhance its power.

IMPLEMENTING CHANGE IN TROUBLED TIMES

Enrique Peña Nieto had pledged to improve competitiveness and growth across the Mexican economy. The country's two trillion dollar economy had become the fifteenth largest in the world (and the second in Latin America). Its trade under NAFTA had more than tripled and accounted for about 35 percent of GDP. More than three-quarters of its exports, primarily manufactured products, but also silver, fruits, vegetables, coffee, and cotton, went to the United States. Mexico was the world's eighth largest producer of oil, at nearly three million barrels per day, but production had been falling and PEMEX was seen as bureaucracy-ridden and inefficient. At the beginning of Peña Nieto's term, Mexican officials estimated that the economic reforms in the energy and telecommunications sectors could net 4 to 5 percent annual growth for the country.

Optimism ran high. In the state of Guanajuato, for example, automobile manufacturers and other multinationals employed many thousands of workers at pay rates higher than those of the border maquiladoras. Most all of the major US automotive companies opened up plants running along a corridor from Puebla to Zacatecas, eventually employing nearly a million workers, an increase of 40 percent in the industry. Mexico had become the world's fourth largest car exporter, having attracted substantial foreign investment with fiscally conservative policies that cut debt and inflation.

Nonetheless, the economy as a whole did not pick up, registering just above one percent GDP in 2013. In late 2013 and 2014, Peña Nieto pushed through a constitutional change to further open up the oil sector to private investment, breaking up PEMEX's state-run oil company's seventy-six-year-old monopoly. The reform, opposed by over half of Mexicans who saw it as a giveaway to foreigners, also included the gas and electricity sectors. The partial privatization of energy began to take place in stages. Offshore oil assets first went on sale in July 2015 but netted bids for only two out of fourteen available oil fields. By September 2015, Mexico's GDP growth had risen slightly to 2.1 percent, a far cry from the glowing predictions made at the beginning of Peña Nieto's term. Salaries were stagnant for many across

In a moment of optimism, *Time Magazine* featured the new Mexican President Peña Nieto on the February 24, 2014 cover.

A very different image of Peña Nieto from a November 14 protest against the killing of the students.

diverse sectors. Since nearly a third of the government's budget came from oil, the global decline in oil prices was one factor explaining poor economic performance, but structural issues such as low productivity, high inequality, a large informal sector employing over half of the workforce, the weak rule of law, and corruption also played a role.

By late 2014, the Peña Nieto administration faced serious charges of corruption and extra-judicial killings. On September 26, 2014, some one hundred students from the normal school in Ayotzinapa in the state of Guerrero, tried to commandeer several buses in the nearby city of Iguala to take them to Mexico City to participate in protests commemorating the Tlatelolco massacre of 1968. In the past, such actions by students were commonplace and without reprisals, but this time an appalling tragedy ensued. The buses were attacked by gunfire from municipal police. Some died on the buses and others were killed as they fled in terror. By dawn the next morning, 43 students had disappeared, not to be found to this day. The initial investigation by Mexico's attorney general attributed the disappearances to the actions of the mayor of Iguala and his wife (both with connections to drug traffickers). The mayor was alleged to have called in the local police who then turned the students over to a drug gang called the Guerreros Unidos. The heroin traffickers supposedly proceeded to kill the students at the edge of a garbage dump where they burned the bodies and then dumped the ashes into a nearby river.

The official report quickly came under fire as more details emerged about the involvement of other security forces (both state and federal). The search for the missing students turned up many unrelated mass graves; these events triggered protests in Guerrero and across Mexico, as well as international condemnation. In the following days, both the attorney general and the governor of Guerrero were forced to resign. On several occasions, hundreds of thousands of people marched in Mexico City in solidarity with the mostly poor rural families of the disappeared, demanding that their children be returned. They chanted: "The government took our sons alive; now we want them back alive." Federal officials resorted to the customary tactic of planting provocateurs in the crowds to carry out acts of violence intended to discredit the peaceful protests. When the arrests of local police and cartel members failed to assuage the protesters, the Mexican government acceded to demands of parents and the public by allowing the Inter-American Commission on Human Rights of the Organization of American States to send a commission of five world-recognized legal experts to investigate the case in

Hundreds of thousands participated in a series of marches in November and December of 2014 to protest the disappearances and murders in Iguala on September 26, 2017.

March 2015. They spent many months in Mexico during which they faced interference in their attempts to question federal and military officials, constant stonewalling, and intimidation.

Their five hundred-page report was presented on September 6, 2015. For six months the experts had interviewed survivors, the abductees' family members, many of the men and women who had been detained in the case, police and legal officials, and others. They conducted their own evidentiary or forensic examinations and studied the case files. The report was inconclusive in that it did not solve the mystery of the missing 43 students, but it did criticize the government investigations as flawed and, in effect, a cover up. But, it left unanswered the question of federal involvement, in particular by the army which has a crematorium at its nearby headquarters, the only facility in the area with the power to dispose of the bodies in the way the state claims.

Many Mexicans received the report with what the writer Francisco Goldman has called the folkloric cynicism that pervades the myriad unsolved cases of political murders. Still the families of the missing, along with other human rights advocates, did not cease their protests, and the horrific affair continued to dog the president and members of his government. In many ways, the Ayotzinapa case represents the untold number of Mexicans searching for disappeared loved ones, despairing that social justice will ever be achieved in a climate of entrenched institutional impunity. Ayotzinapa is just the tip of the iceberg. After the discovery of many mass graves in the region of Iguala during the search for the forty-three, recently others have been uncovered in Durango and other states. The 43 have become a symbol for the many murdered and disappeared in the last decade.

¡PORQUE VIVOS SE LOS LLEVARON, VIVOS LOS QUEREMOS!

Protesters erected this monument to the 43 on the Paseo de la Reforma and planted corn, beans, and other plants as an example of a familiar refrain at protests, "They tried to bury us. They didn't know we were seeds."

A month after the Ayotzinapa disappearances, Peña Nieto, whose popularity had sunk to a historic low, faced another scandal. In November, the respected and prize-winning investigative reporter, Carmen Aristegui who also hosts a show on CNN en Español, broke the story of a conflict of interest scandal in Peña Nietos's inner circle. The report centered on a seven-million dollar mansion (which became known as the Casa Blanca) in the luxurious Lomas de Chapultepec neighborhood, purchased by first lady Angélica Rivera on credit from a company owned by Juan Armando Hinojosa Cantú, which had received millions of dollars in contracts from Peña Nieto when he was governor of the state of Mexico. The company had also won a contract to build a high-speed train between Mexico City and Querétaro, about 120 miles northwest of the capital. Rivera later returned the mansion, and a government investigation subsequently found no wrongdoing by Peña Nieto or his wife, but the president apologized for the incident and the rail contract was canceled. In the maelstrom that followed, Aristegui was fired by MVS Communications because, she alleged, the owner Joaquín Vargas was pressured by the government to do so in retaliation against her. From other platforms, she continued to report on Peña Nieto, revealing that he had plagiarized much of his master's thesis.

The intimidation of a reporter was nothing new in Mexico. At least thirty-four journalists, covering crime, drug trafficking, corruption, and human rights, were murdered between 1992 and 2017. Ninety percent of these murders which occurred throughout Mexico went unsolved. One of the most dangerous places for journalists was the state of Veracruz where Governor Javier Duarte had ties to cocaine trafficking. Rubén Espinosa, the thirteenth victim of reporting on organized crime in Veracruz, was killed in the summer of 2015. After receiving repeated death threats, he had fled to hide in the apartment of his friend and social activist Nadia Vera, in Mexico City. She and three other women were shot in the head along with him; their bodies showed signs of torture and sexual violence. Despite no resolution of this case, Governor Duarte was later charged with embezzlement, drug trafficking, and murders of journalists, but he along with governors from Tamaulipas, Chihuahua, Quintana Roo, Durango, and Coahuila accused of graft and corruption have yet to be prosecuted in mid-2017.

While corruption at the highest levels continued to be fueled by narco dollars and drug-related crime including extortion rose, the homicide rate increased by 20 percent under Peña Nieto whose promises to increase security had not been realized. Emblematic of the government's inability to rein in the cartels, El Chapo (Joaquín Guzmán), boss of the Sinaloa cartel arrested in July 2015 for multi-million-dollar cocaine trafficking, escaped for the second time from a maximum security prison, allegedly through a tunnel under his cell. Most Mexicans actually surmised that he had walked out the front door of the prison. Recaptured by federal police and marines in January 2016, he was finally extradited to the United States a year later. The capture of El Chapo and other cartel kingpins did little to stop organized crime and extrajudicial killings by the government. Cartels splintered and new leaders jockeyed for control of drug production areas and trafficking routes. Violence spiked again; by the middle of 2017 the number of homicides surpassed the previous high recorded during the presidency of Calderón. In the quagmire of official collusion in the drug trade, only the naive wondered why the more than 2 billion dollars spent on fighting the drug trade since the Merida Initiative began in 2008 seemed to have had little influence in dismantling drug organizations that had managed to move into extractive industries like mining, diversifying even further. Nor did the visit of Pope Francis to Mexico in February 2016 do much to improve Mexico's image in the eyes of the world. As the pope addressed hundreds of thousands in the Mexico City slum of Ecatepec, home to Mexicans who had little access to health care and social services, newspapers reported that Mexico's poverty rate had risen to just under 50 percent. The pontiff's thinly veiled references to the government's failure to help the poor were matched on his visit to the border where he prayed for compassion for migrants, criticizing the US government for turning a blind eye to the human tragedy of forced migration.

More trouble surfaced in the summer of 2016 as teachers' strikes escalated in the state of Oaxaca. Teachers and their supporters had protested across the country when the reforms were proposed in 2013—in massive marches and the occupation of the Zócalo in Mexico City—but the resistance had slowed in the intervening years. Resurfacing in 2016 Oaxaca, teachers' protests over new certification requirements and low pay culminated in clashes with federal police forces that left nine people dead. Although most Mexicans favored major changes in a system riddled with favoritism and graft, in Oaxaca the strikes inspired sympathy from those who saw the education reforms as another attempt by Mexico City to marginalize the poor and deprive them of their rights and dignity.[1] Once again international observers decried excessive force and human rights violations directed at ethnic minorities and women. These actions seemed to fit a pattern of civil and military oppression that plagued the Peña Nieto government.

Pope Francis, an Argentine who is the first Latin American pope, visited Mexico in February 2016. Here he greets some of the many thousands who came to see him in Ecatepec in the State of Mexico.

---

1   See the assessment of Peña Nieto's "flagship" educational policy by reporter Nina Lakhani, "'The help never lasts': Why has Mexico's educational policy failed?" The Guardian, August 15, 2017.

Mexico City, however, provided the exception to the rule. Mexico's federal constitution was reformed in January of 2016 to allow for the emergence of Mexico City state (CDMX), an entity with its own congress, constitution, local governments, and fiscal rules, effectively making it the 32nd state of Mexico's federation. Up to this time, the official designation for Mexico City was Distrito Federal/D.F. (Federal District), a territory that hosted Mexico's federal administration but lacked the political rights of other Mexican states. The new entity is more autonomous from federal control. In the summer, elections were held in Mexico City to select sixty members of a constituent assembly who, along with forty members appointed by the congress, the president, and the mayor Miguel Mancera, debated and discussed provisions of a document drafted by experts. Approved in early 2017, the new constitution is scheduled to go into effect in September 2018. The charter reflects the social democratic orientation of Mexico City's dominant parties, the PRD and MORENA. Since the 1990s the leftist governments have legalized gay marriage, abortion, recreational marijuana, among other progressive, but contentious, issues.

At the national level, if some still held out hope for change four years into the Peña Nieto administration, the US election of Donald Trump in November 2016 threw another curve ball at Mexico. Trump had campaigned on an anti-immigrant platform, accusing undocumented Mexicans of rape and murder. He promised to build a "great wall" all along the Mexico-US border, to be paid for by Mexico, and to renegotiate NAFTA. The Mexican government felt a brief respite in December when its offers for drilling in deep water oil fields yielded contracts totally nearly 4 billion dollars. The privatization of telecommunications had brought some new competition (for example, AT&T entered the market controlled by Carlos Slim), but Televisa still dominated the television market.

By the time of Trump's inauguration in January 2017, the Mexican peso had suffered a devaluation from thirteeen pesos to the dollar in late 1914 to twenty pesos, given slow economic development and less probability of foreign investment. Efforts to defuse the "Trump" crisis before the US election had not paid off. Apparently on the advice of his finance minister, Luis Videgaray, Peña Nieto invited Trump to make a friendly visit to Mexico in August 2016. Mexicans were appalled by the invitation to the northern bully that only succeeded in making their president less popular (with ratings below 25 percent) and pleasing Trump's xenophobic followers. While Peña Nieto seemed awkward and submissive during the meeting, he continued to assert that Mexico would not pay for the wall although in less forceful language than that of former president Vicente Fox who tweeted that Mexico would not pay for the "f...ing" wall. As the war of words continued to escalate and Mexicans became more outraged, the president sacked his finance minister but subsequently named him as ambassador to the United States.

Trump's threats to deport millions of undocumented migrants, build a wall, and scrap NAFTA raised momentous concerns. If Mexico would not pay for the wall, Trump vowed to stop the flow of remittances from the United States to Mexico (which exceeded oil revenues in 2015) and to impose tariffs on Mexican imports in the United States. The costs of building a continuous wall (topographically unfeasible in some places) were estimated to fall between ten and fifteen billion dollars.

The US president had attacked NAFTA for months during the campaign, alleging that it was a disaster for "millions" of Americans who had lost their jobs when companies relocated

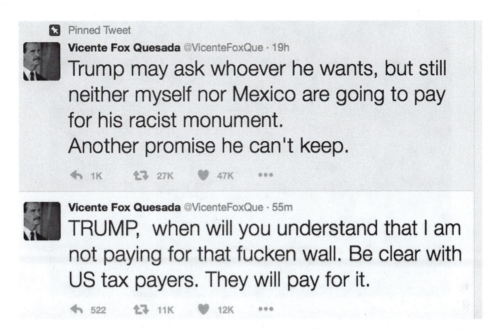

Pinned Tweet

Vicente Fox Quesada @VicenteFoxQue · 19h
Trump may ask whoever he wants, but still neither myself nor Mexico are going to pay for his racist monument.
Another promise he can't keep.

↩ 1K   ⟲ 27K   ♥ 47K   •••

Vicente Fox Quesada @VicenteFoxQue · 55m
TRUMP, when will you understand that I am not paying for that fucken wall. Be clear with US tax payers. They will pay for it.

↩ 522   ⟲ 11K   ♥ 12K   •••

Former Mexican President Vicente Fox uses Twitter to confront the new president of the United States in 2017.

to Mexico. Even before he was inaugurated, he put pressure on Carrier and Ford to cancel plans for new plants in Monterrey and San Luis Potosí although not all the manufacturers he threatened actually acceded. Economists on both sides of the border agreed that NAFTA had benefited consumers with lower prices, but Trump whipped up to a frenzy the issue of job losses in the United States and ignored the degree to which NAFTA had harmed small farmers in Mexico. How the deeply entwined Mexican, US, and Canadian manufacturing economies would be unraveled remained to be seen, but projections for direct foreign investment in Mexico were slashed.

On the issue of undocumented migrants, Trump moved early in his administration to reverse policies of the Obama presidency. Although Obama had deported millions of migrants, in 2012 he implemented DACA (the Dreamers' Act), the measure allowing migrant children not born in the United States (potentially 1.7 million) to remain, attend college, and obtain work permits on a deferred basis if they had no criminal record. Furthermore, he had restricted deportations to undocumented migrants with criminal records and recent border crossers. In spite of the fact that the number of Mexican migrants had dropped significantly, a huge influx of Central Americans fleeing violence in Honduras, Guatemala, and El Salvador flooded the border after 2014. They comprised primarily women and children, as well as unaccompanied minors whose parents were desperate to keep their children from rising violence acoss Central America that often included forced recruitment into gangs. Most requested political asylum allowing them to remain while their cases were investigated, but most asylum requests were denied.

Although Trump vacillated on what he would do about Dreamers, he initially indicated he would not deport them; their fate hung in the balance. However, he authorized ICE

While the Dreamers' Act brought hope to undocumented youth in the United States, it caused frustration for young people who recently returned or had been deported to Mexico. "Los Otros Dreamers" are organizing to support large numbers of return migrants as they struggle to access education, social services, and find jobs in their new country.

(Immigration and Customs Enforcement) agents to step up raids on all migrants, regardless of their time of residence or whether they had committed crimes. Sixty percent of the undocumented had lived and worked in the United States for more than a decade and more than 30 percent owned their homes. Moreover, they paid their taxes; a 2016 study demonstrates that undocumented workers contributed $11.74 billion in state and local tax revenue.[2] This initial move terrified many of the undocumented who feared the break-up of families. Some of them crossed the border into Canada where they would have a better chance to avoid deportation.

Urban centers throughout the United States, including New York, San Francisco, Los Angeles, Chicago, and Washington, DC, declared themselves to be "sanctuary" cities or counties where local law enforcement does not ask or report the immigration status of people they come into contact with. They also typically refuse requests from federal immigration authorities to detain undocumented immigrants apprehended for low-level offenses such as driving without a license. In addition, churches of all denominations began organizing to provide sanctuary although in this case they would not be sheltering Central Americans who had arrived during the wars of the 1980s, but rather undocumented migrants already contributing to their communities. The Mexican Ministry of Foreign Relations stepped up efforts to help in March of 2017 by establishing "defense centers" for immigrants in the fifty consulates across the United States.

---

2   Lisa Christensen Gee, et al., "Undocumented Immigrants' State & Local Tax Contributions," (Washington, DC, 2017), 2.

In Mexico, officials and newspapers denounced the xenophobia of the Trump policies, perhaps muting criticisms of Enrique Peña Nieto. Overall, however, the rebirth of the PRI had not brought major improvements to Mexico in the areas of social, economic, and political reform, instead signaling a renewal of authoritarianism and growing social inequity. In the mid-term elections of June 2015, the PRI barely retained its majority in the Chamber of Deputies in coalition with the Green Party while MORENA scored the largest gains. The elections, in which nearly half of the electorate voted, were marred by murders and violence throughout the country and increased intervention by local cartels. The PRI lost gubernatorial elections in seven states while a few independent candidates won governorships. The 2015 elections begged the question of continued PRI dominance in 2018 although in 2017 the party narrowly won the governorship of the state of Mexico where high levels of poverty and violence persisted.

As this book goes to press, Mexico's 130 million people live in a time of economic uncertainty with rising inflation. Many struggle below the poverty line, especially in rural areas. Unemployment and underemployment remain high. The world Organisation for Economic Cooperation and Development (OECD) surveys its thirty-five member countries regarding how satisfied citizens are with their lives. While Mexico falls near the bottom in income per capita, low in gender inequality, and below the middle in social inequality, it ranks just above the middle in life satisfaction. These statistics reflect hopefulness perhaps because some conditions have changed for the better. More people receive health care, and environmental groups work to promote sustainable development throughout the country. Civil society groups persist in promoting democratic and social justice reforms. The cultural resilience of Mexico's evolving pluriethnic, multicultural society continues to offer testimony to the idea that from tradition springs the passion for creativity.

RECOMMENDED FOR FURTHER STUDY

Anderson, Jill, and Nin Solís. *Los Otros Dreamers*. Mexico City, Mexico: Jill Anderson & Nin Solis, 2014.

Bender, Steven W. *Run for the Border: Vice and Virtue in the U.S.-Mexico Border Crossings*. New York: New York University Press, 2012.

Boullosa, Carmen, and Mike Wallace. *A Narco History: How the United States and Mexico Jointly Created the "Mexican Drug War"*. New York: OR Books, 2016.

Christensen Gee, Lisa, et al. "Undocumented Immigrant' State & Local Tax Contributions." Washington, DC: The Institute on Taxation & Economic Policy, 2017. Accessed March 14, 2017. http://www.itep.org/immigration/.

Dear, Michael. *Why Walls Won't Work: Repairing the US-Mexico Divide*. New York: Oxford University Press, 2013.

De Leon, Jason, with Michael Wells. *The Land of Open Graves: Living and Dying on the Migrant Trail*. Berkeley: University of California Press, 2015.

Espinosa, David. *Jesuit Student Groups, the Universidad Iberoamericana, and Political Resistance in Mexico, 1913–1979*. Albuquerque: University of New Mexico Press, 2014.

Foley, Neil. *Mexicans and the Making of America*. Cambridge, MA: Harvard University Press, 2014.

González de Bustamante, Celeste, and J. E. Relly. "Journalism in Times of Violence: Social Media Use by U.S. and Mexican Journalists Working in Northern Mexico." *Digital Journalism* 2/4 (2014): 507–523.

Hellman, Judith Adler. *The World of Mexican Migrants: The Rock and the Hard Place*. New York: New Press, 2008.

Hernández, Kelly Lytle. *Migra! A History of the U.S. Border Patrol*. Berkeley: University of California Press, 2010.

Hernández-León, Rubén. *Metropolitan Migrants: The Migration of Urban Mexicans to the United States*. Berkeley: University of California Press, 2008.

Holmes, Cameron W. *Organized Crime in Mexico: Assessing the Threat to North American Economies*. Lincoln: University of Nebraska Press, 2014.

Lakhani, Nina. "'The help that never comes': Why has Mexico's educational revolution failed?" *The Guardian*, August 15, 2017. Accessed August 28, 2017. https:/www.the guardian.com/inequality.

Miller, Todd. *Border Patrol Nation: Dispatches from the Front Lines of Homeland Security*. San Francisco, CA: City Lights Publishers, 2014.

Ochoa O'Leary, Ana, Colin Deeds, and Scott Whitefield, eds. *Uncharted Terrains: New Directions in Border Research Methodology, Ethics, and Practice*. Tucson: University of Arizona Press, 2013.

Overmyer-Velázquez, Mark, ed. *Beyond La Frontera: The History of México-U.S. Migration*. New York: Oxford University Press, 2011.

Payan, Tony, Kathleen Staudt, and Z. Anthony Kruszewski. *A War that Can't be Won: Binational Perspectives on the War on Drugs*. Tucson: University of Arizona Press, 2013.

Regan, Margaret. *The Death of Josseline: Immigration Stories from the Arizona Borderlands*. Boston, MA: Beacon Press, 2010.

————. *Detained and Deported: Stories of Immigrant Families Under Fire*. Boston, MA: Beacon Press, 2016.

Rubio-Goldsmith Raquel, Celestino Fernández, Jessie K. Finch, and Araceli Masterson-Algar, eds. *Migrant Deaths in the Arizona Desert: La vida no vale nada*. Tucson: University of Arizona Press, 2016.

Santa Ana, Otto, and Celeste González de Bustamante, eds. *Arizona Firestorm: Global Realities, National Media, and Provincial Politics*. Lanham, MD: Rowman & Littlefield Publishers, 2012.

Schwartzman, Kathleen C. *The Chicken Trail: Following Workers, Migrants, and Corporations across the Americas*. Ithaca, NY: Cornell University Press, 2013.

Segura, Denise A., and Patricia Zavella, eds. *Women and Migration in the U.S.-Mexico Borderlands: A Reader*. Durham, NC: Duke University Press, 2007.

Sheridan, Lynnaire M. *"I Know It's Dangerous:" Why Mexicans Risk their Lives to Cross the Border*. Tucson: University of Arizona Press, 2009.

Smith, Michael Peter, and Matt Bakker. *Citizenship across Borders: The Political Transnationalism of El Migrante*. Ithaca, NY: Cornell University Press, 2008.

Spener, David. *Clandestine Crossings: Migrants and Coyotes on the Texas-Mexico Border*. Ithaca, NY: Cornell University Press, 2010.

CHAPTER 40

SOCIETY AND CULTURE IN AN ERA OF CRISES AND GLOBAL ENTANGLEMENTS

In the 1980s, called the lost decade by some, Mexico faced acute challenges with the debt crisis and the 1985 earthquake. When the government failed to answer adequately after the earthquake, civil society emerged in Mexico as a powerful force. Neighborhood associations, women's groups, and other popular organizations stepped in to respond to grievances and assist in the organization and rebuilding of communities. Emblematic of community organizing was *Superbarrio* who dressed as a superhero and invigorated local residents and groups to pressure the government to take action and to participate in renewal projects. Following the tragedy of the earthquake, political assassinations and corruption led to serious divisions within the PRI. Cuauhtémoc Cárdenas and other leaders left the party to found the PRD (Party of the Democratic Revolution). The Zapatista movement emerged in the 1990s to confront inequities in Chiapas as well as other indigenous areas and to protest Salinas's signing of NAFTA. Taken together, these developments signaled greater popular participation as PRI hegemony declined. As the PRD took control in Mexico City, many saw a democratic opening. Their dreams seemed to come true when the PRI lost the presidential election to PAN's Vicente Fox in 2000. However, economic issues outside of Mexico's control, escalating drug wars, and other dark forces combined to create a new obstacle course for the people. As always, they responded with the historical resilience that seems inbred in the Mexican psyche.

Against the backdrop of killings, kidnappings, corruption, and drug cartels, Mexico City, with its 21.2 million inhabitants, presented a contrast, one in which women, some indigenous, played an impressive role in commerce. As heads of 80 percent of street vendor organizations, they dominated the informal economic sector which produces nearly a quarter of GDP. Their commercial associations solicit permissions from the government to sell merchandise in street markets, supplied by wholesalers in the neighborhoods of Tepito and La Merced. The largest of approximately one hundred street vendor organizations, with six thousand members, is the Asociación Legítima Cívica Comercial founded in 1982, and now run by Alejandra Barrios. In some cases, these associations have initiated self-produced

Superbarrio leads a protest in the Zócalo, after the 1985 earthquake.

housing developments. Street vendors are not immune from threats, corruption, and crime, but they do have collective backing.

Less fortunate are Mexico City's domestic workers who live with the families they work for or spend several hours each day traveling to and from the sprawling state of Mexico which surrounds the capital. Studies suggest that verbal, physical, and sexual abuse of domestic workers is common, and many are accused of stealing or dismissed unfairly. Paid under the table, they have no health benefits, and their low income perpetuates poverty. Attempts to unionize to secure a minimum wage and health care benefits are still in their infancy.

Despite legislation that mandates gender parity in electoral candidacies (50 percent of candidates from all parties in all federal and state elections must be women), gender inequality persisted in the political sphere where women hold 31.7 percent of political posts. At the national level, they hold nearly 43 percent of seats in the Chamber of Deputies and 36.7 percent in the Senate. Women have far exceeded parity in the field of education.

Perhaps one of the most disheartening factors for Mexico is that almost 50 percent of the population still falls into the poverty classification, earning less than fourteen dollars per day due to Mexico's poor infrastructure, inefficient bureaucracy, corruption, lack of education, and a plethora of other factors. Twelve million people work in the black market economy and have no social security or health benefits. Twenty-five percent of the total adult population fall into the underemployed category while another 10 percent are unemployed.

POPULATION

By 2017, the population of Mexico soared to 130 million, three-fourths of them urban dwellers. With 9 million inhabitants in 1980, Mexico City's greater metropolitan area had swelled to over 21 million by 2015 and covered 779 square miles. Like a giant magnet, it drew people from the countryside, adding hundreds of thousands to its population each year. In the process, the capital became a bit less uniquely Mexican and more like New York, Paris, or London. Those who enthusiastically approved of the changes argued that the nation's capital had at last become cosmopolitan; those who preferred the simplicity and charm of earlier days suggested that, as each colonial structure was torn down (despite

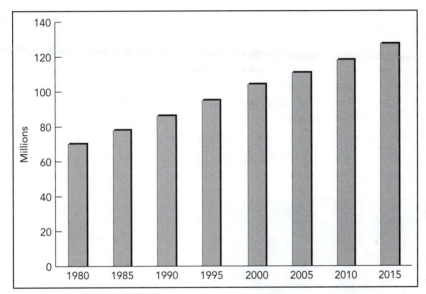

Mexican Population Growth, 1980–2015

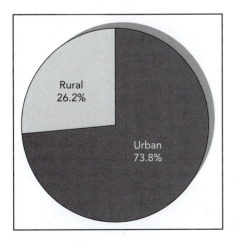

Urban-Rural Population Distribution, 2015

protective legislation) to make room for a skyscraper or a freeway, and as cellular phones, that quintessential yuppie symbol, rang during high mass at the main cathedral, the capital had—alas!—ceased to be Mexican.

Since the 1980s, the sprawling capital city with one-fifth of Mexico's total population has numbered among the ten largest metropolitan areas on earth, and until recently had the most acute traffic and smog problems in the Western Hemisphere. To relieve traffic congestion on the main north-south thoroughfare of Avenida Insurgentes, the Federal District government of Andrés Manuel López Obrador had inaugurated a rapid transit bus line in 2005. More Metrobus lines were added under Marcelo Ebrard and finally reached a total of five. The subway and buses transport approximately 15 million people a day. In 2010, Ebrard created a bike-sharing program called Ecobici, which expanded by 2015 to include four hundred forty bicycle stations, six thousand bicycles and one hundred thousand users making five thousand trips a day in an area of thirty-five square kilometers. The program not only contributes to reducing pollution, but it also offers exercise and recreation. During the years of PRD control, Mexico City has substantially decreased its greenhouse gas emissions but pollution continues to be a problem. In 2016, city officials declared ozone alerts several times and restricted the number of days automobiles could be driven. Nonetheless, in 2017, more than 3.5 million automobiles traveled the crowded streets daily.

Over the years, huge working-class housing projects in Mexico City brought hundreds of thousands together into closer proximity than they would have imagined possible. Crimes

Bicycle stands with Mexico City's ecobicis can be accessed in multiple sites around the central areas of the city.

On Sundays the capital's major avenue, *Paseo de la Reforma*, is closed to vehicular traffic so that families of cyclists can enjoy an outing. Here they circle around El Ángel, the statue that commemorates Mexico's independence heroes and is also a main gathering place for protesters and sports enthusiasts celebrating soccer victories.

averaged 242 robberies and thirteen murders a day in 1988, but under PRD management crime rates declined. By 2010, the murder rate was down 26 percent and amounted to one-fourth of that of Washington, DC. Despite the spiraling narco violence in other areas of Mexico, Mexico City's homicide rates have remained low, although kidnapping and extortion continue to be a problem. Nationally, however, in 2016 Mexico's homicides with firearms escalated to a new high, attributable primarily to organized crime.

Despite the difficulties of modernization, Mexico City has continued to dominate the entire country, with half of the country's industries and over 70 percent of daily banking transactions. Provincial Mexicans resent not only the exaggerated centralism emanating from Mexico City but also what they believe to be the arrogant attitudes of those from the nation's capital. They have coined the derogatory epithet *chilango* to describe them. While the provincial capitals were slightly more successful in retaining some of their local flavor, they, too, fell victim to the homogeneity of technological proficiency conditioned by electronic circuitry, pocket calculators, cell phones, and computers. Guadalajara, Monterrey, and Ciudad Juárez followed Mexico City along the path of seemingly uncontrollable pollution, and even the citizens of León, Guanajuato, worried about their health in 1995 when tens of thousands of birds migrating from Canada and the United States died after drinking contaminated water in a local reservoir. They had a right to be concerned as scientific tests soon revealed that human sewage flowing into the reservoir had turned it into a huge incubator for botulism bacteria.

1.	Valley of Mexico	20.89
2.	Guadalajara	4.80
3.	Monterrey	4.48
4.	Puebla	2.94
5.	Toluca	2.12
6.	Tijuana	1.84
7.	León	1.77
8.	Ciudad Juárez	1.39
9.	Torreón	1.28
10.	Querétaro	1.26
11.	San Luís Potosí	1.13
12.	Mérida	1.06
13.	Aguascalientes	1.04

METROPOLITAN AREAS OF MEXICO WITH POPULATIONS OVER A MILLION (2015)*

*In millions, rounded.

Five years later, a much more sinister and callous ecological disaster was reported in Michoacán. Loggers using chemical pesticides purposely killed 22 million migrating monarch butterflies. They reasoned that if there were no butterflies there would be no reason to continue setting aside a protected forest as the site of the annual butterfly migration.

Since the 1990s, Mexico has seen the proliferation of groups advocating environmental reforms. The environmental movement is strongest in Mexico City and the border area, but local communities throughout Mexico have mobilized to protect their forests and other natural resources. Cuatro Ciénegas in northern Mexico, one of the world's desert wetlands regions with huge biological diversity, is a focus of environmental efforts because it is under threat from stock breeders and tourists. Some of the worst environmental conditions exist in the northern Mexico border cities. In 2009, fully 10 percent of the border population lacked access to potable water and a third had no access to wastewater treatment. Air, water, and soils are heavily contaminated by industrial pollution, pesticides, and raw sewage.

Lack of clean water plagues the entire country, but Mexico City in particular faces a whole host of water issues. Always short of water, the city keeps drilling for more. The enormous volume of water that is pumped up from the diminishing aquifers causes sinking on an average of seven cm. per year. This problem is exacerbated by climate change. More heat and drought produce greater evaporation and mounting demand for water. The dilemma is whether to tap distant reservoirs at overwhelming costs or to further drain underground aquifers and accelerate the city's collapse. In the city's historic center, one can become dizzy just from looking at the tilting buildings with their slanted windows and doors that do not fit their frames.

Mexico City has been forced to import about 40 percent of its water from outside the valley, but it loses that much or more to leaking pipes and pilfering. The shortage of water is most acutely felt in the sprawling slums outside the city where some people get tap water only once a week and must have it brought in on trucks called *pipas*. They generally pay more for water than middle class consumers who have running water most of the time, a lamentable inequity. The effects of pumping water from surrounding areas is nowhere more visible than at Xochimilco on the southeastern edge of the city, all that remains of the Aztec canal system. Farmers grow corn, chard, rosemary and flowers on shrinking chinampa wetlands. On weekends, thousands of tourists picnic and party on brightly painted barges, or *trajineras*, that ply the canals. In early 2017, a twenty-feet-deep hole opened in the canal bed, draining even more water and causing more subsidence.

In addition, drainage problems are omnipresent and sewers often become blocked, whereupon the city's sewage divers go to work dredging up all manner of organic and inorganic paraphernalia, despite the fact that rhirteen thousand metric tons of garbage are collected daily from the streets. The city's grand canal built to move wastewater in the late nineteenth century is now inadequate to the task; thirty miles long and wide open, it stinks of methane and sulphuric acid. Finding solutions for Mexico City's environmental problems is a monumental task facing city planners, but a small contribution can be seen in the

On Avenida Chapultepec in Mexico City, a part of the ancient aqueduct is festooned with multi-tonal living greenery, giving it the appearance of a postmodern, cuboid serpent.

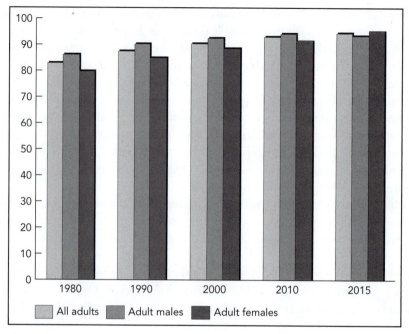

Adult Literacy, 1980–2015

vertical gardens and eco-sculptures that have sprung up to help clean the air and beautify the urban landscape.

One had to travel to a small village to escape the cacophony of big city sounds and to encounter some of the charm of an age now past, but there, behind the façade of what seemed quaint to the foreign eye, the disabilities of underdevelopment remained stark. While the great majority of rural children were in school by 2000, many of those schools had fewer than six grades and only one teacher. They most often served the lowest-income children in Mexico in facilities that lacked even the basic elements for classrooms such as blackboards, desks, and lights. Although improvements have been made in the past decades, rural schools still lack microscopes and computers and are unable to provide quality math and science education; their dropout rates remain high. While Mexico's overall adult literacy had grown to 95 percent by 2015, indigenous literacy lagged behind. Anthropologists concerned with preserving Indian languages applaud the fact that approximately 6.7 million Mexicans still speak their native tongues.

LEISURE AND SPORT

Mexico City is going through a period of transformation. Political changes in the governance of the city can be seen in massive construction projects, rebranding the city in the new signature pink, while tourist facilities multiply. The *New York Times*, with Carlos Slim as its largest individual shareholder, named Mexico City the number one tourist destination of 2016, and tourists have taken notice. Open-top buses ferry tourists to the major museums, public plazas, and other essential attractions. For example, one of these is themed for the lucha libre, having added a night at the Arena de México to the schedule. Festivals, in general, are ubiquitous throughout Mexico, held to celebrate an enormous variety of religious and civic themes, ranging from saints' days and the Día de los Muertos (Day of the Dead) to patriotic holidays inculcated by post-revolutionary leaders. In November 2016, a uniquely

Open-top tour buses are seen all over Mexico City.

The Day of the Dead parade was held on October 29, 2016 in Mexico City, with set pieces from *Spectre* prominently featured.

alien Día de los Muertos procession made its way through the major avenues of the capital toward the Zócalo. The parade, designed to attract tourists, was inspired by the one featured in the James Bond movie *Spectre* the year before. It drew mixed reactions from locals, but no one could deny that this celebration, with the popular, elaborate, public altars to celebrate the dead created each year by businesses, museums, and government offices, has become exceedingly eclectic, mixing indigenous, Catholic, and modern traditions.

While much early Mexican rock was unashamedly derivative (one scholar aptly termed it "Refried Elvis"), it eventually developed distinctive expressions that mixed pop music with traditional forms like *ranchera, banda,* and *norteña.* Along with *rocanrol* came the disco, where salsa and other Latin music coexisted with newer fads. The 2006 Avándaro festival included groups like Café Tacuba, Jaguares, Maldita Vecindad, and Maná. A 2012 film, *Hecho en México,* offers a cinematic mixture of original songs (folk, traditional, and popular), as well as insights from the most iconic artists and performers of contemporary Mexico, including Alejandro

Fantastical creatures called *alebrijes* scrape the treetops and glower over passersby on the Day of the Dead in Mexico City.

Fernández. Popular singers like Thalía, Luis Miguel, Paulina Rubio, Gloria Trevi and Julieta Venegas are well-known outside of Mexico, in part because of their exposure to US audiences in the expanding Spanish-language television networks. Univisión, which gets much of its programming from Mexico's Televisa, became the fifth largest television network in the United States by 2006. The annual Latin Grammy Awards demonstrate the extent to which cultural flows have crossed borders in both directions, bringing attention to many Mexican artists.

Lila Downs, the award-winning Mexican American singer/songwriter who has Zapotec ancestry, incorporates indigenous Mexican influences into her music. *Música norteña* is also highly prized across borders, popularized by such groups as Los Tucanes de Tijuana and Los Tigres del Norte (especially known for *narcocorridos*). 2012 marked the death of Chavela Vargas, a legend in Mexican music (even though she was actually born in Costa Rica). She performed Mexican ranchera songs and other popular genres of Latin American music over a seventy-year period. Her professional career was launched with the support of José Alfredo Jiménez, perhaps the foremost singer/songwriter of Mexican ranchera music. His compositions have been performed for generations by Chavela and many of the groups mentioned above. Juan Gabriel, whose popular music crossed genres, died in 2016. Known to his many fans as JuanGa and "El Divo de Juárez," he was a songwriter and performer, the first popular musician to have his own concert at the Palace of Fine Arts. He was an inspiration to many as he played with gender and sexuality norms, refusing to give in to traditional ideas about masculinity and heteronormative behaviors.

In the twenty-first century, Mexico is known the world over for its filmmakers and actors even if big screen film production in Mexico itself has somewhat subsided. In 2010, Mexico ranked fifth in the world in cinema attendance. Eight-screen multiplexes have squeezed out many independent movie theaters, and there is a huge market for movie DVDs, primarily pirated and sold in street stalls all over Mexico. After three decades of declining interest on the part of producers or audiences, the 1990s saw a resurgence in Mexican film, known internationally as the new wave, or the New Mexican Cinema. El Instituto Mexicano de Cinematografía, (IMCINE), established in 1983, provided scant support for movies until the early 1990s when a series of gifted directors began producing films that appealed to Mexican and international audiences. Among them are Alfonso Arau (whose 1991 *Como agua para chocolate* was an international success), Francisco Athié, Luis Mandoki, and the trio known as the *tres amigos*—Guillermo del Toro, Alfonso Cuarón, and Alejandro González Iñárritu. While the world of film directing is remarkably male dominated in Mexico and around the world, directors like Marisa Sistach, Maria Novarro, and Dana Rotberg also shaped the development of the new wave.

The Tres Amigos offer testimony to both the success of the new wave in and beyond Mexico and the limitations of the Mexican film industry. Cuarón and Iñárritu made their names in Mexico directing films for a national audience using international techniques, while del Toro is best known for his work in the horror genre. His first feature-length film was *Cronos* (1993), a gory vampire narrative, now a cult classic of the category. Cuarón's 2001 film *Y tu mamá también* and *Amores Perros* (2003) directed by Iñárritu flouted the Golden Age focus on revolutionary-era mexicanidad. The first features a road trip by two college-aged boys (played by Diego Luna and Gael García Bernal) that serves as a dual coming of age story

The *tres amigos* in 2007.

Diego Luna and Gael García Bernal at the Golden Globes in 2017. Both actors got their start in telenovelas, were an important part of the new wave cinema in the early 2000s, and now are international stars. Luna starred in the recent *Star Wars* prequel *Rogue One*.

for the boys and for Mexico as it entered a new political chapter in 2000. The latter investigates class difference in Mexico City through the stories of three people all brought together in a car accident. After their initial successes in Mexico, Cuarón and Iñárritu made their way to Hollywood where del Toro had a long-established career as a special effects make-up artist in the horror genre. There they branched out to craft films in US and European contexts, for example, Cuarón's *Harry Potter and the Prisoner of Azkaban* (2004) and *Gravity* (2013), Iñárritu's *Birdman* (2014) and *The Revenant* (2015), along with del Toro's films in the *Hellboy* franchise. Mexicans proudly claim these films, made for international audiences, and cheer when these directors win major awards for their work. For the first time in many years, in 2017 Cuarón returned to film a family drama set in Mexico City called *Roma*.

Movies and television for a Mexican market are still thriving, despite less support from government agencies. A particular favorite was the 2013 *Nosotros los Nobles* that told the story of a *fresa* (Mexican slang for superficial upper middle class "preppies") family patriarch who forces his children to do without his money and work for their keep. The popular comedy,

Nosotros los Nobles is one of the most popular Mexican films of all time.

one of the highest grossing Mexican films of all time, launched the careers of its leads: Karla Souza in Mexican films and a US television series, and Luis Gerardo Méndez who stars in *Club de Cuervos*, Netflix's first original series for the Mexican market. Streaming services are growing in Mexico, with Netflix enlarging the catalog of original Mexican series and other content that includes an expanding Korean selection for this growing immigrant population, while Televisa launched BLIM in 2016 for the Latin American market. BLIM, despite providing the only access to a huge catalog of Televisa-produced *telenovelas* (the Latin American version of US soap operas), has had little success against the bigger international providers. Telenovelas filmed across Latin America continue to draw large audiences in Mexico. The current First Lady of Mexico, Angélica Rivera, got her start as an actor in telenovelas; she is often referred to as "la Gaviota" after her character in the 2007 *Destilando amor* set in the tequila-producing region of Jalisco.

Televisa, the politically affiliated source of much criticism in the 2012 elections, dominated Mexican television for decades, but finally got a rival of sorts when TV Azteca was privatized in 1993. Since then cable television networks have moved into Mexico, making US and other foreign programs and networks available, including CNN, BBC, HBO, and even the NFL Network. Mexican children are treated not only to Disney productions but also to *Bob Esponja (Spongebob Squarepants)* and *Dora la Exploradora*, while the rest of the family watch *Los Simpson*. Some of the cable networks and both Televisa and Azteca feature reruns of American television series, but they also produce many original news, variety, and sports shows, in addition to the most popular genre, telenovelas. The latter fall into

Angélica Rivera as the character "la Gaviota" in the telenovela *Destilando amor*, before she married Enrique Peña Nieto.

several subgenres, including the historical romance, the teen drama, and the pop music story. Perhaps the most popular is the working-class melodrama, which typically features a poor young woman falling in love with a wealthy man whose haughty family spurns her. Beginning in the 1990s, Televisa found a huge market for its telenovelas in Eastern Europe and Asia. More recently telenovelas have aired social criticism, addressing themes of poverty, political corruption, drug smuggling, and immigration. In addition, Mexico's National University and its Polytechnic Institute produce cultural and educational programs on their own networks.

Sports continued to offer diversion, predominantly in soccer. Mexico has qualified consecutively since 1994 for the World Cup competition, making it one of six countries to do so. The Mexico national team, along with Brazil and Germany, are the only nations to make it out of the group stage over the last six world cups. In terms of success, Mexico reached the quarter-finals in both the 1970 and 1986 world cups, both of which were staged on Mexican soil. The Tricolor won the Olympic gold medal in 2012 (London) but disappointed its fans in the 2014 World Cup and the 2016 Río Olympics. Top Mexican players recruited by European teams include Hugo Sánchez, Rafa Márquez, Guillermo Ochoa, and Javier Hernández (Chicharito).

The Internet has been eagerly embraced in Mexico, which counted 60 million users by 2016. Video games are another source of entertainment; a recent study showed that nearly a fourth of Mexicans spent half of their leisure time playing them. Internet cafes are found everywhere. By 2015, 80 percent of the population owned mobile phones while only 40 percent possessed landlines. Rural areas, where few wired telephones exist, are better served by

A popular meme superimposed Guillermo Ochoa's face on the infamous *Time Magazine* cover after his performance at the 2014 World Cup. Goalie Ochoa was named "man of the match" in their semifinal loss to the Dutch. Mexicans still lament the loss with the cry "no era penal," or "that was no penalty!"

cell phones, heavily used to link migrants with their families. Three-quarters of the mobile phone market has been controlled by América Movil (Telcel in Mexico), the multinational company owned by Carlos Slim Helú. As opposed to the high rates charged by his company Telmex, América Movil offers relatively cheap fixed plans and has concentrated on attracting customers en masse, but the new telecommunications reform has allowed competition from AT&T and other providers. Mexico and the USA are closely linked by telephone. More than 90 percent of the international calls from Mexico go to the United States whereas roughly 13 percent of all US international calls go to Mexico. Cell-phone users are ubiquitous on the streets, in restaurants, and more annoyingly in the audiences at public performances.

Yet, according to one newspaper commentator, as a means of communication the telephone is very cold (*muy frío*) and not the most important. In an amusing 2007 editorial in *La Reforma*, cultural critic Juan Villoro maintained that in Mexico the principal means of communication is the *comida*, the main "midday" meal. Other forms of communication are important only for arranging the comida, which is rarely served before 3:00 p.m., lasts at least two hours, and often spills over into dinner and breakfast. The comida is only authentic when performed in the company of others: it is the venue for conducting business most efficiently and certainly in the most civilized manner. According to Villoro, "The only way to reach an agreement—either emotional or professional—involves sharing the table from the aperitif (tequila) to the after-dinner liqueur. Phone calls and e-mails are simply attempts to get to the moment when the dish of maguey worms means that we have begun to understand each other. . . . In some exotic countries the main meal is considered a necessity or a delight. In Mexico it's virtually a legal act. We only know that someone is making a deal or really cares for us if it happens when our mouths are deliciously full."[1]

Mexicans are funny. As in humorous. Humor is central to daily interactions, cultural expressions, and political critique. For example, the *albur* is a complicated form of word play, pun, or double entendre that often has a sexual connotation and Mexicans, men and women alike, constantly try to one-up each other with better albures. While these tend to be a competition among friends, political jokes are a form of public resistance. Mexican political scientist Samuel Schmidt demonstrates that these jokes often direct pointed attacks at politicians and public figures, serving as an outlet for protest not always afforded by the political establishment. One such joke during the Fox sexenio went:

In a message to the nation, Fox says, "Citizens, I have good news and bad news for you."

"What's the good news?"
"Our foreign debt has been settled."
"And the bad news?"
"We have seventy-two hours to leave the country."[2]

Jokes and political cartoons, while still common, have given way to a new generation of memes and hashtags. For example, Mexicans took great pleasure in mocking the government

---

1   "El teléfono es muy frío," *La Reforma*, June 1, 2007.
2   Quoted in Samuel Schmidt, *Seriously Funny: Mexican Political Jokes as Social Resistance*. trans. by Adam Schmidt (Tucson, AZ, 2014), 206.

Two of the many memes that mocked the Mexican President and First Lady during their official visit to the United Kingdom, March 2015. The first, "What kind of gel do these dudes use?" and the second, "Hey Liz: what's the name of the builder who gave you this palace?" (in reference to the Casa Blanca scandal).

when El Chapo escaped for a second time in 2015; many memes suggested that the mayor of Mexico City should hire the workers who built the escape tunnel to fix the newest Mexico City metro line that had been plagued with problems since its opening. Memes circulate through Twitter and Facebook, finding their most popular targets in President Peña Nieto and his wife, other Mexican politicians, and of course Donald Trump. It should also be noted that piñata makers got a boon when they started crafting Trump effigies.

Their political humor notwithstanding, many Mexicans are also religious, as evidenced by the mass turnouts for Pope Francis's visit in 2016. After Vatican II, elements of the church hierarchy and countless parish priests became more outspoken in favor of social reform. Mexican Catholics are eclectic in their ties to the church, and some certainly chose to ignore Mexican Archbishop Norberto Rivera Carrera's warnings in 2007 about the sin of abortion or same-sex marriage, for example. They could not overlook the scandal that beset the Mexican church at the turn of the twenty-first century. Allegations began to surface about the improprieties and sexual abuse perpetrated by Marcial Maciel Degollado who had founded a Mexican order, the Legionaries of Christ, in 1941. While Maciel was protected by Pope John Paul II, the charges were suppressed until they became so public in 2005 that Pope Benedict XVI ordered the priest to resign and offered a public apology from the Vatican for his crimes. Not all Mexicans are Catholics of course. In the 2010 census, 83 percent of Mexicans self-identified as Catholic, about 12 percent as Protestant, Jewish, or Islamic, and 5 percent as having no religion. Many who said they were Catholic did not practice the religion, and thousands have left the church: at least 4 million people between 2000 and 2015.

Despite the anticlericalism embodied in revolutionary ideology, the faithful continued their pilgrimage to the Basílica de Guadalupe in the postwar period. Today you can watch masses through the "Transmisiones en vivo" from their webpage.

SCHOLARSHIP AND INTELLECTUAL ACTIVISM

It took a long time for professional, less polemical scholarship to reach the public, but it finally did in dramatic fashion late in 1992. Mexico's mandatory school textbooks underwent a major revision. Porfirio Díaz emerged not as a despotic megalomaniac but as a positive actor in the creation of modern Mexico. The revolutionary icons on the other hand, especially Emiliano Zapata, surfaced as rather less heroic and not entirely free of warts. In general harmony with the post-revolutionary political ethic, the textbooks no longer attributed Mexico's serious national problems solely to the imperialistic United States. For the first time, Mexican schoolchildren were allowed to read a reasonable and accurate accounting of what happened on October 2, 1968, at Tlatelolco. They deserved to know. But the textbook revisions were controversial as many recoiled at the thought that Mexican history should be rewritten to harmonize with the contemporary political and economic proclivities. In the most recent reincarnation of the idea that historical interpretation reflects the social milieu of the writer, the Fox administration proposed new changes in school curriculum that de-emphasized the study of Mexico's past in favor of texts that would point Mexico in a more modern, technological direction.

Contributing to the maturation of historical scholarship over time, beginning in 1949 Mexican historians came together with their US, Canadian, and European counterparts in conferences held every four years to discuss the state of the field. In 2010, the thirteenth meeting convened in Querétaro to exchange ideas during the bicentennial of Mexico's revolution for independence and the centennial of the Mexican revolution. Aspiring historians submitted the fruits of their research to one another, tested new ideas, pinpointed lacunae, and disputed the latest revisionist interpretations. The Mexican government had been preparing for years to celebrate these centenaries, spending millions of dollars in revitalizing historical places, staging pageantry, and subsidizing research and publication on these watersheds in Mexican history. The historical vision of the PAN governments did not match the revolutionary ideology so long espoused by the PRI. Symbols of national identity were fiercely contested along civil, religious, moral, and philosophical lines, confirming that no one had a monopoly on defining *lo mexicano* in the twenty-first century.

In a move that facilitated access to original historical sources, in 2002 during the presidency of Vicente Fox, a new transparency law changed the political landscape in Mexico. In fact, social science scholars have argued that the Mexican law became a global model for good government practice. For historians, it produced the opening of the collection of documents from the Dirección Federal de Seguridad (DFS) that shed new light on post-World War II Mexico, especially for the 1960s and 1970s. Colloquially known as the secret police, the intelligence agency went through multiple iterations during the twentieth century, becoming what is today known as Centro de Investigación y Seguridad Nacional (CISEN). Initially modeled after the FBI, the agents and their informants were deployed to spy on Mexican citizens, a practice that was ramped up in the 1970s. Political analyst Sergio Aguayo, who gained access to the collection before it officially opened to researchers in 2002, estimated that the one hundred twenty DFS agents in 1965 had swelled to approximately three thousand in 1981, with ten thousand informants. The agency relied on journalists, politicians, businessmen, and academics as informers, and collected substantial raw data on Mexican citizens. Most of those surveilled were involved in a spectrum of reformist and left-leaning political movements considered subversive by the government; they included student activists, Communist party members, intellectuals, and indigenous rights activists. The documents in this collection, available to researchers for twelve years, have been used to write critically revealing historical studies.

In 2012, with the return of the PRI to the presidency, the transparency law was amended. New regulations, under the guise of privacy protections, require that all CISEN documents be redacted of personal information for seventy years. While it is not unusual for governments to establish a period of time before they release documents, reclassifying and redacting documents that had been accessible for twelve years reminded many in Mexico of the censorship of earlier PRI administrations. While researchers are allowed to see redacted versions, individual Mexican citizens can go to the National Archive to see their own files. In late 2016, Elena Poniatowska did just this, consulting her file of one hundred eighty-three pages that included reports on speeches she gave, protests she attended, and analysis of her writings. She commented, "I never thought that going to a student protest was a sin." In 2017, the PRI intends to further restrict access to collections of sources critical to writing the history of post-World War II Mexico by enacting a new law governing archives. The twelve-year window of transparency opened under the PAN may well collapse further as the

Elena Poniatowska, well known Mexican writer and social critic, consulted her own DFS file at the National Archive in November 2016.

PRI tries to obscure past missteps and rights violations. More alarming still, in June 2017, Mexican media outlets reported that the Peña Nieto government was violating the law by using sophisticated surveillance software to spy on prominent journalists and activists critical of the government.

Among the most widely read authors at the turn of the century were the cultural critics Elena Poniatowska and Carlos Monsiváis, writing in the *crónica* style that crosses the borders between fiction and nonfiction. Poniatowska has continued to focus on social and human rights issues, especially those involving women and the poor, in her many novels and essays. She has won several international literary awards, including Spain's 2013 Cervantes award for lifetime literary achievement, the fourth woman to do so. Monsiváis, who garnered Mexico's prestigious Juan Rulfo literary prize in 2006, has been described as a kind of "public trickster" who brilliantly described urban popular culture and sought to empower his readers through his critiques of official policies.

Carlos Monsiváis died in 2010, followed by Carlos Fuentes in 2012, and José Emilio Pacheco in 2014, leaving few literary giants to compellingly carry on the tradition of political satire and cultural commentary. Elena Poniatowska continues to write on Mexico's twentieth century cultural legacy, penning biographies and memoirs about intellectuals, literary figures, and artists whom she knew, including her husband, the astronomer Guillermo Haro. Also among the leading contemporary creative writers are the essayist and novelist Juan Villoro and crime fiction writer Paco Ignacio Taibo II. Sub-Comandante Marcos once again captured public attention in 2004 when he offered Taibo the opportunity to coauthor a novel with him. Entitled *Muertos incómodos*, the novel was published in installments in the leftist newspaper *La Jornada* as the authors alternated chapters in this crime novel featuring a Zapatista detective and a cynical private investigator who expose injustices.

CULTURAL HYBRIDITIES

US cultural influences overwhelmed Mexico in the postwar period, for better or worse. To the chagrin of those who prize traditional Hispanic values, advertisements and commercials assumed a distinct US flavor, and hundreds of Anglicisms invaded the language. Somehow *el jit, el jonron, el extra inin* seemed more palatable than *okay, bay-bay, chance, jipi, biznes, parquear, lonche,* and *Twittear*. Nobody could explain why Mexican teenagers in Gap jeans began calling up their *suiti* for a date. Linguistic syncretism bequeathed its share of amusing redundancies, such as the cocktail lounge that displayed a sign reading "4:00–5:00, La Hora de Happy Hour" and the tourist restaurant whose menu proudly advertised "Chile con Carne with Meat." Beer supplanted pulque as the favorite alcoholic drink of the lower classes, while Scotch whisky took the place of cognac among the middle and upper classes, only to be rivaled by a return to expensive tequila as a status symbol. For the first time, Halloween, complete with plastic pumpkins and trick-or-treating, made inroads into Mexico's traditional celebration of the Day of the Dead, and hand-carved folk toys lost favor to the latest imported crazes.

American-style football did not really challenge the preeminence of soccer, but thousands of Mexicans became enthralled with professional football, telecast to Mexico City on

Sundays. The January 1988 spectacular Superbowl XX, between the Osos de Chicago and the Patriotas de Nueva Inglaterra especially captivated the Mexican sports fan. Mexican businessmen joined the Rotary and the Lions Club. Installment buying on Mexican versions of Visa and MasterCard made possible an orgy of consumption and placed families in a new kind of debt but gave them the opportunity to acquire furnishings and accoutrements for the home that would have been unusual two decades before. Supermercados with plastic packaging and individually priced items began to replace the traditional marketplace in all the larger cities. Stocked with corn flakes, Campbell's soup, Gatorade, Cap'n Crunch cereal, and Coca-Cola, Mexican supermarkets were distinguished from their North American counterparts only by the absence of huge parking lots. Upscale supermarkets emerged to offer elites a variety of international products, and smaller stores catered to the growing Asian market. Mexico's Zona Rosa, after losing its cachet for the rich, is again an up and coming neighborhood where many Koreans have established communities and one can find a Korean grocery outlet or restaurant on every block, selling products like K-pop, imported cosmetics, and bimimbap.

Multinational chains carpeted Mexico City. Residents and tourists alike could rent a car from Avis, Hertz, Budget, or Thrifty; drive on Goodyear, Firestone, or Uniroyal tires to a fast-food outlet called Burger King, KFC, Subway, or Pizza Hut. When the McDonald's chain opened its first restaurant on the southern edge of the sprawling capital in October 1985, eight Mexico City policemen were kept busy for days directing traffic in front of the golden

Korean shops in the Zona Rosa.

arches. In 1992, in the most bizarre example of gastronomical entrepreneurship, one US corporation decided it could think of nothing better than to offer Mexicans an example of exquisite Mexican cuisine. Yes, Taco Bell opened its first Mexico City franchise, nearly gagging Mexicans. By the 1980s, however, Mexican products were being distributed in the United States. Pan Bimbo (originally a Mexican Wonder Bread clone) entered the US market in 1984, producing, distributing, and selling bread, tortillas, and Mexican snack food. Any US city of substantial Hispanic population today boasts supermarkets and *tiendas* that sell a variety of Mexican labels.

In the twenty-first century, no foreign import to Mexico could rival Wal-Mart, which operated over 1400 stores and restaurants. Having bought up several Mexican supermarket chains, it became Mexico's largest retailer and employer. Many Mexicans were outraged when Wal-Mart, despite loud protests, opened a store in San Juan Teotihuacán, less than a half-mile from the ancient "City of the Gods." Local retailers who decried the desecration that figuratively imposed Mickey Mouse on top of pyramids were forced out of business. Costco and Starbucks number among hundreds of recent additions to foreign retailers.

In 2010 UNESCO (United Nations Educational, Scientific and Cultural Organization) designated thirty-one Mexican locations on its list of World Heritage Sites and named a number of Mexican cultural traditions and expressions as part of its project on the Intangible Cultural Heritage of Humanity. Mariachi music, a variety of indigenous cultural practices and festivals, the Day of the Dead celebrations, and traditional Mexican cuisine appear on the list. The latter includes farm production, preparation, and cooking techniques. Food is ever-present in any Mexican city or village, with the smells of tacos, quesadillas, and grilled meat wafting through the streets while refreshing drinks of hot *atole* for breakfast or freshly-squeezed juice and fruit-flavored aguas can be purchased at corner stands.

Diversity and history abound in Mexican cuisine. The north is known for beef—grilled or dried and salted—while seafood dominates the fare of Veracruz along the Gulf coast, as well as Pacific port cities. Oaxaca and Puebla are known for *mole*, a sauce made of any number of ground ingredients (the name comes from the Spanish word *moler,* to grind), most famously including chocolate, but also chilies, spices, fruits, and even flowers, combined in a dark, rich sauce usually served with chicken or turkey. One must take care when ordering a *michelada*, a drink that features additions to beer. In Mexico City, it simply consists of lime with a salted rim, but in many places Worcestershire or hot sauce is added, while along the coast, shrimp might complement the thirst-quenching concoction! The diversity of Mexican food has also been recognized in the rarefied world of international haute cuisine. Mexican chef Mónica Patiño has received recognition as one of the top chefs in the country with high-end restaurants that serve Mexican food with international influences, and more modest eateries that serve the fresas and hipsters in affluent neighborhoods in Mexico City. Three Mexico City establishments made the list of the Fifty Best Restaurants in the World in 2016.

Mexican cuisine has taken on a life of its own well beyond the confines of national borders. Tacos, burritos, and fajitas, in a myriad of styles and forms, have long been available in places around the globe. Foreign chefs like Diana Kennedy and Rick Bayless played a significant role in popularizing high-end Mexican food—through cookbooks, television shows, and restaurants—in the United States. But, in their search for an "authentic" cuisine, they leave little space for a food culture that is constantly changing, within Mexico and beyond. Upscale restaurants from San Francisco to Copenhagen feature creative dishes that use cacao, cactus, prehispanic varieties of tomatoes, squash, and pumpkins, along with corn and chiles. Cultural critic Gustavo Arellano argues that the hard-shelled taco (which got its start at the Los Angeles cafe Cielito Lindo), Arizona-favorite Sonora Dogs, and the food trucks serving Korean-Mexican fusion tacos are as Mexican as *nopales, huitlacoche,* and avocados.

Tequila, mezcal, and pulque, all made from the agave plant but processed differently, have a long and storied history in Mexico. Before the arrival of the Spaniards, they were produced largely for ritual consumption by elites. In the colonial period, the colonizers imposed prohibitions designed to curb the lower classes from drinking so much; one such attempt required that pulquerías have no more than three walls and no chairs to ensure that no one got too comfortable and that officials could keep watch. During the nineteenth century, snobby Porfirians agreed that such drinks were beneath their sophisticated tastes, but this changed with the Mexican revolution. Tequila, made in the region of Jalisco and named after the town, became symbolically linked with the idea of mexicanidad and ideals of social

A late 1960s José Cuervo tequila advertisement for th United States market. Note the image of pyramid of Chichen Itza in the background.

justice. Pancho Villa, imagined as a hard-drinking revolutionary despite the fact that he was a teetotaler, came to be associated with tequila, linking this alcoholic drink with a certain kind of revolutionary masculinity. Amusingly, the 1999 edition of *The New American Bartender's Guide*, suggests that the original way to order a shot of tequila was to say "Tequila, Pancho Villa style, please."[3] Exports of tequilas and Mexican beers, grew steadily throughout the twentieth century; advertising campaigns in the United States elevated the minor Mexican holiday of Cinco de Mayo to a day dedicated to selling these beverages.

Mexican spirits have risen in popularity in the twenty-first century. In fact, mezcal and pulque have come back into fashion and are popular with fresas and hipsters alike. Bars in Mexico City serve artisanal, small batch versions of tequila and mezcal, while pulquerías that were once only found in working class barrios are now fashionable for middle class Mexicans and foreigners. Tourists can visit the Museo del Tequila y El Mezcal (MUTEM), built in 2010 as part of the refurbishment of the Plaza Garibaldi, famous for the mariachi groups who gather there. And just as tequila became a transnational product in the twentieth century, *mezcalerías* are popping up in major cities across the United States. The distribution and sale of tequila and mezcal are fraught with contradictions as locally produced versions from Jalisco, Oaxaca, and Durango struggle against large commercial enterprises. Dispute over regulation speaks to the new-found popularity of mezcal in the last twenty years; while tequila may epitomize mexicanidad for foreigners, Mexicans are finding their autonomous niche by drinking mezcal. As the saying goes, "Para todo mal, mezcal; para todo bien, tambien." (For everything bad, [drink] mezcal; for everything good, [do] the same).

The concept of the "raza cósmica" promulgated by José Vasconcelos in the 1920s proposing that the mestizos of Mexico combined the best of their indigenous and European heritage, has persisted as the primary image of Mexican ethnicity. Mexican society is often understood, by both Mexicans and foreigners, as largely homogeneous. However, this ignores the more than a million Afro-Mexicans or the waves of European, Middle Eastern, and Asian immigrants who began arriving in the nineteenth century. Today, it is difficult to count the number of immigrants living in Mexico as few are officially registered as permanent residents but rather extend their stay on generous tourist visas. For example, statistics from 2009 claimed that just over 260,000 foreigners resided in Mexico, but unofficially most sources agree that at least a million US citizens live or work in the country, not to mention at least an equal number who have emigrated from other parts of the world, like the Koreans mentioned above.

In 2015, for the first time the Mexican census included the category of Afro-Mexican. News outlets reported that this simple act prompted 1.4 million Mexican citizens to self-identify as being of African descent. While clearly not a discovery, it marked the first time in Mexican history that this population was acknowledged as part of the national fabric. Although scholars have devoted energy to understanding the populations of African descent in the colonial period, as slaves and free blacks, in militias and cofradías, and as a significant part of the labor force, these studies are absent for the nineteenth and twentieth centuries.

---

3   Quoted in Marie Sarita Gaytán, ¡Tequila! *Distilling the Spirit of Mexico* (Stanford, CA, 2014), 43.

Mexicans express their frustrations through graffiti throughout the country. In the first, the president is portrayed as Pinocchio, his nose grown long from too many lies (Mexico City); the second says, "Here we unleash the battle" (Oaxaca City); and finally the third portrays an iconic Lázaro Cárdenas taking a stand against the exorbitant rise in gas prices, called the "Gasolinazo," implemented at the start of 2017 by the federal government.

Mid-twentieth-century ethnographies of Afro-Mexicans along the coasts tended to impose ideas about blackness and African origins on populations that saw themselves as Mexican and prefer to identify as *moreno*. Mexicanidad leaves little room for the African component of this identity, but the UNESCO designation and activists who pushed for such a recognition in the federal census have brought the issue back into the nation's consciousness.

The task of reconciling Mexico's pluriethnic past in the twenty-first century became more complicated as scientists compiled data from the Mexico Genome Diversity Project that showed a stunning range of genetic diversity across the indigenous populations. One thing was certain, however: mexicanidad could no longer be summed up in the homogeneous myths of the revolution. The concepts of cultural hybridity and multiculturalism offered better fits for explaining the co-existence of traditional and modern practices and interpretations of culture, as well as the Mexican diaspora to the United States. However disparate their concepts of what it meant to be Mexican, the vision of the future for most was to create a more just and prosperous nation.

This ideal, however, remained a figment of the imagination. Unfortunately, the fresh experiments in democracy after 2000 have been frustrated by an entrenched legal and political culture resistant to change, no matter the party affiliation, by global economic factors beyond Mexico's control, and by the drug trade. The future is scarcely predictable, but the potential for overcoming these setbacks is vast as anyone familiar with the rich and complex history of Mexico cannot fail to appreciate.

RECOMMENDED FOR FURTHER STUDY

Arredondo, Isabel. *In Our Own Image: An Oral History of Mexican Female Filmmakers 1988–1994*. Translated by Mark Schafer, Jim Heinrich, Elissa Rashkin, and Isabel Arredondo. Plattsburgh, NY: Digital Commons @ SUNY Plattsburgh, 2012.

Arellano, Gustavo. *Taco USA: How Mexican Food Conquered America*. New York: Simon & Schuster, 2012.

Boyer, Christopher. *A Land between Waters: Environmental Histories of Modern Mexico*. Tucson: University of Arizona Press, 2012.

Bowen, Sarah. *Divided Spirits: Tequila, Mezcal, and the Politics of Production*. Berkeley: University of California, 2015.

Chorba, Carrie C. *Mexico, from Mestizo to Multicultural: National Identity and Recent Representations of the Conquest*. Nashville, TN: Vanderbilt University Press, 2007.

Corona, Ignacio, and Beth E. Jorgensen. *The Contemporary Mexican Chronicle: Theoretical Perspectives on the Liminal Genre*. Albany: State University of New York Press, 2002.

Davidson, Miriam. *Lives on the Line: Dispatches from the U.S.-Mexico Border*. Tucson: University of Arizona Press, 2000.

De la Dehesa, Rafael. *Queering the Public Sphere in Mexico and Brazil: Sexual Rights Movements in Emerging Democracies*. Durham, NC: Duke University Press, 2010.

Fitting, Elizabeth. *The Struggle for Maize: Campesinos, Workers, and Transgenic Corn in the Mexican Countryside*. Durham, NC: Duke University Press, 2011.

Gaytán, Marie Sarita. *¡Tequila! Distilling the Spirit of Mexico*. Stanford, CA: Stanford University Press, 2014.

Gilbert, Dennis. "Rewriting History: Salinas, Zedillo, and the 1992 Textbook Controversy." *Mexican Studies* 13/2 (1997): 271–98.

Gutiérrez, Natividad. *Nationalist Myths and Ethnic Identities: Indigenous Intellectuals and the Mexican State*. Lincoln: University of Nebraska Press, 1999.

Jorgensen, Beth E. *The Writings of Elena Poniatowska: Emerging Dialogues*. Austin: University of Texas Press, 1994.

Joseph, Gilbert M., Anne Rubenstein, and Eric Zolov, eds. *Fragments of a Golden Age: The Politics of Culture in Mexico since 1940*. Durham, NC: Duke University Press, 2001.

Lewis, Laura. *Chocolate and Corn Flour: History, Race, and Place in the Making of "Black" Mexico*. Durham, NC: Duke University Press, 2012.

Lomnitz, Claudio. *Death and the Idea of Mexico*. Brooklyn, NY: Zone Books, 2005.

Martin, Michael T., Bruce Paddington, and Francisco Athié. "Mexican Cinema and the 'Generation of the 1990s' Filmmakers: A Conversation with Francisco Athié." *Framework: The Journal of Cinema and Media* 45/1 (Spring 2004): 115–128.

McCrossen, Alexis. *Land of Necessity: Consumer Culture in the United States–Mexico Borderlands*. Durham, NC: Duke University Press, 2009.

Padilla, Tanalís, and Louise E. Walker. "In the Archives: History and Politics." *Journal of Iberian and Latin American Research* 19/1 (2013): 1–10.

Pierce, Gretchen, and Áurea Toxqui, eds. *Alcohol in Latin America: A Social and Cultural History*. Tucson, University of Arizona, 2014.

Pilcher, Jeffrey. *Planet Taco: A Global History of Mexican Food*. New York: Oxford University Press, 2012.

Rabasa, José. *Without History: Subaltern Studies, The Zapatista Insurgency, and the Specter of History*. Pittsburgh, PA: University of Pittsburgh Press, 2010.

Ragland, Cathy. *Música Norteña: Mexican Migrants Creating a Nation between Nations*. Philadelphia, PA: Temple University Press, 2009.

Rubenstein, Anne. "Mass Media and Popular Culture in the Postrevolutionary Era." In *The Oxford History of Mexico*, edited by Michael C. Meyer and William H. Beezley, 598–633. New York: Oxford University Press, rev. 2010.

Shaw, Deborah. *The Three Amigos: The Transnational Filmmaking of Guillermo del Toro, Alejandro González Iñárritu and Alfonso Cuarón*. Manchester, UK: Manchester University Press, 2013.

Schmidt, Samuel. *Seriously Funny: Mexican Political Jokes as Social Resistance*. Translated by Adam Schmidt. Tucson: University of Arizona Press, 2014.

Tutino, John, ed. *Mexico and Mexicans in the Making of the United States*. Austin: University of Texas Press, 2012.

Van Young, Eric. *Writing Mexican History*. Stanford, CA: Stanford University Press, 2012.

APPENDIX

MEXICAN HEADS OF STATE

The Aztecs

Acamapichtli	1372–91
Huitzilíhuitl	1391–1417
Chimalpopoca	1417–27
Itzcóatl	1427–40
Moctezuma Ilhuicamina (Moctezuma I)	1440–68
Axayácatl	1468–81
Tizoc	1481–86
Ahuítzotl	1486–1502
Moctezuma Xocoyótzin (Moctezuma II)	1502–June 1520
Cuitláhuac	June–October 1520
Cuauhtémoc	October 1520–August 1521

Immediate Post-Conquest Period

Fernando Cortés	1521–24
Crown Officials	1524–26
Residencia Judges	1526–28
First Audiencia	1528–31
Second Audiencia	1531–35

Viceroys of the Colonial Period

Antonio de Mendoza	1535–50
Luis de Velasco (the elder)	1550–64

Source: Adapted from Richard E. Greenleaf and Michael C. Meyer, eds., *Research in Mexican History: Topics, Methodology, Sources and a Practical Guide to Field Research* (Lincoln, 1973), 221–24; and David P. Henige, *Colonial Governors from the Fifteenth Century to the Present* (Madison, 1970), 312–13.

Gastón de Peralta	1566–68
Martín Enríquez de Almanza	1568–80
Lorenzo Suárez de Mendoza	1580–83
Luis de Villanueva y Zapata	1582–83
Pedro Moya de Contreras	1584–85
Alvaro Manrique de Zúñiga	1585–90
Luis de Velasco (the younger)	1590–95
Gaspar de Zúñiga y Acevedo	1595–1603
Juan Manuel de Mendoza y Luna	1603–07
Luis de Velasco (the younger)	1607–11
Fray Francisco García Guerra	1611–12
Diego Fernández de Córdoba	1612–21
Diego Carrillo de Mendoza y Pimentel	1621–24
Rodrigo Pacheco y Osorio	1624–35
Lope Díaz de Armendáriz	1635–40
Diego López Pacheco Cabrera y Bobadilla	1640–42
Juan de Palafox y Mendoza	1642
García Sarmiento y Sotomayor	1642–48
Marcos de Torres y Rueda	1648–49
Matías de Peralta	1649–50
Luis Enríquez y Guzmán	1650–53
Francisco Fernández de la Cueva	1653–60
Juan de Leyva y de la Cerda	1660–64
Diego Osorio de Escobar y Llamas	1664
Antonio Sebastián de Toledo	1664–73
Pedro Nuño Colón de Portugal	1673
Fray Payo Enríquez de Rivera	1673–80
Tomás Antonio Manrique de la Cerda y Aragón	1680–86
Melchor Portocarrero Lasso de la Vega	1686–88
Gaspar de Sandoval Silva y Mendoza	1688–96
Juan de Ortega y Montañez	1696
José Sarmiento Valladares	1696–1701
Juan de Ortega y Montañez	1701
Francisco Fernández de la Cueva Enríquez	1701–11
Fernando de Alencastre Noroña y Silva	1711–16
Baltasar de Zúñiga y Guzmán	1716–22
Juan de Acuña	1722–34
Juan Antonio Vizarrón y Eguiarreta	1734–40
Pedro de Castro y Figueroa	1740–41
Pedro Cebrián y Agustín	1742–46
Francisco de Güemes y Horcasitas	1746–55
(subsequently first Count Revillagigedo)	

Agustín Ahumada y Villalón	1755–60
Francisco Cajigal de la Vega	1760
Joaquín de Monserrat	1760–66
Carlos Francisco de Croix	1766–71
Antonio María de Bucareli	1771–79
Martín de Mayorga	1779–83
Matías de Gálvez	1783–84
Vicente de Herrera y Rivero	1784–85
Bernardo de Gálvez	1785–86
Eusebio Sánchez Pareja y Beleño	1786–87
Alonso Núñez de Haro y Peralta	1787
Manuel Antonio Flores	1787–89
Juan Vicente de Güemes Pacheco y Padilla (second Count Revillagigedo)	1789–94
Miguel de la Grúa Talamanca y Branciforte	1794–98
Miguel José de Azanza	1798–1800
Félix Berenguer de Marquina	1800–1803
José de Iturrigaray	1803–08
Pedro Garibay	1808–09
Francisco Javier de Lizana y Beaumont	1809–10
Francisco Javier de Venegas	1810–13
Félix María Calleja del Rey	1813–16
Juan Ruiz de Apodaca	1816–21
Francisco Novella	1821
Juan O'Donojú	did not assume office

Independence Period and Early Republic

Emperor Agustín de Iturbide	1822–23
Guadalupe Victoria (Félix Fernández)	1824–29
Vicente Guerrero	1829
José María Bocanegra (interim)	1829
Pedro Vélez, Luis Quintanar, and Lucas Alamán, triumvirate	1829
Anastasio Bustamante	1830–32, 1837–39, and 1842
Melchor Múzquiz (interim)	1832
Manuel Gómez Pedraza	1833
Antonio López de Santa Anna	variously from 1833 to 1855
Valentín Gómez Farías	1833, 1834, and 1847
Miguel Barragán	1835–36
José Justo Corro	1836–37
Nicolás Bravo	variously from 1839 to 1846
Javier Echeverría	1841
Valentín Canalizo	1844

José Joaquín Herrera (interim)	1844, 1845, and 1848–51
Mariano Paredes Arrillaga	1846
Mariano Salas	1846
Pedro María Anaya	1847 and 1848
Manuel de la Peña y Peña	1847 and 1848
Mariano Arista	1851–53
Juan Bautista Ceballos (interim)	1853
Manuel María Lombardini	1853
Martín Carrera (interim)	1855
Rómulo Díaz de la Vega	1855

The Reform and the French Intervention

Juan Alvarez	1855
Ignacio Comonfort	1855–58

Liberal Government

Benito Juárez	1855–72

Conservative Government

Félix Zuloaga	1858 and 1859
Manuel Robles Pezuela	1858
Miguel Miramón	1859–60
Ignacio Pavón	1860
Conservative Junta	1860–64
Emperor Maximilian von Hapsburg	1864–67

Post-Reform Period

Sebastián Lerdo de Tejada	1872–76
Porfirio Díaz	1876–80 and 1884–1911
Juan N. Méndez	1876
Manuel González	1880–84

Revolutionary Period

Francisco León de la Barra (interim)	1911
Francisco I. Madero	1911–13
Pedro Lascuraín (interim)	1913
Victoriano Huerta (interim)	1913–14
Francisco S. Carbajal (interim)	1914
Venustiano Carranza	1914 and 1915–20
Eulalio Gutiérrez (interim, named by Convention)	1914
Roque González Garza	1914
Francisco Lagos Cházaro	1915
Adolfo de la Huerta (interim)	1920

Alvaro Obregón	1920–24
Plutarco Elías Calles	1924–28
Emilio Portes Gil (interim)	1928–30
Pascual Ortiz Rubio	1930–32
Abelardo L. Rodríguez (interim)	1932–34
Lázaro Cárdenas	1934–40

Post-Revolutionary Period

Manuel Avila Camacho	1940–46
Miguel Alemán Valdés	1946–52
Adolfo Ruiz Cortines	1952–58
Adolfo López Mateos	1958–64
Gustavo Díaz Ordaz	1964–70
Luis Echeverría Alvarez	1970–76
José López Portillo	1976–82
Miguel de la Madrid	1982–88
Carlos Salinas de Gortari	1988–94
Ernesto Zedillo	1994–2000
Vicente Fox	2000–2006
Felipe Calderón Hinojosa	2006–2012
Enrique Peña Nieto	2012–2018

SOURCES OF ILLUSTRATIONS

We gratefully acknowledge the following persons and institutions for the photographs and illustrations in this book.

List of Abbreviations

AMNH	American Museum of Natural History, New York
AIA	Archaeological Institute of America, New York
ASHS	Arizona State Historical Society, Tucson
BL	Bancroft Library, University of California, Berkeley
HRC	Humanities Research Center, University of Texas, Austin
HL	Henry E. Huntington Library, San Marino, California
IADB	Interamerican Development Bank, Washington, D.C.
INAH	Instituto Nacional de Antropología e Historia
LC	Library of Congress, Washington, D.C.
MMA	Metropolitan Museum of Art, New York
MNA	Museo Nacional de Antropología, Mexico
MNTC	Mexican National Tourist Council, New York
NA	National Archive, Washington, D.C.
NYPL	New York Public Library
OAS	Organization of American States, Washington, D.C.
SMM	Science Museum of Minnesota, St. Paul
UAL	University of Arizona Library, Tucson

Chapter 1. p. 6, AMNH; 8, left—MMA, Michael C. Rockefeller Mem. Coll. of Primitive Art, right—MNA; 9, LC. *Chapter* 2. p. 12, MMA, Rockefeller Coll; 15, above, AMNH; below, left—AMNH, below, right—MMA, Rockefeller Coll; 17, MNTC; 18, AIA; 19, MNTC; 20, MNA; 21, Leslie Hughes; 23, Jeffrey House; 25, MMA, Rockefeller Coll; 26, above left—AMNH, above right—MNTC, below, MNA; 27, left—MNA, right—Dumbarton Oaks, Washington, D.C. *Chapter* 3. p. 32, AIA; 34, above—NYPL, below—Alan Bates; 35, left—MMA, Rockefeller Coll, right—MNTC; 36, CONACULTA-INAH-MEX; 37, 38, Leslie Hughes; 39, above—AIA, below—Bradley Smith; 40, above—AMNH, below—MNTC; 41, Thomas Laging. *Chapter* 4. p. 46, LC; 49, 50, AMNH. *Chapter* 5. 54, Biblioteca, MNA; 55, Foto Marburg/Art Resource, NY; 56, Dumbarton Oaks, Washington, D.C.; 60, 62, 63, LC; 64, 65, MNA; 66, LC; 68, AMNH; 69, Bradley Smith. *Chapter* 6. p. 76, J.B. Handelsman; 80, above left—MMA, Rogers Fund, 1904, right—MMA, Gift William H. Riggs, 1913, below left— MMA, Gift Abraham Silberman, 1937, right—MMA, Rogers Fund, 1921; 81, Hospital de Jesús, México; 85, NYPL.; 88, above—Los Angeles County Museum of Natural History, below—MMA, Gift William H. Riggs, 1913; 92, Biblioteca, MNA; 93, above—after a model in the John W. Higgins Armory, Worcester, MA. *Chapter* 7. p. 98, MNTC; 101, Casa Popenoe, Antigua, Guatemala; 103, 105, from Justo Sierra, *Mexico, Its Social Revolution*; 106, BL. *Chapter* 8. p. 122, LC; 124, MMA, Gift William H. Riggs, 1913. *Chapter* 9. p. 129, Pan Amer. Development Foundation; 132, Weidenfeld & Nicolson, London; 133, NA; 136, upper left—Philadelphia Museum of Art, upper right and below—MMA, Gift Mrs. Robert W. de Forest, 1911; 138 top, Roger (New Zealand) Morris/ National Geographic Creative, below, from Carlos Nebel, *Viaje pintoresco y arqueológico sobre...la República Mexicana...1839*; 140, American Numismatic Society, N.Y. *Chapter* 10. p. 143, LC; 145, Programa Nacional de Arte Popular; 147, LC; 148, Jeffrey House; 149, LC; 151, 152, Vicente Riva Palacios, *México a través de los siglos*, 1887–89; 153, CONACULTA-INAH-MEX. *Chapter* 11. p. 164, CONACULTA-INAH-MEX; 168, Album/Art Resource, NY; 169, ART Collection/Alamy Stock Photo; 170, www.correodelmaestro.com. *Chapter* 12. pp. 177, 179, from Justo Sierra, *Mexico, Its Social Revolution*, 1900; 184, LC; 185, BL; 186, MMA; 187, Leslie Hughes; 189, 190, Hispanic Society of America, N.Y.; 192, from *México y sus alrededores*, Editorial Valle de México, 1980. *Chapter* 13. p. 198, Bruckman Art Reference Bureau; 205, from *México y sus alrededores*, Editorial Valle de México, 1980. *Chapter* 14. p. 209, OAS; 210, LC; 211, from Carlos Nebel, *Viaje pintoresco y arqueológico sobre...la República Mexicana...*, *1839*; 212, Weidenfeld & Nicolson, London; 214, The Brooklyn Museum; 215, BL; 219, MMA, Bequest Mrs. H. O. Havemeyer, 1929; 221, BL. *Chapter* 15. p. 225, LC; 229, Bettmann Archive. *Chapter* 16. p. 237, from *Gobernantes de México*, 1325–1911, *Artes de México*, No. 175, año XXI, p. 59. *Chapter* 17. p. 247, from Justo Sierra, *México, Its Social Revolution*, 1900. *Chapter* 18. p. 253, BL; 257, BL; 262, NA; 267, NYPL. *Chapter* 19. pp. 273, 274, from Vicente Riva Palacios, *México a través de los siglos*, 1887–89; 275, 277, from B. Mayer, *Mexico, Aztec, Spanish and Republican*, 1852. *Chapter* 20. p. 285, BL; 289, BL; 291, ASHS; 293, 297, from M. de los Torres, *El archiduque Maximiliano de Austria en México*, 1867. *Chapter* 21. p. 303, HRC; 304, NYPL; 306, HL. *Chapter* 22. p. 311, Vicente Riva Palacios, *México a través de los siglos*, 1887–89; 312, BL; 313, *México y sus alrededores*, Editorial Valle de México, 1980; 315, NYPL; 316, from Justo

Sierra, *México, Its Social Revolution, 1900. Chapter* 23. p. 326, HRC; 327, BL; 328, SMM; 330, ASHS. *Chapter* 24. p. 336, SMM; 337, UAL; 342, HL; 343, SMM. *Chapter* 25. p. 348, ASHS; 350, HRC. *Chapter* 26. p. 360, Hemeroteca Nacional de México; 361 top http://archivomagon. net/category/sin-categoria/page/3/; 364, bottom, Catherine Tracy Goode BL; 369, UAL; 371, HRC; 372, ASHS; p. 375, HRC. *Chapter* 27. p. 382, NA; 385, HL; 390, LC. *Chapter* 28. p. 393, HRC; 394, 396, LC; 400, HRC; p. 403, HRC. *Chapter* 29. p. 412, ASHS; 414, LC; 416, above—HL, below—HRC. *Chapter* 30. p. 427, NYPL; 430, Fideicomiso Archivos Calles y Torreblanca. *Chapter* 31. pp. 440, 444, NA; pp. 447, 448, 450, NA. *Chapter* 32. p. 459. Daniel Sambraus/Contributor/Getty Images; 460, Catherine Tracy Goode 462, LC; 463, Pan Amer. Development Foundation; 464, LC; 466, Dartmouth College Museum, Hanover, NH; 467, National Preparatory School, México. *Chapter* 33. pp. 474, 475, Editorial Photocolor Archives; 476, NA. *Chapter* 34. p. 483, MNTC; 483, OAS; 486, MNTC; 492, James W. Wilkie; 493, https://commons .wikimedia.org/wiki/File:John_Carlos,_Tommie_Smith,_Peter_Norman_1968cr.jpg/Angelo Cozzi (Mondadori Publishers). *Chapter* 35. p. 503, Diego Goldberg/Sygma. *Chapter* 36. p. 509, Lourdes Grobet; 510, 511, MMTC; 512, MNTC; 513, RKO/Kobal/REX/Shutterstock; 514, Films Mundiales Metro-Goldwyn-Mayer; 515, Photo 12/Alamy Stock Photo; 516, Ed Clark/Contributor/Getty Images; 517, World History Archive/Alamy Stock Photo. *Chapter* 37. p. 528, Secretaría de Información y Propaganda del Partido Revolucionario Institucional; 529, coin courtesy of Michael M. Brescia; 530, Alejandro Castañeda, México, D.F., 1985; 533, Sergio Dorantes/Contributor/Getty Images; 538, Juan Miranda, *Proceso;* 541, Archive photos/Daniel Aguilar/Reuters 542, Dan Fitzsimmons, *Arizona Daily Star. Chapter* 38. p. 550, *Proceso;* 557, Ronaldo Schemidt/AFP/Getty Images. *Chapter* 39. p. 565, Beth Henson; 568, left—Celeste González de Bustamante, right—Cristóbal Pereyra; 571, Tribune Content Agency LLC/Alamy Stock Photo; 572, Catherine Tracy Goode 575, AP Photo/Dario Lopez-Mills; 577, Vicente Fox Quesada; 578, frenys.com/post/10678152-tambien-de-este-lado-hay-suenos/. *Chapter* 40. p. 582, Photo by Sergio Dorantes/Corbis/VCG via Getty Images; 584, 585, 587, 589, 590, Catherine Tracy Goode; 591, Photo by Nick Wall/WireImage; 592, Photo by Steve Granitz/WireImage; 593, Warner Brothers; 594, http://www.televisa.com/home-entertainment/cata-logs/telenovelas/contemporaneas-juveniles/026910/dvd-destilando-amor-televisa-home-entertainment/; 598, aerialarchives.com/Alamy Stock Photo; 600, Berenice Fregoso/GDA/El Universal/MÃ©xico/ASSOCIATED PRESS; 602, Catherine Tracy Goode 604, http://pzrser-vices.typepad.com/vintageadvertising/2007/01/jose_cuervo_teq.html; Ashley Black.

CREDITS FOR ILLUSTRATIONS IN COLOR INSERT, FOLLOWING P. xxx

Pre-Columbian Classic Period. (1) Palenque (North Courtyard of the Palace): Photo by David Hixson. (2) Death Mask (Jade) of Pacal: SECRETARIA DE CULTURA-INAH-MEX: Reproducción Autorizada por el Instituto Nacional de Antropología e Historia; Photo by Ignacio Guevara/Raíces/INAH. (3) Anthropomorphic female figurine: SECRETARIA DE CULTURA-INAH-MEX: Reproducción Autorizada por el Instituto Nacional de Antropología e Historia; Photo by Marco Antonio Pacheco/Raíces/INAH. (4) Cacaxtla mural: Photo by David Hixson. **Colonial.** (5) Cathedral of Oaxaca: Photo by David Hixson. (6) Santa María Tonantzintla church exterior: Photo by Carlos García Calzada. (7) Santa María Tonantzintla church interior: Photo by Carlos García Calzada. (8) Portrait of Sor Juana Inés de la Cruz by Miguel Cabrera, ca.1750: SECRETARIA DE CULTURA-INAH-MEX: Reproducción Autorizada por el Instituto Nacional de Antropología e Historia (9) Casta painting by Miguel Cabrera, *De chino cambujo y de india, loba*, 1763: Photo by Camilo Garza (Museo de América, Madrid), oil on canvas. **Nineteenth Century.** (10) José Agustín Arrieta, *La sorpresa*, 1850: SECRETARIA DE CULTURA-INAH-MEX: Reproducción Autorizada por el Instituto Nacional de Antropología e Historia, oil on canvas. (11) Salvador Murillo, *El Puente de Chiquihuite*, ca. 1875: Colección Banco Nacional de México, oil on canvas. (12) Luis Coto, *La Colegiata de Guadalupe*, 1859: REPRODUCCIÓN AUTORIZADA POR EL INSTITUTO NACIONAL DE BELLAS ARTES Y LITERATURA, 2017, oil on canvas. (13) José María Velasco, *The Valley of Mexico from the Cerro del Tepeyac*, 1894: REPRODUCCIÓN AUTORIZADA POR EL INSTITUTO NACIONAL DE BELLAS ARTES Y LITERATURA, 2017, oil on canvas. **Twentieth Century.** (14) Diego Rivera, from *Día de los Muertos*, 1923–24: Mural, Secretaría de Educación Pública; D.R. © 2006 Banco de México, Fiduciario en el Fideicomiso relativo a los Museos Diego Rivera y Frida Kahlo; Archivo Fotográfico CENIDIAP/INBA, Artists Rights Society. (15) José Clemente Orozco, *Zapata*, 1930: Joseph Winterbotham Collection, "Photography © The Art Institute of Chicago," Artists Rights Society oil on canvas. (16) David Alfaro Siqueiros, from *El tormento de Cuauhtémoc*, 1951: Mural, Palacio de Bellas Artes; CENIDIAP/INBA, Biblioteca de las Artes, CENART (México), Artists Rights Society. (17) Diego Rivera, *Paisaje zapatista*, 1915: Museo Nacional de Arte; D.R. © 2006 Banco de México, Fiduciario en el Fideicomiso relativo a los Museos Diego Rivera y Frida Kahlo; Archivo Fotográfico CENIDIAP/INBA, Artists Rights Society. (18) Rufino Tamayo, *Dos figuras en rojo*,1973: Couple in Red © Phoenix Art Museum, Arizona/Friends of Mexican Art/The Bridgeman Art Library; D.R. Rufino Tamayo/Herederos/ México/2017, Fundación Olga y Rufino Tamayo A.C.

INDEX

Page numbers followed by *f* indicate illustrations; page numbers followed by *m* indicate maps; page numbers followed by *t* indicate tables, charts, or graphs.

A

Abascal, Carlos, 546
abbreviations, 614–15
Abelardo Rodríguez Market, 458, 460*f*
abortion, 506, 546, 598
Academia de Música, 278
Academia de San Juan de Letrán, 278
Acamapichtli, 47
Acapulco, 122*f*, 137, 167, 199, 284
Acolman, 185
Act of Consolidation of 1804, 217
Acteal massacre, 537–38
Actopan, 185
Africans, 165–67
Afro-mestizos. *See* mulatos
Afro-Mexicans, 166, 167, 172, 605, 607
agrarian reform, 379–80
  by administration, 438*f*
  under Avila Camacho, 451–52
  under Calles, 425, 432
  under Cárdenas, 437–38
  under Carranza, 402
  under Díaz, 323, 329*n*.1
  under Díaz Ordaz, 494
  under Huerta, 388
  under López Mateos, 483, 483*f*
  under Obregón, 406
  Plan de Ayala, 378, 392
  Plan Orozquista, 379

  under Zapata, 393, 401
  See also land ownership and distribution
Agricultural School at Chapingo, 463*f*, 464
agriculture
  Aztecs, 47, 61
  Classic period, 13
  colonial era, 132–34, 200
  and drought in early 19th century, 225
  first half of 19th century, 272
  Formative Period, 4*t*, 5–7
  Green Revolution, 479, 494
  impact of wars of independence on, 238
  under López Portillo, 501, 503
  Maya, 22
  Mexican contribution to United States, 449
  value of New Spain's annual production, 201*t*
Aguascalientes, convention of, 391–92
Aguascalientes Metal Company, 330, 331
Aguayo, marqués de, 209–10
Aguayo, Sergio, 599
Aguilar, Jerónimo de, 79
Aguilar Zinser, Adolfo, 551
Agustín I (emperor of Mexico). *See* Iturbide, Agustín de
Ahuítzotl, 48–49, 51
Air Force Squadron 201, 449
Alamán, Lucas, 227, 267–68, 279
Alameda, 314
Alameda Park, Mexico City, 191, 192*f*

Alamo, 255–56
Albuquerque, 258
Alburquerque, Duque de, 116–17, 199
albur, 596
alcabala, 139
alcaldes mayores, 117
alcaldes ordinarios, 118
alcohol use, 59–60, 349, 350, 458
alcoholic beverages, 604–5
Aldama, Juan de, 225, 226
alebrijes, 590*f*
Alegre, Francisco Javier, 179
Alemán, Miguel, 448, 487, 488
  institutional revolution (1946–52), 473–77
  relations with United States, 475, 476
Alfonso XIII (king of Spain), 367
Alhóndiga de Granaditas, 227
Allá en el Rancho Grande (de Fuentes), 457, 457*f*
Allegories of Music and Song (Tamayo), 462*f*
Allende, Hortensia, 497
Allende, Ignacio, 225–28
almanacs, 279
Almazán, Juan Andreu, 445
almojarifazgo, 139
Almonte, Juan, 294
alms, 312
Altamirano, Ignacio Manuel, 315
altepetl, 47, 49, 58
Alvarado, Pedro de, 89, 93, 100–101, 101*f*, 109, 162
Alvarado, Salvador, 415
Alvarez, Juan, 248, 284, 285
Alvarez Bravo, Lola, 521